THE ST PAUL'S BIBLIOGRAPHIES 14

THE FOULIS PRESS

A BIBLIOGRAPHY OF
THE FOULIS PRESS

Second edition

PHILIP GASKELL

ST PAUL'S BIBLIOGRAPHIES
1986

ST PAUL'S BIBLIOGRAPHIES 14

First published in the Soho Bibliographies by Rupert Hart-Davis in 1964, this second edition is published in 1986 by St Paul's Bibliographies, West End House, 1 Step Terrace, Winchester, Hampshire SO22 5BW, England

British Library Cataloguing in Publication Data

Gaskell, Philip
Bibliography of the Foulis Press.—2nd ed.—(St Paul's Bibliographies; 14)
1. Foulis Press—Catalogs
I. Title
015.414'43   Z2069

ISBN 0 906795 13 3

THIS EDITION IS LIMITED TO 450 COPIES

Printed in Great Britain by
Henry Ling Ltd,
The Dorset Press,
Dorchester, Dorset

INTRODUCTION TO THE ADDITIONS
AND AMENDMENTS (1986)

WHEN the first edition of this *Bibliography of the Foulis Press* appeared in the spring of 1964 it already included on p. 401 addenda and corrigenda to 14 of its entries; and since then I have kept a file of further additions and amendments, which has grown as I have come across them, or (as has usually been the case) have been told of them. The contents of this file is presented here as a total of 221 additions and amendments to the original 724 entries (that is, the original entries numbered 1–706, plus 18 entries with 'A' numbers) of the bibliography. These 221 new addenda and corrigenda consist of 56 completely new entries; 21 entries for editions previously 'not seen' but since discovered; and 144 amendments to other existing entries (including the 14 amendments from p. 401).

The additions and amendments form pages 401–463 of this edition. Entries in the main body of the text to which the additions and amendments refer are now flagged with a †.

There would have been even more amendments if certain categories of minor variation had not been excluded. Where I encountered minor differences of signing not affecting the formula (such as 'D3 not signed', etc.), or occasional variants in series of press-figures, or the occurence of different but similar papers in some of the signatures of a book, I have as a rule not recorded them, especially where recording them would have resulted in an extra entry.

When I was working on the bibliography in 1951–63 I personally examined all the copies of all the Foulis books that I could get hold of (though under COPIES I located only a minority of those that I had examined; see p. 62). For this revision I have as far as possible personally examined at least one example of each new edition or variant; but I have not seen all the new editions, etc., that are located abroad, and I have not systematically checked the holdings of the major collections of Foulis books for the new material.

The index has been reset to include all the new material along with the old; and, as before, it refers to page numbers, not to entry numbers.

For the great majority of the new entries and amendments I am indebted to the correspondents and other sources named in them. I must nevertheless make special mention of the labours of Dr B. J. McMullin of Monash University, Victoria, Australia, and Mr Brian Gerrard of Mount Waverley, Victoria, Australia, who have between them alerted me to the existence of a sizable proportion of the new material presented here, and who have most generously provided me with a stream of locations, descriptions, notes, and advice. Without the continuing support of their enthusiastic but always meticulous scholarship, this revision of my bibliography would have been very much the poorer.

PHILIP GASKELL

TRINITY COLLEGE, CAMBRIDGE
April 1985

FOREWORD

In October 1951 I read a paper to the Bibliographical Society on the early work of the Foulis Press and the Wilson Foundry, and in the following year the text of this paper and a bibliography of the Foulis Press up to the year 1749 were published in successive numbers of *The Library*. I said then that the bibliography would eventually be completed, and completed it is; but only just. The full bibliographical treatment of seven hundred different editions is a lengthy and often tedious business, and I would probably have abandoned it had I not been given an unexpected opportunity to do a further eighteen months of full-time research on Foulis. For this opportunity so considerately given – which is yet but a small part of my debt – I am deeply grateful to the College of which I have the honour and the happiness to be a member.   PHILIP GASKELL

KING'S COLLEGE, CAMBRIDGE,
        July 1960

During the years in which this book has been printing a certain amount of new Foulis material has come to light. While I have incorporated in proof all that I have found or have been told of, I have not been able completely to recheck the holdings of the British Museum, Bodleian, Cambridge University or Mitchell Libraries, which may have been increased here and there by acquisitions made since 1959–60.   PHILIP GASKELL

THE UNIVERSITY LIBRARY, GLASGOW
        October, 1963

7

ACKNOWLEDGEMENTS

OF the many people who have helped me during the past thirteen years with the preparation of this book I am especially grateful to Dr A. N. L. Munby of King's College, and Mr J. C. T. Oates of the University Library, Cambridge; Mr J. L. Weir of Glasgow University Library; Mr A. G. Hepburn of the Mitchell Library, Glasgow, and Mr G. C. Emslie, late of the same Library; Mr L. W. Hanson and Mr D. G. Neill of the Bodleian Library, Oxford; Professor William A. Jackson of Harvard University Library; Dr William Beattie of the National Library of Scotland; Mr Bernard Barr of the Dean and Chapter Library, York Minster; and Professor A. F. Falconer of St Andrews University.

NOTE ON THE TYPE

This book is set in Monotype Fontana, a type-face based on Alexander Wilson's English Roman of 1760, the ' RE 3 ' of the present bibliography. Produced in 1935-6 by Dr Giovanni Mardersteig of the Officina Bodoni, it is a fairly close copy of Wilson's finest design. It was commissioned originally by Messrs Collins, the printer-publishers of London and Glasgow, and until 1962 was reserved for their exclusive use.

ABBREVIATIONS

The following abbreviations are used:

GENERAL

Berry and Johnson	Berry, W. Turner, and Johnson, A. F., *Catalogue of Specimens of Printing Types* (London : Oxford University Press, 1935).
BQ	*A Catalogue of Books, being the entire stock, in Quires, of the late Messrs. R. and A. Foulis* (Glasgow, 1777). No. 614 in the present bibliography. References are to page numbers.
CP	*A Catalogue of Pictures . . . offered . . . by Robert Foulis* (3 vols., London, 1776). No. 595 in the present bibliography. References are to page numbers in sigs. A–C^8 D^2 of Volume iii (' BOOKS ').
Duncan	Duncan, W. J., *Notices and Documents Illustrative of the Literary History of Glasgow, during the Greater Part of the Last Century* (Glasgow, 1831) ; reprinted with appendix additional (Glasgow, 1886).
' Early Work '	Gaskell, Philip, ' The Early Work of the Foulis Press and the Wilson Foundry ', *The Library*, Fifth Series, Vol. vii (1952), pp. 77–110, 149–77.
GC	*The Glasgow Courant.*
GJ	*The Glasgow Journal.*
Maclehose	Maclehose, James, *The Glasgow University Press 1638–1931* (Glasgow, 1931).
Murray, *R. & A. Foulis*	Murray, David, *Robert & Andrew Foulis and the Glasgow Press with some account of the Glasgow Academy of the Fine Arts* (in *Records of the Glasgow Bibliographical Society*, Vol. ii, Glasgow, 1913).

9

ABBREVIATIONS

Spotiswood
    Books Printed by the late Mess. Robert &
Andrew Foulis, . . . Now the property of
James Spotiswood (in *Bibliotheca Moori-*
ana . . . venales prostant, Edinburgi, Apud
. . . Jacobum Spotiswood . . . Id. Feb. A.D.
1779, Edinburgh 1779, pp. 85–92).

LANGUAGES
    E   English
    F   French
    G   Greek
    I   Italian
    L   Latin

WATERMARKS AND TYPE
    See ' Explanation of the Bibliography ', pp. 59-60 below, *s.v.*
' PAPER ' and ' TYPE '.

LIBRARIES
    Aberystwyth, College of Librarianship Library
    C   The University Library, Cambridge
    C^2 Trinity College, Cambridge
    C^4 King's College, Cambridge
    C^5 St. John's College, Cambridge
    Canberra, The National Library of Australia
    D   Trinity College, Dublin
    E   The National Library of Scotland, Edinburgh
    E^2 Edinburgh University Library
    G   The Hunterian Library, University of Glasgow
    G^2 The University Library, Glasgow
    G^4 The Mitchell Library, Glasgow
    Glasgow, Baillie's Library
    Glasgow, The Royal College of Physicians and Surgeon's
        Library
    Glasgow, The University of Strathclyde Library
    HD   Harvard University Library, Cambridge, Mass.
    L   The British Library
    L^{30} University of London Library
    LC   The Library of Congress, Washington, D.C.
    McMaster University Library, Hamilton, Ont.
    MEL The State Library of Victoria
    Melbourne University Library, Vict.
    Monash University Library, Clayton, Vict.
    O   The Bodleian Library, Oxford
    Sydney University Library, N.S.W.

INTRODUCTION

§ 1. Sources

A. *Foulis Press books.* The largest single collection of books printed by or for the Foulises is at the Mitchell Library, Glasgow (G⁴), where most of them are kept in the Glasgow Room, together with a separate catalogue[1] of the whole Foulis collection. Near by is a fine collection at Glasgow University Library (G²), including a number of Hunterian (G) books in their original wrappers, and the Murray Collection (separately catalogued). Almost as numerous are the Foulis books at the British Museum (L); and there is a less complete, but still substantial, collection of Foulis books at the Bodleian Library (O). I know of no other British Library, public or private, which is strong in Foulis books, but this is hardly surprising when it is considered that the least extensive of the collections mentioned above contains about 300 separate editions.

B. *Bibliography.* William James Duncan (1811-85), banker and antiquary, made the first and – until the present work – only attempt to list the whole output of the Foulis Press. His Maitland Club volume of 1831 included a short-title catalogue of 516 Foulis books of the period 1741-76, and a further 75 titles were added as an appendix to the reprint of 1886, including the work of Andrew Foulis the younger

1. Microfilm in C.

and bringing the total to 591.[1] A number of
Duncan's items are not separate editions, however,
but are variant issues of books already listed or are
individual parts of collections, while others are certainly ghosts; a further considerable group of titles
(his Nos. 442-98) were not seen by him, but were
taken from the stock-in-trade catalogue of 1777 (*BQ*).
Duncan himself, therefore, probably saw no more
than about 450 Foulis Press editions. While it would
be rash to claim that the present bibliography is
complete, it is at least a good deal more nearly so
than was Duncan's list; it contains entries for 724
separate editions (counting such things as the collected Shakespeare, 1766, as only one edition), of
which I have seen copies of 632.

Saving errors of identification, cataloguing, etc.,
I have seen all the Foulis books at the Mitchell
Library, Glasgow, Glasgow University Library,
the British Museum, the Bodleian Library and
Cambridge University Library; and I have checked
for missing items at the National Library of
Scotland, Edinburgh University Library, the Sig-
net Library, Edinburgh and Harvard University
Library.

C. *Other major sources.* i. *Manuscript.* In 1808 the
eccentric Earl of Buchan[2] collected materials for a
history of the Foulis Press, but it was never written;
they are now MS. 32225 in the library of Baillie's
Institution, Glasgow.[3] The Archives of Glasgow
University contain a considerable number of docu-

1. W. J. Duncan, *Notices and Documents Illustrative of the
Literary History of Glasgow, during the Greater Part of the Last
Century* (Glasgow, 1831); reprinted with appendix additional,
(Glasgow, 1886).
2. David Steuart Erskine, 11th Earl of Buchan (1742-1829).
3. Microfilm in C.

ments relating to the activities of the Foulises; few of them are of bibliographical interest, but there are some vouchers for books bought by them, as University Booksellers, for the University. Edinburgh University, Laing MSS. III. 363, directly concerns the Foulis Press; while in the Glasgow University Library, Murray Collection, are a number of papers concerning the Wilson Foundry.[1]

ii. *Printed.* In April 1913 the Glasgow Bibliographical Society held a Foulis Exhibition in the University, of which the remarkable *Catalogue* was reprinted in the second volume of the Society's *Records* (Glasgow, 1913). Included in the same volume of the *Records* – also known as *The Book of the Foulis Exhibition* – is David Murray's *Robert & Andrew Foulis and the Glasgow Press with some account of the Glasgow Academy of the Fine Arts*; this is still the major work on its subject, though Murray's references are inadequate. Murray also edited *Some Letters of Robert Foulis* (Glasgow, 1917). James Maclehose, *The Glasgow University Press 1638-1931* (Glasgow, 1931), contains a good section on the Foulis Press; one can only wish that it were longer. My ' The Early Work of the Foulis Press and the Wilson Foundry' (*The Library*, Fifth Series, Vol. vii, pp. 77–110 and 149–77) deals with its period (1740–9) in greater detail than Murray or Maclehose, but its bibliography of the output of the Foulis Press, 1740–9, is now superseded. Finally, there was another Foulis Exhibition held in Glasgow University in March 1958, of manuscripts and printed books, for which there was a good duplicated catalogue by the Archivist, Mr D. J. Wilson Reid.

1. Microfilm in C.

§ 2. The Extent and Character of the Output of the Foulis Press

In the absence of precise information about the edition-sizes of Foulis Press books, estimates of the productivity of the Press cannot be exact;[1] but some idea of its activity may be gained from a count of the editions put out each year.[2] It has been mentioned that the bibliography contains over seven hundred entries. They are arranged in three major divisions:

1. Editions printed for Robert Foulis, 1740–2   13

2. Editions printed by Robert Foulis, and by Robert
   and Andrew Foulis, 1742–76   589*

3. Editions printed by Andrew Foulis the younger,
   1776–1800[3]   103*

The editions actually printed at the Foulis Press may be further divided as follows:

1. It is known that R. and A. Foulis were allowed drawback of duty on about 5000 reams of paper that they had used for printing books in Greek and Latin from 1742 to 1765 (Duncan, p. 138). In this period they printed about 100 editions in Greek and Latin, averaging 15 sheets each in length (longer than their average edition in English), which gives an edition-size for the classics of about 1500.

2. I am sure to have missed a number of Foulis editions, but some of the entries taken over from Duncan are probably ghosts, while others refer to ephemera ; it is hoped that the variables cancel each other out.

3. The books dated ' 1806 ' were reissues ; the last separate edition was dated ' 1800 '.

* See footnote on following page.

TABLE

FOULIS EDITIONS PER ANNUM, 1742–97

Part II : Printed by Robert Foulis and by Robert and
Andrew Foulis, 1742–76

1742	.	13	1754	.	10	1766	.	15
1743	.	16	1755	.	31	1767	.	11
1744	.	14	1756	.	18	1768	.	12
1745	.	14	1757	.	13	1769	.	14
1746	.	9	1758	.	20	1770	.	20
1747	.	19	1759	.	15	1771	.	18
1748	.	24	1760	.	10	1772	.	13
1749	.	14	1761	.	14	1773	.	13
1750	.	40	1762	.	13	1774	.	12
1751	.	43	1763	.	13	1775	.	18
1752	.	29	1764	.	9	1776	.	10
1753	.	21	1765	.	11			

Part III : Printed by Andrew Foulis the younger,
1776–1800

1776	.	5	1785	.	4	1794	.	2
1777	.	16*	1786	.	3	1795	.	3
1778	.	8	1787	.	4	1796	.	2
1779	.	4	1788	.	2	1797	.	1
1780	.	4	1789	.	1	1798	.	0
1781	.	3	1790	.	1	1799	.	0
1782	.	2	1791	.	2	1800	.	1
1783	.	10	1792	.	2			
1784	.	12	1793	.	2			

It is immediately apparent how much less productive was Andrew Foulis the younger than were his father and uncle. In thirty-five years Robert and Andrew Foulis produced an average of nearly 17 editions a year, with a maximum in one year of 43

* Not included in the table are 8 entries taken from *BQ*, the stock catalogue of 1777 ; the books concerned were probably printed at various dates over the previous thirty years. Also omitted are the Foulis-Tilloch books of 1783–4, and all the books with 'A' numbers and No. 706.

and a minimum of 9; whereas Andrew the younger averaged only 4·1 editions a year for twenty-five years, maximum 16, minimum 0.[1]

A chart of two-year averages shows even more clearly than the bare figures the pattern of development as the century progressed (see pp. 24-5).[2] With the exception of the spectacular peak of the early seventeen-fifties, the curve for Robert and Andrew Foulis does not move very far away from 15 editions per annum. At first sight there might appear to be evidence of some sort of cyclical movement, but the peaks are not regularly spaced and I am inclined to doubt whether they have any significance. I am not able to explain the surge of 1750–1; it was over well before the Academy was established and took up so much of Robert's time, though it is possible that Robert's departure for the continent in 1751 (following the death of his first wife) may have been partly responsible for the sharp drop in activity in 1752.

Following the death of the brothers in 1775 and 1776, Andrew Foulis the younger took over the Press and found it to be in a state of financial chaos; the subsequent drop is very marked and, save for a brief resurgence in the early seventeen-eighties, it continued until the Press finally expired in 1800.

The Foulises' choice of titles was influenced chiefly by their position as University Printers. The first

1. Samuel Richardson – whose printing house was a large one by London standards – printed 588 editions in the forty-three years 1720–62, averaging 13 a year, maximum 31, minimum 3 (Sale, William M., Jr, *Samuel Richardson : Master Printer* (Cornell University Press, 1950), pp. 229–50).

2. Two-year averages are plotted rather than annual totals in order to iron out variations due to the issue of books after the end of the calendar years in which they were printed.

need was text-books, of which they produced a wide range, prominent among them being an extensive series of Greek texts with Latin translations, a Greek grammar, various manuals of philosophy and some interesting lecture-notes. In addition to text-books there were of course works of learning, of piety (which became fewer in number as the century advanced), and of general literature. Among their projects were a series of duodecimo English poets retailing at a shilling a volume (from 1766), and books in French (from 1753), Gaelic (one example, 1750) and Italian (from 1753).

A useful indication of the main lines followed by the Press may be given by listing the authors and books which were most often printed. Of authors who appeared in ten or more Foulis editions, Francis Hutcheson, Professor of Philosophy at Glasgow, comes first with 28; after him are Cicero (24), Milton (20), James Moor, Professor of Greek (17), Addison (16), William Leechman, Professor of Divinity and Principal (14), Fénelon (13), Gay (12), and Anacreon, Epictetus, Xenophon and Young (10 each). Of the most popular single works, Moor's *Greek Grammar* heads the list with 11 editions; then come *Paradise Lost* (9), Hutcheson's *Synopsis Metaphysicae* and *Introduction to Moral Philosophy* (7 each), and two sermons by Leechman (7 and 6).

The practice of issuing some copies of an edition on special paper was not uncommon in the eighteenth century, but the Foulises carried the multiplication of variant issues to greater lengths than any other eighteenth-century printer known to me. When allowance is made for the fact that I have not seen enough copies of each Foulis edition to have seen all the possible variants, it is clear that variant issues were the rule rather than the exception at the Foulis Press. Neither were the Foulises always content with a single special-paper issue: to take an extreme case, the *Iliad* of 1747 (No. 84) was issued in Foolscap 8°, Greek with Latin translation; Pot 8°, Greek and Latin; Foolscap 8°, Greek alone; Pot 8°, Greek; Foolscap 4°, Greek; Pot 4°, Greek; and on vellum folded in 8°, Greek.[1]

Several Foulis books were illustrated with copperplates. It is unlikely that a rolling press was ever part of the equipment of the Press; but the copperplate facilities available at the Academy were certainly made use of from the seventeen-fifties until the seventies. Woodcut diagrams were freely used in technical works.

1. On the subject of variant issues, see also the other sections in this introduction.

§ 3. Methods of Printing

The methods of printing employed at the Foulis Press do not seem to have been exceptional. Printing is a craft in which improvisation must often be resorted to, but Foulis books do not show more than their fair share of eccentricities.

In spite of the considerable number of editions printed there, the Foulis Press was not necessarily a large establishment in terms of plant and employees. Twenty editions printed in a year, averaging 10 sheets in 1500 copies, consist of only 300,000 printed sheets, which was within the annual capacity of two journeymen working a single press. It is quite possible, therefore, that the Foulises normally used no more than two presses and a proofing press; and it should be remarked in this connection that when ' press-figures ' began to be used regularly at the Press from 1768 they appear generally to have referred to only two journeymen (and so to two press teams) at a time. Similarly, 200 sheets may be said – as a generalisation within wide limits – to have been a year's work for a single compositor, though in fact a university press, needing compositors with special skills (especially the ability to set Greek) would certainly employ more than one. Nevertheless it is probable that the Foulis Press normally had a staff of no more than about ten, including the owners.

The presses themselves were probably of average size, or even smaller than average: Printing Demy was the largest size of paper in normal use, though very occasionally larger sizes were used, up to Printing Royal. Even type seems to have been short, at any rate in the early years, when the Foulises had an unusual fondness for ' half-sheet imposition ', the object of using which is generally to economise in standing type.

Press-work was above average, but not startlingly so, in the time of the brothers; in the hands of Andrew the younger there was a marked falling off in the quality of the work as a whole. Cancels were a rarity, the brothers apparently preferring to reprint the whole sheet wherever possible. Ink was of a good commercial grade.

The signing of sections followed normal practice, with the addition of sigla (usually asterisks or obeli) to mark runs printed on special paper; as a rule the finer paper was so marked. The few indications that I have found of the order of printing the variant parts of an edition combine to suggest that octavos were printed before quartos or duodecimos, and quartos before folios;[1] that fine paper preceded common; and that Greek texts with Latin translations were printed before the plain Greek; and so they are arranged in the bibliography. No doubt, however, there were exceptions to these rules.

For eccentricities and other notable points, see the Index at 'Printing, methods of'.

1. See for instance Nos. 162 and 419 (mis-signing of the quarto issues).

§ 4. PAPER

Two general impressions result from an examination of all the paper used at the Foulis Press. First, all the Foulises – but especially the brothers – used a higher proportion of fine-quality paper in their printing than did most of their contemporaries. Secondly, and possibly as a consequence of the first point, they consistently printed on smaller sheets than was usual in the mid-eighteenth century. The typical sheet sizes of the eighteenth-century book-printer were Crown and Printing Demy; but at the Foulis Press it was Foolscap.

These impressions are borne out by the only detailed list we have of paper used at the Foulis Press. This is the list of 'Paper made ufe of in printing Greek and Lat. Claffics from the year 1742 to 1765', printed by Duncan (p. 138). A total of 4983 reams 4½ quires are specified, with details of sizes and qualities. Of the total, 87% are of 'fine', as opposed to 'second', quality; and 65% are of Foolscap size, as opposed to all other sizes. A further conclusion which may be drawn from these figures is that the Foulises' common-paper issues – of the classics, at least – tended to be printed in smaller numbers than their fine-paper issues.

Blue-tinted paper was used occasionally as early as 1771, but more commonly from 1778; wove paper, however, was not used at the Press until just before its end. This was in 1795, when everybody else was going over to wove; and it is surprising that none

23

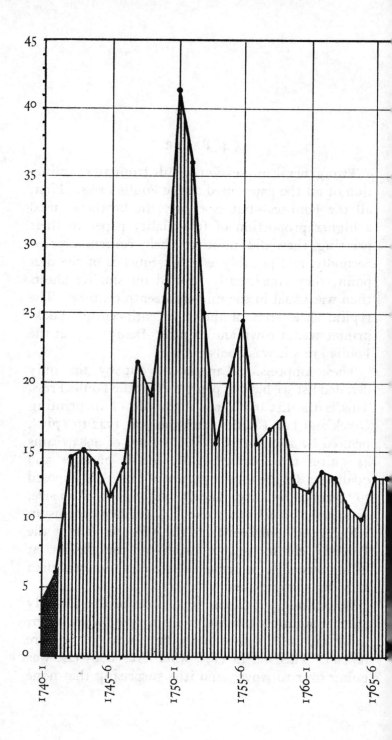

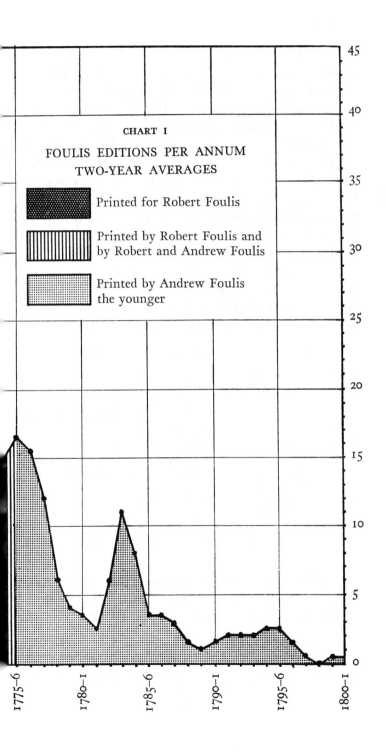

CHART I

FOULIS EDITIONS PER ANNUM
TWO-YEAR AVERAGES

Printed for Robert Foulis

Printed by Robert Foulis and
by Robert and Andrew Foulis

Printed by Andrew Foulis
the younger

of the Foulises, who were conscious innovators in their typography, should have experimented with wove paper before this date. Resort was occasionally made to exotic materials other than paper for printing special issues. These were: vellum (Nos. 81, 'Cebes', 1747; 84, Homer, 1747; 108, Epictetus, 1748; 162, Minucius Felix, 1750)[1]; silk or satin (Nos. 181, Anacreon, 1751; 274, Pindar, 1754; 552, Glasgow University Academy, 1773); and linen (Nos. 101, Cicero, 1748–9; 108, Epictetus, 1748).

The paper itself that was used at the Foulis Press was in no way extraordinary. As usual, watermarks and countermarks indicated specific sizes and qualities; and almost all the Foulises' papers bore one of the following nine marks, or were unmarked.[2]

Mark	Group	Size
1. British Royal Arms	Writing	Pot
2. City of London Arms	Writing	Pot
3. Britannia	Writing	Foolscap; also, from the seventeen-sixties, Pot
4. Pro Patria	Writing	Foolscap
5. Vryheit Lion	Writing	Foolscap
6. Post-horn	Writing	Post
7. Fleur-de-lis in a crowned shield	Writing	Demy; Medium
8. Strasbourg Bend	Writing and Printing	Royal
9. Plain Fleur-de-lis	Printing	Crown; Demy; Medium

Until the later years of the Press, there is not much certain evidence as to which mills the Foulises' paper came from. From 1747 the IW or JW of the

1. There was also a vellum issue of No. 8, Phaedrus, 1741, printed for Robert Foulis by Robert Urie.
2. See also Philip Gaskell, 'Notes on Eighteenth-century British Paper', *The Library*, Fifth Series, Vol. xii, pp. 34–42.

Whatman mill began to appear[1]; and in the seven-teen-eighties Andrew Foulis the younger used a good deal of Writing Demy paper marked with the names of I. Taylor and others. Andrew Foulis the younger certainly bought some of his paper from the Glasgow firm of Edward Collins, and it is likely that the brothers had done so too.[2] My impression is that none of the Foulises bought their paper exclusively from any single source, but patronised several mills or warehouses.

See the Index at ' Printing paper ' for a number of individual points of interest.

1. See the Index, s.v. 'Printing paper'. The first appearances of the IW countermark in 1747, and of JW in 1750, accord exactly with Mr Thomas Balston's conclusions in his *James Whatman Father and Son* (1957), p. 157

2. See Murray, *R. & A. Foulis*, pp. 116–19 ; ' Early Work ', p. 96 n.

§ 5. TYPE

Although, as we have seen, the printing techniques and the papers used at the Foulis Press were generally unremarkable, the Foulises' typography departed considerably, both in choice of type-faces and in style, from the standards of the average eighteenth-century printer. Their admirable text layouts and their influential title-pages have been discussed elsewhere, as has the development of the Wilson Foundry from which they bought practically all their type;[1] here I shall be concerned chiefly with describing the typographical equipment of the Press, which was probably always unique, and which is therefore a reliable guide to the recognition of Foulis books which do not have the Foulis Press imprint.

It has become clear in the course of examining the founts in use at the Foulis Press over periods of more than half a century not only that – as one would expect – these founts were constantly added to and renewed in the printers' cases, but also that the founder as constantly touched up sorts and groups of sorts, with the result that the character of the founts tended gradually to change as the years passed. Sometimes the change was slight; the Great Primer Greek, for example, which first appeared in 1743, was equipped with a new set of

1. ' Early Work ', pp. 89–93 ; and Philip Gaskell, ' Printing the Classics in the Eighteenth Century ', *The Book Collector*, Vol. i, No. 2 (Summer, 1952), pp. 98–111.

capitals in 1747, but its lower case remained virtually unaltered right through until 1797. The second Pica Roman, on the other hand, first used in 1751, was progressively revised and from its general appearance in the sixties and seventies might be taken

CHART II. CHRONOLOGICAL LIST OF

Year	GDP 2	GDP 1	GGP	GP	GB	RDP	RGP 2	RGP 1	RE 4	RE 3	RE 2	RE 1	RP 4	RP 3	RP 2	RP 1	RPX	RSP 2	RSP 1	RLP 2	RLP 1	RLP Cas	RB 2	RB 1
1742											×					×	×						×	
3	×										×					×	×						×	×
4	×	×									×					×							×	×
5	×	×						×			×					×							×	×
6	×	×									×												×	×
7	×	×						×			×												×	×
8	×	×	×					×			×	×											× ×	× ×
9	×		×					×			×	×											× ×	× ×
1750	×	×	×								×	×											× ×	× ×
1	×		×	×				×			×	×			×					×			× ×	× ×
2											×	×			×					×			× ×	× ×
3	×	×	×	×							×	×			×					×			× ×	× ×
4				×							×	×			×					×			× ×	× ×
5	×	×	×	×			×	×			×	×			×					×			× ×	× ×
6	×		×		×			×			×				×					×			×	× ×
7	×		×	×			×	×			×				×					×			×	× ×
8	×		×					×			×				×					×			×	× ×
9	×		×	×	×			×			×				×					×			×	
1760										×	×				×					×			×	×
1		×	×	×						×	×				×					×			×	
2		×	×							×	×				×				×	×			×	
3		×	×	×	×	×		×			×				×					×			×	
4		×		×						×					×					×			×	
5			×	×						×	×				×					×			×	
6		×	×	×		×				×	×				×				×	×			×	
7		×									×				×				×	×			×	×
8		×	×		×	×				×	×				×				× ×	×			×	×
9		×								×					×			×		×			×	×

Each cross indicates that the fount concerned was used in such and such a year for setting more than two or three words of text. Doubtful cases are not included.

for a new fount. This is the extreme case, but a similar process of revision is evident in many of Wilson's founts.

The following chart displays the chronology more fully:

TYPE-FACES USED AT THE FOULIS PRESS[1]

	GDP 2	GDP 1	GGP	GP	GB	RDP	RGP 2	RGP 1	RE 4	RE 3	RE 2	RE 1	RP 4	RP 3	RP 2	RP 1	RPX	RSP 2	RSP 1	RLP 2	RLP 1	RLP Cas	RB 2	RB 1
1770	×		×	×		×				×				×				×			×			×
1	×		×	×		×	×			×				×				×			×			×
2					×						×			×				×			×			×
3			×	×		×	×	×						×				×			×			×
4						×		×	×					×				×			×			×
5	×		×	×		×			×					×				×			×			×
6			×					×	×					×				×	×		×			×
7	×		×	×	×	×	×	×						×				×			×			×
8				×		×		×						×				×			×			×
9	×			×				×	×					×				×			×			×
1780			×	×		×								×				×			×			×
1				×										×						×	×			×
2				×																				×
3	×		×	×	×		×		×	×			×								×			×
4				×			×	×	×				×	×			×		×	×				×
5	×						×		×				×	×			×			×				×
6							×		×				×				×		×					
7	×						×		×								×	×						
8			×	×			×		×				×										×	
9			×															×						
1790			×	×														×						
1							×				×													
2	×		×												×				×				×	
3			×	×						×							×	×						
4			×		×				×								×	×						
5	×		×	×					×		×							×						
6			×	×	×				×							×								
7			×	×														×	×				×	

1. The abbreviations for founts of type are explained on p. 60 below.

Each text fount from Brevier to Double Pica is illustrated and its characteristics are detailed, beginning with the smallest, Greeks following Romans. Where possible identification is made with the founts shown in Wilson's specimens;[1] and dates are given of the first and last appearances (in more than a mere word or two) of each fount in the Foulises' books.

Confusion amid a bewildering array of closely similar founts may be partly unconfounded by the following division of the Wilson Romans into three groups or families.

Group 1 :

RE 1 (1742)	Crude, vigorous founts, of medium colour
RP 1 (1742)	and large x-height. Note that all the
RB 1 (1743)	founts in this group were cut before John
RGP 1 (1745)	Baine parted from Wilson in 1747 ; and
	that Baine's *A Specimen* (Edinburgh, 1787 ;
	Berry and Johnson, p. 57) shows a number
	of similarly crude and vigorous founts
	(though not the same ones).

Group 2 :

RLP 1 (1744)	More restrained than Group 1 ; light in
RE 2 (1748)	colour and very narrow. RE 2 is small
[RB 2 (1748)]	in the face as well. RB 2 belongs chrono-
RP 2 (1751)	logically to this group, but is of medium
RSP 1 (1751)	weight and normal width.
RGP 2 (1755)	

Group 3 :

RE 3 (1760)	A series of transitional faces, obviously in-
RDP (1763)	fluenced by Baskerville. Wide and heavily
RSP 2 (1766)	stressed, and generally dark in colour.
RP 3 (1769)	RE 3, the prototype, is also exceptionally
RP 4 (1772)	large. RP 4 goes some way towards a
RE 4 (1772)	return to the narrower style of Group 2.
RLP 2 (1772)	

1. *A Specimen of . . . Printing Types* (Glasgow, 1772 ; Berry and Johnson, p. 52) ; *A Specimen of Printing Types* (Glasgow, 1786 ; Berry and Johnson, p. 53).

Chap. I. *Of human nature and its various parts or powers.* p. 1.
1. How moral philofophy an art fuperior to others. *ib.*
derived from the ftructure of our nature. 2. the method
of treating it. *ib.*
2. The human body its dignity. 3.
3. The powers of the foul, *underftanding* and *will.* 4. the
fenfes *external* and *internal*, whence our notions of good
and evil. *ib.* 5. Senfations of a middle kind, their *ufe.*
fenfations *direct* and *reflex.* 6.
4. Internal fenfe, confcioufnefs, or reflection. *ib.* Reafon.
ib. the knowledge of God and his will. 7.
5. The fublimer fenfes. *ib.* The will and its calm moti-

1753 : No. 259, Hutcheson

RB 1. The first Brevier Roman, and almost certainly a Wilson
fount. Large x-height ; narrow ; caps with typical
Wilson barbed and cusped serifs. Cap ' Q ' with a short
rounded tail ; l.c. ' g ' with a large loop, matching the
bowl ; lig. ' ct ' with flattened top. Introduced 1743,
gradually superseded in the fifties by RB 2, not used after
1760. Not shown by Wilson.

HORATIUS FLACCUS, Venufinus, patre, ut ipfe tra-
dit, libertino, et exactionum coactore: ut vero creditum
eft, falfamentario, quum illi quidam in altercatione exprobraf-
fet: Quoties ego vidi patrem tuum cubito fe emungentem?
Bello Philippenfi, excitus a M. Bruto imperatore, tribunus mi-
litum meruit: victifque partibus, venia inpetrata, fcriptum quae-
ftorium comparavit. Ac primo Maecenati, deinde Augufto in-
finuatus, non mediocrem in amborum amicitia locum tenuit.
Maecenas quantopere eum dilexit, fatis monftratur illo epigram-
mate, ubi inquit:

1760 : No. 383, Horace ; 1758 caps

RB 2. The second Brevier Roman, introduced 1748, though
little used until 1751 onwards. Differences from RB 1 :
smaller ; lower x-height ; wider ; cleaner cut. L.c. ' g '
with flat loop and more markedly upturned ear than
RB 1 ; lig. ' ct ' with smaller, rounded top. Caps : originally the RB 1 series, but a new set of cleaned-up, narrow
caps was substituted *c.* 1758 (' Q ' has a longer, but still
rounded, tail) ; in the late sixties the caps were again
changed to a wider series, and some changes were also
made to the lower case. In this form the fount appears
as ' Brevier Roman No. 2 ' in Wilson's 1772 specimen.
Further small changes were made in later years ; for
instance, a l.c.' g ' with a downturned ear appeared *c.* 1774.
Still in use in 1797.

ΕΔΕΙ μὲν, ὦ ἄνδρες Ἀθηναῖοι τὰς λέγοντας ἅπαντας ἐν ὑμῖν, μήτε πρὸς ἔχθραν ποιεῖσθαι λόγον μηδένα, μήτε πρὸς χάριν. ἀλλ᾽ ὃ βέλτιστον ἕκαστος ἡγεῖτο, τοῦτ᾽ ἀποφαίνεσθαι. ἄλλως τε καὶ περὶ κοινῶν πραγμάτων καὶ μεγάλων ὑμῶν βουλευομένων. ἐπειδὴ δὲ ἔνιοι τὰ μὲν, φιλονεικίᾳ, τὰ δὲ, ἥ τινι δήποτ᾽ αἰτίᾳ, προάγονται λέγειν, ὑμᾶς, ὦ ἄνδρες Ἀθηναῖοι, τοὺς πολλοὺς δεῖ, πάντα τἄλλ᾽ ἀφέντας, ἃ τῇ πόλει νομίζετε συμφέρειν, ταῦτα καὶ ψηφίζεσθαι καὶ πράττειν· ἡ μὲν οὖν σπουδὴ, περὶ τῶν ἐν Χερρονήσῳ, πραγμάτων ἐστι, καὶ τῆς σρατείας, ἣν ἐνδέκατον μῆνα τουτονὶ, Φίλιππος ἐν Θρᾴκῃ ποιεῖται· τῶν δὲ λόγων οἱ πλεῖστοι, περὶ ὧν Διοπείθης πράττει καὶ μέλλει

1786: Wilson's specimen

GB. Greek Brevier, the third and last of Wilson's ' Stephen's Greek ' series (the others being GP and GGP). First appeared in 1748, still in use in 1797. The ' Brevier Greek No. 2 ' of Wilson's specimen of 1786. For characteristics, see GGP below.

ENTIS DIVISIONES, &c.

ris modis, magis erat connexus: aliorum, igitur, ejufdem generis, modorum, non pariter capax eſſet; nec, eos quoſvis pariter admitteret. Corpus, autem, omne, aliquem locum, aliquam figuram, atque ſtatum vel movendi vel quieſcendi, neceſſario habet; neque, abſque aliqua harum affectionum, eſſe poteſt. Ad omnia, tamen, loca, eſt indifferens; omnes figuras, & motum omnem vel quietem, pa-

1742: No. 21, Hutcheson

RLP Cas. The Long Primer Roman which was original equipment at the Foulis Press in 1742. Apparently a Caslon fount (probably the Long Primer Roman No. 2 of Caslon's broadside specimen of 1742 [1]). Used by Foulis in books until 1749, latterly mixed with RLP 1; used in No. 65 until 1755.

1. *A Specimen by W. Caslon* (London, 1742; Berry and Johnson, plate 1).

34

et me fequere. [22] His verbis auditis adolefcens abiit,
dolens: quippe qui multas facultates haberet. [23] At
Jefus fuos difcipulos alloquens: Hoc vobis, inquit,
confirmo, divitem difficulter in coelefte regnum ingre-
di. [24] Iterumque hoc vobis dico, facilius effe rudentem
per foramen acus trajici, quam divitem in Dei regnum intrare. [25] Hoc audito, admodum ftupefacti ejus
difcipuli, dicere, Quis ergo fervari poteft? [26] Quos in-
tuitus Jefus, dixit eis: Ab hominibus hoc fieri non poteft: at a Deo fieri poffunt omnia. [27] Tum Petrus ita lo-

1758 : No. 344, Bible; second-series caps

RLP 1. Wilson's first Long Primer Roman, and the most
successful of his smaller romans. Appeared in 1744 and
was still in use in 1797. Used more often than any other
type by the Foulises. Average x-height, but very narrow;
light in colour, but cut with typical Wilson vigour. The
earliest caps were rather crude ; they were replaced in the
late fifties by a smoother series (with a straight-tailed
instead of a round-tailed ' Q '), which was itself much
altered before the fount appeared in the 1772 specimen as
' Long Primer Roman No. 2 '. The lower case suffered
few changes, ' g ' with a down-turned instead of up-turned
ear being the most noticeable ; at the time of the change
(c. 1762) both forms are sometimes found side by side.

Quoufque tandem abutere, Catilina, patientia noftra ? quamdiu
nos etiam furor ifte tuus eludet ? quem ad finem fefe effrenata
jactabit audacia ? nihilne te nocturnum præfidium palatii, nihil
urbis vigiliæ, nihil timor populi, nihil confenfus bonorumomnium
nihil hic munitiffimus habendi fenatus locus, nihil horum ora
vultufque moverunt ? patere tua confilia non fentis ? conftrictam
jam omnium horum confcientia teneri conjurationem tuam non
vides ? quid proxima, quid fuperiore nocte egeris, ubi fueris,
quos convocaveris, quid confilii ceperis, quem noftrum ignorare
arbitraris ? O tempora, o mores ! Senatus hoc intelligit, conful

1772 : Wilson's specimen; note two forms of ' g '

RLP 2. A transitional face, wide and fairly heavily-stressed, this
second Long Primer first appeared in 1769 and remained in
occasional use until 1797. It was the Long Primer
Roman No. 1 ' of the 1772 specimen.

35

Quoufque tandem abutere, Catilina, patientia noftra? quamdiu nos etiam furor ifte tuus eludet? quem ad finem fefe effrenata jactabit audacia? nihilne te nocturnum præfidium
palatii, nihil urbis vigiliæ, nihil timor populi, nihil confenfus bonorum omnium, nihil hic munitiffimus habendi fenatus locus, nihil horum ora vultufque moverunt? patere tua
confilia non fentis? conftrictam jam omnium horum confcientia teneri conjurationem tuam non vides? quid proxima,
quid fuperiore nocte egeris, ubi fueris, quos convocaveris,

1772 : Wilson's specimen

RSP 1. Wilson's first Small Pica Roman, shown – with new
caps – in the 1772 specimen as ' Small Pica Roman No. 2 '.
Appeared first in 1751–2 (see NOTES to No. 231 below), and
was used as late as 1796, so outlasting RSP 2 (1766–86).
A large-faced type, fairly pale and narrow.

Quoufque tandem abutere, Catilina patientia noftra? quamdiu nos etiam furor ifte tuus eludet? quem ad finem fefe effrenata jactabit audacia? nihilne te nocturnum præfidium
palatii, nihil urbis vigiliæ, nihil timor populi, nihil confenfus bonorum omnium, nihil hic munitiffimus habendi fenatus locus, nihil horum ora vultufque moverunt? patere tua
confilia non fentis? conftrictam jam omnium horum confcientia teneri conjurationem tuam non vides? quid proxima,
quid fuperiore nocte egeris, ubi fueris, quos convocaveris,

1772 : Wilson's specimen

RSP 2. The second Small Pica Roman followed RSP 1 in 1766,
but was not used by Andrew Foulis after 1790. One of
the wide, heavily-stressed transitionals. Shown in the
specimen of 1772 as ' Small Pica Roman No. 1 '.

Paſſions they apply, theſe they endeavour to raiſe, and look upon as the Springs of their Suc-ceſs. Now when the Paſſions are not under the Government of a well informed Judgment, but gratified without the Approbation of Conſcience, they drive Men to all Follies; the Man is like a Ship at Sea in a Storm, without Helm, Captain, Compaſs, Sun or Stars; in ſuch a Caſe ſudden Tranſports, ſtrong Cryings, Convulſions and Floods of Tears are not ſtrange.

1742 : No. 17, Caldwell

RP X. A poor Pica Roman, original equipment at the Press in 1742, but used only in that and the following year. A narrow, ill-cut fount with a large x-height, inaccurately justified and already badly worn when Foulis acquired it. Origin uncertain, but probably late seventeenth-century Dutch or German.

Chriſt the Mediator, and the Holy Ghoſt the Guide and Sanctifier of mankind? Is it not be-yond all contradiction, a matter of unſpeakable importance, to have it confirmed to us by an in-fallible revelation, that this whole Univerſe is one vaſt and immortal empire, of which God is the King and Head; and that virtue and devoti-on are the great, the ſtanding, and everlaſting laws of this great kingdom, to which all rational be-ings ought to pay a voluntary ſubjection? Can

1742 : No. 23, Leechman

RP 1. Wilson's first Pica Roman. Original equipment in 1742, probably preceding RE 1 by a month or two, and therefore the first Wilson type ; although Wilson did not show it in a specimen, it can hardly have come from any other foundry. The least successful of the early group of founts, it was withdrawn from use after 1745. Uneven in cut, with serifs fiercely beaked and barbed, and strongly-stressed caps.

37

ſub eo defunctorum oſſa proponunt;
et unuſquiſque ſuo cadaveri inferias
affert, ſi quas velit. Quum autem
funeris efferendi dies venit, plauſ-
tra ' adducuntur, quae arcas ex cu-
preſſo factas ex ſingulis Tribubus
ſingulas portant. In his aut́em in-
ſunt oſſa ſingularum Tribuum, ex

1755 : No. 309, Thucydides ; early form

ubique ſequeremur. Quum vero editorum
alios, Lectionum ſanitatis nimis ſecuros, a-
lios conjecturis ſuis nimium indulgentes in-
venimus ; mutato conſilio, quae ubique op-
timae videbantur Lectiones undique collegimus ; ita tamen ut nullas admiſerimus

1760 : No. 383, Horace ; revised form

RP 2. A trim, restrained Pica Roman that was introduced in
1751, after a gap of five years during which no Roman of
this size had been used at the Foulis Press. During the
fifties it was much modified – especially in 1758 – was
equipped with new caps, and was apparently cast on a
slightly narrower body, with the result that when it
appears as ' Pica Roman No. 2 ' in the specimen of 1772
it scarcely seems to be the same type. And indeed it was
perhaps no more the same type than was George Washing-
ton's axe the same axe when it had been equipped first
with a new head and then with a new haft ; but, since
the process of change appears to have been gradual rather
than abrupt, it seems right to treat it as one fount rather
than several.
Original ' g ' with upturned ear replaced by one with a
downturned ear in 1758 ; new caps about a year later.
In regular use at the Press until 1767, and occasionally
later ; last seen in 1778.

38

Quoufque tandem abutere, Catilina, patientia noftra? quamdiu nos etiam furor ifte tuus eludet?
quem ad finem fefe effrenata jactabit audacia? nihilne te nocturnum præfidium palatii, nihil urbis
vigiliæ, nihil timor populi, nihil confenfus bonorum omnium, nihil hic munitiffimus habendi fenatus locus, nihil horum ora vultufque moverunt?
patere tua confilia non fentis? conftrictam jam
omnium horum confcientia teneri conjurationem

1772 : Wilson's specimen

RP 3. One of the wide, heavy transitionals. This Pica appeared
in 1769, and was last used in 1785 ; it matches the RE 3
of 1760. Shown in the 1772 specimen as ' Pica Roman
No. 1 '.

Quoufque tandem abutere, Catilina, patientia noftra? quamdiu etiam furor ifte tuus eludet? quem
ad finem fefe effrenata jactabit audacia nihilne te
nocturnum præfidium palatii, nihil urbis vigiliæ, nihil timor populi, nihil confenfus bonorum omnium,
nihil hic munitiffimus habendi fenatus locus, nihil
horum ora vultufque moverunt? patere tua confilia
non fentis? conftrictam jam omnium horum confcientia teneri conjurationem tuam non vides? quid

1772 : Wilson's specimen

RP 4. Shown in 1772 as ' Pica Roman No. 3 ', this fount was
first used at the Foulis Press in 1782 and continued to
appear until 1795. Still essentially a transitional, it is
considerably lighter and narrower – altogether less extreme
– than had been RP 3.

ΕΔΕΙ μέν, ὦ ἄνδρες Ἀθηναῖοι, τὰς λέγοντας ἅπαντας ἐν ὑμῖν,
μήτε πρὸς ἔχθραν ποιεῖσθαι λόγον μηδένα, μήτε πρὸς χάριν. ἀλλ'
ὃ βέλτιστον ἕκασός ἡγεῖτο, τοῦτ' ἀποφαίνεσθαι. ἄλλως τε κỳ περὶ
κοινῶν πραγμάτων κỳ μεγάλων ὑμῶν βκλευομένων, ἐπειδὴ δέ ἔνιοι
τὰ μὲν, φιλονικίᾳ, τὰ δὲ ἢ τινι δήποτ' αἰτίᾳ, προάγονται λέγειν,
ὑμᾶς, ὦ ἄνδρες Ἀθηναῖοι, τὰς πολλὰς δεῖ, πάντα τἄλλ' ἀφέντας,
ἅ τῇ πόλει νομίζετε συμφέρειν, ταῦτα κỳ ψηφίζεσθαι κỳ πράτζειν.
ἡ μὲν οὖν σπυδὴ, περὶ τῶν ἐν Χερρονήσω πραγμάτων ἐσὶ, κỳ τῆς

1786 : Wilson's specimen

GP. Pica Greek, the second of Wilson's 'Stephen's' Greeks.
Introduced in 1744, it was used frequently until 1795.
Shown in the specimen of 1786 as 'Pica Greek'. For
characteristics, see GGP, below.

239. Scire autem oportet, non dictionis
quoddam genus solum, sed res praeterea quaf-
dam epistolis unice congruere, Aristoteles
sane, qui praeter caeteros videtur consecutus
formam epistolarum, haec verba [in episto-
la quadam] habet, *Hoc autem ad te non scribo;*
non enim erat epistolae aptum.

1743 : No. 31, Demetrius

RE 1. This English Roman, probably Wilson's second type,
first appeared in 1742, a few months after RP 1. The best
of the early group of founts, it is strong and direct, at its
best set solid. Ruggedly cut, with a very large x-height.
Discontinued after 1755, and never shown by Wilson,
although it must have come from his Foundry.

great minds, your Grace may be blind to
your own merit, and imagine I am com-
plimenting, or doing fomething worfe,
whilft I am only giving your juft character; for which reafon, however fond
I am of fo noble a theme, I fhall de-
cline attempting it. Only this I muft
beg leave to fay, your Grace cannot be
enough admired for the univerfal learn-

1758 : No. 343, Aubert

RE 2. Something of a comedown after RE 1, the second English
Roman is a small-faced fount, narrow and lacking the
power of its predecessor. The letters sit uneasily together,
and the general effect is rather weak. Appeared first in
Foulis books in 1748, was used fairly regularly until 1772,
then not again until the period 1793–6. Not shown by
Wilson, but certainly from his Foundry.

Quoufque tandem abutere, Catilina, patientia noftra? quamdiu nos etiam furor
ifte tuus;eludet? quem ad finem fefe effrenata jactabit audacia? nihilne te nocturnum præfidium palatii, nihil urbis vigiliæ, nihil timor populi, nihil confenfus
bonorum omnium, nihil hic munitiffimus
habendi fenatus locus, nihil horum ora

1772 : Wilson's specimen

RE 3. This startling English Roman first appeared in 1760.
Baskerville's influence is obvious, but Wilson has outdone
the master in the width, the weight and even the size of
the face. (It hardly seems possible that RE 2 and RE 3
can even technically be the same size of type, although such
is in fact the case.) I think myself that, with its large
x-height, generous width and clean execution, this elegant
fount carries out Baskerville's ideas better even than did
Baskerville himself ; certainly I find it the most beautiful
of Wilson's Romans, with the exception of its direct
descendant RDP, which is equally fine. Shown in 1772
as ' English Roman No. 1 ' ; not used at the Foulis Press
after 1783.

Quoufque tandem abutere, Catilina, patientia noftra? quamdiu nos etiam furor ifte tuus eludet? quem ad finem fefe effrenata jactabit audacia? nihilne te nocturnum præfidium palatii, nihil urbis vigiliæ, nihil timor populi, nihil confenfus bonorum omnium, nihil hic munitiffimus habendi fenatus locus, nihil horum ora vultufque moverunt? patere tua confilia non

1772: Wilson's specimen

RE 4. Essentially a scaled-down RE 3, this fount has lost the assurance and elegance of its prototype. (Possibly RE 3 was felt to be too extreme in its approach for general use, and RE 4 was cut to replace it.) L.c. 'g' very large. Shown by Wilson as 'English Roman No. 2' in his specimen of 1772, but not used at the Foulis Press until 1773; continued there until 1794.

latera ab angulis trianguli
ipſis oppoſitis, parallelae ⟨
eveniet ſi vice rectarum B
quae per punctum quodvis
tur ipſis BC, BG, ſc. ductis
CR parallelis, erit HK ad

1749 : No. 125, Apollonius

RGP 1. The first Great Primer Roman, and the last of the
crudely-cut faces of Group 1. Without the distinction of
RE 1, but nevertheless a pleasant, vigorous type. Medium-
large x-height. Used at the Foulis Press from 1745 to
1757 ; not shown by Wilson, but it must have come from
his foundry.

Quouſque tandem abutere, Catilina, patientia noſtra? quamdiu nos etiam furor iſte tuus eludet? quem ad finem ſe-
ſe effrenata jactabit audacia? nihilne te
nocturnum praeſidium palatii, nihil urbis vigiliae, nihil timor populi, nihil
A B C D E F G H I J K L M N O

1772 : Wilson's specimen ; revised form

RGP 2. The second Great Primer Roman, which appeared in
1755, was very different from the first, but also good in
its own way. A clean, light-coloured type of average
width, it already gives a hint of the ' modernity ' that was
to burst out five years later in RE 3 ; had Wilson seen the
Great Primer shown by Baskerville in his various *Virgil*
specimens of 1754 ? Shown, considerably refined, as
' [Great Primer Roman] No. 2 ' in the specimen of 1772 ;
used at the Foulis Press until 1784. (Note that the Foulises
never bought Wilson's transitional ' Great Primer
[Roman] No. 1 ', shown in the 1772 specimen, and also,
as ' Paragon Roman ', in the specimen of 1786.)

44

ΕΔΕΙ μὲν, ὦ ἄνδρες Ἀθηναῖοι τὺς λέγοντας ἅ-
παντας ἐν ὑμῖν, μήτε πρὸς ἔχθραν ποιεῖσθαι λόγον μηδένα, μήτε πρὸς χάριν· ἀλλ', ὃ βέλτιςον
ἕκαςος ἡγεῖτο, τοῦτ' ἀποφαίνεσθαι· ἄλλως τε κỳ
περὶ κοινῶν πραγμάτων κỳ μεγάλων ὑμῶν βυλε-
υομένων. ἐπειδὴ δ᾽ ἔνιοι, τὰ μὲν, φιλονικία, τὰ
ΑΒΓΔΕΖΗΘΙΚΛΜΝΞΟΠΡΣΤ

1786 : Wilson's specimen; smaller caps

GGP. Appearing in 1743, Great Primer was the first and perhaps the best of the three ' Stephen's ' Greeks cut by
Wilson for the Foulis Press (the other two being GP, 1744
and GB, 1748). They are spidery but well-disciplined ren-
derings of Garamond's *grec du roi* introduced by Robert
Estienne in 1544. In Wilson's founts ligatures, etc. are
relatively few : in GP – the fount that has most of them
– there are only 8 alternative sorts and 18 ligatures and
contractions. GGP was shown in 1786 as ' Great Primer
Greek ', and was used regularly at the Foulis Press for
fifty-five years, from 1743 until 1797. The original capitals, which were too large, were replaced by a smaller set
in 1746–7, but there were no other major changes.

45

Quoufque tandem abutere, Catilina, patientia noftra? quamdiu nos etiam furor ifte tuus e-
ludet? quem ad finem fefe effrenata jactabit audacia? nihilne te nocturnum præfidium palatii, nihil urbis vigiliæ, nihil ti-

1772 : Wilson's specimen; revised form

RDP. With his two Double Picas, Roman and Greek, Wilson
reached the height of his achievement. An attempt at
the RDP was made by 1763 ; but after one brief showing
in that year, the type was withdrawn, to reappear –
altered in various details – in 1768. In design the face
descends directly from the RE 3 of 1760, q.v. Shown in
1772 as ' D. Pica Roman ', and used at the Foulis Press
until 1796.

λοποννησίων, ἡ νόσος ἤρ-
ξατο εὐθὺς. ᾗ ἐς μὲν Πε-
λοπόννησον ἐκ ἐσῆλθεν,
ὅ,τι ᾗ ἄξιον ἐπεῖν, ἐπενέ-
ματο δὲ Ἀθήνας μὲν μά-
λιϛα, ἔπειτα δὲ ᾗ τῶν ἄλ-
λων χωρίων τὰ πολυαν-
θρωπόταλα. ταῦτα μὲν τὰ
κατὰ τ᾿ νόσον γενόμενα.

1755: No. 309, Thucydides

GDP 1. As with the Roman Double Pica, a Greek type of this size was attempted unsuccessfully and later altered ; but, whereas RDP was only touched-up here and there, GDP 1 was entirely recut from end to end to become GDP 2. It may be seen, however, that this was done more to improve the detail of the fount than to alter its character. GDP 1 first appeared in 1751, and was withdrawn five years later in favour of GDP 2, q.v.

ΕΔΕΙ μὲν, ὦ ἄνδρες Ἀθηναῖοι, τὺς
λέγοντας ἅπαντας ἐν ὑμῖν, μήτε
πρὸς ἔχθραν ποιεῖσθαι λόγον μηδένα,
μήτε πρὸς χάριν. ἀλλ', ὃ βέλτιςον
ἕκαςος ἡγεῖτο τοῦτ' ἀποφαίνεςθαι·
ἄλλως τε κ̀ περὶ κοινῶν πραγμάτων
ΑΒΓΔΕΖΗΘΙΚΛΜΝΞΟΠ

1786 : Wilson's specimen

GDP 2. The recut Double Pica Greek was first used in the
Foulis folio Homer (1756–8), and sporadically thereafter
until 1795. Shown in Wilson's 1786 specimen as ' Glaſgow
Homer Greek '. A magnificent achievement, showing in
its heavy stress a ' modern ' approach to type design which
was unique when the prototype (GDP 1) appeared in 1751.
Very few ligatures and contractions by eighteenth-century
standards ; upright caps. (Note that the Wilson Foundry
later produced six other sizes of Greek of related design –
the English, Small Pica, Long Primer, Brevier No. 1,
Minion and Nonpareil Greeks of the 1786 specimen – none
of which were bought for the Foulis Press.)

Wilson's italics need not be described in detail. The earlier ones were more or less faithful copies of Caslon's designs; and later on a thinner, more refined italic was developed to accompany the later romans. None of them, however, showed any radical departure from tradition.

Ornament of any kind was rarely used at the Foulis Press, except in the period 1742–7; then a couple of varieties of printers' flowers and a handful of blocks (mostly of poor quality) were used in a few books. They are described on p. 61 below.

The following points may also be mentioned. Catchwords: from 1747 the Foulises printed many books without catchwords; catchwords were never dropped altogether at the Press, but they became thereafter the exception rather than the rule, appearing chiefly in the more conventionally-printed English books. Long ſ: a few books, mostly Latin classics, were printed without long ſ; the first book to be so set was the *Virgil* of 1758 (No. 360), but this interesting innovation never became the Foulises' regular practice.[1] Late appearance of RE 1 and RP 2, possibly standing type (No. 526, Foulis, 1771). Andrew Foulis the younger and the stereotype process of Alexander Tilloch (No. 658, 1783–4). See also the Index, s.v. ' Printing type '.

1. Note that the experiments of dropping catchwords and long ſ were both made before the appearance of Capell's *Prolusions* in 1760.

§ 6. Publication, etc.

Robert Foulis set up as a university bookseller in the College before he became a printer; and he and his brother continued as booksellers for the rest of their lives. Andrew Foulis the younger also sold books in the College until he was turned out in 1795–6. A large part of their stock presumably consisted of books they had printed themselves, but they also retailed and auctioned books printed elsewhere. Likewise, their bookshop and auction-room were probably the major outlets for their own books.

I know of only one book printed for, but not by, Foulis after 1742. This is a Celsus, *De Re Medica*, L, 1766, of which the imprint reads in shortened form: ' Glasguae: Excudebat Gulielmus Bell. Veneunt apud Foulis, Gilmour et Duncan: Edinburgi, Kincaid et Bell, Balfour, Fleming, Drummond, et Donaldson: Londini, apud Eundem, Millar, et Wilson. MDCCLXVI.' [1]

As was usual at the time, the Foulises sometimes shared the costs of publication of the books they printed with other booksellers. In only a minority of their books were the names of such partners

1. ' Eundem ' presumably refers to [Alexander] Donaldson, who operated as a bookseller in both Edinburgh and London (H. R. Plomer, G. H. Bushnell and E. R. McC. Dix. *A Dictionary of the Printers and Booksellers . . . 1726 to 1775* (Oxford, 1932), pp. 77–8, 299–300). The printer William Bell is more of a puzzle; he does not appear in the *Dictionary*, or in R. H. Carnie and R. P. Doig, ' Scottish Printers and Booksellers 1668–1775: A Supplement ', *Studies in Bibliography*, Vol. xii (Charlottesville, Virginia, 1959), pp. 131–159.

mentioned in the imprints,[1] but it is clear from newspaper advertisements that in a number of other cases Foulis books were published and sold by other booksellers not named in the imprints.

Publication by subscription was practised by the Foulises (more often by the insolvent Andrew the younger than by his father and uncle), but it does not seem to have been more than an occasional resort. No separate Proposals for such subscription books appear to have survived, although some were certainly printed.[2] Details of subscription arrangements will be found in Appendix A, and in Nos. 375 and 480. For the Thucydides of 1759 (No. 375) subscriptions were invited *after* publication.

Title-pages cannot always be relied upon. Two ' old poems ' of 1755 (*Gill Morice* and *Young Waters*, Nos. 301 and 302) both have second issues which are called on the title-pages ' second edition '; while Boswell's *Dorando* (No. 462) not only had ' second edition ' printed on the title-page of part of the first edition, but also had a London imprint which was intended to mislead.[3]

Many Foulis books were advertised in the Glasgow newspapers, and a few further afield,[4] but no consistent advertising policy appears to have been followed. The brothers advertised a considerable num-

1. See Index, s.v. ' Booksellers and printers '.
2. See Index, s.v. ' Proposals ', and Appendix A. It is reasonable to assume that all the subscription books were preceded by printed Proposals, but I have not made separate entries for Proposals unless I have found other evidence for their existence.
3. See Appendix B, Letter 2, below; and Index, s.v. ' Publication, methods of, false imprint ', etc., for further examples.
4. For instance in the London newspapers and magazines ; and I have also come across Foulis advertisements in Dublin and Norwich papers.

ber of their books during the later seventeen-forties in the *Glasgow Courant* – of which they were almost certainly the printers – but the volume of their advertising declined gradually thereafter until, by the seventeen-sixties, it had reached negligible proportions. The *Courant* advertisements of the late seventeen-forties and the early seventeen-fifties were occasionally displayed in ' title-page style ', sometimes printed from the actual type used for printing the title-page of the book concerned (see, for instance, Nos. 128, Davies, 1749 and 267, Theocritus, 1753). I have found scarcely any advertisements for books printed by Andrew Foulis the younger.

A good deal of evidence survives of both the wholesale and the retail prices of Foulis books, which is incorporated in the bibliography.[1] It is clear that the Foulises' prices varied very much indeed. Expressed in terms of pence per sheet, ordinary books – that is to say, books that were neither ' luxury ' editions nor especially difficult to set – retailed in the middle of the century for as much as $3\frac{1}{2}d$. and for as little as $\frac{2}{3}d$. Naturally the fine-paper copies were at the top of the scale and the common-paper at the bottom; fine- and common-paper copies of the same book were generally separated in price by a factor of

1. The chief sources are: *Wholesale:* the catalogue of the Foulises' stock-in-trade prepared in 1777 after the death of Robert and Andrew Foulis (*BQ*, No. 614). *Retail:* (1) The Foulises' newspaper advertisements, chiefly in *GJ* and *GC*. (2) Robert Foulis's retail catalogue of 1776 in *CP* (No. 595). (3) The catalogue of Foulis books published in 1779, as part of *Bibliotheca Mooriana*, by the Edinburgh bookseller and paper-warehouseman James Spotiswood (or Spottiswood), who bought most if not all of the stock listed in *BQ*. Spotiswood's prices are in many cases different from the Foulises' retail prices, and I have not listed them in the bibliography unless other sources have failed.

approximately two. By the end of our period, when it had become fashionable to collect the classics on large paper, the Press's ' luxury ' editions sometimes reached fantastic prices: Andrew Foulis's folio *Aeschylus* of 1795 (No. 699) retailed at 8*d*. per sheet for the ordinary paper, and at 2*s*. 2¾*d*. for the fine.[1] The discount allowed to the trade also fluctuated widely; but for the more substantial books it was generally around 25%. On one occasion Foulis announced that the retail price of a book would be increased after a certain period of time had elapsed (No. 77, Steele, 1746).

Robert and Andrew Foulis habitually carried a large stock of their own books. The stock catalogue of 1777 is a document of formidable length, which begins with 9815 volumes of English poets in duodecimo, fine, at 9*d*. wholesale and 17,501 volumes, common, at 7*d*.; these first two entries alone represent a capital investment of £880. Moreover, many of the books still in stock in the seventeen-seventies had been printed thirty and more years earlier. The extent and character of its stock-in-trade goes far to explain why the firm was insolvent at the time of Robert Foulis's death.

As well as printing and selling books, the Foulises bound them. By 1770 their bindery occupied two College rooms, which suggests a considerable volume of work. Although the prices quoted for their books generally referred, except in the early years, to copies in sheets or quires, it is nevertheless most likely that they followed the normal eighteenth-century practice of selling copies over the counter in ' trade '

1. The cost of living had of course begun to rise by the seventeen-nineties, but not to anything like the extent suggested by these prices.

bindings. I have come across no signed example of a Foulis binding, but it is possible that a certain design involving crosses in spine panels was commonly used at the Foulis bindery; at any rate it is found on the covers of a suggestively large number of mid-century Foulis books.[1]

1. There is a plate illustrating a few such bindings in Part 1 of ' Early Work '.

EXPLANATION OF THE BIBLIOGRAPHY

Arrangement. The bibliography, which is generally chronological in plan, is divided into three main parts:

Part I: Books printed for Robert Foulis, 1740–2
Part II: Books printed by Robert Foulis, and by Robert and Andrew Foulis, 1742–76
Part III: Books printed by Andrew Foulis the younger, 1776–1806

The entries are ordered chronologically by years, and then alphabetically by authors within each year. (It will be seen that there are two alphabetical sequences for each of the years of change, 1742 and 1776.)

The entries are numbered consecutively from 1 to 706 (including 18 extra entries and 1 deleted entry), each entry referring as a rule to a single edition; in certain special cases more than a single edition is included in one entry,[1] but no entry refers only to the subdivision of an edition.

As far as possible the information contained in each entry is presented in the same way and in the same order. There is one exception: in Part I (books printed for but not by Robert Foulis) I have not given detailed descriptions of the paper and type used.

To turn now to the individual sections within the entries:

HEADLINE. This consists of the number of the

1. See, for instance, Nos. 65, 75, 319, 460 and 658.

57

entry, together with the author or other heading, short title and date of the book concerned. Also indicated here is the main language of the book, if other than English, or if translated into English from another language. The following abbreviations are used: E (English), F (French), G (Greek), I (Italian), L (Latin).

TITLE-PAGE. Full quasi-facsimile transcriptions, according to the rules laid down in Fredson Bowers, *Principles of Bibliographical Description* (Princeton, New Jersey, 1949), chapter 4. Measurements of the lengths of rules, of plate-marks, etc., are given in millimetres. Swash italic caps are not transcribed. Quotations are not transcribed, but a note is given of the total number of lines involved, *including the reference if any*. The following brackets are used:

[ ] Inserted matter, not in the original.
( ), [ ] Brackets used in the original.
⟨ ⟩ Matter conjecturally restored.

FORMULA. The format is given first in the eighteenth-century terminology which is still in use today (paper size + folding). This followed by a detailed statement of the construction of the book expressed in Bowers's adaptation of Greg's formulary (*Principles*, chapter 5). Half-titles, errata and advertisement leaves, etc., often removed by binders, are noted separately, as are any special signatures; and brief descriptive notes are given wherever the algebra becomes particularly complex.

Also included in this section are complete registers of *Press-figures*. They are presented in an abbreviated form, and the following two conventions are used (in this sub-section *only*): (1) all press-figures are assumed to be on the verso of the leaf unless the contrary is stated (*N.B.* Elsewhere, as usual, the recto of the leaf is referred to unless the contrary is stated). (2) The abbreviation ' A1 . . . D1 ' (etc.) means that a certain press-figure occurs on the versos of each of the leaves A1, B1, C1 and D1 (etc.).

Still under *Formula* is included a note of any plates inserted in addition to the letterpress sections.

PAPER. Noted here are (1) quality; (2) watermarks, if any; and (3) dimensions. The name of the size of the paper, which has already been given at the beginning of *Formula*, is not repeated. All paper is assumed to be laid; white; and not unusually thin, unless the contrary is stated.

(1) The following five terms are used to indicate quality: good (really fine, and usually heavy, writing papers, rarely used); medium-good (the normal ' fine quality ' writing paper); medium (middle-grade papers, including printings, such as were widely used in eighteenth-century book printing); medium-poor (rougher papers, often of poor colour, standard in ' common-paper ' issues); and poor (really bad papers, full of fluff and heavily discoloured). Estimation of paper quality is a subjective affair, but I have tried to be consistent; and I hope that users of the bibliography will come to see what I mean by these terms.

(2) The main watermark is indicated by an arabic figure, which is separated by a shilling stroke from a roman figure indicating the countermark. The following key includes Heawood numbers to indicate in a general way the *most usual* forms taken by the marks.[1]

1. See Edward Heawood, *Watermarks* (Hilversum, 1950).

Main watermarks

1. British Royal Arms (Heawood 448)
2. City of London Arms (Heawood 461)
3. Britannia (Heawood 201, 208, 209, 214)
4. Pro Patria (Heawood 3700, 3702)
5. Vryheit Lion (Heawood 3148).
6. Post-horn (Heawood 2686, 2722)
7. Fleur-de-lis in a crowned shield (Heawood 1810)
8. Strasbourg Bend (Heawood 72, 73)
9. Plain Fleur-de-lis (Heawood 1540)

Countermarks

    i. I V
    ii. L V G
    iii. G R
    iv. G R, crowned
    v. G R, crowned, in wreath and circle
    vi. I V, crowned, in wreath and circle
    vii. J W, monogram, in circle

Watermarks and countermarks not included in this list are described in words, again separated by a shilling stroke.

(3) Dimensions are given in inches of the *uncut, unfolded* sheet; no dimensions are given unless an uncut copy has been seen.

TYPE. Noted here are all the text types used in each book for setting more than a word or two of matter, the main text type first. The following abbreviations are used:

RB	Brevier Roman	RE	English Roman
GB	Brevier Greek	RGP	Great Primer Roman
RLP	Long Primer Roman	GGP	Great Primer Greek
RSP	Small Pica Roman	RDP	Double Pica Roman
RP	Pica Roman	GDP	Double Pica Greek
GP	Pica Greek		

Descriptions of the individual founts of type (RB 1, RB 2, etc.) will be found in the Introduction, pp. 33-48 above.

The two sorts of printers' flowers and the 15

blocks used (almost exclusively in the seventeen-forties) are noted here; and, finally, there are notes on any other points of typographical interest (e.g. the position of the Latin translation in a Greek text; lack of long ſ; and, for the year 1747 only, the use of catchwords).

Flowers[1] 1 Circular flower-head, 4½ mm. diameter, 1 sort.
       2 Vignette arabesque, 7×8 mm., 2 sorts (mirror images).

Blocks   1 Rectangular headpiece, a head in the centre, in double frame, 21 × 65 mm.
       2 Vignette tailpiece, a basket of fruit, 23 × 27 mm.
       3 Crude rectangular headpiece, wavy white line on black, dotted frame, 13 × 61 mm.
       4 Small factotum in dotted frame, 13½ mm. square, dots on right-hand side wearing away.
       5 Vignette tailpiece, festoon with swags and side tassels, 23 × 30 mm.
       6 Tailpiece, 90° segment, conventional leaves with swag, 37 × 46 mm.
       7 Vignette tailpiece, similar to Block 5, but smaller and coarser, the right-hand tassel broken, 19 × 24 mm.
       8 Vignette headpiece, trumpet motif, 21 × 17 mm.
       9 Rectangular headpiece in double frame, conventional foliage with cherubs, 36 × 123 mm.
      10 Drop-capital S, 19 mm. square.
      11 Drop-capital R, 19 mm. square.
      12 Drop-capital W, 10 mm. square.
      13 Drop-capital P, 20 mm. square.
      14 British Royal Arms, vignette, 59 × 78 mm.
      15 Rectangular headpiece, in double frame, central thistle-motif, 32 × 85 mm.

VARIANTS. Variant issues and states of the edition are described next, with further notes as necessary on *Title-page*, *Formula*, *Paper* and *Type*; the lack of further notes indicates no change in the sections concerned. The variants are arranged in what appears to have been the usual order of printing:

1. See No. 423, TYPE, for another flower not used elsewhere by Foulis.

octavo before quarto or duodecimo; quarto before folio; fine paper before common; and Greek texts with Latin translations before plain Greek.

NOTES. Details, where available, of publication dates, prices and stock; the abbreviations most frequently used are *GC* (*The Glasgow Courant*), *GJ* (*The Glasgow Journal*), *BQ* (*Books in Quires*, the stock catalogue of 1777, No. 614), *CP* (*Catalogue of Pictures*, 1776, No. 595) and Duncan (W. J. Duncan, *Notices and Documents* [etc.], 1886).[1] For editions of which no copies have been seen, entries necessarily consist only of *Headline* and *Notes*.

Where the reference ' (*GJ*) ' or ' (*GC*) ' is given without a date, the date of the issue concerned is to be taken from the immediately preceding note. The series of duodecimo ' English Poets ', which appears to have begun with the *Paradise Lost* of 1766 (No. 454) and to have ended with the editions of Collins and Hammond, Gray, Lyttelton and Mason of 1777 (Nos. 612, 618, 620 and 622), does not have the prices given in the Notes to each edition; but it is known from *BQ* (p. 1) that the issues on fine and common paper wholesaled at 9*d*. and 7*d*. per volume respectively; and from numerous advertisements that the fine-paper issues retailed at 1*s*. per volume.

COPIES. At least one copy of each edition, and of each variant where there are any, is located. *All* the Foulis books in the Mitchell Library, Glasgow, and in the British Museum are listed here; but if a particular edition or variant is not in either of these libraries, then the location of a copy elsewhere is given.

Standard abbreviations from the revised *S.T.C.* are used, which are listed above on p. 10.

1. For full details, see the list of abbreviations, p. 9 above.

PART I

BOOKS PRINTED

FOR

ROBERT FOULIS

1740-1742

1740   Foulis, Robert, *A Catalogue of Books Imported* **1**

A | CATALOGUE | OF | BOOKS | Newly imported from abroad: Containing | THE fcarceft Editions of almoft all | the GREEK and ROMAN AU-|THORS; and likewife many of | the beft PHILOLOGICAL, MA-|THEMATICAL, FRENCH, ITALIAN and SPANISH Authors. | THE BOOKS are moftly printed by R. and H. | STEPHENS, VASCOSAN, TURNEBUS, COLI-|NÆUS, MOREL, CRAMOISSY, the ALDI, GJUN-|TÆ, WECHELS, Typis REGIIS, LOUVRE Edi-|tions, PLANTIN, ELZEVIR, &c. | THE loweft Price of each BOOK is printed, and any Gentlemen | who want to purchafe, are defired to give in, or direct fpeedily | their Com miffions to Baillie GAVIN HAMILTON, Bookfeller | in *Edinburgh*, or to ROBERT FOULIS, at his Chamber in the | College of *Glafgow*. | [*plain rule, 81*] | ALSO a CATALOGUE of Ancient MANU-| SCRIPTS, chiefly LATIN and ARABICK; and 600 | or 800 *Roman* MEDALS, all Copper, except an | *Otho*, which is in Silver. | [*plain rule, 80*] | Printed in the Year MDCCXL. | *The Price of the* CATALOGUE *is Sixpence, which will be dif-|compted to any who buy to the Value of a Crown.*]

FORMULA: Small Crown 8⁰ in fours: π1 A–P⁴(-P4).

NOTES: An ' advertisement ' on π1ᵛ reads: ' The Books are upheld perfect, and in good Order, and are to be paid upon Delivery. Thofe who buy to the Value of 10 *L.* may, if required have three Months Credit, upon granting Bills.

' Bookfellers who purchafe, fhall have all the Encourage-ment the Seller can afford.'

This appears to be a catalogue of part of the collection of books, etc., made by Robert and Andrew Foulis during their journey abroad in 1739.

Price: 6*d*. (title-page).

COPIES: G4.

1741   Burnet, Gilbert, *Life of Rochester* **2** †

NOTES: Not seen. Listed by Duncan (p. 49, No. 4) as ' Bifhop Burnet's Life of John, Earl of Rochefter, 12mo.' Advertised in *GJ* for 26 October 1761 at 1*s.* 2*d*., bound.

† 3 Cicero, *De Natura Deorum*, L 1741

M. TULLII CICERONIS | DE | NATURA DEORUM | *LIBRI TRES.* | ACCEDUNT | Boherii, Davisii & aliorum | Infigniores LECTIONES variantes | Et Conjecturae. | [*plain double rule, 76 and 77*] | *GLASGUAE,* | Typis Academicis. | Cura & fumptibus Roberti Foulis; proftant Lon-|dini apud Andream Millar Bibliopolam in | vico dicto *The Strand* exadverfum D. Clementis aedem. | M DCC XLI.

FORMULA: [? Crown] 8⁰: π^2 A–I⁸ K⁶ (C4 *signed* 'D4', D4 *signed* 'D3'; A3 *unsigned*).

VARIANTS: Issued on three sizes of paper. *BQ* (p. 3) specifies Demy, Crown and Pot; but in fact the largest size, of which I have seen an uncut copy, is certainly Printing Medium, while the other two are, to judge from cut dimensions, Printing Demy and Small Crown. All these papers are of medium to poor quality, the largest being the worst, and the middle size the best.

NOTES: Presumably printed by Alexander Miller, Foulis's predecessor at the University Press.

Prices: Wholesale: 'd[emy]', 9*d.*; 'c[rown]', 8*d.*; 'p[ot]', 6*d.* (*BQ* 3). Retail: (? size), 1*s.* 6*d.* bound ; large paper, 2*s.* bound (advertisement in No. 21 (Hutcheson, 1742)).

Stock in 1777: Demy, 33 copies; Crown, 14 copies; Pot, 44 copies (*BQ* 3).

COPIES: G4 (largest issue), L (the other two issues).

4 Leechman, William, *The Temper of a Minister,* 1741 *a Sermon*

The Temper, Character, *and* Duty | *of a* Minister *of the* Gospel. | [*plain rule, 76*] | A | SERMON | Preached before the | SYNOD | OF | *GLALGOW* [*sic*] *and AIR*; | At Glasgow, *April 7th,* 1741. | [*plain rule, 76*] | By *WILLIAM LEECHMAN* M.A. | Minister of *Beith.* | [*plain rule 78*] | *GLASGOW,* | Printed for Robert Foulis, within the | College, and fold by him and the | Bookfellers in *Edinburgh* and *Glafgow.* | Price Six-Pence.

FORMULA: [? Crown] 8⁰ in fours: π1 A–F4.

NOTES: *Publication*: published between 7 April 1741 (the date of the sermon) and 5 October 1741 (the date of an advertisement for the second edition).

Price: Retail: 6*d.* (title-page).

COPIES: G4, L.

1741   Leechman, William, *The Temper of a Minister*, **5**
a Sermon

The TEMPER, CHARACTER, *and* DUTY | *of a* MINISTER *of the*
GOSPEL. | [*plain rule, 75*] | A | SERMON | PREACHED BEFORE
THE | SYNOD | of | *GLASGOW and AIR*; | At GLASGOW,
April, 7th 1741. | [*plain rule, 75*] | By *WILLIAM LEECHMAN*
M.A. | MINISTER *of Beith.* | [*plain rule, 77*] | The SECOND
EDITION. | [*plain double rule, 75 and 74*] | *GLASGOW,* | Printed
for ROBERT FOULIS, within the | COLLEGE, and fold by him
and the | Bookfellers in *Edinburgh* and *Glafgow.* | [PRICE SIX-
PENCE.]
FORMULA: [? Crown] 8⁰ in fours: A–F⁴ (A2 *signed* ' A ', A3
sometimes signed ' A2 ').
NOTES: *Publication*: published by 5 October 1741 (*GJ*).
Price: Retail: 6*d.* (title-page).
COPIES: L.

1741   Mears, John, *A Catechism* **6**
A | CATECHISM: | OR, AN | INSTRUCTION | In the
CHRISTIAN | RELIGION, | By Way of | QUESTION and ANSWER.
| [*plain rule, 75*] | In THREE PARTS. | [*plain rule, 75*] | [*two columns
of contents, 5 lines each, separated by a vertical plain double rule,
15*] | [*plain rule, 77*] | To which is added, | A Short CATECHISM
for the Ufe of Children, | being an Abridgment of the larger
one. | [*plain rule, 77*] | By the Revᵈ JOHN MEARS, M.A. an eminent
Mi-|nifter of a Diffenting Congregation at *Dublin.* | *GLASGOW:*
| Printed for ROBERT FOULIS, within the College; and | fold,
at *Edinburgh*, by Meff. *Hamilton* and *Balfour*; and, at | *London*,
by *A. Miller*, in the *Strand.* M DCC XLI.
FORMULA: [? Pot] 8⁰: A–C⁸ D².
NOTES: *Publication*: published by 26 October 1741 (*GJ*).
Price: Retail: 3*d.* stitched (*GJ* 26 October 1741).
COPIES: L.

1741–2   Mears, John, *A Catechism* **7**
NOTES: Not seen. Foulis published the first edition of this
book in October 1741 and the third sometime in 1742; presumably he also published a second edition.

8 Phaedrus, *Aesop's Fables,* L   1741

PHAEDRI, | AUGUSTI LIBERTI, | FABULARUM | AESOPIARUM | LIBRI QUINQUE: | Ex Editione | BUR MANNI. | [*plain double rule, 56*] | *GLASGUAE:* | Typis Roberti Urie & Soc. Curâ & im-|penfis Roberti Foulis. Proftant apud | Gavinum Hamilton & Johannem | Balfour, Biblio polas *Edinburgenfes.* | [*plain rule, 16*] | MDCCXLI.

FORMULA: [? Post] 12⁰: πI A–C¹² (–C12; B8 *signed* ' C2 ', B10 *signed* ' C4 ', C9 *signed* ' D3 ', *presumably relics of signing for the issues in* 18⁰).

VARIANTS: Issue in 18⁰, fine paper, not seen (advertisement No. 21).

Issue in 18⁰, small paper:
Formula: (?) Foolscap 18⁰ πI A¹² B⁶ C¹² D⁶(–D6).
Issue on vellum, in 18⁰:
Formula: (*as 18⁰ on paper*).
Vellum: Rather stiff and heavy, size of sheet at least $16\frac{1}{2}$ × $13\frac{1}{4}$ in.

NOTES: *Prices:* Retail: 12⁰, fine paper, bound, 1s.; 18⁰, fine paper, bound, 8d.; 18⁰, small paper, bound, 6d. (advertisement in No. 21).

COPIES: G⁴ (12⁰), L (12⁰, and 18⁰ vellum), G² (18⁰).

9 Ramsay, Andrew Michael, *A Plan of Education* 1741

A | PLAN | OF | EDUCATION | [*plain rule, 74*] | By the Chevalier *RAMSAY.* | [*plain rule, 76*] | *The Third EDITION, correƈted accord-*|*ing to a genuine Manufcript.* | [*plain double rule, 74*] | *GLASGOW,* | Printed for ROBERT FOULIS, | within the College; and fold by Meff. | Hamilton and Balfour, in *Edin-*|*burgh.* MDCCXLI.

FORMULA: Crown 12⁰ in fours (*sic*): A–C⁴ E².

NOTES: *Publication:* published by 26 October 1741 (*GJ*).
Price: Retail: 3d. (*GJ* 26 October 1741).
COPIES: G⁴.

10 Juvenal, *Satires,* with Persius, *Satires,* L   1742

D. JUNII JUVENALIS | ET | A. PERSII FLACCI | SATYRÆ, | Ex Editionibus emendatiffimis | HENNINII & CASAU BONI. | Ad finem adjiciuntur Lectiones varian-|tes in

JUVENALE, ex Codicibus MSS. & | Excufis. | [*plain double rule, 72 and 70*] | *GLASGUAE,* | Sumptibus ROBERTI FOULIS; venales proftant *Edin-|burgi* apud G. HAMILTON & J. BALFOUR, *Londoni* | apud A. MILLAR, exadverfum D. Clementis Ædem, | in vico dicto *The Strand.* M DCC XLII.

FORMULA: Foolscap 8⁰: π1 A–X⁴ Y² (A3 *signed* 'A4'; X2 *unsigned*).

VARIANTS: An advertisement in No. 21 (Hutcheson, 1742) mentions issues on fine and coarse paper. One issue only seen, on a medium-good quality Amsterdam Arms paper, which is probably fine.

There is another setting of the title-page, reading as follows:

D. JUNII JUVENALIS | ET | A. PERSII FLACCI | SATYRAE | Ex EDITIONIBUS emendatiſſimis | HENNINII ET CASAU BONI. | Ad finem adjiciuntur LECTIONES VARIANTES in | JUVENALE, ex Codicibus MSS. et Excufis. | GLASGUAE: | Sumptibus ROBERTI FOULIS; venales proftant | *Edinburgi* apud G. HAMILTON et J. BALFOUR, | LONDINI apud A. MILLAR, exadverfum D. Cle-|mentis Aedem, in vico dicto *The Strand.* 1742.

NOTES: Printed in a Small Pica italic. *BQ* (p. 1) lists 386 copies remaining in stock in 1777, the entry reading 'Juvenalis et Perfii fatyrae, f. 8vo. (Italic)'; price 1*s.* in Spotiswood (p. 87).

COPIES: G⁴ (second title-page), L (first title-page).

1742   Mears, John, *A Catechism* **11** †

A | CATECHISM: | OR, AN | INSTRUCTION | In the CHRISTIAN | RELIGION, | By Way of | QUESTION and ANSWER. | [*plain rule, 73*] | In THREE PARTS. | [*plain rule, 73*] | [*two columns of contents, 5 lines each, separated by a vertical plain double rule, 15*] | [*plain rule, 70*] | To which is added, | A Short CATECHISM for the Ufe of Children, | being an Abridgment of the larger one. | [*plain rule, 77*] | By the Rev. JOHN MEARS M.A. an eminent Mini-|nifter [*sic*] of a Diſſenting Congregation in *Dublin.* | [*plain rule, 73*] *The THIRD EDITION.* | [*plain rule, 73*] | *GLASGOW:* | Printed for ROBERT FOULIS within the College; and | fold, at *Edinburgh,* by Meſſ. *Hamilton* and *Balfour*; and, | at *London,* by A. *Millar* in the *Strand.* M DCC XLII.

FORMULA: Small Crown 8⁰ in fours: A–F⁴ G².

NOTES: *Price*: Retail: 3*d.* (advertisement in No. 28 (Burnet, 1743)).

COPIES: G².

12 Nepos, Cornelius, *Lives of the Emperors*, L 1742

CORNELII NEPOTIS | VITAE | EXCELLENTIUM | IM
PERATORUM; | Ex EDITIONE emaculatiſſima | AUGUSTINI
VAN STAVEREN | EMENDATAE. | ACCEDUNT | FRAG
MENTA, quæ reperiri | potuerunt, omnia; olim SCHOTTI |
ſtudio collecta, poſtea emendata & | ſubinde aucta ab ANDREA
BOSIO. | [*plain double rule, 63*] | *GLASGUAE*, | Sumptibus
ROBERTI FOULIS, apud quem pro-|ſtant; *Edinburgi* proſtant
apud GAVINUM HA-|MILTON & JOAN. BALFOUR, *Londini* apud |
ANDREAM MILLAR exadverſum D. Clementis | Ædem. M DCC
XLII.

FORMULA: [? Crown] 12⁰ in sixes: π1 A–S⁶ (A1 *signed* ' A2 ',
A2 *unsigned*, A3 *signed* ' A4 ').

VARIANT: Issue in 8⁰, probably on better paper, not seen
(advertisement in No. 21 (Hutcheson, 1742)).

NOTES: The text is printed in what appears to be RP X, and
Foulis owned the type used for the title-page, at least in 1743
(the title-page may of course be a cancel). Just possibly printed
by Foulis.

COPIES: G⁴.

† **13** Terence, *Comedies*, L 1742

PUBLII | TERENTII | AFRI | COMOEDIAE SEX: | Ex
EDITIONE | *WESTERHOVIANA* | Recenſita ad Fidem duodecim
amplius | MSſtorum Codicum & pluſcularum | optimae Notae
Editionum. | [*two plain rules, 69*] | *GLASGUAE:* | Cura &
impenſis ROBERTI FOULIS, Typis ROBERTI | URIE & SOC. Pro
ſtant *Edinburgi* apud GAVI|NUM HAMILTON & JOANNEM
BALFOUR Bibli-|opolas, & *Londini* apud ANDREAM MILLER, |
in vico vulgo dicto *the Strand*. | [*plain rule, 20*] | MDCCXLII.
[*There is another state of this title-page in which* ' MILLER ' *in the
imprint is corrected to* ' MILLAR '.]

FORMULA: Large Crown 8⁰ in fours: π1 A–2I⁴(± 2I4) 2K–2M⁴
(–2M4; C1 *sometimes signed* ' B '; 2B3 *signed* ' R3 ', *probably a
relic of signing for* 12⁰; 2K1, 2K2 *sometimes signed* ' Ii ', ' Ii2 ',
and corrected in MS).

VARIANTS: Issue in 12⁰, coarse paper, not seen (advertisement
in No. 21 (Hutcheson, 1742). Not to be confused with the 12⁰
edition – a completely different setting – printed by Urie in
1742 for himself, Hamilton and Balfour, and Millar. The
mis-signing of sig. 2B3 in the 8⁰, mentioned above, is good
evidence that this book did actually appear as a 12⁰.)

Issue of forty copies on ' Grand Royal Paper ' (? 8⁰), not seen (advertisement in No. 21).

The Crown 8⁰ is also found with one of two other title-pages, in place of the title-page transcribed above. These other title-pages, which were probably cancels, may be called the ' Carlile ' title-page and the ' Robert & Andrew Foulis ' title-page.

The ' Carlile ' title-page is printed in black and red, in a style similar to that of the original Urie title-page, and reads: PUBLII | [*red*] TERENTII | CARTHAGINIENSIS | [*red*] COMOEDIAE SEX: | Ad Optimam EDITIONEM | [*red*] *WES TERHOVIÎ* | ACCURATE EXPRESSAE. | [*two plain rules, 68 and 67*] | [*red*] *GLASGUAE:* | Typis ALEXANDRI CARLILE Bibliopolae. | [*plainrule 23*] | [*red*] MDCCX LII.
This is presumably Urie's work, since Carlile is not otherwise known as a printer.

The ' Robert & Andrew Foulis ' title-page (to judge from its typographical style, the Wilson type used and the inclusion of Andrew Foulis's name in the imprint) was printed at the Foulis Press in the late seventeen-forties. It is hard to see why it should have proved necessary to print it, since Urie's title-page suits Urie's book as well as, if not better than, Foulis's cancel. C⁴ has a copy which contains both the ' MILLER ' state of the original title-page and the ' Robert & Andrew Foulis ' title-page, which reads as follows:
PUBLII | TERENTII | AFRI | COMOEDIAE SEX: | EX EDITIONE | WESTERHOVIANA | RECENSITA AD FIDEM DUODECIM AMPLIUS MANUSCRIPTORUM | CODICUM ET PLUSCULARUM OPTIMAE NOTAE EDITONUM. | G L A S G U AE: | CURA ET IMPENSIS ROBERTI & ANDREAE FOULIS MDCCXLII.

Murray (*R. & A. Foulis*, p. 9) says ' It . . . was issued in three forms: (1) for R. Urie & Company themselves; (2) for Robert Foulis; and (3) for Alexander Carlile, a bookseller in Glasgow, with the imprint *Typis Alexandri Carlile*.' Murray's (1) may have been Urie's own 12⁰.

NOTES: 2I4 was cancelled chiefly to correct the misprint ' omneis ' for ' omnes ' in line ' 19 ', p. 258.

Prices: Retail: 8⁰, fine paper, bound, 3*s.* 6*d.*; 12⁰, coarse paper, bound, 1*s.* 3*d.*; Grand Royal paper, 8*s.* (advertisement in No. 21).

COPIES: G⁴, L (8⁰ with ' Urie ' title-page); C⁴ (8⁰, both ' Urie ' and ' Robert & Andrew Foulis ' title-pages); G² (8⁰, ' Carlile ' title-page).

PART II

BOOKS PRINTED BY

ROBERT FOULIS

AND BY ROBERT AND

ANDREW FOULIS

1742-1776

1742   Aurelius Antoninus, Marcus, *Meditations*, E **14**

THE | MEDITATIONS | OF THE EMPEROR | MARCUS AURELIUS | ANTONINUS. | [*plain rule, 66*] | Newly tran ſlated from the Greek: | With Notes, and an Account of his Life. | [*plain rule, 67*] | *GLASGOW:* | Printed by Robert Foulis; and ſold by him at | the College; by Mess. Hamilton and | Balfour, in Edinburgh; and by Andrew | Millar, over againſt St. *Clements* Church, | London. MDCCXLII.

FORMULA: [? Crown] 12° in sixes: π1 A–D⁶(±D1) E–2A⁶ 2B⁴ 2C⁶ 2D1.

PAPER: Medium-poor quality; marks 9/i.

TYPE: RP i, RLP Cas.

NOTES: Sigs. 2C and 2D (containing Thomas Gataker's *Maxims of the Stoics* and *Apology*) appear to have been added after the rest of the book was completed.

Publication: on 8 June 1742 (*G J* 7 June 1742).
Price: Retail: 3*s.*, bound (*G J loc. cit.*).

COPIES: G⁴, L.

1742 Barnard, John, *A Zeal for Good Works, a Sermon* **15**

A | ZEAL | FOR | GOOD WORKS | EXCITED and DIREC TED: | IN A | SERMON | AT THE | Publick Thursday-Lecture, *in Boſton,* | *March* 25th, 1742. | Printed at the general Deſire of the Hearers. | [*plain rule 81*] | *By* John Barnard, A.M. | Paſtor of a Church in *Marblehead.* | [*plain rule 82*] | [*quotation, 3 lines*] | [*plain rule 83*] | BOSTON | Printed, and *Glaſgow* Re-printed, and Sold by Robert Fou⟨lis⟩, | and by the Book ſellers in *Edinburgh, London, Dublin,* ⟨and⟩ | *Belfaſt.* M.D.CC.XLII. | Price, Six Pence.

FORMULA: [? Printing Demy] 8° in fours: π1 A–F⁴ (A2 *and* E2 *signed*).

PAPER: Medium quality: marks 9/i.

TYPE: RP X, RLP Cas.

VARIANT: Issue on common paper, [? Crown] 8⁰:
Title-page: [*lines 2 and 3 of the imprint complete; the last line reads:*] Price, Four Pence.
Paper: Medium-poor quality; no marks.
NOTES: *Publication:* published on 20 October 1742 (*GJ* 18 October 1742).
Prices: Retail: fine, 6*d.*; common, 4*d.* (*GJ* 18 October, 1742).
Stock in 1777: 108 copies (*BQ* 12, as ' Barnard's fermon, 8vo.', quality and wholesale price unspecified).
COPIES: G² (both issues).

16 Burnet, Gilbert, *Select Sermons*   1742

SELECT | SERMONS | On the following SUBJECTS, | [*two columns of contents, 4 lines each, separated by a vertical double rule, 13*] | AND | A SERMON at the FUNERAL of the | Honourable *ROBERT BOYLE.* | [*plain rule, 60*] | BY | GILBERT BUR NETT *D.D.* | Sometime Profeſſor of Divinity in the Univer-| ſity of *Glaſgow,* afterwards Biſhop of *Sarum.* | [*plain double rule, 61 and 60*] | *GLASGOW,* | Printed by ROBERT FOULIS, and ſold by him | within the College, and by Meſſ. HAMILTON | and BALFOUR, and the other Bookſellers in | *Edinburgh.* MDCCXLII.
FORMULA: [? Crown] 12⁰ in 6s: π1 A–R⁶ S⁴ *T*1 (O2 *signed* ' O3 ', R1 *signed* ' S ').
PAPER: Medium quality; marks 9/i.
TYPE: RLP Cas; RE 1 used for headlines, etc.
VARIANT: Issue on common paper:
Paper: Medium-poor quality; no marks. Size uncertain, but probably not larger than Foolscap.
NOTES: *Publication:* in the press, 7 June 1742; published by 13 September 1742 (*GJ*).
Prices: Retail: fine, 2*s.*; common, in calf, 1*s.* 6*d.*, in sheep, 1*s.* 3*d.* (advertisement in No. 17).
COPIES: G⁴ (fine); L (common).

17 Caldwell, John, *An Impartial Trial of the Spirit,*   1742
a Sermon

An Impartial Trial of the Spirit operating in this | *Part of the World; by comparing the Nature,* | *Effects and Evidences of the preſent ſuppoſed* | *Converſion, with the Word of God.* |[*plain rule, 83*] | A | SERMON | PREACHED AT | *New London-derry.* | *OCTOBER* 14th, 1741. | On 1 JOHN iv. 1. | [*plain rule, 82·5*] | *By* JOHN CALDWELL, A.M. | [*plain rule, bent, 82*] | Publiſhed at the Defire of the OLD CONGREGATION in the faid | TOWN. | [*plain rule, 82*] | PROVERBS XXX. 12. | [*quotations, 9 lines*] | [*plain rule, 82·5*] | *BOSTON* | Printed, and *Glafgow* Re-printed, and Sold by ROBERT FOULIS, | and by the Bookfellers in *Edinburgh*, *London*, *Dublin*, and | *Belfaft*. M.D.CC.XLII. [Price, Six Pence.]

FORMULA: [? Crown] 8⁰ in fours: π^2 a⁴ A–G⁴ (C2, E2, F2, G2 *unsigned;* π1 *half-title*).

PAPER: Medium-poor quality; marks 9/i.

TYPE: RP X, RLP Cas.

VARIANT: Issue on inferior paper:

   Title-page: Reads ' Four Pence ' for ' Six Pence ' in the last line.

   Paper: Poor quality; marks indecipherable; size uncertain, but at least Foolscap.

NOTES: *Publication:* in the press, 20 September 1742; published by 6 October 1742 (*GJ* 20 September and 4 October 1742).

   Prices: Retail: fine, 6*d.*; common, 4*d.* (title-pages and *GJ* 4 October 1742).

   Stock in 1777: 192 copies, quality unspecified (*BQ* 12).

COPIES: G⁴ (fine); L (common).

1742 (published 1743)   ' Cebes ', *Table*, E **18** †

THE | TABLATURE | OF | CEBES | The *Theban*, a Difciple· of *Socrates*. | (Being an *Allegorical Picture of Humane Life*.) | [*plain rule, 60*] | [*quotation, 1 line*] | [*plain rule, 59*] | [*block 7*] | [*plain rule, 60*] | *GLASGOW*, | Printed by ROBERT FOULIS, and fold by | him, and other Bookfellers in *Glafgow* and | *Edinburgh*. 1742.

FORMULA: [? Crown] 18⁰: A¹² B⁶ (B6 *blank*).

PAPER: Medium quality; no marks.

TYPE: RLP Cas. Three words on the title-page (quotation) in GGP. Block 7.

NOTES: *Publication*: published by 7 March 1743 (*GJ*, ' This Day is Published ').

   Price: Retail: 9*d.* sewed in blue paper (*GJ*, 7 March 1743).

COPIES: G⁴.

1742   Chauncy, Charles, *The Wonderful Narrative* **19**

THE | Wonderful Narrative: | OR, A FAITHFUL | ACCOUNT | OF THE | *FRENCH PROPHETS*, | THEIR | AGITA

TIONS, EXTASIES, | and INSPIRATIONS. | To which are added, | Several other remarkable inſtances of PERSONS | under the Influence of the like Spirit, in va-|rious Parts of the World, particularly in NEW-|ENGLAND. | [*plain rule, bent, 83*] | In a LETTER to a FRIEND. | [*plain rule, 83*] | With an INTRO DUCTION, directing to the pro-|per Uſe of ſuch EXTRAORDIN ARY APPEAR-|ANCES, in the Courſe of PROVIDENCE. | I JOHN iv. I. | [*quotation, 3 lines*] | [*plain rule, 83*] | *GLASGOW:* | Printed by ROBERT FOULIS, Sold by him; and by the | Bookſellers in *Edinburgh, London,* and *Dublin.* 1742. | [Price, ONE SHILLING.]

FORMULA: [? Crown] 8⁰ in fours: π1 a–b⁴ A–L⁴ M^2 ($2 unsigned: M2 advertisements).

PAPER: Medium quality; thin; marks 9/i.

TYPE: RP X, RLP Cas.   A badly-printed book.

VARIANT: Issue on inferior paper, [? Crown] 8⁰:
  Title-page: [*last line reads:*] [Price SIX-PENCE.]
  Paper: Medium-poor quality; no marks.

NOTES: *Publication*: published by 20 September 1742 (*GJ*).
  Prices: Retail: fine, 1*s.*; common, 6*d.* (title-pages).

COPIES: G⁴ (both issues), L (fine).

20 Hale, Sir Matthew, *Some Thoughts on True*   1742
  Religion, etc.

SOME | THOUGHTS | ON THE | NATURE OF TRUE | RELIGION. | [*plain rule, 60*] | *By* Sir MATTHEW HALE, *Lord* | *Chief Juſtice of the King's Bench.* | [*plain rule, 61*] | To which is added, A | LETTER | FROM | Sir WALTER RAWLEIGH to his | Lady, after his Condemnation. | [*plain rule, 61*] | *GLASGOW:* | Printed by ROBERT FOULIS, Sold by | him, and ROBERT SMITH, in *Glaſ.* | *gow*; and by Meſſieurs HAMILTON and | BALFOUR, and other Bookſellers in *Edinburgh.* | M.D.CC.XLII. | [*Price Bound, Eight Pence.*]

FORMULA: [? Crown] 12⁰ in sixes: a⁶ A–H⁶.

PAPER: Medium-poor quality; no marks.

TYPE: RP X, RLP Cas.

NOTES: *Publication*: published by 4 October 1742 (*GJ*).
  Price: Retail : 8*d.*, bound in sheep (*GJ* 4 October 1742).

COPIES: G⁴.

1742   Hutcheson, Francis, *Metaphysicae Synopsis*, L **21**

METAPHYSICAE | SYNOPSIS: | ONTOLOGIAM, | ET, | PNEUMATOLOGIAM, | COMPLECTENS. | [*plain rule, 79*] | *GLASGUÆ:* | Ex officinâ ROBRRTI [*sic*] FOULIS. venales pro ſtant *Londini* | apud ANDREAM MILLER, ex adverſum D. Clementis | Ædem, in vico vulgo dicto *the Strand. Oxonii* apud | Jacobum Fletcher, Bibliopolam. MDCCXLII.

FORMULA: Half-sheets of [? Crown] 12° in alternate fours and twos: π² A⁴ B² [. . .] O² P⁴ (π1 *half-title*, P4 *advertisements*). (This is probably the imposition shown in Stower, Caleb, *The Printer's Grammar*, London, 1808, p. 176, where he calls it ' *Half Sheet of Twelves with Two Signatures – being 8 concluding pages of a work, and 4 of other matter* '.)

PAPER: Medium quality; marks 9/i.

TYPE: RLP Cas.

VARIANT: Issue on coarse paper not seen (advertisement in No. 41).

NOTES:
Prices: Retail: fine paper 1s. 6d.; coarse 1s. (advertisement in No. 41).

COPIES: G4 L (both (?) fine).

1742   Hutcheson, Francis, *Philosophiae Moralis* **22**
Institutio Compendiaria, L

PHILOSOPHIAE | MORALIS | INSTITUTIO COMPEN DIARIA, | Ethices & Juriſprudentiae Naturalis | ELEMENTA continens. | LIB. III. | [*plain rule, 67*] | Auctore FRANCISCO HUTCHESON | in Academia Glaſguenſi P.P. | [*plain rule, 67*] | [*plain rule, 67*] | *GLASGUAE*, | Typis ROBERTI FOULIS, apud quem venales | proſtant. M DCC XLII.

FORMULA: [? Crown] 12° in sixes: π1 a⁴ b² *² A–2D⁶ 2E² 2F1.

PAPER: Medium-poor quality; marks 9/i.

TYPE: RP 1, RLP Cas, Wilson's Two-line Great Primer roman caps.

NOTES:
Price: Retail: 3s. 6d. (advertisement in No. 41).

COPIES: G4, L.

† **23** Leechman, William, *The Temper of a Minister,*   1742
a Sermon

The TEMPER, CHARACTER, *and* DUTY | *of a* MINISTER *of the*
GOSPEL. | [*plain rule, 71*] | A | SERMON | PREACHED BEFORE
THE | SYNOD | OF | *GLASGOW and AIR,* | At GLASGOW,
April 7th, 1741. | [*plain rule, 75*] | By *WILLIAM LEECHMAN,*
M.A. | MINISTER of *Beith.* | [*plain rule, 75*] | The THIRD EDITION
| [*two plain rules, 71 and 73*] | *GLASGOW,* | Printed by ROBERT
FOULIS, within the | COLLEGE, and fold by him, and at *London*
| by AND. MILLER overagainſt St. *Clement's* | Church, and the
Book-fellers in *Edinburgh* | and *Glaſgow.* MDCCXLII. | [PRICE,
SIX-PENCE.]

FORMULA: Small Crown 8⁰ in fours: A–F⁴.
PAPER: Medium-poor quality; marks 9/i, and no marks. Size
of sheet 18 × 14 in.
TYPE: RP 1.
VARIANT: Issue on different paper, not seen.
NOTES: *Publication*: by 13 September 1742 (*GJ*).
   Prices: Retail: fine, 6*d.*; common, 4*d.* (*GJ* 13 September
1742).
COPIES: G⁴, L (both as above).

24 Ramsay, Andrew Michael, *A Plan of Education*   1742

A | PLAN | OF | EDUCATION: | [*plain rule, 72*] | By The
CHEVALIER RAMSAY. | [*plain rule, 71*] | The FOURTH EDITION.
| [*plain rule, 72*] | From a genuine MANUSCRIPT. | [*plain double
rule, 70 and 71*] | *GLASGOW,* | Printed by ROBERT FOULIS, and
fold by | him within the College; at *Edinburgh* by | Meſſ.
HAMILTON and BALFOUR; and at | *London* by A. MILLAR.
MDCCXLII.

FORMULA: [? Printing Demy] 12⁰ in sixes: A–B⁶ C² (B1
signed ' C ').
PAPER: Medium-poor quality; marks 9/i.
TYPE: RP 1.
COPIES: G⁴.

† **25** A.M., *The State of Religion in New England,*   1742

THE | State of Religion | IN | *NEW-ENGLAND,* | Since the
Reverend | Mr. *George Whitefield's* ARRIVAL there | IN | A

LETTER from a Gentleman in *New-|England* to his Friend in *Glafgow*. | To which is fubjoined an | APPENDIX, *con taining* ATTESTATIONS | *of the principal* FACTS *in the LETTER,* | By The Reverend | [*Two columns, 6 lines each; left:*] Mr. CHAUNCY, Paftor of the | firft *Church of Chrift* in | *Bofton,* | Mr. JOHN CALDWELL, in | *New-Londonderry,* | Mr. JOHN BAR NARD Paftor | [*right:*] of a Church in *Marblehead,* | Mr. TURRELL, | Mr. JONATHAN PARSONS | Minifter at *Lyme,* and | Dr. BEN JAMIN COLMAN, | Minifter in *Bofton.* | [*plain rule, ? length*] | *GLASGOW,* | Printed by ROBERT FOULIS, and fold by | him and other Bookfellers in *Edinburgh* | and *Glafgow.* MDCCXLII.

FORMULA: [N.B. Original not seen; the following collation, taken from photographs, is conjectural.] [? size] 8° in fours: π1 A⁴ B–E⁴ F².

PAPER: [Not seen].

TYPE: RP X.

VARIANT: Two issues, on fine and coarse paper (*GJ* 23 August 1742).

NOTES: *Publication*: in the press, 9 August 1742; published by 23 August 1742 (*GJ*).

Prices: Retail: fine, 3*d*.; coarse, 2*d*. (*GJ* 23 August 1742).

COPIES: New York Public Library (photostat at E); HD (microfilm only seen).

1742　　A.M., *The State of Religion in New England,* 26 †
second edition

THE | STATE | OF | RELIGION | IN | *NEW ENGLAND,* fince the Reverend Mr. | *George Whitefield*'s Arrival there, | In a LETTER from a Gentleman in *New-|England* to his friend in *Glafgow:* | With an APPENDIX, | Containing Proofs of the principal Facts, and far-|ther Accounts of the Diforders in Matters of | Religion, lately introduced into Various Parts of | *New-England* and *Carolina.* | Thefe FACTS are attefted and con firmed by the Authority of | the Reverend Dr. *Chauncey,* Mr. *Caldwell,* Mr. *Barnard,* Mr. | *Turrel,* Mr. *Parfons,* Dr. *Colman,* Mr. *Gilbert Tennent,* Mr. | *Appleton,* Mr. *Mather,* &c. | To which is prefixed | A REPLY to Mr. *Whitefield*'s REMARKS on the firft | EDITION. | [*plain rule, 79*] | *GLASGOW,* | Printed by R. FOULIS, and fold by him and the Bookfellers | in *Glafgow* and Edinburgh; At *London,* by A. MILLAR, o-|ver-againft *Katherine*'s Street in the *Strand* MDCCXLII. | Price Six Pence.

FORMULA: Small Crown 8⁰ in fours: π1 a⁴ B1 b⁴ A⁴(–A1)
C–Q⁴ (a2 *signed* ' A3 ', D2 . . . Q2 *unsigned*).

PAPER: Poor quality; no marks; size of sheet 18 × 14 in.

TYPE: RP X, RP 1, RLP Cas.

VARIANT: Issue on fine paper, not seen (*GJ* 29 November
1742).

NOTES: *Publication*: in the press, 18 October 1742; published
by 29 November 1742 (*GJ*). 40 copies remained in 1777 (*BQ*, 12).
   Prices: Retail: fine, 1*s.*; coarse, 6*d.* (*GJ* 29 November, 1742).

COPIES: G⁴, L (both coarse).

27 Bossuet, Jacques-Bénigne, *An Account of the* 1743
Education of the Dauphine, etc., E

AN | ACCOUNT | OF THE | EDUCATION | OF THE |
DAUPHINE, | In a LETTER to | Pope *INNOCENT* XI. | [*plain
rule, 60*] | By JAMES BENIGNUS BOSSUET, | Bifhop of *Meaux*,
Preceptor to the *Dauphine.* | [*plain rule, 61*] | To which is added,
| [*two columns of contents, 5 lines each, separated by a vertical double
rule, 15*] | [*plain rule, 63*] | Tranflated by J. T. PHILLIPS, | Pre
ceptor to his Royal Highnefs, Prince | WILLIAM, Duke of
Cumberland. | [*plain rule, 63*] | *GLASGOW:* | Printed by R.
FOULIS, and Sold by him; and | by Meffieurs HAMILTON and
BALFOUR, at | *Edinburgh.* MD. CC. XLIII.

FORMULA: [? Foolscap] 12⁰ in sixes: π1 A–E⁶.

PAPER: Medium-poor quality; no marks.

TYPE: RP X, RLP Cas, RE 1. Block 4.

NOTES: *Price*: Wholesale: 1*d.* (*BQ* 11).
   Stock in 1777: 178 copies (*BQ* 11).

COPIES: G².

28 Burnet, Gilbert, *A Treatise concerning the Truth* 1743
of the Christian Religion, with Locke, John, *A
Discourse on Miracles*

A | TREATISE | Concerning the TRUTH of the | CHRISTIAN
RELIGION. | [*plain rule, 60*] | By GILBERT BURNET *D.D.*
| Sometime Profeffor of Divinity in the Univerfity | of *Glafgow*,
afterwards Bifhop of *Sarum.* | [*plain rule 61*] | To which is added,
A DISCOURSE on | MIRACLES, by JOHN LOCKE Efq; [*plain rule,*

60] | *GLASGOW*, | Printed by ROBERT FOULIS, and fold by him | there, and at *Edinburgh* by Meff. G. HA-|MILTON and J. BALFOUR. MDCCXLIII.

FORMULA: [? Crown] 12⁰ in sixes: πι A–G⁶ H⁴ χι ²A² ²B⁶ ²C⁴ (*the second alphabet signed with italic capitals*; χι *title to* Locke's *Discourse*, ²C3ᵛ–4ᵛ *advertisements*).

PAPER: Medium quality; marks 9/i.

TYPE: RP I, RLP Cas. Block 5.

VARIANT: Issue on inferior paper, small Crown 12⁰:
   Paper: Poor quality; no marks; size of sheet 18 × 14 in.

NOTES: *Publication*: published by 28 February 1743 (*GJ*).
   Prices: Retail: large paper, 1s., sewed; ditto, 1s. 6d. bound and titled; ordinary paper, 6d., sewed in blue paper; ditto, 10d., bound (*GJ* 28 February 1743).

COPIES: G⁴ (large paper); G² (ordinary).

1743   Campbell, Archibald, Marquis of Argyll, 29
                      Instructions to a Son, etc.

INSTRUCTIONS | To a | SON, | Containing | RULES of CONDUCT in publick | and private LIFE, | Under the following Heads: | [*two columns of contents, 4 and 3 lines, separated by a vertical rule, 11·5*] | By ARCHIBALD Marquis of *ARGYLE*. | Addrefs'd to his Children, and to his eldeft Son in | particular. | Written in the Year 1660, during his Confinement. | To which are added by the fame Noble AUTHOR: | [*two columns of contents, 4 and 3 lines, separated by a vertical rule, 11·5*] | GLASGOW: | Printed by R. FOULIS, and fold by him there; at *Edin-|burgh*, by Meff. HAMILTON and BALFOUR. 1743.

FORMULA: [? Crown] 8⁰ in fours: πι A–P⁴ Q² *R*i.

PAPER: Medium-good quality; marks 9/i.

TYPE: RE I.

VARIANT: Issue in Printing Demy 12⁰:
   Formula: Printing Demy 12⁰ in sixes: πι A–K⁶ L² *M*i.
   Paper: Medium-poor quality; marks 9/i; size of sheet 21¾ × 16½ in.

NOTES: *Publication*: published on about 29 July 1743 (*GJ* 25 July 1743).

COPIES: G⁴ (12⁰), L (8⁰).

† **30** Cooper, Anthony Ashley, Lord Shaftesbury, 1743–5
Characteristics

[*Vol.* I:] *CHARACTERISTICKS.* | VOLUME I. | A Letter con
cerning ENTHUSIASM. | *Senfus Communis;* an Effay on the
Free-|dom of WIT and HUMOUR. | *Soliloquy*, or Advice to an
AUTHOR. | PRINTED in the YEAR M.DCC.XLIV.
[*Vol.* II:] *CHARACTERISTICKS.* | VOLUME II. AN | IN
QUIRY | CONCERNING | VIRTUE and MERIT. | THE
MORALISTS; | A | PHILOSOPHICAL RHAPSODY. | PRINTED in
the YEAR MDCCXLIII.
[*Vol.* III:] *CHARACTERISTICKS* | VOLUME IIII. | MISCEL
LANEOUS REFLECTIONS | ON THE PRECEDING | TREATISES
| AND OTHER | CRITICAL SUBJECTS. | A | NOTION
OF THE TABLATURE | OR | JUDGMENT OF HERCULES. |
PRINTED IN THE YEAR | M DCC XLV.

FORMULA: [Printing Demy] 12° in sixes:
   Vol. I: π1 A–2D⁶ 2E1 (H3 *sometimes signed* ' G3 ', S3 *signed*
' S2 ', Z3 *signed* 'Z5 ', 2A2 *signed* ' A2 ', 2C3 *sometimes signed*
' Cc5 '; D2 *unsigned*).
   Vol. II : π2 a⁴ (–a1) A–M⁶ χ² ²A–S6(π1 *title page,* π2 *sub-title to*
An Inquiry, χ1 *blank,* χ2 *sub-title to* The Moralists).
   Vol. III: π1 A⁴ B–2M⁶ 2*N*² (G3 *signed* ' G5 ', 2K2, 2K3 *signed*
' K2 ', ' K3 ';* I2 *and sometimes* 2M3 *unsigned*).
   (*There is also a complicated system of signing parts and sections
of the works used on both versos and rectos.*)

PAPER: Medium and medium-poor quality; marks 9/i.

TYPE: RLP Cas, RB 1; GP (Vols I and III, 1744–5). Blocks 11
and 12 (Vol. II, 1743) and 13 (Vol. III, 1745).

VARIANT: Issue in [? Crown] 12°:
   Paper: Medium and medium-poor quality; no marks.

NOTES: Without imprints, but probably Foulis Press.   The
early advertisements and *BQ* refer to three volumes, but an
advertisement in No. 135 (Lucretius, 1749) speaks of four
volumes, and it may be that Shaftesbury's *Letters*, 1746 (No.
73) was used as a fourth volume.   Note that No. 613 (Shaftesbury, *The Moralists*, by 1777) is probably an extract from Vol. II
of this book.
   Publication: published by 23 December 1745 (*GC*).
   Prices: Wholesale: (probably): fine, 1s. 6d. per volume ;
common, 1s. per volume (*BQ* 12). Retail: large paper, 9s.
the set; common, 7s. 6d. the set, bound and lettered (*GC* 23
December 1745 and 31 March 1746).

Stock in 1777: Vols. II and III only, 60 volumes in all (*BQ* 12).
COPIES: L (common), O (both issues).

1743   Demetrius ' of Phalerum ', *De Elocutione*, 31
                                    G and L

ΔHMHTPIOΥ ΦΑΛHPEΩΣ | Περὶ | ΕΡMHNEIAΣ. | DE
METRII PHALEREI | DE | ELOCUTIONE, | SIVE, |
DICTIONE RHETORICA. | In hac editione, contextus
Graecus ex optimis Ex-|emplaribus emendatur, Verſio Latina
paſſim ab | erroribus repurgatur; & loca à Demetrio laudata, |
quae hactenus Graecè tantum extabant, nunc | primùm Latini
tate donantur. | [*quotation, 3 lines*] | *G L A S G U AE:* | Ex
Officina ROBERTI FOULIS. MDCCXLIII.
FORMULA: [? Crown] 8º in fours: π1 A–2A⁴ 2B² 2C1.
PAPER: Medium quality; marks 9/i.
TYPE: GGP, RE 1. Greek and Latin on facing pages (Greek
on the versos, Latin on the rectos).
VARIANT: Issue on inferior paper, [? Small Crown] 8º:
  Paper: Medium-poor quality; no marks.
  Issue in Foolscap 4º:
  Formula: Foolscap 4º in twos: π1 *A*² B–2B² ²A–²G²($\pm$²G2)
²H–²Z² (*A*1 *half-title, usually placed before* π1, *which is the title-
page*).
  Paper: Good quality; marks 4/iv.
  Type: Latin follows Greek in the second signature alphabet;
and, since the Greek and Latin pages no longer have to tally,
extra spacing has been closed up, resulting in new page divi-
sions.
NOTES: *Publication*: published on about 4 April 1743 (*GJ*
7 April 1743). It was the first Greek text to be printed at
Glasgow.
  Prices: Wholesale: 8º (? issue), 1*s*. (*BQ* 5). Retail: 8º (?
fine), 3*s*. (*CP* 4).
  Stock in 1777: 8º (? issue), 14 copies (*BQ* 5).
COPIES: G⁴, L (each has 4º, and 8º fine), O (8º common).

1743   Epictetus, *Manual*, E 32

THE | MANUAL | OF | *EPICTETUS*, | Containing | AN
ABRIDGEMENT | OF HIS | PHILOSOPHY. | [*two plain rules,
58 and 60*] | Printed in the Year MDCCXLIII.

FORMULA: [? Crown] 18° and [? Pot] 12°: A¹² B⁶ C¹² (A *and* B *have vertical chain lines, and together make an 18° sheet; C has horizontal chain lines, and makes a 12° sheet*).

PAPER: Medium-poor quality; marks 9/i (Crown), no marks (Pot).

TYPE: RLP Cas, Wilson titling.

NOTES: A companion to No. 18, ' Cebes ', with which it is usually found bound up. An advertisement in No. 14, published in the Summer of 1742, for a new translation of Epictetus which ' will ere long be publifhed ' may refer to this book. Almost certainly printed by Foulis.

COPIES: G⁴.

33 Fleming, Robert, *The Confirming Work of Religion*   1743

THE | CONFIRMING WORK | OF | RELIGION: | OR, | Its great Things made plain, | By their Primary | EVIDENCES and DEMONSTRATIONS. | Whereby the meaneft in the Church, may | foon be made able to render a rational | Account of their Faith. | [*plain rule, 68*] | By the late Reverend Mr. ROBERT | FLEMING, Author of *the Fulfilling | of the Scriptures*. | [*plain rule, 67*] | [*plain double rule, 69 and 68*] | *GLASGOW*, | Printed by ROBERT FOULIS, and fold by him, | and other Bookfellers in *Glafgow* and *Edinburgh*. | MD.CC.XLIII.

FORMULA: [? Crown] 12° in sixes: a–b⁶ A–L⁶ (F2 *signed* ' F3 ').

PAPER: Poor quality; no marks.

TYPE: RP X, RE i, RLP Cas, RP i. Blocks 1-5.

VARIANT: Issue on fine paper, not seen (*GJ* 7 February 1743).

NOTES: *Publication*: in the press, September 1742 (advertisement in No. 19); published by 7 February 1743 (*GJ*).
    Prices: Retail: fine, 1s.; common, 9d. (*GJ* 7 February, 1743).

COPIES: G⁴, L (both common).

34 Fleming, Robert, *A Description of the Confirmed State of a Christian*   1743

A | DESCRIPTION | OF THE | Confirmed State | OF A | CHRISTIAN. | [*plain rule, 67*] | By the late Reverend Mr. ROBERT | FLEMING, Author *of the Fulfilling | of the Scriptures*. |

[*plain rule, 65*] | [*plain double rule, 67 and 68*] | *GLASGOW*, |
Printed by ROBERT FOULIS, and fold by him, | and other Book
fellers in *Glafgow* and *Edinburgh*. | MD.CC.XLIII.

FORMULA: [? Crown] 12⁰ in sixes: A–G^6(–G6) (F2 *signed* ‘ F3 ’).

PAPER: Poor quality; no marks.

TYPE: RP X, RE I. Blocks 1, 4, 5 and 6.

NOTES: Probably issued with Fleming's *Confirming Work of
Religion* (No. 33). All three copies seen are bound up with
copies of No. 33; the co-incident mis-signing ‘ F3 ’ for F2
suggests that skeleton formes were taken over intact from one
book to the other; and the two books are closely related in
subject, paper and typography.

COPIES: G⁴, L.

1743   Leechman, William, *The Nature of Prayer*,   **35**
                                                  a Sermon

THE | NATURE, | REASONABLENESS, | AND | AD
VANTAGES, | OF | PRAYER, | With an ATTEMPT to anfwer
| The OBJECTIONS againſt it. | A SERMON | BY | WILLIAM
LEECHMAN *M.A.* | MINISTER of *Beith*. | PSALM LXV. 2. |
[*quotation, 2 lines*] | *GLASGOW*, | Printed by ROBERT FOULIS,
and fold by him, at *London* by | ANDREW MILLAR over-againſt
Katherine-ſtreet in the | *Strand*, and by the Bookfellers in *Edin
burgh*. | M DCC XLIII.

FORMULA: [? Crown] 8⁰ in fours: A–H⁴ (A2 *signed* ‘ A ’; B2
unsigned).

PAPER: Medium quality, marks 9/i.

TYPE RP I, RB I.

VARIANT: Issue on small paper, not seen (*GJ* 2 May 1743).

NOTES: *Publication*: in the press, 4 April 1743; published 2
May 1743 (*GJ*).
  Prices: Retail: large paper, 8*d* ; small paper, 6*d*. (*GJ* 2 May
1743).

COPIES: L (large paper).

1743   Leechman, William, *The Nature of Prayer*,   **36**
                                  a Sermon, second edition

THE | NATURE, | REASONABLENESS, | AND | AD
VANTAGES | OF | PRAYER; | With an ATTEMPT to anfwer

| The Objections againſt it. | A SERMON | BY | WILLIAM LEECHMAN *M.A.* | Miniſter of *Beith.* | [*quotation, 2 lines*] | The Second Edition. | *GLASGOW,* | Printed by Robert Foulis, and ſold by him, at *London* by | Andrew Millar over-againſt *Katherine-ſtreet* in the | *Strand,* and by the Bookſellers in *Edinburgh.* | M DCC XLIII.

FORMULA: Printing Demy 8⁰ in fours: A–H⁴.

PAPER: Medium quality; marks 9/i; size of sheet 21½ × 16½ in.

TYPE: RP i, RB i.

VARIANT: Issue on inferior paper [? Crown] 8⁰:
Paper: Medium-poor quality, no marks.

NOTES: *Publication*: published by 18 July 1743 (*GJ*).
Prices: Retail: fine, 8*d.*; common, 6*d.* (*GJ* 18 July 1743).

COPIES: G⁴ (common), L (fine).

37 More, Henry, *Divine Dialogues* 1743

DIVINE | DIALOGUES, | Containing | DISQUISITIONS | Concerning the | ATTRIBUTES | AND | Providence of GOD. | [*plain rule, 68*] | In three Volumes. | [*plain rule, 67*] | By *HENRY MORE,* D.D. | [*plain rule, 67*] | [*quotation, 3 lines*] | [*plain rule, 67*] | *GLASGOW,* | Printed by Robert Foulis, and ſold by him there; | at *Edinburgh,* by Meſſ. Hamilton and Bal-|four, and John Paton. MDCCXLIII.

FORMULA: Printing Demy 12⁰ in sixes: π1 a² A⁴ B–M⁶ N² O⁴ P–2B⁶ 2C² 2D⁴ 2E–2R⁶ 2S⁴ 2T1 (C2, M2, 2B2 *unsigned; also found bound in three volumes, with* N2 *and* 2C2 *as volume titles;* 2T1 *advertisements*).

PAPER: Medium quality; marks 9/i; size of sheet 21¾ × 16½ in.

TYPE: RP i, RE i, RLP Cas, RB i, GGP. With RDP caps and two-line Double Pica as titling.

VARIANT: Issue on common paper:
Paper: Poor qʼality; no marks; size uncertain, but probably Crown.

NOTES: *Publication*: published by 25 July 1743 (*GJ*).
Prices: Wholesale: common, 6*d.* (*BQ* 12). Retail: fine, 1*s.* 6*d.* (*GJ* 25 July 1743).
Stock in 1777: common, 49 copies (*BQ* 12).

COPIES: G⁴ (fine and common), L (common).

1743   Ramsay, Allan, *The Gentle Shepherd* **38**

THE | GENTLE SHEPHERD; | A | *SCOTS* | PASTORAL
COMEDY. | [*plain rule, 73*] | By ALLAN RAMSAY. | [*plain rule, 72*]
| The Seventh Edition with the SANGS. | [*plain rule, 73*] |
[*plain rule, 72*] | *GLASGOW*, | Printed by ROBERT FOULIS, and
fold by him there; | at *Edinburgh*, Meff. HAMILTON and BAL
FOUR. | MDCCXLIII. [Price 1s.]

FORMULA: Post 8⁰ in fours: πı A–K⁴(–K4).
PAPER: Medium quality; thin; marks 6/ ?HR.
TYPE: RLP Cas, RP 1, RB 1. Block 8.
VARIANT: Issue in Small Crown 8⁰:
   ' *Title-page*: [*the same type respaced vertically to include a copper-
plate (unsigned, plate mark 71 × 74) between the last two rules. The
last line reads:*] MDCCXLIII. [Price 6d.]
   Paper: Poor quality; no marks; size of sheet 17¾ × 14¼ in.
NOTES: *Publication*: published after 29 July 1743, since it con-
tains an advertisement for No. 29 (Campbell, 1743).
   Prices: Retail: fine, 1s.; common, 6d. (title-pages).
COPIES: G² (Crown), O (Post).

1743   Shenstone, William, *The Judgment of Hercules,* **39** †
       with the Pythagoreans' *Golden Verses,* E

THE | JUDGMENT of HERCULES, | A | POEM. | [*plain rule, 70*]
| By a STUDENT of *Oxford*. | [*plain rule, 73*] | To which is fub
joined, | The GOLDEN VERSES of PYTHAGORAS, | [*plain rule, 73*]
| Tranflated from the Greek by Mr. ROWE. | [*plain rule, 71*] |
GLASGOW, | Printed and fold by ROBERT FOULIS, | M DCC
XLIII. | Price Four Pence.

FORMULA: Post 8⁰ in fours: πı A–C⁴ D1.
PAPER: Medium quality; thin; marks 6/iii; size of sheet
18¾ × 15 in.
TYPE: RLP Cas, RE italic, RP 1.
NOTES: *Publication*: published by 25 July 1743 (*GJ*).
   Prices: Retail: 3d. (*GJ* 25 July 1743), or 4d. (title-page).
COPIES: G⁴.

1743   Theophrastus, *Characters,* G and L **40** †
ΘΕΟΦΡΑΣΤΟΥ | ΧΑΡΑΚΤΗΡΕΣ | ΗΘΙΚΟΙ. | THEO
PHRASTI | CHARACTERES | ETHICI: | EX RECENSIONE |

PETRI NEEDHAM. | Cum Versione Latina | ISAACI
CASAUBONI. | *GLASGUAE:* | IN AEDIBUS ACA
DEMICIS | Excudebat Robertus Foulis Academiae |
Typographus. MDCCXLIII.

FORMULA: Foolscap 8⁰ in fours: π1 A–G⁴(–G4) ²A–F⁴ ²G².

PAPER: Medium-good quality; marks 4/iii.

TYPE: GGP, RE 1. Latin follows Greek in the second signature alphabet.

VARIANT: Issue in [? Crown] 12⁰:

Title-page: Partly reset. Reads as the 8⁰, except: line 6 ends
with a full point; line 8 ends with a comma; line 9, ' Et ' for
' Cum '; line 14, ' MDCCXLIII.' for ' MDCCXLIII.' (but line 14
sometimes unaltered).

Formula: [? Crown] 12° in sixes: π1 A–H⁶ I⁴.

Paper: Medium-poor quality; marks 9/i.

Type: Greek and Latin on facing pages. The first use of
Foulis's usual parallel-text scheme, of which the typical
arrangement was: A1 blank, A1ᵛ Greek, A2–A2ᵛ Latin,
A3–A3ᵛ Greek, A4–A4ᵛ Latin, and so on. It has the advan-
tage that, although each page of text faces its translation,
the monotony of showing Greek on the left-hand page and
Latin on the right of every opening is avoided.

NOTES: *Publication*: published by 25 July 1743 (advertisement
in No. 37).

This is the first book in which Foulis described himself as
University Printer, to which office he was elected on 31 March
1743 (see ' Early Work ', p. 83 and n. 2).

COPIES: G⁴ (8⁰ and 12⁰), L (8⁰).

41 Theophrastus, *Characters*, E   1743

THE MORAL | CHARACTERS | OF | *THEOPHRASTUS:*
| Tranſlated from the *Greek*, | *By* Eustace Budgell, *Eſquire.*
| [*quotation, 2 lines*] | Printed in the Year MDCCXLIII. | Price
eight Pence.

FORMULA: [? Printing Demy] 12⁰ in sixes: π1 a–b⁶ c1 A–D⁶ E⁴.

PAPER: Medium-poor quality; marks 9/?.

TYPE: RP 1, RE 1, RLP Cas, Wilson titling; 2 words (b6ᵛ)
in GP.

VARIANT: Issue on common paper, [? size] 12⁰:

Title-page: [*last line reads:*] Price Sixpence.

Paper: Poor quality; no marks; size uncertain, the only copy seen being heavily cut down, but possibly Crown.

NOTES: Probably a Foulis book, in spite of the lack of imprint (see TYPE, above).

Prices: Retail: fine, 8*d.*; common, 6*d.* (title-pages).

COPIES: G² (common), O (fine).

1743   Thomas More, St, *Utopia*, E **42**

UTOPIA: | OR THE | HAPPY REPUBLIC; | A Philofo phical ROMANCE, | In Two Books. | [*two columns of contents, 6 lines each, separated by a vertical double rule, 19*] | [*plain rule, 82*] | Written in Latin by Sir THOMAS MORE, | Lord High Chancel lor of *England*. | [*plain rule, 82*] | Tranflated into Englifh by GILBERT BURNET D.D. | Sometime Profeffor of Divinity in the Univerfity of | *Glafgow*, afterwards Bifhop of *Sarum*. | [*plain double rule, 82*] | *GLASGOW*, | Printed by ROBERT FOULIS, and fold by him there; and, at | *Edinburgh*, by Meff. HAMILTON and BALFOUR Bookfellers. | [*plain rule, 22*] | M DCC XLIII.

FORMULA: [? Printing Demy] 8⁰ in fours: a–c⁴ A–R⁴ S² (b1 ᵛ *signed* ' b2 ', A2 *signed* ' B2 ').

Frontispiece: mezzotint portrait of More, signed ' *H. Holbein pinx. Sam¹, Taylor fecit.*'

PAPER: Medium-good quality; marks 9/i.

TYPE: RP I, RE I. First appearance of Wilson's Canon roman. Block 15.

VARIANT: Issue on small paper, [? Crown] 8⁰:
Paper: Medium-poor quality, no marks.

NOTES: *Publication*: published by 21 February 1743 (*GJ*).
Prices: Retail: large paper, 2*s.*; small paper, bound in calf, 1*s.* 6*d.* (*GJ* 21 February 1743).

COPIES: G⁴, L (large paper), O (small).

1744 Anacreon, *Lyrics*, with Sappho, *Lyrics*, G and L **43**

ΤΑ ΤΟΥ | ΑΝΑΚΡΕΟΝΤΟΣ | ΚΑΙ | ΣΑΠΦΟΥΣ | ΜΕΛΗ. | ANACREONTIS | ET | SAPPHONIS | CARMINA. | [*quotation, 3 lines*] | *GLASGUAE*, | In AEDIBUS ACA DEMICIS | Excudebat ROBERTUS FOULIS Academiae Typo graphus | M DCC XLIV.

FORMULA: Foolscap 8º in fours: a² A–N⁴ O².
PAPER: Medium quality; marks 5/v, 4/iv.
TYPE: GGP, GP, RB I, RLP I. GDP caps as titling. Latin translation as footnotes to the text.
VARIANT: Issue in [? Crown] 12º:
  Formula: [? Crown] 12º in sixes: a² A–I⁶.
  Paper: Medium quality; marks 9/i.
COPIES: G⁴, L (both 12º), O (8º).

44 Aurelius Antoninus, Marcus, *Meditations*,   1744
G and L

[Vol. 1:] MAPKOY | ANTΩNINOY | AYTOKPATOPOΣ | TΩN EIΣ EAYTON BIBΛIA ιβ'. | MARCI | ANTONINI | IMPERATORIS | EORUM QUAE AD SEIPSUM LIBRI XII. | *Poſt Gatakerum, ceteroſque, recogniti, et notis illuſtrati*; | *a doctiſſimo viro* R. I. Oxonienſi. | GLASGUAE: | IN AEDIBUS ACADEMICIS, | Excudebat R. FOULIS Academiae Typo graphus. | M DCC XLIV [Vol. II, from a different setting, reads the same, except that the four lines of Greek are omitted, and ' LIBRI XII. ' is placed on a separate line.]
FORMULA: Foolscap 8º in four:
  Vol. I: π² A–Q⁴.
  Vol. II: π² A–2E⁴ (π2 *advertisements*).
PAPER: Medium-good quality; marks 5/iv, 5/v, 4/iv, 4/v.
TYPE: GP, RLP Cas, RB I. Greek in Vol. I, Latin in Vol. II.
VARIANT: Parallel-text issue in one volume, Foolscap 8º:
  Formula: Foolscap 8º in fours: π² A–2X⁴ 2Y² (2Y² *advertise-ments ; Vol.* II *title-page omitted*).
  Paper: Same as the two-volume issue.
  Type: Greek and Latin on facing pages.
NOTES: Comparison of the arrangement of the various lots of paper in the two issues shows that they were in all probability printed in parallel, doubtless in order to liberate the type for re-setting.
  Price: Retail: 3s. 6d. sewed for either issue (advertisement in No. 48).
COPIES: G⁴ (both issues); L (parallel-text issue).

† **45** Cicero, *Tusculanae Quaestiones*, L   1744

M. TULLII CICERONIS | TUSCULANARUM | DISPUTA TIONUM | LIBRI QUINQUE. | ACCEDUNT | LECTIONES

VARIANTES, | ET | DOCTORUM, | PRAECIPUE | Cl. BOUHERII | CONJECTURAE. | *GLASGUAE:* | IN AEDIBUS ACADEMICIS | Excudebat ROBERTUS FOULIS, Academiae Typo-|graphus. MDCCXLIV.

FORMULA: Foolscap 8° in fours: a⁴ A–2D⁴ 2E² (2C1 *and* 2C2 *each signed* ' c '; 2E2 *advertisements*).

PAPER: Medium-good quality; marks 4/i, foolscap/(?)i.

TYPE: RB 1, RLP 1.

VARIANT: Issue in [? small Crown] 12°:
    Formula : [? small Crown] 12° in sixes: a⁴ A–R⁶ *S*² ‡⁶ (*S*2 *advertisements*).
    Paper: Medium-poor quality; no marks.

COPIES: G⁴ (12°), G² (8°).

1744   Cudworth, Ralph, *The Life of Christ, a Sermon* **46**

THE | LIFE of CHRIST | THE | PITH and KERNEL | OF ALL | RELIGION: | A SERMON | Preached before the Honourable | HOUSE of COMMONS, | AT | *WEST MINSTER,* | *March* 31. 1647. | By R. CUDWORTH, B.D. | [*quotations, 3 lines*] | *CAMBRIDGE,* | Printed by ROGER DANIEL Printer to the Univerſity. 1647. | AND | *GLASGOW,* | Reprinted and ſold by ROBERT FOULIS. 1744. | PRICE Eight PENCE.

FORMULA: [? Demy] 8° in fours: π⁴ A–G⁴ (π2 *signed* ' * ' ; π4 *advertisements*).

PAPER: Medium-good quality; marks eagle/CM over T.

TYPE: RP 1, RLP Cas.

NOTES: *Price*: Retail: 8*d.* (title-page).
    Stock in 1777: 56 copies (*BQ* 12).

COPIES: G⁴.

1744 Epictetus, *Manual*, with ' Cebes ', *Table*; Prodicus, **47** † *The Choice of Heracles*; Cleanthes, *Hymn to Zeus*, G and L

ΕΠΙΚΤΗΤΟΥ | ΕΓΧΕΙΡΙΔΙΟΝ, | ΚΗΒΗΤΟΣ | ΠΙΝΑΞ, | ΠΡΟΔΙΚΟΥ ΗΡΑΚΛΗΣ, | ΚΑΙ | ΚΛΕΑΝΘΟΥΣ ΥΜΝΟΣ. | EPICTETI | ENCHIRIDION, | CEBETIS | TABULA, | PRODICI HERCULES, | ET | CLEANTHIS HYMNUS. | Omnia Græce & Latine. | *G L A S G UAE:* | IN AEDIBUS ACADEMICIS | Excudebat ROBERTUS FOULIS, Academiae | Typographus. M DCC XLIV.

FORMULA: Foolscap 12⁰ in sixes: π1 A–C⁶ D⁴ E1 F1 G–I⁶ K⁴ L1 χ² ²A–C⁶ ²D⁴ ²E² ²F–H⁶ ²I⁴ (²A4 *signed* ' B2 '; χ² *Latin half-title and title-page*).

PAPER: Medium-good quality; marks 4/v, 5/v; size of sheet 16¾ × 13 in.

TYPE: GP, RLP Cas. Latin follows Greek in the second alphabet.

VARIANTS: Parallel-text issue in Foolscap 12⁰:
    Formula: Foolscap 12⁰ in sixes: π² A–G⁶ H⁴ I² K–Q⁶ R⁴ (–R4; π1 *half-title*).
    Paper: Medium quality; no marks; size of sheet 16¾ × 13½ in.
    Type: Greek and Latin on facing pages.
    Both the Foolscap issues are also found on smaller paper:
    Paper: Medium quality; marks 6/?, 5/v; in spite of the Post and Foolscap marks, the cut dimensions of the copies seen are so small as to suggest Pot.

COPIES: G⁴ (both issues on small paper), G (Foolscap, Latin following Greek), G² and L (Foolscap, parallel text).

48 Epictetus, *Manual*, L   1744

EPICTETI | ENCHIRIDION | LATINIS VERSIBUS | ADUMBRATUM | Per EDVARDUM IVIE A.M. *Aedis Chriſti* Alumn. | et Rev. Dom. Epiſc. *Briſtol.* a Sacris Domeſticis. | [*quotation, two lines*] | *GLASGUAE*: | IN AEDIBUS ACADE MICIS | Excudebat ROBERTUS FOULIS, Academiae Typographus. | M DCC XLIV.

FORMULA: Post 12⁰ in sixes: π² A–C⁶.

PAPER: Medium-good quality; marks 6/i.

TYPE: RB 1, RE 1, RLP 1.

VARIANT: Issue on inferior paper, not seen (*BQ* 11).

NOTES: *Prices*: Wholesale: [fine], 4*d.*, [common], 2*d.* (*BQ* 11).
    Stock in 1777: [fine], 30 copies; [common], 48 copies (*BQ* 11). The entry in *BQ* (' Epicteti Enchiridion, f[oolscap]. 12mo.') probably, but not certainly, refers to this book.

COPIES: G⁴ (fine).

49 Foulis, Robert, *A Catalogue of Books Imported*   1744–5

A | CATALOGUE | OF | BOOKS | IMPORTED from ABROAD, | PART I. | CONSISTING OF | ANTIENT GREEK

AUTHORS; | VIZ. | [*two columns of contents, 4 lines each, separated by a vertical plain double rule, 16·5*] | Printed by The ALDI, JUNTAE, COLINAEUS, | ROBERT, CHARLES and HENRY STEPHENS, | TURNEBUS, WILLIAM and CL. MORELS, BENE-|NATUS, SONNIUS, CRAMOISY, LIBERT, WECHEL, | FROBEN, PLANTIN, ELZEVIR, and in the LOUVRE, | and OXONIAN THEATRE. | N.B. GENTLEMEN are defired to direct their Commiffions to | ROBERT FOULIS Book feller and Printer to the UNIVERSITY of *Glafgow*. | *GLASGOW:* M DCC XLIV [*The title-page to Part* II (χ1), *which refers to books by Antient Latin Authors, is similar but is dated* ' *GLASGOW:* M DCC XLV.']

FORMULA: Small Crown 8⁰ in fours: π1 A–F⁴ χ1 G–M⁴ N1 (*N*1 *advertisements; the only copy seen contains this leaf in two different settings*).

PAPER: Medium-poor quality;   no marks;   size of sheet 18¾ × 14¼ in.

TYPE: RLP 1, RB 1, RP 1, RE 1.

NOTES: The following note is printed on the versos of π1 and χ1: ' Advertifement. That the Books are warranted perfect, fold for ready money only, and to no-body below the price marked.' This may be compared with the advertisement quoted in the NOTES to No. 1, above.

COPIES: G⁴.

1744   Horace, *Works*, L **50**

QUINTUS | HORATIUS | FLACCUS | Ad lectiones pro batiores diligenter emendatus, et | interpunctione nova faepius illuftratus. | *GLASGUAE:* | IN AEDIBUS ACADEMICIS | Excudebat ROBERTUS FOULIS, Academiae Typographus. | M DCC XLIV.

FORMULA: Foolscap 8⁰ in fours: π2 A–2E⁴ (2E4 *advertisements*).

PAPER: Good quality; marks 5/v, 4/iv.

TYPE: RB 1, RLP 1.

VARIANTS: Issue in [? Demy] 12⁰:
  Formula: π2 A–S⁶ T⁴ (T4 *advertisements*).
  Paper: Medium and medium-good quality;   marks 9/i, eagle/CM over T, no marks.
  Issue on inferior paper, 12⁰:
  Formula: as [? Demy] 12⁰.
  Paper: Medium-poor quality; no marks; size uncertain, but probably small Crown.

NOTES: The 'immaculate' Horace. The proofs are said to have been hung up in the College, and a reward of £50 (Scots, presumably) offered for the discovery of an error. Several mistakes were overlooked, however; Duncan (p. 14) lists six of them.

COPIES: G⁴ (8⁰ and 12⁰, both issues), L (8⁰).

51 Hutcheson, Francis, *Synopsis Metaphysicæ*, L   1744

SYNOPSIS | METAPHYSICAE, | ONTOLOGIAM et PNEUMA-| TOLOGIAM complectens. | [*plain rule, 62*] | Editio altera auctior. | [*plain rule, 62*] | [*plain rule, 39*] | A.D. MDCCXLIV.

FORMULA: [? Printing Demy] 12⁰ in sixes: a⁴ A–K⁶ L².

PAPER: Medium quality, marks 9/i.

TYPE: RLP Cas, RB 1.

NOTES: *Stock in 1777:* BQ lists 56 copies of 'Hutchefon's fynopfis metaph. d[emy]. 12mo. (1743.)' (*BQ* 12). There was an edition in 1742, but not, so far as I know, in 1743; the entry may, therefore, refer to this book.

COPIES: L.

52 Leechman, William, *The Temper of a Minister,*   1744
a Sermon

THE | TEMPER, | CHARACTER, | AND | DUTY | OF A | MINISTER of the GOSPEL. | A SERMON | PREACHED BEFORE THE | SYNOD OF GLASGOW AND AIR, | At GLASGOW, *Aprile* [*sic*] *7th, 1741.* | By WILLIAM LEECHMAN *M.A.* | now PROFESSOR of DIVINITY in the UNIVERSITY of | *Glafgow.* | The FOURTH EDITION. | *GLASGOW,* | Printed by ROBERT FOULIS, and fold by him and Meff. HAMILTON | and BALFOUR, Book fellers in *Edinburgh.* | M DCC XLIV.

FORMULA: [? Demy] 8⁰ in fours: A–G⁴.

PAPER: Medium good quality; marks eagle /T; size of sheet 21 × 17 in.

TYPE: RP 1, RLP Cas, RB 1.

COPIES: L.

1744   Locke, John, *Essay concerning Human Under-* **53**
standing, abridged by John Wynne

AN | ABRIDGMENT | OF | Mr. *LOCKE's* | ESSAY | Concerning | *HUMAN UNDERSTANDING.* | The Sixth EDITION Corrected. | *GLASGOW:* | Printed and fold by ROBERT FOULIS | M, DCC, XLIV. [*There are two settings of this title-page, reading the same.*]

FORMULA: Post 8º in fours: π^2 A–2D⁴ 2E^2.

PAPER: Medium-good quality; thin; marks 6/?HR, 6/i.

TYPE: RP 1, RLP Cas, RB 1.

VARIANT: Issue on inferior paper, [? Small Crown] 8º:
Paper: Poor quality; no marks.

COPIES: G⁴ (both issues).

1744   Pindar, *Works*, G and L **54**

ΠΑΝΤΑ ΤΑ | ΠΙΝΔΑΡΟΥ | ΣΩΖΟΜΕΝΑ. | [*two columns of two lines each, separated by a vertical rule, 8; left:*] ΟΛΥΜΠΙΑ, | ΠΥΘΙΑ, | [*right:*] ΝΕΜΕΑ, | ΙΣΘΜΙΑ. | OMNIA | PINDARI | QUAE EXTANT. | [*two columns of two lines each, separated by a vertical rule, 6; left:*] | OLYMPIA, | PYTHIA, | [*right:*] NEMEA, | ISTHMIA. | CUM INTERPRETATIONE LATINA. | TOMUS I [II]. | *GLASGUAE:* | IN AEDIBUS ACADEMICIS | Excudebat ROBERTUS FOULIS, Academiae Typogra-|phus. MDCCXLIV.

FORMULA: Foolscap 8º in fours:
Vol. I: π^2 A–2G⁴ 2H1 (O4 *signed* ' K2 ' , 2D3 *signed* ' S ').
Vol. II: π1 2H⁴(–2H1) 2I–3C⁴ (–3C4) ‡² †⁴ (†4 *advertisements*).

PAPER: Good quality; marks 5/v, 4/v.

TYPE: GGP, GP, RB 1, RE 1; two-line Great Primer Greek caps as titling. Latin translation as footnotes to the text.

VARIANTS: Issue in [? Demy] 12º:
Formula: [? Demy] 12º in sixes: Vol. I: π^2 A–U⁶ X1.
Vol. II: π1 X⁶(–X1) Y–2I⁶ 2K² 2L1 ‡⁶ (‡6 *advertisements*).
This issue sometimes has as a frontispiece a copper-plate portrait of Pindar, signed ' *R. Strange Sculpt Edinr* ', plate-mark 112×71.
Paper: Good quality, marks 9/i, eagle/CM over T, no marks.
Common-paper issue in 12º:
Formula: As [? Demy] 12º.

Paper: Poor quality; no marks; size uncertain, but probably Crown.

COPIES: G⁴ (12⁰ fine and common), L (8⁰ and 12⁰ fine); the copy at O is a monster, consisting of Vol. I of the 12⁰ and Vol. II of the 8⁰ bound in contemporary calf (possibly by Foulis) as one volume.

55 Plutarch, *De Superstitione*, with Xenophon,   1744
Socrates and Aristodemus; Plato, *Alcibiades secundus*, G and L

ΠΛΟΥΤΑΡΧΟΣ | ΠΕΡΙ ΔΕΙΣΙΔΑΙΜΩΝΙΑΣ· | ΞΕΝΟ ΦΩΝΤΟΣ | ΣΩΚΡΑΤΗΣ *καὶ*[*ligature*] ΑΡΙΣΤΟΔΗΜΟΣ | ΠΕΡΙ ΠΡΟΝΟΙΑΣ· | ΠΛΑΤΩΝΟΣ | ΑΛΚΙΒΙΑΔΗΣ ΔΕΥΤΕΡΟΣ | ΠΕΡΙ ΠΡΟΣΕΥΧΗΣ. | PLUTARCHUS | De SUPERSTITIONE; | XENOPHONTIS | SOCRATES ET ALCIBIADES [*sic*] | De PROVIDENTIA; | PLATONIS | ALCIBIADES SECUNDUS | De NUMINE ORANDO. | *GLASGUAE:* | IN AEDIBUS ACADEMICIS | Excudebat ROBERTUS FOULIS, Academiae | Typographus. M DCC XLIV.

FORMULA: Post 12⁰ in sixes: π1 A–M⁶(–M4. *Only one copy of this issue seen, which did not contain the 1756 insertion.*)

PAPER: Medium-good quality; marks 6/i; size of sheet 18¾ × 14½ in.

TYPE: (1744) GP, RLP Cas, RB 1; (1756) RLP 1, GB. Greek and Latin on facing pages.

VARIANTS: Issue in [? Crown] 12⁰ in sixes:
Formula: (*as Post 12⁰ issue, also without the 1756 insertion*).
Paper: Medium quality; no marks; size of sheet 18¾ × 14 in.
Issue in Foolscap 12⁰:
Formula: Foolscap 12⁰ in sixes: π1 a1 b1 A–C⁶(±C3) D⁶ (±D2, D4) E–F⁶ ²A–F⁶ (±²F4, –(?)²F6. a1, *which is signed* '*a2*' *and* b1 *were inserted in 1756.* π1 *title-page*).
Paper: Medium-good quality; marks 4/v, 5/v.
Type: Latin follows Greek in the second alphabet.

NOTES: A Latin preface, dated 17 April 1756, was inserted in some copies of this book. Foulis confesses in it that he had been unable to attend personally to the correction of the text when it was printed, but had had to leave it to the care of a young and faltering compositor, who, being unversed in the business, had let many errors pass. On realising this, Foulis had decided to suppress the whole book; but recently he had been asked to allow it to circulate, purged of its errors, amongst the junior members of the University; and, almost against his will, he had consented.

The ' purgation ' was effected by inserting a list of errata with the Preface; but, even so, a good many copies of both issues remained on his hands for more than twenty years.

Stock in 1777: fine, 246 copies; common, 562 copies (*BQ* 12).

COPIES: G⁴ (Post), G² (Crown), C (Foolscap).

1744   Steele, Sir Richard, *The Conscious Lovers* 56

THE | CONSCIOUS LOVERS. | A | COMEDY. | Written by | Sir RICHARD STEELE. | [*quotation, 7 lines*] | *GLASGOW*, | Printed and fold by ROBERT FOULIS. | MDCCXLIV.

FORMULA: [? small Crown] 12⁰ in sixes: π1 ‡² A–F⁶ G²(–G4).

PAPER: Medium-poor quality; no marks.

TYPE: RB 1, RLP 1. Flowers 1.

COPIES: G².

c. 1745   Addison, Joseph, *Cato* 57 †

NOTES: Not seen. Advertised in No. 69 (1745) below; and in *GC* for 10 and 31 March 1746, the latter giving the prices 4*d.* and, fine, 6*d.*

1745   Aristotle, *Poetics*, G and L 58 †

ΑΡΙΣΤΟΤΕΛΟΥΣ | ΠΕΡΙ | ΠΟΙΗΤΙΚΗΣ. | ARISTOTELIS | DE | POETICA. | Accedunt Verfio Latina THEODORI GOULSTONI | et infigniores Lectiones variantes. | *GLASGUAE:* | IN AEDIBUS ACADEMICIS | Excudebat ROBERTUS FOULIS Academiae Ty-|pographus. MDCCXLV.

FORMULA: Foolscap 8⁰ in fours: π² χ1 A–Q⁴ R1 (*signed*) ' * ' on Q 1; π1 *title-page*, π2–χ1 *argument*).

PAPER: Medium-good quality; marks 4/v, 5/v; size of sheet 16½ × 13¼ in.

TYPE: GGP, GP, RB 1, RP 1, RLP Cas. The GGP has few of the small capitals that were to be substituted for the large ones in 1747. Latin follows Greek.

VARIANT: Issue in Pot 8⁰:

Paper: Poor quality; marks 2/i; size of sheet 14¾ × 12¼ in.

NOTES: *Price*: Wholesale: foolscap, 8*d*. (*BQ* 5).

Stock in 1777: foolscap, 7 copies, one imperfect (*BQ* 5).

COPIES: G⁴ (foolscap), L (both issues).

59 ' Aristotle ', *De Mundo*, G and L   1745

ΑΡΙΣΤΟΤΕΛΟΥΣ | ΠΕΡΙ | ΚΟΣΜΟΥ, | ΠΡΟΣ | ΑΛΕΞ
ΑΝΔΡΟΝ. | ARISTOTELIS | DE | MUNDO | LIBER,
AD | ALEX ANDRUM. | Cum Versione Latina | GULIELMI
BUDAEI. | *GLASGUAE:* | IN AEDIBUS ACADEMICIS |
Excudebat R. Foulis, Academiae Typographus, | MDCCXLV.

FORMULA: Foolscap 8⁰ in fours: π1 A–K⁴ L1 (C2 *signed* ' C3 ';
L1 *advertisements*).

PAPER: Medium-good quality; marks 4/i, 5/v.

TYPE: GGP, GP, RB 1, RP 1, RLP Cas.   Latin follows Greek.

VARIANT: Issue in [? Crown] 12⁰:

Formula: [? Crown] 12⁰ in sixes: π1 A–F⁶ G⁴ H1 (*H1
advertisements*).

Paper: Medium-poor quality; no marks.

NOTES: *Price*: Wholesale: 12⁰, 3*d*. (*BQ* 5).

Stock in 1777: 12⁰, 87 copies (*BQ* 5).

COPIES: G⁴ (8⁰), L (12⁰).

60 Buchanan, George, *Francisci Valesii et*   *c.* 1745
Maria Stuartae Epithalamium

NOTES: Not seen.   Advertised in No. 69 (Wardlaw, 1745) as
being ' *In the Preſs, and will ſpeedily be publiſh'd* '.

† 61 Hoadly, Benjamin, *An Abridgment of the Plain*   1745
Account of the Lord's Supper

AN | ABRIDGMENT | OF THE | PLAIN ACCOUNT | OF
THE | *NATURE and END* | OF THE | SACRAMENT |
OF THE | Lord's Supper; | Deſigned principally | *For the uſe
of Proteſtant Diſſenters.* | IN WHICH | All the texts in the
New Testament, relat-|ing to it, are produced and explained:
and | the whole doctrine about it, drawn from | them alone.
| To which are added, | FORMS of PRAYER. | *GLASGOW:* |
Printed and ſold by R. Foulis. Mdccxlv.

FORMULA: Pot 12⁰ in sixes: a⁶ A–P⁶ Q⁴ (signed ' * ' on A–Q $1).

PAPER: Medium quality; marks 1/iv.

TYPE: RB 1, RLP 1.

VARIANT: Issue on inferior paper, not seen (' * ' signatures; *GC* 10 March 1746).

NOTES: *Prices*: Retail: fine, 1*s*. 6*d*.; common, 6*d*. (*GC* 10 March 1746).

COPIES: G⁴ (fine).

1745   Hutcheson, Francis, *Philosophiae Moralis* **62**
                        Institutio Compendiaria, L

PHILOSOPHIAE | MORALIS | INSTITUTIO COMPEN DIARIA, | LIBRIS III. | Ethices et Jurifprudentiae Naturalis | ELEMENTA continens. | Auctore FRANCISCO HUTCHESON | in Academia Glafguenfi P.P. | [*plain rule, 68*] | Editio altera auctior et emendatior. | [*plain rule, 64*] | [*quotation, 2 lines*] | *GLASGUAE*, | Typis ROBERTI FOULIS, Academiae Typographi; | apud quem venales proftant. | M DCC XLV.

FORMULA: Foolscap 8⁰ in fours: a⁴ A–2Z⁴ (*with cancels at* A2, B4, G1 *and* 2Y2; *cancellans* B4 *signed* 'i B2'; Q1, Q2 *signed* ' P ', ' P2 ', *but with* Q*s stamped in*).

PAPER: Medium-good quality; marks 4/v; size of sheet 16½ × 13¼ in.

TYPE: RP 1, RLP Cas, RB 1.

VARIANT: Issue in [? Crown] 12⁰:
    Formula: [? Crown] 12⁰ in sixes: *a*² *b*² A–2G⁶ 2H⁴.
    Paper: Medium-poor quality; marks 9/i.

COPIES: G⁴ (both issues), L (8⁰).

1745   Leechman, William, *The Nature of Prayer*, **63**
                                    a Sermon

THE | NATURE, | REASONABLENESS, | AND | AD VANTAGES | OF | PRAYER; | With an ATTEMPT to anfwer | The OBJECTIONS againft it. | A SERMON | BY | WILLIAM LEECHMAN, | Profeffor of Divinity in the Univerfity of *Glafgow*. | PSALM LXV. 2. | [*quotation, 1 line*] | THE THIRD EDITION. | *GLASGOW*, | Printed by ROBERT FOULIS, and fold by him, at *London* | by ANDREW MILLAR over-againſt *Katherine-ſtreet* in | the *Strand*, and by the Bookſellers in *Edinburgh*. | M DCC XLV.

FORMULA: Small Crown 8⁰ in fours: A–H⁴.

PAPER: Medium quality; no marks; size of sheet 18½ × 14¼ in.

TYPE: RP I, RLP Cas.

COPIES: L.

64 Otway, Thomas, *The Orphan*   1745

THE | ORPHAN: | OR, THE | UNHAPPY MARRIAGE. | A | TRAGEDY. | [*quotation, 7 lines*] | *GLASGOW:* | Printed and ſold by ROBERT FOULIS. | MDCCXLV.

FORMULA: Pot 8⁰ in fours: A–K⁴ (K4 *advertisements*).

PAPER: Medium-poor quality; marks I/iii, I/iv, I/v.

TYPE: RB I, RLP Cas, RGP I. Flowers I and 2.

VARIANT: Issue on better paper, not seen (*GC* 23 March 1747).

NOTES: *Prices*: Retail: fine, 6*d*., [common], 4*d*. (*GC* 23 March 1747).

COPIES: G².

65 Periodical. *The Glasgow Courant*   1745–60

HEADING (OF EARLIEST NUMBER SEEN): NUMB. 6. | THE | GLASGOW COURANT. | [*plain rule, 204*] | From MONDAY, NOVEMBER 18, to MONDAY, NOVEMBER 25, 1745. | [*plain rule, 205*] [*The second of the two dates was the date of issue.*]

COLOPHON: Printed for MATTHEW SIMSON. Subſcriptions and Advertiſements are taken in by JOHN GILMOUR Stationer, at his | Shop, oppoſite to *Gibſon's* Land, *Salt-mercat*; To whoſe Care, all Propoſals and Letters from Correſpondents | are deſired to be directed. Poſtages paid by the Publiſher. [*The heading and colophon remained substantially unchanged throughout the life of the newspaper.*]

FORMULA: [? Crown] 2⁰: π².

Note: horizontal chain-lines, which means that the sheets were probably Double Crown originally, measuring 27 × 20¼ in. (a reasonable size for Double Crown at this period, and matching quite well with the Small Crown used by Foulis in 1745, which measured about 18¾ × 14¼ in.). It is of course possible that Foulis was printing *GC* as Double Crown 4⁰ in twos, but, since in his book-printing he never used any paper larger than Royal up to 1760, it seems much more likely that he was cutting the sheets in half and printing them as Crown folio. (See Nos. 83 and 201 below for books printed on half-sheets of Double Crown in 1747 and 1751.)

PAPER: Medium-poor quality (though good by the standards of contemporary newspapers); no marks; size of half-sheet $20\frac{1}{4} \times 13\frac{1}{2}$ in.

TYPE: *Text*: 1745–55 RLP Cas; as the fount became worn, it gradually replaced by RLP 1, the last of the RLP Cas being discarded in 1755. Mid-1755–1760: RLP 1.

Headline: Wilson's two-line Double Pica, with date line and colophon in RE 1 (RE 2 from 1755).

Several blocks were regularly used in advertisements; some of them may have been the property of the advertisers, and none was used in any book printed by Foulis.

NOTES: *Publication*: No. 1 must have appeared on 21 October 1745; thereafter the paper appeared weekly on Mondays until 9 October 1760 (No. 782), when the following announcement appeared: ' The PUBLISHER begs leave to acquaint his READERS, that as his other concerns engage him to a cloſe attendance, and as the time for publiſhing the COURANT, by the alteration in the courſe of the POST, renders him unable to accompliſh it by reaſon of his health, he is obliged to ſtop further publication of the ſame.' An extra number reporting the battle of Culloden appeared at the end of April 1746 (No. 30).

Foulis's advertisements normally appeared on p. 4, sometimes displayed in a 'title-page' layout printed from the same type as the title-page of the book advertised.

Price: (?) 2*d*. a copy, including $\frac{1}{2}d$. tax.

COPIES: G⁴ (Nos. 6, 11, 12, 29, 30, 34, 38–9, 41–55, 76–7; then a complete run from No. 92, 20 July 1747, to No. 782, 9 October 1760, with the sole exception of No. 718, 23 July 1759). The following numbers not at G⁴ have been found at other libraries: G² (Nos. 17, 28, 31, 33), L (Nos. 10, 13–28), LC (Nos. 36, 40, 56–60, 62, 64, 66, 69, 74, 80, 81, 87).

The remaining numbers which I have *not* examined are Nos. 1–5, 7–9, 32, 35, 37, 61, 63, 65, 67–8, 70–73, 75, 78–9, 82–6, 88–91, 718.

1745   Ramsay, Allan, *The Gentle Shepherd* **66**

THE | GENTLE SHEPHERD. | A | *SCOTS* | PASTORAL COMEDY. | [*plain rule, 65*] | By ALLAN RAMSAY. | [*plain rule,*

64] | The Eighth Edition with the SANGS. | [*plain rule, 68*] | *GLASGOW,* | Printed by ROBERT FOULIS | MDCCXLV.

FORMULA: Post 12⁰ in sixes: A–G⁶.

PAPER: Medium quality; thin; marks 6/i, 6/HR.

TYPE: RB i, RLP Cas.   Flowers i and 2.

VARIANT: Issue in Small Crown 12⁰:
Paper: Medium-poor quality; no marks; size of sheet 18¾ × 14 in.

COPIES: G⁴ (Crown), O (Post).

67 Smith, John, *The Excellency and Nobleness of*   1745
True Religion

THE | EXCELLENCY | AND | NOBLENESS | OF | TRUE RELIGION, | In its ORIGINAL, NATURE, PROPERTYS, | OPERA TIONS, PROGRESS and END. | [*plain rule, 75*] | BY | *JOHN SMITH*, fometime Fellow of | *Queen's* [*sic*] *College* in *Cambridge.* | [*plain rule, 75*] | GLASGOW, | Printed by ROBERT FOULIS, and fold by him there. | M DCC XLV.

FORMULA: [? Printing Demy] 8⁰ in fours: π1 A–K⁴ L1.

PAPER: Medium-poor quality; marks 9/i.

TYPE: RP i, RB i.

VARIANT: Issue in Crown 8⁰:
Paper: Medium-poor quality, no marks, size of sheet *c.* 19 × 14½ in.

COPIES: G⁴, L (both Demy), O (Crown).

† **68** Sophocles, *Tragedies*, G and L   1745

ΑΙ ΤΟΥ | ΣΟΦΟΚΛΕΟΥΣ | ΤΡΑΓΩΔΙΑΙ | ΣΩΖΟΜΕΝΑΙ | ΕΠΤΑ. | SOPHOCLIS | T R A G OE D I AE | QUAE EX TANT | SEPTEM; | CUM VERSIONE LATINA. | ADDITAE SUNT LECTIONES VARIANTES; ET NOTAE VIRI | DOCTISSIMI T. JOHNSON IN QUATUOR TRAGOEDIAS. | TOM. I [II]. | *G L A S G U AE:* | IN AEDIBUS ACADEMICIS | Excudebat R. FOULIS Academiae Typographus, apud quem ve- | nales proftant; Edinburgi, apud G. HAMILTON et J. BALFOUR, | et A. KINCAID. | M DCC XLV. [*with the misprint* ' DOCISSIMI ' *for* ' DOCTISSIMI ' *in Vol.* II.]

FORMULA: Foolscap 8⁰ in fours:
Vol. I: π1 a² A–2X⁴ 2Y² (*signed* 'VOL. I.' *on* B–2Y $1; 2T4 *advertisements*).
Vol. II: π1 A–31⁴ 3K² 3L⁴ (*signed* 'VOL. II.' *on* A–3L $1).

PAPER: Medium quality; marks 4/v, 4/i, 4/iii, 5/v.

TYPE: GP, RLP Cas, RB 1. Greek and Latin on facing pages.

VARIANTS: The Foolscap 8⁰ is sometimes found with variant title-pages:
Title-pages: [*Reset, reading as before down to line 15, except no misprint* 'DOCISSIMI'; *then:*] EXCUDEBAT ROBERTUS FOULIS ACADEMIAE TYPOGRAPHUS. | M DCC XLV.
Issue in two volumes, Pot 8⁰, Greek and Latin:
Title-pages: [*Found with the* '*Edinburgh*' *versions only.*]
Formula and Type: Same as the Foolscap 8⁰
Paper: Medium-poor quality; marks 1/v.
Issue in one volume, Foolscap 4⁰, Greek only:
Title-page: ['*Edinburgh*' *version, Vol. I, minus line 10* ('CUM VERSIONE LATINA.') *and line 13* ('TOM. I.'); *sometimes with misprint* 'DOCISSIMI']
Formula: Foolscap 4⁰ in twos: π1 A–5O² 5P1.
Paper: Good quality; marks 4/v.
Type: Greek only.
Issue in one volume, Pot 4⁰, Greek only:
Title-page, Formula and Type: Same as the Foolscap 4⁰.
Paper: Medium-good quality; marks 1/v.

NOTES: *Prices*: Wholesale: 8⁰, Foolscap and Pot mixed, 3s. (*BQ* 5). Retail: 4⁰, G and L, 10s. 6d. in 1779 (Spotiswood, p. 85).
Stock in 1777: 8⁰, Foolscap and Pot mixed, 6 copies; ditto, Vol. II, 5 copies; Foolscap 4⁰, imperfect, 5 copies (*BQ* 5).

COPIES: G⁴ (Foolscap 8⁰, second title-pages, Foolscap 4⁰), L (Pot 8⁰, Pot 4⁰), O (Foolscap 8⁰, 'Edinburgh' title-pages).

1745   Wardlaw, Elizabeth Lady, *Hardyknute* **69**

HARDYKNUTE. | A | FRAGMENT | OF AN | ANTIENT SCOTS POEM. | GLASGOW: | Printed and fold by ROBERT FOULIS. 1745 | [Price Six-Pence.]

FORMULA: Pot 4⁰ in twos: A² B–G² (*signed* '*·*' *on* B–G $1).

PAPER: Medium-good quality; marks 1/iv.

TYPE: RGP 1.

VARIANT: Issue on inferior paper, Pot 4⁰:
  Title-page: [*Last line*:] [Price Four-pence.]
  Formula: (*Without* ' * ' *signatures.*)
  Paper: Medium quality; marks, 2/1.
NOTES: *Prices*: Retail: fine, 6*d.*; common, 4*d.* (title-pages).
COPIES: G⁴ (fine); L (common).

† **70** Xenophon, *Hieron*, G and L 1745

ΞΕΝΟΦΩΝΤΟΣ | ΙΕΡΩΝ, | ἢ ΤΥΡΑΝΝΙΚΟΣ. | ΧΕΝΟ
PHONTIS | HIERO, | SIVE | DE REGNO. | Accedit verſio
Latina JOANNIS LEUNCLAVII. | *G L A S G U AE*: | IN AEDIBUS
ACADEMICIS | EXCUDEBAT ROBERTUS FOULIS ACADEMIAE
TYPOGRAPHUS. | M DCC XLV.

FORMULA: Foolscap 8⁰ in fours: π² A–F⁴ G² (A2 *signed* ' A3 ';
π2 *advertisements*).

PAPER: Medium-good quality; marks 4/v; size of sheet
16½ × 13¼ in.

TYPE: GP, RLP 1. Latin follows Greek.

NOTES: *Price*: Wholesale: 6*d.* (*BQ* 5).
  Stock in 1777: 1 copy (*BQ* 5).

COPIES: G⁴, L.

† **71** Aeschylus, *Tragedies*, G and L 1746

ΑΙ ΤΟΥ | ΑΙΣΧΥΛΟΥ | ΤΡΑΓΩΔΙΑΙ | ΣΩΖΟΜΕΝΑΙ |
ΕΠΤΑ. | AESCHYLI | T R A G O E D I AE | Q U A E E X
T A N T | SEPTEM. | CUM VERSIONE LATINA, | ET |
LECTIONESVARIANTIBUS. | TOM. I [II]. | *G L A S G U A E*:
| IN AEDIBUS ACADEMICIS | EXCUDEBAT ROBERTUS FOULIS
ACADEMIAE TYPOGRAPHUS,|apud quem proſtant. M DCC XLVI.

FORMULA: Foolscap 8⁰ in fours:
  Vol. I: a⁴ b² A–2R⁴ 2S1.
  Vol. II: π1 A–2O⁴.

PAPER: Medium-good quality; marks 4/v.

TYPE: GP, GGP, RLP 1, RB 1. Greek and Latin on facing
pages. Pagination: a separate series in each volume.

VARIANTS: Issue in two volumes, Pot 8⁰, Greek and Latin:
  Title-pages, Formula and Type: Same as the Foolscap 8⁰.
  Paper: Medium-poor quality; marks 1/v, 1/iv.
  Issue in two volumes, Pot 4⁰, Greek and Latin:

Title-pages: [*Vol.* I *omits* ' TOM. I.'] [*Vol.* II: *reads as the 8°*
issues, Vol. II, *down to* ' . . . ACADEMICIS | ', *line 15; then:*]
Excudebat Robertus Foulis Academiae Typographus. |
M DCC XLVI.

Formula: Pot 4° in twos: Vol. I: a^2 b–c^2 A–4L^2 4MI.
Vol. II: πI $^2\pi$I 4N–7Q^2 7RI.

Paper: Good quality; marks 5/v, 5/iv.

Type: Greek and Latin on facing pages as in the 8° issues, but
pagination runs through both volumes in a single series.

Issue in one volume, Foolscap 4°, Greek only:

Title-page: [*As the 8° issues, Vol.* II, *down to* ' SEPTEM. | ',
line 8; then:] CUM | LECTIONIBUS VARIANTIBUS. |
G L A S G U AE: [*etc., as before.*]

Formula: Foolscap 4° in twos: πI a–b^2 A–4L^2 4MI.

Paper: Good quality; marks 4/v; size of sheet 16¾ × 13 in.

Type: Greek only.

NOTES: On 7R1^v of the Pot 4° issue is an advertisement for
books of which Andrew as well as Robert Foulis is named as
printer.

Prices: Wholesale: Pot 8°, 3s.; Foolscap 4°, 6s. (*BQ* 4).
Retail: Foolscap 4°, 8s. (*CP* 3).

Stock in 1777: Pot 8°, 6 copies; Foolscap 4°, 4 copies (*BQ* 4).

COPIES: G⁴ (Foolscap 8°, Pot 4°, Foolscap 4°), L (all four issues).

1746   Bennet, Benjamin, *The Persecution and Cruelty* 72
                    of the Church of Rome

THE | PERSECUTION | AND | CRUELTY | OF THE |
CHURCH of ROME. | IN A | DISCOURSE | On Rev. xvii. 6. |
[*quotation, 3 lines*] | By BENJAMIN BENNET. | *GLASGOW:* |
Printed in the Year, MDCCXLVI.

FORMULA: Pot 8° in fours: a^2 A–D^4.

PAPER: Medium quality; marks 1/v; size of sheet 15 × 12 in.

TYPE: RLP I RB I.

VARIANT: Issue on inferior paper, [? Crown] 8°:
  Paper: Poor quality; no marks.

NOTES: *Stock in 1777*: fine, 118 copies; common, 258 copies
(*BQ* 12). Ascribed to the Foulis Press on the evidence of the
typography and of the entry in *BQ*.

COPIES: L (fine), G² (both issues).

73 Cooper, Anthony Ashley, Lord Shaftesbury,   1746
Letters

LETTERS | OF THE EARL OF | SHAFTESBURY, | AUTHOR OF THE | CHARACTERISTICKS, | COLLEC TED INTO ONE VOLUME. | PRINTED M DCC XLVI.

FORMULA: Writing Demy 12⁰ in sixes: π^2 A–K⁶.

PAPER: Good quality; marks eagle/T; size of sheet 21 × 16½ in.

TYPE: RLP 1, RB 1.

VARIANT: Issue on inferior paper, [? Crown] 12⁰:
   Paper: Medium quality; no marks.

NOTES: A companion volume to Shaftesbury's *Characteristics*, 1743–5 (No. 30), and probably also printed at the Foulis Press; see the NOTES to that entry.

COPIES: L (both issues).

74 Fénelon, *Letters to the Duke of Burgundy*, E   1746

LETTERS | TO THE | DUKE OF BURGUNDY, | FROM | Mᴿ DE FENELON | ARCHBISHOP OF CAMBRAY. | GLASGOW: | PRINTED AND SOLD BY ROBERT FOULIS. | M DCC XLVI.

FORMULA: Foolscap 4⁰ in twos: A^2 B–G².

PAPER: Medium quality; marks 4/v.

TYPE: RE 1, RLP Cas (with RLP 1 mixed in). Two-line English capitals as titling.

VARIANTS: Issues in [? Demy] and [? Pot] 4⁰, not seen (*BQ* 11).

NOTES: *Publication*: published by 22 October 1746 (*GC* 20 October 1746).
   Prices: Wholesale: Demy 4⁰, 3*d*.; Foolscap 4⁰, 2½*d*.; Pot 4⁰, 2*d*. (*BQ* 11).
   Stock in 1777: Demy 4⁰, 72 copies; Foolscap 4⁰, 18 copies; Pot 4⁰, 26 copies (*BQ* 11).

COPIES: G⁴ (Foolscap 4⁰).

† **75** Foulis, Robert and Andrew, *Auction*   1746–1770
Catalogues

NOTES: The Foulis brothers held regular evening book auctions, some of which were advertised in *GC* and (after

1760) in *GJ*. Nine such notices appeared in *GC* between 14 January 1746 (advertised on 23 December 1745) and 1 January 1750. From March 1750 until October 1760 auction notices appeared much more frequently in *GC*, being repeated every week for considerable periods. After the demise of *GC* in 1760, the notices continued to appear in *GJ*, though not nearly so often; it appears, nevertheless that the sales were still normally held at least once a week. The last advertisement I have seen occured in *GJ* for 15 March 1770.

It is clear from these advertisements that a catalogue was usually printed for each sale, copies of which were given away on the same or on the preceding day. Only one copy of any of these catalogues is known to have survived; it is described below.

Occasionally complete libraries would be auctioned. The following libraries were specifically mentioned:

> William Forbes, Professor of Law, Glasgow University (*GC* 3 November 1746).
> Patrick Maxwell (*GC* 26 March 1750).
> Robert Murdoch (*GC* 16 December 1754).
> William M'Ilhose (*GJ* 28 January 1768).
> Capt. Thomas Walker (*GJ* 18 February 1768).

The sole surviving catalogue was for the auction of the library of the Reverend Alexander Campbell in 1765:

A | CATALOGUE | OF THE VALUABLE | LIBRARY | OF THE REVEREND | Mr. ALEXANDER CAMPBELL, | Late Minifter of the Gofpel at INVERERA; | WHICH BEGINS TO BE SOLD | BY AUCTION | At R. and A. FOULIS'S AUCTION-ROOM | In the OLD-COFFEE-HOUSE, | On Monday the 4th of March, 1765, | at 7 o'clock at Night. | Commiffions directed to R. and A. FOULIS, will be carefully | obferv'd. | GLASGOW, M.DCC.LXV.

FORMULA: Pot 4° in twos: π1 A–H².

PAPER: Poor quality; marks (?) 1/v.

TYPE: RP 2.

COPIES: G².

1746　　Montgomery, Capt. Alexander, *The Cherrie* 76 †
　　　　　　　　　　　　　　　　　　　　　　　and the Slae

THE | CHERRIE | AND THE | SLAE, | COMPYLT INTO | SCOTTIS MEETER, | BY CAPTAIN | ALEX. MONT

109

GOMERY. | FIRST PRINTED M D XCVII BY | ROBERT
WALGRAVE PRINTER | TO KING JAMES VI. | GLAS
GOW: | PRINTED AND SOLD BY ROBERT FOULIS |
M DCC XLVI.

FORMULA: Post 12⁰ in sixes: A–D⁶(–D6).

PAPER: Medium quality; marks 6/i.

TYPE: RB 1.

COPIES: L.

† 77 Steele, Sir Richard, *The Guardian*   1746

THE | GUARDIAN. | VOL. I [II]. | GLASGOW: | PRINTED
AND SOLD BY ROBERT FOULIS. | M DCC XLVI. [*Both title-pages
from the same setting.*]

FORMULA: Foolscap 8⁰ in fours:

Vol. I: a² b1 A–2U⁴(–2U4; b1 *signed* ' b3 ').
Vol. II: π² A–2X⁴ 2Y² (*signed* ' VOL 2.' *on* A–2U $1 *and* 2Y1).

PAPER: Medium-good quality; marks 4/v; size of sheet
16½ × 13 in.

TYPE: RLP 1, RE 1, RB 1.

VARIANT: Issue in [? Crown] 12⁰:
Formula: [? Crown] 12⁰ in sixes: Vol. I a² *b1* A–2E⁶ 2F⁴(–2F4).
Vol. II: π² A–2F⁶ 2G⁴ (*signed* ' VOL 2.' *on* A–2G $1).
Paper: Poor quality; marks 9/i.

NOTES: *Publication*: in the press 31 March 1746; published by
22 September 1746 (*GC*).
Prices: Retail: 8⁰, 6s. neatly bound and lettered, 5s. in sheets;
12⁰, 4s. neatly bound and lettered, 3s. in sheets. ' The Price of
the Common Paper will be raiſed after Martinmaſs next [i.e.
11 November 1746] to 4s. 6d.' (*GC* 22 September 1746).

COPIES: G⁴ (8⁰ and 12⁰).

† 78 Theocritus, *Works*, G and L   1746

ΤΑ ΤΟΥ | ΘΕΟΚΡΙΤΟΥ | ΣΕΣΩΣΜΕΝΑ. | THEOCRITI |
QUAE EXTANT. | Ex Editione DANIELIS HEINSII expreſſa.
| – nec erubuit Sylvas habitare Thalia. VIRG. | GLASGUAE,
| IN AEDIBUS ACADEMICIS | EXCUDEBANT RO
BERTUS ET ANDREAS FOULIS | ACADEMIAE TYPO
GRAPHI | M. DCC. XLVI.

FORMULA: Foolscap 8⁰ in fours: π² *⁴ A–Z⁴ 2A² 2B–2H⁴ (π1 *half-title*).

PAPER: Good quality; marks 4/iv, 4/v, 5/iv.

TYPE: GP, GGP, RB I, RLP I. A complete alphabet of two-line Great Primer Greek capitals in the scholia. Canon Greek initials. The Latin translation as footnotes to the text.

VARIANTS: Issue in Pot 8⁰, Greek and Latin:
Paper: Medium quality; marks 1/v, 1/iv, 2/iv; size of sheet 14¾ × 12¼ in.
Issue in Foolscap 4⁰, Greek only:
Formula: Foolscap 4⁰: π² *⁴ A–P⁴ Q² R–Z⁴ (E2 *signed* ' ʒE ').
Paper: Good quality; marks 4/ii, 4/v, 4/iv, 5/v.
Type: Greek only, re-imposed without footnotes.
Issue in [? Pot] 4⁰, Greek only, not seen (*BQ* 3–4).

NOTES: Andrew Foulis's name appears for the first time in the imprint as University Printer.
Prices: Wholesale: 8⁰, fine, 2s. 6d.; 8⁰, common, 2s.; 4⁰, fine, 4s. 6d.; 4⁰, common, 3s. (*BQ* 3–4). Retail: 8⁰, fine, 3s.; 4⁰, fine, 5s. 6d. (*CP* 3–4).
Stock in 1777: 8⁰, fine, 8 copies; 8⁰, common, 183 copies; 4⁰, fine, 17 copies; 4⁰, common, 86 copies (*BQ* 3–4).
(These details of prices and stock are assumed to apply to this book, and not to a Theocritus which *may* have appeared in 1753. See No. 267 below.)

COPIES: G⁴ (Foolscap 8⁰, Pot 8⁰, Foolscap 4⁰), L (ditto).

1746   [Anon.], *True Religion, a Mystery* **79**

NOTES: Not seen. Listed by Duncan (p. 52, No. 46) as ' True Religion, a Myſtery, 8vo.'

1747   Butler, Samuel, *Hudibras* **80**

NOTES: Not seen. Advertised in *GC*, 7 September 1747 as ' *Lately Printed, and ſold,*' ' *with Cutts*'.

1747   ' Cebes ' *Table*, G and L **81**

Ὁ' ΤΟΥ | ΚΕΒΗΤΟΣ | ΠΙΝΑΞ. | ACCEDIT | INTERPRE TATIO LATINA, | EX EDITIONE | JACOBI GRONOVII. | GLASGUAE, | IN AEDIBUS ACADEMICIS | EXCUDE BAT ROBERTUS FOULIS, | ACADEMIAE TYPOGRA PHUS. | MDCCXLVII. [*cancellans*]

III

FORMULA: Foolscap 12⁰ in sixes: a⁶(±a1) b–f⁶ g² A⁶ B⁴

PAPER: Medium-good quality; marks 5/v.

TYPE: GGP with smaller capitals, GP, RB 1, Latin follows Greek. Without catchwords.

VARIANTS: Issue in Pot 12⁰, Greek and Latin:
Paper: Medium quality; marks 1/v.
Issue on vellum, Greek only:
Title-page: [*uncancelled; reads as above down to line 4* (' ACCE DIT | ')*; then:*] INTERPRETATIO | JACOBI GRONOVII. | GLASGUAE, [*etc., as before.*]
Formula: 12⁰ in sixes: a–f⁶.
Vellum: size of sheet at least 15¼ × 11¾ in.
Type: Greek only.

NOTES: Edited by Professor James Moor (Irving, David, *Lives of Scotish Writers* (Edinburgh, 1839), ii. p. 301).

COPIES: G⁴ (Pot 12⁰), L (Pot 12⁰, vellum), O (Foolscap).

82 Congreve, William, *The Mourning Bride* 1747

NOTES: Not seen. Advertised in *GC*, 23 March 1747.
Prices: Retail: fine, 6*d*.; common, 4*d*.

83 Demosthenes, *Philippics and Olynthiacs,* G and L 1747

ΛΟΓΟΙ ΤΟΥ | ΔΗΜΟΣΘΕΝΟΥΣ | ΚΑΤΑ | ΦΙΛΙΠΠΟΥ | ΤΕΣΣΑΡΕΣ, | ΟΛΥΝΘΙΑΚΟΙ | ΤΡΕΙΣ, | CUM LATINA VERSIONE ADJECTA. | GLASGUAE: | IN AEDIBUS ACADEMICIS, | EXCUDEBAT R. FOULIS, ACADEMIAE TYPOGRA phus, | APUD QUEM VENALES PROSTANT. | MDCCXLVII.

FORMULA: Crown 12⁰ in sixes: π1 A⁴ χ² B–I⁶ K⁴, ²A–D⁶ ²E⁴ ³A–C⁶ ³D², ⁴A⁴ ⁴B⁶ (*vertical chain-lines; an unopened copy at G⁴ proves it to have been printed by half-sheet imposition on half double-sized sheets of paper*).

PAPER: Medium-poor quality; no marks; size of half sheet, 19½ × 14¾ in.

TYPE: GGP with smaller capitals, RB 1, RLP 1. Latin follows Greek in the third and fourth signature alphabets.

NOTES: In the press in October 1746 (advertisement in No. 74).

COPIES: G⁴.

Η ΤΟΥ | 'ΟΜΗΡΟΥ | ΙΛΙΑΣ. | HOMERI | ILIAS. | Inter
pretatio Latina adjecta est, | ex editione S. Clarke. |
VOL. I [II]. | GLASGUAE, | IN AEDIBUS ACADEMICIS |
EXCUDEBANT ROBERTUS ET ANDREAS FOULIS |
ACADEMIAE TYPOGRAPHI. | M.DCC.XLVII. [*Vol.* II
reads ' 'Η ΤΟΥ ' in line 1; different settings]

colophon: [*Vol.* II 2L4ᵛ only] EXCUDEBATUR APUD
FRATRES | ROBERTUM ET ANDREAM FOULIS, |
ACADEMIAE GLASGUENSI | TYPOGRAPHOS, ANN.
M.DCC.XLVII. | PRIDIE NONAS SEPTEMBRIS [4 Septem-
ber 1747].

formula: Foolscap 8⁰ in fours:
Vol. I: π² A–2H⁴ 2I², ²A–U⁴ ²X².
Vol. II: π² A–2L⁴, ²A–Y⁴ ²Z² (signed ' Vol. 2 ' on $1 except π1;
π2 blank).

paper: Good quality; marks 4/ii, 4/i, 5/v, 4/v, 4/iv.

type: GP, RB 1, RLP 1. Latin follows Greek in the second
signature alphabets of each volume. (A copy seen in which all
the Greek is collected in the first volume and all the Latin in
the second, which makes nonsense of the ' Vol. 2 ' signings.)
Without catchwords.

variants: Issue in Foolscap 8⁰, Greek only:
Title-pages: [From the same type as the Greek and Latin Foolscap
8⁰ issue, but ' 'Η ΤΟΥ ' in line 1 of Vol. I as well as of Vol. II; and
with the omission of lines 6 and 7, ' Interpretatio ... Clarke.'
There are also alternative settings of both title-pages in slightly
larger type, emended as above and with the further alteration that the
' GLASGUAE ' of the imprint is followed by a colon instead of a
comma.
Finally, the original title-pages are also found unaltered with this
issue.]
Colophon: [Same as Greek and Latin issue.]
Formula: Foolscap 8⁰ in fours: Vol. I: π² A–2H⁴ 2I².
Vol. II: π² A–2L⁴ (π2 blank; signed ' Vol. 2.' on $1 except π1).
Paper: Good quality; marks 4/ii, 4/1, 5/v, 4/v.
Type: Greek only.
Issues in Pot 8⁰, with and without the Latin, not seen; their
existence inferred from the usual practice of the Press at this
period (cf. Nos. 68, 71), and from the fact that *BQ* (p. 3) refers
to common paper 8⁰, Greek only.
Issue in 8⁰ on vellum, Greek only:

Title-pages, Colophon, Formula and Type: Same as Foolscap 8⁰, Greek only.

Vellum: Poor quality; size of sheet at least 13¾ × 11½ in.

Issue in Foolscap 4⁰, Greek only:

Title-pages, Colophon, Formula and Type: Same as Foolscap 8⁰, Greek only.

Paper: Good quality; marks 4/ii, 4/i, 5/v, 4/v.

Issue in Pot 4⁰, Greek only:

Title-pages, Colophon, Formula and Type: Same as Foolscap 8⁰, Greek only.

Paper: Good quality, thin; marks 1/v.

NOTES: *Publication*: probably published on about 15 February 1747 (*GC*), in spite of the date given in the Colophon.

Prices: Wholesale: 8⁰, Greek only, common (probably = Pot), 2s. 6d.; 8⁰, Greek only, vellum, 10s.; Foolscap 4⁰, Greek only, 6s. (*BQ* 3, 5). Retail: 8⁰, Greek only, (?) Foolscap, 4s. (*CP* 4).

Stock in 1777: 8⁰, Greek only, common, 2 copies; 8⁰, vellum, 3 copies; 8⁰, fine and common mixed, 4 copies; Foolscap 4⁰, 32 copies. (*BQ* 3, 5.)

COPIES: G⁴ (Foolscap 8⁰ with and without Latin, Foolscap 4⁰), L (all issues except Pot 8⁰s).

---

† **85** Hutcheson, Francis, *A Short Introduction to* 1747
Moral Philosophy

A SHORT | INTRODUCTION | TO | MORAL PHILO SOPHY, | IN THREE BOOKS; | CONTAINING THE | ELEMENTS OF ETHICKS | AND THE | LAW OF NATURE. | BY FRANCIS HUTCHESON, LLD. | LATE PROFESSOR OF PHILOSOPHY IN | THE UNIVERSITY OF GLASGOW. | TRANSLATED FROM THE LATIN. | GLASGOW, | PRINTED AND SOLD BY ROBERT FOULIS. | PRINTER TO THE UNIVER SITY. | MDCCXLVII.

FORMULA: Foolscap 8⁰ in fours: a^2 b–c^4 A–2U⁴ 2X².

PAPER: Medium quality; marks 5/iv; size of sheet 16½ × 13¼ in.

TYPE: RLP Cas, RB 1, RE 1.

VARIANT: Issue in [? Printing Demy] 12⁰:

Formula: [? Printing Demy] 12⁰ in sixes: a⁶ c⁴ A–2F⁶ (a3 as well as a2 *signed* ' a2 '; B2 *signed* ' A2 ').

Paper: Medium-poor quality, marks 9/IW.

NOTES: *Publication*: published by 7 September 1747 (*GC*).

COPIES: 8⁰: G⁴, L; 12⁰: O.

1747   Longinus, *On the Sublime*, (?) G and L **86**

NOTES: Not seen. Listed by Duncan (p. 53, No. 56) simply as
' Longinus '.

1747   Milton, John, *Paradise Lost* **87**

NOTES: Not seen. Advertised in *GC*, 7 September 1747 as
' *Lately Printed, and fold,*' ' *with Cutts* '.

1747   Milton, John, *Paradise Regained, etc.* **88**

PARADISE REGAIN'D. | A | POEM, | IN | FOUR BOOKS.
| TO WHICH IS ADDED | SAMSON AGONISTES; | AND |
POEMS UPON SEVERAL OCCASIONS, | WITH A
TRACTATE OF | EDUCATION. | THE AUTHOR | JOHN
MILTON. | GLASGOW: | PRINTED AND SOLD BY ROBERT
FOULIS | M DCC XLVII.

FORMULA: Pot 12⁰ in sixes: π1 χ1 A–E⁶ F⁴ ²χ1 ²A–E⁶ ²F² ³χ1
³A–R⁶(–³R6) (π1 general title-page; χ1, ²χ1 and ³χ1 are separate
title-pages each dated 1747, to *Paradise Regained*, *Samson* and
Poems on Several Occasions respectively; the title-page to *A
Tractate* is on ³P5).

PAPER: Medium-poor quality; marks 1/iv, 1/v.

TYPE: RB 1, RLP 1. Without catchwords.

VARIANT: Issue on better-quality paper, not seen (*GC* 23
March 1747).

NOTES: *Publication*: published by 23 March 1747 (*GC*).
   Prices: Retail: fine, 6*d*.; common, 4*d*. (*GC* 23 March 1747;
these prices probably refer to the first alphabet only, containing
Paradise Regained).

COPIES: G⁴, L (both common).

1747–9   Milton, John, *L'Allegro and il Penseroso* **89**

NOTES: Not seen. '*Milton's Allegro and Penferofo. Price 3d.*' is
advertised as '*This Day publifhed and fold by* ROBERT FOULIS '
in *GC* for 23 March 1747. A quarto edition of *L'Allegro and il
Penseroso* is advertised in No. 123 (1749), though this may not
be the same one. Cf. No. 198 below (1751).

90 Milton, John, *Comus* 1747

COMUS. | A | MASK | PRESENTED | At LUDLOW-CASTLE, M DC XXXIV. | BEFORE | THE EARL OF BRIDGE WATER, | THEN PRESIDENT | OF WALES. | GLASGOW: | Printed and sold by Robert Foulis. | M DCC XLVII.

FORMULA: Pot 12⁰ in sixes: A⁴ B–D⁶(–D6).

PAPER: Medium-poor quality; marks 1/v.

TYPE: RB 1.   Without catchwords.

NOTES: Uniform with No. 88.

COPIES: L.

91 Milton, John, *A Tractate of Education* 1747

A | TRACTATE | OF | EDUCATION. | TO | SAMUEL HARTLIB. | BY | JOHN MILTON. | GLASGOW: | Printed and sold by Robert Foulis. | M DCC XLVII.

FORMULA: Foolscap 12⁰ in sixes: A–B⁶ C² (C² *advertisements; an extra leaf of advertisements bound at the end of the G² copy does not appear to have been printed at the Foulis Press*).

PAPER: Medium quality; marks 5/v.

TYPE: RLP 1.   Without catchwords.

NOTES: *Price*: Wholesale: ½d. (*BQ* 11).
Stock in 1777: 48 copies (*BQ* 11).

COPIES: G².

† **92** Old Poem.   *Chevy Chace* 1747

CHEVY-CHACE, | THE | CELEBRATED | OLD POEM | ON THE | MEMORABLE HUNTING | OF THE EARLS | PIERCY AND DOUGLAS. | [*quotation, 6 lines*] | GLASGOW, | PRINTED BY ROBERT FOULIS, | ACCORDING TO ALL THE ENGLISH EDITIONS. | M DCC XLVII.

FORMULA: Pot 4⁰ in twos: A² B–E².

PAPER: Medium quality; marks 1/v.

TYPE: RGP 1, RLP 1.

VARIANT: *Title page* [*in another state, reading* 'DOUGLAS AND PIERCY.' *in line 8, and* 'SCOTTISH' *for* 'ENGLISH' *in the penultimate line.*]

COPIES: G⁴, L (title-page as transcribed), O (variant title-page).

1747   Otway, Thomas, *Venice Preserved* **93**

NOTES: Not seen. Advertised in *GC*, 23 March 1747.
Prices: Retail: fine, 6*d*.; common, 4*d*.

1747   Philips, Ambrose, *The Distressed Mother* **94** †

NOTES: Not seen. Advertised in *GC*, 23 March 1747.
Prices: Retail: fine, 6*d*.; common, 4*d*.

1747   Ramsay, Allan, *The Gentle Shepherd* **95**

THE | GENTLE SHEPHERD: | A | *SCOTS* | PASTORAL
COMEDY. | BY | ALLAN RAMSAY. | THE NINTH
EDITION WITH THE SANGS. | GLASGOW, | PRINTED
AND SOLD BY ROBERT FOULIS. | M DCC XLVII.

FORMULA: [? Printing Demy 18⁰]: A–C¹² D–E⁶(–E6). (*Horizontal chain-lines. Another possible arrangement is* ' Small Crown 12⁰
in twelves and sixes ', *printed on half double-sized sheets.*)

PAPER: Poor quality; no marks; size of sheet (if Printing
Demy 18⁰), 22 × 18¾ in., or (if Small Crown 12⁰) of half sheet,
18¾ × 14¾ in.

TYPE: RB I, RLP I.

COPIES: G⁴.

1747   Relph, Josiah, *A Miscellany of Poems* **96**

A | MISCELLANY | OF | POEMS, | CONSISTING OF |
[*two columns of contents, 4 lines each, separated by two plain vertical
rules, 17·5*] | BY THE LATE REVEREND | JOSIAH RELPH OF SEBERG
HAM, CUMBERLAND. | WITH A PREFACE AND A GLOS
SARY. | [*quotation, 5 lines*] | GLASGOW, | PRINTED BY
ROBERT FOULIS | FOR MR. THOMLINSON | IN
WIGTON. | M DCC XLVII.

FORMULA: [? Printing Demy] 8⁰: a–c⁸ d² A–L⁸.

PAPER: Medium-poor quality; marks 9/i.

TYPE: RE I, RGP I. Flowers 1 and 2.

NOTES: The typography is more traditional than was usual
at the Foulis Press at this time.

COPIES: G⁴, L.

97 Steele, Sir Richard and Addison, Joseph,   1747–9
The Tatler

THE | LUCUBRATIONS | OF | *Iſaac Bickerſtaff*, Efq; | VOL.
I [II] [III] [IV]. | [*quotation, 2 lines*] | GLASGOW, | PRINTED
AND SOLD BY ROBERT FOULIS. | M DCC XLVII.
[*different settings*; *Vol.* III *dated* ' M DCC XLVIII.', *Vols.* II and IV,
' M DCC XLIX.']

FORMULA: Foolscap 8⁰
    Vol. I: A–T⁸ (Q5 *signed* ' M5 ').
    Vol. II: A^2 B–Y⁸ Z² (K4 *signed* ' K6 '; Z2 *advertisements*).
    Vol. III: A–U⁸ (U8 *advertisements*).
    Vol. IV: A–U⁸.

PAPER: Medium-good quality; marks 5/v; size of sheet
$16\frac{3}{4} \times 13\frac{1}{4}$ in.

TYPE: RLP 1, RB 1, RE 1.

VARIANT: Issue in [? Printing Demy] 12⁰:
    Title-pages: [*Vol.* II *dated* ' M DCC XLVII.']
    Formula: [? Printing Demy] 12⁰: Vol. I: A–F¹² H–N¹² O⁸.
    Vol. II: A² B–O¹² P⁶ (P6 *advertisements*).
    Vol. III: A–N¹² O⁴ (O4 *advertisements*).
    Vol. IV: A–N¹² O² P².
    Paper: Poor quality; marks 9/i, no marks.

NOTES: *Prices*: Wholesale: 8⁰, 7s. 6d. (*BQ* 6). Retail: 8⁰, 10s.
(*CP* 7).
    Stock in 1777: 8⁰, 7 copies.   (*BQ* 6.)

COPIES: G⁴ (12⁰), G (8⁰).

† **98** Worthington, John, *A Scripture Catechism*   1747

NOTES: Not seen. Advertised in *GC*, 23 March 1747.
    Prices: Retail: fine, 3d.; common, 2d.

99 Addison, Joseph, *Cato*   1748

CATO. | A | TRAGEDY. | BY | JOSEPH ADDISON, Efq; | [*quota-
tion, 8 lines*] | *GLASGOW*, | Printed and fold by ROBERT and
ANDREW FOULIS. | M DCC XLVIII.

FORMULA: Foolscap 8⁰: A–E⁸ (B3 *signed* ' B4 ').

PAPER: Medium-good quality; marks 5/iv.

TYPE: RB 2.

COPIES: L.

1748   Cicero, [Proposals for *Works*, 1748–9] **100**

NOTES: Not seen. The following advertisement appeared in *GC* for 15 February 1748: ' *Propoſals for printing all* CICERO'*s Works in* 20 *Vol. of a Pocket Size.*

' *As this Work is now going on with all the Expedition, confiſtent with Correctneſs; any Gentlemen willing to encourage this Edition, are deſired to ſend in their Names to the Printers.*'

The Proposals were to be had of Robert and Andrew Foulis in Glasgow.

1748–9   Cicero, *Works*, L **101** †

[*General title-page, Vol.* I *only*:] M. TULLII | CICERONIS | OPERA | QUAE SUPERSUNT | OMNIA. | AD | FIDEM OPTIMARUM EDITIONUM | DILIGENTER | EXPRES SA. | VOLUMINIBUS | XX. | GLASGUAE, | IN AEDIBUS ACADEMICIS | EXCUDEBANT ROB. ET AND. FOULIS | ACA DEMIAE TYPOGRAPHI | M. DCC. XLIX. [*There are two settings of the general title-page, in one of which the last line reads* ' M DCC XLIX.']

[*In Vols.* I–III *and* XI–XX *there are half-titles followed by full titles, after the manner of the following examples from Vol.* II*: half-title*:] M. TULLII | CICERONIS | OPERUM OMNIUM | VOL. II. | RHETORICORUM | VOL. II. [*title-page*:] M.T. | CICERONIS | ORATOR | AD M. BRUTUM. | EX EDITIONE J. OLIVETI. | GLASGUAE, | IN AEDIBUS ACADEMICIS | EXCUDE BANT ROB. ET AND. FOULIS | MDCCXLVIII.
[*In Vol.* IV–X *the half-title and full title-page are combined; the following example is from Vol.* IV:] M. TULLII | CICERONIS | OPERUM OMNIUM | VOL. IV. | ORATIONUM | VOL. I. | EX EDITIONE J. OLIVETI. | GLASGUAE, | IN AEDIBUS ACADEMICIS | EXCUDEBANT ROB. ET AND. FOULIS | ACA DEMIAE TYPOGRAPHI | M DCC XLIX.
[*Dates*: 1748: *Vols.* I, II, IV–VII, X–XVI; 1749: III, VIII, IX, XVII–XX.]
[*Colophons: Vols.* I, II, XII–XV:] EXCUDEBANT GLASGUAE | ROB. ET AND. FOULIS FRATRES | ACADEMIAE TYPOGRAPHI | M.DCC.XLVIII. [*Similar colophons in Vols.* III, VIII, IX, XVII, XVIII, XX, *but dated* ' M.DCC.XLIX.'*; the colophon of Vol.* IV *dated*:] ANN. M.DCC.XLVIII. | IDUUM MENSIS MARTII, | DIE SEPTIMO. [*9 March 1748 (cf. the colophon of No. 105 above). No colophons in Vols.* V–VII, X, XI, XVI, XIX.]
FORMULA: Foolscap 12°:
      Vol. I: π^6 $^2\pi^2$ a^2 bI $^2a^4$ ^2bI A–Q^{12} R^6 S–T^{12} U^4 (πI *general half-title,* π2 *general title,* π3 *dedication,* π4–6 *contents,* $^2\pi$I *part*

half-title, $^2\pi2$ *volume half-title,* a1 *volume title,* a2 (*signed* ' a ') *to* b1 *argumentum,* ^{2}a1 *volume sub-title,* ^{2}a2–^{2}b1 *preface*).

Vol. II: π^2 A–L^{12} ^{2}A–G^{12}.

Vol. III: π^2 A^8 B–I^{12} K^6 ^{2}A–H^{12}(–^{2}H12).

Vol. IV: π^4 A–O^{12} P^{12}(–P6–12).

Vol. V: π^2 χ1 P^{12}(–P1–5) Q–2H^{12} 2I^{12}(–2I8–12) $^2\chi$1.

Vol. VI: π1 2I^{12}(–2I1–7) 2K–3B^{12} 3C^6.

Vol. VII: π^2 A–R^{12}.

Vol. VIII: π^2 A–R^{12} S^2.

Vol. IX: π^2 A–Q^{12} R^8.

Vol. X: π^2 A–R^{12}.

Vol. XI: π^2 a^6 A–I^{12} K^6 χ1 ^{12}A–F^{12} ^{2}G^8.

Vol. XII: π^2 A^2 B–O^{12} P^4.

Vol. XIII: π^2 A^8(A1 + a4) B–O^{12} P^4.

Vol. XIV: π^2 A–K^{12} L^4 ^{2}A^4 ^{2}B–F^{12}.

Vol. XV: π^2 a^4 A–F^{12} ^{2}A–I^{12} ^{2}K^6.

Vol. XVI: π^2 A^4 B–Q^{12}.

Vol. XVII: π^2 A–R^{12} S^6.

Vol. XVIII: π^2 A–R^{12} S^2.

Vol. XIX: π^2 A^{10} B–R^{12} S^6.

Vol. XX: π^2 A–H^{12} ^{2}A–F^{12} ^{2}G^6 $^2H^2$.

PAPER: Good quality; marks 5/iv, 5/ii, 5/v, 4/iv, 4/i.

TYPE: RLP 1, RB 2, GB.

VARIANTS: Issue in Pot 12º:
Formula: (signed ' ✳ ' on most gatherings).
Paper: Medium and medium-good quality; marks 1/v.
Issue on a third quality of paper, not seen (*BQ* 12).
Issue of part of Vol. XI on linen:
Title-page: M.T. | CICERONIS | LAELIUS, | SIVE | DE AMICITIA. | DIALOGUS. | AD TITUM POMPONIUM | ATTI cum. | GLASGUAE: | IN AEDIBUS ACADEMICIS | EXCUDEBANT ROB. ET AND. FOULIS. | M DCC XLVIII.
Formula: [*From the same type, pagination and signatures altered, as* ^{2}C5–^{2}E10^v *of Opera Vol.* XI.] π^2 A^8 D^{12} C^8 ^{2}D^2 (sic; π1 blank).
Linen: medium weight white linen, sewn round the edges with yellow thread; folded dimensions, 133 × 78 mm.

NOTES: *Publication*: published by 11 December 1749 (*GC*).
Prices: Wholesale: fine, 40*s.*; middle, 25*s.*; common, 17*s.* (*BQ* 12).   Retail: (?) middle, 2*l.*   (*CP* 5.)
Stock in 1777: fine, 3 copies; middle, 1 copy; common, 3 copies (*BQ* 12, which also lists various imperfect copies, and groups of volumes which appear to belong to this edition).
See the Note on the Duodecimo Ciceros, below.

COPIES: G⁴ (Foolscap), L (Foolscap and linen), O (Pot with ' * ' signatures).

A Note on the Duodecimo Ciceros, 1748-9

Confusion may be caused by the fact that some of the volumes, groups of volumes or parts of volumes of the twenty-volume Cicero of 1748-9 (No. 101) are sometimes found separately, and have consequently been listed as separate editions. Confusion is worse confounded by the existence of at least four editions of separate works by Cicero which appeared in duodecimo in 1748 and which are not from the same settings of type as the equivalent sections of the collected edition; these are Nos. 102, 103, 105 and 106; while No. 104 (not seen) may be a similar case. That there may be yet more separate duodecimo editions of works by Cicero dating from 1748-9, as yet unfound, is suggested by *BQ*. Most of the Ciceros listed on pp. 12-13 of *BQ* can be identified with some confidence with parts of the collected edition; but the following works, which do not have their own signature series in the collected edition, may have been separate editions:

ORATIONS: *de Lege Agraria, etc.; in M. Antonium; in Vatinium.*
PHILOSOPHICA: *Lucullus.*

1748   Cicero, *Cato Major, etc.,* L **102** †

M.T. | CICERONIS | CATO MAJOR, | SIVE DE | SENEC TUTE. | EX EDITIONE J. OLIVETI. | GLASGUAE: | IN AEDI BUS ACADEMICIS | EXCUDEBANT ROB. ET AND. FOULIS | M DCC XLVIII.

FORMULA: Foolscap 12⁰: π1 A–C¹²(C4 + χ1) D–F¹² G⁸ (χ1 *is a title-page to* Laelius, *which, with* Paradoxa *and* Somnium Scipionis, *immediately follows* Cato Major.)

PAPER: Medium quality; marks 4/vi.

TYPE: RLP I.

VARIANTS: Issue in Pot 12⁰:
Paper: Medium quality; marks 1/v; size of sheet $15\frac{1}{2} \times 11\frac{3}{4}$ in.
Issue on inferior paper, not seen (*BQ* 2, which speaks of three issues, fine, middle and common paper).

NOTES: See the Note on the Duodecimo Ciceros, above.
Prices: Wholesale: fine, 9*d.*; middle, 6*d.*; common, 6*d.* (*BQ* 2).
Stock in 1777: fine, 27 copies; middle, 11 copies; common, 70 copies (*BQ* 2).

COPIES: G⁴ (Pot), C⁴ (Foolscap).

† **103** Cicero, *De Finibus Bonorum et Malorum*, L   1748

M. T. | CICERONIS | DE | FINIBUS | BONORUM ET MALORUM, | AD | MARCUM BRUTUM, | LIBRI QUIN QUE. | EX EDITIONE J. OLIVETI. | GLASGUAE: | IN AEDIBUS ACADEMICIS | EXCUDEBANT ROB. ET AND. FOULIS | M DCC XLVIII. [*Colophon:*] EXCUDEBANT GLASGUAE | ROB. ET AND. FOULIS FRATRES, | ACADEMIAE TYPO GRAPHI | M.DCC.XLVIII.

FORMULA: Pot 12⁰: A¹² B⁴ C–O¹² P⁴.

PAPER: Medium quality; marks 1/iv.

TYPE: RLP 1, RB 2.

VARIANT: Issue in (?) Foolscap 12⁰, not seen (*BQ* 2).

NOTES: See the Note on the Duodecimo Ciceros, p. 121.
   Prices: Wholesale: fine, 1*s*. 2*d*.; common, 1*s*. (*BQ* 2).
   Stock in 1777: fine, 22 copies; common, 21 copies; imperfect, 15 copies (*BQ* 2).

COPIES: L (Pot).

† **104** Cicero, *De Inventione*   1748

NOTES: Not seen. Duncan (Appendix, p. 145) lists it as ' De Inventione Rhetorica, 18mo.' It may have been this book of which 17 copies remained in 1777, price 3*d*. (*BQ* 12, format unspecified). Spotiswood, however, lists a duodecimo *De Inventione*, fine, at 1*s*. 6*d*. (p. 91).
   See the Note on the Duodecimo Ciceros, p. 121.

† **105** Cicero, *De Officiis*, L   1748

M.T. | CICERONIS | DE | OFFICIIS | AD | MARCUM FILIUM | LIBRI TRES. | EX EDITIONE Z. PEARCE. | GLAS GUAE: | IN AEDIBUS ACADEMICIS | EXCUDEBANT ROB. ET AND. FOULIS. | MDCCXLVIII.

COLOPHON: EXCUDEBANT | ROB. ET AND. FOULIS FRATRES, | ACADEMIAE GLASGUENSIS | TYPOGRAPHI | ANN. M.DCC [.]XLVIII. | IDUUM MENSIS MARTII, | DIE SEPTIMO [*9 March 1748*].

FORMULA: Pot 12⁰: a⁶ b² A–I¹² K⁶ (a1 *half-title*).

PAPER: Medium quality; marks 1/iv; size of sheet 15½ × 11¾ in.

TYPE: RLP 1.

VARIANT: Issue in (?) Foolscap 12⁰, not seen (*BQ* 2).
NOTES: See the Note on the Duodecimo Ciceros, p. 121.
  Price: Wholesale: fine, 1*s*. 2*d*. (*BQ* 2).
  Stock in 1777: fine, 6 copies (*BQ* 2).
COPIES: G⁴ (Pot).

1748   Cicero, *Orator*, L **106** †

M.T. | CICERONIS | ORATOR | AD | M. BRUTUM. | EX
EDITIONE J. OLIVETI. | GLASGUAE: | IN AEDIBUS ACA
DEMICIS | EXCUDEBANT ROB. ET AND. FOULIS |
M DCC XLVIII.
FORMULA: Foolscap 12⁰: A–E¹² F⁴ (F4 *blank*; A3 *signed* ' A2 ').
PAPER: Medium-good quality; marks 4/vi, 4/v; size of sheet
16¾ × 13¼ in.
TYPE: RLP 1, RB 2.
VARIANT: Issue in Pot 12⁰:
  Paper: Medium-poor quality; marks 1/v, 1/iv; size of sheet
15½ × 11¾ in.
NOTES: See the Note on the Duodecimo Ciceros, p. 121.
COPIES: G⁴ (Foolscap and Pot).

1748   Drummond, William, *Polemo-Middinia* **107**

POLEMO-MIDDINIA | INTER | VITARVAM | ET |
NIBERNAM. | *GLASGOW*, | PRINTED AND SOLD BY
ROBERT FOULIS. | MDCCXLVIII.
FORMULA: Pot 4⁰ in twos: A1 B–D².
PAPER: Medium quality; marks 1/v.
TYPE: RGP 1.
COPIES: L.

1748   Epictetus, *Manual*, G and L **108**

TO TOY | ΕΠΙΚΤΗΤΟΥ | ΕΓΧΕΙΡΙΔΙΟΝ. | EX EDI
TIONE | JOANNIS UPTON | ACCURATE EXPRESSUM.
| GLASGUAE, | IN AEDIBUS ACADEMICIS | EX
CUDEBAT ROBERTUS FOULIS, | ACADEMIAE TYPO
GRAPHUS. | MDCCXLVIII.

123

FORMULA: Foolscap 12⁰ in sixes: π1 A–E⁶ F⁴ G1 ²A–B⁶.

PAPER: Good quality; marks 4/iv, 5/iv.

TYPE: GGP, GP, RB 1.   Latin follows Greek.

VARIANTS: Issue in Pot 12⁰, Greek and Latin:
   Paper: Medium quality; marks 1/v.
   Issue on linen, 12⁰, Greek only:
   Formula: (–²A–B⁶).
   Linen: White, of the weight used nowadays for good-quality handkerchiefs; size of sheet at least 15 × 12 in. (or of half-sheet 12 × 7½ in.).
   Murray (*R. & A. Foulis*, p. 40) mentions an issue on vellum.*

NOTES: *Publication*: Published by 16 May 1748 (*GC*).

COPIES: G⁴ (Foolscap and Pot), L (Foolscap); C⁵, E (linen).

109 Geddes, James, *An Essay on the Composition*   1748
of the Antients

AN ESSAY | ON THE | COMPOSITION | AND | MANNER OF WRITING | OF THE | ANTIENTS, PARTICULARLY PLATO. | BY THE LATE | JAMES GEDDES, ESQ ; ADVO CATE. | [copper-plate head, plate mark 76 × 68] | *GLASGOW*, | PRINTED AND SOLD BY ROBERT FOULIS. | M DCC XLVIII.

FORMULA: [? Writing Demy] 8⁰ in fours: π1 a⁴ A–I⁴(±I4) K–Y⁴ (±Y4) Z–2Z⁴ 3A1 (Z2, 2S2 *unsigned;* π1, *title-page, sometimes placed after* a1, *half-title*).

PAPER: Good quality; marks Eagle/T.

TYPE: RE 1, GGP, RB 1, GP, RE 2.   Copper-plates on I4ᵛ (*cancellans*) and 2P4ᵛ.

VARIANTS: Issue in [? Printing Demy] 8⁰:
   Formula: (*signed* ' * ' *on* a2, 3A1ᵛ *and* A–2Z $1 *except* (*sometimes*) B1).
   Paper: Medium-poor and medium quality; marks 9/i (cancels on 'Eagle' paper).
   Issue in [? Crown] 8⁰:
   Formula: (*without* ' * ' *signatures except on* G1, R1, S1).
   Paper: Medium-good quality; marks 9/1.

NOTES: *Publication*: in the press in 1745 (advertisements in Nos. 63 and 68, which speak of two volumes octavo); published by 27 June 1748 (*GC*).

   * Addendum, 1963: Mr Bernard Barr reports a vellum copy at the John Rylands Library, Manchester.

Price: Wholesale: (? issue), 3*s*. (*BQ* 11, which refers to ' d[emy]. 8vo.').

Stock in 1777: (? issue), 1 copy (*BQ* 11).

COPIES: G⁴, L (Crown); C (Writing Demy); O (Printing Demy).

1748   Hamilton, William, *Poems on Several* **110** †
Occasions

POEMS | ON | SEVERAL | OCCASIONS. | GLASGOW: Printed and fold by ROBERT & ANDREW FOULIS | M.D.CC.XLVIII.

FORMULA: Foolscap 8⁰ in fours: π⁴(–π4) A–S⁴ T² (*signed* ' * ' *on* $1 *except* π1, B1, F1, H1, Q1, R1 *and* T1).

PAPER: Good quality; marks 4/v, 5/v.

TYPE: RLP 1, RB 2.

VARIANT: Issue on inferior paper, Post 8⁰:
Formula: (*without the* ' * ' *signatures*).
Paper: Medium quality; thin; marks 6/iii.

NOTES: *Publication*: Adam Smith's Preface is dated 21 December 1748, so the advertisement for Hamilton's *Poems* in *GC* for 23 January 1749 probably refers to this and not to the second edition (No. 131 below).

COPIES: G⁴ (Foolscap), O (Post).

1748   ' Hippocrates ', *Aphorisms*, G and L **111**

ΟΙ ΤΟΥ | ΙΠΠΟΚΡΑΤΟΥΣ | ΑΦΟΡΙΣΜΟΙ. | HIPPO CRATIS | APHORISMI. | EX EDITIONE | THEODORI JANSSONII | AB Almeloveen, M.D. | GLASGUAE, | IN AEDIBUS ACADEMICIS | EXCUDEBANT ROB. ET AND. FOULIS | MDCCXLVIII.

FORMULA: Foolscap 12⁰ in sixes: A–K⁶.

PAPER: Medium-good quality; marks 4/1, 5/ii; size of sheet 17 × 13 in.

TYPE: GP, RB 1. Latin follows Greek.

VARIANT: Issue in Pot 12⁰;
Paper: Medium quality; marks 1/v, 1/iv; size of sheet 15¼ × 12 in.

NOTES: *Publication*: published by 19 September 1748 (*GC*).

COPIES: G⁴, L (both Pot), O (Foolscap).

112 [Anon.], *A Lady's Religion*　　　　　1748

A | LADY's | RELIGION: | IN A | LETTER | TO THE HON
OURABLE | MY LADY HOWARD. | TO WHICH IS
ADDED, | A ſecond LETTER to the ſame LADY, | concerning
the import of FEAR in | RELIGION. | By a Divine of the Church
of England. | GLASGOW, | PRINTED AND SOLD BY
R. AND A. FOULIS. | MDCCXLVIII. | *

FORMULA: Pot 12° in sixes: A–I⁶ (*signed '* * *' on* $1 *except* H1).

PAPER: Medium quality; marks 1/v.

TYPE: RE 1, RLP 1, RLP Cas.

VARIANT: Issue on inferior paper, not seen (inferred from the
'*' signatures).

NOTES: *Publication*: published by 23 May 1748 (*GC*).

COPIES: G⁴.

113 Miscellany.　*Poems in the Scottish Dialect*　　　1748

POEMS | IN THE | SCOTTISH DIALECT | BY SEVERAL
| CELEBRATED POETS, | VIZ. | [*two columns of contents, 10
lines each, separated by a vertical plain rule, 46*] | GLASGOW, |
PRINTED AND SOLD BY ROBERT FOULIS. |
MDCCXLVIII.

FORMULA: [? Pot] 4°: *A*² B–G⁴ (C4ᵛ *signed* 'C'; B2, D2
*unsigned; A*1 *advertisements*).

PAPER: Medium-poor quality; no marks.

TYPE: RE 1.

COPIES: L.

114 [Anon.], *Ode to the Duke of Cumberland*, L,　　*c.* 1748

[*No full title-page;* A1, *the half- or sub-title, reads:*] AD | GU
LIELMUM | CUMBRIAE DUCEM | ODE.

FORMULA: Pot 4° in twos: A–B².

PAPER: Medium-good quality, marks 1/?.

TYPE: RE 1, and Wilson titling.

NOTES: This looks as if it was printed at the Foulis Press, and
it is probably the book — or part of the book — advertised as
Odes by a Lady, inscribed to the Duke of Cumberland, 4°, in Lady
Wardlaw's *Hardyknute*, 1748 (No. 121) and in *Poems in the
Scottish Dialect*, 1748 (No. 113).

A leaf at L (11602, i. 5 (6)) may have been printed at the Foulis Press:

[*begins*] AN ODE, | Addreſſed to his Royal Highneſs *William* | Duke of *Cumberland.* | *By a LADY.* | [*followed by 9 stanzas and postscript*].

Formula: [? size] 2⁰: [*single leaf*].

Paper: Medium-poor quality; no marks.

Type: RE 1; lines 2 and 3 in an unknown Double Pica, which could be by Wilson; Five-line Pica ' R '; Two-line English caps.

The typographical evidence is ambiguous, but on the whole I am inclined to think that this leaf was *not* printed at the Foulis Press.

COPIES: L (both the pamphlet and the single leaf).

1748   Old Poem. *The Battle of Harlaw*, with **115**
The Red Squair

TWO | OLD HISTORICAL | SCOTS POEMS, | GIVING AN ACCOUNT OF THE | BATTLES OF HARLAW, | AND THE | REID-SQUAIR. | *GLASGOW*, | PRINTED AND SOLD BY ROBERT FOULIS. | MDCCXLVIII.

FORMULA: Pot 8⁰ in fours: π1 A–B⁴ C1 (sometimes signed ' ＊ ' on A1).

PAPER: Medium quality; marks 1/v.

TYPE: RLP 1.

VARIANT: Issue in (?) Foolscap 8⁰, fine paper, not seen (*BQ* 12).

NOTES: *Prices*: Wholesale: fine, 2*d.*; common, 1*d.* (*BQ* 12).
Stock in 1777: fine, 24 copies; common, 56 copies (*BQ* 12).

COPIES: G⁴, L (Pot).

1748–9   Ramsay, Andrew Michael, *The Philosophical* **116**
Principles of Natural and Revealed Religion

[*Vol.* 1:] THE | PHILOSOPHICAL | PRINCIPLES | OF | NATURAL AND REVEALED | RELIGION, | UNFOLDED | IN | A GEOMETRICAL ORDER | BY | THE CHEVALIER RAMSAY | AUTHOR OF THE TRAVELS OF CYRUS. | GLASGOW: | PRINTED AND SOLD BY ROBERT FOULIS. | M DCC XL VIII.

[*Vol.* II:] THE | PHILOSOPHICAL PRINCIPLES | OF | NATURAL AND REVEALED | RELIGION. | PART SECOND. | BY | THE CHEVALIER RAMSAY, | AUTHOR OF THE TRAVELS OF CYRUS. | GLASGOW, | PRINTED AND SOLD BY ROBERT AND ANDREW FOULIS. | MDCCXLIX.

FORMULA: [? Writing Demy] 4⁰:
   Vol. I: a⁴ A–3Y⁴(–3Y4).
   Vol. II: A–3M⁴.

PAPER: Good quality; marks 7/i, 9/i.

TYPE: RE 2, RLP 1; also RGP 1, RB 2 in Vol. II.

VARIANT: Issue in Foolscap 4⁰:
   Paper: Medium quality; marks 4/iv, 5/iv, 5/v; size of sheet $16\frac{3}{4} \times 14\frac{1}{4}$ in.

NOTES: Duncan (p. 53, No. 61) says, ' Some copies are marked, London, 1749–51'.
   Prices: Wholesale: Writing Demy, 21*s.*; Foolscap, 10*s.* 6*d.* (*BQ* 11). Retail: (? Foolscap) 1*l.* (*CP* 6, *sic*).
   Stock in 1777: Writing Demy, 1 copy; Foolscap, 2 copies; Foolscap, imperfect, 1 copy (*BQ* 11).

COPIES: G⁴ (both issues), L (Foolscap).

117 Rowe, Nicholas, *The Fair Penitent*   1748

NOTES: Not seen. Advertised as ' *Lately printed and fold* ' by Robert Foulis in *GC*, 16 May 1748.

118 Rowe, Nicholas, *Jane Shore*   1748

THE | TRAGEDY | OF | JANE SHORE, | WRITTEN BY | NICHOLAS ROWE, Efq; | [*quotation, 2 lines*] | GLASGOW, PRINTED AND SOLD BY ROBERT FOULIS. | MDCCXLVIII.

FORMULA: [? Crown] 12⁰ in sixes: A² B–F⁶ (*sig.* D *signed* ' C ' (D1 *sometimes correct*); *vertical chain lines, presumably printed on half double-sized sheets of Crown*).

PAPER: Poor quality; no marks.

TYPE: RB 1, RLP 1.

NOTES: *Publication*: published by 16 May 1748 (*GC*).

COPIES: L.

1748   Rowe, Nicholas, *Lady Jane Gray* **119** †

THE | TRAGEDY | OF THE LADY | JANE GRAY. | WRITTEN
BY | NICHOLAS ROWE Efq; | [*quotation, 2 lines*] | GLAS
GOW, | PRINTED AND SOLD BY ROBERT FOULIS |
MDCCXLVIII. | *

FORMULA: Pot 8⁰ in fours: A–I⁴ (signed ' * ' on A–G $1).

PAPER: Medium quality; marks 1/v.

TYPE: RB 1, RB 2, RLP Cas.

VARIANT: Issue on inferior paper, not seen (inferred from
' * ' signatures).

COPIES: G².

1748   Theophrastus, *Characters*, G and L **120**

ΘΕΟΦΡΑΣΤΟΥ | ΧΑΡΑΚΤΗΡΕΣ | ΗΘΙΚΟΙ. | THEO
PHRASTI | CHARACTERES | ETHICI. | EX RECENSIONE
| PETRI NEEDHAM, | ET VERSIONE LATINA | ISAACI
CASAUBONI. | GLASGUAE, | EXCUDEBAT ROBERTUS
FOULIS, | ACADEMIAE TYPOGRAPHUS. | MDCCXLVIII

FORMULA: Foolscap 12⁰ in sixes: A–D⁶ E² ²A–C⁶ (²C6 *blank*).

PAPER: Medium-good quality; 4/iv, 4/i, 5/iv.

TYPE: GP, RB 1.   Latin follows Greek.

NOTES: *Price*: Wholesale: 6d. (*BQ* 5).
   Stock in 1777: 44 copies (*BQ* 5).

COPIES: G⁴, L.

1748   Wardlaw, Elizabeth Lady, *Hardyknute* **121**

HARDYKNUTE, | A | FRAGMENT | OF AN | ANTIENT
SCOTS POEM. | GLASGOW, | Printed and fold by ROBERT
FOULIS. 1748. | [Price Six-pence.]

FORMULA: Pot 4⁰ in twos: A² B–G².

PAPER: Medium-good quality; marks 1/v; size of sheet
15¼ × 12 in.

TYPE: RGP 1, RE 1.

VARIANT: Issue on inferior paper, Pot 4⁰:
   Paper: Poor quality; marks, 1/v.
   Title-page: [*last line reads:*] [Price Four-pence.]

NOTES: *Publication*: Published by 19 September 1748 (*GC*).
  Prices: Wholesale: fine, 3*d*. (*BQ* 10). Retail: fine, 6*d*.; common, 4*d*. (title-pages).
  Stock in 1777: fine, 20 copies (*BQ* 10).
COPIES: G⁴ (both issues), L (fine).

122 Xenophon, *Agesilaus*, G and L 1748

Ό ΤΟΥ | ΧΕΝΟΦΩΝΤΟΣ | ΛΟΓΟΣ, ΕΙΣ | ΑΓΗΣΙΛΑΟΝ | ΤΟΝ ΒΑΣΙΛΕΑ. | XENOPHONTIS | DE | AGESILAO REGE | ORATIO. | ADJECTA EST VERSIO LATINA. | EX EDITIONE T. HUTCHINSON. | GLASGUAE, | IN AEDIBUS ACADEMICIS, | EXCUDEBANT ROB. ET AND. FOULIS | M DCC XLVIII.
FORMULA: Foolscap 8⁰ in fours: π1 A–P⁴(–P4).
PAPER: Medium-good quality; marks 5, 4/i, ii, iv, v.
TYPE: GGP, RE 1. Latin follows Greek.
NOTES: *Publication*: published by 23 January 1749 (*GC*).
COPIES: G⁴, L.

123 Addison, Joseph, *The Drummer* 1749

THE | DRUMMER; | OR, THE | HAUNTED-HOUSE. | A | COMEDY. | BY THE LATE RIGHT HONOURABLE | JOSEPH ADDISON, Efq; | [*quotation, 2 lines*] | GLASGOW, | PRINTED AND SOLD BY R. & A. FOULIS. | M.DCC.XLIX.
FORMULA: Foolscap 8⁰: A–D⁸ E⁶ *F*² (*F*² advertisements).
PAPER: Medium quality; marks 4/v.
TYPE: RB 2, RLP 1.
NOTES: *Publication*: published by 23 October 1749 (*GC*).
COPIES: G⁴, L.

124 Addison, Joseph, *Rosamond* c. 1749

NOTES: Not seen. *GC*, 23 October 1749, advertised ' *Addifon's 3 Plays* ' as just published by R. and A. Foulis. *Cato* appeared in 1748 (No. 99) and *The Drummer* in 1749 (No. 123), so that there was probably an edition of *Rosamond* put out at about the same time.

1749   Apollonius of Perga, *Plane Loci*, L **125** †

APOLLONII PERGAEI | LOCORUM PLANORUM | LIBRI II. | *RESTITUTI* | A | ROBERTO SIMSON M.D. | Matheseos in Academia Glasguensi Professore. | GLAS GUAE, | IN AEDIBUS ACADEMICIS, | Excudebant Rob. et And. Foulis Academiae Typographi. | A.D. MDCCXLIX.

FORMULA: [? Demy) 4⁰: a^2 b–d² eɪ A–D² E–F⁴($\pm$F2) G–M⁴ ($\pm$M4) N–2H⁴ 2Iɪ.

PAPER: Good quality; marks eagle/T, no marks. The copy at O has sigs. a–e on a poorer-quality paper, no marks.

TYPE: RGP ɪ, RE ɪ, RLP ɪ, GGP. Blocks 9 and 10. Numerous woodcut diagrams.

VARIANT: Issue on inferior paper, [? Crown] 4⁰:
  Paper: Poor quality; marks 9/i.

COPIES: G⁴ (mixed, but mostly common paper), L (Demy).

1749   Aurelius Antoninus, Marcus, *Meditations*, E **126** †

THE | MEDITATIONS | OF THE EMPEROR | MARCUS AURELIUS | ANTONINUS. | newly tranflated from the greek: with | notes, and an account of his life. | SECOND EDITION. | GLASGOW, | Printed by Robert & Andrew Foulis, | printers to the University. | M D CC XLIX. [*Vol.* ɪɪ, *from a different setting, substitutes* ' VOLUME SECOND.' *for lines 6–8* (' newly . . . EDITION.'); *and reads in the last line* ' M DCC XLIX.']

FORMULA: Foolscap 8⁰:
  Vol. ɪ: A–P⁸ Q⁴.
  Vol. ɪɪ: A–O⁸ P⁴.

PAPER: Medium-good quality; marks 5/iv, 4/v, 5/v.

TYPE: RE 2, RB 2.

NOTES: *Publication*: published on about 13 September 1749 (*GC* 11 September 1749).

COPIES: G⁴, L.

by 1749   Chandler, Samuel, *Plain Reasons for* **127**
                                       being a Christian

NOTES: Not seen. Advertised as ' Plain reafons for being a Chriftian ' in No. 123 (published October 1749). It continued to appear in Foulis's advertisements, without the author's name, for many years; then in 1766 it becomes 'Dr. Nettleton's Plain Reafons for being a Chriftian' (No. 454). Thomas Nettleton, however, does not appear to have written a book of this title, whereas Samuel Chandler certainly did, the first of many anonymous editions being published in London in 1730.

BQ (p. 11) lists 45 copies of the book as a crown octavo, wholesale price 2*d.*, as one of a considerable group of titles dating from the late seventeen-forties.

† **128** Davies, Sir John, *The Original, Nature and*   1749
Immortality of the Soul

THE | ORIGINAL, | NATURE, | AND | IMMORTALITY | OF THE | SOUL. | A | POEM | BY | SIR *JOHN DAVIES,* | ATTORNEY-GENERAL TO | Q. ELIZABETH. | GLASGOW, PRINTED AND SOLD BY R. & A. FOULIS. | MDCCXLIX.

FORMULA: Foolscap 8⁰ in fours: π^2 χ1 A–M⁴(–M4, =χ1) (π1 *half-title*, χ1 *contents*).

PAPER: Medium-good quality; marks 5/v, 5/iv, 4/v.

TYPE: RLP 1.

NOTES: *Publication*: published by 9 October 1749 (*GC*, in which the title-page, slightly re-arranged, is used for the advertisement).

COPIES: G⁴, L.

129 Amory, Thomas, *A Dialogue on Devotion*   1749

NOTES: Not seen. Advertised in No. 123 (published October 1749) as 'A dialogue on devotion after the manner of Xenophon'.

130 Gay, John, *The What d'ye Call it*   1749

THE | WHAT D'YE CALL IT: | A | *Tragi-Comi-Paftoral* | FARCE. | BY | MR. JOHN GAY. | [*quotation, 2 lines*] | GLASGOW. | PRINTED AND SOLD BY ROB. AND A. FOULIS. M DCC XLIX.

FORMULA: Pot 8⁰ in fours: π1 A–E⁴ F1 (π1 *half-title*).

PAPER: Medium quality; marks 1/iv.

TYPE: RB 2, a few words in GB on A4.
NOTES: *Publication*: published by 10 April 1749 (*GC*).
COPIES: G².

1749   Hamilton, William, *Poems on Several Occasions* **131** †
POEMS | ON | SEVERAL | OCCASIONS. | GLASGOW: | PRINTED BY ROBERT AND ANDREW FOULIS, | M.DCC.XLIX.
FORMULA: Foolscap 8⁰: π² χι A–I⁸ T² (*the compositor, setting from No. 110 has mistakenly taken over signature ' T ' for the last gathering.*)
   Plate: copper-plate portrait of the author, unsigned, plate-mark 91 × (?), faces the title-page.
PAPER: Medium good quality; marks 5/v, 5/iv, 4/v; size of sheet 16½ × 13¼ in.
TYPE: RLP I (with a few RLP Cas sorts), RB 2.
VARIANT: Another setting of the title-page, lacking the comma after ' FOULIS '.
NOTES: *Publication*: see *Notes* to No. 110 above.
COPIES: G⁴, L (one of the G⁴ copies with the variant title-page).

1749   Hutcheson, Francis, *Synopsis Metaphysicae*, L **132**
SYNOPSIS | METAPHYSICAE, | ONTOLOGIAM | ET | PNEUMATOLOGIAM | COMPLECTENS. | EDITIO TERTIA, AUCTIOR ET EMENDATIOR. | GLASGUAE, | IN AEDIBUS ACADEMICIS | EXCUDEBANT ROBERTUS ET ANDREAS FOULIS. | M DCC XLIX.
FORMULA: Foolscap 8⁰: a⁴ A–H⁸ I⁴ (I4 *advertisements*).
PAPER: Medium-good quality; marks 5/v, 5/iv.
TYPE: RLP I, RB I, RB 2.
NOTES: *Publication*: published by 11 December 1749 (*GC*).
COPIES: G⁴.

1749   Leechman, William, *The Nature of Prayer,* **133**
                                       a Sermon
THE | NATURE, | REASONABLENESS, | AND | ADVANTAGES | OF | PRAYER; | WITH AN ATTEMPT TO ANSWER | THE OBJECTIONS AGAINST IT. | A |

SERMON | By WILLIAM LEECHMAN | PROFESSOR OF DIVINITY IN THE | UNIVERSITY OF GLASGOW. | [*quotation, 2 lines*] | THE FOURTH EDITION. | Printed and fold by ROBERT and ANDREW FOULIS, | PRINTERS TO THE UNIVERSITY. | GLASGOW: M DCC XLIX.

FORMULA: Foolscap 8⁰ in fours: A–I⁴.

PAPER: Medium quality; marks 5/iv.

TYPE: RLP 1.

VARIANT: An issue in 4⁰, not seen (*GC* 24 April 1749).

NOTES: *Publication*: in the press 24 April 1749 (*GC*).

COPIES: G⁴ (8⁰).

134 Leechman, William, *The Temper of a Minister,*   1749
a Sermon

THE | TEMPER, | CHARACTER, | AND | DUTY | OF A | MINISTER OF THE GOSPEL. | A | SERMON. | By WILLIAM LEECHMAN | PROFESSOR OF DIVINITY IN THE | UNIVERSITY OF GLASGOW. | The FIFTH EDITION. Printed and fold by ROBERT and ANDREW FOULIS, | AT GLAS GOW: M.DCC.XLIX.

FORMULA: Foolscap 8⁰ in fours: A–G⁴.

PAPER: Medium-good quality; marks 5/iv.

TYPE: RLP 1, RB 2.

VARIANT: An issue in 4⁰, not seen (*GC*, 24 April 1749).

NOTES: *Publication*: published by 6 February 1749 (*GC*).

COPIES: G⁴ (8⁰).

135 Lucretius, *De Rerum Natura*, L   1749

TITI | LUCRETII | CARI | DE | RERUM NATURA | LIBRI SEX. | EX EDITIONE THOMAE CREECH. | GLAS GUAE, | IN AEDIBUS ACADEMICIS | EXCUDEBANT ROBER TUS ET ANDREAS FOULIS | M.DCC.XLIX.

FORMULA: Foolscap 8⁰: a⁸(–a1, a8) A–N⁸ O² (a3, a4 *signed* ' a ', ' a2 ' ; *watermarks suggest that* a1.8 = O²; O2 *advertisements*).

PAPER: Medium-good quality; marks, 5/iv.

TYPE: RB 2, RLP 1.

NOTES: *Publication*: published by 11 December 1749 (*GC*).

COPIES: G⁴, L.

1749   Nepos, Cornelius, *Lives of the Emperors*, L **136**

CORNELII | NEPOTIS | EXCELLENTIUM | IMPERA TORUM | VITAE | EX EDITIONE OXONIENSI | FIDELITER EXPRESSAE. | GLASGUAE, | IN AEDIBUS ACADEMICIS | EXCUDEBANT ROB. ET AND. FOULIS | M.DCC.XLIX.

FORMULA: Foolscap 12⁰: a¹² A–I¹² (a12 *advertisements*).

PAPER: Medium-good quality; marks 5/iv, 5/v.

TYPE: RLP 1, RB 1, RB 2.

NOTES: *Publication*: published by 23 October 1749 (*CG*). Two issues of a duodecimo Cornelius Nepos were offered by Spotiswood in 1779 in addition to two of an octavo (pp. 87–8, 90).

COPIES: G⁴, L.

1750   Anacreon, *Odes*, with Sappho and Alcaeus, **137**   *Remains*, G

NOTES: Not seen. Listed by Duncan (p. 56, No. 92) as ' Anacreon, Sappho et Alcæus, Gr. fools. 8vo.'

1750   Baxter, Richard, *A Call to the Unconverted*, **138**   Gaelic

GAIRM | AN | DE MHOIR | DO'NT SLUAGH | NEIMH-IOMPOICHTE, | IOMPOCHADH AGUS BITH BEO. | LE RICHARD BAXTER. | EIDIR-THEANGAICHT' O GHAILL-BHEARLA CHUM | GAOIDHEILG ALBANNAICH, AIR IARTAS AGUS | COSTAS EIRIONNAICH DHEAG-RUNAICH | OIRDHEIRC, CHUM LEASS COITCHEANN | GAOIDHEALTACHD ALBA. | CLO-BHUAILT' ANN | GLASSACHA | LE ROIB. AGUS AIND. FOULIS CLOI-|FHEARA AN OILL-TIGH. | M.DCC.L.

FORMULA: Pot 8⁰ in fours: a–h⁴ A–2L⁴ (*signed ' * ' on* a2 *and* $1 *except* a1, e1, D1: ' * ' *signatures in* A–2L *only in the* L *copy*).

PAPER: Medium-good quality; marks 1/v, i/iv.

TYPE: RLP 1.

VARIANT: Issue on inferior paper, not seen (inferred from the ' * ' signatures).

NOTES: ' The translator was Rev. Alexander Macfarlane of Kilninver, Argyllshire. This was the first work of English Divines published in Gaelic.' (Maclean, Donald, *Typographica Scoto-Gadelica*, Edinburgh 1915, p. 9). For Macfarlane, who also translated *The Psalms of David* into Gaelic (Glasgow, 1753), see Scott, Hew, *Fasti Ecclesiae Scoticanae*, Edinburgh 1920, Vol. III, pp. 325-6.

COPIES: G⁴, L.

139 Caesar, *Works*, L   1750

C. JULII | CAESARIS | ET | A. HIRTII | DE REBUS A CAESARE GESTIS | COMMENTARII. | CUM FRAG MENTIS. | ACCESSERUNT | INDICES LOCORUM RERUMQUE ET VERBORUM. | OMNIA, EX RECEN SIONE SAMUELIS CLARKE, | FIDELITER EXPRESSA. | GLASGUAE: | IN AEDIBUS ACADEMICIS | EXCUDE BANT ROBERTUS ET ANDREAS FOULIS ACADEMIAE TYPOGRAPHI | MDCCL.

FORMULA: Foolscap 4^0: π^2 A–3T⁴ (C1 *signed* ' B ', X2 *signed* ' Y2 '; π1 *half-title*, 3T4 *advertisements*).

PAPER: Good quality; marks 5/ii, 5/iii, 5/iv.

TYPE: RLP 1, RB 2, RB 1, GP.

VARIANT: Issue in Foolscap 2^0:

   Title-page: [*reset; reads as the* 4^0, *except* ' CAII JULII ' *in line 1.*]

   Formula: Foolscap 2^0: π^2 A–5F² (3B1 *signed* ' Bb '; π1 *half-title*).

   Paper: Same as the 4^0.

   Type: The same type re-arranged in longer pages.

NOTES: *Publication*: published by 3 September 1750 (*GC*).

   Prices: Wholesale: 4^0, 8*s.*; 2^0, 10*s.* (*BQ* 2). Retail: 2^0, 14*s.* (*CP* 3).

   Stock in 1777: 4^0, 2 copies; 2^0, 10 copies (*BQ* 2).

COPIES: G⁴ (both issues), L (both issues).

† **140** Caesar, *Works*, L   1750

C. JULII | CAESARIS | ET | A. HIRTII | DE | REBUS A CAESARE GESTIS | COMMENTARII. | CUM FRAG MENTIS. | EX RECENSIONE SAMUELIS CLARKE | FIDELITER EXPRESSI. | VOL. I [II] [III]. | GLASGUAE: | IN AEDIBUS ACADEMICIS | EXCUDEBANT ROB. ET AND. FOULIS | ACADEMIAE TYPOGRAPHI | MDCCL. [*from the same setting*]

FORMULA: Foolscap 12^0:

   Vol. I: *6 A–Q¹² (Q12 *blank*).

   Vol. II: †4 A–L¹²(– L4–12).

   Vol. III: ‡6 L¹²(– L1–3) M–Z¹².

PAPER: Medium and medium-good quality; marks 5/iv, 5/v, 3/iv.

TYPE: RLP 1, RB 2.

VARIANT: Issue on coarse paper for schools, not seen (*GC* 5 November 1750).

NOTES: *Price*: Wholesale: 2 vols. only, 1s. 9d. (*BQ* 2).
Stock in 1777: 2 vols. only, 4 copies (*BQ* 2).

COPIES: G⁴, L.

1750   ' Cebes ', *Table*, E **141**

THE | TABLATURE | OF | CEBES | THE THEBAN, | A DISCIPLE OF SOCRATES. | BEING AN | ALLEGORICAL PICTURE | OF | HUMAN LIFE. | TRANSLATED FROM THE GREEK | BY SAMUEL BOYSE M.A. | THE THIRD EDITION. | GLASGOW: | PRINTED AND SOLD BY ROBERT AND ANDREW FOULIS | MDCCL.

FORMULA: Foolscap 8⁰ in fours: A–F⁶ G² (G2 *advertisements*).

PAPER: Medium-good quality; marks 5/iv, 4/iv.

TYPE: RE 2, RLP 1.

VARIANT: Issue in Pot 8⁰:
Paper: Medium-good quality; marks 1/v, 1/iv; size of sheet 15½ × 12½ in.

NOTES: *Publication*: published by 15 October 1750 (*GC*). The entry in *BQ* (p. 9) ' Cebes ' table, (Englifh) p[ot]. 12mo. common.' may refer to this book; 550 copies were offered at 2½d. wholesale.

COPIES: G⁴, L (both Pot), O (Foolscap).

1750   Demosthenes, *De Pace, etc.*, (?) G and L **142**

NOTES: Not seen. Listed by Duncan (p. 56, No. 90) as ' Demofthenes de Pace Cherfonefi, fools. 8 vo.' This may refer to the fifth section of No. 143 (1750), ⁵A–I⁸ ⁵K², although no copy has been seen with a separate title-page to this section.

1750   Demosthenes, *Philippics, Olynthiacs, etc.*, **143**
                                    G and L

ΟΙ ΤΟΥ | ΔΗΜΟΣΘΕΝΟΥΣ | ΛΟΓΟΙ | ΦΙΛΙΠΠΙΚΟΙ | ΔΩΔΕΚΑ. | ADJECTA EST IN FINE | VERSIO LATINA WOLFII. | GLASGUAE, | IN AEDIBUS ACADEMICIS | EXCUDEBANT ROBERTUS ET ANDREAS FOULIS, | ACADEMIAE TYPOGRAPHI. | M.DCC.L. [*no general title-page found*]

FORMULA: Foolscap 8⁰ in fours: a⁴ A–O⁴ P², ²A–G⁴, ³A–E⁴, ⁴A–B⁴ ⁴C², ⁵A–I⁸ ⁵K² (²G4 *blank;* ⁵K2 *advertisements; for the contents, see* TYPE *below*).

PAPER: Medium-good quality; marks 4/v, 5/v, iv.

TYPE: GGP, GP, GB, RB I, RLP I. The contents of the five alphabets of the formula are as follows: 1: *Philippics* (Greek); 2: *Olynthiacs* (Greek); 3: *Philippics* (Latin); 4: *Olynthiacs* (Latin); 5: *de Pace, de Haloneso, de Chersoneso, Literae Philippi, ad Philippi Epistolam Oratio* (Greek followed by Latin).

VARIANT: Also found containing the Greek only (i.e. alphabets 1, 2 and 5 to ⁵G6).

COPIES: L (G and L); G (G, with MS notes by James Moor).

144 Drummond, William, *Polemo-Middinia*   1750

NOTES: Not seen. Listed by Duncan (p. 56, No. 111) as an octavo.

145 Dunbar, William, *The Thistle and the Rose,*   1750
with Bellenden, John, *Virtue and Vice*

[*General half-title:*] THE THISTLE | AND | THE ROSE. | VERTUE | AND | VYCE. | TWO ANTIENT | *ALLEGORI CAL* | SCOTS POEMS. | PRICE SIX-PENCE. [*Each poem has a separate sub-title with imprints reading:*] GLASGOW: | PRIN TED BY ROBERT AND ANDREW FOULIS. | MDCCL.

FORMULA: [? Printing Demy] 8⁰ in fours: π1 A–E⁴(–E1, = π1, *half-title*).

PAPER: Medium-poor quality; marks 9/i, no marks.

TYPE: RE I.

NOTES: *Publication*: published by 5 November 1750 (*GC*).
 Price: Retail: 6d. (*half-title*).

COPIES: G⁴, L.

146 Epictetus, *Manual*, E   1750

THE | MANUAL | OF | EPICTETUS, | CONTAINING AN ABRIDGMENT OF HIS | PHILOSOPHY. | TRANSLATED FROM THE GREEK BY GEORGE | STANHOPE, D.D. LATE DEAN OF CANTER–|BURY. | GLASGOW: | PRINTED AND SOLD BY R. AND A. FOULIS | M.DCC.L.

FORMULA: Foolscap 8⁰ in fours: π^2 A–L⁴ M² (π1 *half-title*, M2 *advertisements*.

PAPER: Medium quality; marks 5/ii, iv, v, 4/iv, v.

TYPE: RE 2, RLP 1.

VARIANT: *BQ* (p. 11) lists 58 copies of 'Epictetus' manual, p[ot]. 12mo. common. 1½*d* [wholesale] ', which may be another issue of this edition, not seen.

NOTES: *Publication*: published possibly by 8 January, certainly by 12 March 1750 (*GC*).

COPIES: G⁴, L.

1750   Fénelon, *Advice for a Person in Distress of* **147**
                              Mind, E

ADVICE | AND | CONSOLATION | FOR A | PERSON IN DISTRESS | AND DEJECTION OF MIND, | WITH SOME THOUGHTS ON THE | REMEDYS OF DISSIPATION. | *WROTE FOR THE USE OF A FRIEND,* | BY M. DE FENE LON, | ARCHBISHOP AND DUKE | OF CAMBRAY. | TRANSLATED FROM THE FRENCH. | GLASGOW, | PRINTED AND SOLD BY R. & A. FOULIS | MDCCL.

FORMULA: Foolscap 8⁰ in fours: π^2 A–D⁴ (π1 *half-title*).

PAPER: Medium-good quality; marks 4/iv, size of sheet 16½ × 13¼ in.

TYPE: RE 1.

NOTES: *Publication*: published by 3 September 1750 (*GC*).
  Price: Wholesale: 3*d*. (*BQ* 10).
  Stock in 1777: 32 copies (*BQ* 10).

COPIES: G⁴, L.

1750   Fénelon, *Dialogues concerning Eloquence*, with **148**
                      A Letter on Rhetoric and Poetry, etc., E

DIALOGUES | CONCERNING | ELOQUENCE: | WITH A LETTER TO THE | FRENCH ACADEMY, | CONCERN ING | RHETORIC, | AND | POETRY. | BY | M. DE FENE LON | ARCHBISHOP OF CAMBRAY. | To which is added, | A DISCOURSE PRONOUNCED BY THE AUTHOR | AT HIS ADMISSION INTO THE ACADEMY; | with a new Tranſlation of his Dialogues | BETWEEN DEMOSTHENES

AND CICERO, | VIRGIL AND HORACE. [*Each of the four parts has a sub-title, with the imprint of Robert and Andrew Foulis, dated 1750. For a transcription of one of them, see* VARIANT, *below.*]

FORMULA: Foolscap 8⁰: a⁸ A–S⁸ T².

PAPER: Medium-good quality; marks 5/iv, 4/v.

TYPE: RLP 1, RB 1, RE 1, RE 2, GP, GB.

VARIANTS: Issue in Pot 8⁰:
   Paper: Medium-good quality; marks 1/v.
Separate issue of the *Letter concerning Rhetoric*, Foolscap 8⁰:
   Title-page: A | LETTER | FROM THE | ARCHBISHOP | OF | CAMBRAY | TO THE | FRENCH ACADEMY; | CONCERNING | RHETORIC, POETRY, HISTORY: | AND | A COMPARISON BETWEEN THE ANTIENTS | AND MODERNS. | GLASGOW: | PRINTED AND SOLD BY ROBERT AND ANDREW FOULIS. | M.DCC.L.
   Formula: Foolscap 8⁰: A⁴ B–G⁸ (*these are the type pages* K5–Q8 *of the Collection described above, re-imposed and with new pagination*).
   Paper: Medium-good quality; marks 5/iv, 4/v; size of sheet 16¾ × 13¼ in.

NOTES: *Publication*: Collection: in the press 3 September 1750 (*GC*, with a note stating that the Foulis brothers had no previous knowledge of any other bookseller's intention to reprint the book); published, 15 October 1750 (*GC*).
   Price: Letter concerning Rhetoric: 6d. (*BQ* 6).
   Stock in 1777: Letter: 47 copies (*BQ* 6).

COPIES: G⁴, L (both Pot), O (Foolscap); G⁴, L (*Letter concerning Rhetoric*).

149 Fénelon, *Instructions for the Education of*   1750
   Daughters, E

INSTRUCTIONS | FOR THE | EDUCATION | OF | DAUGHTERS, | BY | M. FENELON | ARCHBISHOP | OF | CAMBRAY. | TRANSLATED FROM THE FRENCH, | AND REVISED BY | GEORGE HICKES, D.D. | GLASGOW: | PRINTED AND SOLD BY R. & A. FOULIS | M.DCC.L.

FORMULA: Foolscap 8⁰ in fours: a² A–2B⁴ (a2 *signed on* a2ᵛ; 2B4 *advertisements*).

PAPER: Good quality ; marks 5/iv, 5/v; size of sheet 16½ × 13 in.

TYPE: RLP 1, RB 2.

VARIANT: Issue in Pot 8⁰:
Paper: Medium quality; marks 1/v.
NOTES: *Publication*: in the press 3 September 1750; published 10 December 1750 (*GC*).
Price: Wholesale: common, 1s. (*BQ* 6).
Stock in 1777: common, 5 copies (*BQ* 6).
COPIES: G⁴ (both issues), L (Pot).

1750　　　　　　　Garth, Sir Samuel, *The Dispensary* **150** †

THE | DISPENSARY. | A | POEM | IN | SIX CANTO'S. | BY | SIR SAMUEL GARTH. | [*quotation, 2 lines*) | THE FOUR TEENTH EDITION. | GLASGOW, | PRINTED AND SOLD BY ROBERT AND ANDREW FOULIS. | EDINBURGH, | SOLD BY JOHN ROSSE IN THE PARLIAMENT CLOSS. | MDCCL.
FORMULA: Foolscap 8⁰ in fours: A–L⁴ M².
PAPER: Medium quality; marks 4/v.
TYPE: RLP 1, RE 2, RB 2.
COPIES: G⁴.

1750　　　　　　Gay, John, *The Beggar's Opera* **151**

NOTES: Not seen. Listed by Duncan (p. 56, No. 108) as ' Gray's [*sic*] Beggar's Opera.'

1750　　　　　　　　　　Gay, John, *Fables* **152** †

FABLES. | IN TWO PARTS. | By the late Mr. GAY. | Printed in the Year MDCCL.
FORMULA: [N.B. Original not seen; the following collation, taken from microfilm, is conjectural.] [? size 8⁰ in fours]: π⁴ A–N⁴ O⁴ P–2A⁴.
PAPER, TYPE: [Not seen.]
NOTES. Duncan (p. 56, No. 107) lists ' Gray's [*sic*] Fables, pot. 8vo. common, 6d.' under the year 1750; he has taken format and price from *BQ* (p. 11), but the *BQ* entry probably refers to the Pot 8⁰ edition of 1761 (No. 394).
Looks like a Foulis book, though without imprint.
COPIES: HD (microfilm only seen).

† **153** Gee, Joshua, *The Trade and Navigation of* 　　1750
Great Britain

THE | TRADE | AND | NAVIGATION | OF | GREAT-
BRITAIN | CONSIDERED: | SHEWING, | [*two columns of
contents, 9 lines each, separated by a vertical plain rule, 29*] | BY
JOSHUA GEE. | THE FIFTH EDITION. | GLASGOW: |
PRINTED AND SOLD BY ROBERT AND ANDREW
FOULIS | MDCCL.

FORMULA: Foolscap 8⁰ in fours: a–c⁴ A–Y⁴ Z².

PAPER: Medium-good quality; marks 5/iv, 5/v.

TYPE: RLP 1, RE italic, RB 2.

NOTES: *Publication*: in the press, 4 June 1750; published by
6 August 1750 (*GC*).

COPIES: G⁴, L.

154 Herodotus, [Proposals for an edition] 　　　c. 1750

NOTES: Not seen. ' Speedily will be Publifhed, Propofals for
printing by fubfcription an edition of Herodotus, in 3 vol.
8vo.' (advertisement on ²*H*2 of Vol. xx of Cicero, *Works*, 1748–9
(No. 101, published December 1749).

The Foulis Herodotus actually appeared in 9 volumes, 8⁰,
in 1761 (No. 395).

155 Horace, *Works* 　　　　　　　　　　　1750

QUINTUS | HORATIUS | FLACCUS | AD | LECTIONES
PROBATIORES | DILIGENTER EMENDATUS, | ET
INTERPUNCTIONE NOVA | SAEPIUS ILLUSTRATUS. |
EDITIO ALTERA. | GLASGUAE: | IN AEDIBUS ACA
DEMICIS | EXCUDEBANT ROBERTUS ET ANDREAS
FOULIS | ACADEMIAE TYPOGRAPHI | M.DCC.L.

FORMULA: Pot 8⁰: π² A–P⁸ Q⁴.

PAPER: Medium quality; marks 1/v.

TYPE: RB 2, RLP 1.

VARIANT: Issue in Foolscap 8⁰:
Paper: Medium-good quality; marks 5/v, 5/iv.

NOTES: *Publication*: published by 3 September 1750 (*GC*).

COPIES: G² (both issues).

1750   Hutcheson, Francis, *Thoughts on Laughter* **156**

NOTES: Not seen. Listed by Duncan (p. 56, No. 104) as 'Hutchefon on Laughter.'

1750   Jerningham, Edward, *The Epistle of Yarico to* **157** †
                                                   Inkle

THE EPISTLE | OF | YARICO | TO | INKLE. | A | POEM. | GLASGOW, | PRINTED FOR JOHN ROSS BOOKSELLER | IN THE PARLIAMENT CLOSS, EDINBURGH. | M.DCC.L. | Price Sixpence.
FORMULA: [? Printing Demy] 8⁰ in fours: *A*⁴ B–D⁴.
PAPER: Medium-poor quality; marks 9/i.
TYPE: RE I, RLP I.
NOTES: A pair to Musaeus, *Hero and Leander*, 1750 (No. 163); almost certainly printed at the Foulis Press.
    Price: Retail: 6*d*. (title-page).
COPIES: L.

1750   Juvenal, *Satires*, with Persius, *Satires* **158**

[*Separate title-pages for Juvenal and Persius, preceded by a half-title reading:*] D. JUNIUS | JUVENALIS | AQUINAS, | ET | AULUS | PERSIUS | FLACCUS.
[*Title-page to Juvenal:*] DECII JUNII | JUVENALIS | AQUI NATIS | SATIRAE; | EX RECENSIONE | HENRICI CHRISTIANI HENNINII | FIDELITER EXPRESSAE. | GLASGUAE, | IN AEDIBUS ACADEMICIS | EXCUDE BANT ROBERTUS ET ANDREAS FOULIS | ACADEM IAE TYPOGRAPHI | M.DCC.L. [*and a similar title-page to Persius on* H1.]
FORMULA: Foolscap 8⁰: π² A–H⁸ I⁴ (πI *half-title*, I4 *advertisements*).
PAPER: Good quality; marks 4/v, 5/iv; size of sheet $16\frac{1}{2} \times 13\frac{1}{4}$ in.
TYPE: RB 2, RLP I.
VARIANT: issue in Pot 8⁰:
    Paper: Medium quality; marks I/v.
NOTES: *Publication*: published by 3 September 1750 (*GC*).
COPIES: G⁴ (Foolscap), L (Pot).

1750   Law, John, *Money and Trade Considered* **159**

MONEY | AND | TRADE | CONSIDERED: | WITH A PROPOSAL FOR SUPPLYING | THE NATION WITH

MONEY. | FIRST PUBLISHED AT EDINBURGH MDCCV. | BY THE CELEBRATED | JOHN LAW, Esq; | AFTERWARD | DIRECTOR TO THE MISSISIPI [sic] COMPANY. | GLASGOW. | printed and sold by r. & a. foulis | MDCCL.

formula: Foolscap 8⁰ in fours: A^4 B–2E⁴ 2F² (M2 *signed* ' M3 '; 2F2 *advertisements*).

paper: Medium-good quality; marks 5/v.

type: RE 2, RLP 1.

variant: Issue in Pot 8⁰:
 Paper: Medium quality; marks 1/v; size of sheet 16 × 12½ in.

notes: *Publication*: published by 4 June 1750 (*GC*).

copies: G⁴ (Pot), L (Foolscap).

160 Milton, John, *Paradise Lost* 1750

PARADISE | LOST, | A | POEM | IN | TWELVE BOOKS. | *THE AUTHOR* | JOHN MILTON. | ACCORDING TO THE AUTHOR'S LAST | EDITION, IN THE YEAR 1672. | GLASGOW, | printed and sold by r. & a. Foulis | PRIN TERS TO THE UNIVERSITY. | M.DCC.L.

formula: Foolscap 8⁰: a⁸ A–U⁸ (a3 *signed* ' *a ', a4 *signed* ' a2 '; a1 *half-title*, U8 *advertisements*).

paper: Good quality; marks 5/iv, 4/v.

type: RB 2, RLP 1.

variant: Issue in Pot 12⁰:
 Formula: Pot 12⁰: π² a⁶ A–G¹² H⁶ I–P¹² Q⁴(–Q 3–4; π1 *half-title*).
 Paper: Medium quality; marks 1/iv, 1/v.

notes: *Publication*: in the press January or March 1750 (No. 146); published by 26 November 1750 (*GC*).

copies: G⁴ (8⁰), L (8⁰), G² (12⁰).

161 Milton, John, *Paradise Lost Book I* 1750

MILTON'S | PARADISE | LOST, | BOOK I. | [*quotation, 3 lines*] | GLASGOW: | PRINTED AND SOLD BY ROBERT AND ANDREW FOULIS | PRINTERS TO THE UNIVER SITY. | M.DCC.L.

formula: Foolscap 4⁰: π² A–X⁴.

paper: Good quality; marks 3/iv, 5/v; size of sheet 16½ × 13 in.

type: RE 1, RE 2, RLP 1, GB, RB 1, RB 2.

NOTES: With a commentary by John Callander of Craigforth.
Publication: published by 3 December 1750 (*GC*).
Prices: Wholesale: 1s. 6d. (*BQ* 6). Retail: 2s. 6d. (*CP* 7).
Stock in 1777: 179 copies (*BQ* 6).
COPIES: G⁴, L.

1750   Minucius Felix, *Octavius*, L **162**

MARCI | MINUCII | FELICIS | OCTAVIUS. | EX RECEN
SIONE | JOHANNIS DAVISII. | GLASGUAE, | IN AEDI
BUS ACADEMICIS | EXCUDEBANT ROBERTUS ET
ANDREAS FOULIS | ACADEMIAE TYPOGRAPHI, |
M.DcC.L.
FORMULA: Foolscap 8⁰: π^2 A–G⁸ H⁴ I² (π1 *half-title*; I2
advertisements).
PAPER: Medium-good quality; marks 4/vi.
TYPE: RE 2, RB 2, RLP 1.
VARIANT: Issue in Foolscap 4⁰:
    Formula: Foolscap 4⁰: π^2 A–P⁴ ²I² (P2 *signed* ' H2 '; π1
half-title, ²I2 *advertisements; note the signatures in the last two
sections taken over unaltered from the 8⁰*).
    Paper: Same as the 8⁰.
    Murray (*R. & A. Foulis*, p. 40) mentions an issue on vellum.
NOTES: *Publication*: published by 6 August 1750 (*GC*).
COPIES: G⁴ (both issues), L (8⁰).

1750   Musaeus Grammaticus, *Hero and Leander*, E **163**

HERO | AND | LEANDER: | A | POEM | BY | MUSAEUS,
| TRANSLATED FROM THE GREEK BY | L. EUSDEN |
OF TRINITY-COLLEGE, CAMBRIDGE. | GLASGOW:|
PRINTED BY ROBERT AND ANDREW FOULIS, | AND
SOLD BY JOHN ROSS, IN EDINBURGH, | MDCCL. |
PRICE SIX-PENCE.
FORMULA: [? Crown) 8⁰ in fours: A–D⁴.
PAPER: Medium quality; marks 9/i.
TYPE: RE 1.
VARIANT: Issue on inferior paper, [? Crown] 8⁰:
    Paper: Medium-poor quality, no marks (Note: the price on
the title-page unchanged).
NOTES: *Price*: Retail: 6d. (title-page).
COPIES: L (fine), O (common).

† **164** Plato, [Proposals for editions, E and L, with   1750–51
specimens]

NOTES: Not seen. Listed by Duncan (p. 54, No. 79) under the
year 1749, quoting a letter from John Wilkes to Robert Foulis
dated 3 December 1746 (*sic*) concerning a proposed edition in ten
volumes octavo.

Proposals for editions in Greek and Latin, in four volumes
small folio and twenty volumes small octavo, dated 15 June
1750, appeared in *GC* for 18 June 1750; in *GC* for 3 September
1750 it was announced that specimens were available from the
printers; and we know that a Double Pica Greek was cut for
this purpose (Maclehose, p. 168). This must have been GDP 1,
which was used in the following year to print Archimedes's
Sand-reckoner (No. 182).

An altered and expanded form of the proposals, which now
referred to editions in nine volumes quarto and six volumes
folio, were printed on M11–M12ᵛ of the duodecimo *De Imitatione* (No. 218), published by 27 May 1751; they are dated 7
January 1751. A Latin version of these later proposals appeared
in *The Gentleman's Magazine* for September 1751 (Vol. xxi,
pp. 430–1). William Hunter wrote to William Cullen on 1
August 1751, ' I received first the English and then the Latin
proposals for Plato ' (Murray, *R. & A. Foulis*, p. 54).

Several sets, therefore, of proposals and specimens were
issued in 1750 and 1751. The proposals dated 7 January 1751,
(English version) are reprinted below in Appendix A.

165 Pythagoreans, *Golden Verses*, E, with Pope,   1750
Alexander, *The Universal Prayer*

THE | GOLDEN VERSES | OF | PYTHAGORAS. | TRANS
LATED FROM THE GREEK | BY | NICHOLAS ROWE
Efq; | TO WHICH IS ADDED, | THE | UNIVERSAL
PRAYER, | BY | ALEXANDER POPE Efq; | GLASGOW⟨:⟩
| PRINTED AND SOLD BY ROBERT AND ANDREW
FO⟨ULI⟩S. M.DCC.L. | Price Three-pence.

FORMULA: [? Crown] 8⁰ in fours: π1 A⁴.

PAPER: Medium-poor quality; no marks.

TYPE: RE 2.

VARIANT: Possibly an issue on better-quality paper, not seen
(*BQ* 10 mentions a *wholesale* price of 3*d*., which is the same
as the *retail* price given on the title-page above).

NOTES: *Prices*: Wholesale: (?) fine, 3*d*. (*BQ* 10). Retail: (?) common, 3*d*. (*title-page*).
COPIES: G⁴.

1750   Ramsay, Allan, *A Collection of Scots Proverbs* **166**

A | COLLECTION | OF | *SCOTS* | PROVERBS. | ACCORD
ING TO THE EDITION PUBLISHED | BY | *ALLAN
RAMSAY.* | EDINBURGH, | SOLD BY W. GORDON IN
THE PARLIAMENT CLOSS, | AT GLASGOW BY R. AND
A. FOULIS, | M DCC L.
FORMULA: Pot 8⁰ in fours: A–R⁴(–R₄; A2 *signed* ' A ', Q2
signed ' Q 3 ').
PAPER: Medium-poor quality; marks 1/v.
TYPE: RLP I, RB I.
NOTES: The typography strongly suggests that this book was
printed as well as sold by Robert and Andrew Foulis; and it
appears among a list of books lately printed and sold by them
in *GC* for 3 September 1750.
COPIES: G².

1750   Ramsay, Allan, *The Gentle Shepherd* **167**

THE | GENTLE SHEPHERD: | A | *SCOTS* | PASTORAL
COMEDY. | BY | ALLAN RAMSAY. | THE TENTH EDI
TION WITH THE SANGS. | GLASGOW. | PRINTED AND
SOLD BY R. & A. FOULIS. | M.DCC.L.
FORMULA: [? Crown 12⁰ in sixes): A–G⁶.
PAPER: Medium-poor quality; thin; no marks; vertical
chain-lines (probably half-sheets of Double Crown); size of
half-sheet 19¼ × 14¾ in.
TYPE: RB I, RLP I.
NOTES: Publication: published by 12 March 1750 (*GC*).
COPIES: L.

1750   Rowe, Nicholas, *Tamerlane* **168**

NOTES: Not seen. Advertised as ' lately printed ' by Robert
and Andrew Foulis in *GC* for 5 November 1750.

169 Sherlock, Thomas, *A Letter on Occasion of the*　1750
late Earthquakes

A | LETTER | ON OCCASION OF THE LATE | EARTH
QUAKES, | FROM THE | LORD BISHOP | OF | LONDON,
| TO THE | CLERGY AND PEOPLE | OF | LONDON and
WESTMINSTER. | GLASGOW, | PRINTED AND SOLD BY R. & A.
FOULIS | PRINTERS TO THE UNIVERSITY | MDCCL. |
PRICE THREE PENCE.

FORMULA: Foolscap 8⁰: A–B⁸ (B3 *signed* ' B2 ').

PAPER: Medium quality; marks 3/iv.

TYPE: RE 2.

VARIANT: Issue on common paper, not seen (*GC* 2 April 1750).

NOTES: *Publication*: published by 2 April 1750 (*GC*).
　Prices: Retail: fine, 3*d*.; common, 2*d*. (*GC* 2 April 1750).

COPIES: L (Foolscap).

170 Smith, Edmund, *Phaedra and Hippolitus*　1750

PHAEDRA | AND | HIPPOLITUS, | A | TRAGEDY. | BY
EDMUND SMITH, Efq; | THE FOURTH EDITION. |
GLASGOW, | PRINTED AND SOLD BY ROBERT & ANDREW
FOULIS | MDCCL.

FORMULA: Post 12⁰ in sixes: A–F⁶.

PAPER: Medium quality; marks 6/JW.

TYPE: RB 1, RLP 1.

NOTES: *Publication*: published by 5 November 1750 (*GC*).

COPIES: G².

171 Steel, William, *Memorial concerning Small*　1750
Stipends in Scotland

NOTES: Not seen. Advertisement for books to be had of
Robert and Andrew Foulis, *GC* 9 April 1750: ' MEMORIAL,
Shewing the Reafonablenefs and Neceffity of an immediate
Application to the King and Parliament, for augmenting
fmall Stipends in Scotland. BY WILLIAM STEEL of Waygate
fhaw, Minifter in Dalferf.'

This advertisement may refer to the edition printed by
Sands, Murray and Cochrane, Edinburgh 1750.

1750   Thomas More, St, *Utopia*, L **172**

DE | OPTIMO | REIPUBLICAE | STATU, | DEQUE | NOVA INSULA | UTOPIA, | LIBRI II. | *AUCTORE* | THOMA MORO EQUITE, | ANGLIAE CANCELLARIO. | EX PRIORIBUS EDITIONIBUS COLLATIS | ACCU RATE EXPRESSI. | *GLASGUAE,* | IN AEDIBUS ACADE MICIS | Excudebant ROBERTUS et ANDREAS FOULIS | M DCC L.

FORMULA: Foolscap 8⁰: a⁴ A–R⁸ S⁴ (H4, N3, S2 *unsigned;* S4 *advertisements*).

PAPER: Medium-good quality; marks 5/v; size of sheet 16½ × 13 in.

TYPE: RE 2, RLP 1, RB 2.

NOTES: *Publication*: published by 3 September 1750 (*GC*). *Prices*: Wholesale: 1s. 6d. (*BQ* 11). Retail: 2s. 6d. (*CP* 5). *Stock in 1777*: 2 copies (*BQ* 11).

COPIES: G⁴, L.

1750   Webb, Bernard, *De Imperii Civilis origine et* **173** *causis*, L

DISSERTATIO | PHILOSOPHICA INAUGURALIS | DE | IMPERII CIVILIS | ORIGINE et CAUSIS. | QUAM | FAVENTE SUMMO NUMINE | *Auctoritate Digniſſimi Vice-Cancellarii* | NIGELLI CAMPBELL V.D.M. | S.S.T. PROFES SORIS PRIMARII ET ACADEMIAE PRAEFECTI; | NEC NON | *Ampliſſimi* SENATUS ACADEMICI *confenſu* | *et celeberrimae* FACULTATIS ARTIUM *decreto,* | PRO GRADU MAGIS TERII, | SUMMISQUE IN PHILOSOPHIA ET ARTIBUS LIBERALIBUS, | PRIVILEGIIS, ET HONORIBUS, | RITE AC LEGITIME CONSEQUENDIS, | In auditorio publico Academiae Glafguenfis, | Ad diem Maii 22, hora [' 4ta ' *in MS*] poft meridiem, | PROPUGNABIT | BERNARDUS WEBB, HIBERNUS. | [*Quotation, 1 line*] | GLASGUAE, | IN AEDIBUS ACADEMICIS | EXCUDEBANT ROB. ET AND. FOULIS ACADEMIAE TYPOGRAPHI | MDCCL.

FORMULA: [? Writing Demy] 4⁰ in twos: A² B–G².

PAPER: Medium-good quality; marks 7/1.

TYPE: RE 2.

NOTES: *Publication*: published by 22 May 1750 (the date of the dissertation).

COPIES: G⁴, L.

174 Xenophon, *Hieron*, E 1750

HIERO, | OR THE | CONDITION | OF A | TYRANT. | TRANSLATED FROM | XENOPHON. | FIRST PRINTED MDCCXIII. | THE SECOND EDITION. | GLASGOW, | PRINTED AND SOLD BY R. & A. FOULIS | MDCCL.

FORMULA: Foolscap 8⁰ in fours: π^2 A–B⁴($\pm$B4) C–I⁴ K² (πI *half-title*).

PAPER: Medium-good quality; marks 5/ii, iv, v, 4/iv, v.

TYPE: RE 2.

NOTES: *Price*: Wholesale: 3*d*. (*BQ* 12).
   Stock in 1777: 14 copies (*BQ* 12).

COPIES: G⁴, L.

175 Xenophon, *Symposium*, E 1750

THE | BANQUET | OF | XENOPHON. | DONE FROM THE GREEK, | WITH AN | INTRODUCTORY ESSAY | TO | LADY JEAN DOUGLASS, | CONCERNING THE | DOCTRINE, AND DEATH | OF | SOCRATES. | BY JAMES WELWOOD, M.D. | FELLOW OF THE ROYAL COLLEGE OF PHYSICIANS, | *LONDON*. | GLASGOW, | PRINTED AND SOLD BY ROBERT AND ANDREW FOULIS | MDCCL.

FORMULA: Foolscap 8⁰ in fours: A–2G⁴ (2G4 *advertisements*).

PAPER: Medium-good quality; marks 5/iv, 5/v.

TYPE: RE 2, RB 2, RLP 1.

VARIANT: Issue in Pot 8⁰:
   Paper: Medium quality; marks 1/v.

NOTES: *Publication*: in the press 3 September 1750; published by 17 September 1750 (*GC*).
   Prices: Wholesale: Foolscap, 1*s*. 2*d*. (*BQ* 6). Retail: (?) Foolscap, 2*s*. (*CP* 9).
   Stock in 1777: Foolscap, 4 copies (*BQ* 6).

COPIES: G⁴ (Pot), L (Pot), G (Foolscap).

† **176** Young, Edward, *Love of Fame* 1750

LOVE OF FAME, | THE | UNIVERSAL PASSION. | IN | SEVEN CHARACTERISTICAL | SATIRES. | [*quotation, 2 lines*) | BY THE REVEREND | EDWARD YOUNG, LL.D. | RECTOR OF WELLWYN IN HARTFORDSHIRE, | AND

CHAPLAIN IN ORDINARY TO HIS MAJESTY. | GLAS
GOW: | PRINTED AND SOLD BY ROBERT AND AN
DREW FOULIS. | M.DCC.L.
FORMULA: Pot 8⁰ in fours: a⁴ b² A–M⁴.
PAPER: Medium quality; marks 1/v.
TYPE: RLP 1, RE 2.
NOTES: *Publication*: in the press 3 September 1750; published
by 15 October 1750 (*GC*).
COPIES: G⁴.

1751   Abélard, Pierre, *Letters of Abélard and Héloïse,*   **177**
          with Pope, Alexander, *Eloisa to Abelard*

LETTERS | OF THE CELEBRATED | ABELARD | AND
| HELOISE. | WITH THE HISTORY OF THEIR | LIVES |
PREFIXED. | In both of which are defcribed their various
MISFORTUNES, | and the fatal confequences of their AMOURS.
| TRANSLATED BY MR. JOHN HUGHES. | To which is added, |
ELOISA TO ABELARD; | A POEM | BY | ALEXANDER POPE Efq; |
GLASGOW; | PRINTED AND SOLD BY ROBERT AND
| ANDREW FOULIS | M.DCC.LI.
FORMULA: Foolscap 8⁰ in fours: π⁴ ᵖA–D⁴ A–2B⁴ ²2A⁴ ²2B²
(*sub-title with imprint to Pope's poem on* ²2A1).
PAPER: Medium-good quality; marks 5/iv; size of sheet
16½ × 13 in.
TYPE: RE 2, RB 2, RLP 1.
VARIANT: Issue in Pot 8⁰:
Paper: Medium quality; marks 1/v.
NOTES: *Publication*: published by 4 March 1751 (*GC*).
   Price: Wholesale: Foolscap, 1*s.* 6*d.* (*BQ* 11).
   Stock in 1777: Foolscap, 2 copies (*BQ* 11).
COPIES: G⁴ (Pot), G (Foolscap).

1751   Addison, Joseph, *Poems on Several Occasions* **178**

POEMS | ON | SEVERAL OCCASIONS. | BY | THE RIGHT
HONOURABLE | JOSEPH ADDISON, ESQ.; | GLASGOW,
| PRINTED AND SOLD BY ROBERT & ANDREW FOULIS | M.DCC.LI.
[*there are two settings of the title-page, reading the same*]
FORMULA: Foolscap 8⁰ in fours: π1 A–2B⁴.

PAPER: Medium-good quality; marks 4/v, 5/v; size of sheet 16½ × 13 in.

TYPE: RB 2.

VARIANT: Issue in Pot 8⁰:

Paper: Medium-poor quality; marks 1/v.

COPIES: G⁴ (Foolscap), L (Pot).

179 Addison, Joseph, *The Drummer* 1751

THE | DRUMMER; | OR, THE | HAUNTED-HOUSE. | A | COMEDY. | BY THE LATE RIGHT HONOURABLE | JOSEPH ADDISON, Efq; | [*quotation, 2 lines*] | GLASGOW, | PRINTED AND SOLD BY R. & A. FOULIS | M.DCC.LI.

FORMULA: Foolscap 8⁰ in fours: A–I⁴ K².

PAPER: Medium-good quality; marks 5/v.

TYPE: RB 2, RLP 1.

VARIANT: Issue in Pot 8⁰:

Paper: Medium quality; marks 1/v; size of sheet 15 × 12¼ in.

COPIES: G⁴ (Foolscap), L (Pot).

180 Addison, Joseph, *Rosamond* 1751

ROSAMOND. | AN | OPERA. | INSCRIB'D TO HER GRACE, | THE DUTCHESS OF | MARLBOROUGH. | [*quotation, 4 lines*] | BY THE LATE RIGHT HONOURABLE | JOSEPH ADDISON EsQ; | GLASGOW, | PRINTED AND SOLD BY ROBERT & ANDREW FOULIS | M.DCC.LI.

FORMULA: Foolscap 8⁰ in fours: A–D⁴ E².

PAPER: Medium-good quality; marks 4/v.

TYPE: RB 2, RE 2.

COPIES: L.

181 Anacreon, *Odes*, with Sappho and Alcaeus, 1751 *Remains*, G

ΑΙ ΤΟΥ | ΑΝΑΚΡΕΟΝΤΟΣ | ,ΩΔΑΙ. | Καὶ τὰ τῆς | ΣΑΠ ΦΟΥΣ, | Καὶ τὰ τοῦ[*lig.*] | ΑΛΚΑΙΟΥ | ΛΕΙΨΑΝΑ. | [*quotation, 1 line* | GLASGUAE: | EXCUDEBANT R. & A. FOULIS. | M.DCC.LI.

FORMULA: Foolscap 32⁰ in eights: π² A–D⁸ E⁶.

PAPER: Good quality; marks 5/iv.

TYPE: GB.

VARIANT: Issue printed on silk:
  Silk: Each gathering of four conjugate pairs printed on silk of four different colours, sewn round the edges. This could have been done in one of three ways: (1) separate imposition of each conjugate pair; (2) imposition by colours with subsequent re-sorting; (3) normal imposition on white silk which was afterwards cut up and dyed.

NOTES: *Publication*: published by 21 January 1751 (*GC*, which mentions a few copies on silk).

COPIES: G4 (paper), L (paper and silk).

1751   Archimedes, *The Sand-reckoner*, G **182**

[*The following title-page relates, not to the* Arenarius *as a whole, but only the theorem given in the first two pages, said to have been used by Archimedes:*] ΘΕΩΡΗΜΑ | 'Ωι ΚΕΧΡΗΤΑΙ, ΕΝ ΤΩι ΨΑΜΜΙΤΗι | 'Ο ΑΡΧΙΜΗΔΗΣ· | 'ΩιΤΕ, ΚΑΙ ΠΟΛ ΛΑΚΙΣ, | ΑΡΙΣΤΑΡΧΟΣ | 'Ο ΣΑΜΙΟΣ | ΕΝ ΤΩι ΠΕΡΙ ΤΩΝ ΜΕΓΕΘΩΝ | ΚΑΙ ΑΠΟΣΤΗΜΑΤΩΝ· | 'ΥΠΟ ΜΕΝ ΤΟΥ | ΕΥΔΟΞΟΥ, | 'ΩΣ ΕΟΙΚΕΝ, ΕΞΕΥΡΕΘΕΝ· | ΣΕ ΣΩΣΜΕΝΟΝ ΔΕ ΕΙΣ 'ΗΜΑΣ | 'ΥΠΟ ΤΟΥ | ΠΤΟΛΕ ΜΑΙΟΥ, | ΕΝ ΤΩι, ΤΟΥ ΠΡΩΤΟΥ ΤΗΣ ΜΕΓΑΛΗΣ ΣΥΝ-|ΤΑΞΕΩΣ, ΠΕΡΙ ΤΩΝ ΕΝ ΤΩι ΚΥΚΛΩι, ΕΥΘΕΙΩΝ.

FORMULA: Foolscap 2^0: π^2 A–H^2 (π1 *title-page to* The Theorem, π1^v–π2 The Theorem of Eudoxus, π2^v *blank*, A1–A2^v The Sand-Reckoner).

PAPER: Medium-good quality; marks 5/v; size of sheet $16\frac{1}{2} \times 13$ in.

TYPE: GDP 1; several woodcut diagrams.

NOTES: Edited by Professor James Moor, and printed in the early part of 1751 from a manuscript borrowed from the Bibliothèque du Roi, Paris. Part of the edition seems to have been remaindered, although it is not mentioned in *BQ*. Spotiswood (p. 85) offers copies at 5s. in 1779. (See the long note in the L copy (715.k.2; also in O, 2905.c.2) by C. F. Barnwell, dated 1833, quoting Moor's letter of 26 July 1751; and Murray, *R. & A. Foulis*, p. 24.)

COPIES: G4, L.

183 Berkeley, George, *The Querist*, with *A Word*   1751
to the Wise

THE | QUERIST, | OR, | SEVERAL QUERIES | PROPOSED
TO THE | CONSIDERATION | OF THE | PUBLIC. | BY
THE RIGHT REVEREND | Dr. GEORGE BERKLEY, |
LORD BISHOP OF CLOYNE. | [*quotation, 4 lines*] | GLAS
GOW: | Printed and sold by Robert & Andrew Foulis, |
printers to the University. | M.DCC.LI.

FORMULA: Foolscap 8⁰ in fours: *A⁴ B–N⁴ ×N⁴ O² (signed ' ✱ '
on A3 and $1 except A1, F1 (sometimes), L1 and N1. The whole
of section N is sometimes omitted, so that, although the signatures
appear to run correctly, eight pages of text are left out between pp. 88
and ²89. Since sections N and ×N are both numbered 89–96, the
page numbers 97–104 are missing whether or not section N is in
place; A1 half-title, M2 sub-title to* A Word to the Wise).

PAPER: Good quality; marks 4/v, 5/iv; size of sheet 16½ × 13 in.

TYPE: RLP 1, RB 2, RP 2.

VARIANT: Issue on inferior paper, Foolscap 8⁰:
   Formula: (*without ' ✱ ' signatures*).
   Paper: Medium quality; marks 4/v; size of sheet 16¼ × 13 in.

NOTES: *Publication*: the printers preface is dated 10 January
1751; published by 21 January 1751 (*GC*).
   Price: Wholesale: (? issue, ' fome fullied '), 9d. (*BQ* 6).
   Stock in 1777: (? issue, ' fome fullied '), 18 copies (*BQ* 6).

COPIES: G⁴ (fine), L (common).

184 Boethius, *De Consolatione Philosophiae*, L   1751

ANICII MANLII | SEVERINI | BOETII | CONSOLA
TIONIS | PHILOSOPHIAE | LIBRI QUINQUE. | GLAS
GUAE: | IN AEDIBUS ACADEMICIS | EXCUDEBANT
ROBERTUS ET ANDREAS FOULIS, | ACADEMIAE
TYPOGRAPHI, | M.DCC.LI.

FORMULA: Foolscap 8⁰ in fours: a² A–U⁴ (U4 *advertisements*).

PAPER: Medium-good quality; marks 4/v, 5/iv.

TYPE: RP 2, RE 2, RB 2, RLP 1.

VARIANT: Issue in Foolscap 4⁰:
   Formula: Foolscap 4⁰: (*as* 8⁰).
   Paper: Same as 8⁰.

NOTES: *Publication*: in the press, 3 September 1750; published by 25 February 1751 (*GC*).
  Prices: Wholesale: 8⁰, 1s. 6d. (*BQ* 2). Retail: 8⁰, 2s. (*CP* 5).
  Stock in 1777: 8⁰, 55 copies (*BQ* 2).
COPIES: G⁴ (8⁰ and 4⁰), L (8⁰).

1751   Child, Sir Josiah, *A New Discourse of Trade, etc.* **185**

A NEW | DISCOURSE | OF | TRADE: | WHEREIN ARE RECOMMENDED | SEVERAL WEIGHTY POINTS; | RELATING TO | [*two columns of contents, 10 and 12 lines, separated by a vertical plain rule, 39*) | BY SIR JOSIAH CHILD, BARONET. | To which is added, | A SMALL TREATISE AGAINST USURY. | BY THE SAME AUTHOR. | THE FIFTH EDITION. | GLASGOW: | PRINTED AND SOLD BY ROBERT AND ANDREW FOULIS. | M.DCC.LI.

FORMULA: Foolscap 8⁰: a–b⁸ A–L⁸ M⁴.

PAPER: Medium-good quality; marks 4/v, 5/v; size of sheet 16½ × 13 in.

TYPE: RLP 1, RB 2.

VARIANT: Issue in Pot 8⁰:
  Paper: Medium quality; marks 1/v.

NOTES: *Publication*: in the press, 26 November 1750; published by 25 March 1751 (*GC*).
  Prices: Wholesale: Pot, 1s. (*BQ* 10). Retail: (?) Foolscap, 2s. (*CP* 9).
  Stock in 1777: Pot, 29 copies (*BQ* 10).

COPIES: G⁴ (both issues) L (1 copy, missing).

1751   Congreve, William, *Dramatic Works* **186**

THE | DRAMATIC | WORKS | OF | Mr. WILLIAM CON GREVE. | VOL. I [II]. | GLASGOW, | PRINTED BY ROBERT & ANDREW FOULIS | M DCC LI. [*Both title-pages from the same setting. Each play has its own sub-title with imprint.*]

FORMULA: Pot 8⁰:
  Vol. I: π² A–Y⁸ Z⁴ (Z4 *blank*).
  Vol. II: π² A–P⁸ Q² (F4 *signed* ' F3 ').

PAPER: Medium-good quality; marks 1/v, 2/?.

TYPE: RB 1, RE 2, RLP 1.

NOTES: *Publication*: published by 7 October 1751 (*GC*).

COPIES: G⁴.

187 Daniel, Samuel, *Cleopatra*   1751

THE | TRAGEDY | OF | CLEOPATRA. | BY MR. SAMUEL
DANIEL. | [*quotation, 1 line*] | GLASGOW, | PRINTED AND SOLD
BY ROBERT & ANDREW FOULIS | M.DCC.LI.

FORMULA: Post 12⁰ in sixes: A–E⁶ (E6 *advertisements*).

PAPER: Medium-good quality; marks 6/monogram.

TYPE: RB 1, RLP 1.

VARIANT: Issue on inferior paper, [? Crown 12⁰]:
Formula: (as above, but vertical chain lines, suggesting the
use of half double-sized sheets of Crown).
Paper: Medium-poor quality; no marks.

NOTES: *Publication*: published by 25 February 1751 (*GC*).

COPIES: G² (Post), L (Crown).

188 Denham, Sir John, *Poems and Translations,*   1751
with The Sophy

POEMS | AND | TRANSLATIONS; | WITH THE | SOPHY,
| A | TRAGEDY. | WRITTEN BY THE HONOURABLE | SIR JOHN
DENHAM, | KNIGHT OF THE BATH. | GLASGOW: | PRINTED
BY ROBERT AND ANDREW FOULIS | M DCC LI.

FORMULA: Foolscap 8⁰ in fours: A–2H⁴ (H2 *signed* ' G2 '; 2H4
advertisements).

PAPER: Medium-good quality; marks 5/v.

TYPE: RLP 1, RB 2.

VARIANT: issue in Pot 8⁰:
Paper: Medium quality; marks 2/iv, 2/v; size of sheet
$15 \times 12\frac{1}{2}$ in.

NOTES: *Publication*: published by 3 February 1752 (*sic, GC*).
Price: Wholesale: Pot, 1s. (*BQ* 11).
Stock in 1777: Pot, 2 copies (*BQ* 11).

COPIES: G⁴ (Foolscap), G (Pot).

189 Duncan, John, *The Defects of a Pharisaical*   1751
Righteousness, a Sermon

THE | DEFECTS | AND | DANGER | OF A | PHARISAICAL
| RIGHTEOUSNESS. | A SERMON | PREACHED | AT
GLASGOW JULY 7th, 1751. | BY JOHN DUNCAN M.A. | FEL

LOW OF ST. JOHN BAPTIST'S COLLEGE OXON, |
AND CHAPLAIN TO COLONEL RICH'S REGIMENT. |
GLASGOW: | Printed by robert and andrew foulis |
M DCC LI.

FORMULA: Foolscap 8⁰ in fours: π1 A⁴($\pm$A4) B–D⁴.

PAPER: Medium-good quality; marks 5/v.

TYPE: RE 2.

NOTES: *Publication*: published by 9 September 1751 (*GC*).
  Price: Wholesale, 2*d*. (*BQ* 9).
  Stock in 1777: 186 copies (*BQ* 9).

COPIES: G⁴, L.

1751   Epictetus, *Manual*, G **190**

ΤΟ ΤΟΥ | ΕΠΙΚΤΗΤΟΥ | ΕΓΧΕΙΡΙΔΙΟΝ. | EX EDI
TIONE | JOANNIS UPTON | ACCURATE EXPRESSUM.
| GLASGUAE, | Excudebant Robertus et | Andreas Foulis, |
MDCCLI.

FORMULA: Foolscap 32⁰ in eights: A–F⁸.

PAPER: Medium-good quality; marks 5/iv.

TYPE: GB.

NOTES: Publication: published by 29 July 1751 (*GC*).

COPIES: G⁴, L.

1751   Fénelon, *Fables*, E **191**

FABLES | COMPOSED | FOR THE USE OF THE | DUKE
OF BURGUNDY. | BY | M. FENELON, | ARCHBISHOP |
OF | CAMBRAY. | NEWLY TRANSLATED FROM THE
FRENCH | BY MR. ELPHINGSTON. | GLASGOW: | PRIN
TED AND SOLD BY ROBERT AND ANDREW FOULIS
| M. DCC.LI.

FORMULA: Foolscap 8⁰ in fours: A² B–O⁴ P².

PAPER: Medium-good quality; marks 4/v.

TYPE: RLP 1.

COPIES: G⁴.

192 Foulis, Robert and Andrew, *A Catalogue of* 1751
Books. with Prices, Parts 1 and 2

NOTES: Not seen. Advertisements in *GC* for 16 September 1751: ' *This Day is publiſhed, By* R. *and* A. FOULIS *Bookſellers in Glaſgow*, A Catalogue of Curious and valuable BOOKS with the Prices printed. Part Iſt.'; and, for 21 October 1751, for ' PART II.' of the same Catalogue.

† **193** Gay, John, *Poems on Several Occasions* 1751

POEMS | ON | SEVERAL OCCASIONS. | BY | Mr. JOHN GAY. | VOLUME I. | [*quotation, 4 lines*] | GLASGOW, | PRINTED AND SOLD BY ROBERT AND ANDREW FOULIS | M DCC LI. [*Vol. II reads ' VOLUME II.' in line 6; omits the quotation; and reads in the last two lines:* ' PRINTED AND SOLD BY ROBERT & ANDREW FOULIS | M.DCC.LI.']

FORMULA: Foolscap 8° in fours:
Vol. I: A–F⁴(–F4) G–2A⁴ (H4 *signed* ' F2 ', L2 *sometimes signed* ' L ').
Vol. II: π² A–P⁴ ˣP⁴ Q–Y⁴ Z² (*signed* ' VOL. II. *on* $1 *except* A1, M1; Z2 *advertisements*).

PAPER: Medium-good quality; marks 4/v, 5/v, 5/iv.

TYPE: RLP 1, RB 2, RE 2.

VARIANT: Issue in [? Crown] 12°:
Title-pages: [*Both from the same settings as the 8°, but Vol.* I *puts the quotation immediately after line 5.*]
Formula: [? Crown] 12° in sixes: Vol. I: A–D⁶(–D6) E–Q⁶.
Vol. II: π² A–P⁶ Q⁴ (*signed* ' VOL. II.' *on* $1 *except* A1; Q4 *advertisements*).
Paper: Medium-poor quality; no marks.

NOTES: *Publication*: published by 9 September 1751 (*GC*).

COPIES: G⁴ (8°), L (12°).

194 ' Law, John ', *Proposals for a Council of Trade* 1751
in Scotland

PROPOSALS AND REASONS | FOR CONSTITUTING A | COUNCIL OF TRADE | IN | *SCOTLAND*. | BY THE CELE BRATED | JOHN LAW Esǫ; | AFTERWARDS | COMP TROLLER OF THE FINANCES IN FRANCE. | FIRST PUBLISHED AT EDINBURGH IN THE 1700. [*sic*] | IN

WHICH | MANY NATIONAL IMPROVEMENTS | OF
GREAT IMPORTANCE ARE POINTED OUT, VIZ. | [*two columns of
contents, 17 lines each, separated by a vertical plain rule, 48*] |
GLASGOW, | PRINTED AND SOLD BY ROB. & AND. FOULIS
MDCCLI.

FORMULA: Foolscap 8° in fours: a^2 b–c⁴ A–2M⁴ 2N² (2N2
advertisements).

PAPER: Medium-good quality; marks 4/v, 5/v; size of sheet
$16\frac{1}{2} \times 13$ in.

TYPE: RE 2, RB 1, RLP 1.

VARIANT: Issue in Pot 8°:
Paper: Medium-good quality; marks 1/v.

NOTES: Probably by William Paterson, not by Law.
Publication: in the press, 6 August 1750, 26 November 1750;
published by 29 July 1751 (*GC*).
Prices: Wholesale: Pot, 1s. 6d. (*BQ* 11). Retail: (? Pot), 2s.
(*CP* 9).
Stock in 1777: Pot, 20 copies (*BQ* 11).

COPIES: G⁴ (Pot), L (Foolscap).

1751   Locke, John, *Elements of Natural Philosophy, etc.*   **195**

ELEMENTS | OF | NATURAL | PHILOSOPHY. | BY |
JOHN LOCKE Esq; | TO WHICH IS ADDED | SOME
THOUGHTS | CONCERNING | READING AND STUDY,
| FOR A | GENTLEMAN, | BY THE SAME AUTHOR. |
GLASGOW, | PRINTED AND SOLD BY R. AND A. FOULIS |
M DCC LI.

FORMULA: Foolscap 8° in fours: a⁴ A–I⁴ (a2 *signed* ' 2a ';
I4 *blank*).

PAPER: Medium quality; marks 4/v.

TYPE: RE 1, RE 2, RLP 1.

NOTES: Publication: published by 18 February 1751 (*GC*).

COPIES: L.

1751   Longinus, *On the Sublime*, G and L   **196**

ΤΟ ΤΟΥ | ΔΙΟΝΥΣΙΟΥ | ΛΟΓΓΙΝΟΥ | ΠΕΡΙ | ΥΨΟΥΣ |
ΥΠΟΜΝΗΜΑ. | EX EDITIONE TERTIA | ZACHARIAE
PEARCE, | EPISCOPI BANGORIENSIS, | EXPRESSUM. | GLAS
GUAE: | IN AEDIBUS ACADEMICIS | EXCUDEBANT
ROBERTUS ET ANDREAS FOULIS | ACADEMIAE
TYPOGRAPHI, | M.DCC.LI.

FORMULA: Foolscap 8⁰ in fours: π^4 A–T⁴ U² (G2 *signed;* ' D2 ' π1 *half-title*).

PAPER: Medium-good quality; marks 5/v.

TYPE: GP, RB 2, RLP 1. Latin follows Greek.

VARIANT: Issue in Pot 8⁰:

 Paper: Medium quality; marks 1/v.

COPIES: G⁴ (Foolscap, imperfect), L (Foolscap), G² (Pot).

197 Lucan, *Pharsalia* 1751

NOTES: Not seen. Listed by Duncan (p. 57, No. 119) as ' Lucanus, ex editione Burmanni.'

198 Milton, John, *L'Allegro and il Penseroso* 1751

L' ALLEGRO, | AND | IL PENSEROSO. | THE AUTHOR | JOHN MILTON. | GLASGOW, | PRINTED AND SOLD BY ROBERT AND ANDREW FOULIS | MDCCLI.

FORMULA: Foolscap 4⁰ in twos: π1 A–E² ˣE1.

PAPER: Medium-good quality; marks 5/iv, 5/v.

TYPE: RGP 1.

NOTES: *Price*: Wholesale: 3*d*. (*BQ* 10).

 Stock in 1777: 34 copies (*BQ* 10).

COPIES: G⁴, L.

199 Miscellany. *Poems on Moral and Divine Subjects* 1751

POEMS | ON | MORAL AND DIVINE | SUBJECTS, | BY SEVERAL CELEBRATED | ENGLISH POETS, | *VIZ.* | [*three columns of names, 7 lines each, separated by vertical plain rules, 25 and 24*] | [*quotation, 8 lines*] | GLASGOW, | PRINTED BY ROBERT & ANDREW FOULIS | M.DCC.LI.

FORMULA: [? Printing Demy] 8⁰ in fours: π^2 A–3C⁴ (π1 *half-title*).

PAPER: Medium-poor quality; marks 9/i, no marks.

TYPE: RE 2, RLP 1, RB 2, RSP 1.

NOTES: *Publication*: an advertisement in *GC* for what appears to be this book says that it will be published a few days after 21 May 1753; but of course this advertisement, and the *BQ* and *CP* entries (see below), may refer to a later edition, not seen.

Prices: Wholesale: 2*s*. 6*d*. (*BQ* 7).   Retail, 3*s*. 6*d*. (*CP* 7).
Stock in 1777: 28 copies (*BQ* 7).
COPIES: G⁴.

1751   Miscellany.   *The Speech of a Fife Laird, etc.* **200**

THE SPEECH | OF A | FIFE LAIRD | NEWLY COME
FROM THE GRAVE. | THE | MARE | OF | COLLING
TOUN. | THE | BANISHMENT | OF | POVERTY. | *THREE
SCOTS POEMS.* | GLASGOW. | PRINTED AND SOLD BY ROBERT
& ANDREW FOULIS, | M.DCC.LI.
FORMULA: [? Crown] 8⁰ in fours: π1 A–F⁴ G1.
PAPER: Medium-poor quality; no marks.
TYPE: RE 1.
NOTES: *Publication*: published by 11 March 1751 (*GC*).
COPIES: G⁴.

1751   Montgomery, Capt. Alexander, *The Cherry and* **201**
                                       the Slae, etc.

THE | CHERRY | AND THE | SLAE, | WITH OTHER
| POEMS. | BY CAPTAIN | ALEXANDER MOUNT
GOMERY. | GLASGOW, | PRINTED AND SOLD BY ROBERT AND
ANDREW FOULIS | M DCC LI.
FORMULA: Post 8⁰ in fours: π2 A–L⁴ M² (π1 *half-title*).
PAPER: Medium-good quality; 6/i.
TYPE: RE 1, RLP 1.
VARIANT: Issue on inferior paper, Crown 8⁰:
   Paper: Medium-poor quality; no marks; horizontal chain
lines, printed on half sheets of Double Crown; size of half-
sheet, 19½ × 14¼ in.
NOTES: *Prices*: Wholesale: fine, 9*d*.; common, 4½*d*. (*BQ* 9).
   Stock in 1777: fine, 4 copies; common, 100 copies (*BQ* 9).
COPIES: G⁴ (both issues), L (Post).

1751   Nettleton, Thomas, *Treatise on Virtue and* **202**
                                       Happiness

NOTES: Not seen. Listed by Duncan (p. 57, No. 125), without
further details.

203 Otway, Thomas, *The Orphan*   1751

THE | ORPHAN: | OR, THE | Unhappy marriage. | A | TRAGEDY. | [*quotation, 7 lines*] | GLASGOW, printed and sold by robert & andrew foulis | M.DCC.LI.

formula: Post 12⁰ in sixes: A–G⁶.

paper: Medium quality; marks 6/i.

type: RB 2.

copies: G².

204 Ovid, [? *Works*] in three volumes, L   *c.* 1751

notes: Not seen. Advertised as being in the press in No. 139 (Caesar, 1750), No. 149 (Fénelon, 1750), No. 184 (Boethius, 1751) and No. 208 (Pliny, 1751). No advertisement for its publication has been found in *GC*, and it may never have been completed. Cf. No. 212 (Quintilian, 1751).

205 Petty, Sir William, *Political Arithmetic*, with   1751
Xenophon, *Ways and Means*, E

POLITICAL | ARITHMETIC; | OR, A | DISCOURSE | CONCERNING | [*two columns of contents, 9 and 8 lines separated by a vertical plain rule, damaged, 29*] | By Sir WILLIAM PETTY, | LATE FELLOW OF THE ROYAL SOCIETY. | GLAS GOW, | printed and sold by Robert and Andrew foulis | MDCC LI.

formula: Foolscap 8⁰ in fours: π1 A–S⁴(–S4, = π1; π1 *half-title; on* N2 *is a sub-title with imprint to Xenophon,* Discourse upon improving the Revenue of Athens, *E* (*trs. Walter Moyle*), *which follows* Political Arithmetic.)

paper: Medium quality; marks 5/iv, 5/v.

type: RLP 1, RB 2, RP 2, RE 2.

variant: Issue in Pot 8⁰:

Paper: Medium-poor quality; 9/[initials, dated ' 1742 ']; size of sheet, 15½ × 12¼ in.

notes: *Publication*: in the press July 1751 (No. 194); published by 30 September 1751 (*GC*).

Prices: Wholesale: Foolscap, 4½*d.* (*BQ* 6; this price would be low even for common paper). Retail: (? Foolscap), 1*s.* 6*d.* with No. 269 (Tucker's *Letter concerning Naturalisations*, 1753; *CP* 10).

Stock in 1777: Foolscap, 137 copies (*BQ* 6).

copies: G⁴ (both issues); L (Foolscap).

1751   Phaedrus, *Aesop's Fables*, L **206**

PHAEDRI, | AUGUSTI LIBERTI, | FABULARUM | AESO
PIARUM | LIBRI QUINQUE: | EX RECENSIONE | PETRI
BURMANNI | GLASGUAE: | IN AEDIBUS ACADEMICIS
| EXCUDEBANT ROBERTUS ET ANDREAS FOULIS |
ACADEMIAE TYPOGRAPHI, | M.DCC.LI. [*the first ' c ' is
lower case.*]

FORMULA: Foolscap 8⁰: A–E⁸ (A2, A3, A4 *signed* ' A ', ' A2 ',
' A3 ').

PAPER: Medium-good quality; marks 5/v; size of sheet
$16\frac{1}{2} \times 12\frac{3}{4}$ in.

TYPE: RB 2.

COPIES: G⁴, L.

1751   Pliny the Younger, *Works*, L **207**

CAII | PLINII | CAECILII SECUNDI | OPERA | QUAE
SUPERSUNT; | OMNIA. | AD | FIDEM OPTIMARUM
EDITIONUM | DILIGENTER EXPRESSA. | GLASGUAE,
| IN AEDIBUS ACADEMICIS | EXCUDEBANT ROBER
TUS ET ANDREAS FOULIS | ACADEMIAE TYPO
GRAPHI | M.DCC.LI.

FORMULA: Foolscap 4⁰: π^2 A–2M⁴(2M2 + χ^2) ᵡ2M⁴ 2N–2T⁴
2U² 2X⁴.

PAPER: Medium-good quality; marks 5/iv.

TYPE: RLP 1, RB 2.

NOTES: *Prices:* Wholesale: 7s. 6d. (*BQ* 2). Retail: 9s. (*CP* 3).
Stock in 1777: 18 copies (*BQ* 2).

COPIES: G⁴, L.

1751   Pliny the Younger, *Works*, L **208** †

CAII | PLINII | CAECILII SECUNDI | OPERA | QUAE
SUPERSUNT; | OMNIA. | AD | FIDEM OPTIMARUM
EDITIONUM | DILIGENTER EXPRESSA. | VOL. 1 [II]. |
GLASGUAE, | IN AEDIBUS ACADEMICIS | EXCUDE
BANT ROBERTUS ET ANDREAS FOULIS, | ACADEM
IAE TYPOGRAPHI | M.DCC.LI. [*different settings.*]

FORMULA: Foolscap 12⁰:
   Vol. 1: π^2 A–L¹² M⁶.

Vol. II: π^2 N–X^{12} Y^6 Z–2D^{12} 2E^6 2F^{12} (*signed* 'VOL. II.' *on* N–Y \$1 *and* 'VOL. III.' *on* Z–2E \$1; *clearly it was intended that sections* Z *to the end should comprise a third volume, but no copy has been seen with a separately-bound Vol.* III, *nor one with a Vol.* III *title-page between* Y *and* Z; 2F11–12 *advertisements*).

PAPER: Medium-good quality; marks 5/iv.

TYPE: RLP 1.

VARIANT: Issue in Pot 12°:
Paper: Medium quality; marks 1/iv.

NOTES: *Publication*: in the press 3 September 1750; to be published a few days after 21 January 1751 (*GC*).

COPIES: G^4 (both issues), L (Pot).

209 Pomfret, John, *Poems on Several Occasions*　　1751

POEMS | ON | SEVERAL | OCCASIONS. | BY THE REVER END | MR. JOHN POMFRET. | THE ELEVENTH EDI TION. | GLASGOW, | PRINTED AND SOLD BY ROBERT AND ANDREW FOULIS | MDCC LI.

FORMULA: Foolscap 8° in fours: a^4 A–T^4 (L2 *signed* 'K2'; T4 *blank*).

PAPER: Medium quality; marks 4/ii.

TYPE: RLP 1, RE 2.

VARIANT: Issue in Pot 8°:
Paper: Medium-good quality; marks 1/v.

COPIES: G^4 (Pot), L (Foolscap).

† **210** Pope, Alexander, *An Essay on Man*　　1751

AN | ESSAY | ON | MAN. | IN FOUR EPISTLES. | BY | ALEXANDER POPE Efq; | GLASGOW, | PRINTED AND SOLD BY R. & A. FOULIS | M DCC LI.

FORMULA: Foolscap 8° in fours: a^4 A–G^4.

PAPER: Medium-good quality; marks 5/v.

TYPE: RLP 1, RB 2.

NOTES: Advertisements for what appears to be this book in No. 175 (Xenophon, 1750) and No. 141 ('Cebes', 1750), which appeared in September and October 1750 respectively, may possibly refer to an earlier edition, not seen.

COPIES: G^4, L.

1751   Prior, Matthew, *Poems on Several Occasions* **211** †

POEMS | ON | SEVERAL OCCASIONS. | BY | MATTHEW
PRIOR, Efq; | VOL. I [II]. | GLASGOW, | PRINTED AND SOLD
BY ROBERT & ANDREW FOULIS. | M.DCC.LI. [*different settings*]
FORMULA: Foolscap 8⁰ in fours:
    Vol. I: A–2D⁴ 2E².
    Vol. II: A–2E⁴ (*signed ' VOL. II.' on* B–2D $1; 2E3–4 *advertise-
ments*).
PAPER: Medium-good and medium quality; marks 5/v.
TYPE: RB 1, RLP 1.
VARIANT: Issue in [? Crown] 12⁰:
    Formula: [? Crown) 12⁰ in sixes: Vol. I: A–S⁶ T²(H2 *sometimes
signed ' H ', K3 signed ' B3 ', N2 signed ' 2N '*).
    Vol. II: A⁴ B–T⁶ (*signed ' VOL. II.' on* B–S $1 *except* D1; T5–6
advertisements).
COPIES: G⁴, L (both 12⁰), O (8⁰ and 12⁰).

c. 1751   Quintilian, [? *Works*], L **212**

NOTES: Not seen. Advertised as being in the press in No. 149
(Fénelon, 1750), No. 184 (Boethius, 1751) and No. 208 (Pliny
1751). No advertisement for its publication has been found in
GC, and it may never have been completed. Cf. No. 204
(Ovid, 1751).

1751   Sallust, *Opera*, L **213**

C. CRISPI | SALLUSTII | OPERA | QUAE SUPERSUNT,
| OMNIA. | EX RECENSIONE | GOTTLIEB CORTII. |
| GLASGUAE: | IN AEDIBUS ACADEMICIS | EXCUDE
BANT ROBERTUS ET ANDREAS FOULIS | ACADEMIAE
TYPOGRAPHI | M.DCC.LI. [*There are two settings of this
title-page, reading the same.*]
FORMULA: Foolscap 8⁰ in fours: π² A–2X⁴ (π1 *half-title*, 2X4
    advertisments.)
PAPER: Medium-good quality; marks 5/ii, 5/v; size of sheet
16½ × 13 in.
TYPE: RP 2, RB 2.
NOTES: *Price*: Retail: 2s. 6d. (*CP* 5). Spotiswood (p. 90) offers
two issues of a *duodecimo* Sallust in 1779.
COPIES: G⁴.

214 Scougal, Henry, *Discourses on Important Subjects,* 1751
with Gairden, George, *Scougal's Funeral Sermon*

DISCOURSES | ON | IMPORTANT | SUBJECTS. | BY | HENRY SCOUGAL A.M. | and S.T.P. | To which is added, | A SERMON preached at his Funeral, | By GEORGE GAIRDEN, D.D. | *GLASGOW:* | Printed and fold by R. and A. FOULIS | MDCCLI.

FORMULA: Foolscap 12⁰ in sixes: $\pi^2 \chi$I A–2L⁶ 2M²(–2M2, =χI, *dedication*).

PAPER: Medium-good quality; marks 5/v, 4/v.

TYPE: RLP I, RB 2.

VARIANT: Issue in Pot 12⁰:
  Paper: Medium-good quality; marks 2/iii.

COPIES: G⁴ (Foolscap), L (Pot).

215 Scougal, Henry, *The Life of God in the Soul of* 1751
Man, with Leighton, Robert, *Rules and Instructions*

THE | LIFE OF GOD | IN THE | SOUL OF MAN: | OR, THE | *NATURE and EXCELLENCY* | OF THE | CHRISTIAN RELIGION. | By HENRY SCOUGAL, late PROFESSOR of | DIVINITY in the UNIVERSITY | of ABERDEEN. | With a PREFACE by G. BURNET, PROFES-|SOR of DIVINITY in the UNIVERSITY of | GLASGOW, afterwards BISHOP of SARUM. | [*quotation, 1 line*] | GLASGOW, | PRINTED AND SOLD BY R. & A. FOULIS | M DCC LI. [*Separate title-page on* MI *for Leighton, Dr Robert*, Rules and Instructions for a Holy Life.]

FORMULA: Formula: Foolscap 12⁰ in sixes: a⁶ b⁴ A–K⁶ L⁴ M² N–O⁶ P² (aI *half-title*).

PAPER: Medium-good quality; marks 4/v, 5/v.

TYPE: RLP I, RB 2.

NOTES: *Publication*: published by 29 July 1751 (*GC*).

COPIES: G⁴.

† **216** Steele, Sir Richard, *The Conscious Lovers* 1751

NOTES: Not seen. Listed by Duncan (p. 58, No. 142) without further details.

1751   Temple, Sir William, *Letter of Consolation* **217** †

NOTES: Not seen. Listed by Duncan (p. 57, No. 120) as ' Letter of Confolation to the Countefs of Effex on the lofs of her only Daughter, by Sir William Temple, fools. 8vo. fine, 2½ '.

Price : Foolscap 8⁰, 2½*d.* (*BQ* 10).

Stock in 1777: 210 copies (*BQ* 10).

1751   Thomas à Kempis, St, *De Imitatione* **218** *Christi*, L

DE | IMITATIONE | CHRISTI, | LIBRI QUATUOR, | AUCTORE THOMA A KEMPIS. | RECENSITI AD FIDEM AUTOGRAPHI | ANNI M.CCCC.XLI. | CUM VITA EJUSDEM THOMAE, | PER | HERIBERTUM ROSWEYDUM | SOCIETATIS IESU. | GLASGUAE, | IN AEDIBUS ACADEMICIS | EXCUDEBANT ROBERTUS ET ANDREAS FOULIS, | ACADEMIAE TYPOGRAPHI. | M.DCC.LI.

FORMULA: Foolscap 12⁰: a¹² A–M¹² (M10 *advertisements*; M11–12 Proposals *for editions of Plato* [v. No. 164]).

PAPER: Medium-good quality; marks 5/iv, 4/v; size of sheet 16¾ × 13 in.

TYPE: RB 2, RLP 1.

VARIANT: Issue on inferior paper, not seen (*BQ* 2).

NOTES: *Publication*: published by 27 May 1751 (*GC*).

Prices: Wholesale: fine, 1*s*. 6*d*.; common, 1*s*. (*BQ* 2). Retail: (?) fine, 2*s*.

Stock in 1777: fine, 148 copies; common, 2 copies (*BQ* 2).

COPIES: G⁴, L (both Foolscap).

1751   Young, Edward, *The Force of Religion* **219**

THE | FORCE | OF | RELIGION; | OR, | VANQUISH'D | LOVE. | A | POEM. | IN TWO BOOKS. | [*quotation, 1 line*] | GLASGOW: | PRINTED AND SOLD BY ROBERT AND ANDREW FOULIS | M.DCC.LI.

FORMULA: Foolscap 8⁰ in fours: a⁴ A–C⁴ (*signed* ' * ' *on* A1, B1 *and* C1).

PAPER: Medium-good quality; marks 5/v; size of sheet 17 × 13¼ in.

TYPE: RLP 1, RE 2.

VARIANT: Issue on inferior paper, not seen (*GC* 28 January 1751).

NOTES: *Publication*: published on about 30 January 1751 (*GC* 28 January 1751).

Prices: Wholesale: common, 1*d*. (*BQ* 9). Retail: fine, 4*d*.; common, 3*d*. (*GC* 28 January 1751).

Stock in 1777: common, 62 copies (*BQ* 9).

COPIES: G (Foolscap).

220 Addison, Joseph, *Dramatic Works* (Title) 1752

THE | DRAMATIC | WORKS | OF | THE RIGHT HONOUR ABLE | JOSEPH ADDISON, Esq.; | GLASGOW, | PRINTED AND SOLD BY R. AND A. FOULIS | M DCC LII.

FORMULA: Foolscap 8⁰: π^2 (*title-page and contents*).

PAPER: Medium-good quality; marks 5/?.

TYPE: RLP 1.

NOTES: This title-page and contents leaf were used for binding up together various Foulis Press editions of Addison's *Cato*, *The Drummer* and *Rosamond*. In the copies at G4 and O, for instance, the editions are *Rosamond*, 1758 (No. 342); *Cato*, 1765 (No. 436); and *The Drummer*, 1749 (No. 123). In my own copy the editions are *Cato*, 1753 (No. 249); *The Drummer*, 1751 (No. 179); and *Rosamond*, 1751 (No. 180).

COPIES: G4.

221 Aurelius Antoninus, Marcus, *Meditations*, E 1752

THE | MEDITATIONS | OF THE EMPEROR | MARCUS AURELIUS | ANTONINUS. | NEWLY tranflated from the GREEK: with | NOTES, and an account of his LIFE. | THIRD EDITION. | GLASGOW, | PRINTED BY ROBERT AND ANDREW FOULIS, | PRINTERS TO THE UNIVERSITY, | M DCC LII.

FORMULA: Foolscap 8⁰ in fours: A–2N4.

PAPER: Medium-good quality; marks 5/v.

TYPE: RLP 1, RB 2, RE 2.

VARIANT: Issue in Pot 8⁰:

Paper: Medium-good quality; marks 1/v.

NOTES: *Publication*: advertised as this day published on 23 April 1753 (*sic*, *GC*).

COPIES: G⁴ (both issues), L (Pot).

1752   Boileau-Despréaux, Nicolas, *Le Lutrin*, E **222**

THE | LUTRIN: | AN | Heroi-Comical POEM. | In SIX CANTOS. | By Monſieur *BOILEAU*. | To which is Prefix'd, | Some ACCOUNT of the Author's WRITINGS, and | this TRANSLATION: | By N. ROWE, Eſq; | The FOURTH EDITION, Corrected and Revis'd by | the laſt PARIS Edition. | GLASGOW, | PRINTED BY ROBERT & ANDREW FOULIS | MDCC LII.

FORMULA: Foolscap 8⁰ in fours: A–I⁴ K² (E2 *signed* ' C2 '; *signed* ' * ' on $1 except* A1 *and, occasionally*, B1, D1, K1).

PAPER: Medium quality; marks 5/ii.

TYPE: RLP 1, RB 1.

VARIANT: Issue on common paper, not seen (*BQ* 9).

NOTES: *Prices*: Wholesale: fine, 4*d*.; common, 3*d*. (*BQ* 9). *Stock in 1777*: fine, 184 copies; common, 252 copies (*BQ* 9).

COPIES: G⁴, L (both Foolscap).

1752   Burnet, Gilbert, *Life of Rochester*, etc. **223**

SOME | PASSAGES | OF THE | *LIFE AND DEATH* | OF | JOHN | EARL OF ROCHESTER. | [*plain rule, 66*] | *Written at his Deſire, on his Death-bed, by* | GILBERT BURNET, D.D. | Sometime *Profeſſor of Divinity* in the Univerſity | of *Glaſgow*, and afterwards Biſhop of *Sarum*. | [*plain rule, 62*] | Containing more amply their Converſations | on the great Principles of NATURAL and | REVEALED RELIGION. | [*plain rule, 66*] | To which is ſub joined, a further Account of his | CONVERSION, and Penitential Sentiments, by | *Robert Parſons*, M.A. Chaplain to the Counteſs | Dowager of *Rocheſter*. | [*plain rule, 66*] | GLASGOW, | PRINTED AND SOLD BY ROBERT & ANDREW FOULIS | MDCCLII.

FORMULA: Pot 8⁰ in fours: π1 A–L⁴ M1 (*signed* ' * ' on $1 except* π1, M1).

PAPER: Medium-good quality; marks 1/v.

TYPE: RLP 1.

VARIANT: Issue on common paper, Pot 8⁰:
 Formula: (*without* ' * ' *signatures*).
 Paper: Poor quality; marks 1/v.
NOTES: *Publication*: published by 20 January 1752 (*GC*).
COPIES: L (common), O (fine).

224 Congreve, William, *Poems upon Several Occasions*   1752

POEMS | UPON | SEVERAL OCCASIONS. | BY | Mr.
WILLIAM CONGREVE. | [*quotation, 2 lines*] | GLASGOW,
| PRINTED AND SOLD BY R. AND A. FOULIS | M DCC LII.
FORMULA: Foolscap 8⁰ in fours: A–2A⁴.
PAPER: Medium-good quality; marks 5/v; size of sheet
16½ × 13 in.
TYPE: RB 1, RLP 1.
VARIANT: Issue in Pot 8⁰:
 Paper: Medium quality; marks 1/v.
NOTES: *Prices*: Wholesale: Pot, 9*d*. (*BQ* 11). Retail: (?)
Foolscap, 2*s*. (*CP* 7).
 Stock in 1777: Pot, 3 copies (*BQ* 11).
COPIES: G⁴ (Pot), G (Foolscap).

† **225** Denham, Sir John, *The Sophy*   1752

NOTES: Not seen. Listed by Duncan (p. 59, No. 176) as ' The
Sophy, a Tragedy, 8vo.' Possibly an extract from Denham,
Poems, 8⁰, 1751 (No. 188), in which U2 is a sub-title to *The
Sophy*, with the imprint ' GLASGOW: | Printed in the YEAR
MDCCLI.'

226 Dryden, John, *Fables Ancient and Modern, etc.*   1752

FABLES | ANCIENT & MODERN; | TRANSLATED INTO
| VERSE, | FROM | HOMER, OVID, | BOCCACE, &
CHAUCER: | WITH | ORIGINAL POEMS. | BY JOHN
DRYDEN, Efq; | VOL. I, | [*quotation, 3 lines*] | GLASGOW, |
PRINTED BY ROBERT & ANDREW FOULIS | * M DCCLII.
[*Vol.* II:] FABLES | *ANCIENT* and *MODERN;* | TRANSLATED
INTO VERSE, | FROM | HOMER, OVID, | BOCCACE, AND
CHAUCER, | WITH | ORIGINAL POEMS. | BY JOHN
DRYDEN, Efq; | VOL. II. | GLASGOW, | PRINTED BY ROBERT
AND ANDREW FOULIS | * M DCC LII.

FORMULA: Pot 8⁰:
  Vol. I: a–b⁸ c² A–L⁸ M⁴ N² (*signed ' ＊ ' on $1 except A1*).
  Vol. II: A–N⁸ O⁴ (*signed ' ＊ ' on $1; signed ' Vol. II.' on A2 and $1 except A1, G1 and sometimes B1*).
PAPER: Medium-good quality; marks 1/v.
TYPE: RLP 1, RB 2.
VARIANT: Issue on slightly poorer paper, Pot 8⁰:
  Formula: (*without ' ＊ ' signatures*).
  Paper: Medium quality; marks 1/v.
NOTES: *Publication*: published a few days after 15 January 1753 (*GC*).
  Price: Retail: (? fine), 3s. (*CP* 7).
COPIES: G⁴ (common), O (fine).

1752   Dryden, John, *Aureng-Zebe* **227**

NOTES: Not seen. Listed by Duncan (p. 59, No. 170) as 'Aureng-Zebe: or the Great Mogul, a Tragedy by John Dryden, Efq. 12mo.'

1752   Dryden, John, *The Spanish Friar* **228** †

THE | SPANISH FRYAR: | OR, THE | DOUBLE DIS COVERY. | A | TRAGI-COMEDY. | BY | JOHN DRYDEN Esq; | [*quotations, 3 lines*] | GLASGOW, | PRINTED AND SOLD BY R. AND A. FOULIS | M DCC LII.
FORMULA: [? Crown] 12⁰ in sixes: A^2 B–I⁶ K⁴(–K4).
PAPER: Medium-poor quality; no marks.
TYPE: RB 2.
COPIES: G⁴.

1752   Fénelon, *Dialogues of the Dead and Fables*, **229**

NOTES: Not seen. Listed by Duncan (p. 59, No. 160) as 'Fenelon's Dialogues of the Dead and Fables, 2 vols. 8vo. fine, 2s. 3d.' As usual Duncan takes his price from *BQ* (here from p. 6), but in this case the *BQ* entry probably refers to the edition of 1754 (No. 270, q.v.), which was not included in his original list. Nevertheless there may have been an edition of 1752, since the book is advertised as being in the press as early as 15 October 1750 (*GC*).

230 Garden, James, *Comparative Theology*   1752

COMPARATIVE | THEOLOGY; | OR, | The true and folid grounds of pure | and peaceable THEOLOGY. | *A fubject very neceffary, though hitherto | almoft wholly neglected.* | Propofed in an Univerfity-Difcourfe. | And now Tranflated from the printed *Latin* | copy, with fome few enlargements by the | Author. | [*quotation, 1 line*] | *GLASGOW,* | PRINTED AND SOLD BY R. & A. FOULIS | M.DCC.LII.

FORMULA: Foolscap 12⁰ in sixes: A–L⁶.

PAPER: Medium quality; marks 5/ii; size of sheet 17 × 13 in.

TYPE: RE 2; RSP 1, RLP 1 and RB 1 on the title-page.

VARIANT: Issue on inferior paper, not seen (*BQ* 9).

NOTES: *Publication*: published by 4 May 1752 (*GC*).
  Prices: Wholesale: fine, 4½*d.*; common, 3*d.* (*BQ* 9). Retail: (?) fine, 6*d.* (*CP* 11).
  Stock in 1777: fine, 68 copies, common, 224 copies (*BQ* 9).

COPIES: G⁴ (Foolscap).

231 Gillies, John, [Proposals for *Historical Collections*, 1754]   1752

NOTES: Not seen. The following ' ADVERTISEMENT ' appeared on a2 of Vol. 1 of Gillies's *Historical Collections*, 1754 (No. 272):
  ' *THE Recommendation annexed to the Propofals, December 19th, 1752, refers to Book* IV. *Chapters 2d, 5th, 6th, 7th, which would have been a more confiderable Part of the Whole, had the two Volumes been of no larger Size than what was promifed in the Propofals: But they now contain as much as would have made about three Volumes and a Half of that Size. The Type is the fame; but the Paper (being a great Deal larger) is almoft a third dearer; yet this additional Expence of Paper and Print, as well as that of Binding, is fufficiently anfwered by the numerous Subfcription with which Providence has favoured the Undertaking.*'
  This notice suggests that RSP 1, the text type of the book as published, was available in December 1752. No. 199 (Miscellany, 1751), in which the fount is first noted, may be misdated; see the NOTES to that entry. It was used several other times in 1752.

1752   Granville, George, Baron Lansdowne, *Plays* **232**

NOTES: Not seen. Listed by Duncan (p. 59, No. 164) as ' Lanſdowne's Plays, 8vo.'

1752   Locke, John, *Essay concerning Human Under-* **233**
standing, abridged

AN | ABRIDGEMENT | OF | Mr. *LOCKE*'s | ESSAY | CON CERNING | HUMAN UNDERSTANDING. | THE SEVENTH EDITION. | *GLASGOW,* | PRINTED AND SOLD BY ROBERT AND ANDREW FOULIS | M DCC LII.

FORMULA: Foolscap 8⁰ in fours: A–2L⁴.

PAPER: Medium-good quality; marks 5/ii; size of sheet 17 × 13 in.

TYPE: RLP 1, RSP 1, RB 1.

VARIANT: Issue in [? small Crown] 12⁰:
Formula: [? small Crown] 12⁰ in sixes: A–Z⁶ (Z5–6 *advertisements*).
Paper: Medium-poor quality; thin; no marks.

NOTES: *Publication*: published by 4 December 1752 (*GC*).
Price: Retail: 8⁰, 2*s*. 6*d*. (*CP* 9).

COPIES: G⁴, L (12⁰), G (8⁰).

1752   Milton, John, *Paradise Lost* **234**

PARADISE | LOST, | A | POEM | IN | TWELVE BOOKS. | *THE AUTHOR* | JOHN MILTON. | ACCORDING TO THE AUTHOR'S LAST | EDITION, IN THE YEAR 1674. | GLASGOW, | PRINTED AND SOLD BY R. & A. FOULIS | PRIN TERS TO THE UNIVERSITY | M DCC LII. [*There is a separate sub-title on I1 so that Books vii–xii could be bound as a separate volume.*]

FORMULA: Pot 12⁰: a⁸ A–G¹² H⁶ I–P¹² Q⁴ (a1 *half-title*, Q 3–4 *advertisements*).

PAPER: Medium quality; marks 1/v.

TYPE: RB 2, RLP 1.

NOTES: *Publication*: published by 1 June 1752 (*GC*).

COPIES: G⁴.

235 Milton, John, *Paradise Regained, etc.*   1752

PARADISE REGAIN'D. | A | POEM, | IN | FOUR BOOKS. | TO WHICH IS ADDED | SAMSON AGONISTES; | AND | POEMS UPON SEVERAL OCCASIONS, | WITH A TRAC TATE OF | EDUCATION. | THE AUTHOR | JOHN MIL TON. | GLASGOW, | Printed and fold by ROBERT and ANDREW FOULIS | M DCC LII.

FORMULA: Pot 12^0 in sixes: π^2 A–2H⁶ 2I⁴ (U3 *signed on the verso*).

PAPER: Medium quality; marks 1/v.

TYPE: RB 2, RLP 1.

NOTES: *Publication*: published by 15 June 1752 (*GC*).

COPIES: G⁴, L.

236 Milton, John, *Poems on Several Occasions*   1752

NOTES: Not seen. Listed by Duncan (Appendix, p. 145) with the note ' [Foulis ? no imprint].' Probably an extract from *Paradise Regained, etc.*, (No. 235) in which the section of *Poems on Several Occasions* has a sub-title, dated 1752 but without the printers' names.

237 Miscellany. *Poetae Latini Minores*, L   1752

POETAE | LATINI | MINORES, | EX EDITIONE | PETRI BURMANNI | FIDELITER EXPRESSI. | GLASGUAE, | IN AEDIBUS ACADEMICIS | EXCUDEBANT ROBERTUS ET ANDREAS FOULIS | M.DCC.LII.

FORMULA: Foolscap 8^0: π^2 A–I⁸ K⁴.

PAPER: Medium-good quality; marks 5/v; size of sheet $16\frac{1}{2} \times 12\frac{1}{2}$ in.

TYPE: RB 2.

VARIANT: Issue in Pot 8^0:
   Paper: Medium quality; marks 2/iv.

NOTES: *Publication*: published by 11 December 1752 (*GC*).
   Prices: Wholesale: Foolscap, 1s. 6d.; Pot, 1s. (*BQ* 1). Retail: (?) Foolscap, 2s. (*CP* 5).
   Stock in 1777: Foolscap, 154 copies; Pot, 121 copies (*BQ* 1).

COPIES: G⁴ (both issues).

1752   Nye, Stephen, *A Discourse concerning Natural* **238**
           and Revealed Religion

A | DISCOURSE | CONCERNING | NATURAL AND RE
VEALED | RELIGION; | EVIDENCING | The TRUTH, and
CERTAINTY of | both; by Confiderations (for the moſt | part)
not yet touched by any. | RECOMMENDED | (Purſuant to
the deſign of Mr. BOYLE's Lecture) | To the conſideration of
ATHEISTS, DEISTS, and SCEP-|TICS; and uſeful to confirm and
nouriſh the | FAITH and PIETY of others. | BY STEPHEN NYE.
| FIRST PRINTED IN THE YEAR M.DC.XCVI. | GLAS
GOW: | PRINTED AND SOLD BY ROBERT AND
ANDREW FOULIS | M.DCC.LII.

FORMULA: Post 12° in sixes: a6 A–2B6.

PAPER: Medium-good quality; thin; marks 6/?.

TYPE: RLP I, RE 2.

VARIANT: Issue on inferior paper, [? small Crown] 12°:
   Paper: Medium-poor quality; no marks.

NOTES: *Publication*: in the press, 30 September 1751; published by 23 December 1751 (*GC*).

COPIES: G4 (Post), L (small Crown).

1752   Otway, Thomas, *Venice Preserved* **239**

VENICE PRESERV'D: | OR, A | PLOT DISCOVER'D. | A |
TRAGEDY. | [*plain rule, 63*] | By THOMAS OTWAY. | [*plain rule,
61*] | GLASGOW, | PRINTED AND SOLD BY R. & A. FOULIS |
M.DCC.LII.

FORMULA: Small Crown 12° in sixes: A–G6 H4(–H4).

PAPER: Medium quality; no marks; size of sheet 18¾ × 14¾ in.

TYPE: RB 2.

COPIES: G4.

1752   Philips, Ambrose, *The Distressed Mother* **240**

THE | DISTREST | MOTHER. | A | TRAGEDY. | BY |
AMBROSE PHILIPS. | GLASGOW, | PRINTED AND SOLD BY
ROBERT & ANDREW FOULIS | M DCC LII.

FORMULA: Pot 8° in fours: A–H4.

PAPER: Medium-poor quality; marks I/v.

TYPE: RB I, RLP I.

COPIES: G4, L.

241. Pomponius Mela, *De Situ Orbis*, L   1752

POMPONII | MELAE | DE SITU ORBIS, | LIBRI TRES. | EX RECENSIONE | JACOBI GRONOVII. | GLASGUAE, | IN AEDIBUS ACADEMICIS | EXCUDEBANT ROBER TUS ET ANDREAS FOULIS | ACADEMIAE TYPO GRAPHI | M.DCC.LII.

FORMULA: Foolscap 8° in fours: π1 A–X⁴ Y1.

PAPER: Medium-good quality; marks 5/v; size of sheet 16½ × 13 in.

TYPE: RP 2, RB 1.

NOTES: *Publication*: published by 9 March 1752. (*GC*).
   Prices: Wholesale: 1s. 6d. (*BQ* 2). Retail: 2s. (*CP* 5).
   Stock in 1777: 73 copies (*BQ* 2).

COPIES: G⁴, L.

242 Pope, Alexander, *Poems on Several Occasions*   1752

POEMS | ON | SEVERAL OCCASIONS | BY | ALEXANDER POPE, ESQ.; | VOL. I [II] [III]. | [*quotation, 4 lines, Vol. 1 only*] | GLASGOW, | PRINTED AND SOLD BY R. AND A. FOULIS | M DCC LII.

FORMULA: Foolscap 8°:
   Vol. I: a–b⁸ c⁴ A–L⁸ M⁴ N² (N2 *blank*).
   Vol. II: a² A–N⁸ O⁴ P² (*signed* ' VOL. II.' *on* $1 *except* a1, A1; P2 *blank*).
   Vol. III: π² A–K⁸ M⁴ (*signed* ' VOL. III.' *on* $1 *except* π1, A1).

PAPER: Medium quality; marks 5/ii, 4/v.

TYPE: RLP 1, RB 2, RP 2.

NOTES: *Publication*: published by 27 July 1752 (*GC*).

COPIES: G⁴.

243 Ramsay, Allan, *The Gentle Shepherd*   1752

THE | GENTLE SHEPHERD: | A | *SCOTS* | PASTORAL COMEDY. | BY | ALLAN RAMSAY. | THE ELEVENTH EDITION WITH THE SANGS. | *GLASGOW,* | PRINTED AND SOLD BY ROBERT AND ANDREW FOULIS | M DCC LII.

FORMULA: [N.B. Original not seen; the following collation, taken from a microfilm of a copy which is dissected and mounted, is conjectural.] [? size 12° in sixes]: A–H⁶(?–H6).

PAPER, TYPE: [Not seen.]

COPIES: Henry E. Huntington Library, California (microfilm only seen).

1752   Sheffield, John, Duke of Buckingham, *Poems* **244** †
          on Several Occasions, etc.

POEMS | ON | SEVERAL OCCASIONS. | To which are
added, | THE | TRAGEDIES | OF | JULIUS CAESAR, and
MARCUS BRUTUS. | BY | JOHN SHEFFIELD, | DUKE of
BUCKINGHAM. | [*quotation, 3 lines*] | GLASGOW, | Printed
by Robert and Andrew Foulis | M DCC LII.

FORMULA: Foolscap 8⁰ in fours: a⁴ A–2M⁴ (A2 *sometimes
signed ' A '*).

PAPER: Medium-good quality; marks 5/iv, 5/ii; size of sheet
16¾ × 13¼ in.

TYPE: RLP 1, RB 1.

VARIANT: Issue in Pot 4⁰:
  Formula: Pot 4⁰: [*as the 8⁰*]
  Paper: Medium-good quality; marks 2/iii.
  Separate issue of *Marcus Brutus*, in Pot 8⁰:
  Title-page: THE | TRAGEDY | OF | MARCUS BRUTUS.
  | WITH THE | PROLOGUE, | AND THE | TWO LAST
  CHORUS'S. | WRITTEN BY HIS GRACE | JOHN DUKE
  OF BUCKINGHAM. | GLASGOW, | Printed by Robert
  and Andrew Foulis | M DCC LII.
  Formula: Pot 8⁰ in fours: A⁴ B–K⁴ (A1 *half-title*).
  Paper: Medium-poor quality; marks 1/v.
  Type: These are the same type pages, with new signatures,
pagination and title-page, used in the complete *Poems, etc.*
  Other possible issues, not seen: *Poems, etc.*, complete, in
Pot 8⁰; *Marcus Brutus* in Foolscap 8⁰; *Julius Caesar* in Pot 8⁰
and Foolscap 8⁰.

NOTES: *Publication*: to be published a few days after 13 July
1752 (*GC*).
  Price: Wholesale: *Poems, etc.*, 8⁰, 1s. 6d. (*BQ* 6).
  Stock in 1777: *Poems, etc.*, 8⁰, 9 copies (*BQ* 6).

COPIES: G⁴ (*Poems, etc.*, Foolscap 8⁰, Pot 4⁰; *Marcus Brutus*,
Pot 8⁰); L (*Poems, etc.*, Foolscap 8⁰).

1752   Velleius Paterculus, *Historiae Romanae*, L **245**

CAII VELLEII | PATERCULI | QUAE SUPERSUNT | EX
| HISTORIAE ROMANAE | VOLUMINIBUS DUOBUS.
| EX EDITIONE | PETRI BURMANNI | FIDELITER
EXPRESSA. | GLASGUAE, | IN AEDIBUS ACADEMICIS
| EXCUDEBANT Robertus et Andreas foulis | M.DCC.LII.

FORMULA: Foolscap 8⁰ in fours: π1 A–2H⁴ 2*I*1.

PAPER: Medium-good quality; marks 5/ii, 5/v; size of sheet 16½ × 13 in.

TYPE: RP 2, RLP 1.

VARIANT: Issue on inferior paper, Foolscap 8⁰:
Paper: Medium-poor quality, marks GROSBON/[?] DAN GON . . ., size of sheet 16½ × 12¾ in.

NOTES: *Publication*: published by 18 December 1752 (*GC*).
Prices: Wholesale: fine, 1*s*. 6*d*.; common, 1*s*. 2*d*. (*BQ* 2). Retail: (?) fine, 2*s*. (*CP* 5).
Stock in 1777; fine, 74 copies; common, 190 copies (*BQ* 2).

COPIES: G⁴, L (both fine), O (common).

246 Vischard de St Réal, César, *The Conspiracy of*   1752
the Spaniards, E

THE | HISTORY | OF THE | CONSPIRACY | OF THE | SPANIARDS | Againſt the | *Republick of* VENICE. | In the Year MDCXVIII. | Tranſlated from the *French* Original | OF THE | ABBOT de St. REAL. | GLASGOW, | PRINTED & SOLD BY ROB. & A. FOULIS | M DCC LII.

FORMULA: Foolscap 12⁰ in sixes: A–L⁶ M².

PAPER: Medium quality; marks 5/v; size of sheet, 16¾ × 12¾ in.

TYPE: RLP 1.

VARIANT: Issue in Pot 12⁰;
Paper: Medium-poor quality; marks 1/v.

NOTES: *Publication*: published by 27 November 1752 (*GC*).
Prices: Wholesale: Foolscap, 6*d*.; Pot, 4*d*. (*BQ* 9).
Stock in 1777: Foolscap, 68 copies; Pot, 224 copies (*BQ* 9).

COPIES: G⁴ (Foolscap), L (Pot).

† **247** Waller, Edmund, *Works*   1752

THE | WORKS | OF | EDMUND WALLER, Eſq; | IN | VERSE AND PROSE. | PUBLISHED | By Mr. FENTON. | GLASGOW, | PRINTED BY ROBERT AND ANDREW FOULIS | M DCC LII.

FORMULA: Foolscap 8⁰: A–T⁸ U⁴ (A4, C3, M4, S2, U2 *unsigned;* U4 *advertisements*).

PAPER: Medium-good quality; marks 5/v, 5/ii.

TYPE: RLP 1, RB 2, RSP 1.

VARIANT: Issue in Pot 8⁰:
 Paper: Medium-poor quality; marks 5/v.

NOTES: *Publication*: published by 18 May 1752 (*GC*).
 Price: Wholesale: Foolscap, 1s. (*BQ* 11).
 Stock in 1777: Foolscap, 1 copy (*BQ* 11).

COPIES: G⁴ (Foolscap), L (Pot).

1753 Young, Edward, *A Poem on the Last Day* **248**

A | POEM | ON THE | LAST DAY. | IN THREE BOOKS. |
BY | EDWARD YOUNG, | FELLOW OF ALL-SOULS COLLEGE,
OXON. | [*quotation, 1 line*] | GLASGOW, | PRINTED AND SOLD
BY R. AND A. FOULIS | M DCC LII.

FORMULA: Foolscap 8⁰ in fours: A–G⁴ H^2 (*signed '* $*$ *' on* \$1
except A1; *H2 advertisements*).

PAPER: Medium-good quality; marks 5/v; size of sheet
$17 \times 13\frac{1}{4}$ in.

TYPE: RLP 1, RP 2.

VARIANT: Issue on inferior paper, not seen (inferred from the
' $*$ ' signatures).

NOTES: *Publication*: published by 9 March 1752 (*GC*).

COPIES: G (Foolscap).

1753 Addison, Joseph, *Cato* **249**

CATO. | A | TRAGEDY. | BY | JOSEPH ADDISON, Efq; |
[*quotation, 8 lines*] | *GLASGOW*, | Printed and fold by ROBERT
and ANDREW FOULIS | M DCC LIII.

FORMULA: Foolscap 8⁰ in fours: A–K⁴.

PAPER: Medium-good quality; marks 5/v.

TYPE: RB 2.

COPIES: G⁴, L.

1753 Addison, Joseph, *Of the Christian Religion* **250 †**

OF THE | CHRISTIAN | RELIGION. | BY | JOSEPH
ADDISON, ESQ.; | GLASGOW, | PRINTED AND SOLD BY R. AND
A. FOULIS | M DCC LIII.

FORMULA: Foolscap 8⁰ in fours: π1 A–H⁴(–H4).

PAPER: Medium-good quality; marks 5/v.

TYPE: RSP 1.

VARIANT: Issue on inferior paper, possibly 12⁰ (*BQ* 10, *CP* 11).

NOTES. *Prices*: Wholesale: fine, $4\frac{1}{2}d$.; common, $2\frac{1}{2}d$. (*BQ* 10). Retail: 12⁰, 6*d*. (*CP* 11).
   Stock in 1777: fine, 72 copies; common, 210 copies (*BQ* 10).

COPIES: G⁴ (Foolscap 8⁰).

251 Cornaro, Luigi, *Sure Methods of Attaining a*   1753
Long Life, E

SURE | METHODS | OF ATTAINING A | LONG | AND HEALTHFUL | LIFE. | With Means of correcting a | BAD CONSTITUTION. | Written originally in ITALIAN, | By LEWIS CORNARO, | a Noble Venetian, when he was near | an Hun dred Years of Age. | GLASGOW, | PRINTED AND SOLD BY R. & A. FOULIS. | MDCC LIII.

FORMULA: Foolscap 12⁰ in sixes: a⁶ b⁴ A–K⁶ (a1 *half-title with a quotation only*).

PAPER: Medium-good quality; marks 5/v.

TYPE: RSP 1, RLP 1, RP 2.

VARIANT: Issue in [? Pot] 12⁰:
   Paper: Medium-poor quality; marks 9/GROSBON.

NOTES: *Publication*: published by 23 April 1753 (*GC*).
   Price: Wholesale: Foolscap, fine, 6*d*. (*BQ* 11).
   Stock in 1777: Foolscap, fine, 4 copies (*BQ* 11).

COPIES: G⁴ (Foolscap), L (Pot).

252 Coypel, Charles, *Dialogue sur la Con-*   1753 or 1754
noissance de la Peinture, F

NOTES: Not seen. *GC* 3 December 1753: ' In a few Days will be publifhed, And fold by R. and A. FOULIS. DIALOGUE SUR LA CONNOISSANCE DE LA PEINTURE. Par M. CHARLES COYPEL, Premier Peintre de Monfeigneur le Duc d'Orleans.'
   Price: Foolscap 8⁰, fine, $2\frac{1}{2}d$. (*BQ* 10).
   Stock in 1777: 288 copies (*BQ* 10).

1753   Dillon, Wentworth, Earl of Roscommon, **253**
Works

THE | WORKS | OF | THE RIGHT HONOURABLE | WENTWORTH DILLON, | EARL of ROSCOMMON. | GLASGOW: | Printed by Robert and Andrew Foulis | MDCCLIII.

FORMULA: Foolscap 8⁰ in fours: a^2 b⁴ A–2D⁴ 2E² (X2 *signed* 'U2').

PAPER: Medium-good quality; marks 5/v, 4/?; size of sheet $16\frac{3}{4} \times 13$ in.

TYPE: RLP i, RB 2.

VARIANT: Issue in Pot 8⁰:
Formula: (X2 *correctly signed*).
Paper: Medium quality; marks 1/v.

NOTES: *Publication*: published by 3 September 1753 (*GC*).
Prices: Wholesale: Foolscap, 1s. 6d.; Pot, 1s. 2d. (*BQ* 6).
Retail: (?) Foolscap, 2s. (*CP* 7).
Stock in 1777: Foolscap, 7 copies, 'fome fullied'; Pot, 163. copies (*BQ* 6).

COPIES: G⁴ (Foolscap), L (Pot).

1753   Euripides, *Orestes*, G and L **254**

'Ο ΤΟΥ | ΕΥΡΙΠΙΔΟΥ | ΟΡΕΣΤΗΣ. | EURIPIDIS | ORESTES. | ADJECTA EST AD FINEM | VERSIO LA TINA, EX EDITIONE | J. BARNES. | [*quotations, 6 lines*] | GLASGUAE, | IN AEDIBUS ACADEMICIS | EXCUDE BANT ROBERTUS ET ANDREAS FOULIS | ACADE MIAE TYPOGRAPHI | M.DCC.LIII.

FORMULA: Foolscap 8⁰ in fours: π1 A–U⁴ (*signed* '*' on $1 *except* π1, E1).

PAPER: Medium-good quality; marks 5/v.

TYPE: GGP, RSP i. Latin follows Greek.

VARIANT: Issue in Pot 8⁰:
Formula: (*without the* '*' *signatures*).
Paper: Medium quality; marks 1/v.

NOTES: *Publication*: published by 7 May 1753 (*GC*).
Prices: Retail: 2s. (No. 546, 1772), or 3s. (*CP* 4): these prices may refer to the Pot and Foolscap issues respectively.

COPIES: G⁴ (Pot), L (Foolscap).

255 Gay, John, *The Beggar's Opera* 1753

THE | BEGGAR's | OPERA. | AS IT IS ACTED AT THE | THEATRE-ROYAL | IN | LINCOLNS-INN-FIELDS. | Written by MR. GAY. | [*quotation, 1 line*] | GLASGOW, | PRINTED AND SOLD BY ROBERT & ANDREW FOULIS | M DCC LIII.

FORMULA: Foolscap 8⁰ in fours: A^4 B–I^4.

PAPER: Medium-good quality; marks 5/v.

TYPE: RB 2.

COPIES: L.

256 Glasgow University. [*Vacation exercise for* 1753 *students*], L

[*No title-page; headed:*] E SCHOLA GLASCUENSI | ANNO M.DCC.LIII.

FORMULA: [? Pot] 8⁰ in fours: A–B^4.

PAPER: Medium quality; marks ?/v.

TYPE: RLP 1.

NOTES: Without the imprint of the Foulis Press, but both content and typography make it certainly a Foulis book.

The text begins: ' Pro materia vernacula, quam difcipulis noftris, vacationis tempore Latine vertendam, praefcribere folemus, hoc anno, materiam Latinam vernacule reddendam in hanc fchedulam collegimus.' (Instead of the vernacular material which we are accustomed to prescribe to our students for translation into Latin during the vacation, we have this year collected in this pamphlet Latin material to be translated into the vernacular.)

COPIES: G^4.

257 Glasgow University, Academy. *A Proposal* [? 1753] *for Encouraging an Academy*

[*Begins:*] A | PROPOSAL | FOR ENCOURAGING, | BY SUBSCRIPTION, | An ACADEMY for PAINTING and SCULPTURE, | Now inftituted at GLASGOW. [*followed by text.*]

FORMULA: Foolscap 2⁰: π^2.

PAPER: Medium-good quality; marks 4/iv.

TYPE: RP 2.

NOTES: Bound in the G4 copy of the *Catalogue of Pictures, etc.*, of 1758 (No. 352). Duncan (p. 77, No. 503) lists it as ' [cir. 1758] ', but it seems more likely to be the Proposals agreed to by the University on 23 October 1753 (v. *Records of the Glasgow Bibliographical Society*, Vol. ii (Glasgow, 1913), p. 33).

COPIES: G4.

1753   Heliodorus, *Theagenes and Chariclea*, E **258**

AETHIOPIAN | ADVENTURES: | OR, THE | HISTORY | OF | THEAGENES | AND | CHARICLEA. |WRITTEN ORIGINALLY IN GREEK, | BY | HELIODORUS. | In TEN BOOKS. | The Firſt Five tranſlated by a *Perſon of Quality*, | The Laſt Five by N. TATE. | To which are prefixed, | *The* TESTIMONIES *of* WRITERS, *both* Ancient *and* | Modern, *concerning this* WORK. | Reprinted in the Year MDCCLIII.

FORMULA: Foolscap 8⁰: A4 B–U8 X2 (*signed ' * ' on $1 except* A1, D1).

PAPER: Medium-good quality; marks 5/ii; size of sheet 17 × 13 in.

TYPE: RLP 1.

VARIANT: Issue in Pot 8⁰:
    Formula: (*without ' * ' signatures except on* M1).
    Paper: Medium-good quality; thin; marks 1/v.

NOTES: Without the imprint of the Foulis Press, but the typography makes it fairly certain that this is the book to which the advertisements, etc., refer.
    Publication: published by 16 April 1752 (*GC*).
    Prices: Wholesale: fine, 2s.; common, 1s. 4d. (*BQ* 5). Retail: (?) fine, 2s. 6d. (*CP* 9).
    Stock in 1777: fine, 58 copies; common, 52 copies (*BQ* 5).

COPIES: G (Foolscap), O (Pot).

1753   Hutcheson, Francis, *A Short Introduction to* **259**
                          Moral Philosophy, E

A SHORT | INTRODUCTION | TO | MORAL PHILO SOPHY, | IN THREE BOOKS; | CONTAINING THE | ELEMENTS OF ETHICKS | AND THE | LAW OF NATURE. | BY FRANCIS HUTCHESON, LL D. | LATE PROFESSOR OF PHILOSOPHY IN |THE UNIVERSITY OF GLASGOW.|

TRANSLATED FROM THE LATIN. | SECOND EDITION. | GLASGOW, | PRINTED AND SOLD BY ROBERT & ANDREW FOULIS, | PRINTERS TO THE UNIVERSITY | MDCCLIII.

FORMULA: Foolscap 8⁰ a² b⁸ A–U⁸ X⁶.

PAPER: Medium quality; marks 5/v.

TYPE: RLP 1, RE 1, RB 1, RB 2.

NOTES: *Price*: Wholesale: 1*s*. 6*d*. (*BQ* 11, recording a single copy of what seems to be a single-volume edition of this book; later editions were in two volumes).

COPIES: G⁴, L.

260 Hutcheson, Francis, [Proposals for *A System of*   1753 *Moral Philosophy*, 1755]

NOTES: Not seen. Robert Foulis to John Leslie, 6 February, 1753: ' The Proposals for Mʳ. Hutcheson's System of Moral Philosophy, are published.' (Murray, David, *Some Letters of Robert Foulis*, Glasgow, 1917, p. 30).

261 Moor, James, *De Analogia Contractionum*   1753 *Linguae Graecae Regulae Generales*, L

DE ANALOGIA | CONTRACTIONUM | LINGUAE GRAECAE | REGULAE GENERALES. | PRÆMISSÆ SUNT NOMINUM DECLINATIONES. | IN USUM TIRONUM JUNIORUM CLASSIS | GRÆCÆ IN ACADEMIA GLASGUENSI. | GLASGUAE, | IN AEDIBUS ACADEMICIS | EXCUDE BANT ROBERTUS ET ANDREAS FOULIS | ACADEMIAE TYPOGRAPHI | M.DCC.LIII.

FORMULA: [? small Crown] 8⁰ in fours: π1 A–E⁴(–E4).

PAPER: Medium-poor quality; no marks.

TYPE: RE 1, RLP 1, GGP, GB.

COPIES: King's College, London.

262 Plutarch, *How the Young should hear Poetry*,   1753 G and L

ΤΟ ΤΟΥ | ΠΛΟΥΤΑΡΧΟΥ | ΧΑΙΡΩΝΕΩΣ | ΒΙΒΛΙΟΝ | ΠΩΣ ΔΕΙ ΤΟΝ ΝΕΟΝ | ΠΟΙΗΜΑΤΩΝ | ΑΚΟΥΕΙΝ. | PLUTARCHI | CHAERONENSIS | LIBER | QUOMODO

Juveni audienda sint | POEMATA. | CUM INTERPRE
TATIONE | HUGONIS GROTII. | Variantes Lectiones et
Notas | Adjecit | JOHANNES POTTER, A.B. | (postea
Archiepiscopus Cantuariensis.) | Oxoniae 1694. 8ᵛᵒ. | [*plain
rule, 65*] | EDITIO ALTERA. | In usum Juventutis Aca
demicae. | GLASGUAE, | IN AEDIBUS ACADEMICIS |
EXCUDEBANT | ROBERTUS ET ANDREAS FOULIS |
ACADEMIAE TYPOGRAPHI | M.DCC.LIII.

FORMULA: Foolscap 8⁰ in fours: π^2 A–L⁴ M² N–2B⁴ 2C² (2C2 *advertisements*).

PAPER: Medium-good quality; marks 5/v.

TYPE: GGP, GP, GB, GDP 1, RP 2, RE 2, RLP 1, RB 2.   Latin follows Greek.

VARIANT: Issue on inferior paper, not seen (*BQ* 4).

NOTES: *Prices*: Wholesale: fine 1s. 9d.; common, 1s. 2d. (*BQ* 4). Retail: (?) fine, 2s. 6d. (*CP* 4).

Stock in 1777: fine, 106 copies; common 216 copies (*BQ* 4).

COPIES: G⁴, L (Foolscap).

1753   Southerne, Thomas, *Oroonoko* **263**

OROONOKO | A | TRAGEDY, | As it was acted at the |
THEATRE ROYAL, | By His Majesty's Servants. | In the
Year 1699. | By THO. SOUTHERN. | [*quotations, 3 lines*] |
GLASGOW, | printed and sold by robert & andrew
foulis. | MDCCLIII.

FORMULA: Post 12⁰ in sixes: A–G⁶ H² (G3 *signed* ' F3 ').

PAPER: Medium quality; marks 6/?.

TYPE: RB 1, RB 2.

COPIES: G².

1753   Steele, Sir Richard, *The Funeral* **264** †

THE | FUNERAL: | OR, | GRIEF A-LA-MODE. | A |
COMEDY. | Written by | Sir RICHARD STEELE. | [*quotation,
3 lines*] | GLASGOW, | printed and sold by robert & andrew
foulis | MDCCLIII.

FORMULA: Foolscap 8⁰ in fours: A–L⁴.

PAPER: Medium-good quality; marks 5/v.

TYPE: RB 2, RLP 1.

COPIES: G².

† **265** Tacitus, *Works*, L   1753

C. CORNELII | TACITI | OPERA | QUAE SUPERSUNT. | EX EDITIONE | JACOBI GRONOVII | FIDELITER EXPRESSA. | VOL. I [II] [III] [IV]. | GLASGUAE: | IN AEDIBUS ACADEMICIS | EXCUDEBANT ROB. ET AND. FOULIS | M DCC LIII. [*All from the same setting.*]

FORMULA: Foolscap 12⁰:
   Vol. I: π^2 χ1 A–Q^{12} (*signed* ' TOM. I,' *on* A–Q $1; χ1 *dedication*, Q11–12 *advertisements*).
   Vol. II: π^2 A–N^{12} O^6 (*signed* ' TOM. II.' *on* A–O $1).
   Vol. III: π^2 A–L^{12} M^4 N1 (*signed* ' TOM. III.' *on* A–M $1).
   Vol. IV: π^2 A–M^{12} N–P^6 Q^4 (*signed* ' TOM. IV.' *on* A–Q $1).

PAPER: Medium-good and medium quality; marks 5/v, 4/iv; size of sheet 16¾ × 13 in.

TYPE: RLP 1, RB 2.

VARIANT: Issue on different, probably inferior, paper, not seen (*BQ* 1).

NOTES: *Publication*: published by 5 November 1753 (*GC*).
   Prices: Wholesale: fine, 5*s*. 6*d*.; common, 3*s*. 6*d*. (*BQ* 1). Retail: (?) fine, 8*s*. (*CP* 6).
   Stock in 1777: fine, 3 copies; common, 87 copies; odd volumes, 43 (*BQ* 1).

COPIES: G^4, L (both Foolscap).

266 Tasso, Torquato, *Aminta*, I   1753

AMINTA; | FAVOLA BOSCARECCIA | DI | TORQUATO | TASSO. | IN GLASGUA, | DELLA STAMPA DI ROBERTO ED ANDREA FOULIS | MDCCLIII.

FORMULA: Foolscap 8⁰ in fours: π1 A–I^4 K^2 (K2 *blank*).
   Plates: seven plates, variously placed, numbered ' I ' to ' VII ' and signed ' *Se. le Clerc f.*' on No. 1. Plate marks average 80 × 50.

PAPER: Medium quality; marks 5/v, 5/ii. Plates: marks 4/?.

TYPE: RB 2.

NOTES: *Publication*: in the press May 1752 (No. 247); published by 25 June 1753 (*GC*).

COPIES: G^4, L.

1753   Theocritus, *Works*, G and L **267**

NOTES: Not seen. *GC*, 5 November 1753 has the following Foulis advertisement laid out in the style of one of their title-pages:

ΤΑ ΤΟΥ | ΘΕΟΚΡΙΤΟΥ | ΣΕΣΩΣΜΕΝΑ. | THEOCRITI | QUAE EXTANT. | Ex Editione DANIELIS HEINSII expreſſa. | – nec erubuit Sylvas habitare Thalia. VIRG.

However, since at least some of the type used for printing this advertisement, and probably all of it, is the same as had been used for the title-page of the Foulis *Theocritus* of 1746 (No. 78), it seems likely that it refers to the original book, still in stock, rather than to a new edition. For some reason the original setting of the title-page must have been kept set up for seven years. (Another argument against a new edition is that it is most unlikely to have disappeared so completely; the Foulis classics of this period have survived in large numbers.)

1753   Tibullus, *Works*, with Propertius, *Works*, L **268**

TIBULLI | ET | PROPERTII | OPERA. | EX EDITIONE J. BROUKHUSII | FIDELITER EXPRESSA. | GLASGUAE, | EXCUDEBANT ROBERTUS & ANDREAS FOULIS | M DCC LIII.

FORMULA: Foolscap 8°: π^2 A–O⁸ P⁴ Q² (π1 *half-title*, Q2 *advertisements*).

PAPER: Medium-good quality; marks 5/v.

TYPE: RB 2, RLP 1.

VARIANT: Issue in Pot 8°:
Paper: Medium-good quality; marks 1/v.

NOTES: *Prices*: Wholesale: Foolscap, 1*s.* 9*d.*; Pot, 1*s.* 2*d.* (*BQ* 2). Retail: (?) Foolscap, 2*s.* 6*d.* (*CP* 5).
Stock in 1777: Foolscap, 54 copies; Pot, 188 copies (*BQ* 2).

COPIES: G⁴, L (both Foolscap), Philip Gaskell (Pot).

1753   Tucker, Josiah, *A Letter concerning* **269**
                              Naturalisations

A | LETTER | TO A | FRIEND | CONCERNING | NATUR ALIZATIONS: | SHEWING, | [*two columns of contents, 13 and 11 lines, separated by a vertical plain rule, 42*] | By *JOSIAH TUCKER*, M.A. | Rector of St. STEPHEN's in BRISTOL, | AND

| Chaplain to the Rt. Rev. the Lord Biſhop of BRISTOL. | GLAS GOW, | PRINTED AND SOLD BY R. AND A. FOULIS | MDCCLIII. | Price Four-pence.

FORMULA: Foolscap 8⁰ in fours: A–D⁴.

PAPER: Medium-good quality; marks 4/iv; size of sheet $16 \times 12\frac{1}{4}$ in.

TYPE: RLP I.

NOTES: *Publication*: published by 8 October 1753 (*GC*).

Prices: Retail: 4*d*. (title-page); 1*s*. 6*d*. with No. 205 (Petty's *Political Arithmetic*, 1751; *CP* 10. The G copy, in wrappers, is stitched up with No. 205).

COPIES: G.

270 Fénelon, *Dialogues of the Dead, and Fables*, E   1754

DIALOGUES | OF THE | DEAD; | TOGETHER WITH SOME | FABLES, | COMPOSED FOR THE | EDUCATION OF A PRINCE. | BY THE LATE | M. DE FENELON, | PRECEPTOR TO THE INFANTS OF FRANCE, AND | AFTERWARDS ARCHBISHOP-DUKE OF CAMBRAY. | NEWLY TRANSLATED FROM THE FRENCH | BY MR. ELPHINGSTON. | VOL. I. | CONTAINING THE | DIA LOGUES OF THE ANCIENTS. | GLASGOW: | PRINTED AND SOLD BY ROBERT AND ANDREW FOULIS | MDCCLIV.

[*Vol.* II: *from a different setting, reads the same, except: omits lines 12–13; changes* 'VOL. I.' *to* 'VOL. II.'; *reads instead of line 16* ('DIALOGUES OF THE ANCIENTS.'): 'DIALOGUES OF THE MODERNS, | AND THE FABLES,']

FORMULA: Foolscap 8⁰ in fours:
   Vol. I: *A*1 B–2I⁴.
   Vol. II: A–N⁴ O² (*signed* 'VOL. II.' *on* D–O $1).

(*Note*: This collation does not include the *Fables* mentioned on the title-pages. It was evidently intended that a separate edition of the *Fables* should be bound up with this book, originally, no doubt, that of 1751 (No. 191); but it is more often found with the *Fables* of 1760 (No. 381).

PAPER: Medium-good quality; marks 4/v, iv, ii, 5/v; size of sheet $16\frac{1}{2} \times 12\frac{3}{4}$ in.

TYPE: RLP I.

VARIANT: Issue in Pot 8⁰:
Paper: Medium quality; marks 1/v.

NOTES: *Publication*: published by 26 August 1754 (*GC*).
Prices: Wholesale: Foolscap, 2*s*. 3*d*. (*BQ* 6). Retail: (?)
Foolscap, 3*s*. (*CP* 8).
Stock in 1777: Foolscap, 39 copies (*BQ* 6).

COPIES: G⁴ (both issues).

1754   Foulis, Robert and Andrew, *A Catalogue of* **271**
                          Books (*Greek Authors*)

NOTES: Not seen. Advertisement in *GC* for 7 January 1754:
' *On Wednefday firft* [9 January 1754] *will be publifhed*, A CATA
LOGUE, *Containing* Many of the BEST, And alfo the moft
UNCOMMON GREEK AUTHORS, Either in the old and rare
Editions, Or in the lateft. The loweft Price of each Book is
printed : | Gentlemen are defired to give in, or direct their
Commiffions to Robert and Andrew Foulis.'

1754   Gillies, John, *Historical Collections* **272**

HISTORICAL   COLLECTIONS | RELATING   TO |
REMARKABLE PERIODS | OF | THE SUCCESS | OF
| THE GOSPEL, | AND | EMINENT INSTRUMENTS |
EMPLOYED IN PROMOTING IT. | IN TWO VOLUMES.
| [*quotation, 2 lines*] | COMPILED BY | JOHN GILLIES, |
ONE OF THE MINISTERS OF GLASGOW. | *IN MAGNIS*
VOLUISSE. | VOL. I [II]. | GLASGOW, | PRINTED BY
ROBERT AND ANDREW FOULIS | MDCLIV. [*Same*
settings.]

FORMULA: [? Printing Demy] 8⁰ in fours:
   Vol. I: a–b⁴ A–3M⁴ (*signed* ' VOL. I.' *on* $1 *except* a1, 2L1).
   Vol. II: a⁴ b² A–3M⁴ 3N² (*signed* ' VOL. II.' *on* $1 *except* a1 b1).

PAPER: Poor quality; no marks.

TYPE: RSP 1, RB 1, RB 2, RE 1 italic.

NOTES: A subscription book, issued bound; see the *Proposals*,
1752 (No. 231).

COPIES: G⁴, L.

273 Phaedrus, *Aesop's Fables*, L 1754

FABULARUM | AESOPIARUM | LIBRI QUINQUE. | [*quotation, 2 lines*] | GLASGUAE: | IN AEDIBUS ACADEMICIS | EXCUDEBANT ROBERTUS ET ANDREAS FOULIS | M DCC LIV.

FORMULA: Foolscap 8⁰: a⁸ b² A–F⁸ G⁴ H² (*with* b² *in original position as central conjugate pair of section* H *in the* L *copy*).

PAPER: Medium-good quality; marks 5/v.

TYPE: RLP 1, RP 2.

NOTES: *Price*: Retail: 1*s.* 6*d.* (*CP* 5).

COPIES: G⁴, L.

274 Pindar, *Works*, G 1754–8

ΤΑ ΤΟΥ | ΠΙΝΔΑΡΟΥ | ΣΕΣΩΣΜΕΝΑ. | [*two columns of 2 lines each; left:*] ΟΛΥΜΠΙΑ, | ΠΥΘΙΑ, | [*right:*] ΝΕΜΕΑ, | ΙΣΘΜΙΑ. | EX EDITIONE OXONIENSI. | GLASGUAE: | EXCUDEBANT R. & A. FOULIS | M.DCC.LIV. [*With volume titles dated as follows:* 1: *Olympia*, 1754; 11: *Pythia*, 1754; 111: *Nemea*, 1757; 1V: *Isthmia*, 1758.]

FORMULA: Foolscap 32⁰ in eights:
Vol. 1: π1 A–K⁸ (K8 *blank*).
Vol. 11: A–M⁸ (M6–8 *blank*).
Vol. 111: A–H⁸.
Vol. 1V: A–E⁸.

PAPER: Vols. 1 and 11: Medium-good quality; marks 5/v; vols. 111 and 1V: Medium-good quality; marks 4/iv; size of sheet 16½ × 13¼ in.

TYPE: GB.

VARIANT: Vol. 1 (*Olympia*, 1754) printed on silk:
Formula: (–π1).
Silk: White, bound round the edges with thread in some copies.

NOTES: *Publication*: Vols. 1 and 11 published by 9 September 1754 (*GC*).
Prices: Wholesale: paper, 2*s.* 3*d.* (*BQ* 3, specifying three volumes, but Vols. 111 and 1V were normally bound up together). Retail: paper, 3*s.* (*CP* 3, ditto).
Stock in 1777: complete, paper, 587 copies; vol. 11, 187 copies; vol. 111 (i.e. 111 and 1V) 176 copies.

COPIES: G⁴ (paper, complete; silk, Vol. 1); L (as G⁴).

1754   Pope, Alexander, *An Essay on Man* **275**

AN | ESSAY | ON | MAN. | IN | FOUR EPISTLES. | BY |
ALEXANDER POPE Efq; | GLASGOW, | PRINTED BY
ROBERT AND ANDREW FOULIS, AND SOLD | BY THEM
AND ANDREW STALKER. | M DCC LIV.

FORMULA: Foolscap 8⁰: A–D⁸.

PAPER: Medium-good quality; marks 4/ii.

TYPE: RLP 1, RB 2.

COPIES: L.

1754   Raleigh, Sir Walter, *Instructions to a Son, etc.* **276**

INSTRUCTIONS | OF A | FATHER | TO HIS | SON, |
Under the following heads: | [*two columns of contents, 6 and 5
lines, separated by a plain vertical rule, 16*] | To which are added;
| A loving Son's ADVICE to an aged Father, | AND | SELECT
LETTERS on interefting Subjeɗts. | BY | SIR WALTER RAW
LEIGH. | GLASGOW, | PRINTED AND SOLD BY ROBERT AND
ANDREW FOULIS | M DCC LIV. | [Price ONE SHILLING.]

FORMULA: Foolscap 8⁰ in fours: π1 A–L⁴ M1 (*signed* ' * ' *on
$1 except* π1, B1, F1, H1, I1, K1, M1).

PAPER: Medium quality; marks 4/v, iv.

TYPE: RE 2, RB 1.

VARIANT: Issue on inferior paper, not seen (inferred from the
' * ' signatures).

NOTES: *Publication*: published by 28 January 1754 (*GC*).
    Price: Retail, 1s. (title-page).

COPIES: G⁴.

1754   Vanbrugh, Sir John, *The Provoked Husband* **277**

THE | PROVOK'D HUSBAND; | OR, A JOURNEY TO
LONDON. | A | COMEDY. | As it is Aɗted at the | THEATRE-
ROYAL, | By His MAJESTY's Servants. | Written by the Late
| Sir JOHN VANBRUGH, and Mr. CIBBER. | [*quotation, 1 line*) |
GLASGOW, | PRINTED AND SOLD BY R. AND A. FOULIS |
M DCC LIV.

FORMULA: Pot 8⁰ in fours: A–N⁴ O² (*signed* ' * ' *on* D1, F1, G1,
I1 . . . N1).

PAPER: Medium quality; marks 1/v.

TYPE: RB 1, RB 2, RLP 1.

VARIANT: Issue on inferior paper, not seen (inferred from the '*' signatures).

COPIES: G⁴.

† **278** Vanbrugh, Sir John, *The Provoked Wife* 1754

THE | PROVOK'D WIFE; | A | COMEDY. | BY | SIR JOHN VANBRUGH. | GLASGOW, | PRINTED AND SOLD BY R. AND A. FOULIS | M DCC LIV.

FORMULA: Pot 8⁰ in fours: A–L⁴.

PAPER: Medium-poor quality; marks 1/v; size of sheet 15 × 12½ in.

TYPE: RB 1.

COPIES: G².

† **279** Young, Edward, *Love of Fame* 1754

NOTES: Not seen. Listed by Duncan (p. 61, No. 199) as 'Young's Satyres, fools. 8vo. fine, 6d., common, 4d.' These prices, which come from *BQ* (p. 9), probably refer to the edition of 1758 (No. 361).

280 Addison, Joseph, *Remarks on Several Parts* 1755
of Italy

REMARKS | ON SEVERAL | PARTS | OF | ITALY, &c. | In the Years 1701, 1702, 1703. | By the late Right Honourable | JOSEPH ADDISON, Efq; | [*quotation, 4 lines*] | GLASGOW, | PRINTED AND SOLD BY ROBERT AND ANDREW FOULIS | M.DCC.LV.

FORMULA: Foolscap 8⁰ in fours: a⁴ A–2M⁴.

Plate: folding plate of 12 medals, unsigned, plate-mark not seen, variously placed.

PAPER: Medium-good quality; marks 5/ii.

TYPE: RLP 1, RP 2, RB 1.

VARIANT: Issue in [? Crown] 12⁰:

Formula: [? Crown] 12⁰ in sixes: a⁴ A–Z⁶ 2A² (with plate as 8⁰).

Paper: Poor quality; no marks.

COPIES: G⁴ (both issues), L (12⁰).

1755   Aristophanes, *Clouds*, G and L **281** †

ʿΑΙ ΤΟΥ | ΑΡΙΣΤΟΦΑΝΟΥΣ | ΝΕΦΕΛΑΙ· | ΚΩΜΩιΔΙΑ. | ARISTOPHANIS | NUBES, | COMOEDIA. | GRAECE; | EX EDITIONE KUSTERI. | LATINE; | EX VERSIONE VIRI ERUDITI, LONDINI 8VO. 1695. | [*quotation, 2 lines*] | GLASGUAE: | IN AEDIBUS ACADEMICIS | EXCUDEBANT ROBER TUS ET ANDREAS FOULIS | ACADEMIAE TYPO GRAPHI | M.DCC.LV. [*There are three settings of the title-page, all reading the same, except that in one of them the two-line quotation is set in roman, not italic, type. They are distributed indiscriminately among the issues.*]

FORMULA: Foolscap 8⁰ in fours: π1 A–Q⁴ (*signed* 'Tom. 1.' *on* A–Q $1).

PAPER: Medium-good quality; marks 5/ii, 4/v; size of sheet 16½ × 13 in.

TYPE: GP, RLP 1. Greek and Latin on facing pages.

VARIANTS: Issue in (?) Pot 8⁰, Greek and Latin, not seen (*BQ* 3).
Issue in Pot 4⁰, Greek and Latin:
Formula: Same as the 8⁰.
Paper: Medium-good quality; marks 1/v.
Issue in Foolscap 4⁰, Greek only:
Title-page: [*does not omit the reference to the translation.*]
Formula: Foolscap 4⁰: π1 A–H⁴ (*the same type pages, reimposed*).
Paper: Medium-good quality; marks 5/v, 4/vi, 3/?.

NOTES: *Prices*: Wholesale: 8⁰, G and L, fine, 1s. 2d.; ditto, common, 9d.; Pot 4⁰, G and L, 2s.; Foolscap 4⁰, G, 2s. 6d. (*BQ* 3). Retail: 8⁰, G and L, (?) fine, 1s. 6d. (*CP* 4).
Stock in 1777: 8⁰, G and L, fine, 283 copies; ditto, common, 400 copies; Pot 4⁰, G and L, 93 copies; Foolscap 4⁰, G, 138 copies; 8⁰, G and L, fine, imperfect, 94 copies. (*BQ* 3).

COPIES: G⁴ (Foolscap 8⁰, Pot 4⁰, Foolscap 4⁰), L (Foolscap 8⁰, Foolscap 4⁰).

1755   Boileau-Despréaux, Nicolas, *L'Art Poétique*, E **282** †

THE | ART | OF | POETRY, | Written in FRENCH by | MON SIEUR DE BOILEAU | IN FOUR CANTO'S. | TRANSLATED | BY | SIR WILLIAM SOAMES, | Since Revis'd by JOHN DRYDEN, ESQ. | GLASGOW: | PRINTED AND SOLD BY R. AND A. FOULIS | M DCC LV. | *

FORMULA: Pot 8⁰ in fours: A–E⁴ F² (*signed ' * ' on* $1 *except* D1).

PAPER: Medium-good quality; marks 1/v; size of sheet 15¾ × 12½ in.

TYPE: RLP 1.

VARIANT: Issue on inferior paper, not seen (' * ' signatures; *BQ* 6).

NOTES: *Prices*: Wholesale: fine, 4*d*.; common, 3*d*. (*BQ* 6).
   Stock in 1777: fine, 90 copies; common, 317 copies (*BQ* 6).

COPIES: G².

† **283** Callimachus, *Hymns and Epigrams*, G   1755

ΟΙ ΤΟΥ | ΚΑΛΛΙΜΑΧΟΥ | ΚΥΡΗΝΑΙΟΥ | ΥΜΝΟΙ | ΤΕ, ΚΑΙ | ΕΠΙΓΡΑΜΜΑΤΑ. | GLASGUAE: | IN AEDIBUS ACADEMICIS | EXCUDEBANT ROBERTUS ET AND REAS FOULIS | ACADEMIAE TYPOGRAPHI | MDCCLV.

FORMULA: Post 4⁰: a⁴(a1 + χ1) A–I⁴ K² (χ1 *dedication*).
   Plates: Three plates of Greek statues, variously placed; unnumbered, unsigned; plate marks not seen.

PAPER: Good quality; marks 6/i; size of sheet 19 × 14¾ in.

TYPE: GGP, GDP 1, RGP 2.

VARIANTS: Issue in Foolscap 4⁰:
   Paper: Medium-good quality; marks 4/ii.
   Issue in [? Post] 2⁰, not seen (*BQ* 3, which actually specifies Writing Demy 2⁰; but it also specifies Writing Demy for the fine-paper 4⁰, which is in fact Post 4⁰).
   Issue in Foolscap 2⁰:
   Title-page: [*The same lines of type spaced out vertically, with the addition of an extra line after line 6:*]
PALMAM CALLIMACHUS—MART. |
   Formula: Foolscap 2⁰: π(*4 disjunct leaves*) A² B–Q² (Q2 *blank*).
   Paper: Medium-good quality; marks 4/iv, 4/ii; size of sheet 16½ × 13 in.
   Type: The same type made up into longer pages.
   Awarded the silver medal of the Select Society of Edinburgh (Murray, *R. & A. Foulis*, p. 29).

NOTES: *Prices*: Wholesale: Post 4⁰, 4*s*.; Foolscap 4⁰, 2*s*. 6*d*.; Post 2⁰, 5*s*.; Foolscap 2⁰, 4*s*. (*BQ* 3). Retail: (?) Foolscap 4⁰, 3*s*.; (? size) 2⁰, 6*s*. (*CP* 3).

Stock in 1777: Post 4⁰, 65 copies; Foolscap 4⁰, 15 copies; Post, 2⁰ 1 copy; Foolscap 2⁰, 228 copies (*BQ* 3).
COPIES: G⁴ (Post 4⁰, Foolscap 4⁰, Foolscap 2⁰), L (Post 4⁰, Foolscap 2⁰).

1755   Congreve, William, *The Mourning Bride* **284**

THE | MOURNING | BRIDE. | A | TRAGEDY. | BY | WILLIAM CONGREVE. | [*quotation, 3 lines*] | *GLASGOW*: | PRINTED AND SOLD BY ROBERT AND ANDREW FOULIS. | M.DCC.LV.
FORMULA: Pot 8⁰ in fours: A–F⁴ G1.
PAPER: Medium-poor quality; marks 1/v.
TYPE: RB 1, RLP 1.
COPIES: G².

by 1755   Dryden, John, ' *The Conquest of Mexico* ', **285**

NOTES. Not seen. Advertised in No. 286 (Dufresnoy, 1755). The title is probably a mistake for *The Conquest of Granada*.

1755   Dufresnoy, Charles-Alphonse, *A Judgment on* **286**
                                                Painters, E

A | JUDGMENT | ON THE | WORKS | OF THE | PRINCIPAL AND BEST | PAINTERS | OF THE | TWO LAST AGES. | BY | CHARLES ALPHONSE DU FRESNOY. | GLASGOW: | PRINTED AND SOLD BY ROBERT & ANDREW FOULIS | M.DCC.LV.
FORMULA: Foolscap 8⁰ in fours: A–D⁴ E² (E2 *advertisements*).
PAPER: Good quality; marks 3/iv.
TYPE: RE 2, RLP 1.
NOTES: *Price* : Wholesale: 3*d*. (*BQ* 10).
   Stock in 1777: 120 copies (*BQ* 10).
COPIES: G².

1755   Euclid, [Proposals for Simson's edition, 1756] **287**

NOTES: Not seen. *GJ*, 28 April 1755: ' *This day were publi∫hed*, PROPOSALS for printing by ∫ub∫cription, in *quarto*, A new edition of the fir∫t ∫ix, the eleventh and twelfth books of

EUCLIDS ELEMENTS. By *ROBERT SIMSON*, Profeſſor of Mathematics in the univerſity of Glaſgow. . . . Subſcriptions are taken in, and receipts given by William Sands, Bookſeller in the Parliament cloſe, Edinburgh, and by Robert and Andrew Foulis, Bookſellers in Glaſgow.' See Nos. 315, 316.

† **288** Farquhar, George, *The Beaux' Stratagem*   by 1755

NOTES: Not seen.   Advertised in No. 286 (Dufresnoy, 1755).

289 Farquhar, George, *Love and a Bottle*   1755

LOVE AND A BOTTLE. | A | COMEDY. | AS IT IS ACTED AT THE | THEATRE-ROYAL | IN | DRURY-LANE, | By Her MAJESTY's Servants. | [*quotation, 2 lines*] | GLASGOW: | PRINTED AND SOLD BY ROBERT AND ANDREW FOULIS | M.DCC.LV.

FORMULA: Pot 8⁰ in fours: A–K⁴ L².

PAPER: Medium-poor quality; marks 1/v; size of sheet 14½ × 12 in.

TYPE: RB 1, RB 2.

COPIES: G⁴.

290 Farquhar, George, *The Recruiting Officer*   1755

THE | RECRUITING OFFICER: | A | COMEDY. | BY | MR. GEORGE FARQUHAR. | [*quotation, 2 lines*] | GLASGOW: | PRINTED AND SOLD BY ROBERT AND ANDREW FOULIS | M.DCC.LV.

FORMULA: Pot 8⁰ in fours: A–L⁴.

PAPER: Medium-poor quality; 1/v.

TYPE: RB 1, RLP 1.

COPIES: G⁴.

291 Farquhar, George, *The Twin Rivals*   1755

THE | TWIN-RIVALS: | A | COMEDY. | BY | MR. GEORGE FARQUHAR. | [*quotation, 1 line*] | GLASGOW: | PRINTED AND SOLD BY ROBERT AND ANDREW FOULIS | M.DCC.LV.

FORMULA: Pot 8⁰ in fours: a⁴ B–K⁴ L².

PAPER: Medium-poor quality; marks 1/v; size of sheet $14\frac{1}{2} \times 12$ in.

TYPE: RB 1.

COPIES: G⁴.

1755   Fénelon, *A Demonstration of the Existence of* **292**
God, E

A | DEMONSTRATION | OF THE | EXISTENCE | AND | ATTRIBUTES | OF | GOD, | DRAWN FROM THE KNOW LEDGE OF NATURE. | BY THE LATE | M. DE FENELON, | ARCHBISHOP OF CAMBRAY. | Tranflated from the French, | BY A. BOYER. | GLASGOW, | PRINTED AND SOLD BY R. AND A. FOULIS | MDCCLV. ✲

FORMULA: Foolscap 8⁰ in fours: a⁴ A–Z⁴ (*signed* '✲' *on* $1 *except* S1).

PAPER: Medium-good quality; marks 5/v, 5/vi; size of sheet $16\frac{3}{4} \times 13\frac{1}{2}$ in.

TYPE: RSP 1, RB 2, RLP 1.

VARIANT: Issue on inferior paper, Foolscap 8⁰:
Formula: (*Without* '✲' *signatures*).
Paper: Medium-poor quality; marks 5/v; size of sheet $16\frac{3}{4} \times 13\frac{1}{2}$ in.

NOTES: *Prices*: Wholesale: fine, 1s. 3d. (*BQ* 6). Retail: (?) fine, 1s. 6d. (*CP* 8).
Stock in 1777: fine, 6 copies (*BQ* 6).

COPIES: G⁴ (common), L (fine).

1755   Fénelon, *Télémaque*, E **293**

THE | ADVENTURES | OF | TELEMACHUS, | THE | SON OF ULYSSES. | WRITTEN BY THE | ARCHBISHOP OF CAMBRAY. | DONE INTO ENGLISH | BY | MR. LITTLE BURY AND MR. BOYER. | VOLUME FIRST [SECOND]. | GLASGOW, | PRINTED AND SOLD BY R. & A. FOULIS | MDCCLV. [*Same settings.*]

FORMULA: Pot 12⁰ in sixes:
Vol. I: a–d⁶ A–Z⁶ (*signed* 'VOL. I.' *on* $1 *except* a1; Z6 *blank; the whole of sig*. L *missing in the only copy seen*).
Vol. II: A–2F⁶ SG² (*signed* 'VOL. II.' *on* $1 *except* A1).

PAPER: Medium quality; marks 1/v.

TYPE: RB 2.

COPIES: G⁴.

† **294** Gay, John, *Dione*   by 1755

NOTES: Not seen.   Advertised in No. 286 (Dufresnoy, 1755).

295 Gordon, Sir Adam, *Edom of Gordon*   1755

EDOM OF GORDON; | AN ANCIENT | SCOTTISH POEM. | NEVER BEFORE PRINTED. | GLASGOW: | PRINTED AND SOLD BY ROBERT AND ANDREW FOULIS | M.DCC.LV.

FORMULA: Pot 4⁰ in twos: A–C².

PAPER: Medium quality; marks 1/v; size of sheet $15\frac{1}{2} \times 12$ in.

TYPE: RGP 2.

NOTES: Edited by Sir David Dalrymple, Lord Hailes (*The Percy Letters*, vol. iv (ed. Falconer, A. F.), Louisiana, 1954, *passim*).

COPIES: G⁴, L.

296 Hutcheson, Francis, *Philosophiae Moralis*   1755
          Institutio Compendiaria, L

PHILOSOPHIAE | MORALIS | INSTITUTIO COMPEN DIARIA, | LIBRIS III. | ETHICES | ET | JURISPRUDEN TIAE NATURALIS | ELEMENTA | CONTINENS. | AUC TORE | FRANCISCO HUTCHESON | IN ACADEMIA GLASGUENSI P.P. | EDITIO TERTIA. | [*quotation, 2 lines*] | GLASGUAE: | IN AEDIBUS ACADEMICIS | EXCUDEBANT ROBER TUS ET ANDREAS FOULIS | M DCC LV.

FORMULA: Foolscap 8⁰: b⁴ A–S⁸ (b2 *signed* ' b ').

PAPER: Medium-good quality; marks 4/vi, 4/ii.

TYPE: RLP 1, RP 2, RB 2, GP.

VARIANT: Issue in Pot 8⁰:
   Paper: medium quality, marks 1/v.

COPIES: G⁴ (Foolscap), L (Pot).

1755   Hutcheson, Francis, *A System of Moral* **297** †
                                         Philosophy

A | SYSTEM | OF | MORAL | PHILOSOPHY, | IN THREE
BOOKS; | WRITTEN BY THE LATE | FRANCIS HUT
CHESON, L.L.D. | PROFESSOR OF PHILOSOPHY | IN
THE UNIVERSITY OF GLASGOW. | PUBLISHED FROM
THE ORIGINAL MANUSCRIPT, | BY HIS SON FRANCIS
HUTCHESON, M.D. | To which is prefixed | SOME
ACCOUNT OF THE LIFE, WRITINGS, AND CHARAC
TER OF THE AUTHOR, | BY THE REVEREND WILLIAM
LEECHMAN, D.D. | PROFESSOR OF DIVINITY IN THE
SAME UNIVERSITY. | VOLUME I [II]. | GLASGOW:
PRINTED AND SOLD BY R. AND A. FOULIS PRINTERS
TO THE UNIVERSITY. | LONDON, | SOLD BY A. MILLAR
OVER - AGAINST KATHARINE - STREET IN THE
STRAND, | AND BY T. LONGMAN IN PATER-NOSTER
ROW. | M.DCC.LV. [*Same setting.*]

FORMULA: Printing Demy 4⁰:
 Vol. I: π^2 χ^2 $^2\chi^2$ a–f⁴ A–2Y⁴ (*signed* ' VOL. I.' *on* A–2Y $1;
2Y4 *blank;* χ^2 *and* $^2\chi$1—*subscribers—and* $^2\chi$2—*contents—are
sometimes found elsewhere*).
 Vol. II: π^2 A–3A⁴ 3B² (*signed* ' VOL. II.' *on* A–3B $1).

PAPER: Medium quality; no marks; size of sheet $22\frac{1}{2} \times 17\frac{1}{2}$ in.

TYPE: RGP 2, RSP 1, RE 2, RLP 1, RB italic.

NOTES: *Publication*: Proposals, early in 1753 (No. 260);
published by 12 May 1755 (*GC*, *GJ*).
 Prices: Wholesale: 15s. (*BQ* 11). Retail: 21s. (*CP* 6).
 Stock in 1777: 13 copies (*BQ* 11).

COPIES: G⁴, L. The manuscript copy is in G².

1755   Leechman, William, *The Temper of a Minister,*   **298**
       a Sermon, with *The Nature of Prayer, a Sermon*

THE | TEMPER, | CHARACTER, | AND | DUTY | OF A |
MINISTER OF THE GOSPEL. | A | SERMON. | By WILLIAM
LEECHMAN | PROFESSOR OF DIVINITY IN THE | UNIVER
SITY OF GLASGOW. | The SIXTH EDITION. | Printed and fold
by ROBERT and ANDREW | FOULIS, AT GLASGOW: | M.DCC.LV.
[*There is a separate sub-title to the fifth edition of* The Nature of
Prayer *on* G1.]

FORMULA: Foolscap 12⁰ in sixes: A–O⁶ (O6 *blank*).

PAPER: Medium quality; marks 4/vi.
TYPE: RLP I.
COPIES: G⁴, L.

299 Moor, James, *De Analogia Contractionum*   1755
Linguae Graecae Regulae Generales

DE ANALOGIA | CONTRACTIONUM | LINGUAE
GRAECAE | REGULAE GENERALES. | PRAEMISSAE
SUNT NOMINUM DECLINATIONES; | ET ADJECTAE
REGULAE DE TEMPORIBUS | FORMANDIS. | In usum
Tironum juniorum Classis | Graecae in Academia Glas
guensi. | GLASGUAE, | IN AEDIBUS ACADEMICIS |
EXCUDEBANT ROBERTUS ET ANDREAS FOULIS |
ACADEMIAE TYPOGRAPHI | M DCC LV.

FORMULA: [? Crown] 8⁰ in fours: A–I⁴.
PAPER: Medium quality; thin; no marks.
TYPE: RE 2, GGP, RLP I, GB.
COPIES: G⁴.

300 Mun, Thomas, *England's Treasure by Foreign*   1755
Trade

ENGLAND's | TREASURE | BY | FOREIGN TRADE. | OR,
THE | BALANCE OF OUR FOREIGN TRADE | IS THE |
RULE OF OUR TREASURE. | WRITTEN BY | THOMAS
MUN of London, Merchant. | FIRST PUBLISHED BY HIS
SON IN THE YEAR | M.DC.LXIV. | GLASGOW: | PRIN
TED AND SOLD BY R. AND A. FOULIS | M.DCC.LV.

FORMULA: Foolscap 8⁰ in fours: a⁴ A–P⁴ Q².
PAPER: Medium-good quality; marks 4/vi; size of sheet
$16\frac{1}{2} \times 13$ in.
TYPE: RSP I, RP 2, RB I.
VARIANT: Issue in 12⁰ on inferior paper, probably Crown, not
seen (*BQ* 7).
NOTES: *Publication*: published by 26 May 1755 (*GC*).
  Prices: Wholesale: 8⁰, 9*d.*; 12⁰ 6*d.* (*BQ* 7). Retail: 8⁰, 1*s.* 6*d.*
(*CP* 9).
  Stock in 1777: 8⁰, 4 copies; 12⁰, 348 copies (*BQ* 7).
COPIES: G⁴, L (both 8⁰).

1755   Old Poem.   *Gill Morice* **301**

GILL MORICE, | AN ANCIENT | SCOTTISH POEM. |
GLASGOW, | PRINTED AND SOLD BY ROBERT AND
ANDREW FOULIS | M.DCC.LV.

FORMULA: Pot 4⁰ in twos: A^2 B–D^2.

PAPER: Medium-good quality; marks 1/v.

TYPE: RGP 1, RE 2, RLP 1.

VARIANT: Another issue, called ' Second edition ':
    Title-page: [*adds* ' SECOND EDITION ' *after line 3; otherwise
same setting.*]
    Formula: (*the same setting of type; but, since the position of the
signature letters is disturbed, probably re-imposed.*)

NOTES: *Publication*: published by 20 January 1755 (*GC*).

COPIES: G², L (first issue); G⁴ (second issue).

1755   Old Poem.   *Young Waters* **302**

YOUNG WATERS, | AN ANCIENT | SCOTTISH POEM.
NEVER BEFORE PRINTED. | GLASGOW, | PRINTED
AND SOLD BY ROBERT AND ANDREW FOULIS |
M.DCC.LV.

FORMULA: Pot 4⁰ in twos: A^2 B².

PAPER: Medium-good quality; marks 1/v.

TYPE: RGP 2.

VARIANT: Another issue, called 'Second edition ':
    Title-page: [*Altered to read* ' SECOND EDITION ' *instead of*
' NEVER BEFORE PRINTED '; *otherwise same setting
throughout.*]

NOTES: *Publication*: published by 10 February 1755 (*GC*).
    Price: Wholesale: 1d. (*BQ* 10).
    Stock in 1777: 144 copies (*BQ* 10).

COPIES: G⁴ (both issues), L (first issue).

1755   Parnell, Thomas, *Works* **303**

THE | WORKS | IN | VERSE AND PROSE, | OF | Dᴿ.
THOMAS PARNELL, | LATE ARCH-DEACON OF
CLOGHER. | ENLARGED WITH VARIATIONS AND
POEMS, | NOT BEFORE PUBLISH'D. | GLASGOW, |
PRINTED AND SOLD BY R. AND A. FOULIS | MDCCLV.

FORMULA: Foolscap 8⁰ in fours: π⁴ A–2F⁴.

PAPER: Medium-good quality; marks 4/ii; size of sheet 16½ × 13¼ in.

TYPE: RLP 1, RB 2, RB 1.

VARIANT: Issue in Pot 8⁰:
  Paper: Medium quality; marks 1/iv, v.

NOTES: *Publication*: published by 10 February 1755 (*GC*).

COPIES: G⁴ (Pot), G² (Foolscap).

304 Ramsay, Andrew Michael, *The Travels of*   1755
Cyrus, etc.

THE | TRAVELS | OF | CYRUS. | To which is annexed, | A DISCOURSE | UPON THE | THEOLOGY AND MYTHO LOGY | OF THE PAGANS. | BY THE | CHEVALIER RAMSAY. | VOL. I [II]. | GLASGOW, | PRINTED AND SOLD BY R. & A. FOULIS | M.DCC.LV. [*Same settings.*]

FORMULA: Pot 12⁰ in sixes:
  Vol. I: a⁶(–a1) b–c⁶ d² A–T⁶(–T5–6).
  Vol. II: T⁶(–T1–4) U–2S⁶ 2T⁴ (2M3 *signed* ' Mm ', 2T2 *signed* ' T2 '; 2T4 *advertisements*).

PAPER: Medium-poor quality; marks 1/v; size of sheet 15½ × 12¼ in.

TYPE: RB 2, RLP 1.

COPIES: G⁴.

305 Selden, John, *Table-talk*   1755

TABLE-TALK: | BEING THE | DISCOURSES | OF | JOHN SELDEN ESQ. | OR HIS | SENSE | OF VARIOUS MATTERS OF WEIGHT | AND HIGH CONSEQUENCE RELA-|TING ESPECIALLY TO RELI-|GION AND STATE. | DISTINGUE TEMPORA. | GLASGOW: | PRINTED AND SOLD BY R. AND A. FOULIS | M.DCC.LV.

FORMULA: Foolscap 12⁰ in sixes: a⁶ A–T⁶.

PAPER: Medium-good quality; marks 4/vi, 3/v, 3/iv, no marks; size of sheet 16½ × 13¼ in.

TYPE: RLP 1, RB 2, RE 2.

NOTES: *Prices*: Wholesale, 9d. (*BQ* 9). Retail: 1s. 6d. (*CP* 10).

COPIES: G⁴, L.

1755   Somerville, William, *The Chace* **306** †

THE | CHACE. | A | POEM. | BY | WILLIAM SOMER
VILLE, Esq; | [*quotations, 5 lines*] | GLASGOW: | PRINTED
AND SOLD BY R. AND A. FOULIS | M.DCC.LV.

FORMULA: Pot 8º in fours: A–K⁴ L² (L2 *advertisements*).

PAPER: Medium quality; marks 1/v; size of sheet 15½ × 12¼ in.

TYPE: RLP 1, RP 2.

VARIANT: Issue in [? small Crown] 12º, not seen (*BQ* 9).

NOTES: *Price*: Wholesale: 12º, 3*d*. (*BQ* 9).

COPIES: G⁴ (8º).

1755   Somerville, William, *Hobbinol* **307**

HOBBINOL, | OR THE | RURAL GAMES. | A | BUR
LESQUE POEM, | IN BLANK VERSE. | BY | WILLIAM
SOMERVILLE Esq. | [*quotation, 6 lines*] | GLASGOW: |
PRINTED AND SOLD BY R. AND A. FOULIS | M DCC LV.

FORMULA: Pot 8º in fours: *A*⁴ B–F⁴ G² (G2 *advertisements*).

PAPER: Medium quality; marks 1/v.

TYPE: RLP 1, RE 1, RB 1.

VARIANT: Issue in [? small Crown 12º]:
   Formula: [? small Crown 12º] in sixes: A–D⁶ E² (E2 *advertisements*).
   Paper: Medium-poor quality; thin; no marks; vertical
chain-lines (probably half-sheets of Double Crown).

NOTES: *Price*: Wholesale: 8º, 4*d*.; 12º, 3*d*. (*BQ* 9).

COPIES: G⁴ (8º); L (12º).

by 1755   Steele, Sir Richard, *The Tender Husband* **308** †

NOTES: Not seen. Advertised in No. 286 (Dufresnoy, 1755).

1755   Thucydides, *Funeral Orations, etc., from the* **309**
                   Peloponnesian War, G and L

ΕΚ ΤΟΥ | ΘΟΥΚΥΔΙΔΟΥ· | ʽΟ ΝΟΜΟΣ | ΕΠΙΤΑΦΙΟΥ
| ΛΟΓΟΥ | ΠΑΡΑ ΤΟΙΣ ΑΘΗΝΑΙΟΙΣ· | ΚΑΙ ʽΟ ΤΟΥ |
ΠΕΡΙΚΛΕΟΥΣ | ΛΟΓΟΣ ΕΠΙΤΑΦΙΟΣ· | ΕΤΙ ΔΕʼ, | ʽΟ

ΕΝ ΤΗι ΠΟΛΕΙ | ΛΟΙΜΟΣ. | ΠΑΝΤΑ 'ΕΞΗΣ ΕΚ ΤΟΥ
ΔΕΥΤΕΡΟΥ | ΤΗΣ ΣΥΓΓΡΑΦΗΣ. | GLASGUAE: | IN
AEDIBUS ACADEMICIS | EXCUDEBANT ROBERTUS
ET ANDREAS FOULIS | ACADEMIAE TYPOGRAPHI. |
M DCC LV.

FORMULA: Writing Demy 12⁰ in sixes: π^4 A–E⁶ F²(F1 + χ1)
G–I⁶ K1 (π1 *Greek title-page*, π2 *sub-title to Funeral Orations*,
π3–4 *pp. i–iv;* χ1 *Latin title-page*).

PAPER: Medium-good quality; marks 7/ monogram ? JW.

TYPE: GDP 1, RP 2.   Latin follows Greek.

VARIANT: Issue in [? Crown] 12⁰:
   Paper: Medium quality; marks 9/CM, IS.

NOTES: *Price*: Wholesale: (?) Crown, 1*s*. (*BQ* 4).
   Stock in 1777: (?) Crown, 287 copies (*BQ* 4).

COPIES: G⁴ (both issues), L (both issues, Demy lacks Latin).

† **310** Young, Edward, *Revenge*   by 1755

NOTES: Not seen.   Advertised in No. 286 (Dufresnoy, 1755).

311 Cicero, *In Catilinam I-IV*, L   1756

MARCI TULLII | CICERONIS | IN CATILINAM | ORA
TIONES IV. | Ex EDITIONE J. OLIVETI. | GLASGUAE: | IN
AEDIBUS ACADEMICIS | EXCUDEBANT ROB. ET AND.
FOULIS | M DCC LVI.

FORMULA: Foolscap 8⁰ in fours: π1 A–N⁴.

PAPER: Medium-good quality; marks 4/ii.

TYPE: RP 2.

VARIANT: Issue in Pot 8⁰:
   Paper: Medium quality; marks 1/v; size of sheet $15\frac{1}{2} \times 12\frac{1}{4}$
in.

NOTES: *Prices*: Wholesale: Foolscap, 9*d*.; Pot, 6*d*. (*BQ* 2).
   Stock in 1777: Foolscap, 70 copies; Pot, 216 copies (*BQ* 2).

COPIES: G⁴ (Foolscap), G² (Pot).

312 Dryden, John, *Original Poems*   1756

ORIGINAL | POEMS, | BY | JOHN DRYDEN, Esq. | In
TWO VOLUMES. | VOLUME I [II]. | GLASGOW: | PRINTED
AND SOLD BY ROB. & AND. FOULIS | M.DCC.LVI. [*Same settings.*]

FORMULA: Foolscap 8⁰:

Vol. I: π⁴ A–P⁸ (*signed* ' VOL. I.' *on* A–P $1; π1 *half-title*, P8 *blank*).

Vol. II: a⁴ A–P⁸ (*signed* ' VOL. II.' *on* A–P $1).

PAPER: Medium-good quality; marks 4/vi; size of sheet 16½ × 13 in.

TYPE: RLP 1, RB 2.

VARIANT: Issue in Pot 8⁰:

Paper: Medium-poor quality; marks 1/v.

COPIES: G⁴ (Pot), L (Foolscap).

1756   Dublin Society, Royal, *Weekly Observations* **313**

THE | DUBLIN | SOCIETY'S | WEEKLY | OBSERVA
TIONS | FOR THE ADVANCEMENT OF | AGRICUL
TURE AND MANUFACTURES. | GLASGOW: | PRINTED
AND SOLD BY ROBERT & ANDREW FOULIS | M.DCC.LVI.

FORMULA: Foolscap 8⁰ in fours: a² A–2R⁴ 2S².

Plates: Four folding plates inserted at 2E3, 2F2, 2H1, 2I4, unsigned, plate marks c. 132 × 175.

PAPER: Medium quality; marks 5/ii; size of sheet 16½ × 13 in.

TYPE: RSP 1, RB 1.

VARIANT: Issue in [? Crown) 12⁰:

Formula: [? Crown] 12⁰ in sixes: a² A–2D⁶ (*vertical chain lines; probably printed on half sheets of Double Crown*).

Plates: at T2, T6, X1, Y2.

Paper: Medium-poor quality; no marks.

NOTES: *Publication*: in the press, 8 March 1756; published by 7 June 1756 (*GC*).

Prices: Wholesale: 8⁰, 2s. 3d.; 12⁰, 1s. 2d. (*BQ* 6). Retail: 8⁰, 3s. (*CP* 9).

Stock in 1777: 8⁰, 20 copies; 12⁰, 208 copies (*BQ* 6).

COPIES: G⁴ (12⁰), L (8⁰).

1756   Dublin Society, Royal, *The Flax-husbandman* **314**
                                                          Instructed

THE | FLAX-HUSBANDMAN | AND | FLAX-DRESSER
| INSTRUCTED: | OR, THE | BEST METHODS | OF |
Flax-Husbandry and Flax-Dreſſing | EXPLAINED, | *In*

feveral LETTERS, *by the Gentlemen of the* | DUBLIN SOCIETY. | GLASGOW: | PRINTED AND SOLD BY ROBERT & ANDREW FOULIS | M.DCC.LVI.

FORMULA: Foolscap 8⁰ in fours: π^2 A–S⁴ T² (π2 *advertisements*).

PAPER: Medium-poor quality; marks 5/v.

TYPE: RSP 1.

NOTES: *Publication*: in the press 8 March 1756; published by 7 June 1756 (*GC*).
  Price: Wholesale: 8*d*. (*BQ* 6).
  Stock in 1777: 152 copies (*BQ* 6).

COPIES: G⁴.

† **315** Euclid, *Elements I-VI, XI-XII*, L   1756

EUCLIDIS | ELEMENTORUM | LIBRI PRIORES SEX, | ITEM | UNDECIMUS ET DUODECIMUS, | EX VERSIONE LATINA | FEDERICI COMMANDINI; | Sublatis iis quibus olim Libri hi a THEONE, aliifve, Vitiati funt, | Et quibufdam EUCLIDIS Demonftrationibus Reftitutis, | A ROBERTO SIMSON, M.D. | In Academia Glafguenfi Mathefeos Pro feffore. | GLASGUAE, | IN AEDIBUS ACADEMICIS | EXCUDEBANT ROBERTUS ET ANDREAS FOULIS | ACADEMIAE TYPOGRAPHI | M.DCC.LVI.

FORMULA: [? Writing] Royal 4⁰: π^4 A–3E⁴ 3F².

PAPER: Medium quality; marks 8/JW.

TYPE: RGP 2, RE 2, GGP, RLP 1. Numerous woodcut diagrams.

VARIANT: Issue in [? Printing Demy] 4⁰:
  Paper: Medium-poor quality; no marks.

NOTES: *Publication*: published (by subscription) by 20 December 1756 (*GC*). Proposals issued in April 1756 (No. 287).

COPIES: G⁴ (Demy), L (both issues).

† **316** Euclid, *Elements I-VI, XI-XII*, E   1756

THE | ELEMENTS | OF | EUCLID, | VIZ. | THE FIRST SIX BOOKS, | TOGETHER WITH THE | ELEVENTH AND TWELFTH. | In this Edition, the Errors, by which THEON, or others, have long | ago Vitiated thefe Books, are Corrected, | And fome of EUCLID's Demonftrations are Reftored. | BY | ROBERT SIMSON, M.D. | Profeffor of Mathematics

in the Univerfity of Glafgow. | GLASGOW, | PRINTED BY
ROBERT AND ANDREW FOULIS | PRINTERS TO THE
UNIVERSITY | M.DCC.LVI.

FORMULA: [? Writing] Royal 4⁰: π⁴ A–3H⁴.

PAPER: Medium quality; marks 8/JW.

TYPE: RGP 2, RE 2, GGP, RLP 1, RB 2. Numerous woodcut
diagrams.

VARIANT: There may have been an issue in Demy 4⁰, as there
was of the Latin edition (No. 315).

NOTES: *Publication*: published (by subscription) by 20 December 1756 (*GC*). Proposals issued in April 1755 (No. 287).

COPIES: G⁴, L (Royal).

1756   Farquhar, George, *The Constant Couple* **317**

THE | CONSTANT COUPLE; | OR, | *A Trip to the Jubilee.*
| A | COMEDY. | BY | MR. GEORGE FARQUHAR. | [*quotation, 3 lines*] | GLASGOW: | PRINTED AND SOLD BY ROBERT &
ANDREW FOULIS | M DCC LVI. | *

FORMULA: Pot 8⁰ in fours: A–K⁴ L² (*signed ' * ' on* $1).

PAPER: Medium quality; marks 1/v.

TYPE: RB 1.

VARIANT: Issue on inferior paper, Pot 8⁰:
  Formula: (*without ' * ' signatures*).
  Paper: Medium-poor quality; marks 1/v.

COPIES: G⁴ (both issues).

1756   Hierocles, *Commentary on the Pythagoreans'* **318**
                                   Golden Verses, E

HIEROCLES | UPON THE | GOLDEN VERSES | OF THE
| PYTHAGOREANS. | TRANSLATED IMMEDIATELY
OUT OF THE | GREEK INTO ENGLISH. | With a PREFACE
concerning the Morality of the | Heathens in Theory and
Practice. | [*quotation, 4 lines*] | FIRST PRINTED IN THE
YEAR M.DC.LXXXII. | GLASGOW: | PRINTED AND SOLD
BY ROB. & AND. FOULIS | M.DCC.LVI.

FORMULA: Foolscap 8⁰: A–S⁸ T⁴ U².

PAPER: Medium-good quality; marks 5/ii, 5/v; size of sheet
16½ × 13 in.

TYPE: RE 2, GGP, RLP 1.

VARIANT: Issue in Pot 8⁰:
Paper: Medium-poor quality; marks 1/v.

NOTES: *Publication*: published by 13 December 1756 (*GC*).
Prices: Wholesale: Foolscap, 2*s*.; Pot 1*s*. 2*d*. (*BQ* 7). Retail:
(?) Foolscap, 2*s*. 6*d*. (*CP* 9).
Stock in 1777: Foolscap, 26 copies; Pot, 338 copies (*BQ* 7).

COPIES: G⁴ (Pot), G² (Foolscap).

† **319** Homer, *Works* 1756–8

[*General title-page*:] ΤΩΝ ΤΟΥ | ΟΜΗΡΟΥ | ΣΕΣΩΣΜΕΝΩΝ
| ΑΠΑΝΤΩΝ | ΤΟΜΟΙ ΤΕΣΣΑΡΕΣ. | [*quotation, 2 lines*]
GLASGUAE; | IN AEDIBUS ACADEMICIS, | EXCUDE
BANT ROBERTUS ET ANDREAS FOULIS|ACADEMIAE
TYPOGRAPHI, | M DCC LVIII.
[*Volume title-pages:* Iliad:] ΤΗΣ ΤΟΥ | ΟΜΗΡΟΥ | ΙΛΙΑΔΟΣ
| Ο ΤΟΜΟΣ ΠΡΟΤΕΡΟΣ [ΔΕΥΤΕΡΟΣ]. | [*quotation, 2 lines*]
| GLASGUAE; | IN AEDIBUS ACADEMICIS, | EXCUDE
BANT ROBERTUS ET ANDREAS FOULIS, | ACADE
MIAE TYPOGRAPHI, | M DCC LVI.
[Oddysey:] ΤΗΣ ΤΟΥ | ΟΜΗΡΟΥ | ΟΔΥΣΣΕΙΑΣ | Ο ΤΟ
ΜΟΣ ΠΡΟΤΕΡΟΣ [ΔΕΥΤΕΡΟΣ]. | [*quotation, 2 lines*] |
GLASGUAE; | IN AEDIBUS ACADEMICIS, | EXCUDE
BANT ROBERTUS ET ANDREAS FOULIS | ACADE
MIAE TYPOGRAPHI, | M DCC LVIII.

FORMULA: Writing Demy 2⁰: π^2 (π1 *blank*, π2 general title-
page; rarely found).
Iliad, Vol. I: a–b^2 c^2 A–4I² (a1 *half-title*). Vol. II: π^2 a–4p²
(π1 *half-title*).
Odyssey, Vol. I: π^2 $^2\pi^2$ A–4F² (π1 *half-title;* 4F2 *blank*). Vol. II
π^2 a–4p² (π1 *half-title*).

PAPER: Good quality; marks 7/IV, 7/JW, 7/vii; size of sheet
$19\frac{1}{4} \times 15\frac{1}{4}$ in.

TYPE: GDP 2, RGP 2, RLP 1.

VARIANTS: Issue in Foolscap 2⁰:
Paper: Medium-good quality; marks, *Iliad*: 4/ii, 5/ii;
Odyssey: 4/ii, 5/ii, 4/iv, 5/v, 4/vi, 4/v over DURHAM. Size of
sheet $16\frac{1}{2} \times 13$ in.
A copy of the large paper *Odyssey* in C (S706.a.75.1) has
variant half-title and title page, lacks $^2\pi^2$ of Vol. II, and appears

to be the copy presented for judgment as a specimen of typography by the Select Society of Edinburgh:
[*Vol.* I *Half-title reads*:] ΤΩΝ ΤΟΥ | ΟΜΗΡΟΥ | Ο ΤΟΜΟΣ ΤΡΙΤΟΣ. [*instead of*:] Η ΤΟΥ | ΟΜΗΡΟΥ | ΟΔΥΣΣΕΙΑ.
[*Vol.* I: *title-page reads as usual, except that the quotation begins* '— QUID [*etc.*]' *instead of* 'RURSUS, QUID [*etc.*]', *and that the date is* 'M DCC LVII.']
[*Vol.* II *half-title and title page as usual. A manuscript note on the fly-leaf reads as follows:* 'We are of opinion this edition of Homer's Odyssey is entitled to the prize for the best printed & most correct Greek Book. [signed] Alex^r Boswel Jac: Burnett'. *A third signature,* 'John Davidson', *appears to be that of an owner.*]

PROOFS: Complete sets of first proofs and revises of the whole of the *Iliad*, 1756, are preserved at E. Printed on medium-good Foolscap paper similar to that used for the Foolscap issue, each sheet of the first proof is endorsed 'Corrected and revised. Ja. Tweedie.' Tweedie used standard proof-correcting symbols. Most of his corrections were of literal errors, though he (or another ?) was also concerned to get rid of lingering GDP I sorts. (We know in fact that the proofs were read by Andrew Foulis and by the editors, Professors Moor and Muirhead, as well as by Tweedie. See Maclehose, pp. 176–7, for a full account of the proof-reading technique employed for this book.)

Amongst Tweedie's more personal notes are the following: 'Remember to speak to Sandy Duncan about the Regularity of the spaces' (A1); and 'N.B. I keep, or endeavour to keep, strictly to my Copy, right or wrong: According to orders. A⟨nd⟩ leave it to my Betters to correct both *it* & *me*: *neither* of whom, I plainly see, are without our faults. J.T.' (I1).

NOTES: Edited by Professors James Moor and George Muirhead, whose prefaces are dated Ides November 1756 (*Iliad*) and Ides May 1758 (*Odyssey*). Awarded the Silver Medals of the Select Society of Edinburgh in 1756 and 1757 (Murray, *R. & A. Foulis*, p. 29; and see *Variants* above).

Prices: Wholesale: 4 vols., Demy, 50*s.*; Foolscap, 34*s.* (*BQ* 5). *Retail*: 4 vols., Demy, 63*s.*; Foolscap, 42*s.* (*CP* 3).

Stock in 1777: Demy, *Odyssey* only, 21 copies; Foolscap, complete, 160 copies; Foolscap, *Odyssey* only, 16 copies; odd volumes of the *Odyssey*, imperfect, 8 (*BQ* 5).

COPIES: G⁴ (both issues), L (both issues), C (both issues, with the general title-page in a Foolscap copy), E (both issues, and proofs of the *Iliad*).

† **320** Horace, *Works*, L   1756

QUINTUS | HORATIUS | FLACCUS; | AD | LECTIONES
PROBATIORES | DILIGENTER EMENDATUS, | ET |
INTERPUNCTIONE NOVA | SAEPIUS ILLUSTRATUS.
| EDITIO TERTIA. | GLASGUAE: | IN AEDIBUS ACA
DEMICIS | EXCUDEBANT ROBERTUS ET ANDREAS
FOULIS | ACADEMIAE TYPOGRAPHI | M.DCC.LVI.

FORMULA: Foolscap 8º: a⁸(a2 +χ1) A–R⁸ (a1 *half-title*, χ1
dedication).

PAPER: Medium-good quality; marks 4/ii.

TYPE: RB 2, RE 2, RLP 1.

NOTES: Awarded the silver medal of the Select Society of
Edinburgh (Murray, *R. & A. Foulis*, p. 29).

COPIES: G⁴, L.

321 Hutcheson, Francis, *De Naturali Hominum*   1756
Socialitate (*Oratio Inauguralis*), L

DE | NATURALI | HOMINUM | SOCIALITATE. | AUC
TORE | FRANCISCO HUTCHESON LL.D. | PHILOSO
PHIAE PROFESSORE | IN ACADEMIA GLASGUENSI.
| GLASGUAE: | IN AEDIBUS ACADEMICIS | EXCUDE
BANT ROBERTUS ET ANDREAS FOULIS | M DCC LVI.

FORMULA: Foolscap 8º in fours: π² A–E⁴ (π2 *advertisements*).

PAPER: Medium-good quality; marks 5/?, 4/ii.

TYPE: RSP 1.

NOTES: *Price*: Wholesale: 9*d*. (*BQ* 5, as ' oratio inauguralis ').
Retail: 2*s*. 6*d*. with ' metaphyfica ' (*CP* 5).
    Stock in 1777: 114 copies (*BQ* 5).

COPIES: G⁴, L.

322 Hutcheson, Francis, *Logicae Compendium*, L   1756

LOGICAE | COMPENDIUM. | PRAEFIXA EST | DISSER
TATIO | DE | PHILOSOPHIAE ORIGINE, | EJUSQUE |
INVENTORIBUS AUT EXCULTORIBUS | PRAECIPUIS.
| GLASGUAE: | IN AEDIBUS ACADEMICIS | EXCUDE
BANT ROBERTUS ET ANDREAS FOULIS | ACADEMIAE
TYPOGRAPHI | M.DCC.LVI.

FORMULA: Foolscap 8⁰: π^2 A–F⁸ G⁴ (π1 *half-title*).
PAPER: Medium-good quality; marks 5/v; size of sheet
$16\frac{1}{2} \times 13$ in.
TYPE: RE 2, GGP.
NOTES: *Publication*: published by 13 December 1756 (*GC*).
COPIES: G⁴.

1756   Hutcheson, Francis, *Synopsis Metaphysicae*, L **323**

SYNOPSIS | METAPHYSICAE, | ONTOLOGIAM | ET |
PNEUMATOLOGIAM | COMPLECTENS. | EDITIO
QUARTA. | GLASGUAE, | IN AEDIBUS ACADEMICIS
| EXCUDEBANT ROBERTUS ET ANDREAS FOULIS |
M DCC LVI.
FORMULA: Foolscap 8⁰: a⁴ b² A–S⁸ (S8 *blank*).
PAPER: Medium-good quality; marks 4/ii; size of sheet
$16\frac{1}{2} \times 13$ in.
TYPE: RE 2, RSP 1, RB 2.
VARIANT: Issue in [? Crown] 12⁰:
   Formula: [? Crown] 12⁰: a⁶ A–M¹² (–M12).
   Paper: Medium-poor quality; vertical chain-lines; no
marks (probably half sheets of Double Crown).
COPIES: G⁴ (8⁰), O (12⁰).

1756   More, Henry, *An Essay on Disinterested Love* **324**

AN ESSAY | ON | DISINTERESTED | LOVE; | IN A
LETTER TO | BISHOP STILLINGFLEET, | BY | HENRY
MORE, D.D. | GLASGOW: | PRINTED AND SOLD BY
R. AND A. FOULIS | M DCC LVI.
FORMULA: Crown 12⁰ in sixes: π^2 (*outset*) A–B⁶ (*the outset on
paper with horizontal chain lines; the rest of the book on a different
paper with vertical chain lines; printing was on half sheets of
Double Crown;* π1 *title-page,* π2 *last page of text*).
PAPER: Medium-poor quality; no marks. The outset on a
better-quality paper. Size of sheet 20×15 in. (A–B).
TYPE: RE 2.
NOTES: *Price*: Wholesale: $1\frac{1}{2}d$. (*BQ* 9, specifying ' p[ot]. 12 mo.
common.')
   Stock in 1777: 340 copies (*BQ* 9).
COPIES: G⁴.

325 Vanbrugh, Sir John, *Aesop* 1756

ESOP; | A | COMEDY. | BY | Sɪʀ JOHN VANBRUGH. | GLASGOW: | PRINTED AND SOLD BY ROBERT AND ANDREW FOULIS | M DCC LVI. | *

FORMULA: Pot 8⁰ in fours: A–L⁴ (*signed '* * ' on* $1; *L4 blank*).

PAPER: Medium quality; thin; marks 1/v.

TYPE: RB 1, RLP 1.

VARIANT: Issue on common paper, Pot 8⁰:
  Formula: (*without '* * ' *signatures*).
  Paper: Medium-poor quality; marks 1/v.

COPIES: G⁴ (common), O (fine).

326 Vanbrugh, Sir John, *The Relapse* 1756

THE | RELAPSE; | OR, | VIRTUE ɪɴ DANGER: | BEING THE SEQUEL OF | THE FOOL IN FASHION. | A | COMEDY | WRITTEN BY | SIR JOHN VANBRUGH. | GLASGOW, | PRINTED IN THE YEAR M.DCC.LVI.

FORMULA: Pot 8⁰ in fours: A–N⁴ O² (*signed '* * ' on* G1).

PAPER: Medium-poor quality; marks 1/v.

TYPE: RB 1, RB 2.

VARIANT: Possibly an issue on better paper, of which the sole ' * ' signature is a relic.

NOTES: Without the Foulis Press imprint, but almost certainly printed there.

COPIES: G⁴.

327 Voltaire, *La Pucelle d'Orléans*, F 1756

NOTES: Not seen. Listed by Duncan (p. 77, No. 506) as ' La Pucelle d Orleans, Poeme Heroi-Comique, 18mo. *Chez les Frères Follis*, [1756].'

328 Xenophon, *Polity of the Lacedaemonians*, 1756
G and L

ʻΗ ΤΟΥ | ΞΕΝΟΦΩΝΤΟΣ | ΤΩΝ | ΛΑΚΕΔΑΙΜΟΝΙΩΝ | ΠΟΛΙΤΕΙΑ. | XENOPHONTIS | LACEDAEMONIORUM | RESPUBLICA. | ACCEDIT INTERPRETATIO LATINA | LEUNCLAVII. | GLASGUAE: | IN AEDIBUS ACA DEMICIS | EXCUDEBANT ROBERTUS ET ANDREAS FOULIS | ACADEMIAE TYPOGRAPHI | M.DCC.LVI.

FORMULA: Foolscap 8º in fours: πI A–M⁴ N1.
PAPER: Medium-good quality; marks 4/ii, 5/ii.
TYPE: GGP, RE 2.   Latin follows Greek.
VARIANT: Issue on inferior paper, not seen (*BQ* 4).
NOTES: *Prices*: Wholesale: fine, 1*s*. 2*d*.; common, 9*d*. (*BQ* 4).
  Stock in 1777: fine, 231 copies; common, 64 copies (*BQ* 4).
COPIES: G⁴, L (both Foolscap).

1757   Anacreon, *Odes*, with Sappho and Alcaeus, **329** †
                              Remains, G

ΑΙ | ΤΟΥ | ΑΝΑΚΡΕΟΝΤΟΣ | ΩιΔΑΙ. | ΚΑΙ ΤΑ ΤΗΣ |
ΣΑΠΦΟΥΣ, | ΚΑΙ ΤΑ | ΤΟΥ | ΑΛΚΑΙΟΥ | ΛΕΙΨΑΝΑ.
| [*quotation, 1 line*] | GLASGUAE: | IN AEDIBUS ACA
DEMICIS | EXCUDEBANT ROBERTUS ET ANDREAS
FOULIS | ACADEMIAE TYPOGRAPHI | M DCC LVII.
FORMULA: Foolscap 8º: A–E⁸ (A1 *half-title*).
PAPER: Medium-good quality; marks 4/ii; size of sheet
16½ × 13¼ in.
TYPE: GDP 2.
NOTES: *Publication*: published by 11 April 1757 (*GC*).
COPIES: G⁴, L

1757   ' Cebes ', *Table*, G and L **330**

Ὁ ΤΟΥ | ΚΕΒΗΤΟΣ | ΠΙΝΑΞ. | ACCEDIT | INTERPRE
TATIO LATINA, | EX EDITIONE | JACOBI GRONOVII. |
GLASGUAE: | IN AEDIBUS ACADEMICIS | EXCUDE
BANT ROBERTUS ET ANDREAS FOULIS | ACADE
MIAE TYPOGRAPHI | M DCC LVII.
FORMULA: Foolscap 8º: A–E⁸ F⁴ G².
PAPER: Medium-good quality; marks 4/ii; size of sheet
16¾ × 13 in.
TYPE: GDP 2, GGP, GP, RLP 1.   Latin follows Greek.
COPIES: G⁴, L.

1757 Cervantes Saavedra, Miguel de, *Don Quixote*, E **331**
THE | HISTORY | OF THE RENOWNED | DON QUIXOTE
| DE LA MANCHA. | WRITTEN IN SPANISH BY |
MIGUEL DE CERVANTES SAAVEDRA. | TRANSLATED

BY SEVERAL HANDS: | And PUBLISHED by | THE LATE
MR. MOTTEUX. | Revis'd a-new from the beſt SPANISH
Edition, | BY MR. OZELL: | Who has likewiſe added EXPLANA
TORY NOTES | from *Jarvis, Oudin, Sobrino, Pineda, Gregorio,* |
and the *Royal Academy Dictionary* of *Madrid.* | VOL. I [II] [III]
[IV]. | GLASGOW: | PRINTED AND SOLD BY R. AND A.
FOULIS | M.DCC.LVII. * [*Same setting.*]

FORMULA: Pot 8º:
   Vol. I: a⁸ b² A–Q⁸ R⁴.
   Vol. II: π1 A–Q⁸ R².
   Vol. III: A–R⁸ S⁴ (S4 *advertisements*).
   Vol. IV: π1 A–T⁸ U⁴ X² (X2 *advertisements*).
   (*Signed* ' * ' *on* \$1 *except Vol.* I N1, *Vol.* II L1; *signed* ' VOL. I
   [. . . IV].' *on* \$1 *except title-pages*).
PAPER: Medium-good quality; marks 1/v, 1/iv.
TYPE: RB 2, RLP 1.
VARIANT: Issue on common paper, Pot 8º:
   Formula: (*without the* ' * ' *signatures*).
   Paper: Medium-poor quality; marks 1/v; size of sheet
   15¼ × 12¼ in.
COPIES: G⁴ (common), O (fine).

† **332** Cicero, *De Officiis,* L   1757
MARCI TULLII | CICERONIS | DE | OFFICIIS | AD |
MARCUM FILIUM | LIBRI TRES. | GLASGUAE: |
EXCUDEBANT ROB. ET AND. FOULIS | M.DCC.LVII.
FORMULA: Foolscap 8º: a² b⁴ A–R⁸ S⁶.
PAPER: Good quality; marks 4/iv, 4/vi.
TYPE: RP 2, RLP 1, RB 2.
NOTES: *Prices*: Wholesale: 2*s.* 6*d.* (*BQ* 1). Retail: 3*s.* (*CP* 5).
   Stock in 1777: 69 copies (*BQ* 1).
COPIES: G⁴, L.

333 Derham, William, *Astro-theology*   1757
ASTRO-THEOLOGY: | OR A | DEMONSTRATION | OF
THE | BEING AND ATTRIBUTES | OF | GOD, | FROM A
SURVEY OF THE | HEAVENS. | ILLUSTRATED WITH
COPPER-PLATES. | BY | W. DERHAM, | CANON OF
WINDSOR, RECTOR OF UPMINSTER | IN ESSEX, AND
F.R.S. | The Seventh EDITION. | GLASGOW, | Printed in the
Year M DCC LVII.

FORMULA: [? Crown) 12⁰ in sixes: a–g⁶ A–M⁶ (F1, M2 *unsigned;* g6 *blank*).

Plates: three folding copper-plates, the second and third signed ' *T: Smith fculp* ', placed in sig. M.

PAPER: Medium quality; marks 9/i and no marks.

TYPE: RP 2, RSP 1, RGP 1, RB 2.

NOTES: Without the Foulis Press imprint, but is most probably the edition of *Astro-theology* advertised in No. 389 (Charteris, 1761) as printed by R. and A. Foulis.

COPIES: O.

1757   Drummond, William, *Polemo-Middinia* **334**

POLEMO–MIDDINIA | INTER | VITARVAM | ET | NEBERNAM. | GLASGOW, Printed in the Year MDCCLVII.

FORMULA: Foolscap 4⁰ in twos: *A*² B–C² D1.

PAPER: Medium-good quality; marks 5/?, 4/?.

TYPE: RGP 1.

NOTES: Without the Foulis Press imprint, but closely similar to Foulis's other editions of the book, and most probably printed by him.

COPIES: G².

1757   Gay, John, *Poems on Several Occasions* **335**

POEMS | ON | SEVERAL OCCASIONS. | BY | MR. JOHN GAY | [*quotation, 4 lines, vol.* 1 *only*] | VOLUME I [II]. | GLAS GOW: | PRINTED AND SOLD BY R. AND A. FOULIS | M.DCC.LVII. [*Same setting, respaced.*]

FORMULA: Pot 8⁰:

Vol. I: A–M⁸ (*signed* ' VOL. I.' *on* B–M $1).

Vol. II: π² A–L⁸ M⁴ N² (*signed* ' VOL. II.' *on* A–N $1).

PAPER: Medium quality; marks 1/v.

TYPE: RLP 1, RB 2, RE2.

COPIES: G⁴, L.

1757   Gray, John, *The Art of Land-measuring* **336**
                                                  Explained

THE | ART | OF | LAND-MEASURING | EXPLAINED. | IN FIVE PARTS. | VIZ. | [*two columns of contents, 3 lines each,*

separated by a vertical double plain rule, 15] | WITH AN APPEN
DIX CONCERNING INSTRUMENTS. | BY JOHN GRAY,
| TEACHER OF MATHEMATICS IN GREENOCK, | AND
LAND-MEASURER. | GLASGOW: | PRINTED BY
ROBERT AND ANDREW FOULIS FOR THE AUTHOR.
| SOLD BY D. WILSON AND J. DURHAM IN THE
STRAND, LONDON; | G. HAMILTON AND J. BALFOUR,
EDINBURGH; | AND R. AND A. FOULIS, GLASGOW,
| M.DCC.LVII.

FORMULA: [? Printing Demy] 8⁰: a⁶ A–T⁸ U².
Plates: Nine plates at D1, D2, N8, O5, S1, S3, S4, S6, U2;
unsigned, various sizes.

PAPER: Medium quality; no marks.

TYPE: RE 2, RGP 2, RLP 1. Numerous woodcut diagrams.

COPIES: G⁴, L.

337 Huygens, Christiaan, *Cosmotheoros*, E   1757

COSMOTHEOROS: | OR | CONJECTURES | CONCERN
ING THE | PLANETARY | WORLDS, | AND THEIR |
INHABITANTS. | WRITTEN IN LATIN BY | CHRIS
TIANUS HUYGENS. | *Illuſtrated with plates.* | This Tranſla
tion was firſt publiſhed in 1689. | In the preſent Edition many
places have been corrected. | GLASGOW, | PRINTED AND SOLD
BY ROB. & AND. FOULIS | M.DCC.LVII.

FORMULA: Foolscap 8⁰: a² A–N⁸ O⁴ P².
Plates: Five folding plates: Fig. 1, p. 15, plate mark 141 × 139;
Fig. 2, p. 20, 121 × 118; Fig. 3 (numbered ' 5 '), p. 152, 165 × 307;
Fig. 4, p. 168, 96 × 139; Fig. 5, p. 189, 118 × 96. All unsigned.

PAPER: Medium-good quality; marks 5/v; size of sheet 16½ × 13
in. Plates on medium-good quality papers with marks 4 and 1.

TYPE: RE 2, RB 2.

VARIANT: Issue in Pot 8⁰:
Paper: Medium-poor quality; marks 1/v.

NOTES: *Publication*: to be published 'in a few days', 13
December 1756 (*GC*).
Prices: Wholesale: Foolscap, 1s. 6d.; Pot, 1s. 2d. (*BQ* 7).
Retail: (?) Foolscap, 2s. (*CP* 9).
Stock in 1777: Foolscap, 60 copies; Pot, 274 copies (*BQ* 7).

COPIES: G⁴ (Pot), L (Foolscap).

1757 Osterwald, Jean-Frédéric, *Theologiae* **338**
Christianae Compendium, L

THEOLOGIAE | CHRISTIANAE | COMPENDIUM; |
AUTHORE | JOHANNE FRIDERICO OSTERWALDIO,
| CELEBERRIMO THEOLOGO NEOCOMENSI. | EDITIO
SECUNDA. | GLASGUAE: | IN AEDIBUS ACADEMICIS
| EXCUDEBANT ROBERTUS ET ANDREAS FOULIS |
M.DCC.LVII. | *

FORMULA: Pot 12⁰ in sixes: π^4 A–2E⁶ $2F^2$ (*signed* ' * ' *on* $1
except E1, H1, O1, 2D1, 2F1; $2F2$ *advertisements*).

PAPER: Medium-good quality; marks 6/1, 6/HR; size of sheet
$19\frac{3}{4} \times 15\frac{1}{2}$ in.

TYPE: RLP 1, RSP 1, RB 1.

VARIANT: Issue on inferior paper, in [? Crown] 12⁰:
Formula: (*without* ' * ' *signatures*).
Paper: Medium-poor quality; no marks.

NOTES: *Publication*: published by 11 April 1757 (*GC*).
Prices: Wholesale: fine, 2s.; common, 1s. 6d. (*BQ* 5).
Stock in 1777: fine, 12 copies; common, 86 copies (*BQ* 5).

COPIES: G⁴ (both issues), L (Crown).

1757 Pomfret, John, *Poems on Several Occasions* **339**

POEMS | ON | SEVERAL OCCASIONS. | BY THE REVER
END | MR. JOHN POMFRET. | THE TWELFTH EDITION.
| GLASGOW, | PRINTED AND SOLD BY R. AND A.
FOULIS | M DCC LVII.

FORMULA: Foolscap 8⁰ in fours: a⁴ A–R⁴ (R4 *blank*).

PAPER: Medium-good quality; marks 4/ii, 5/v.

TYPE: RLP 1, RE 2, RB 2.

COPIES: G⁴, L.

1757 Saint John, Henry, Lord Bolingbroke, *The* **340**
Freeholder's Political Catechism

THE | FREEHOLDER'S | POLITICAL | CATECHISM. |
Printed in the Year M.DCC.LVII.

FORMULA: Foolscap 8⁰ in fours: A–D⁴ E².

PAPER: Medium-good quality; marks 5/ii.

TYPE: RE 2, RB 2.

VARIANT: Issue on common paper, not seen (*BQ* 9).

NOTES: Without imprint, but looks like a Foulis book of the period, and is probably ' The freeholder's political catechiſm' listed in *BQ* as a Foolscap 8°.

   Prices: Wholesale: fine, 2½*d*.; common, 2*d*. (*BQ* 9).

   Stock in 1777: fine, 48 copies; common, 216 copies (*BQ* 9).

COPIES: O (Foolscap).

341 [Anon.], *Virtue's Expostulation with the Poets*   1757

NOTES: Not seen. *GC*, 11 April 1757: ' On *Wedneſday next* [i.e. 13 April] *will be published*, And ſold by R. and A. FOULIS, VIRTUE's EXPOSTULATION WITH THE BRITISH POETS. AN ODE.'

342 Addison, Joseph, *Rosamond*   1758

ROSAMOND. | AN | OPERA. | INSCRIB'D TO HER GRACE, | THE DUTCHESS OF | MARLBOROUGH. | [*quotation, 3 lines*] | BY THE LATE RIGHT HONOURABLE | JOSEPH ADDISON, Esǫ; | GLASGOW, | PRINTED AND SOLD BY ROB. & AND. FOULIS. | M.DCC.LVIII.

FORMULA: Foolscap 8° in fours: A–D⁴ E².

PAPER: Medium-good quality; marks 4/v.

TYPE: RB 2, RE 2.

VARIANTS: Issue in Pot 8°, fine:
   Formula: (*signed* ' ＊ ' *on* $1).
   Paper: Medium quality; marks 1/v.
   Issue in Pot 8°, common:
   Formula: (*without* ' ＊ ' *signatures*).
   Paper: Medium-poor quality; marks 1/v.

COPIES: G⁴ (Pot, fine), G² (Pot, common), O (Foolscap).

343 Aubert de Vertot d'Aubeuf, René,   1758
The Revolutions of Portugal, E

THE | HISTORY | OF THE | REVOLUTIONS | OF | PORTUGAL. | BY | M. L'ABBE DE VERTOT, | MEMBER OF THE ROYAL ACADEMY OF INSCRIP-|TIONS, AND OF THE BELLES LETTRES. | REVISED, AND CONSID ERABLY ENLARGED, BY | THE AUTHOR. | TRANS

LATED INTO ENGLISH FROM THE LAST | PARIS EDITION. | [*quotation, 7 lines*] | GLASGOW: | PRINTED IN THE YEAR MDCCLVIII.

FORMULA: Pot 8⁰: a⁸ A–K⁸.

PAPER: Medium quality; marks 1/v.

TYPE: RSP 1, RE 2, RP 2, RB 2.

VARIANT: Issue on better paper, (?) Foolscap 8⁰, not seen (*BQ* 6).

NOTES: Without the Foulis Press imprint, but certainly printed there.
   Prices: Wholesale: fine 1*s*. 2*d*.; common, 8*d* (*BQ* 6). Retail: (?) fine, 1*s*. 6*d*. (*CP* 9).
   Stock in 1777: fine, 34 copies; common, 275 copies (*BQ* 6).

COPIES: G⁴, L (both Pot).

1758   Bible, *New Testament*, L 344

NOVUM | TESTAMENTUM | EX | SEBASTIANI CASTA LIONIS | INTERPRETATIONE. | TOM. I [II]. | GLAS GUAE: | EXCUDEBANT ROBERTUS ET ANDREAS FOULIS | M.DCC.LVIII. [*Vol.* II, *from a different setting, lacks the point at the end of line 5*.]

FORMULA: Foolscap 8⁰:
   Vol. I: π² A–R⁸ S². (π1, S2 *blank*).
   Vol. II: π² S–2Q⁸ 2R² (π1 *blank*).

PAPER: Medium-good quality; marks 5/v, 4/ii, 4/v.

TYPE: RLP 1.

VARIANT: Issue in Pot 8⁰:
   Paper: Medium-poor quality, marks 1/iv, 1/v.

NOTES: *Prices*: Wholesale: fine, 3*s*. 6*d*.; common, 2*s*. 3*d*. (*BQ* 2). *Retail*: (?) fine, 5*s*. (*CP* 5).
   Stock in 1777: fine, 41 copies; common, 104 copies (*BQ* 2).

COPIES: G⁴, L (both Foolscap), O (Pot).

1758   Boileau-Despréaux, Nicolas, *L'Art Poétique*, F 345

NOTES: Not seen. Listed by Duncan (p. 64, No. 246) as ' L'Art Poetique de M. de Boileau Defpreaux. fools. 8vo. fine, 3d.' *BQ* (p. 9) lists 55 copies in 1777 at a wholesale price of 3*d*.

346 Campbell, Archibald, 3rd Duke of Argyll,   1758
Catalogus Librorum, L

CATALOGUS | LIBRORUM | A. C. D. A. | GLASGUAE: | IN AEDIBUS ACADEMICIS | EXCUDEBANT ROBER TUS ET ANDREAS FOULIS, | ACADEMIAE TYPO GRAPHI, | MDCCLVIII.

FORMULA: Foolscap 4⁰: π^2 A–2P^4 (π1 *blank*).

PAPER: Medium-good quality; marks 4/iv, 4/v.

TYPE: RLP 1.

VARIANT: Some copies pulled on one side of the paper only. The pages of each sheet were re-imposed in the formes, with pp. 1, 2, 7 and 8 in one forme and pp. 3, 4, 5 and 6 in the other, with the result that, with the book quired in eights, every other opening is blank. The purpose of this arrangement was no doubt to enable additions to be made to the catalogue. Copies with ordinary binder's interleaving are also found.

COPIES: G^4, L (both ordinary), G (special imposition).

347 Cappe, Newcome, *The Voice of Rejoicing*,   1758
a Sermon

THE | VOICE OF REJOICING | IN THE | TABERNACLES | OF THE | RIGHTEOUS. | A SERMON | PREACHED AT YORK, TO A CONGREGATION OF | PROTESTANT DISSENTERS, ON THE 27TH | OF NOVEMBER, 1757, JUST UPON RE-|CEIVING THE ACCOUNT OF THE | KING OF PRUSSIA'S VICTORY, | ON THE FIFTH OF THAT MONTH. | BY NEWCOME CAPPE, | LATE OF THE UNIVERSITY OF GLASGOW. | PUBLISH'D AT THE REQUEST OF THE AUDIENCE. | THE SIXTH EDITION. | GLASGOW: | RE-PRINTED BY ROBERT AND ANDREW FOULIS | AT THE DESIRE OF THE PUBLIC. | M.DCC.LVIII. | Price Four-pence.

FORMULA: Foolscap 8⁰ in fours: π1 A^4 B–C^4 D^2 E1 (π1 *half-title*).

PAPER: Medium quality; marks 4/v over DURHAM.

TYPE: RGP 2, RP 2.

VARIANT: Issue on (?) inferior paper, not seen (*BQ* 9).

NOTES: *Publication*: published by 27 February 1758 (*GC*).
  Prices: Wholesale: fine, 3*d.*; common, 2*d.* (*BQ* 9). Retail:
(?) fine, 4*d.* (title-page).
  Stock in 1777: fine, 82 copies; common 70 copies (*BQ* 9).
COPIES: G⁴, L (both Foolscap).

1758   Dalrymple, Sir John, *An Essay towards a* **348**
              General History of Feudal Property

NOTES: Not seen. *GC*, 24 April 1758: ' This day publiſhed,
And to be ſold by R. and A. FOULIS, AN ESSAY towards a
Genral Hiſtory of FEUDAL PROPERTY in Great-Britain. The
Second Edition correĉted and enlarged. By JOHN DALRYMPLE,
Eſq; '.

1758   Epictetus, *Manual*, G and L **349**

ΤΟ ΤΟΥ | ΕΠΙΚΤΗΤΟΥ | ΕΓΧΕΙΡΙΔΙΟΝ. | EX EDITIONE
| JOANNIS UPTON | ACCURATE EXPRESSUM. | GLAS
GUAE: | IN AEDIBUS ACADEMICIS | EXCUDEBANT
ROBERTUS ET ANDREAS FOULIS | ACADEMIAE
TYPOGRAPHI | M DCC LVIII.
FORMULA: Foolscap 8⁰: A–D⁸ E² F–G⁸ H².
PAPER: Medium quality; marks 4/iv.
TYPE: GDP 2, GGP, RP 2, RLP 1. Latin follows Greek.
NOTES: *Price*: Retail: 3*s.* 6*d.*, together with No. 359 (Theo-
phrastus, 1758) and No. 520 (' Cebes ', 1771) as a set of three
(advertisement in No. 546, Hutcheson, 1772).
COPIES: G⁴, L.

1758   Fordyce, James, *The Spirit of Popery, a Sermon* **350**

THE | DELUSIVE AND PERSECUTING | SPIRIT | OF |
POPERY. | A | SERMON | PREACHED BEFORE THE |
SYNOD OF PERTH AND STIRLING | AT PERTH,
OCTOBER 16, 1754. | BY | JAMES FORDYCE, | MINISTER
AT ALLOA. | THE SECOND EDITION. | GLASGOW: |
PRINTED BY R. & A. FOULIS, | FOR ROBERT BANKS BOOK
SELLER IN STIRLING | M.DCC.LVIII.
FORMULA: Foolscap 8⁰ in fours: A–D⁴.

PAPER: Medium-good quality; marks 5/iv.

TYPE: RLP i, RB 2.

NOTES: Two other sermons by Fordyce advertised on D4, *The Eloquence of the Pulpit*, and *The Methods of Promoting Edification by Public Institutions*, were printed at Glasgow for Banks in 1755, no printer named. They are set in RLP i, and may have been printed at the Foulis Press, though from their appearance they might as well be Urie's work.

COPIES: G4.

† **351** Frederick II of Prussia, *La Délassement de la*   1758
Guerre, F and E

NOTES: Not seen. *GC*, 12 June 1758: ' *To-morrow will be publifhed*, And fold by R. and A. FOULIS, THe RELAXATION from WAR, or the HERO's PHILOSOPHY. a poem in French and Englifh, wrote by The KING of PRUSSIA, During his refidence at Breflau.'

352 Glasgow University, Academy. *A Catalogue*   1758
of Pictures, etc.

A CATALOGUE | OF | PICTURES, DRAWINGS, PRINTS, | STATUES and BUSTS in PLAISTER of PARIS, | DONE AT THE | ACADEMY IN THE UNIVERSITY OF GLASGOW. | [*copper-plate with legend* 'ARS LONGA | VITA BREVIS', *unsigned, plate mark 199 × 141*] | In this Catalogue is inferted a Colleαion of Prints, the plates of which | are the property of R. and A. FOULIS. | Publifhed for the ufe of SUBSCRIBERS.

FORMULA: Foolscap 2⁰: π1 A–C² D1 (π1, *title-page, and* D1 *probably a conjugate outset; the only copy seen* (G4) *has the* Proposal for Encouraging an Academy (No. 257) *bound in between* π1 *and* A1).

PAPER: Medium-good quality; marks 4/v.

TYPE: RLP i.

COPIES: G4.

353 Gordon, George, *Quaestiones Philosophicae*, L   1758

DE | NATURA | RERUM | QUAESTIONES | PHILO SOPHICAE. | AUTHORE | GEORGIO GORDONO. | [*quotation, 2 lines*] | GLASGUAE, | Veneunt apud A. STALKER, R. et A. FOULIS; | EDINBURGI, ap. J. YAIR et R. FLEMING. | M.DCC.LVIII.

FORMULA: [? Printing Demy] 8⁰: π² A–O⁸ (π1 *half-title*).

PAPER: Medium quality; no marks.

TYPE: RE 2, RB 2. Woodcut diagrams.

NOTES: *Publication*: published by 20 February 1758 (*GJ*). Almost certainly a Foulis book.

COPIES: G⁴, L.

1758   Hamilton, William, *Poems on Several Occasions* 354 †

POEMS | ON | SEVERAL | OCCASIONS. | BY | WILLIAM HAMILTON ESQ; | THE SECOND EDITION. | GLAS GOW: | Printed and fold by ROBERT and ANDREW FOULIS | M.D.CC.LVIII.

FORMULA: Foolscap 8⁰: a⁴ A–I⁸ K².

Plate: sometimes found with a copper-plate portrait of the author, unsigned, plate-mark 98 × ?, facing the title-page; it is a reverse copy of the plate in No. 131 (Hamilton, 1749).

PAPER: Medium-good quality; marks 4/vi, 4/iv.

TYPE: RLP 1, RP 2, RB italic.

VARIANT: Issue on another quality of paper, not seen (*BQ* 7).

NOTES: *Publication*: published by 27 February 1758 (*GC*).

Prices: Wholesale: fine, 1s.; common, 9d. (*BQ* 7). Retail: (?) fine, 2s. (*CP* 8).

Stock in 1777: fine, 43 copies; common, 419 copies (*BQ* 7).

COPIES: G⁴, L (both Foolscap), O (Foolscap with plate).

1758   Hutcheson, Francis, *Thoughts on Laughter* 355

THOUGHTS | ON | LAUGHTER, | AND | OBSERVA TIONS | ON THE | FABLE OF THE BEES. | IN SIX LET TERS. | BY | FRANCIS HUTCHESON LL.D. | PROFESSOR OF PHILOSOPHY IN THE UNIVER-|SITY OF GLAS GOW. | GLASGOW: | PRINTED BY ROBERT AND ANDREW FOULIS | M DCC LVIII.

FORMULA: Foolscap 8⁰ in fours: π1 A–P⁴ Q².

PAPER: Medium quality; marks 4/vi; size of sheet $16\frac{3}{4} \times 13\frac{1}{4}$ in.

TYPE: RE 2, RLP 1.

COPIES: L.

356 Leechman, William, *The Wisdom of God*,   1758
a Sermon

NOTES: Not seen. *GC*, 12 June 1758: ' R. and A. FOULIS . . .
Of whom may be had, price one ſhilling, The Wiſdom of God in
the Goſpel Revelation. a Sermon by Dr. William Leechman,
Profeſſor of Divinity in the Univerſity of Glaſgow.' This
advertisement may refer to the edition printed by Hamilton,
Balfour and Neill, Edinburgh, 1758.

357 Otway, Thomas, *The Orphan*   1758

THE | ORPHAN: | OR, THE | UNHAPPY MARRIAGE. |
A | TRAGEDY. | [*quotation, 7 lines*] | GLASGOW: | PRINTED
AND SOLD BY R. AND A. FOULIS | * M.DCC.LVIII.
FORMULA: Pot 8⁰ in fours: A–I⁴ K² (*signed* ' * ' *on* $1 *except* C1,
F1; H2 *signed* ' 2H ').
PAPER: Medium quality; marks 1/v.
TYPE: RB 1, RLP 1.
VARIANT: Issue on inferior paper, not seen (' * ' signatures).
COPIES: L.

358 Rowe, Nicholas, *Tamerlane*,   1758

TAMERLANE, | A | TRAGEDY, | WRITTEN BY | NICO
LAS [*sic*] ROWE, ESQ. | [*quotation, 4 lines*] | THE SEVENTH
EDITION. | GLASGOW, | PRINTED AND SOLD BY ROB. & AND.
FOULIS | M.DCC.LVIII.
FORMULA: Pot 8⁰ in fours: A–K⁴.
PAPER: Medium-poor quality; marks 1/v.
TYPE: RB 2.
COPIES: G⁴.

359 Theophrastus, *Characters*, G and L   1758

ΘΕΟΦΡΑΣΤΟΥ | ΧΑΡΑΚΤΗΡΕΣ | ΗΘΙΚΟΙ. | THEO
PHRASTI | CHARACTERES | ETHICI. | EX RECENSIONE
| PETRI NEEDHAM, | ET VERSIONE LATINA | ISAACI
CASAUBONI. | GLASGUAE: | IN AEDIBUS ACADE
MICIS | EXCUDEBANT ROBERTUS ET ANDREAS
FOULIS | ACADEMIAE TYPOGRAPHI | M DCCL VIII.

FORMULA: Foolscap 8⁰: A–H⁸ I².

PAPER: Medium quality; marks 4/iv.

TYPE: GDP 2, RP 2.   Latin follows Greek.

NOTES: *Prices*: Wholesale: 1s. 2d. (*BQ* 3). Retail: 3s. 6d., together with No. 349 (Epictetus, 1758) or No. 583 (Epictetus 1775) and No. 520 (' Cebes ', 1771) as a set of three (advertisement in No. 546, Hutcheson, 1772; *CP* 4).

   Stock in 1777: 192 copies (*BQ* 3).

COPIES: G⁴, L.

1758   Virgil, *Works*, L **360** †

PUBLII | VIRGILII | MARONIS | BUCOLICA, | GEOR
GICA, | ET | AENEIS. | EX EDITIONE | PETRI BUR
MANNI. | GLASGUAE: | IN AEDIBUS ACADEMICIS |
EXCUDEBANT ROBERTUS ET ANDREAS FOULIS |
ACADEMIAE TYPOGRAPHI | M.DCC.LVIII.

FORMULA: Foolscap 8⁰: π²(π1 + χ²) A–2B⁸ (π1 *title-page*, χ1 *dedication*, χ2 *blank*, π2 *note from Quintilian*).

PAPER: Medium good quality; marks 4/ii, iii, vi.

TYPE: RB 2, RLP 1.   Without long f.

NOTES: *Publication*: to be published in a few days, 9 April 1759 (*GJ*); and 16 April 1759 (*GC*).

   Prices: Wholesale: 2s. 6d. (*BQ* 1). Retail: 4s. 6d. (*CP* 5).

   Stock in 1777: 1 copy (*BQ* 1).

COPIES: G⁴, L.

1758   Young, Edward, *Love of Fame* **361**

LOVE OF FAME, | THE | UNIVERSAL PASSION. | IN |
SEVEN CHARACTERISTICAL | SATIRES. | [*quotation, 2
lines*] | BY THE REVEREND | EDWARD YOUNG, LL.D.
| RECTOR OF WELLWYN IN HARTFORDSHIRE [*sic*], |
AND CHAPLAIN IN ORDINARY | TO HIS MAJESTY.
| GLASGOW: | PRINTED AND SOLD BY ROB. AND
AND. FOULIS | M DCC LVIII.

FORMULA: Foolscap 8⁰ in fours: a⁴ b² A–L⁴ (L4 *blank*).

PAPER: Medium-good quality; marks 4/v; size of sheet 16¾ × 13 in.

TYPE: RLP 1, RB 2, RE 2.

P   225

VARIANT: Issue on inferior paper, Pot 8⁰:
Paper: Medium-poor quality; marks 1/iv.

NOTES: *Prices*: Wholesale: Foolscap, 6*d.*; Pot, 4*d.* (*BQ* 9).

COPIES: G⁴ (Pot), G (Foolscap).

† **362** Addison, Joseph, *A Discourse on Ancient and* 1759
Modern Learning

A | DISCOURSE | ON | ANCIENT AND MODERN |
LEARNING. | BY THE LATE RIGHT HONOURABLE |
JOSEPH ADDISON, Esq; | Firſt publiſhed from an Original
MANUSCRIPT of | Mr. ADDISON's, prepared and correˊeted by
him-|felf. | THE FOURTH EDITION. | GLASGOW: |
PRINTED BY ROBERT AND ANDREW FOULIS |
M DCC LIX.

FORMULA: Foolscap 8⁰ in fours: A–C⁴.

PAPER: Medium-good quality; marks 4/v.

TYPE: RLP 1.

VARIANT: Issue on inferior paper, not seen (*BQ* 10).

NOTES: *Publication*: To be published in a few days, 16 April
1759 (*GC*).
 Prices: Wholesale: fine, 3*d.*; common, 2*d.* (*BQ* 10).
 Stock in 1777: fine, 84 copies; common, 96 copies (*BQ* 10).

COPIES: G⁴ (Foolscap).

363 Bible, *New Testament*, G 1759

'H | KAINH | ΔIAΘHKH. | NOVUM | TESTAMENTUM.
| EX EDITIONE | WETSTENIANA | M DCC XI. | GLAS
GUAE: | EXCUDEBANT R. ET A. FOULIS ACADEMIAE
TYPOGRAPHI | SUMPTIBUS GULIELMI CHARNLEY
BIBLIOPOLAE NOVOCASTRENSIS, | APUD QUEM
VENALES PROSTANT; | M DCC LIX.

FORMULA: Foolscap 4⁰: π^2 A–2C⁴ (π1 *half-title*, 2C4 *blank*).

PAPER: Medium-good quality; marks 4/ii; size of sheet
16¾ × 13 in.

TYPE: GB.

NOTES: *Prices*: Wholesale: 3*s.* (*BQ* 5). Retail: 5*s.* (*CP* 3).

COPIES: G⁴, L.

1759   Boileau-Despréaux, Nicolas, *Works*, F **364**

OEUVRES | DE | M. BOILEAU | DESPREAUX. | TOME
PREMIER [SECOND]. | A GLASGOW: | DE L'IMPRI
MERIE DE R. ET A. FOULIS | M.DCC.LIX. [*Same settings.*]

FORMULA: Foolscap 8⁰:
  Vol. I: a–b⁸ c² A–X⁸ Y² (*signed '* TOME. I.*' on* $1 *except* a1; a1
half-title].
  Vol. II: a⁸ A–X⁸ (*signed '* TOME. II.*' on* $1 *except* a1; a1 *half-
title*).

PAPER: Medium-good quality; marks 4/iv; size of sheet
16¾ × 13¼ in.

TYPE: RLP 1, RB 2.

NOTES: *Publication*: published by 9 April 1759 (*GJ*).
  Prices: Wholesale: 4s. (*BQ* 8). Retail: 5s. (*CP* 6); 6s. bound
(*GJ*, 9 April 1759).
  Stock in 1777: 11 copies (*BQ* 8).

COPIES: G⁴, L.

1759   Butler, Joseph, *Fifteen Sermons* **365**

FIFTEEN | SERMONS | PREACHED AT THE | ROLLS
CHAPEL | Upon the following SUBJECTS. | [*two columns, 6 lines
each, separated by a vertical plain rule, 20*] | BY | JOSEPH
BUTLER, LL.D. | According to the Edition of 1729. | GLAS
GOW: | PRINTED IN THE YEAR M.DCC.LIX.

FORMULA: Foolscap 8⁰: a⁴ A–P⁸ Q⁴ R².

PAPER: Medium quality; marks 4/ii; size of sheet 16¾ × 13¼ in.

TYPE: RLP 1, RB 2, RGP 2.

NOTES: Without the Foulis Press imprint, but most probably
printed there.

COPIES: G⁴.

1759   Cicero, *Laelius*, E **366**

LAELIUS: | OR A | DISCOURSE | UPON | FRIENDSHIP.
| BY | MARCUS TULLIUS CICERO. | TRANSLATED
FROM THE LATIN. | Firſt printed in 1700. | GLASGOW,
| PRINTED IN THE YEAR | M.DCC.LIX.

FORMULA: Foolscap 8⁰ in fours: π² A–H⁴ (π1 *half-title*).

PAPER: Medium-good quality; marks 5/v; size of sheet $16\frac{1}{2} \times 13$ in.
TYPE: RLP 1.
VARIANT: Issue in Pot 8⁰:
  Paper: Medium quality; marks 1/?.
NOTES: Without the Foulis Press imprint, but certainly a Foulis book.
  Prices: Wholesale: Foolscap 4*d*.; Pot, 3*d*. (*BQ* 6).
  Stock in 1777: Foolscap, 126 copies; Pot, 134 copies (*BQ* 6).
COPIES: L (Pot), G (Foolscap).

367 Davies, Sir John, *The Original, Nature and*   1759
Immortality of the Soul

THE | ORIGINAL, | NATURE, | AND | IMMORTALITY | OF THE | SOUL. | A | POEM | BY | SIR *JOHN DAVIES,* | ATTORNEY-GENERAL TO | Q. ELISABETH [*sic*]. | GLAS GOW, | PRINTED AND SOLD BY R. & A. FOULIS | MDCCLIX.
FORMULA: Foolscap 8⁰ in fours: π^2 A–M⁴ (π1 *half-title*, M4 *contents*).
PAPER: Medium-good quality; marks 4/iv, v, vi; size of sheet $16\frac{1}{2} \times 13\frac{1}{4}$ in.
TYPE: RLP 1, RB 2.
NOTES: *Prices*: Wholesale: 9*d*. (*BQ* 10). Retail: 1*s*. (*CP* 8).
  Stock in 1777: 186 copies (*BQ* 10).
COPIES: G⁴.

368 Hoadly, Benjamin, *Discourses concerning the*   1759
Terms of Acceptance with God

SEVERAL | DISCOURSES | CONCERNING THE | TERMS OF ACCEPTANCE | WITH | GOD. | IN WHICH | I. The Terms themfelves are diftinctly laid down; as they are | propofed to Chriftians in the New Teftament. And | II. Several falfe Notions of the Conditions of Salvation are | confidered. | PARTICULARLY, | [*two columns, 9 lines each, separated by a vertical plain double rule, 31*] | BY BENJAMIN HOADLY, M.A. | Rector of St. *Peter's Poor* (now Lord Bifhop of *Winchefter*.) | GLASGOW: | PRINTED IN THE YEAR M.DCC.LIX.
FORMULA: Foolscap 8⁰: π^4 A–R⁸ S⁴ (π1 *half-title*).

PAPER: Medium quality; marks 4/v, 3/?; size of sheet 16¾ × 13 in.

TYPE: RLP 1, RB 2.

VARIANT: Issue on another quality of paper, not seen (Spotiswood, p. 89).

NOTES: Advertised in No. 374 (Prior, 1759).
  Prices: Wholesale: 1s. 2d. (*BQ* 6). Retail: 2s. 6d. (*CP* 8). These prices suggest that there may be two issues involved here, which is confirmed by Spotiswood, p. 89.

COPIES: G⁴.

1759   Hutcheson, Francis, *Logicae Compendium*, L **369**

LOGICAE | COMPENDIUM. | PRAEFIXA EST | DISSER TATIO | DE | PHILOSOPHIAE ORIGINE, | EJUSQUE | INVENTORIBUS AUT EXCULTORIBUS | PRAECIPUIS. | GLASGUAE: | IN AEDIBUS ACADEMICIS | EXCUDE BANT ROBERTUS ET ANDREAS FOULIS | ACADE MIAE TYPOGRAPHI | MDCCLIX.

FORMULA: Foolscap 8⁰: π² A–F⁸ G⁴ (π1 *half-title*).

PAPER: Medium-good quality; marks 3/iv, 4/ii; size of sheet 16½ × 13 in.

TYPE: RE 2, RLP 1, RSP 1.

COPIES: G⁴.

1759   Lucretius, *De Rerum Natura*, L **370** †

TITI | LUCRETII | CARI | DE | RERUM NATURA | LIBRI SEX. | EX EDITIONE THOMAE CREECH. | [*quotation, 2 lines*] | GLASGUAE: | IN AEDIBUS ACADEMICIS | EXCUDEBANT ROBERTUS ET ANDREAS FOULIS | ACADEMIAE TYPOGRAPHI | MDCCLIX.

FORMULA: Foolscap 8⁰: a⁸ A–R⁸ (a1 *half-title*, R8 *blank*).

PAPER: Medium-good quality; marks 4/ii, 4/v; size of sheet 16¾ × 13¼ in.

TYPE: RLP 1.

VARIANTS: Issue on inferior paper in 8⁰, not seen (*BQ* 1).
  Issue in Foolscap 4⁰;
  Formula: Foolscap 4⁰: a⁴ b⁴ A–2L⁴ (a1 *half-title*, 2L4 *blank*).
  Paper: Medium-good quality; marks 4/ii, 4/v.

NOTES: A copy of the Foolscap 8⁰ issue, bound in contemporary red morocco, in the library of Sir Geoffrey Keynes contains the following MS note: ' This Book in the Roman Character is given in to the Edinburgh Society to compete for the Prize. It was begun to be printed in October 1759 and was finish'd in Novr. The number of copys exceed 250.

Robert Foulis
Andrew Foulis '

Prices: Wholesale: 8⁰, fine, 2*s*. 6*d*.; 8⁰ common, 1*s*. 4*d*.; 4⁰, 5*s*. (*BQ* 1). Retail: 8⁰, (?) fine, 3*s*.; 4⁰, 6*s*. (*CP* 3).

Stock in 1777: 8⁰, fine, 3 copies; 8⁰, common, 10 copies; 4⁰, 85 copies (*BQ* 1).

COPIES: G⁴ (Foolscap 8⁰ and 4⁰), L (Foolscap 8⁰ and 4⁰).

371 Moor, James, *De Analogia Contractionum*   1759
Linguae Graecae Regulae Generales, L

DE ANALOGIA | CONTRACTIONUM | LINGUAE GRAECAE | REGULAE GENERALES. | PRAEMISSAE SUNT NOMINUM DECLINATIONES; | ET ADJECTAE REGULAE DE TEMPORIBUS | FORMANDIS. | IN USUM TIRONUM JUNIORUM CLASSIS | GRAECAE IN ACADEMIA GLASGUENSI. | GLASGUAE, | IN AEDIBUS ACADEMICIS | EXCUDEBANT ROBERTUS ET ANDREAS FOULIS | ACADEMIAE TYPOGRAPHI | M DCC LIX.

FORMULA: Crown 8⁰ in fours: A–E⁴ a–i⁴ F–I⁴ (*sections a–i, containing additions to the original Grammar, which interrupt the pagination and which are printed on a different sort of paper from the rest of the book, were clearly an afterthought.*)

PAPER: A–E, F–I: Medium-poor quality; mark VA only; size of sheet 18½ × 14½ in.
      a–i: Poor quality; no marks; size of sheet 18¾ × 15½ in.

TYPE: RE 2, GGP 1, RLP 1, GP, GB.

COPIES: G⁴.

372 Moor, James, *Essays read to a Literary Society*   1759

ESSAYS; | READ TO A | LITERARY SOCIETY; | AT THEIR | WEEKLY MEETINGS, | WITHIN THE | COL LEGE, AT GLASGOW. | [*two columns of contents, 5 lines each, separated by a vertical plain rule, 17*] | EXEMPLARIA GRAECA. | GLASGOW: | PRINTED BY ROBERT AND ANDREW FOULIS | M.DCC.LIX.

FORMULA: Foolscap 8⁰: π^2 χ1 A–B⁸ ²χ1 C–L⁸ M² (L4 *unsigned;* π1 *title-page,* π2 *dedication,* χ1 *sub-title to the first essay,* ²χ1 *sub-title to the second essay,* M2 *errata*).

PAPER: Medium-good quality; marks 4/v, 4/vi; size of sheet 17¼ × 13¼ in.

TYPE: RE 2, RLP 1, GGP, GP.

NOTES: *Publication*: to be published on 4 July 1759 (*GJ* 2 July 1759).

COPIES: G⁴, L.

1759   Mottershead, Joseph, *Religious Discourses*   **373**

RELIGIOUS | DISCOURSES, | ON VARIOUS, | USEFUL | AND | IMPORTANT | SUBJECTS. | BY | JOSEPH MOT TERSHEAD. | GLASGOW: | PRINTED BY ROBERT AND ANDREW FOULIS | M.DCC.LIX.

FORMULA: Foolscap 8⁰: π^4 A–X⁸ Y⁴ Z².

PAPER: Medium quality; marks 4/v.

TYPE: RP 2, RLP 1, RE 2.

VARIANT: Issue on inferior paper, Foolscap 8⁰:
Paper: Medium-poor quality; marks 5/v.

NOTES: Duncan lists an edition under 1760 and none under 1759 (see No. 385 below). If, as seems possible, there was no 1760 edition, the following notes from *BQ* and *CP* refer to this book:
Prices: Wholesale: fine, 2s.; common, 1s. 2d. (*BQ* 7). Retail: (?) fine, 2s. 6d. (*CP* 9).
Stock in 1777: fine, 4 copies; common, 99 copies (*BQ* 7).

COPIES: G⁴, L (common); O (fine).

1759   Prior, Matthew, *Poems on Several Occasions*   **374**

POEMS | ON | SEVERAL | OCCASIONS. | BY | MATTHEW PRIOR, Esǫ. | IN | TWO VOLUMES. | VOL. I [II]. | GLAS GOW, | PRINTED BY ROBERT & ANDREW FOULIS | M DCC LIX. [*Lines 7–8 omitted in Vol.* II.]

FORMULA: Foolscap 8⁰:
Vol. I: A–Q⁸ (*signed* ' VOL. I.' *on* B–Q $1; Q 7 *advertisements,* Q8 *blank*).
Vol. II: A–O⁸ (*signed* ' VOL. II.' *on* B–N $1).

PAPER: Medium-poor quality; marks 4/v.

TYPE: RLP 1, RB 2.

VARIANT: Issue in Pot 8⁰:

Paper: Medium quality; marks 1/v.

NOTES: *Price*: Wholesale: Foolscap, 2*s*. (*BQ* 10).

Stock in 1777: Foolscap, 4 copies, plus 3 odd volumes (*BQ* 10).

COPIES: G⁴ (Foolscap), L (Pot).

† **375** Thucydides, *The Peloponnesian War*, G and L   1759

'Ο ΤΟΥ | ΘΟΥΚΥΔΙΔΟΥ | ΠΟΛΕΜΟΣ | ΠΕΛΟΠΟΝΝΗ
ΣΙΑΚΟΣ. | THUCYDIDIS | BELLUM | PELOPONNE
SIACUM. | Ex editione WASSII et DUKERI. | TOM. I [II . . .
VIII]. | GLASGUAE: | IN AEDIBUS ACADEMICIS | EX
CUDEBANT ROBERTUS ET ANDREAS FOULIS | ACA
DEMIAE TYPOGRAPHI | MDCCLIX. [*Different settings.*]

FORMULA: Foolscap 8⁰:

Vol. I: a²(a1 + χ1) A–Z⁸ (A4 *unsigned;* χ1 *dedication,* Z8 *blank*).
(*The remaining 7 volumes signed* 'TOM. II.' . . . 'TOM. VIII.'
on $1 *except the title-pages.*)

Vol. II: π1 A–S⁸ T⁶ (T6 *blank*).

Vol. III: A–T⁸ (T8 *blank*).

Vol. IV: A–Y⁸ Z² (S3 *unsigned*).

Vol. V: A–Q⁸ R⁴ S².

Vol. VI: A–T⁸ (F3, H3, P3, R3 *unsigned;* T8 *blank*).

Vol. VII: A–R⁸.

Vol. VIII: A–T⁸ (N3 *unsigned*).

PAPER: Medium-good quality; marks 4/v, 4/vi.

TYPE: GGP, RP 2.   Greek and Latin on facing pages.

VARIANT: Issue on similar paper, Latin at the end:

Formula: Foolscap 8⁰ in fours:

Vol. I: a²(a1 + χ²) A–Z⁴ ²A–Z⁴ (A2ᵛ *signed* 'A3'; a1 *title-page,*
χ1 *dedication,* χ2 *blank,* a2 *Life*).

Vol. II: π1 A–T⁴(–T4) ²A–T⁴ (*signed* 'TOM. II' *on* $1 *except*
π1; ²T4 *blank*).

Vol. III: A–T⁴ U² ²A–T⁴ (*signed* 'TOM. III.' *on* $1 *except* A1,
U1; U2 *blank*).

Vol. IV: A–Y⁴ Z² ²A–Y⁴ ²Z² (²A2 *signed* 'A3'; ²S2 *unsigned;*
signed 'TOM. IV.' *on* $1 *except* A1; ²Z2 *blank*).

Vol. V: A–R⁴ ²A–R⁴ (*signed* 'TOM. V.' *on* $1 *except* A1;
²R4 *blank*).

Vol. VI: A–T⁴ U² ²A–T⁴ (²H2, ²R2 *unsigned; signed* 'TOM.
VI.' *on* $1 *except* A1, T1, U1; *signed* 'VOL. VI.' *on* T1, U1; U2
blank).

Vol. VII: A–R⁴ S² ²A–R⁴ (*signed* 'TOM. VII.' *on* $1 *except* A1;
S2 *blank*).

Vol. VIII: A–T⁴ U² ²A–T⁴ (²N2 *unsigned; signed* 'TOM. VIII.' *on* $1 *except* A1; U2 *blank*).
Latin follows Greek in the second alphabets.

Paper: As parallel text issue, plus 5/v.

Issues on common paper, parallel text and Latin at end, not seen (*BQ* 4).

NOTES: *GJ*, 22 January 1761: '*GLASGOW, Auguſt* 15th, 1760, ROBERT and ANDREW FOULIS, Printers to the Univerſity of Glaſgow, HAVING finiſhed at the preſs a correct edition of THUCYDIDES, Greek and Latin, in eight volumes, ſmall Octavo, on fine writing paper, propoſe to publiſh it by ſub ſcription.

' The price to ſubſcribers will be one pound in ſheets; or one pound one ſhilling, ſewed in blue paper.

' Thoſe who are inclined to favour this undertaking, are deſired to give their names to the printers at Glaſgow, or to T. Becket, bookſeller, at Tully's Head, near Surry-ſtreet, London, where a ſpecimen of the work is to be ſeen, and by whom the ſubſcription books will be delivered.

' Some copies are printed with the Greek and Latin on oppoſite pages, and ſome with the transſlation ſeparately. Subſcribers are deſired to mention, at the time of ſubſcribing, which ſort they chuſe.

' N.B. No money required but on delivery of the work.'

Prices: Wholesale: either issue, fine, 17*s*. (*BQ* 4). Retail: fine, 20*s*. in sheets; 21*s*. sewed in blue paper (*GJ* advertisement quoted above; *CP* 4).

Stock in 1777: parallel text, fine, 60 copies; Latin at the end, fine, 52 copies; odd volumes, fine and common, 114 (*BQ* 4).

COPIES: G⁴, L (both fine, parallel text).

1759   Tyrtaeus, *Spartan Lessons*, G and L **376**

SPARTAN LESSONS; | OR, | THE PRAISE OF VALOUR; | IN THE VERSES OF | TYRTAEUS; | AN ANCIENT ATHENIAN POET, | ADOPTED BY THE | REPUBLIC OF LACEDAEMON, | AND EMPLOYED | TO INSPIRE THEIR YOUTH | WITH WARLIKE SENTIMENTS. | [*quotations, 4 lines*] | GLASGOW: | PRINTED BY ROBERT AND ANDREW FOULIS. | M DCC LIX.

FORMULA: Foolscap 4⁰ in twos: *a*² b–g² *h*² A–E² χ1 F–G² H1 (*a*1 *title-page, a*2 *dedication, h*1 *Greek sub-title, h*2 *plate,* χ1 (*printed as* H2) *Latin sub-title*).

PAPER: Medium-good quality; marks 4/vi, 4/ii, 4/v.

TYPE: GDP 2, RE 2, RGP 2, GGP, RLP 1, GP, RB 2. Plates printed on *h*2 and C2, unsigned. Latin follows Greek.

NOTES: There is a proof copy in G (Cy.2.1) annotated by the editor, Professor James Moor. It is made up from unperfected whole sheets of ' half-sheet imposition ', so that every other opening is blank.

Publication: published by 9 April 1759 (*GJ*).

Prices: Wholesale: 1*s*. 6*d*. (*BQ* 4). Retail: 2*s*. (*CP* 3). These are the prices which obtained nearly twenty years later; at publication the retail price was 1*s*. 6*d*. in boards (*GJ*, 9 April 1759).

Stock in 1777: 88 copies (*BQ* 4).

COPIES: G⁴, L.

† 377 Anderson, John, *A Compend of Experimental*   1760 *Philosophy*

A | COMPEND | OF | EXPERIMENTAL | PHILOSOPHY; | CONTAINING | PROPOSITIONS | PROVED BY A | COURSE OF EXPERIMENTS | IN | NATURAL PHILO SOPHY, | AND THE | GENERAL HEADS OF LECTURES | WHICH ACCOMPANY THEM. | GLASGOW: | PRINTED BY ROBERT AND ANDREW FOULIS | M.DCC.LX.

FORMULA: Foolscap 8⁰ in fours: a⁴ A–G⁴ (*watermarks in the only copy seen prove that the two conjugate pairs of sig. A are not part of the same half sheet, which suggests that one or other of them is a cancel*).

PAPER: Medium-good quality; marks 4/v.

TYPE: RLP 1, RB 1.

COPIES: G².

378 Brekell, John, *Remarks on Mottershead's*   1760 *Discourse*

FREE | AND | CANDID | REMARKS | UPON THE REVEREND | MR. MOTTERSHEAD'S DISCOURSE, | OF | BAPTIZING SICK AND DYING INFANTS. | [*quotations, 3 lines*] | BY THE AUTHOR OF PAEDO-BAPTISM, | IN TWO PARTS. | GLASGOW: | Printed by R. and A. FOULIS for the AUTHOR, | And Sold by T. BECKET, at Tully's Head, near Surrey-|ſtreet, in the Strand, London; and by R. FLEET WOOD, Bookſeller in Liverpool. M. DCC. LX. | Price 6*d*.

FORMULA: Foolscap 8⁰ in fours: π1 A–D⁴ (D4 *advertisement*).

PAPER: Medium quality; marks 4, 5/?.
TYPE: RLP 1, RB 2.
NOTES: Price: 6*d.* (title-page).
COPIES: York Minster Library.

1760   [Anon.], *An Essay on the Theory of Agriculture* **379**

AN | ESSAY | ON THE | THEORY | OF | AGRICUL
TURE, | INTENDED AS AN | INTRODUCTION | TO A
| RATIONAL SYSTEM | OF THAT | ART. | [*quotation,
3 lines*] | BY A FARMER. | LONDON: | Sold by T. BECKET,
at Tully's Head, near Surry-ftreet, in the | Strand; and, at
Glafgow, by R. and A. FOULIS. | M.DCC.LX.
FORMULA: [? Writing] Royal 12⁰ in sixes: π1 A–D⁶ E⁴.
PAPER: Medium-good quality; marks 8/?.
TYPE: RE 2.
NOTES: Almost certainly printed at the Foulis Press, in spite
of the imprint.
  Publication: published by 19 June 1760 (*GC*).
  Duncan (p. 66, No. 282) lists the book under 1761 and not
under 1760, but this may be a mistake.
COPIES: G².

1760   Fénelon, *Dialogues concerning Eloquence, etc.*, E **380**

DIALOGUES | CONCERNING | ELOQUENCE: | WITH
A LETTER TO THE | FRENCH ACADEMY, | CONCERN
ING | RHETORIC, | AND | POETRY. | BY | M. DE FENE
LON | ARCHBISHOP OF CAMBRAY. | To which is added,
| A DISCOURSE PRONOUNCED BY THE AUTHOR |
AT HIS ADMISSION INTO THE ACADEMY; | with a new
Tranflation of his Dialogues | BETWEEN DEMOSTHENES
AND CICERO, | VIRGIL AND HORACE. [*Also found with lines
13–18 omitted.*]
  [*Each of the four parts has a sub-title, with the imprint of Robert
and Andrew Foulis, dated 1760. The first one reads as follows:*]
DIALOGUES | CONCERNING | ELOQUENCE | IN
GENERAL; | AND PARTICULARLY THAT KIND |
WHICH IS FIT FOR THE PULPIT: | BY THE | ARCH
BISHOP | OF | CAMBRAY, | TRANSLATED FROM THE
FRENCH, AND ILLUS-|TRATED WITH NOTES AND
QUOTATIONS; | BY WILLIAM STEVENSON M.A. |

RECTOR OF MORNINGTHORP IN NORFOLK. | GLAS
GOW: | PRINTED AND SOLD BY R. AND A. FOULIS |
M.DCC.LX.

FORMULA: Foolscap 8⁰: a⁸ A–X⁸ Y⁴.

PAPER: Medium-good quality; marks 5/v, 4/vi; size of sheet
$16\frac{3}{4} \times 13$ in.

TYPE: RLP 1, RB 2, RE 2.

VARIANT: Issue in Pot 8⁰;
  Paper: Medium quality; marks 1/v.

NOTES: *Prices*: Wholesale: Foolscap. 3s.; Pot 1s. 6d. (*BQ* 6).
Retail: (?) Foolscap, 3s. 6d. (*CP* 8).
  Stock in 1777: Foolscap, 8 copies; Pot, 11 copies (*BQ* 6).

COPIES: G⁴, L (both Pot), G (Foolscap).

381 Fénelon, *Fables*, E   1760

FABLES, | COMPOSED | FOR THE USE OF THE | DUKE
OF BURGUNDY. | BY | M. FENELON, | ARCHBISHOP |
OF | CAMBRAY. | NEWLY TRANSLATED FROM THE
FRENCH | BY MR. ELPHINGSTON. | GLASGOW: |
PRINTED AND SOLD BY R. AND A. FOULIS | M.DCC.LX.

FORMULA: Foolscap 8⁰ in fours: A² B–O⁴ P² (P² *actually printed
as the central conjugate fold of A*).

PAPER: Medium-good quality; marks 4/v, vi; size of sheet
16 × 13 in.

TYPE: RLP 1.

VARIANT: Issue on inferior paper, not seen (*BQ* 6).

NOTES: *Prices*: Wholesale: fine, 9d.; common, 4d. (*BQ* 6).
Retail: (?) fine, 1s. (*CP* 8).
  Stock in 1777: fine, 178 copies; common, 56 copies (*BQ* 6).

COPIES: G⁴, L (both Foolscap).

382 Gee, Joshua, *The Trade and Navigation of*   1760
Great Britain

THE | TRADE | AND | NAVIGATION | OF | GREAT-
BRITAIN | CONSIDERED: | SHEWING, | [*two columns of
contents, 9 lines each, separated by a vertical plain rule, 31*] | BY
JOSHUA GEE. | THE SIXTH EDITION. | GLASGOW: |
PRINTED AND SOLD BY R. AND A. FOULIS | M.DCC.LX.

FORMULA: Foolscap 8⁰ in fours: a–c⁴ A–Y⁴ Z².

PAPER: Medium quality; marks 5/v, 4/v; size of sheet, 16½ × 13 in.
TYPE: RLP 1, RP 2, RB 2.
VARIANT: Issue in Pot 8⁰:
  Paper: Medium quality; marks 1/iv; size of sheet 15¼ × 12 in.
NOTES: *Prices*: Wholesale: Foolscap, 1s. 4d.; Pot, 1s. (*BQ* 6). Retail: (?) Foolscap, 2s. (*CP* 9).
  Stock in 1777: Foolscap, 164 copies, Pot, 104 copies (*BQ* 6).
COPIES: G⁴, L (both Foolscap), G² (Pot).

1760   Horace, *Works*, L **383** †

QUINTUS | HORATIUS | FLACCUS; | AD | LECTIONES PROBATIORES | DILIGENTER EMENDATUS, | ET | INTERPUNCTIONE NOVA | SAEPIUS ILLUSTRATUS. | EDITIO QUARTA. | GLASGUAE: | IN AEDIBUS ACA DEMICIS | EXCUDEBANT ROBERTUS ET ANDREAS FOULIS | ACADEMIAE TYPOGRAPHI | M.DCC.LX.

FORMULA: Foolscap 8⁰: $\pi^6(\pi 2 + \chi 1)$ A–T⁸ U² ($\pi 1$ *half-title*, $\chi 1$ *dedication*).
PAPER: Medium-good quality; marks 4/v.
TYPE: RLP 1, RP 2, RB 2, RE 3.
VARIANT: Issue in Foolscap 4⁰:
  Formula: Foolscap 4⁰: a^2 $\chi 1$ b⁴ A–2P⁴ 2Q² (a1 *half-title*, $\chi 1$ *dedication*).
  Paper: Medium-good quality; marks 4/v.
NOTES: *Prices*: Wholesale: 8⁰, 2s. 6d.; 4⁰, 5s. (*BQ* 1). Retail: 8⁰, 3s.; 4⁰, 6s. (*CP* 3).
COPIES: G⁴ (8⁰ and 4⁰), L (8⁰ and 4⁰).

1760   Law, John, *Money and Trade considered* **384**

MONEY | AND | TRADE | CONSIDERED: | WITH A PROPOSAL FOR SUPPLYING THE | NATION WITH MONEY. | FIRST PUBLISHED AT EDINBURGH MDCCV. | BY THE CELEBRATED | JOHN LAW, Esq.; | AFTERWARD | COMPTROLLER-GENERAL OF THE FINANCES | OF FRANCE. | GLASGOW, | PRINTED AND SOLD BY R. AND A. FOULIS | M.DCC.LX.

FORMULA: Foolscap 8⁰ in fours: A–2E⁴ 2F² (Y2 *unsigned;* 2F2 *advertisements*).
PAPER: Medium-good quality; marks 4/v; size of sheet 16 × 13¼ in.

TYPE: RE 2, RLP 1.

NOTES: *Prices*: Wholesale: 1*s.* 6*d.* (*BQ* 6). Retail: 2*s.* (*CP* 9).
 Stock in 1777: 184 copies, of which 34 were imperfect (*BQ* 6).

COPIES: G⁴, L.

385 Mottershead, Joseph, *Religious Discourses*   1760

NOTES: Not seen. Listed by Duncan (p. 65, No. 271), with
details from *BQ*. Possibly listed by mistake for No. 373 (q.v.),
which he omits.

386 Southerne, Thomas, *Oroonoko* (adapted by   1760
Francis Gentleman)

OROONOKO: | OR THE | ROYAL SLAVE. | A | TRAGEDY.
| ALTERED FROM | SOUTHERNE, | BY | FRANCIS
GENTLEMAN. | As it was Performed at the THEATRE in
EDINBURGH, | with univerſal Applauſe. | GLASGOW: |
PRINTED BY ROBERT AND ANDREW FOULIS |
M.DCC.LX.

FORMULA: Foolscap 8⁰: A–E⁸ F⁴ (A1 *half-title*).

PAPER: Medium-good quality; marks 4/vi.

TYPE: RLP 1, RB 2.

COPIES: L.

387 Anacreon, *Odes*, with Sappho and Alcaeus,   1761
Remains, G

ΑΙ ΤΟΥ | ΑΝΑΚΡΕΟΝΤΟΣ | Ω,ΔΑΙ. | Καὶ τὰ τῆς | ΣΑΠ
ΦΟΥΣ, | Καὶ τὰ τοῦ [*lig.*] | ΑΛΚΑΙΟΥ | ΛΕΙΨΑΝΑ. | [*quotation,
1 line*] | GLASGUAE: | EXCUD. R. & A. FOULIS | M. DCC. LXI.

FORMULA: Foolscap 32⁰ in eights: A–E⁸ F². (A1 *half-title*).

PAPER: Medium-good quality; marks 4/v.

TYPE: GB.

VARIANT: Issue with indexes, not seen (*BQ* 3).

NOTES: *Prices*: Wholesale: without indexes, 9*d.*; with indexes,
1*s.* (*BQ* 3). Retail: (?) with indexes, 1*s.* 6*d.* (*CP* 3).
 Stock in 1777: without indexes, 240 copies; with indexes, 134
copies (*BQ* 3).

COPIES: G⁴, L (without indexes).

1761   Butler, Samuel, *Hudibras* **388** †

HUDIBRAS. | IN THREE PARTS. | WRITTEN IN THE | TIME | OF THE | LATE WARS. | BY | SAMUEL BUTLER. | WITH | Annotations, and a complete Index. | VOL. I [II]. | GLASGOW: | printed by rob. & and. foulis | M.DCC.LXI. [*Same setting.*]

FORMULA: Pot 12⁰:
 Vol. I: a⁸ A–I¹² K⁶.
 Vol. II: L–U¹² X⁴.

PAPER: Medium quality; marks 1/v, 1/iv; size of sheet 15½ × 12¼ in.

TYPE: RB 2, RLP 1.

COPIES: G⁴, L.

1761 Charteris, Laurence, *The Corruption of this Age,* **389**
                    etc.

THE | CORRUPTION | OF | THIS AGE, | AND THE | REMEDY THEREOF. | OR, THE | CHIEF HINDERANCES OF THE | growth of true Christianity, | AND | THE WAY OF GROWING | IN GRACE, WISDOM, AND ALL | Christian virtue; | Reprefented in two letters to a friend. | Written by the Reverend | Mr. LAURENCE CHARTERIS, | Sometime Profeffor of Theology in | the College of Edinburgh. | To which is added, | PREPARATION for DEATH; | Written by the fame author for the ufe | of a young Gentleman. | GLASGOW: | Printed by robert and andrew foulis | M.DCC.LXI.

FORMULA: Pot 12⁰ in sixes: π1 A–O⁶ (O6 *advertisements*).

PAPER: Medium quality; marks 1/iv.

TYPE: RLP 1.

NOTES: *Price*: Wholesale: 4*d.* (*BQ* 7).
 Stock in 1777: 244 copies (*BQ* 7).

COPIES: L.

1761   Cicero, *Pro Milone*, L **390**

MARCI TULLII | CICERONIS | PRO | T. ANNIO MILONE | ORATIO. | Ex editione J. Oliveti. | GLASGUAE: | IN AEDIBUS ACADEMICIS | EXCUDEBANT ROBERTUS ET ANDREAS FOULIS | M.DCCLXI.

FORMULA: Pot 8⁰ in fours: π1 A–K^4 L1.

PAPER: Medium-good quality; marks 1/v; size of sheet 14¾ × 12 in.

TYPE: RP 2.

NOTES: An entry in *BQ* (p. 3) for a *Pro Milone*, ' f[oolscap]. 8vo. common ', of which 71 copies remained in 1777, may refer to this book.

COPIES: G².

391 Craig, William, *The Reverence due to the Name*   1761
of God, a Sermon

THE | REVERENCE | WHICH | IS DUE | TO | THE NAME | OF | GOD. | A | SERMON. | BY | WILLIAM CRAIG, M.A. | ONE OF THE MINISTERS OF GLASGOW. | [*quotation, 2 lines*] | GLASGOW: | PRINTED AND SOLD BY. R. AND A. FOULIS | M.DCC.LXI.

FORMULA: Foolscap 8⁰ in fours: π² A–E^4 F² (π1 *half-title*).

PAPER: Medium-good quality; marks 4/v.

TYPE: RP 2 RB 2.

NOTES: *Publication*: preached on 13 January 1761 (half-title); published on 24 January 1761 (*GJ* 22 January 1761).

   Prices: Wholesale: 4*d*. (*BQ* 9, probably referring to this book and not to No. 429). Retail: 6*d*. (half-title).

   Stock in 1777: 162 copies (*BQ* 9).

COPIES: G^4, L.

392 Eugene Francis, Prince of Savoy, *Prince*   by 1761
Eugene's Prayer, with *King Henry's Prayer*

NOTES: Not seen. Advertised in No. 389 (Charteris, 1761) as printed by R. and A. Foulis. *BQ* (p. 10) lists 190 copies of ' Prince Eugene and King Henry's Prayer, f[oolscap]. 8vo. fine. 3*d*. [wholesale] '.

393 [Anon.], *Extract of Orders and Regulations*   1761

EXTRACT | OF | ORDERS | AND | REGULATIONS | FOR | GARRISON AND CAMP DUTIES, | FROM THE YEAR 1743. | TO THE | CONCLUSION OF THE PEACE | AT | AIX LA CHAPELLE, | IN THE YEAR 1748. | &c. &c. &c. | GLASGOW: | PRINTED BY ROBERT AND ANDREW FOULIS | M.DCC.LXI.

FORMULA: Foolscap 4⁰: π² A–K⁴ L² (I2, K2 *unsigned*).
PAPER: Medium-good quality; marks 3/v, 4/?; size of sheet
16½ × 13¼ in.
TYPE: RLP 1, RB 2.
NOTES: The Murray copy (G²) is inscribed on the title-page
' Cardrofs | *Fort. Augustus* | *July 8ᵗʰ 1761* '. This is the Foulises'
friend Lord Buchan, whose title was Lord Cardross until he
succeeded his father as the eleventh Earl in 1767.
COPIES: G².

1761   Gay, John, *Fables* **394**

FABLES | IN | TWO PARTS. | WROTE FOR THE | AMUSE
MENT OF HIS ROYAL HIGHNESS | WILLIAM | DUKE
OF CUMBERLAND. | BY THE LATE | Mʀ. JOHN GAY.
| GLASGOW: | PRINTED BY ROBERT & ANDREW FOULIS |
| M.DCC.LXI.

FORMULA: Foolscap 8⁰: π⁴ A–K⁸ L⁴ (H3 *unsigned*).
PAPER: Medium quality; marks 4/v.
TYPE: RLP 1.
VARIANT: Issue in Pot 8⁰:
  Paper: Medium quality; marks 1/iv.
NOTES: *Prices*: Wholesale: Pot, 6*d.* (*BQ* 11). Retail: (?)
Foolscap, 1*s.* 6*d.* (*CP* 8).
  Stock in 1777: Pot, 1 copy (*BQ* 11).
COPIES: G⁴ (Pot), L (Foolscap).

1761   Herodotus, *History*, G and L **395 †**

'Η ΤΟΥ | Η'ΡΟΔΟΤΟΥ | 'ΑΛΙΚΑΡΝΑΣΣΕΩΣ | 'ΙΣ
ΤΟΡΙΑ. | HERODOTI | HALICARNASSENSIS | HIS
TORIA. | EX EDITIONE JACOBI GRONOVII; | TOMIS
NOVEM. | COELATUMQUE NOVEM MUSIS OPUS. HOR. |
ADJECTUS EST, EX EADEM EDITIONE, LIBER DE | VITA HOMERI;
VULGO SED FALSO, ADSCRIPTUS | HERODOTO. | TOM. I [II . . .
IX]. | GLASGUAE: | IN AEDIBUS ACADEMICIS | EX
CUDEBANT ROBERTUS ET ANDREAS FOULIS | ACA
DEMIAE TYPOGRAPHI | M DCC LXI. [*Different settings.*]

FORMULA: Foolscap 8⁰:
  Vol. I: π² A–2F⁸ 2G⁴ (P2, X4 *unsigned; signed* ' * ' *on* A–I $1,
M1, N1; *Vols.* I *to* IX *signed* ' TOM. I [. . . IX].' *on* $1 *except
title-pages*).

Vol. II: π^2 A–2B^8 (–2B8; I2, K4, O2 *unsigned;* πI *blank*).
Vol. III: π^2 A–Y^8 (A4 *signed* ' B4 '; πI, Y8 *blank*).
Vol. IV: π^2 A–Y^8 Z^4 (πI *blank*).
Vol. V: π^2 A–P^8 Q^4 (K3 *unsigned;* πI *blank*).
Vol. VI: π^2 A–Q^8 R^2 (πI *blank*).
Vol. VII: π^2 A–2E^8 2F^2 (N2, Y4, 2D3 *unsigned;* πI *blank*).
Vol. VIII: π^2 A–R^8 (D2, E3 *unsigned;* πI, R8 *blank*).
Vol. IX: π^2 A–T^8 (Q2 *unsigned;* πI, T8 *blank*).

PAPER: Various qualities from good to medium; marks 4/iv, 4/v, 5/i, 5/v.

TYPE: GGP, GP, GB, RE 2, RLP 1, RB 2. Greek and Latin on facing pages.

VARIANTS: Issue on inferior paper, Foolscap 8⁰, Greek and Latin:

> *Formula*: (*without Vol.* I ' * ' *signatures; usually lacks all initial blanks*).
> *Paper*: Similar to better paper, same marks, but generally of poorer quality.

Issue, probably better paper Foolscap 8⁰, Greek only (*GJ* 22 January 1761).

NOTES: *Publication*: *GJ*, 22 January 1761: ' *Now in the Prefs*, And will be ready to be delivered to fubfcribers againft the firft of March, 1761 . . . a few will be pure Greek. Price to fubfcribers for Greek and Latin 25s. in fheets, 26s. in blue paper, and for the pure Greek 14s. in fheets.'
Prices: Wholesale: G and L, fine, 21*s*.; G, fine, 10*s*. 6*d*. (*BQ* 4–5). Retail: G and L, (?) fine, 25*s*. (*CP* 4; and see above).
COPIES: G^4 (G and L, common), L (G and L, fine and common).

† **396** Milton, John, *Paradise Lost*   1761

NOTES: Not seen. Listed by Duncan (p. 66, No. 280) as ' Milton's Paradife Loft, 2 vols. small 12mo.'

† **397** Nepos, Cornelius, *Lives of the Emperors*, L   1761

CORNELII | NEPOTIS | EXCELLENTIUM | IMPERA TORUM | VITAE. | EX EDITIONE OXONIENSI. | GLAS GUAE: | IN AEDIBUS ACADEMICIS | EXCUDEBANT ROBERTUS ET ANDREAS FOULIS | ACADEMIAE TYPOGRAPHI | M DCC LXI.

FORMULA: [? Writing Demy] 8⁰: a^4 A–G^8($\pm$G4) H–T^8 (T8 *advertisements*).

PAPER: Good quality; marks 7/i.

TYPE: RE 3, RB 2, RLP 1. Without long f.

VARIANTS: Issue in Post 8⁰:
  Paper: Medium-good and good quality; marks 6/none.
  Issue in Foolscap 8⁰:
  Paper: Medium quality; marks 5/ii; size $16\frac{1}{2} \times 13$ in.

NOTES: *Price*: Retail: (? issue), 2s. 6d. (*CP* 5).

COPIES: G⁴ (Post and Foolscap), L (Demy and Foolscap).

by 1761   Ray, John, *The Wisdom of God manifested* **398** †
                      in the works of Creation

NOTES: Not seen. Advertised in No. 389 (Charteris, 1761) as printed by R. and A. Foulis.

by 1761   Sherlock, William, *A Practical Discourse* **399**
                                    concerning Death

NOTES: Not seen. Advertised in No. 389 (Charteris, 1761) as printed by R. and A. Foulis. An edition at HD (Glasgow: printed in the year M.DCC.LXI.), of which I have seen a microfilm, appears on typographical grounds not to be a Foulis book.

1761   Xenophon, *Memorabilia*, G **400**

ΤΑ ΤΟΥ | ΞΕΝΟΦΩΝΤΟΣ | ΠΕΡΙ ΤΟΥ | ΣΩΚΡΑΤΟΥΣ | ΑΠΟΜΝΗΜΟΝΕΥΜΑΤΑ· | ΚΑΙ 'Η ΤΟΥ | ΣΩΚΡΑΤΟΥΣ | ΑΠΟΛΟΓΙΑ. | [*plain rule 30*] | XENOPHONTIS | DE | SOCRATE | COMMENTARII; | ITEM | SOCRATIS | APOLOGIA. | IN HAC EDITIONE EMENDATIONES NONNULLAE | IN IMA PAGINA PROPONUNTUR. | GLASGUAE: | IN AEDIBUS ACADEMICIS | EXCUDE BANT ROBERTUS ET ANDREAS FOULIS | ACADE MIAE TYPOGRAPHI | M DCC LXI.

FORMULA: Foolscap 8⁰ in fours: π^2 A–2O⁴ 2P² (π1 *blank*).

PAPER: Medium-good quality; marks 4/v, 5/v; size of sheet $16\frac{3}{4} \times 13\frac{1}{4}$ in.

TYPE: GGP, GP, GB, RB 2.

VARIANT: Issue in Foolscap 4⁰:
  Formula: Foolscap 4⁰: (*as* 8⁰).
  Paper: Good quality; marks 4/v.

NOTES: *Prices*: Wholesale: 4⁰, 5*s*. (*BQ* 4). Retail: 8⁰, 3*s*.; 4⁰, 6*s*. (*CP* 3–4).

COPIES: G⁴ (both issues), L (both issues).

---

401 Burnet, Gilbert, *A Discourse of the Pastoral*   1762
Care

A | DISCOURSE | OF THE | PASTORAL CARE. | WRITTEN | BY THE RIGHT REVEREND FATHER IN GOD, | GILBERT, | LATE LORD BISHOP OF SARUM. | With a new PREFACE; and fome other additions. | FIRST PRINTED M.DC.XCII. | GLASGOW, | PRINTED BY ROBERT AND ANDREW FOULIS | M DCC LXII.

FORMULA: Pot 8⁰: a–c⁸ A–N⁸.

PAPER: Medium quality; marks 1/v; size of sheet 15¼ × 12¼ in.

TYPE: RLP 1, RP 2.

NOTES: *Prices*: Wholesale: 1*s*. 2*d*. (*BQ* 7). Retail: 1*s*. 6*d*. (*CP* 8).

   Stock in 1777: 240 copies (*BQ* 7).

COPIES: G⁴, L.

---

402 Bushe, Amyas, *Socrates*   1762

SOCRATES, | A | DRAMATIC | POEM. | BY | AMYAS BUSHE, ESQ. A.M. | FELLOW OF THE ROYAL SOCIETY. | GLASGOW: | PRINTED BY ROBERT AND ANDREW FOULIS, | PRINTERS TO THE UNIVERSITY, | M.DCC.LXII.

FORMULA: Foolscap 8⁰: a⁴ A–F⁸ G⁴.

PAPER: Medium quality; marks 5/ii; size 16½ × 13 in.

TYPE: RLP 1, RB 2.

VARIANT: Issue in Pot 8⁰:

   Paper: Medium-poor quality; marks 1/v.

NOTES: *Price*: Retail: (?) Foolscap, 1*s*. (*CP* 8).

COPIES: G⁴ (Foolscap), L (both issues).

---

403 Campbell, Archibald, Marquis of Argyll,   1762
Instructions to a Son, etc.

INSTRUCTIONS | To a | SON, | Containing | RULES of CONDUCT in Publick and | private LIFE, | Under the following Heads: | [*two columns of 3 lines each, separated by a vertical plain rule, 11*] | By ARCHIBALD Marquis of ARGYLE. | Addreſs'd to his Children, and to his eldeſt Son in | particular. | Written in the Year 1660, during his confinement. | To which are added by the ſame Noble Author: | [*two columns of 3 lines each, separated by a vertical plain rule, 11*] | GLASGOW: | PRINTED AND SOLD BY R. & A. FOULIS | MDCCLXII.

FORMULA: Post 12⁰ in sixes: π^2 A–M⁶ N⁴ (A2, A3 *signed* ' B2 ', ' B3 '; π1 *half-title*, N4 *blank*).

PAPER: Medium-good quality; marks 6/i; size of sheet 20 × 14¾ in.

TYPE: RE 2.

VARIANT: Issue on inferior paper, [? Crown] 12⁰:
   Paper: Poor quality; no marks.

NOTES: *Prices*: Wholesale: Post, 1*s*.; Crown, 6*d*. (*BQ* 7). Retail: (?) Post, 1*s*. 6*d*. (*CP* 11).
   Stock in 1777: Post, 36 copies; Crown, 178 copies (*BQ* 7).

COPIES: G⁴ (both issues).

1762   Cicero, *In M. Antonium I-II*, L   **404** †

MARCI TULLII | CICERONIS | IN | M. ANTONIUM | ORATIONES I ET II. | EX EDITIONE J. OLIVETI. | GLASGUAE, | IN AEDIBUS ACADEMICIS | EXCUDEBANT ROBER TUS ET ANDREAS FOULIS | M DCC LXII.

FORMULA: Foolscap 8⁰ in fours: π1 A–I⁴.

PAPER: Medium-good quality; marks 4/vi.

TYPE: RLP 1.

COPIES: G⁴.

1762   Dalrymple, David, Lord Hailes, *Memorials*   **405** †
                                   and Letters: James I

MEMORIALS | AND | LETTERS | RELATING TO THE | HISTORY OF BRITAIN | IN THE | REIGN | OF | JAMES THE FIRST. | PUBLISHED FROM THE ORIGINALS. | GLASGOW: | PRINTED BY ROBERT AND ANDREW FOULIS, | PRINTERS TO THE UNIVERSITY, | M.DCC.LXII.

FORMULA: Post 8⁰: a⁸ b² A–I⁸ K⁴.

PAPER: Good quality; marks 6/i.

TYPE: RLP 1, RB 2, RE 3.

NOTES: See Appendix B, letter 2 (pp. 397-8 below).

COPIES: G⁴ (copy missing), L.

406 Demosthenes, *Philippics*, G   1762

ΟΊ ΤΟΥ | ΔΗΜΟΣΘΕΝΟΥΣ | ΛΟΓΟΙ | ΦΙΛΙΠΠΙΚΟΙ | ΔΩΔΕΚΑ. | DEMOSTHENIS | ORATIONES | PHILIP PICAE | DUODECIM; | EO, JAM, ORDINE EDITAE, | QUO SUNT AB ORATORE DICTAE. | IN IMA PAGINA; SUBJECTAE SUNT | QUAEDAM EX LECTIONIBUS VARIANTIBUS | EDITIONIS APUD BENENATUM; | ET | EMENDATIONES NONNULLAE PROPONUNTUR. | GLASGUAE: | IN AEDIBUS ACADEMICIS | EXCUDE BANT ROBERTUS ET ANDREAS FOULIS | ACADE MIAE TYPOGRAPHI | M DCC LXII.

FORMULA: Foolscap 8⁰ in fours: a⁴ A–I⁴ k⁴ K–2K⁴ 2L1 (*pagination normal up to p.* 74 [k1ᵛ]; *then* '74a' *to* '74h' [k2–K1ᵛ]; *then normal again from p.* 75 [K2]).

PAPER: Medium-good quality; marks 4/v, 5/?; size of sheet $16\frac{1}{2} \times 13\frac{1}{4}$ in.

TYPE: GGP, GP, RE 3, RLP 1.

VARIANT: Issue in Pot 8⁰:
Paper: Medium-poor quality; marks 1/v.

NOTES: *Prices*: Wholesale: Foolscap, 2s. 6d.; Pot 1s. 6d. (*BQ* 3). Retail: (?) Foolscap, 3s. (*CP* 4).
Stock in 1777: Foolscap, 44 copies; Pot, 33 copies (*BQ* 3).

COPIES: G⁴ (both issues), L (Foolscap).

407 Euclid, *Elements I-VI, XI-XII, and Data*, E   1762

THE | ELEMENTS | OF | EUCLID, | VIZ. | THE FIRST SIX BOOKS, | TOGETHER WITH THE | ELEVENTH AND TWELFTH. | The Errors, by which THEON, or others, have long ago Vitiated | thefe Books, are Corrected, | And fome of EUCLID's Demonftrations are Reftored. | Alfo, to this SECOND EDITION is added | THE BOOK OF | EUCLID'S DATA. | In like manner Corrected. | BY | ROBERT SIMSON, M.D. | Emeritus Profeffor of Mathematics in the Univerfity | of Glafgow. | GLASGOW: | PRINTED BY ROBERT AND ANDREW FOULIS | PRINTERS TO THE UNIVERSITY | M.DCC.LXII.

FORMULA: [? Printing Demy] 8⁰: π⁴ A–C⁸(±C5) D–2F⁸ 2G1.

PAPER: Medium-poor quality; mark (?) BAH.

TYPE: RP 2, RSP 1, GP. Numerous woodcut diagrams.

COPIES: G⁴, L.

1762   Gay, John, *Fables* **408**

NOTES: Not seen. Listed by Duncan (p. 66, No. 297) as ' Gray's
[*sic*] Fables, 12mo.', possibly in error for the 8⁰ edition of 1761,
which he omits.

1762   George III, *His Majesty's Speech to Parliament* **409**

HIS | MAJESTY'S | MOST | GRACIOUS SPEECH | TO
BOTH | HOUSES | OF | PARLIAMENT, | ON | THURS
DAY THE TWENTY-FIFTH DAY OF | NOVEMBER,
M.DCC.LXII. | GLASGOW: | PRINTED BY ROBERT AND
ANDREW FOULIS | PRINTERS TO THE UNIVERSITY
| M.DCC.LXII.

FORMULA: Foolscap 4⁰: A–B⁴.

PAPER: Medium quality; marks 4/vi.

TYPE: RE 3.

NOTES: *Price*: Wholesale: 2*d*. (*BQ* 10).
    Stock in 1777: 40 copies (*BQ* 10).
    Spotiswood, p. 86, speaks of ' The King's fpeech, 1776, [4⁰]
3d '; but since BQ, p. 10, lists only ' The King's fpeech 1762 '
this is probably a mistake.

COPIES: G⁴, L.

1762   Hutcheson, Francis, *Synopsis Metaphysicae*, L **410**

SYNOPSIS | METAPHYSICAE, | ONTOLOGIAM | ET |
PNEUMATOLOGIAM | COMPLECTENS. | EDITIO
QUINTA. | GLASGUAE, | IN AEDIBUS ACADEMICIS
| EXCUDEBANT ROBERTUS ET ANDREAS FOULIS |
M.DCC.LXII.

FORMULA: Foolscap 8⁰ in fours: a⁴ A–T⁴.

PAPER: Medium-good quality; marks 4/v, 5/ii; size of sheet
16¾ × 13 in.

TYPE: RLP 1, RB 2.

NOTES: *Price*: Retail: 2*s*. 6*d*. (advertisement in No. 546,
Hutcheson 1772).

COPIES: G⁴

1762   Swift, Jonathan, *Directions to Servants* **411**

NOTES: Not seen. Listed by Duncan (p. 66, No. 293) as
' Directions to Servants in general, &c. By the Rev. Dr Swift,

small fools. 8vo. fine, 6d. common, 3d.' These wholesale prices are taken from *BQ* (p. 10), which lists 150 copies of the fine and 256 of the common remaining in 1777.

† 412 Thomas More, St, *Utopia*, E   1762

UTOPIA: | OR THE | HAPPY REPUBLIC: | A | PHILO SOPHICAL ROMANCE, | IN TWO BOOKS. | [*two columns of contents, 7 and 6 lines, separated by a vertical plain double rule, 24*] | WRITTEN IN LATIN | BY SIR THOMAS MORE, | Lord High Chancellor of England. | TRANSLATED INTO ENGLISH | BY GILBERT BURNET D.D. | Sometime Profeſſor of Divinity in the Univerſity of Glaſgow, | afterwards Biſhop of Sarum. | GLASGOW: | PRINTED BY ROBERT AND ANDREW FOULIS, | M.DCC.LXII.

FORMULA: Foolscap 8⁰ in fours: a–c⁴ A–U⁴.

PAPER: Medium-good quality; marks 4, 5/v, ii; size of sheet 16½ × 13 in.

TYPE: RLP 1, RB 2.

VARIANT: Issue on inferior paper, Foolscap 8⁰:
  Paper: Poor quality; marks 5/v.

NOTES: *Prices*: Wholesale: common, 6*d*. (*BQ* 7). Retail: (? Issue), 1*s*. (*CP* 9).
  Stock in 1777: common, 122 copies (*BQ* 7).

COPIES: G⁴ (common), L (both issues).

† 413 Xenophon, *Hellenica and Agesilaus*, G and L   1762

ΤΑ ΤΟΥ | ΞΕΝΟΦΩΝΤΟΣ | ʽΕΛΛΗΝΙΚΑ· | ΚΑΙ | ʽΟ ΑΓΗΣΙΛΑΟΣ. | [*plain rule, 25*] | XENOPHONTIS | GRAE CORUM | RES GESTAE; [' ;' *sometimes missing in Vol.* I] | ET | AGESILAUS. | CUM ANNOTATIONIBUS EDWARDI WELLS. | TOMIS QUATUOR. | TOM. I [II] [III] [IV]. | GLASGUAE: | IN AEDIBUS ACADEMICIS | EXCUDEBANT ROBER TUS ET ANDREAS FO [sic *in some copies of vol.* I, ' FOULIS ' *elsewhere*] | ACADEMIAE [' ACDAEMIAE ' *in Vol.* IV] TYPO GRAPHI | M.DCC.LXII. [*different settings*].

FORMULA: Foolscap 8⁰:
  Vol. I: π1 A–Q⁸ (*Vols.* I–IV *signed* ' TOM. I [. . . IV].' *on* \$1 *except title-pages*; Q8 *blank*).
  Vol. II: π1 A–U⁸.
  Vol. III: π1 A–X⁸ Y⁴.
  Vol. IV: π1 A–K⁸ L⁴ M–S⁸ T⁴ (T4 *advertisements*).

PAPER: Medium-good quality; marks 4/v, 5/ii.

TYPE: GGP, RP 2, RLP 1. Greek and Latin on facing pages.

VARIANTS : Some copies seem to be on paper that is of slightly inferior quality throughout, same marks; but this may be accidental.

Issue on fine paper, Greek only, not seen (*BQ* 4).

NOTES: *Prices*: Wholesale: fine, G and L, 7*s*. 6*d*.; fine, G only, 4*s*. 8*d*. (*BQ* 4). Retail: G and L, 10*s*. (*CP* 4).

Stock in 1777: G and L, 24 copies; G only, 170 copies; imperfect sets, G and L, 5; odd volumes, some imperfect, 160 (*BQ* 4).

COPIES: G⁴, L (each with copies on the two slightly differing papers).

1763   Barr, James, *An Easy Introduction to Latin* 414
Grammar

AN EASY | INTRODUCTION | TO | LATIN GRAMMAR | BY | JAMES BARR, A.M. | RECTOR OF THE GRAMMAR-SCHOOL | OF GLASGOW. | [*quotations, 4 lines*] | GLASGOW: | PRINTED BY ROBERT AND ANDREW FOULIS | M.DCC.LXIII.

FORMULA: [? Crown] 8⁰ in fours: π² A–2E⁴ 2F².

PAPER: Poor quality; no marks.

TYPE: RLP 1, RB 2, RP 2.

COPIES: G⁴.

1763   Bell, John, *Travels from St Petersburg* 415 †

[*Vol.* 1:] TRAVELS | FROM | Sᵀ. PETERSBURG | IN | RUSSIA, | TO | DIVERSE PARTS | OF | ASIA. | IN | TWO VOLUMES. | BY | JOHN BELL, | OF ANTERMONY. | VOLUME I. | CONTAINING | [*two columns of contents, 4 lines each, separated by a vertical double plain rule, 17*] | GLASGOW: | PRINTED FOR THE AUTHOR BY ROBERT AND ANDREW FOULIS | PRINTERS TO THE UNIVERSITY | M.DCC.LXIII. | Sold by R. & A. FOULIS, and A. STALKER at GLASGOW; KINCAID & BELL | at EDINBURGH; A. MILLER, J. NOURSE, T. BECKET & P. A de HONDT, | and C. HENDERSON in LONDON; J. LEAKE, and J. FREDERICK at BATH; | and T. CADELL at BRISTOL.

[*Vol.* II *omits lines 10–11* ('IN | TWO VOLUMES. | ')*; changes* 'VOLUME I.' *to* 'VOLUME II.'*; has different contents in*

5 lines each, separated by a vertical plain rule, 21; and changes ' BELL ' to ' BELL ' in the fifth line of the imprint.]

FORMULA: [? Writing Demy] 4⁰:

Vol. I: a–b⁴ c² A–2Y⁴ (*signed ' VOL. I.' on b–2Y $1; 2Y4 advertisements*).

Vol. II: π1 A–3G⁴ 3H² (*signed ' VOL. II.' on A–3H $1; 3H2 errata*).

Plate: folding map, signed '*Jo Riddell Sculp* ', no imprint, faces Vol. I A1.

PAPER: Medium-good quality; most of the book on marks 7/i, but 9/i, 6/i and 1 (large)/v also found.

TYPE: RGP 2, RSP 1, RE 3, RLP 1, RB 2.

NOTES: The dedication dated 1 October 1762.

Price: Retail: 21s. (*CP* 7).

COPIES: G⁴, L.

416 Denina, Carlo, *Discorso sopra le vicende della*   1763
Letteratura, I

DISCORSO | SOPRA LE | VICENDE | DELLA | LETTERA TURA, | DEL | SIG. CARLO DENINA, | PROFESSORE DI ELOQUENZA, E UMANE LETTERE | NELLE | REGIE SCUOLE DI TORINO. | EDIZIONE SECONDA. | [*quotation, 1 line*] | IN GLASGUA, | DELLA STAMPA DI ROBERTO ED ANDREA FOULIS | M.DCC.LXIII.

FORMULA: Foolscap 8⁰: A–P⁸ Q⁴ (B3 *signed ' 3 ' in some copies*).

PAPER: Medium-good quality; marks 4/vi; size of sheet 16¾ × 13 in.

TYPE: RLP 1, RB 2, RE 3, GB.

NOTES: *Prices*: Wholesale: 2s. 6d. (*BQ* 8). Retail: 3s. (*CP* 6). *Stock in 1777*: 4 copies (*BQ* 8).

COPIES: G⁴, L.

417 Fénelon, *Pious Thoughts concerning God, etc.*, E   1763

PIOUS THOUGHTS | CONCERNING THE | KNOW LEDGE | AND | LOVE OF GOD, | AND OTHER HOLY EXERCISES: | BY THE LATE | ARCHBISHOP OF CAM BRAY. | TOGETHER WITH A | LETTER | OF | CHRIS TIAN INSTRUCTION | BY A LADY. | TRANSLATED FROM THE FRENCH. | [*quotation, 2 lines*] | FIRST PRINTED IN M.DCC.XX. | GLASGOW: | PRINTED BY ROBERT AND ANDREW FOULIS | M.DCC.LXIII.

FORMULA: Foolscap 8⁰ in fours: π^2 A–O⁴ P².
PAPER: Medium quality; marks 4/vi, 5/vi.
TYPE: RLP 1, RP 2.
VARIANT: Issue in Pot 8⁰:
Paper: Medium-poor quality; marks 1/v.
NOTES: *Prices*: Wholesale: Foolscap, 1*s.* 2*d.*; Pot, 9*d.* (*BQ* 7).
Retail: (?) Foolscap, 1*s.* 6*d.* (*CP* 8).
Stock in 1777: Foolscap, 16 copies; Pot, 96 copies (*BQ* 7).
COPIES: G⁴ (Foolscap), G² (Pot).

1763   Guarini, Giambattista, *Il Pastor Fido*, I **418**

IL | PASTOR FIDO | TRAGICOMMEDIA | PASTORALE | DEL | CAVALIER GUARINI. | IN GLASGUA, | DELLA STAMPA DI ROBERTO ED ANDREA FOULIS, | E SI VENDONO APPRESSO LORO, | E GIOVANNI BALFOUR IN EDINBURGO, | M.DCC.LXIII.
FORMULA: Foolscap 8⁰: A–Q⁸ R⁴.
Plates: Plates numbered ' 1 ' to ' 7 ', variously placed, plate-marks c. 78 × c. 49; the first one (only) signed ' *Se. le Clerc f* '.
PAPER: Medium-good quality; marks 4/vi. Plates on an almost identical paper.
TYPE: RLP 1.
VARIANT: Issue in Pot 8⁰:
Paper: Medium-poor quality; marks 1/v.
NOTES: *Prices*: Wholesale, ' con fig.': Foolscap, 2*s.* 6*d.*; Pot, 1*s.* 6*d.* (*BQ* 8). Retail, ' con fig.': (?) Foolscap, 3*s.* (*CP* 6).
Stock in 1777: Foolscap, 67 copies; Pot, 138 copies (*BQ* 8).
COPIES: G⁴ (Pot), L (both issues).

1763   Longinus, *On the Sublime*, G and L **419**

ΤΟ ΤΟΥ | ΔΙΟΝΥΣΙΟΥ | ΛΟΓΓΙΝΟΥ | ΠΕΡΙ | ΎΨΟΥΣ | ΎΠΟΜΝΗΜΑ. | EX EDITIONE TERTIA | ZACHARIAE PEARCE, | Episcopi Bangoriensis, | EXPRESSUM. | GLASGUAE: | IN AEDIBUS ACADEMICIS | EXCUDEBANT ROBERTUS ET ANDREAS FOULIS | ACADEMIAE TYPOGRAPHI | M.DCC.LXIII.
FORMULA: Foolscap 8⁰: π^4 A–P⁸ (π1 *half-title*, P8 *advertisements*).

PAPER: Medium-good quality; marks 4/vi; size of sheet $16\frac{1}{2} \times 13$ in.

TYPE: GGP, RP 2, GP, RLP 1. Greek and Latin on facing pages.

VARIANTS: Issue in 8⁰ on inferior paper, not seen (*BQ* 3).

Issue in Foolscap 4⁰:

Formula: Foolscap 4⁰: π⁴ A–2G⁴ (2D3 [O3 *of the* 8⁰] *signed* ' O '; π1 *half-title*, 2G4 *advertisements*).

Paper: Same as the 8⁰.

NOTES: *Prices*: Wholesale: 8⁰, fine, 2*s*. 6*d*.; 8⁰, common, 1*s*. 2*d*.; 4⁰, 5*s*. (*BQ* 3). Retail: 8⁰, (?) fine, 3*s*.; 4⁰, 6*s*. (*CP* 3).

Stock in 1777: 8⁰, fine, 2 copies; 8⁰, common, 18 copies; 4⁰, 54 copies (*BQ* 3).

COPIES: G⁴ (Foolscap 8⁰, 4⁰), L (Foolscap 8⁰, 4⁰).

420 Moor, James, *On the End of Tragedy*   1763

ON THE | END | OF | TRAGEDY, | ACCORDING TO | ARISTOTLE; | AN ESSAY, | IN TWO PARTS; | READ TO A LITERARY SOCIETY IN GLASGOW, | AT THEIR WEEKLY MEETINGS WITHIN | THE COLLEGE. | BY JAMES MOOR LLD. PROFESSOR OF GREEK | IN THE UNIVER SITY OF GLASGOW. | GLASGOW, | PRINTED BY ROBERT AND ANDREW FOULIS | PRINTERS TO THE UNIVER SITY | M.DCC.LXIII.

FORMULA: [? Writing Demy] 8⁰ in fours: π² A–E⁴ F² (π1 *half-title*).

PAPER: Medium-good quality; marks 8/i.

TYPE: RGP 2, RE 3, GGP. Text (but not the advertisements on F2ᵛ) without long ſ.

COPIES: G⁴, L.

421 Philips, Ambrose, *Pastorals*   1763

PASTORALS | BY | MR. AMBROSE PHILIPS. | [*quotation, 2 lines*] | GLASGOW: | PRINTED BY ROBERT AND ANDREW FOULIS | M.DCC.LXIII.

FORMULA: Foolscap 8⁰: A–B⁸ C².

PAPER: Medium quality; marks 4/vi.

TYPE: RLP 1.

Also issued with John Philips's *Poems on Several Occasions*, 1763 (No. 422), q.v., ' VARIANTS '.

NOTES: *Prices*: Wholesale: 2*d*. (*BQ* 9). Retail: 6*d*. (*CP* 7).
   Stock in 1777: 13 copies (*BQ* 9).
COPIES: G⁴.

1763   Philips, John, *Poems on Several Occasions* **422**

POEMS | ON | SEVERAL | OCCASIONS. | VIZ. | [*two
columns, 4 and 3 lines, separated by a vertical double plain rule, 14;
left:*) An ODE to Henry Saint | John, Efq; | The SPLENDID
SHIL-|LING. | [*right:*] BLEINHEIM. | And | CYDER. In two Books.
| BY | MR. JOHN PHILIPS, | STUDENT OF CHRIST-
CHURCH, OXON. | To which is added, | HIS LIFE, | By
Mr. GEORGE SEWELL. | GLASGOW: | PRINTED BY ROBERT
AND ANDREW FOULIS | M.DCC.LXIII.
FORMULA: Foolscap 8⁰: π² A⁸(–A1) B–G⁸ H² (π1 *half-title*,
π2 *title-page*).
PAPER: Medium quality; marks 4/vi.
TYPE: RLP 1, RB 2.
VARIANTS: Another state, without half-title:
   Formula: A–G⁸ H² (A1 *title-page, same setting as above*).
   Issue including Ambrose Philips's *Pastorals*, 1763 (No. 421):
   Title-page: [The right-hand column of contents reads:]
BLEINHEIM, | CYDER. In two Books. | Six PASTORALS. |
   Formula: A–G⁸ H² ²A–B⁸ ²C² (i.e. *the second state of this book,
with the title-page reset, plus No. 421. The reset title-page must
refer to No. 421, in spite of the obvious confusion of the two Philipses*).
NOTES: *Prices*: Wholesale: 9*d*. (*BQ* 10). Retail: 1*s*. (*CP* 7).
   Stock in 1777: 7 copies (*BQ* 10).
COPIES: G⁴ (which has all the variants described).

1763   Plato, *Republic*, E **423**

THE | REPUBLIC | OF | PLATO. | IN TEN BOOKS. |
TRANSLATED FROM THE GREEK BY | H. SPENS, D.D.
| WITH A PRELIMINARY DISCOURSE CONCERNING
THE PHILO-|SOPHY OF THE ANCIENTS BY THE
TRANSLATOR. | GLASGOW: | PRINTED BY ROBERT
AND ANDREW FOULIS | PRINTERS TO THE UNIVER
SITY | M.DCC.LXIII.
FORMULA: [? Writing Demy] 4⁰: *a*⁴ b–e⁴ f² A–3H⁴ (2R2
signed ' R2 '; 3H4 *advertisements*).

PAPER: Good quality; marks 6/?, 7/1 (cf. the Post marks in another Demy book, No. 415, Bell 1763.)

TYPE: RE 3, RDP, RSP 1, RLP 1. There is also a row of flowers (Nonpareil crosses) on *a*4, not found elsewhere in Foulis books.

VARIANT: Issue in Foolscap 4º:
Paper: Medium-good quality; marks 4/v, 4/vi.

NOTES: *Prices*: Wholesale: Demy, 9*s.*; Foolscap, 6*s.* (*BQ* 5). Retail: (? issue), 10*s.* 6*d.* (*CP* 7).

Stock in 1777: Demy, 9 copies; Foolscap, 51 copies; imperfect copies, 3 (*BQ* 5).

COPIES: G⁴, L (each has both issues).

---

424 Plautus, *Comedies*, L   1763

MARCI | ACCII | PLAUTI | COMOEDIAE. | EX EDITIONE | JOH. FREDERICI GRONOVII. | TOM. I [II] [III]. | GLAS GUAE: | IN AEDIBUS ACADEMICIS | EXCUDEBANT ROBERTUS ET ANDREAS FOULIS | ACADEMIAE TYPOGRAPHI | M DCC LXIII. [*Largely the same setting.*]

FORMULA: Foolscap 8º:
Vol. I: π² A–S⁸ T² (*signed* ' VOL. I.' *on* T1).
Vol. II: π1 A–S⁸ T⁴ (*signed* ' VOL. II.' *on* A–T $1; N2 *signed* ' M2 '*).
Vol. III: π1 A–Q⁸ R⁶ (*signed* ' VOL. III.' *on* A–R $1; R6 *advertisements*).

PAPER: Medium quality; marks 4/vi 4/v, 5/iv; size of sheet 16½ × 13 in.

TYPE: RB 2, RLP 1. Without long f.

VARIANT: Issue on another quality of paper, not seen (*BQ* 1).

NOTES. *Prices*: Wholesale: fine, 6*s.* 6*d.*; common, 2*s.* 3*d.* (*BQ* 1). Retail: (?) fine, 9*s.* (*CP* 5).

Stock in 1777: fine, 211 copies; common, 127 copies; odd volumes, 26 (*BQ* 1).

COPIES: G⁴, L (both Foolscap).

---

425 Tasso, Torquato, *Aminta*, I   1763

NOTES: Not seen. Listed by Duncan (p. 67, No. 310) as ' Aminta, Favola Bofcareccia di Torquato Taffo, fools. 8vo. fine, 1*s.*' The size and wholesale price are taken from *BQ* (p. 8), which lists 30 copies, remaining in 1777, ' con fig.' Retail price: 1*s.* 6*d.*, ' con fig.' (*CP* 6).

1763   Tasso, Torquato, *La Gierusalemme Liberata*, I **426** †

LA | GIERUSALEMME | LIBERATA | DI | TORQUATO
TASSO: | Con le Figure di Sebastiano Clerc. [*this line omitted
in Vol.* II] | IN DUE VOLUMI. | VOL. I [II]. | IN GLASGUA,
| DELLA STAMPA DI ROBERTO ED ANDREA FOULIS,
| E SI VENDONO APPRESSO LORO, | E GIOVANNI
BALFOUR IN EDINBURGO. | M.DCC.LXIII.

FORMULA: Foolscap 8⁰:
    Vol. I: π^2 a⁴ A–U⁸ X⁴ Y² (π1 *blank*).
    Vol. II: π^2 A–Z⁸ 2A² (*signed* ' Vol. II.' *on* A–2A $1; π1 *blank*).
    Plates: two frontispieces and twenty plates, numbered ' 1 '
to ' 20 ', unsigned, plate marks, c. 79 × c. 50, variously placed.

PAPER: Medium-good quality; marks 5/iv, 4/vi.

TYPE: RLP 1, RB 2.

VARIANT: Issue in Pot 8⁰:
    Title-page: [*Without the line* ' Con le Figure di Sebastiano
Clerc.', *though the plates are in fact present in all copies of this
issue seen.*]
    Paper: Medium quality; marks 1/v.

NOTES: *Prices*: Wholesale: ' con figure ', Foolscap, 5s.; Pot,
3s. 6d. (*BQ* 8). Retail: ' con figure ', (?) Foolscap, 6s. (*CP* 6).

COPIES: G⁴ (Foolscap), L (Pot).

1764   Aurelius Antoninus, Marcus, *Meditations*, E **427** †

THE | MEDITATIONS | OF THE EMPEROR | MARCUS
AURELIUS | ANTONINUS. | NEWLY tranflated from the
GREEK: with | NOTES, and an account of his LIFE. | FOURTH
EDITION. | GLASGOW, | PRINTED BY ROBERT & ANDREW
FOULIS | PRINTERS TO THE UNIVERSITY | M DCC LXIV. [*Vol.* II
title-page reads the same, except ' VOLUME SECOND.' *in place
of lines 6, 7 and 8; some of the same type used.*]

FORMULA: Foolscap 8⁰:
    Vol. I: A–P⁸ Q⁴.
    Vol. II: A–O⁸ P⁴.

PAPER: Medium quality; marks 4/vi; size of sheet $16\frac{1}{2} \times 13\frac{1}{4}$ in.

TYPE: RE 2, RB 2, RLP 1.

VARIANT: Issue on inferior paper, Foolscap 8⁰:
    Paper: Poor quality; no marks; size of sheet $16\frac{1}{2} \times 13$ in.

NOTES: *Prices*: Wholesale: fine, 3*s*.; common, 2*s*. (*BQ* 5). Retail (?) fine, 4*s*. (*CP* 9).

Stock in 1777: fine, 99 copies; common, 9 copies (*BQ* 5).

COPIES: G⁴ (fine; common Vol. I), L (fine), O (common).

428 Butler, Joseph, *The Analogy of Religion*   1764

THE | ANALOGY | OF | RELIGION, | NATURAL AND REVEALED, | TO THE | CONSTITUTION AND COURSE OF NATURE. | IN TWO VOLUMES. | To the firſt of which are added | TWO BRIEF DISSERTATIONS: | I. OF PERSONAL IDENTITY. | II. OF THE NATURE OF VIRTUE. | BY | JOSEPH BUTLER, LL.D. | LATE LORD BISHOP OF DURHAM. | [*quotation, 3 lines*] | VOL. I [II]. | GLASGOW: | PRINTED BY ROBERT AND ANDREW FOULIS | PRINTERS TO THE UNIVERSITY [*this line omitted in Vol.* II] | M.DCC.LXIV.

FORMULA: Foolscap 8⁰:
   Vol. I: π^4 A–N⁸.
   Vol. II: A–N⁸ (*signed* ' VOL. II.' *on* B–N $1; N8 *advertisements*).

PAPER: Medium-good quality; marks 4/vi; size of sheet $16\frac{1}{2} \times 13$ in.

TYPE: RLP 1, RP 2, RB 2, GB.

COPIES: G⁴.

429 Craig, William, *The Character and Obligations*   1764
of a Minister

THE | CHARACTER | AND | OBLIGATIONS | OF A | MINISTER | OF THE | GOSPEL. | A SERMON. | To which is added, | A | CHARGE | TO THE | MINISTER AND THE CONGREGATION. | BY | WILLIAM CRAIG, D.D. | ONE OF THE MINISTERS OF GLASGOW. | GLASGOW: | PRINTED AND SOLD BY R. AND A. FOULIS | M.DCC.LXIV.

FORMULA: Foolscap 8⁰: π^2 A–D⁸ (π1 *half-title;* D8 *blank*).

PAPER: Medium quality; marks 4/vi, 4/v; size of sheet $16\frac{1}{2} \times 13$ in.

TYPE: RP 2.

NOTES: *Publication*: *GJ*, 6 December 1764: ' *This day was Publifhed*, And fold by R. and A. FOULIS, J. GILMOUR. D. BAXTER, and other Bookfellers in Glafgow. . . .'

COPIES: G⁴, L.

1764   [Anon.], *The History of the Feuds and Conflicts* **430** *among the Clans*

THE | HISTORY | OF THE | FEUDS | AND | CONFLICTS | AMONG | THE CLANS | IN THE | NORTHERN PARTS OF SCOTLAND | AND IN THE | WESTERN ISLES; | FROM THE YEAR M.XXXI. UNTO M.DC.XIX. | Now firft publifhed from a MANUSCRIPT, wrote in the | reign of King JAMES VI. | GLASGOW: | PRINTED BY ROBERT AND ANDREW FOULIS | M.DCC.LXIV.

FORMULA: Foolscap 8⁰: π^2 A–I⁸ K².

PAPER: Medium quality; marks 4/vi; size of sheet 16 × 13 in.

TYPE: RP 2, RSP 1.

VARIANT: Issue on inferior paper, [? Pot] 8⁰:
Paper: Poor quality; no marks.

NOTES: *Prices*: Wholesale: ' f[oolscap]. 8vo. common. 9d.' (*BQ* 7). Retail: (? issue), 1*s*. (*CP* 10).
Stock in 1777: (? issue), 194 copies (*BQ* 7).

COPIES: G⁴ (both issues).

1764   Hutcheson, Francis, *Logicae Compendium*, L **431**

LOGICAE | COMPENDIUM. | PRAEFIXA EST | DISSER TATIO | DE | PHILOSOPHIAE ORIGINE, | EJUSQUE | INVENTORIBUS AUT EXCULTORIBUS | PRAECIPUIS. | GLASGUAE: | IN AEDIBUS ACADEMICIS | EXCUDE BANT ROBERTUS ET ANDREAS FOULIS | ACADEMIAE TYPOGRAPHI | M.DCC.LXIV.

FORMULA: Foolscap 8⁰ in fours: π^2 A–N⁴ (N1, N2 *signed* ' G ', ' G2 ', *with the* ' N ' *stamped in over the* ' G ' *on* N1; D2 *unsigned;* π1 *half-title*).

PAPER: Medium quality; marks 5/v; size of sheet $16\frac{1}{2}$ × 13 in.

TYPE: RE 2, RLP 1.

NOTES: Listed by Duncan (p. 68, No. 315) as ' Editio quinta '. This is in fact only the third edition listed by Duncan (or found by me), none of which has the edition number on the title-page.

COPIES: G⁴.

† **432** Hutcheson, Francis, *A Short Introduction to*   1764
Moral Philosophy

A SHORT | INTRODUCTION | TO | MORAL PHILO SOPHY, | IN THREE BOOKS; | CONTAINING THE | ELEMENTS OF ETHICKS | AND THE | LAW OF NATURE. | BY FRANCIS HUTCHESON, LLD. | LATE PROFESSOR OF PHILOSOPHY IN | THE UNIVERSITY OF GLAS GOW. | TRANSLATED FROM THE LATIN. | THIRD EDITION. | VOL. I [II]. | GLASGOW, | PRINTED BY ROBERT & ANDREW FOULIS | PRINTERS TO THE UNIVERSITY. | M DCC LXIV. [*Different settings.*]

FORMULA: Foolscap 8⁰:
Vol. I: a⁸ A–L⁸ M⁶ (M6 *blank*).
Vol. II: π^2 A² B–M⁸ N⁴ (*signed* ' VOL. II.' *on* A–N $1; π1 *blank*, N4 *advertisements*).

PAPER: Medium-good quality; marks 4/vi; size of sheet 16½ × 13 in.

TYPE: RLP 1, RB 2, RP 2.

VARIANT: Issue in Pot 8⁰:
Paper: Medium-poor quality; marks 1/?v.

COPIES: G⁴ (both issues), L (Pot).

433 Hyde, Edward, Earl of Clarendon, *Essays*   1764

NOTES: Not seen. Listed by Duncan (p. 68. No. 314) as ' Clarendon's Effays, 12mo.'

434 Sherlock, William, *A Discourse concerning the*   1764
Happiness of Good Men

A | DISCOURSE | CONCERNING THE | HAPPINESS OF GOOD MEN, | AND THE | PUNISHMENT OF THE WICKED, | IN THE | NEXT WORLD; | Under the following HEADS: Viz. | [*two columns of contents, 10 and 11 lines, separated by a vertical plain rule, 37; in Vol.* II *the line endings are not exactly the same*] | By WILLIAM SHERLOCK, D.D. | LATE DEAN OF ST. PAUL'S. | IN TWO VOLUMES. | VOL. I [II]. | GLAS GOW | PRINTED BY ROBERT AND ANDREW FOULIS | M.DCC.LXIV. [*Different settings.*]

FORMULA: Foolscap 8⁰:
    Vol. I: π^2 A–O⁸ P².
    Vol. II: π^2 A–M⁸ N⁴ (*signed* ' VOL. II.' *on* A–N $1).
PAPER: Medium-good quality; marks ⁴̣/vi.
TYPE: RLP I.
COPIES: G⁴.

1764   Xenophon, *Anabasis*, G and L **435 †**

TOΥ | ΞΕΝΟΦΩΝΤΟΣ | 'Η TOΥ | ΚΥΡΟΥ | ΑΝΑΒΑΣΙΣ. | [*plain rule, 27*] | XENOPHONTIS | EXPEDITIO | CYRI. | TOMIS QUATUOR. | EX EDITIONE T. HUTCHINSON. | [*quotation, 3 lines*] | TOM. I [II] [III] [IV]. | GLASGUAE: | IN AEDIBUS ACADEMICIS | EXCUDEBANT ROBERTUS ET ANDREAS FOULIS | ACADEMIAE TYPOGRAPHI | M.DCC.LXIV. [*Same setting.*]

FORMULA: Foolscap 8⁰:
    Vol. I: π^2 A–Q⁸ R⁴ (*Vols.* I–IV *signed* ' TOM. I [. . . IV].' *on* $1 *except title-pages;* π1 *half-title,* R4 *advertisements*).
    Vol. II: π^2 A–Q⁸ (Q 3 *unsigned;* π1 *half-title*).
    Vol. III: π^2 A–P⁸ Q⁴ (π1 *half-title,* Q 4 *advertisements*).
    Vol. IV: π^2 A–R⁸ (π1 *half-title*).
PAPER: Medium-good quality; marks 4/vi, 5/v.
TYPE: RP 2, GGP, RLP I. Greek and Latin on facing pages.
VARIANTS: Issue on common paper, Greek and Latin not seen (*BQ* 5).
    Issue on fine paper, Greek only, not seen (*BQ* 5).
NOTES: *Prices:* Wholesale: G only, fine, 4*s.* 8*d.* (*BQ* 5). Retail: G and L, (?) fine, 10*s.* (*CP* 4).
    Stock in 1777: G only, fine, 10 copies; odd volumes, 26 (*BQ* 5).
COPIES: G⁴ L (both Foolscap, fine).

1765   Addison, Joseph, *Cato* **436**

CATO | A | TRAGEDY. | BY | JOSEPH ADDISON, Efq; | [*quotation, 9 lines*] | GLASGOW | PRINTED AND SOLD BY ROB. & AND. FOULIS. | * M.DCC.LXV.

FORMULA: Foolscap 8⁰: A–E⁸ (*signed ' * ' on* $1; A4 *unsigned;* E8 *advertisements*). *Also found* (G²) *without the ' * ' signatures on an apparently identical Foolscap paper*).

PAPER: Medium-good quality; marks 4/?v.

TYPE: RB 2, RLP 1.

VARIANT: Issue in Pot 8⁰:
  Title-page: [*Type disturbed in the penultimate line.*]
  Formula: (*without ' * ' signatures*).
  Paper: Poor quality; marks 1/?.

COPIES: G⁴ (Pot); G², O (Foolscap).

437 Barnard, Sir John, *A Present for an Apprentice* 1765

A | PRESENT | FOR AN | APPRENTICE: | OR | A SURE GUIDE to gain both Efteem and Eftate; | WITH | RULES for his conduct to his Mafter, and | in the World. | Under the following Heads: | [*two columns of contents, 14 lines each, separated by a vertical plain double rule, 47*] | By a late LORD MAYOR of London. | GLASGOW: | PRINTED BY ROBERT AND ANDREW FOULIS | M.DCC.LXV.

FORMULA: [? Crown] 12⁰ in sixes: π² A–F⁶ G⁴.

PAPER: Medium-poor quality; no marks.

TYPE: RLP 1, RB 2.

NOTES: *Price*: Wholesale: 3*d.* (*BQ* 9).
  Stock in 1777: 548 copies (*BQ* 9).

COPIES: G⁴.

438 Buchanan, George, *Paraphrasis Psalmorum* 1765
Davidis, L

GEORGII | BUCHANANI | PARAPHRASIS | PSALMO RUM | DAVIDIS | POETICA. | GLASGUAE: | IN AEDI BUS ACADEMICIS | EXCUDEBANT ROBERTUS ET ANDREAS FOULIS | ACADEMIAE TYPOGRAPHI | M.DCC.LXV.

FORMULA: Foolscap 8⁰: π² A–P⁸ Q⁶ (Q6 *advertisements*).

PAPER: Medium-good quality; marks 4/v; size of sheet 16¾ × 13 in.

TYPE: RB 2, RLP 1. Without long f.

VARIANT: Issue in Pot 8⁰:
  Paper: Poor quality; marks 1/?.

NOTES: *Prices*: Wholesale: Foolscap, 2*s*. 6*d*.; Pot, [not given] (*BQ* 2). Retail: (?) Foolscap, 3*s*. (*CP* 5).
Stock in 1777: Foolscap, 27 copies; Pot, 95 copies (*BQ* 2).

COPIES: G⁴ (both issues), L (Foolscap).

1765   Buirette de Belloy, Pierre-Laurent, *Le Siège de* **439**
Calais, F

LE | SIEGE | DE | CALAIS, | TRAGEDIE. | PAR M. DE
BELLOY. | Repréfentée pour la premiere fois, par les Comé
diens | Français ordinaires du Roi, le 13 Février 1765. | SUIVIE
DE NOTES HISTORIQUES. | [*quotation, 2 lines*] | A GLAS
GOW: | DE L'IMPRIMERIE DE R. ET A. FOULIS |
M DCC LXV.

FORMULA: Foolscap 8⁰: a⁸ A–F⁸ G² (G2 *advertisements*).

PAPER: Medium quality; marks 4/v; size of sheet 16½ × 13 in.

TYPE: RLP 1, RB 2, RE 3.

VARIANT: Issue on another, probably inferior, quality of
paper, not seen (*BQ* 9).

NOTES: *Prices*: Wholesale: fine, 9*d*; common, 6*d*. (*BQ* 9).
Retail: (?) fine, 1*s*. (*CP* 6).
Stock in 1777: fine, 31 copies; common, 255 copies (*BQ* 9).

COPIES: G⁴ (Foolscap).

1765, 1766   [Anon.], *The Confession of Faith, etc.* **440**

THE | CONFESSION of FAITH, | THE | LARGER AND
SHORTER | CATECHISMS, | WITH THE | SCRIPTURE-
PROOFS AT LARGE. | TOGETHER WITH | [*two columns of
contents, 6 lines each, separated by a vertical plain double rule, 20*]
| OF | PUBLICK AUTHORITY | IN THE | CHURCH OF
SCOTLAND. | WITH | ACTS OF ASSEMBLY AND PAR
LIAMENT, | RELATIVE TO, AND APPROBATIVE OF
THE SAME. | [*quotation, 4 lines*] | GLASGOW: | PRINTED
BY ROBERT AND ANDREW FOULIS, | FOR JOHN ORR
BOOKSELLER. | MDCCLXV.

FORMULA: [? Printing Demy] 8⁰: A–2P⁸ 2Q⁴ 2R1.

PAPER: Poor quality; no marks.

TYPE: RP 2, RSP 1, RLP 1, RB 2.

VARIANT: Issue dated 1766:

Title-page: [*Re-set; reads as above, with changes of lineation in the Contents and Quotation, down to the imprint, which reads:*] GLASGOW: | PRINTED BY ROBERT AND ANDREW FOULIS, | PRINTERS TO THE UNIVERSITY, | M.DCC.LXVI.

COPIES: G⁴ (both issues).

441 D'Alembert, Jean le Rond, *Sur la Destruction*   1765
des Jésuites, F

SUR LA | DESTRUCTION | DES | JESUITES | EN | FRANCE. | Par un AUTEUR défintéreffé. | [*quotations, 5 lines*] | A EDINBOURG | CHEZ J. BALFOUR LIBRAIRE; | DE L'IM PRIMERIE DE R. ET A. FOULIS | M DCC LXV.

FORMULA: Foolscap 8⁰ in fours: a⁴ A–U⁴.

PAPER: Medium-poor quality; marks 5/v; size of sheet 16 × 13 in.

TYPE: RP 2, RLP 1, RE 2, RE 3.

NOTES: *Price*: Wholesale: 1s. (*BQ* 10).
  Stock in 1777: 4 copies (*BQ* 10).

COPIES: G⁴, L.

442 Epictetus, *Manual*, G   1765

ΤΟ ΤΟΥ | ΕΠΙΚΤΗΤΟΥ | ΕΓΧΕΙΡΙΔΙΟΝ. | EX EDITIONE | JOANNIS UPTON | Accurate Expreffum. | GLASGUAE: | Excudebant R. et A. Foulis | MDCCLXV.

FORMULA: Foolscap 32⁰ in eights: A–F⁸.

PAPER: Medium-good quality; marks 4/v.

TYPE: GB.

NOTES: *Prices*: Wholesale: 9d. (*BQ* 3). Retail: 1s. (advertisement in No. 544, Hutcheson, 1772).
  Stock in 1777: 442 copies (*BQ* 3).

COPIES: G⁴, L.

443 Hales, John, *Works* and *Letters from the*   1765
Synod of Dort

THE | WORKS | OF THE | EVER MEMORABLE | MR. JOHN HALES | OF | EATON. | NOW FIRST COLLECTED TOGETHER. | IN THREE VOLUMES. | [*quotation, 5 lines*]

| VOL. I [II] [III]. | GLASGOW: | PRINTED BY ROBERT AND ANDREW FOULIS. | SOLD BY J. TONSON, A. MILLAR, AND D. WILSON, | LONDON; J. BALFOUR, EDINBURGH; AND | R. AND A. FOULIS, GLASGOW. | M.DCC.LXV.   [*Same settings.   On Vol.* III ²A1 *is a sub-title complete with imprint to Hales's* Letters from the Synod of Dort.]

FORMULA: Post 8⁰:

> Vol. I: a⁸ b² A–O⁸ P⁴ Q⁶ (Q 5 *errata*).
> Vol. II: π^2 A–X⁸ Y² (*signed* ' VOL. II.' *on* A–Y \$1).
> Vol. III: π^2 A–N⁸ O² ²A–I⁸ ²K⁴ (*signed* ' VOL. III.' *on* A–O \$1;
> O2 *half-title to the* Letters from the Synod of Dort.)

PAPER: Medium-good quality; marks 6/?.

TYPE: RSP 1, RP 2, GP, RB 2, GB.

VARIANTS: Issue in Foolscap 8⁰:

> *Paper*: Medium-good quality; marks 4/vi.
> Issue in Pot 8⁰:
> *Formula*: Vol. I (–a2, *dedication*).
> *Paper*: Medium quality; marks 1/v.
> Issue in [? Crown] 8⁰:
> *Paper*: Poor quality; no marks.

COPIES: G⁴ (Post, Foolscap, Pot), L (Post, Pot), C (Crown).

1765   Lactantius, *De Mortibus Persecutorum*, E **444**

A | RELATION | OF THE | DEATH | OF THE PRIMITIVE | PERSECUTORS. | Written originally in Latin by | L. C. F. LACTANTIUS. | Englifhed by | GILBERT BURNET D.D. | To which is prefixed a | DISCOURSE | CONCERNING | PERSECUTION. | GLASGOW: | PRINTED BY ROBERT AND ANDREW FOULIS | M DCC LXV.

FORMULA: [? Printing Demy] 18⁰ in twelves and sixes: A¹² B⁶ C¹² . . . I¹² K⁶ L⁶ M² N1.

PAPER: Medium-poor quality; no marks.

TYPE: RP 2.

NOTES: See No. 453 (Lactantius, 1766), VARIANT and NOTES.

COPIES: G².

1765   Milton, John, *Paradise Regained, etc.* **445**

PARADISE REGAIN'D | A | POEM, | IN | FOUR BOOKS. | TO WHICH IS ADDED | SAMSON AGONISTES; | AND | POEMS UPON SEVERAL OCCASIONS, | WITH A

TRACTATE OF | EDUCATION. | THE AUTHOR | JOHN
MILTON. | GLASGOW, | Printed and fold by ROBERT &
ANDREW FOULIS | M.DCC.LXV.

FORMULA: Pot 12⁰ in sixes: π^2 A–2H⁶ 2I⁴.

PAPER: Medium quality; marks 1/iv; size of sheet $15\frac{1}{4} \times 12\frac{1}{2}$ in.

TYPE: RB 2, RLP 1, GP.

COPIES: G⁴.

446 Milton, John, *Minor Poems*   1765

NOTES: Not seen.   Listed by Duncan (p. 68, No. 323) as
' Milton's Minor Poems, 12mo.' Possibly an extract from
No. 445 (Milton, 1765).

† 447 Dalrymple, David, Lord Hailes, *Memorials and*   1766
Letters: Charles I

MEMORIALS | AND | LETTERS | RELATING TO THE |
HISTORY OF BRITAIN | IN THE | REIGN | OF |
CHARLES THE FIRST. | PUBLISHED FROM THE
ORIGINALS. | GLASGOW: | PRINTED BY ROBERT
AND ANDREW FOULIS, | PRINTERS TO THE UNIVER
SITY, | M.DCC.LXVI.

FORMULA: Small Crown 8⁰: a–c⁸ A–M⁸ (*signed* ' VOL. II.' on
\$1 except a1, b1, c1, A1 and F1, ' VOL.' alone on F1).

PAPER: Medium-poor quality; no marks; size of sheet
$18\frac{3}{4} \times 14\frac{3}{4}$ in.

TYPE: RSP 2, RLP 1, RE 3.

VARIANT: There may have been an issue in Post 8⁰ as there was
of the companion volume, No. 448 (Dalrymple, 1766), but I
have not seen one among ten copies examined.

NOTES: Companion and, presumably, ' VOL. II.' to No. 448
(Dalrymple, 1766).   See Appendix B, letter 2 (pp. 397–8 below).

COPIES: G⁴, L.

448 Dalrymple, David, Lord Hailes, *Memorials and*   1766
Letters: James I

MEMORIALS | AND | LETTERS | RELATING TO THE |
HISTORY OF BRITAIN | IN THE | REIGN | OF | JAMES
THE FIRST. | PUBLISHED FROM THE ORIGINALS. |

THE SECOND EDITION, | CORRECTED AND EN
LARGED. | GLASGOW: | PRINTED BY ROBERT AND
ANDREW FOULIS, | PRINTERS TO THE UNIVERSITY,
| M.DCC.LXVI.

FORMULA: Post 8⁰: a–b⁸ A–M⁸.

PAPER: Medium-good quality; marks 3 dolphins in a crowned
shield over L V GERREVINK/i, 6/i.

TYPE: RSP 2, RLP 1, RE 3.

VARIANT: Issue in small Crown 8⁰:
Paper: Medium-poor quality; no marks; size of sheet
$18\frac{3}{4} \times 14\frac{3}{4}$ in.

NOTES: See Appendix B, letter 2 (pp. 397-8 below).

COPIES: G⁴, L (both Crown), C (Post).

1766   Dalrymple, David, Lord Hailes, *The Preserva-* **449** †
                                              tion of Charles II

AN | ACCOUNT | OF THE | PRESERVATION | OF KING
| CHARLES II. | AFTER THE | BATTLE of WORCESTER,
| DRAWN UP | BY | HIMSELF. | TO WHICH ARE ADDED,
| HIS LETTERS | TO | SEVERAL PERSONS. | GLASGOW:
| PRINTED BY ROBERT AND ANDREW FOULIS, | AND SOLD BY
JOHN BALFOUR BOOKSELLER | IN EDINBURGH. | M.DCC.LXVI.

FORMULA: Printing Demy 8⁰: a⁴ A–M⁸ (M8 *blank*).

PAPER: Medium-good quality; marks 9/i; size of sheet
$21\frac{1}{2} \times 17$ in.

TYPE: RE 3, RSP 2.

VARIANT: State with an altered imprint:
Title-page: [*From the same type as the title-page transcribed
above, but with the imprint altered to read:*] LONDON: | PRINTED
FOR WILLIAM SANDBY, | M.DCC.LXVI.

NOTES: See Appendix B, letter 2 (pp. 397-8 below).

Price: Wholesale: 1s. 6d. (*BQ* 11).
Stock in 1777: 7 copies, 1 of them imperfect (*BQ* 11).

COPIES: G⁴ (Glasgow imprint), L (London imprint).

1766   Dalrymple, William, *Christian Unity* **450**
                                  Illustrated, a Sermon

CHRISTIAN UNITY | ILLUSTRATED | AND | RECOM
MENDED, | FROM THE | EXAMPLE | OF THE | PRIMI

TIVE CHURCH. | A SERMON, | Preached before the synod of glas-|gow and ayr, at glasgow, October | 14th, 1766. | By WILLIAM DALRYMPLE, A.M. | ONE OF THE MINISTERS OF AYR. | GLASGOW, | PRINTED AND SOLD BY R. AND A. FOULIS | PRINTERS TO THE UNIVERSITY | M.DCC.LXVI.

formula: Foolscap 8⁰ in fours: π^2 A–D⁴ E² (π1 *half-title*).

paper: Medium-good quality; marks 4/v; size of sheet $16\frac{1}{2} \times 13$ in.

type: RSP 2.

notes: *Publication*: published by 20 November 1766 (*GJ*).
Price: Wholesale: 4*d*. (*BQ* 9).
Stock in 1777: 168 copies (*BQ* 9).
Duncan (p. 70, No. 357) lists the book under the year 1767 and not under 1766, but no 1767 copies have been seen and this is probably a mistake.

copies: G⁴, L.

† **451** Epictetus, *Discourses*, E   1766

THE | DISCOURSES | OF | EPICTETUS: | Collected and Preferved | BY | ARRIAN, | His Disciple. | IN FOUR BOOKS. | Tranflated from the Greek. | Printed in the Year, MDCCLXVI,

formula: [N.B. Original not seen; the following collation, taken from microfilm, is conjectural.] [? size 12⁰ in sixes]: [6 *leaves, the second signed* ' a2 ', *the third signed* ' Aa2 '] b⁴ A–2I⁶.

paper, type: [Not seen.]

notes: Duncan (p. 69, No. 346) lists ' The Manuel of Epictetus, 12mo.' under the year 1766; although it is not a translation of the *Manual*, this may be the book he refers to. Spotiswood (p. 92) lists ' Epictetus's Manuel ' as a duodecimo at 2*d*.
Looks like a Foulis book, though without imprint.

copies: HD (microfilm only seen).

452 Glasgow University, *Official Papers, etc.*   1766–1790

notes: Five volumes of quarto pamphlets in G² (Yy. b. 19, Yy. b. 20, Education S32 1776–G, Education S32 1778–G and Education S32 1785–G) contain a number of official University reports, briefs, etc., which may have been printed at the Foulis

Press. All are printed in Wilson type with a moderately high standard of press-work and typography; but they are without imprints and, since other Scotch printers owned Wilson material at this period, they are not necessarily Foulis books. Moreover, since most of them concern litigation, they are most likely to have been printed in Edinburgh by order of the Writer to the Signet. Only one of them, which is described below, is in the typographical style of the Foulis Press.

PROCESS | OF | DECLARATOR | M DCC LXXV. | CON CERNING | THE MANAGEMENT | OF | THE REVENUE | OF | GLASGOW COLLEGE: | AND CONCERNING | A VOTE IN THE COMITIA OF THE | UNIVERSITY OF GLASGOW. | WITH AN APPENDIX. | PRINTED JULY M DCC LXXVIII.

FORMULA: [? Crown] 4° in twos: $\pi 1$ $^2\pi^2$ A–4C^2(4C2 + χ1) 4D–4F^2.

PAPER: Medium-poor quality; no marks.

TYPE: RSP 2.

COPIES: G, L.

1766   Lactantius, *De Mortibus Persecutorum*, E **453**

A | RELATION | OF THE | DEATH | OF THE PRIMITIVE | PERSECUTORS. | Written originally in Latin by | L. C. F. LACTANTIUS. | Englifhed by | GILBERT BURNET, D.D. | To which is prefixed a | DISCOURSE | CONCERNING | PERSECUTION. | GLASGOW: | PRINTED BY ROBERT AND ANDREW FOULIS | M.DCC.LXVI.

FORMULA: Writing Medium 18° in twelves and sixes: A^{12} B^6 C^{12} . . . I^{12} K^6 L^6 M^2 N1.

PAPER: Medium-good quality; marks 7/ii; size of sheet $22\frac{1}{4} \times 17\frac{1}{2}$ in.

TYPE: RP 2.

VARIANT: *BQ* (p. 7) lists the book as a ' d[emy]. 18vo.' fine and common. This may refer to the editions of 1766 and 1765 (Nos. 453 and 444) respectively, or to separate issues of one of them.

NOTES: A line-for-line reprint of No. 444 (Lactantius, 1765), but not the same setting.

Prices: Wholesale: fine, 9*d*.; common, 4*d*. (*BQ* 7). Retail: (?) fine, 1*s*. 6*d*. (*CP* 8).

Stock in 1777: fine, 22 copies; common, 448 copies (*BQ* 7).

COPIES: G.

† **454** Milton, John, *Paradise Lost*   1766

PARADISE | LOST, | A | POEM | IN | TWELVE BOOKS. | THE AUTHOR | JOHN MILTON. | ACCORDING TO THE AUTHOR'S LAST | EDITION, IN THE YEAR 1674. | GLASGOW: | PRINTED BY ROBERT AND ANDREW FOULIS | M.DCC.LXVI. [*Vol.* ii *has* ' VOL. II.' *in place of lines 9 and 10.*]

FORMULA: Pot 12⁰:

Vol. i: a⁶ b^2 A–G¹² H⁶ (a1 *half-title*).

Vol. ii: I–P¹² Q⁴ (Q 3–4 *advertisements*).

PAPER: Medium quality; marks 5/iv; size of sheet $15\frac{1}{4} \times 12\frac{1}{2}$ in.

TYPE: RB 2, RLP 1.

COPIES: G⁴.

455 Moor, James, *Elementa Linguae Graecae*, L   1766

ELEMENTA | LINGUAE GRAECAE; | NOVIS, PLERUM QUE, REGULIS | TRADITA; | BREVITATE SUA MEMO RIAE FACILIBUS. | PARS PRIMA. | COMPLECTENS | PARTES ORATIONIS DECLINABILES; | ET | ANALO GIAM | DUAS IN UNAM SYLLABAS | CONTRAHENDI, | EX IPSA VOCALIUM NATURA | DEDUCTAM, | ET REGU LIS UNIVERSALIBUS TRADITAM. | IN USUM TYRONUM JUNIORUM | CLASSIS GRAECAE IN ACADEMIA GLASGUENSI. | EDITIO NOVA PRIORIBUS AUCTIOR ET EMENDATIOR. | STUDIO JACOBI MOOR L.L.D. | IN EADEM ACADEMIA LITT. GRAEC. PROF. | [*quotation, 2 lines*] | GLASGUAE: | IN AEDIBUS ACADEMICIS | EXCUDEBANT ROBERTUS ET ANDREAS FOULIS | ACADEMIAE TYPOGRAPHI | M.DCC.LXVI.

FORMULA: [? Crown] 8⁰ in fours: π^2 A–H⁴(H1 + χ1) I–U⁴ (π1 *half-title*).

Plate of abbreviations and contractions faces A1, unsigned, plate mark 154 × 90.

PAPER: Medium-poor quality; no marks.

TYPE: RGP 2, GGP, GP, GB, RLP 1.

COPIES: L.

456 Moor, James, *On the Praepositions of the Greek Language*   1766

ON THE | PRAEPOSITIONS | OF THE | GREEK | LAN GUAGE; | AN | INTRODUCTORY | ESSAY; | READ TO

A LITERARY SOCIETY IN GLASGOW, | AT THEIR
WEEKLY MEETINGS WITHIN | THE COLLEGE. | By
JAMES MOOR LLD. Professor of Greek | in the UNIVER
SITY of Glasgow. | GLASGOW: | PRINTED BY ROBERT
AND ANDREW FOULIS, | PRINTERS TO THE UNIVER
SITY. | M.DCC.LXVI.

FORMULA: Foolscap 8⁰ in fours: A–D⁴.

PAPER: Medium quality; marks 3/S.LAY.

TYPE: RGP 2, GGP. Without long f.

VARIANT: Issue in [? Crown] 8⁰:
  Paper: Poor quality; no marks.

NOTES: Easily confused with No. 457 below, which follows
(or precedes) it line for line, but is from a different setting.
The following notes from *GJ*, *BQ* (which speaks of ' w[riting].
d[emy]. 8vo.') and *CP* may refer to either edition.
  Publication: published by 20 November 1766 (*GJ*).
  Prices: Wholesale: 9*d.* (*BQ* 10). Retail: 1*s.* (*CP* 10).
  Stock in 1777: 24 copies (*BQ* 10).

COPIES: L (Foolscap), C (Crown).

1766   Moor, James, *On the Praepositions of the Greek* **457**
                              Language (another edition)

[*Title-page reads exactly as that of No. 456 above, except that the
first and third lines of the imprint read* ' GLASGOW,' (*for*
' GLASGOW: ') *and* ' PRINTERS TO THE UNIVERSITY '
(*for* ' PRINTERS TO THE UNIVERSITY.') *respectively.*]

FORMULA: Foolscap 8⁰ in fours: π1 A–D⁴ (π1 *half-title*).

PAPER: Medium-poor quality; marks 4/vi.

TYPE: RGP 2, GGP. Without long f.

NOTES: See NOTES to No. 456 above.

COPIES: G⁴, L.

1766   Moor James, *Vindication of Virgil* **458** †

VINDICATION | OF | VIRGIL, | FROM THE | CHARGE
| OF A | PUERILITY; | IMPUTED TO HIM BY | DOCTOR
PEARCE, | IN HIS NOTES ON | LONGINUS; | AN ESSAY,
| READ TO A LITERARY SOCIETY IN GLASGOW, | AT
THEIR WEEKLY MEETINGS WITHIN | THE COLLEGE.
| By JAMES MOOR LLD. Professor of Greek | in the

UNIVERSITY OF GLASGOW. | [*plain rule, 46*] | [*quotation, 2 lines*] | GLASGOW, | PRINTED BY ROBERT AND ANDREW FOULIS, | PRINTERS TO THE UNIVERSITY. | M.DCC.LXVI.

FORMULA: [? Post] 8º in fours: A⁴ χ² B–D⁴ E1 (A1 *title-page;* A2 *half-title;* A3 ' *note* '; A4—*signed* ' A2 '—*pp.* 3–4; χ² *pp.* 5–8).

PAPER: Medium-good quality; marks ?9/?.

TYPE: RGP 2, RLP 1.   Without long f.

VARIANT: Issue in Foolscap 8º:
Paper: Medium quality; marks 4/vi.

NOTES: *Publication*: published by 20 November 1766 (*GJ*).
Prices: Wholesale: Post, 9*d.*; Foolscap, 4½*d.* (*BQ* 10, which calls the large paper Writing Demy). Retail: (?) Post, 1*s.* (*CP* 10).
Stock in 1777: Post, 72 copies; Foolscap, 184 copies (*BQ* 10).

COPIES: G⁴ (Post), L (Foolscap).

459 Ramsay, Andrew Michael, *A Plan of*   1766
    Education

A | PLAN | OF | EDUCATION: | BY THE | CHEVALIER RAMSAY. | From a genuine MANUSCRIPT. | THE FIFTH EDITION. | GLASGOW: | PRINTED BY ROBERT AND ANDREW FOULIS. | M.DCC.LXVI.

FORMULA: Foolscap 8º in fours: A–D⁴ E².

PAPER: Medium-poor quality; marks 5/v.

TYPE: RE 2.

VARIANT: Issue on (?) better quality paper, not seen (*BQ* 10).

NOTES: *Prices*: Wholesale: fine, 3*d.*; common, 2½*d.* (*BQ* 10).
Stock in 1777: fine, 6 copies; common, 174 copies (*BQ* 10).

COPIES: G⁴ (Foolscap).

460 Shakespeare, William, *[Dramatic] Works*   1766

THE | WORKS | OF | SHAKESPEAR. | IN | EIGHT VOLUMES. | Collated and Corrected by the former Editions, | BY MR. POPE. | PRINTED FROM HIS SECOND EDI TION. | VOLUME I. PART I. | GLASGOW: | PRINTED

BY ROBERT AND ANDREW FOULIS | M.DCC.LXVI.
[*Each of the 16 Parts has a title-page printed from the same type,
with appropriate changes to* 'VOLUME I. PART II.',
'VOLUME II. PART I.', *etc. Each of the two or three plays
in each Part also has a dated title-page, the first of which reads:*]
THE | TEMPEST. | THE AUTHOR | Mr. WILLIAM
SHAKESPEAR. | ACCORDING TO | Mr. POPE's SECOND
EDITION. | GLASGOW, | Printed and sold by R. and A.
Foulis | M DCC LII.

FORMULA: Foolscap 8⁰ in fours: (*Eight volumes in sixteen Parts,
each of which begins:*) π² (π1 *Part title-page*, π2 *Part sub-title*).

Vol. I, Pt. 1: a–f⁴ (*prefatory matter, no separate title-page*); π1
A–K⁴(–K4; *The Tempest*, 1752); π1 A–I⁴ K1 (*A Midsummer
Night's Dream*, 1752)

Vol. I, Pt. 2: A–K⁴ (*The Two Gentlemen of Verona*, 1753); π1
A–M⁴ (*The Merry Wives of Windsor*, 1753); A⁴ B–M⁴ N² (*Measure
for Measure*, 1753).

Vol. II, Pt. 1: A–H⁴ I² (*The Comedy of Errors*, 1765); A² B–M⁴
(*Much Ado about Nothing*, 1765); A–L⁴ M1 (*The Merchant of
Venice*, 1753).

Vol. II, Pt. 2: A–M⁴ (*Love's Labour's Lost*, 1765); A–L⁴ M²
(*As You Like It*, 1765).

Vol. III, Pt. 1: A–M⁴ (*The Taming of the Shrew*, 1765); A–M⁴
N² (N1 *signed* ' I '; M2 *unsigned; All's Well that Ends Well*, 1765);
A–L⁴ (*Twelfth Night*, 1765).

Vol. III, Pt. 2: A–O⁴ (*The Winter's Tale*, 1765); A–P⁴ (*King
Lear*, 1753).

Vol. IV, Pt. 1: A–M⁴ (*King John*, 1765); A–M⁴ N² (*Richard II*,
1765); A–N⁴ O² (O2 *blank; Henry IV Pt. 1*, 1753).

Vol. IV, Pt. 2: A–O⁴ P² (*Henry IV, Pt. 2*, 1754); a² A–O⁴
(*Henry V*, 1760).

Vol. V, Pt. 1: A–M⁴ N² (*Henry VI, Pt. 1*, 1765); A² B–O⁴ P²
(*Henry VI, Pt. 2*, 1765).

Vol. V, Pt. 2: A² B–O⁴ (*Henry VI, Pt. 3*, 1765); A–Q⁴ R²
(*Richard III*, 1758).

Vol. VI, Pt. 1: a² A–N⁴ O² (*Henry VIII*, 1759); A–L⁴ (*Timon of
Athens*, 1765).

Vol. VI, Pt. 2: A–Q⁴ (*Coriolanus*, 1760); A–L⁴ M² (*Julius
Caesar*, 1759).

Vol. VII, Pt. 1: A–P⁴ (*Antony and Cleopatra*, 1765); A–L⁴ M²
(*Titus Andronicus*, 1765).

Vol. VII, Pt. 2: A–L⁴ (L4 *blank; Macbeth*, 1758); A–P⁴
(*Troilus and Cressida*, 1765).

Vol. VIII, Pt. 1: A–P⁴ Q² (*Cymbeline*, 1765); A–N⁴ (*Romeo and
Juliet*, 1765).

Vol. VIII, Pt. 2: A–R⁴ (*Hamlet*, 1756); A–P⁴ Q² (*Othello*, 1757); A–L⁴ M² (*index, etc., no separate title-page;* M2 *advertisements*).

(*Signed* ' VOL. I [. . . VIII].' *on* \$1 *except title pages*.)

Plate: portrait of Shakespeare faces the title-page of Vol. I Pt. I, unsigned, plate mark ?152 × 87.

PAPER: Medium to medium-good quality (the plays printed in 1752–60 generally on better paper than those printed in 1765); marks 5/v, 4/iii, 4/v, 4/vi.

TYPE: RLP 1, RB 2.

VARIANT: Issue in [? Crown] 12⁰:

Title-pages: [*Eight volume title-pages only, re-set, reading the same as the* 8⁰ *Part title-pages, but* ' VOLUME I.', *etc., for* ' VOLUME I. PART I.', *etc.*]

FORMULA: [? Crown] 12⁰ in sixes: (*Eight Volumes, each of which begins:*) π² (π1 *Volume title-page*, π2 *Volume sub-title*).

Vol. I: a–d⁶(*pref.*); A–F⁶ G⁴ (*Temp.*); π1 A² B–G⁶(–G6; *MND*); A–F⁶ G⁴ (*TGV*); π1 A–H⁶ (*MWW*); A–H⁶ I² (*Meas.*).

Vol. II: A–E⁶ F⁴ (*Errors*); A² B–H⁶ I² (*Much Ado*); A–G⁶ H⁴ (H4 *blank; MV*); A² B⁴ C–I⁶ (*LLL*); A–G⁶ H⁴ (*AYLI*).

Vol. III: A–H⁶ (*Shrew*); A–H⁶ I² (*All's Well*); A⁴ B–G⁶ H⁴ (*TN*); A² B–K⁶ (*WT*); A–K⁶ (I3 *signed* ' I2 '; *Lear*).

Vol. IV: A–H⁶ (*John*); A–H⁶ I² (*RII*); A–I⁶ (I6 *blank; 1HIV*); A–I⁶ K⁴ (*2HIV*); A–I⁶ K⁴ (*HV*).

Vol. V: A–H⁶ I² (*1HVI*); A–I⁶ K⁴ (A3 *signed* ' B3 '; *2HVI*); A² B⁴ C–I⁶ K⁴ (*3HVI*); A–L⁶ (*RIII*).

Vol. VI: a² A–I⁶ (*HVIII*); A² B–H⁶ (*Timon*); a² A–K⁶ L² (*Cor.*); A–G⁶ H⁴ (*JC*).

Vol. VII: A⁴ B–K⁶ L² (*AC*); A⁴ B–H⁶ (*Titus*); A–G⁶ H1 (*MacB*); A⁴ B–K⁶ L² (*TC*).

Vol. VIII: A–K⁶ L² (*Cymb.*); A⁴ B–I⁶ (*RJ*); A–L⁶ M² (*Ham.*); A–K⁶ L² (*Oth.*); A–G⁶ H² I² (*index, etc.*).

(*Signed* ' * ' *on* \$1 *passim, but apparently quite erratically, only about two-thirds of all the signatures being so signed. Copies of some plays seen both with and without these* ' * ' *signatures; they appear to be on precisely the same paper. Signed* ' VOL. I [. . . VIII].) *on* \$1 *except title-pages.*)

Press-figures: Merry Wives (Vol. I, *dated* 1753): ' 1 ' *on* C1 E1 . . . G1; ' 3 ' *on* A1 B1 D1 H1. King Lear (Vol. III, *dated* 1753): ' 1 ' *on* D1 E6ʳ I1 K1; ' 3 ' *on* B1 C1 F1 . . . H1. No other press-figures appear in Foulis Press books until 1768; it is just possible that their appearance here indicates a concealed reprint.

Paper: Medium-poor quality; no marks.

NOTES: *Prices*: Wholesale: 8⁰, 24*s*.; 12⁰, 12*s*. (*BQ* 8). Retail: 8⁰, 32*s*.; 12⁰, 16*s*. (*CP* 7, 10).

Stock in 1777: 8⁰, 50 copies (4 imperfect); 12⁰, 29 copies (2 imperfect) (*BQ* 8)

An advertisement on *M*2ᵛ of Vol. viii, Pt. 2 (8⁰ issue, undated but presumably 1766) announces that the printers intend 'foon to publifh Propofals for a NEW EDITION of SPENSER'S FAIRY QUEEN.'

COPIES: G⁴ (8⁰ complete; 12⁰ *MND*, *Much Ado TGV*), G² (12⁰ complete).

1766   Somerville, William, *Poems* **461**

NOTES: Not seen. Listed by Duncan (p. 69, No. 347) as 'Somerville's Poems, 12mo.' *CP* (p. 8) lists the book among the octavos at 1*s*. 2*d*. (retail).

1767   Boswell, James, *Dorando* **462** †

DORANDO, | A | SPANISH TALE. | [*quotation, 10 lines*] | LONDON, | PRINTED FOR J. WILKIE AT THE BIBLE IN ST. PAUL'S | CHURCH-YARD. SOLD ALSO BY J. DODSLEY IN | PALL-MALL, T. DAVIES IN RUSSEL-STREET | COVENT-GARDEN, | AND BY THE BOOKSELLERS OF SCOTLAND. | M.DCC.LXVII.

FORMULA: [? Writing Demy] 8⁰ in fours: *A*⁴ B–F⁴ G² (*A*1 *half-title*, G2 *blank*).

PAPER: Medium quality; marks 7/i.

TYPE: RE 3, RSP 2.

VARIANT: Issue in [? Crown] 8⁰, called 'Second edition':

Title-page: [*Largely from the same setting, but with the addition of* 'SECOND EDITION.' *on a separate line following the quotation.*]

Paper: Medium quality; marks 9/?ii.

NOTES: For a commentary on the negotiations between Boswell and Foulis and of the publication of the book, see Pottle, F. A., *The Literary Career of James Boswell, Esq.*, (Oxford, 1929), pp. 32-7.

Three letters which Foulis wrote to Boswell about the book in the Spring and Summer of 1767 are given in Appendix B, pp. 397-8 below. Seven or eight hundred copies were printed, three hundred of them being the Crown issue; publication in London took place early in June 1767.

Price: Retail: 1*s*. (half-title).

COPIES: G⁴ (Crown), L (Demy).

463 [Anon.], *A Compend of Physics*   1767

NOTES: Not seen. Listed by Duncan (p. 70, No. 359) as ' Compend of Phyſics, 8vo.'

464 Craig, William, *An Essay on the Life of Christ*   1767

AN | ESSAY | ON THE | LIFE | OF | JESUS CHRIST. | BY | WILLIAM CRAIG, D.D. | ONE OF THE MINISTERS OF GLASGOW. | [*quotations, 6 lines*] | GLASGOW, | PRINTED BY ROBERT & ANDREW FOULIS. | SOLD AT EDINBURGH BY J. BALFOUR AND J. | DICKSON, AT LONDON BY T. CADELL. | M.DCC.LXVII.

FORMULA: [Writing Demy] 8⁰: a² A–I⁸ K² (K2 *contents*).

PAPER: Medium-good quality; marks 7/ii.

TYPE: RSP 2.

VARIANT: Issue in Foolscap 8⁰:
    Paper: Medium-good quality; marks 4/v; size of sheet 16¾ × 13 in.

NOTES: *Publication*: published by 12 February 1767 (*GJ*).
    Prices: Retail: large paper, 2s. 6d.; ordinary, 1s. 6d. in boards (*GJ* 12 February 1767).

COPIES: G⁴ (both issues).

465 [Anon.], *An Essay on Religion and Morality*   1767

AN | ESSAY | ON | RELIGION | AND | MORALITY: | OR THE | SUM AND EVIDENCES | OF TRUE | RELIGION. | [*quotation, 5 lines*] | GLASGOW, | PRINTED FOR DANIEL BAXTER | BY ROBERT AND ANDREW FOULIS. | M.DCC.LXVII.

FORMULA: [? Printing Demy] 8⁰ in fours: π² A–K⁴.

PAPER: Medium-poor quality; marks 7/i; size of sheet 21¾ × 17¼ in.

TYPE: RSP 2, RB 2.

COPIES: G⁴, L.

466 Graham, George, *Telemachus*   1767

TELEMACHUS, | A | MASK. | BY | GEORGE GRAHAM, M.A. | FELLOW OF KING's COLLEGE, CAMBRIDGE. | GLASGOW: | PRINTED BY ROBERT AND ANDREW FOULIS | M.DCC.LXVII. | *

FORMULA: Foolscap 8⁰: π^4 A–F^8 (*signed* ' * ' *on* $1; A4 *unsigned*).

PAPER: Medium quality; marks 5/v.

TYPE: RLP 1, RB 2, RE 3.

VARIANT: Issue on inferior paper, Foolscap 8⁰:
Formula: (*without* ' * ' *signatures*).
Paper: Medium-poor quality; marks 5/v.

NOTES: *Publication*: to be published a few days after 9 July 1767 (*GJ*).
Prices: Retail: (?) fine, 1s. (*CP* 8); second paper, 8d. (Spotiswood, p. 88).

COPIES: G⁴ (fine), L (common).

1767 *Pope's Homer*, Iliad, E **467**

THE | ILIAD | OF | HOMER. | TRANSLATED BY | ALEX
ANDER POPE. | VOLUME FIRST [SECOND] [THIRD]
[FOURTH]. | [*quotations, 4 lines (Vol.* I), *4 lines (Vol.* II), *5 lines
(Vol.* III) *and 2 lines (Vol.* IV)] | GLASGOW: | PRINTED BY
ROBERT AND ANDREW FOULIS | M.DCC.LXVII.

FORMULA: Pot 12⁰ in sixes:
Vol. I: π^2 A–O^6 P^4 (F3 *signed* ' C3 '; π1 *half-title*).
Vol. II: π^2 A^2 B–O^6 (π1 *half-title*, O6 *blank*).
Vol. III: π^2 A–P^6 Q^2 (L3 *unsigned*; π1 *half-title*).
Vol. IV: π^2 A^4 B–O^6 (π1 *half-title*).
(*Signed* ' * ' *on* $1 *except Vol.* I B1 . . . N1, *Vol.* II A1 *and Vol.* IV
π1; *signed* ' VOL. I [. . . IV].' *on* $1 *except half-titles and Vol.* I
A1, B1.)
Plate: folding map follows Vol. I π2, 'GRÆCIA | HOMERICA ',
' PHRYGIA | cum | Oris Maritimis ', unsigned, plate mark
166 × 246.

PAPER: Medium quality; marks 1/iv 3/iv.

TYPE: RB 2.

VARIANT: Issue on inferior paper not seen (' * ' signatures; *GJ* 12 May 1768).

NOTES: *Publication*: published by 9 July 1767 (*GJ*).
Prices: see NOTES to No. 476 (Homer, 1768).

COPIES: G⁴ (fine).

1767 Parnell, Thomas, *Works* **468**

THE | WORKS | IN | VERSE AND PROSE, | OF | DR.
THOMAS PARNELL, | LATE ARCH-DEACON OF

CLOGHER. | ENLARGED WITH VARIATIONS AND POEMS, | NOT BEFORE PUBLISH'D. | GLASGOW: | PRINTED BY ROBERT & ANDREW FOULIS. | PRINTERS TO THE UNIVERSITY. | M.DCC.LXVII.

FORMULA: Foolscap 8⁰ in fours: π^4 A–2F⁴ (2C1 *signed* ' C '; I2, U2 *unsigned*).

PAPER: Medium quality; marks 5/v, 4/v.

TYPE: RLP 1, RB 2.

VARIANT: Issue in Pot 8⁰:

Formula: (*signed* ' * ' *on* B1, D1 . . . F1, K1, N1, O1, Q1, R1, X1 . . . 2F1).

Paper: Medium-poor quality; marks 1/v; size of sheet $14\frac{3}{4} \times 12\frac{1}{2}$ in.

NOTES: *GJ*, 12 February 1767: 'In a few Days will be Publiſhed, New Editions of PARNELL and HAMILTON's Poems.' Advertisement repeated, without the mention of Hamilton, in *GJ* for 30 April 1767. The reference is probably to this book; the Hamilton has not been found, and may not have been published.

Prices: Wholesale: Foolscap, 1s. 4d. (*BQ* 8). Retail: (?) 2s. (*CP* 7; both *BQ* and *CP* speak of 8⁰ *Poems*, but most probably refer to this book).

Stock in 1777: Foolscap, 172 copies (*BQ* 8).

COPIES: G⁴ (Pot), L (Foolscap).

469 Ramsay, Andrew Michael, *A Translation of*   1767 *Fénelon on the Love of God*

A | TRANSLATION | OF THE | PHILOSOPHICAL DIS COURSE | ON THE | LOVE OF GOD; | EXPLAINING THE SENTIMENTS | OF THE | ARCHBISHOP OF CAM BRAY. | BY | CHEVALIER RAMSAY. | GLASGOW: | PRINTED BY ROBERT AND ANDREW FOULIS | M.DCC.LXVII.

FORMULA: Foolscap 8⁰: π^2 A–B⁸ C⁴ D² (C2 *unsigned*; π1 half-title, D2 *advertisements*).

PAPER: Medium quality, marks 5/v, size of sheet $16\frac{3}{4} \times 13\frac{1}{4}$ in.

TYPE: RE 3, RLP 1.

VARIANT: Issue on inferior paper, [? Foolscap) 8⁰:

Paper: Poor quality; no marks.

NOTES: *Prices*: Wholesale: fine, 3d.; common, 2d. (*BQ* 10).

Stock in 1777: fine, 102 copies; common, 256 copies (*BQ* 10).

COPIES: G⁴, L (both common), O (fine).

1767   Somerset, Edward, Marquis of Worcester, **470** †
         A Century of Inventions

A | CENTURY | OF THE NAMES | AND | SCANTLINGS
| OF SUCH | INVENTIONS, | As at prefent I can call to mind
to have tried | and perfected, (which my former Notes | being
loft) I have, at the inftance of a | powerful Friend, endeavoured
now in the | Year 1655. to fet thefe down in fuch a | way as
may fufficiently inftruct me to put | any of them in practice. |
[*quotation, 1 line*] | THE AUTHOR THE | MARQUIS OF
WORCESTER. | GLASGOW: | PRINTED BY R. AND A.
FOULIS | M.DCC.LXVII.

FORMULA: Foolscap 12⁰: a¹² b² A–C¹² D⁸ (a4, B5, C5, D4
unsigned; D8 *blank*).

PAPER: Medium quality; marks 5/v; size of sheet $16\frac{1}{2} \times 13$ in.

TYPE: RE 3, RSP 2, RB 2.

VARIANT: Another issue, ' sold by J. Dickson ':
    Title-page: [*Another setting; reads as above, with minor changes
in the lineation of lines 8–14, and with a variant imprint reading:*]
GLASGOW: | PRINTED BY R. AND A. FOULIS, | AND
SOLD BY J. DICKSON, BOOKSELLER | IN EDINBURGH.
| M.DCC.LXVII.
    Formula: (*Neither title-page is found as a cancel*).

NOTES: *Prices*: Wholesale: 9*d*. (*BQ* 9). Retail: 1*s*. (*CP* 11).
    Stock in 1777: 267 copies (*BQ* 9).

COPIES: G⁴ (both issues), L (issue without Dickson's name).

1767   Wight, William, *Heads of a Course on the* **471**
                                 Study of History

HEADS | OF A | COURSE OF | LECTURES | ON THE |
STUDY OF | HISTORY; | GIVEN ANNUALLY | BY
WILLIAM WIGHT, D.D. | PROFESSOR OF HISTORY |
IN THE UNIVERSITY OF GLASGOW. | The COURSE
begins on NOVEMBER firft. | GLASGOW: | PRINTED BY ROBERT
& ANDREW FOULIS, | PRINTERS TO THE UNIVERSITY, |
M.DCC.LXVII.

FORMULA: [? Writing Demy) 8⁰ in fours: π1 A–B⁴ C².

PAPER: Medium quality; marks 7/ii.

TYPE: RLP 1.

NOTES: Concerning prices, etc., see the NOTES to No. 549
(Wight, 1772).

COPIES: L.

472 Xenophon, *Cyropaedia*, G and L 1767

ΤΟΥ | ΞΕΝΟΦΩΝΤΟΣ | ʹΗ ΤΟΥ | ΚΥΡΟΥ | ΠΑΙΔΕΙΑ. | [*plain rule, 37*] | XENOPHONTIS | INSTITUTIO | CYRI. | TOMIS QUATUOR. | ΕΧ EDITIONE T. HUTCHINSON. | TOM. I [II] [III] [IV]. | GLASGUAE: | IN AEDIBUS ACADEMICIS | EXCUDEBANT ROBERTUS ET ANDREAS FOULIS | ACADEMIAE TYPOGRAPHI | M.DCC.LXVII. [*Same setting. Some copies of the fine-paper issue add* ' | * ' *to all title-pages.*]

FORMULA: Foolscap 8⁰:

Vol. I: π^2 A–T⁸ U⁴ (*signed* ' * ' *on* U1; K4 *unsigned;* π1 *half-title*).

Vol. II: π^2 A–R⁸ (I3, R3, R4 *unsigned;* π1 *half-title*, R8 *blank*).

Vol. III: π^2 A–S⁸ T⁴ U² (*some copies signed* ' * ' *on* T1; π1 *half-title*, U2 *advertisements*).

Vol. IV: π^2 A–Z⁸ (I4, K2 *unsigned;* π1 *half-title*).

(*Signed* ' TOM. I [. . . IV].' *on* $1.)

PAPER: Medium-good quality, marks 4/ii; medium quality, marks 5/ii; medium-poor quality, marks 5/v.

TYPE: RP 2, GGP. Greek and Latin on facing pages.

VARIANTS: Issue on inferior-quality paper, Foolscap 8⁰, Greek and Latin:

Formula: (*without* ' * ' *signatures*).

Paper: Poorer quality overall than the issue described above, marks 5/ii, 4/ii.

Fine-paper issue, Greek only, not seen (*BQ* 4).

NOTES: *Prices* : Wholesale: G and L, fine, 7s. 6d.; G and L, common, 3s.; G only, fine, 4s. 8d. (*BQ* 4). Retail: G and L, (?) fine, 10s. (*CP* 4).

Stock in 1777: G and L, fine, 114 copies; G and L, common, 872 copies; G only, fine, 186 copies (*BQ* 4).

COPIES: G⁴ (both issues), L (fine).

† **473** Boswell, James, *An Account of Corsica* 1768

AN | ACCOUNT | OF | CORSICA, | THE JOURNAL OF A TOUR | TO THAT ISLAND; | AND MEMOIRS OF | PASCAL PAOLI. | BY JAMES BOSWELL, Efq; | ILLUS TRATED with a New and Accurate MAP of CORSICA. | [*quotation, 3 lines*] | [*copper-plate vignette, unsigned, plate mark 59 × 83*] | GLASGOW, | PRINTED BY ROBERT AND ANDREW FOULIS FOR | EDWARD AND CHARLES DILLY IN THE POULTRY, LON DON; | M DCC LXVIII.

FORMULA: Printing Demy 8⁰: π1 ²π1 a⁸ b² A–E⁸($\pm$E2) F–Z⁸ ($\pm$Z3) 2A⁸ (π1 *half-title*, ²π1 *title-page*, 2A8 *blank. See F. A. Pottle*, The Literary Career of James Boswell, Esq. (*Oxford, 1929*) *pp. 51–2, for a discussion of the cancels, which were set up in duplicate.*)

Plate: Folding map facing the title-page with imprint: ' *Published Agreeable to Act of Parliament Feb*ʸ. *4. 1768. & Sold by E. & C. Dilly, in the Poultry. & Carrington Bowles, N*⁰. *69 in S*ᵗ. *Pauls Church Yard, London.*' Plate mark 278 × 450.

PAPER: Medium quality; marks 9/i; Pottle (*op. cit.* p. 54) cites a copy of which the sheet measured 21½ × 17¼ in.

TYPE: RE 2, RE3, RDP, RSP 2, RLP 1, RB 2, GGP, GP.

VARIANT: Issue on (?) better quality paper, not seen (letter of Robert Foulis to Boswell of 2 March 1768, p. 400 below).

NOTES: For letters concerning this book between Robert Foulis and Boswell, August 1767 to March 1768, see Appendix B, pp. 399-400 below.

Publication: to be published ' next week ' (*GJ* 18 Feburary 1768, which gives the title as ' THE HISTORY OF CORSICA ').

Price: Retail: 6*s*. bound (Pottle, *op. cit.*, p. 54).

COPIES: G⁴, L

1768   Drummond, William, *Polemo-Middinia* **474**

POLEMO-MIDDINIA | INTER | VITARVAM | ET | NEBERNAM. | GLASGOW, | PRINTED BY ROBERT AND ANDREW FOULIS, | M.DCC.LXVIII.

FORMULA: Pot 4⁰ in twos: A² B–D² (D2 *advertisements*).

Press figures: ' 2 ' on B1, C1.

PAPER: Medium-poor quality; marks i/v; size of sheet 15 × 12½ in.

TYPE: RGP 2. The advertisements (which refer to Old Poems printed and sold by R. and A. Foulis, 1748–1768) are set in a fount of Caslon pica, not found in other Foulis Press books.

NOTES: *Price*: Wholesale: 3*d*. (*BQ* 9).

Stock in 1777: 770 copies (*BQ* 9).

COPIES: G⁴, L.

1768   Gray, Thomas, *Poems* **475** †

POEMS | BY | MR. GRAY. | GLASGOW: | PRINTED BY ROBERT AND ANDREW FOULIS, | PRINTERS TO THE UNIVERSITY, | M.DCC.LXVIII. | *

FORMULA: [? Writing] Royal 4⁰: π^2 A–H⁴ (*signed* ' * ' *on* π–G $1 *and* H2).

PAPER: Good quality; marks 8/none.

TYPE: RDP, RSP 2, GP, RE 3. In an ' advertisement ' on π2 the printers state that ' This is the firſt work in the Roman char-aćter which they have printed with ſo large a type; and they are obliged to DOCTOR WILSON for preparing ſo expeditiouſly, and with ſo much attention, charaćters of ſo beautiful a form.' In fact RDP had made a brief appearance five years earlier in No. 423 (Plato, 1763), when many of the letters were in a slightly cruder state.

VARIANT: Issue on inferior paper, [? Printing) Royal 4⁰:
  Formula: (*without* ' * ' *signatures*).
  Paper: Medium quality; marks 8/i.
  Note: BQ (p. 7) refers to ' medium paper ', which would suggest that there were three issues, since the ' medium ' is more likely to have referred to quality than to size; neverthe-less the wholesale price quoted for ' medium paper ' fits well with the retail price of the ' Superfine Royal ' paper copies advertised in the press.
    The common-paper issue is now a much rarer book than the fine.

NOTES: Edited by Dr James Beattie, whose interesting corre-spondence with Gray concerning the production of the book is printed in *Correspondence of Thomas Gray*, ed. Paget Toynbee and Leonard Whibley (Oxford, 1935), vol. iii, Letters 457, 465, 466, 469, 487. Beattie proposed the idea to Gray late in 1767; the copy was delivered in mid-February 1768 and the book was published on about 4 May 1768 (*GJ*, 28 April 1768; *not* 5 May 1768, as stated by Toynbee and Whibley, *loc. cit.*, Letter 487 n. 1).
    Prices: Wholesale: ' medium paper ', 3s. 6d. (*BQ* 7). Retail : ' Superfine Royal Paper ', 5s. in boards (*GJ* 28 April 1768; *CP* 7).
    Stock in 1777: ' medium paper ', 24 copies (*BQ* 7).
COPIES: G⁴, L (both fine), O (common).

476 Pope's Homer, *Odyssey*, E   1768

THE | ODYSSEY | OF | HOMER. | TRANSLATED BY | ALEXANDER POPE. | VOLUME FIRST [SECOND] [THIRD]. | [*quotation, 2 lines*] | GLASGOW: | PRINTED BY ROBERT AND ANDREW FOULIS | M.DCC.LXVIII. | * [*Same setting.*]

FORMULA: Pot 12⁰ in sixes:
  Vol. I: π^2 A–O⁶ P² (*signed ' † ' on* K2; πI *half-title*).
  Vol. II: π^2 A⁴ B–P⁶ (*signed ' † ' on* B2; πI *half-title*).
  Vol. III: π^2 A–N⁶ (πI *half-title*).
  (*Signed ' * ' On title-pages and* \$I *except half-titles; signed*
  ' VOL. I [. . . III].' *on* \$I *except half-titles*).
PAPER: Medium-good quality; marks I/v, I/iv.
TYPE: RB 2.
VARIANT: Issue on inferior paper, not seen (' * ' and ' † '
signatures; *GJ* 12 May 1768).
NOTES: *Publication*: in the press, 28 January 1768; published
by 12 May 1768 (*GJ*).
  Prices: Retail, with No. 467 (*Iliad*, 1767): fine, ' neatly
bound and gilt ', 10s. 6d.; common, 8s. 6d. (*GJ*, 12 May 1768).
COPIES: G⁴.

1768   James I and Ramsay, Allan, *Christ's Kirk on* **477**
                                              the Green

CHRIST'S KIRK | ON THE | GREEN, | IN | THREE
CANTO'S. | THE FIRST CANTO BY KING JAMES THE FIRST; | THE
OTHER TWO BY ALLAN RAMSAY. | GLASGOW: |
PRINTED IN THE YEAR | M.DCC.LXVIII. | *
FORMULA: [? Foolscap] 8⁰: A–B⁸ C⁴ (*signed ' * ' on* AI, BI).
  Press figures: ' 3 ' on BI CI.
PAPER: Medium-poor quality; marks 5/v; size of sheet
$16\frac{1}{2} \times 13$ in.
TYPE: RSP I, RLP I.
VARIANT: Issue on common paper, [? Foolscap] 8⁰:
  Formula: (*without ' * ' signatures*).
  Paper: Poor quality, no marks.
NOTES: Most probably a Foulis book, though without imprint.
  Prices: Wholesale: fine, 3d.; common, $2\frac{1}{2}d.$ (*BQ* 9).
  Stock in 1777: fine, 48 copies; common, 156 copies (*BQ* 9).
COPIES: L (common), O (fine).

1768   M'Gill, William, *The Prayer of our Saviour*, **478**
                                              a Sermon

THE PRAYER | OF | OUR SAVIOUR | FOR THE | UNION
| OF | HIS FOLLOWERS | CONSIDERED; | A | SERMON,

| BY | WILLIAM M'GILL, A.M. | ONE OF THE MINIS
TERS OF AYR. | [*quotation, 1 line*] | GLASGOW: | PRINTED
BY ROBERT & ANDREW FOULIS, | M.DCC.LXVIII.

FORMULA: Foolscap 8⁰ in fours: A–E⁴ F².

PAPER: Medium-good quality; marks 4/v; size of sheet
16½ × 13 in.

TYPE: RSP 2, RB 2.

NOTES: *Publication*: to be published on 3 February 1768 (*GJ*,
28 January 1768, which names Mr Gilmour and Mr Baxter as
publishers with R. and A. Foulis).

Prices: Wholesale: 4*d.* (*BQ* 9). Retail: 6*d.* (*GJ* 28 January
1768).

Stock in 1777: 264 copies (*BQ* 9).

COPIES: G⁴, L.

479 [Anon.], *Military Instructions for forming a*   by 1768
Partisan

NOTES: Not seen. ' Illustrated with Plans '. Advertised in
No. 481 (Pope, 1768) as printed by R. and A. Foulis. It appears
in *CP* (p. 10) as an octavo, retail price 3*s.*

480 [Anon.], *The Modern Farmer's Guide*   1768

THE | MODERN | FARMERS | GUIDE. | IN TWO VOL
UMES. | A new SYSTEM of HUSBANDRY, from | long experience
in ſeveral Kingdoms; | NEVER BEFORE MADE PUBLIC
| [*contents, 14 lines*] | [*plain rule, 83*] | BY A REAL FARMER.
| [*plain rule, 82*] | VOL. I [II]. | GLASGOW: | PRINTED
FOR THE AUTHOR, | BY ROBERT AND ANDREW
FOULIS, M.DCC.LXVIII. [*Different settings.*]

FORMULA: [? Printing Demy] 8⁰ in fours:

Vol. I: π⁴ †⁴ ††⁴ (–††4) a–i⁴ k² A–2P⁴ 2Q² (*signed* ' VOL. I.'
on †–2Q $1; A2, 2B2, 2C2 *unsigned*).

Vol. II: π⁴ A–3D⁴(–3D4); *signed* ' VOL. II.' *on* A–3D $1; D2,
2D2 *unsigned*).

Press figures: ' 1 ' on Vol. II G1 I1 L1 O1 Q1 S1 U1 X1 Z1
2B1 2E1 2G1 . . . 2I1 2M1 2O1 2Q1 2R1 2T1 2U1 2Y1 3A1 3C1.
' 3 ' on Vol. I a1 . . . i1, Vol. II H1 K1 M1 N1 P1 R1 T1 Y1 2A1
2D1 2F1 2K1 2L1 2P1 2S1 2X1 2Z1 3B1 3D1.

Plates: woodcuts inserted at Vol. I π2ᵛ (' Plate 3 '), 2Q2
(' Plate 2 '); Vol. II 2P2 (' Plate 4 ') and 2U2 (' Plate 1 '). Printed
tables inserted at Vol. II π4ᵛ and 2I3ᵛ.

PAPER: Poor quality; marks 9/1.

TYPE: RE 3, RLP I.

NOTES: The book was advertised in *GJ* for 25 February 1768 as printing by subscription at Glasgow for the Author: ' to Subfcribers 12s. the Set ftitched, half payed at Subfcribing. . . . This Work to be delivered in April next.'

COPIES: G⁴.

1768   Pope, Alexander, *Poetical Works* **481**

THE | POETICAL | WORKS | OF | ALEXANDER POPE, Efq. | VOLUME I. | CONTAINING HIS | JUVENILE POEMS. [II. | CONTAINING | TRANSLATIONS, IMITA TIONS, | EPISTLES, EPITAPHS, etc.] [III. | CONTAINING HIS | MORAL ESSAYS, SATIRES, etc.] [IV. | CONTAIN ING THE | DUNCIAD, | IN | FOUR BOOKS.] | GLASGOW: | PRINTED BY ROBERT & ANDREW FOULIS, | PRINTERS TO THE UNIVERSITY | M.DCC.LXVIII. | † [*The* ' † ' *in Vols.* I *and* II *only.*]

FORMULA: Pot 12⁰ in sixes:

Vol. I: a⁶ A–N⁶ O⁴ (C2, I3 *unsigned;* O4 *blank*).

Vol. II: a⁴ A² B–P⁶ Q² (D2, G2, I3, L2 *unsigned*).

Vol. III: π² A⁴ B–U⁶ X⁴ (P2 *signed* ' M2 '*;* G2 *unsigned;* X4 *blank*).

Vol. IV: π² A–Q⁶ R⁴ (B2, D2, E2, F2, G2, L2, M2, O3, Q1, Q2 *unsigned;* R4 *advertisements*).

(*Signed* ' † ' *on* $1 *except Vol.* I G1, *Vol.* II A1, Q1, *Vol.* III π1, E1, *Vol.* IV π1, Q1*; signed* ' * ' *on Vol.* I G1, *Vol.* II Q1, *Vol.* III E1, K1*; signed* ' VOL. I [. . . IV].' *on* $1 *except title-pages.*)

Press-figures: ' 1 ' on Vol. I A2 B1 . . . D1 F1 G1 I1 L1 N6, Vol. II B1 . . . E1 H1 I1 L1 M1 N2 O1, Vol. III A4 C1 . . . E1 F6 G1 . . . I1 L1 M6 N1 O6 P1 Q6 S1 . . . X1, Vol. IV B1 . . . L1 N1 O1 Q1. ' 3 ' on Vol. I E3 H1 K1 M1 O1, Vol. II F1 G1 K1 P1, Vol. III B1 R1.

Plates: frontispiece to each volume, unsigned, plate marks not seen.

PAPER: Medium quality; marks 3/v.

TYPE: RB 2, RLP I.

VARIANT: Issue on inferior paper, Pot 12⁰ (Vols. II and IV only seen):

Formula: (*Without the* ' † ' *and* ' * ' *signatures*).

Paper: Medium-poor quality; marks 1/v.

NOTES: Publication: published by 24 November 1768 (*GJ*).

COPIES: G⁴ (fine, complete; common, Vols. II and IV only).

† **482** Ramsay, Allan, *The Tea-table Miscellany*   1768

THE | TEA-TABLE | MISCELLANY: | A | COLLECTION | OF | CHOICE SONGS, | SCOTS AND ENGLISH. | FOR MERLY IN FOUR VOLUMES, | NOW COMPRISED IN TWO. | BY | ALLAN RAMSAY. | [*quotation, 7 lines*] | VOL. I [II]. | GLASGOW: | PRINTED BY ROBERT AND ANDREW FOULIS | M.DCC.LXVIII.

FORMULA: [? Foolscap] 8⁰:

Vol. I: a⁸ b⁴ A–T⁸ U² (R1 *and* R2 *missing in the only copy seen, probably accidentally;* a⁴, F3, O2, O4 *unsigned; signed* ' VOL. I.' *on* A–U $1).

Vol. II: A–U⁸ (*signed* ' VOL. II.' *on* B–U $1).

Press-figures: ' 1 ' on Vol. II O1 T1. ' 2 ' on Vol. I A1 E1 F1 H1 K1 . . . N1 Q1 S1 T1, Vol. II B1 . . . D1 F1 . . . N1 P1 . . . S1 U1. ' 3 ' on Vol. I N2 O1 P1.

Plate: portrait frontispiece faces title-page of Vol. I, signed ' *A Ramsay Junᵣ delin* ', plate mark 140 × 80.

PAPER: Medium-poor quality; no marks.

TYPE: RLP 1, RB 2, RSP 2.

VARIANT: Issue on (?) better paper, not seen (*BQ* 5).

NOTES: *Publication*: to be published a few days after 24 November 1768 (*GJ*).

Prices: Wholesale: fine, 3s.; common, 1s. 6d. (*BQ* 5). Retail: (?) fine, 4s. (*CP* 8).

Stock in 1777: fine, 28 copies; common, 105 copies (*BQ* 5).

COPIES: G⁴.

† **483** Shenstone, William, *Select Works*   1768

THE | SELECT | WORKS | IN | VERSE AND PROSE, | OF | WILLIAM SHENSTONE, | ESQUIRE. | GLASGOW: | PRINTED BY ROBERT & ANDREW FOULIS, | PRINTERS TO THE UNIVERSITY. | M.DCC.LXVIII. | *

FORMULA: Pot 12⁰ in sixes:

π² a² A–L⁶ M⁴ (*signed* ' * ' *on* $1; *signed* ' VOL. I.' *on* A1; M4 *advertisements*).

Press-figures: ' 1 ' on A1 F1 K1 M1.

Plate: mezzotint portrait faces title-page, unsigned, plate mark not seen.

PAPER: Medium quality; marks 3/v.

TYPE: RB 2, RLP 1.

VARIANT: Issue on (?) inferior paper, not seen (' * ' *signatures*).

NOTES: *Publication*: to be published a few days after 24 November 1768 (*GJ*).
COPIES: G⁴.

by 1768   Sherlock, William, *A Discourse of the* **484**
                Immortality of the Soul, and a Future State

NOTES: Not seen. Advertised in No. 483 (Shenstone 1768) as printed for R. and A. Foulis (other books in the same list were in fact printed by them). *BQ* (p. 8) lists it as a Foolscap 8⁰ in two volumes.
  Prices: Wholesale: fine, 2*s.* 6*d.*; common, 1*s.* 9*d.* (*BQ* 8).
Retail: (?) fine, 3*s.* (*CP* 8).
  Stock in 1777: fine, 4 copies; common, 37 copies (*BQ* 8).

1769   Bell, John, *A System of English Grammar* **484A**

[*Vol.* I:] A | CONCISE | AND | COMPREHENSIVE | SYS TEM | OF | ENGLISH | GRAMMAR. | IN TWO BOOKS. | DESIGNED for the USE of SCHOOLS and PRIVATE | FAMILIES. | BY J. BELL, | LATE TEACHER OF GRAMMAR AND THE | MATHEMATICS. | GLASGOW: | PRINTED BY R. AND A. FOULIS FOR THE AUTHOR | M.DCC.LXIX.
[*Vol.* II:] THE | CONSTRUCTION | OF | PROSE, | IN | THEORY | AND | PRACTICE: | OR, | AN INTRODUC TION | TO | SPEAKING AND WRITING | ENGLISH, | According to the tafte of the moft judicious Claffic Writers, | Ancient and Modern. | BOOK SECOND. | BY J. BELL, | [*last five lines as Vol.* I]
[*Vol.* III:] THE | CONSTRUCTION | OF | VERSE, | IN | THEORY | AND | PRACTICE: | OR, | THE ART OF POETRY, | OR | POETICAL ORATORY | MADE EASY. | BOOK III. OR APPENDIX TO BOOK II. | BY J. BELL, | LATE TEACHER OF GRAMMAR AND THE | MATHEMATICS. | GLASGOW; | PRINTED IN THE YEAR M.DCC.LXIX.

FORMULA: [? Foolscap] 8⁰ in fours:
  Vol. I: A–2S⁴ (12 *signed* ' 2 ' *or unsigned*, 2A1 *signed* ' A2 ', 2Q2 *signed* ' Q2 '; 2F2, 2S2 *unsigned;* 2S4 *errata*).
  Vol. II: A–2F⁴ 2G1 (*signed* ' Book [BOOK] II.' *on* B–2G \$1, *except* D1; 2G1 *errata*).
  Vol. III: A–P⁴ Q1 (G2 *unsigned; signed* ' Book III.' *on* B–Q1 \$1).
  Press-figures: ' 1 ' on Vol. I C2 F1 L1 . . . N1 R1 T1 X1 Z1 2A1 . . . 2D1 2F1 2G1 2I1 2K1 2K2 2L1 2N1 . . . 2S1; Vol. II C1

Eɪ . . . Gɪ Iɪ Kɪ Mɪ . . . Oɪ Qɪ . . . Tɪ Xɪ . . . Zɪ 2Bɪ . . . 2Fɪ;
Vol. ɪɪɪ Bɪ . . . Hɪ Lɪ . . . Pɪ. ' 2 ' on Vol. ɪ Yɪ. ' 3 ' on Vol. ɪ
A3 Bɪ E3ʳ Hɪ Kɪ.

PAPER: Medium-poor quality; no marks.

TYPE: RSP ɪ, RLP ɪ, RLP 2.

COPIES: L.

† 485   Butler, Samuel, *Hudibras*   1769

HUDIBRAS, [' . ' *in Vol.* ɪɪ] | IN THREE PARTS. | WRITTEN
IN THE | TIME | OF THE | LATE WARS. | BY | SAMUEL
BUTLER. | WITH | Aɴɴᴏᴛᴀᴛɪᴏɴs, and a complete Iɴᴅᴇx. |
VOL. I [II]. | GLASGOW: | ᴘʀɪɴᴛᴇᴅ ʙʏ ʀᴏʙᴇʀᴛ & ᴀɴᴅʀᴇᴡ
ғᴏᴜʟɪs | M.DCC.LXIX. | †

Formula: Pot 12⁰ in sixes:
    Vol. ɪ: a⁸ A–T⁶ (*signed* ' † ' *on* $1).
    Vol. ɪɪ: U–2Q⁶ 2R⁴ (*signed* ' † ' *on* $1; *signed* ' VOL. II.' *on*
X–2R $1; 2R3 *signed,* 2M3 *unsigned*).
    Press-figures: ' ɪ ' on Vol. ɪ Bɪ Cɪ Fɪ Hɪ Kɪ Lɪ Nɪ Oɪ Qɪ Rɪ,
Vol. ɪɪ Xɪ Zɪ 2Cɪ 2Eɪ 2Gɪ . . . 2Iɪ 2Lɪ . . . 2Rɪ. ' 3 ' on Vol. ɪ
Aɪ Dɪ Eɪ Iɪ Mɪ Pɪ Sɪ Tɪ, Vol. ɪɪ Yɪ 2Aɪ 2Bɪ 2Dɪ 2Fɪ 2Kɪ.

PAPER: Medium quality; marks 3/? crown; size of sheet
15¼ × 12½ in.

TYPE: RB 2, RLP ɪ.

VARIANT: Issue on another paper, Pot 12⁰:
    Formula: (*without* ' † ' *signatures*).
    Paper: Medium quality; marks ɪ/v.

NOTES: *Publication*: published by 13 April 1769 (*GJ*).

COPIES: G⁴ (both issues).

† 486   Cicero, *Pro Marcello* and *Pro Ligario*, L   1769

MARCI TULLII | CICERONIS | PRO | M. MARCELLO, |
ET | Q. LIGARIO | ORATIONES. | ᴇx ᴇᴅɪᴛɪᴏɴᴇ J. Oʟɪᴠᴇᴛɪ.
| GLASGUAE, | IN AEDIBUS ACADEMICIS | EXCUDE
BANT ROBERTUS ET ANDREAS FOULIS | M.DCC.
LXIX. | †

FORMULA: Foolscap 8⁰ in fours: πɪ A–D⁴ Eɪ (*signed* ' † ' *on*
π–D $1).
    Press-figures: ' ɪ ' on Aɪ Bɪ.

PAPER: Medium-good quality; marks 5/iv.

TYPE: RLP ɪ.

VARIANT: Issue on (?) inferior paper, not seen (' † ' signatures).
NOTES: *Prices*: Wholesale: fine, 6*d*.; common, 4*d*. (*BQ* 3).
Stock in 1777: fine, 60 copies; common, 180 copies (*BQ* 3).
COPIES: G² (? fine).

1769   Craig, William, *An Essay on the Life of Christ* 487

AN | ESSAY | ON THE | LIFE | OF | JESUS CHRIST. | BY
| WILLIAM CRAIG, D.D. | ONE OF THE MINISTERS OF
GLASGOW. | THE SECOND EDITION, CORRECTED |
AND ENLARGED. | GLASGOW, | PRINTED BY ROBERT &
ANDREW FOULIS. | SOLD AT EDINBURGH BY J. BALFOUR AND
J. | DICKSON, AT LONDON BY T. CADELL. | M.DCC LXIX.

FORMULA: Foolscap 8⁰: a² A–L⁸ M² (M2 *contents*).

PAPER: Medium quality; marks 5/v.

TYPE: RSP 2, RB 2.

VARIANT: Issue on large paper, Writing Demy 8⁰:
Formula: (*an erratum slip pasted onto* M1).
Paper: Medium-good quality; marks 7/?ii, 9/i.

NOTES: *Publication*: published by 30 March 1769 (*GJ*, which
names J. Gilmour, D. Baxter and J. Barry as publishers with
R. and A. Foulis).
Prices: Wholesale: Demy, 1*s*. 8*d*.; Foolscap, 1*s*. 2*d*. (*BQ* 7).
Retail: Demy, 2*s*. 6*d*.; Foolscap, 1*s*. 6*d*. (*CP* 10).
Stock in 1777: Demy, 51 copies; Foolscap, 225 copies (*BQ* 7).

COPIES: G⁴, L (both Foolscap), G² (Demy).

1769   Glover, Richard, *Leonidas* 488

LEONIDAS. | A | POEM. | [*quotation, 4 lines*] | GLASGOW: |
PRINTED BY ROBERT & ANDREW FOULIS, | PRINTERS TO THE
UNIVERSITY, | M.DCC.LXIX. †

FORMULA: Pot 12⁰ in sixes: a–b⁶ c² A–P⁶ (*signed* ' † ' *on* a2 *and*
b–P $1; b3, K2 *unsigned;* a1 *half-title*).
Press-figures: ' 1 ' on b3 A1 B1 D1 F1 H1 K1 M1 O1 P1.
' 3 ' on C1 E1 G1 I1 L1 N1.

PAPER: Medium quality; marks 3/? crown.

TYPE: RLP 1, RB 2, GP.

VARIANT: Issue on inferior paper, Pot 12⁰:
Formula: (*without* ' † ' *signatures*).
Paper: Medium-poor quality; marks 1/v.

NOTES: *Publication*: in the press 13 April 1769 (*GJ*).

COPIES: G⁴ (both issues), L (fine).

489 Hutcheson, Francis, *An Essay on the Nature*   1769
and Conduct of the Passions

AN | ESSAY | ON THE | NATURE AND CONDUCT | OF THE | PASSIONS | AND | AFFECTIONS. | WITH | ILLUS TRATIONS | UPON THE | MORAL SENSE. | BY | FRAN CIS HUTCHESON, LL.D. | LATE PROFESSOR OF MORAL PHILOSOPHY | IN THE UNIVERSITY OF GLASGOW. | [*quotation, 2 lines*] | THE THIRD EDITION. | GLASGOW: | PRINTED BY ROBERT & ANDREW FOULIS, | PRIN TERS TO THE UNIVERSITY, | M.DCC.LXIX.

FORMULA: Foolscap 8⁰: a⁸ A–T⁸(T8 *advertisements*).

PAPER: Medium quality; marks 4/iv.

TYPE: RLP 1, RB 2, RSP 2.

VARIANT: Issue on inferior paper, [? Foolscap] 8⁰:
    Paper: Medium-poor quality, no marks.

COPIES: G⁴ (fine), O (common).

490 Leechman, William, *The Nature of Prayer,*   1769
a Sermon

THE | NATURE, | REASONABLENESS, | AND | ADVAN TAGES | OF | PRAYER; | WITH AN ATTEMPT TO ANSWER | THE OBJECTIONS AGAINST IT. | A | SER MON | BY WILLIAM LEECHMAN, D.D. | PRINCIPAL OF THE COLLEGE OF | GLASGOW. | [*quotation, 2 lines*] | THE SIXTH EDITION. | GLASGOW: | PRINTED BY ROBERT & ANDREW FOULIS, | PRINTERS TO THE UNIVERSITY, | M.DCC.LXIX.

FORMULA: Pot 8⁰: Λ–D⁸ E⁴.

PAPER: Medium quality; marks 1/v.

TYPE: RLP 1.

VARIANT: Issue on fine paper, probably Foolscap, not seen (*BQ* 6, and cf. No. 491).

NOTES: *Publication*: published by 30 March 1769 (*GJ*, which names J. Gilmour, D. Baxter and J. Barry as publishers with R. and A. Foulis).
    Prices: Wholesale: fine, 6*d.*; common, 4*d.* (*BQ* 6). Retail: (?) fine, 1*s.* 6*d.*, together with No. 491 (*CP* 10).
    Stock in 1777: fine, 124 copies; common, 229 copies (*BQ* 6).

COPIES: G².

1769   Leechman, William, *The Temper of a Minister,* **491**
a Sermon

THE | TEMPER, | CHARACTER, | AND | DUTY | OF A |
MINISTER OF THE GOSPEL. | A | SERMON. | BY WIL
LIAM LEECHMAN, D.D. | PRINCIPAL OF THE COL
LEGE OF | GLASGOW. | THE SEVENTH EDITION. |
GLASGOW: | PRINTED BY ROBERT & ANDREW FOULIS, | PRIN
TERS TO THE UNIVERSITY, | M.DCC.LXIX.

FORMULA: Foolscap 8°: A–C⁸ D².

PAPER: Medium quality; marks 5/iv, 4/?.

TYPE: RLP I.

VARIANT: Issue in Pot 8°:
Paper: Medium quality; marks 1/?v.

NOTES: *Prices*: Wholesale: fine, 4½d.; common, 2½d. (*BQ* 6).
Retail: (?) fine, 1s. 6d., together with No. 490 (*CP* 10).
Stock in 1777: fine, 213 copies; common, 237 copies (*BQ* 6).

COPIES: L (Foolscap), G² (Pot).

1769   Old Poem.   *The Death of Artho and the Death* **492**
of Fraoch

THE | DEATH OF ARTHO, | AND THE | DEATH OF
FRAOCH. | TWO | ANCIENT POEMS, | TRANSLATED
FROM | THE GALIC. | GLASGOW: | PRINTED BY ROBERT &
ANDREW FOULIS | M.DCC.LXIX.

FORMULA: Crown 8°: π² A⁸.

PAPER: Medium-good quality; marks 9/?; size of sheet
19¾ × 15 in.

TYPE: RE 3, RSP 2.

NOTES: *Publication*: published by 30 March 1769 (*GJ* which
names J. Gilmour, D. Baxter and J. Barry as publishers with
R. and A. Foulis).

COPIES: G⁴.

1769   Prior, Matthew, *Poems on Several Occasions* **493**

POEMS | ON | SEVERAL OCCASIONS; | BY | MATTHEW
PRIOR, Efq. | VOL. I [II]. | GLASGOW: | PRINTED BY ROBERT
& ANDREW FOULIS, | PRINTERS TO THE UNIVERSITY,
| M.DCC.LXIX. † [*same setting.*]

FORMULA: Pot 12º in sixes:

Vol. I: a⁶ b⁴ A–R⁶ (*signed* ' † ' *on* \$1; *signed* ' VOL. I.' *on* b–R \$1; a2, F3 *unsigned;* R6 *advertisements*).

Vol. II: A–Y⁶ (*signed* ' † ' *on* \$1; *signed* ' VOL. II.' *on* B–Y \$1; A3 *signed* ' R3 ').

Press-figures: ' 1 ' on Vol. I b1, Vol. II F1 G1 I1 ... M1 O1 P1 R1 ... Y1. ' 3 ' on Vol. I B1 ... K1 L6 M1 ... O1 P6 Q1 R1, Vol. II B1 C6ʳ D1 E1. ' 0 ' on Vol. II Q1.

PAPER: Medium quality; marks 1/?v, ?3/?v.

TYPE: RB 2.

VARIANT: Issue on another paper, Pot 12º (Vol. II only seen):
　Formula: (*without* ' † ' *signatures*).
　Paper: medium quality, mark 1/v.

COPIES: G⁴ (with ' † ' *signatures*), O (Vol. I with ' † ' signatures, Vol. II without).

494　Richardson, William, *Corsica*　　　1769

CORSICA: | A | POETICAL | ADDRESS. | THE SECOND EDITION. | GLASGOW: | PRINTED BY ROBERT & ANDREW FOULIS, | M.DCC.LXIX.

FORMULA: Foolscap 8º: A⁸.

PAPER: Medium-good quality; marks 4/iv.

TYPE: RLP 1, RP 3.

COPIES: G⁴, L.

† **495**　Thomson, James, *The Seasons*　　　1769

THE | SEASONS. | BY | JAMES THOMSON. | GLASGOW: | PRINTED BY ROBERT & ANDREW FOULIS, | PRINTERS TO THE UNIVERSITY, | M.DCC.LXIX.

FORMULA: Pot 12º in sixes: π² a–b⁶ c⁴ A–R⁶ (*signed* ' † ' *on* b–R \$1 *except* K1; π1 *half-title*).

Press-figures: ' 1 ' on b1 c1 A4ʳ C1 E1 ... I1 L1 M1 O2 P1 Q1. ' 3 ' on B1 D1 K1 N1 R1.

PAPER: Medium quality; marks 1/v; size of sheet 14¾ × 12½ in.

TYPE: RB 2, RLP 1.

VARIANT: Issue on slightly inferior paper, Pot 12º:
　Formula: (*without* ' † ' *signatures; press-figure* ' 3 ' *on* a4).
　Paper: Medium quality; marks 1/v.

COPIES: G⁴ (fine), O (common).

1769   Thomson, James, *The Seasons* (another edition)   496 †

THE | SEASONS. | BY | JAMES THOMSON. | GLASGOW: | PRINTED BY ROBERT & ANDREW FOULIS, | PRINTERS TO THE UNIVERSITY, | M.DCC.LXIX.

FORMULA: Pot 12⁰ in sixes: a–b⁶ c⁴ A–R⁶.

Press-figures: ' 1 ' on b1 c1 A4ʳ C1 D1 F1 G1 I1 K1 P1 . . . R1.

PAPER: Medium-poor quality; marks 1/vii.

TYPE: RB 2, RLP 1.

NOTES: Follows the other edition of 1769 (No. 495) line for line, but is a different setting throughout.

COPIES: G4.

1769   Dryden's Virgil, *Works*, E   497

THE | WORKS | OF | VIRGIL, | TRANSLATED BY | JOHN DRYDEN, Efq; | IN THREE VOLUMES. | VOL. I [II] [III]. | GLASGOW: | PRINTED BY ROBERT AND ANDREW FOULIS | M.DCC.LXIX. | * [*Different settings.*]

FORMULA: Pot 12⁰ in sixes:

Vol. I: π^2 a–c⁶ d² A–N⁶ O² (*signed* ' * ' *on* a–O $1 *and* π2; *signed* ' VOL. I.' *on* a–O $1; A2, B2, L2, L3 *unsigned*; π1 *half-title*, O2 *advertisements*).

Vol. II: π^2 A–S⁶ T⁴ (*signed* ' * ' *on* A–T $1 *and* π2; *signed* ' VOL. II.' *on* A–T $1; A2, D2, L2, N2, P2, Q2, S2, *unsigned*; π1 *half-title*).

Vol. III: π^2 A–U⁶ X⁴ (*signed* ' * ' *on* A–X $1 *and* π2; *signed* ' VOL. III.' *on* A–X $1; B2 D2 E2, I2, K2, N2, Q2, R2, S2, U2 *unsigned*; π1 *half-title*, X4 *advertisements*).

Press-figures: ' 1 ' on Vol. I b1 A1 . . . E1 G1 H1 I1 M1 N1, Vol. II B1 . . . D1 F1 G1 M1 . . . T1, Vol. III K3 L1 M1 P1 . . . U1. ' 3 ' on Vol. I a1 c1 F1 K1 L1, Vol. II A1 E1 H1 . . . L1, Vol. III A1 . . . D1 F1 G6ʳ H1 I1 N1 O1 X1.

Plates: portrait ' VIRGILIUS.' faces Vol. I title-page, unsigned, plate marks 82 × 65. Folding map at Vol. II A1: ' THE | *Voyage* | of Æneas | *As Defcribed by* | VIRGIL ', unsigned, plate mark c. 165 × 235.

PAPER: Medium quality; marks 1/v, 1/bell.

TYPE: RB 2.

VARIANT: Issue on inferior paper, Pot 12⁰:
   Formula: (*Without* ' * ' *signatures*).
   Paper: Medium-poor quality; marks 2/i, 1/v.

NOTES: *Publication*: published by 30 March 1769 (*GJ*, which names J. Gilmour, D. Baxter and J. Barry as publishers with R. and A. Foulis).

COPIES: G⁴ (fine and common), L (fine and common).

498 Young, Edward, *The Complaint: or Night-*   1769
thoughts, etc.

THE | COMPLAINT: | OR, | NIGHT-THOUGHTS | ON | LIFE, DEATH, | AND | IMMORTALITY. | TO WHICH IS ADDED, | A PARAPHRASE ON PART OF THE | BOOK OF JOB. | [*quotation, 2 lines*] VOL. I [II]. | GLASGOW: | PRINTED BY ROBERT & ANDREW FOULIS, | PRINTERS TO THE UNIVERSITY, | M.DCC.LXIX. † [*Same setting.*]

FORMULA: Pot 12⁰ in sixes:
    Vol. I: π^2 A–T⁶ (*signed* ' † ' *on* \$1; *signed* ' VOL. I.' *on* A–T \$1).
    Vol. II: π1 A–N⁶ O² (*signed* ' † ' *on* \$1; *signed* ' VOL. II.' *on* A–O \$1).
    Press-figures: ' 1 ' on Vol. I A2 B1 E1 G1 I6 K6 L1 ... O1 Q1 R1 T1, Vol. II B1 C1 E1 ... O1. ' 3 ' on Vol. I C1 D1 F1 H1 P3 S1, Vol. II A2 D1.

PAPER: Medium quality; marks 1/v.

TYPE: RB 2.

VARIANT: Issue on (?) inferior paper, not seen (' † ' signatures).

COPIES: G⁴, L.

† **499** Addison, Joseph, *Poems on Several Occasions*   1770

POEMS | ON | SEVERAL | OCCASIONS; | BY | THE RIGHT HONOURABLE | JOSEPH ADDISON, Efq; | GLASGOW, | PRINTED BY ROBERT AND ANDREW FOULIS, | PRINTERS TO THE UNIVERSITY, | M.DCC.LXX.

FORMULA: Pot 12⁰ in sixes: π^2 A–Q⁶ R⁴.
    Press-figures: ' 1 ' on C1 G1 ... L1 P1. ' 2 ' on B1 F1.

PAPER: Medium-poor quality; marks ?1/v.

TYPE: RB 2.

NOTES: Published by 15 March 1770 (*GJ*).

COPIES: G⁴, L.

1770   Anacreon, *Odes*, with Sappho and Alcaeus, **500**
                                    Remains, G and L

'ΑΙ ΤΟΥ | ΑΝΑΚΡΕΟΝΤΟΣ | Ω,ΔΑΙ, | ΚΑΙ ΤΑ ΤΗΣ |
ΣΑΠΦΟΥΣ, | ΚΑΙ ΤΑ ΤΟΥ | ΑΛΚΑΙΟΥ | ΛΕΙΨΣΑΝΑ. |
[*quotation, 1 line*] | GLASGUAE: | IN AEDIBUS ACA
DEMICIS | EXCUDEBANT R. ET A. FOULIS | ACA
DEMIAE TYPOGRAPHI | M.DCC.LXX.

FORMULA: Foolscap 8⁰ in fours: A^4 B–M^4 N^2 (*A1 half-title*).

PAPER: Medium quality; marks 4/iv.

TYPE: GDP 2, RB 2, RSP 2. Without long f. Latin translation
as footnotes to the text.

VARIANT: Issue on common paper, [? Foolscap] 8⁰:
Paper: Medium-poor quality; no marks.

NOTES: *Prices* (? issue): Wholesale: 1s. 2d. (*BQ* 4). Retail:
1s. 6d. (*CP* 4).

COPIES: G^4 (title-page mutilated), O (both fine); G^2 (common).

1770   Collins, William, *Poetical Works*, with **501**
                                    Hammond, James, *Elegies*

THE | POETICAL | WORKS | OF | Mr. WILLIAM COL
LINS. | TO WHICH ARE ADDED, | Mr. HAMMOND'S
ELEGIES. | GLASGOW, | PRINTED BY ROBERT AND
ANDREW FOULIS, | PRINTERS TO THE UNIVERSITY.
| M.DCC.LXX.

FORMULA: Pot 12⁰ in sixes: π^2 A–I^6 (I6 *blank*).
Press-figures: ' 1 ' on B1 D1.

PAPER: Medium-good quality; marks 1/?v, 3/?iv, 4/?iv. The
book certainly belongs to the series of Pot 12⁰ poets in spite of
the Foolscap mark in the third lot of paper.

TYPE: RB 2.

VARIANT: State with a variant title-page:
Title-page: [*Omits lines 6–7* (' TO WHICH ARE ADDED, |
| MR. HAMMOND'S ELEGIES.'). *The rest of the book,
including the press figures, is identical, and Hammond's* Elegies *are
included. The rest of the title-page is apparently printed from the
same type as the fuller version, with altered vertical spacing.*]
COPIES: G^4 (short title-page), L (long title-page).

† **502** [Anon.], *A Compend of Physics*   1770

A | COMPEND | OF | PHYSICS. | [*quotation, 2 lines*] | GLAS
GOW: | Printed by Robert and Andrew Foulis | for T.
CADEL in London, and | John Balfour in Edinburgh. |
M.DCC.LXX.

FORMULA: Foolscap 8° in fours: A–O⁴.
   Press-figures: ' 3 ' on C2 D1 F4 G1 I1 M1 N1.

PAPER: Medium-good quality; marks 5/bell.

TYPE: RLP 1, RB 2.

VARIANT: Issue on inferior paper. [? Crown] 8°:
   Paper: Medium-poor quality; no marks.

COPIES: G⁴ (both issues).

† **503** Dryden, John, *Original Poems*   1770

ORIGINAL | POEMS, | BY | JOHN DRYDEN, Esq. | IN
TWO VOLUMES. | VOLUME I [II]. | GLASGOW, | PRIN
TED BY ROBERT AND ANDREW FOULIS, | PRINTERS
TO THE UNIVERSITY. [' ,' in Vol. II] | M.DCC.LXX.
[*Some of the same type used.*]

FORMULA: Pot 12° in sixes:
   Vol. I: π⁴ A–X⁶ (*signed* ' Vol. I.' *on* A–X $1; C2 *signed* ' C3 ';
   N3 *unsigned*; π1 *half-title*).
   Vol. II: π⁴ A–X⁶ Y⁴ (*signed* ' Vol. II.' *on* A–Y $1).
   Press-figures: ' 1 ' on Vol. I C1 . . . I1 M1 U1, Vol. II B1 C3 D1
   . . . F1 G2 H1 I1 L1 M1 O1 Q1 R1 T1 X1 (*variants*: ' 3 ' on
   Vol. I E1; none on Vol. I X1). ' 3 ' on Vol. I A1 B1 K1 L1 O1
   P1 Q1 R1 S1 X1, Vol. II A6ʳ K3 P1 U6ʳ (*variant*: ' 1 ' on Vol.
   I O1).

PAPER: Medium-poor quality; marks 1/v.

TYPE: RB 2.

COPIES: G⁴, L.

504 Findlay, Robert, *A Vindication of the Sacred*   1770
Books

A | VINDICATION | OF THE | SACRED BOOKS | AND
OF | JOSEPHUS, | ESPECIALLY THE FORMER, | FROM
VARIOUS | MISREPRESENTATIONS and CAVILS | OF
THE CELEBRATED | M. DE VOLTAIRE. | [*quotation, 2 lines*]
| BY | ROBERT FINDLAY, A.M. | ONE OF THE MINIS

TERS OF GLASGOW. | GLASGOW: | PRINTED BY ROBERT AND ANDREW FOULIS, | AND | SOLD BY J. GILMOUR AND SON, J. BARRY, | AND THE PRIN TERS. | M.DCC.LXX.

FORMULA: [? Writing Medium] 8⁰: a–b⁸ A–2N⁸ 2O⁴ 2P² (Z3ᵛ signed ' Z4 '; 2F2 unsigned).

Press-figures: ' 1 ' on a2 A1 . . . C1 E1 . . . 2F1 2G3 2I1 . . . 2M1 2O1.

PAPER: Medium quality; marks 7/i.

TYPE: RP 3, RLP 1, GP, Pica Hebrew.

NOTES: Publication: published by 26 July 1770 (GJ).

Prices: Wholesale: 4s. (BQ 11). Retail: 5s. in boards (GJ 26 July 1770, CP 10).

Stock in 1777: 200 copies (BQ 11).

COPIES: G⁴, L.

1770   Foulis Robert and Andrew, *Books printed by* **505** †
                                         R. and A. Foulis

[*Begins:*] BOOKS printed by ROBERT and ANDREW | FOULIS, printers to the UNIVERSITY | of GLASGOW. | The prices of the books, fewed in blue paper, are affixed.

[*Dated at the end:*] NOVEMBER 6th, 1770.

FORMULA: Single leaf of Foolscap 2⁰; π1.

PAPER: Medium quality; marks 5/GR beneath inverted bell.

TYPE: RSP 2.

NOTES: Reads the same as CP except: (1) Euripides, *Orestes*, 8⁰ (1753) priced 2s., not 3s.; (2) Velleius Paterculus (1752) and Pomponius Mela (1752) listed as 12⁰s, not 8⁰s; (3) Addison, *on the Christian Religion* (1753) and Argyll's *Instructions to a Son* (1763) listed as 8⁰s, not 12⁰s; (4) omits the following: Euripides, *Medea* (1775), Bonarelli, *Filli di Sciro* (1772), Hutcheson, *Inquiry*, (1772), *History of the Feuds among the Clans* (1764), Cervantes, *Don Quixote* (1771); (5) has a smaller list of 12⁰ English poets.

COPIES: Oxford University Press (John Johnson Memorial, 2 copies).

1770   Gay, John, *Poems on Several Occasions* **506** †

POEMS | ON | SEVERAL | OCCASIONS; | BY | MR. JOHN GAY, | [*quotation, 5 lines*] | VOLUME I. | GLASGOW: |

PRINTED BY ROBERT & ANDREW FOULIS, | PRINTERS TO THE UNIVERSITY, | M.DCC.LXX.
[*Vol.* II:] POEMS | ON | SEVERAL | OCCASIONS. | BY | MR. JOHN GAY. | VOLUME II. | GLASGOW: | PRINTED BY ROBERT & ANDREW FOULIS, | M.DCC.LXX.

FORMULA: Pot 12⁰ in sixes:
 Vol. I: A–R⁶ (*signed* ' VOL. I.' *on* B–R $1; I1 *signed* ' G '; G3, I2, Q2 *unsigned*).
 Vol. II: π^2 A–Q⁶ (*signed* ' VOL. II.' *on* A–Q $1; I1, M2 *unsigned*).
 Press-figures: ' 1 ' on Vol. I A2 D1 . . . F1 H1 K1 (*variant:* ' 3 ' on Vol. I E1), Vol. II E1 I1. ' 3 ' on Vol. I B1 C1 G1 L1 . . . N1 O6 P1 . . . R1, *Vol.* II A2 B1 C1 F1 . . . H1 K1 L1 N1 . . . Q1.

PAPER: Medium-poor quality; marks 1/iv.

TYPE: RB 2.

COPIES: G⁴.

507 Glasgow University: Academy. *The Gallery*   1770
of Raphael

THE | GALLERY OF RAPHAEL, | CALLED HIS | BIBLE, | BEING | FIFTY-TWO PRINTS, | AFTER PICTURES | PAINTED BY RAPHAEL | AND HIS DISCIPLES | IN THE LODGES OF THE VATICAN, | ENGRAVED IN THE ACADEMY OF ARTS AT GLASGOW. | GLASGOW: | PRINTED BY ROBERT AND ANDREW FOULIS, | PRINTERS TO THE UNIVERSITY, | M.DCC.LXX.

FORMULA: Writing Royal 1⁰: 2 leaves of letterpress (*title-page and contents*) + (?) 53 plates, unsigned, unnumbered (*the number of plates uncertain: the title-page specifies 52, each of the G⁴ copies has 53 and CP (pp. 16–17) advertises 54*).

PAPER: Title-page and plates: Good quality; marks 8/i, 8/J WHATMAN; size of sheet 24 × 17½ in. Contents leaf on a cut-down sheet of the paper used in *The Seven Cartoons of Raphael* of 1773 (No. 552, q.v.).

TYPE: (Contents leaf) RDP.

NOTES: *Price*: Retail: ' a feries of fifty-four prints ', 42s.; ' The Prints of the above Collection are fold feparately at 1s.' (*CP* 16–17).

COPIES: G⁴ (two copies, one of which lacks the contents leaf, each containing a slightly different series of 53 prints).

1770   Gray, Thomas, *Poems* **508**

NOTES: Not seen. Listed by Duncan (p. 71, No. 392) as 'Gray's Poems, 18mo.' Not in C. S. Northup's *A Bibliography of Thomas Gray* ((New Haven, 1917), nor H. W. Starr's supplement (Philadelphia, 1953).

1770   [Anon.], *Instructions for Officers* **509** †

NOTES: Not seen. Listed by Duncan (p. 71, No. 393) as 'Inſtructions for Officers, with Plates, 8vo.'

1770   Milton, John, *Paradise Lost* **510** †

PARADISE LOST, | A POEM. | THE AUTHOR | JOHN MILTON. | [*copper-plate portrait, unsigned, plate mark 121 × 121*] | GLASGOW: | PRINTED BY ROBERT AND ANDREW FOULIS, | PRINTERS TO THE UNIVERSITY, | M.DCC.LXX.

FORMULA: [? Writing Demy] 2⁰: π⁴ a² A–6D² (π1 *title-page*, π4 '*The Verse*', *probably conjugate;* π2.3 '*Advertisement*' *and subscribers*).

PAPER: Good quality; marks 9/i, 7/ii.

TYPE: RDP, RP 3, RSP 2, RLP 1.

VARIANT: Issue in Foolscap 2⁰:

Paper: Medium quality; marks 4/R crowned, 4/v, 4/vi.

NOTES: *Prices:* Wholesale: Demy, 17s.; Foolscap, 10s. 6d. (*BQ* 5). Retail: Demy, 21s.; Foolscap, 13s. (*CP* 6).

Stock in 1777: Demy, 41 copies; Foolscap, 92 copies (*BQ* 5).

COPIES: G⁴ (Demy), L (Demy), C (Foolscap).

1770   Montgomery Family.   *Memorables of the* **511** †
                                  Montgomeries

MEMORABLES | OF THE | MONTGOMERIES, | A NARRATIVE IN RHYME, | COMPOSED BEFORE THE PRESENT CENTURY. | PRINTED FROM | THE ONLY COPY KNOWN TO REMAIN, | WHICH HAS BEEN PRESERVED ABOVE SIXTY YEARS BY THE | CARE OF HUGH MONTGOMERIE SENIOR AT EAGLESHAM, | LONG ONE OF THE FACTORS OF THE | FAMILY OF EGLINTOUN. | GLASGOW, | PRINTED BY ROBERT AND ANDREW FOULIS, | M.DCC.LXX.

FORMULA: Foolscap 4⁰ in twos: A^2 B^2 C1.

PAPER: Medium quality; marks 3/?iv. C on poor quality, (?) no marks.

TYPE: RE 3.

VARIANT: Issue on another quality of paper, not seen (*BQ* 10).

NOTES: *Prices*: Wholesale: fine, 3*d*.; common, 2*d*. (*BQ* 10).
    Stock in 1777: fine, 44 copies; common, 46 copies (*BQ* 10).

COPIES: G⁴, L.

512   Moor, James, *Elementa Linguae Graecae*, L   1770

NOTES: Not seen. Listed by Duncan (p. 71, No. 387) as ' Moor's Greek Grammar, 8vo.' It is probably this edition that is advertised at a retail price of 1*s*. 8*d*. in No. 546 (Hutcheson, 1772).

513   Pindar, *Works*, G and L   1770

ΤΑ ΤΟΥ | ΠΙΝΔΑΡΟΥ | ΣΩΖΟΜΕΝΑ. | [*two columns of 2 lines each, separated by a vertical plain rule, 9; left:*] ΟΛΥΜΠΙΑ, | ΠΥΘΙΑ, | [*right:*] | ΝΕΜΕΑ, | ΙΣΘΜΙΑ. | PINDARI | QUAE EXTANT. | [*two columns of 2 lines each, separated by a vertical plain rule, 9; left:*] OLYMPIA, | PYTHIA, | [*right:*] NEMEA, | ISTHMIA. | CUM INTERPRETATIONE LATINA. | TOMUS I [II]. | GLASGUAE: | IN AEDIBUS ACADE MICIS, | EXCUDEBANT ROB. ET AND. FOULIS, | ACA DEMIAE TYPOGRAPHI, | M.DCC.LXX. [*Same setting.*]

FORMULA: Foolscap 8⁰: in fours:
    Vol. I: a^4 b^4 A–2L⁴ 2M² (a1 *half-title*).
    Vol. II: $π^4$ A^2 B–X⁴ (signed ' TOM. II.' on A–X \$1; X4 *advertisements*).

PAPER: Medium-good quality; marks 4/?iv, 5/?v.

TYPE: GGP, GP, RB 2, RSP 2, RLP 1. Without long f. Latin translation as footnotes to the text.

VARIANT: Issue on (?) inferior paper, not seen (*BQ* 3).

NOTES: *Prices*: Wholesale: fine, 3*s*. 6*d*.; common, 2*s*. (*BQ* 3). Retail: (?) fine, 5*s*. (*CP* 4).
    Stock in 1777: fine, 303 copies; common, 172 copies (*BQ* 3).

COPIES: G⁴, L (both Foolscap).

1770   Scougal, Henry, *The Life of God in the Soul of* **514**
       Man, with Leighton, Robert, *Rules and*
                                    Instructions

THE | LIFE of GOD | IN THE | SOUL of MAN. | OR, THE
| *NATURE and EXCELLENCY* | OF THE | CHRISTIAN
RELIGION. | By Henry Scougal, late Professor of | Divinity
in the University | of Aberdeen. | With a Preface by G.
Burnet, Profeffor of | Divinity in the Univerfity of Glafgow,
after-|wards Bifhop of Sarum. | [*quotation, 1 line*] | GLASGOW,
| Printed and sold by R. & A. Foulis | M.DCC.LXX. [*Separate
title-page on* L5 *for Leighton, Dr Robert*, Rules and Instructions
for a Holy Life.]

FORMULA: Foolscap 12⁰ in sixes: a⁶ b⁴ A–L⁶ N–O⁶ P² (L6
signed ' M2 '; a1 *half-title*, L4 *blank*).

PAPER: Medium-good quality; marks 4/R crowned, 4/vii.

TYPE: RLP 1, RB 2.

VARIANT: Issue on (?) inferior paper, not seen (*BQ* 11).

NOTES: *Prices*: Wholesale: fine, 9*d.*; common, 4*d.* (*BQ* 11).
Retail: (?) fine, 1*s.* (*CP* 11).
   Stock in 1777: fine, 100 copies; common, 1448 copies (*BQ* 11).

COPIES: G⁴ (Foolscap).

1770   Shenstone, William, *Select Works* **515 †**

THE | SELECT | WORKS | IN | VERSE and PROSE, | OF
| WILLIAM SHENSTONE, | ESQUIRE. | THE SECOND
EDITION. | GLASGOW: | printed by robert & andrew
foulis, | M.DCC.LXX.

FORMULA: Pot 12⁰ in sixes: A–M⁶.
   Press-figures: ' 1 ' on L1. ' 3 ' on B1 . . . K1 M1.

PAPER: Medium quality; marks 1/v.

TYPE: RB 2, RLP 1.

COPIES: L.

1770   Stayley, George, *An Elegy on Mr William Dick* **515A**

AN | ELEGY | ON | MR. WILLIAM DICK. | ADDRESSED
| TO ALL HIS FRIENDS; | PARTICULARLY | TO HIS
WIDOW. | BY GEORGE STAYLEY. | [*quotation, 2 lines*] |
GLASGOW: | PRINTED IN THE YEAR M.DCC.LXX.

FORMULA: Royal 4⁰: π⁴.

PAPER: Medium-good quality; marks 8/J WHATMAN.

TYPE: RDP, RSP 2.

NOTES: Without the Foulis Press imprint, but in their style and can scarcely have been printed elsewhere. Another book by Stayley, *A Moral Inquiry into the Natural Worth and Dignity of Man . . . to which is added an Elegy in memory of the Author by J. Riddell* (Glasgow, no printer, 1778) may also have been printed at the Foulis Press, but here the typographical evidence is ambiguous (see BM 1477. dd. 39).

COPIES: G².

516 Stonhouse, James, *Spiritual Directions*   1770

SPIRITUAL | DIRECTIONS | FOR THE | UNINSTRUC TED; | NOT LESS PROPER | For the Ufe of INFIRMARY PATIENTS, | THAN FOR | The UNINSTRUCTED in all CONDI TIONS. | BY JAMES STONHOUSE, M.D. | Phyfician to the Northampton Infirmary; and | formerly of St. John's College, Oxford. | [*quotations, 4 lines*] | THE TWELFTH EDITION. | GLASGOW: | PRINTED BY ROBERT AND ANDREW FOULIS | M.DCC.LXX.

FORMULA: Foolscap 8⁰ in fours: A–K⁴ (sometimes signed '†' on C1).

Press-figures: '1' on G1. '3' on B1 . . . F1 H1 . . . K1.

PAPER: Medium quality; marks 3/iv; size of sheet 16 × 13 in.

TYPE: RLP 1, RB 2.

VARIANT: Issue on another quality of paper, not seen (*BQ* 7). The appearance of only one '†' signature does not point conclusively to the quality of the copies seen.

NOTES: *Prices*: Wholesale: fine, 4*d*.; common, 3*d*. (*BQ* 7).
Stock in 1777: fine, 78 copies; common 110 copies (*BQ* 7).

COPIES: G⁴ (one of two copies missing).

517 Waller, Edmund, *Poems on Several Occasions*   1770

POEMS | ON | SEVERAL OCCASIONS; | BY | EDMUND WALLER, Efq; | GLASGOW, | PRINTED BY ROBERT AND ANDREW FOULIS, | PRINTERS TO THE UNIVER SITY, | M.DCC.LXX.

FORMULA: Pot 12⁰ in sixes: a⁶ A–Y⁶ (*sometimes signed '†' on* R1; R2 *unsigned*; a1 *half-title*).

Press-figures: ' 1 ' on B1 E1 . . . I1 L1 . . . P1 S1 U1 . . . Y1.
' 2 ' on R1. ' 3 ' on T1.

PAPER: Medium-poor quality; marks 1/v.

TYPE: RB 2.

VARIANT: There was probably an issue on better-quality paper, of which the ' † ' signature in the G4 copy is a relic.

COPIES: G4.

1770   Wight, William, *Heads of a Course on Ancient* **518**
                               and Modern History

NOTES: Not seen. *GJ* 25 October 1770: ' DOCTOR WIGHT will begin his courſe of Lectures *on Ancient and Modern Hiſtory*, in the COLLEGE of Glaſgow, on Monday the fifth Day of November next. – Heads of the Courſe of Lectures, to be had at the Shop of Meſſrs. FOULIS in the COLLEGE.'

For details of prices, etc., see the *Notes* to No. 549 (Wight, 1772).

1771   Akenside, Mark, *The Pleasures of Imagination* **519**

THE | PLEASURES | OF | IMAGINATION. | A POEM. | IN | THREE BOOKS. | BY | DR. AIKENSIDE. | [*quotation, 2 lines*] | GLASGOW: | PRINTED BY ROBERT AND ANDREW FOULIS | M.DCC.LXXI.

FORMULA: Pot 12⁰ in sixes; a^2 b^2 A–H⁶ I⁴ (*signed* ' † ' *on* b–I $1, except – occasionally – B1).

Press-figures: ' 1 ' on b1 A1 . . . F1 H1 I1 (*Variant*: none on b1). ' 3 ' on G1.

PAPER: Medium-poor quality; marks 1/bell, 1/v, 3/v.

TYPE: RB 2.

VARIANT: Issue on another quality of paper, not seen (' † ' signatures).

COPIES: G4, L.

1771   ' Cebes ', *Table*, G and L **520**

ʽΟ ΤΟΥ | ΚΕΒΗΤΟΣ | ΠΙΝΑΞ. | ACCEDIT | INTERPRE TATIO LATINA, | EX EDITIONE | JACOBI GRONOVII. | GLASGUAE: | IN AEDIBUS ACADEMICIS | EXCUDE BANT ROBERTUS ET ANDREAS FOULIS | ACA DEMIAE TYPOGRAPHI. | M.DCC.LXXI.

FORMULA: Foolscap 8⁰ in fours: A–L⁴ M².

  Press-figures: ' 3 ' on A2 B1 . . . L1.

PAPER: Medium quality; marks 4/iv, 3/iv; size of sheet 16½ × 13 in.

TYPE: GDP 2, GGP, GP, RLP 1.   Latin follows Greek.

VARIANT: Issue on inferior paper, [? Foolscap] 8⁰:

  Paper: Medium-poor quality; no marks.

NOTES: *Prices*: Wholesale: fine, 1*s*. 2*d*.; common, 9*d*. (*BQ* 3). Retail: (?) fine, 3*s*. 6*d*., together with No. 349 (Epictetus, 1758) or No. 583 (Epictetus, 1775) and No. 359 (Theophrastus, 1758) as a set of three (advertisement in No. 546, Hutcheson, 1772; *CP* 4).

  Stock in 1777: fine, 174 copies; common, 84 copies (*BQ* 3).

COPIES: G⁴ (both issues), L (fine).

520A   ' Cebes ', *Table*, E   1771

THE | TABLATURE | OF | CEBES | THE THEBAN, | A DISCIPLE OF SOCRATES. | BEING AN | ALLEGORICAL PICTURE | OF | HUMAN LIFE. | Tranſlated from the GREEK | BY SAMUEL BOYSE M.A. | THE FOURTH EDITION. | GLASGOW: | PRINTED AND SOLD BY ROBERT | AND ANDREW FOULIS | M.DCC.LXXI.

FORMULA: Pot 12⁰ in sixes: A–C⁶ (C6 *advertisements*).

PAPER: Medium-poor quality; marks 1/iv.

TYPE: RLP 2, RB 2.

COPIES: G².

† **521**   Cervantes Saavedra, Miguel de, *Don Quixote*, E   1771

THE | HISTORY | OF THE RENOWNED | DON QUIXOTE | DE LA MANCHA. | Written in SPANISH by | MIGUEL DE CERVANTES SAAVEDRA. | TRANSLATED BY SEVERAL HANDS: | And PUBLISHED by | THE LATE MR. MOTTEUX. | Revis'd a new from the beſt SPANISH Edition, | BY MR. OZELL: | Who has likewiſe added EXPLANATORY NOTES | from *Jervas, Oudin, Sobrino, Pineda, Gregorio,* | and the *Royal Academy Dictionary* of *Madrid.* | IN FOUR VOLUMES. | VOLUME I [II] [III] [IV]. | GLASGOW: | PRINTED BY ROBERT & ANDREW FOULIS | M.DCC.LXXI. [*Nearly all from the same setting. Vol.* 1 *has* ' * ' *at the beginning, and Vols.* 11 *and* 1v *have* ' † ' *at the end, of the last line. The word* ' Pineda ' *in line 14 of Vol.* 111 *has had the* ' i ' *supplied in pen and ink in the fine-paper copies seen.*]

FORMULA: [? Crown] 12° in sixes:

Vol. I: a⁶ b⁴ A–2E⁶ 2F² 2G² (*signed ' * ' on $1; C2ᵛ signed ' C3 '; 2G2 advertisements*).

Vol. II: π1 A⁴ B–2E⁶ 2F⁴ (*signed ' * ' on A–R $1; signed ' † ' on π1 and T–X, 2A–2F $1*).

Vol. III: A² B–2G⁶ 2H⁴ (*signed ' † ' on B–2H $1*).

Vol. IV: A–2L⁶ 2M² (*signed ' † ' on $1; E2 unsigned*). (*Signed ' VOL. I [. . . IV].' on $1 except title-pages.*)

Press-figures: ' 1 ' on Vol. I A1 . . . D1 F1 H1 N1 . . . 2E1, Vol. II A1 B1 D1 F1 G1 I1 K1 M1 O1 Q1 . . . T1 X1 Y1 2B1 2E1, Vol. III B1 . . . D1 G1 . . . M1 O1 . . . Q1 S1 T1 X1 . . . 2B1 2D1 2E1 2G1 2H1, Vol. IV A6 B1 . . . F1 H1 I1 N1 Q1 T1 X1 Y1 2C1 2D1 2G1 2I1 2K1 2M1 (*variant*: ' 3 ' on Vol. I N1). ' 3 ' on Vol. I E1 G1 I1 . . . L1 M6, Vol. II C1 E1 H1 L1 N1 P1 U1 Z1 2A1 2C1 2D1 2F1, Vol. III E1 F1 N1 R1 2C1 2F1, Vol. IV G1 K1 . . . M1 O1 P1 R1 S1 U1 Z1 . . . 2B1 2E1 2F1 2H1 2L1 (*variants*: ' 1 ' on Vol. I L1 M6).

Plates: 3 plates, unsigned, plate marks not seen, with directions for placing at Vol. II p. 238, Vol. III p. 146 and Vol. IV p. 398.

PAPER: Poor quality; no marks.

TYPE: RLP 1, RB 2.

VARIANTS: Issue on (?) inferior paper, [? Crown] 12°:

Formula: (*without ' * ' and ' † ' signatures*).

Paper: Poor quality; vertical chain lines; no marks (probably half sheets of Double Crown).

BQ (p. 8) speaks of ' fine,' ' middle ' and ' common ' paper. with middle and common at the same price. (?) Fine not seen,

NOTES: *Prices*: Wholesale: fine, 6s.; middle, 3s. 6d.; common, 3s. 6d. (*BQ* 8). Retail: (?) fine, 8s. (*CP* 11).

Stock in 1777: fine, 106 copies; middle 818 copies; common 650 copies; odd volumes, 60 (*BQ* 8).

COPIES: G⁴, L (with ' * ' and ' † ' signatures), O (without ' * ' and ' † ' signatures).

1771   Collins, William, *Poetical Works*, with   **522** † Hammond, James, *Elegies*

THE | POETICAL | WORKS | OF | Mr. WILLIAM COL LINS. | TO WHICH ARE ADDED | Mr. HAMMOND'S ELEGIES. | GLASGOW: | PRINTED BY ROBERT & ANDREW FOULIS, | M.DCC.LXXI.

FORMULA: Pot 12° in sixes: π² A–I⁶ (*signed ' † ' on $1 except π1, B1; I6 advertisements*).

Press-figures: ' 1 ' on A6 C1 E1 G6ʳ H1 I1.   ' 3 ' on B1 D1 F1.

PAPER: Medium-good quality; blue; marks 3/IO in lozenge. Hammond (from sig G.) on medium quality; marks 1/?vii.

TYPE: RB 2.

VARIANT: Issue on (?) inferior paper, not seen (' † ' signatures).

COPIES: G⁴, L.

523 [Anon.], *Considerations upon a Bankrupt Law for*   1771
Scotland

CONSIDERATIONS | UPON A | BANKRUPT LAW | FOR | SCOTLAND. | GLASGOW: | PRINTED BY ROBERT AND ANDREW FOULIS, | M.DCC.LXXI. | [*plain rule, 50*] | PRICE SIX-PENCE.

FORMULA: Crown 4⁰: π² A–B⁴ (π1 *half-title*, B4 *blank*).

PAPER: Medium-good quality; marks 9/i; size of sheet 19¾ × 14¾ in.

TYPE: RE 3, RSP 2, RGP 2, RDP.

NOTES: *Price*: Retail: 6*d*. (title-page).

COPIES: G⁴.

524 Denham, John, *Poems and Translations, with*   1771
The Sophy

POEMS | AND | TRANSLATIONS; | WITH THE | SOPHY, | A | TRAGEDY. | WRITTEN BY THE HONOURABLE | SIR JOHN DENHAM, | KNIGHT OF THE BATH. | GLASGOW: | PRINTED BY ROBERT & ANDREW FOULIS | M.DCC.LXXI.

FORMULA: Pot 12⁰ in sixes : *a*² b² A–U⁶ X⁴ (*signed* ' † ' *on* A–X$1 *except* S1, U1; *signed* '†' *on* b1ᵛ, S6ᵛ, U6ᵛ; D2 *unsigned*; a1 *half-title*).

Press-figures: ' 1 ' on A6 C1 F1 H1 K1 M1 O1 P1 R1 T1 X1. ' 3 ' on B1 E1 G1 I1 L1 N1 Q1 S1 U1.

PAPER: Medium quality; blue; marks 3/IO in lozenge.

TYPE: RB 2.

VARIANT: Issue on inferior paper, Pot 12⁰:
Formula: (*Without* ' † ' *signatures*; *no press-figures on* A6).
Paper: Medium-poor quality; marks 1/v.

COPIES: G⁴ (both issues), L (fine).

1771   Dryden, John, *Fables Ancient and Modern, etc.* **525**

FABLES | ANTIENT AND MODERN; | TRANSLATED
INTO | VERSE, | FROM | HOMER, OVID, | BOCCACE
AND CHAUCER: | WITH | ORIGINAL POEMS. | BY JOHN
DRYDEN Esq̄ ; | VOL. I [II]. | [*quotation, 3 lines; omitted in
Vol.* II] | GLASGOW: | PRINTED BY ROBERT AND
ANDREW FOULIS | M.DCC.LXXI. [*Much of the same type
used.*]

FORMULA: Pot 12⁰ in sixes:
Vol. I: A–U⁶ X² (A2 *signed* ' A ', A3 *signed* ' A2 ').
    Vol. II: A⁴ B–T⁶.
    (*Signed* ' VOL. I [II].' *on $1 except title-pages.*)
    Press-figures: ' 1 ' on Vol. I A2 (' A ') B1 . . . F1 H1 . . . Q1 R3
U1 X1, Vol. II C1 E1 F1 L1 M1 N1 P2 R1 T1. ' 3 ' on Vol. II
B1 D1 G1 I1 K1 O1 Q1 S1.
PAPER: Medium-poor quality; marks 1/iv.
TYPE: RB 2.
COPIES: G⁴, L.

1771   Foulis, Robert and Andrew, *A Catalogue of* **526**
                                Books of Various Ages

A | CATALOGUE OF BOOKS | OF VARIOUS | AGES, LAN
GUAGES, and SCIENCES; | TO WHICH IS SUBJOINED, | A
CATALOGUE OF MANUSCRIPTS | IN THE | GREEK,
LATIN, ORIENTAL, and other LANGUAGES; | many of which have
not been printed, and the colla-|tion of others which have been
printed, might be | very useful in giving more accurate
editions. | The PRICE of each BOOK and MANUSCRIPT is to be
found at the END of | the CATALOGUE, with a reference to the
Number. | GENTLEMEN, *who choose any Articles of this Catalogue,
are desired to di-|rect their Orders to* ROBERT *and* ANDREW
FOULIS, *Printers to the Uni-|versity of Glasgow.* | G L A S G O W,
M.DCC.LXXI.

FORMULA: Foolscap 4⁰ in twos: π² A–T² X–2G² (B1 *signed* 'A').
PAPER: Medium-poor quality; marks 5/?.
TYPE: A1–Q1 in RE 1; Q1ᵛ–T2ᵛ and 2E2–2G2ᵛ in RLP 1;
X1–2E1ᵛ in RP 2 (early form); π2–π2ᵛ in RE 3. The RE1 and
RP 2 are both very worn.
NOTES: An extraordinary typographical hodge-podge. It is
possible that the sections set in RE 1 and the early form of
RP 2 had been standing in type for many years.
COPIES: G² (3 copies, 2 imperfect).

527 Garth, Samuel, *Poetical Works* 1771

THE | POETICAL | WORKS | OF | Sir SAMUEL GARTH, M.D. | GLASGOW: | PRINTED BY ROBERT AND ANDREW FOULIS | M.DCC.LXXI. †

FORMULA: Pot 12⁰ in sixes: a⁴ A–N⁶ O² (*signed '†' on $1 O2 contents;*).

Press-figures: ' 1 ' on B1 . . . N1.

PAPER: Medium quality; marks 3/v, 3/bell, 1/iv; size of sheet 15¾ × 13¼ in. (i.e. large Pot).

TYPE: RB 2.

VARIANT: Issue on inferior paper, Pot 12⁰:
Formula: (*without ' † ' signatures*).
Paper: Medium-poor quality; marks 1/iv.

COPIES: G⁴ (both issues), L (fine).

528 Pope's Homer, *Iliad*, E 1771

THE | ILIAD | OF | HOMER. | TRANSLATED BY | ALEXANDER POPE. | VOLUME FIRST [SECOND] [THIRD] [FOURTH]. | [*quotations, 4 lines (Vol. I), 4 lines (Vol. II), 5 lines (Vol. III) and 2 lines (Vol. IV)*] | GLASGOW: | PRINTED BY ROBERT AND ANDREW FOULIS | M.DCC.LXXI. | †

FORMULA: Pot 12⁰ in sixes:
Vol. I: π² A–O⁶ P⁴ (E2, M3 *unsigned;* π1 *half-title*).
Vol. II: π² A² B–O⁶ (E2 *unsigned;* π1 *half-title*, O6 *blank*).
Vol. III: π² A–P⁶ Q² (K2 *unsigned;* π1 *half-title*).
Vol. IV: π² A⁴ B–O⁶ (I2, M2, O2, O3 *unsigned;* π1 *half-title*).
(*Signed '†' on title pages and $1 except half-titles and Vol. II M1; signed ' VOL. I [. . . IV].' on $1 except half-titles.*)
Press-figures: ' 1 ' on Vol. I A6 F1 H1 P1, Vol. II B1 C1 E1 . . . G1 H6 L1 M1 N6 O1, Vol. III B6 F1 H1 K1 . . . O1, Vol. IV A4 B1 . . . D1 I1 N1. ' 3 ' on Vol. I B1 . . . E1 G1 I1 . . . O1, Vol. II D6 I1 K1, Vol. III A1 C1 D6ʳ E1 G1 I1 P1, Vol. IV E1 G6 H1 K1 M1.
Plate: folding map follows Vol. I π2, ' GRÆCIA | HOMERICA ', ' PHRYGIA | cum | Oris Maritimis ', unsigned, plate marks 166 × 246.

PAPER: Medium quality; marks 1/vii.

TYPE: RB 2.

VARIANT: Issue on (?) inferior paper, not seen (' † ' signatures).

COPIES: G⁴, L.

1771   Millar, John, *Lectures on Government* **529** †

NOTES: Not seen. There was a copy in G⁴, but it is missing.
The unnumbered catalogue slip reads: '[Millar (John)
Professor.] A course of lectures on government, given annually
in the University. Glasgow: [Printed by R. and A. Foulis?]
1771. 167 × 104 mm. pp. 8.' This sounds like a Foolscap 8⁰,
½ sheet, uncut. Cf. No. 530 below. (G⁴ also has a complete
MS of these lectures, catalogue No. 703558–9.)

1771   Millar, John, *Lectures on the Private Law of* **530**
Scotland

A | COURSE OF LECTURES | ON THE | PRIVATE LAW
| OF | SCOTLAND. | GIVEN ANNUALLY | IN THE |
UNIVERSITY OF GLASGOW. | GLASGOW: | PRINTED BY
ROBERT & ANDREW FOULIS, | PRINTERS TO THE UNIVER
SITY, | M.DCC.LXXI.
FORMULA: Foolscap 8⁰: π^8.
PAPER: Medium quality; marks 3/iv.
TYPE: RE 3, RP 3, RSP 2, RLP 1.
COPIES: G⁴.

1771   Milton John, *Paradise Lost* **531** †

PARADISE | LOST, | A | POEM | IN | TWELVE BOOKS.
| THE AUTHOR | JOHN MILTON. | VOLUME I [II]. |
GLASGOW: | PRINTED AND SOLD BY R. & A. FOULIS | PRIN
TERS TO THE UNIVERSITY, | M.DCC.LXXI. [*Same
setting*.]
FORMULA: Pot 12⁰ in sixes:
    Vol. I: a⁶ b² A–P⁶ Q² (*signed* ' VOL. I.' *on* b–Q $1; a1 *half-title*).
    Vol. II: A–P⁶ (–P5, P6; *signed* ' VOL. II.' *on* B–P $1; C2
signed ' C3 ').
    Press-figures: ' 3 ' on Vol. I b1 A1 . . . Q1. Vol. II A2 B1 . . . P1.
PAPER: Medium quality; marks 1/vii.
TYPE: RB 2, RSP 2.
COPIES: G⁴, L.

1771   Prior, Matthew, *Poems on Several Occasions* **532** †

POEMS | ON | SEVERAL | OCCASIONS; | BY | MATTHEW
PRIOR, Efq. | VOL. I [II]. | GLASGOW: | PRINTED BY ROBERT

& ANDREW FOULIS, | PRINTERS TO THE UNIVERSITY, |
M.DCC.LXXI. | † [*Same setting.*]

FORMULA: Pot 12⁰ in sixes:
    Vol. I: a⁶ b⁴ A–R⁶ (B2 *unsigned;* R6 *advertisements*).
    Vol. II: A–Y⁶ (Y3.4, *contents of Vol. I, may be found bound in
    Vol. I*).
    (*Signed* ' † ' *on* $1; *signed* ' VOL. I [II].' *on* $1 *except title-pages*).
    Press-figures: ' 1 ' on Vol. I bɪ Aɪ Eɪ Fɪ Hɪ Mɪ Oɪ Qɪ Rɪ,
Vol. II Dɪ Fɪ Iɪ Kɪ Mɪ Pɪ Rɪ Uɪ Xɪ. ' 3 ' on Vol. I a2 Bɪ Cɪ
Gɪ Kɪ L6 Nɪ P6, Vol. II A3 Bɪ Eɪ Gɪ Hɪ Lɪ Nɪ Oɪ Qɪ Sɪ Tɪ Yɪ.
PAPER: Medium quality; marks I/iv.
TYPE: RB 2.
VARIANT: Issue on (?) inferior paper, not seen (' † ' signatures).
COPIES: G⁴, L.

533 Steele, Sir Richard, *The Conscious Lovers*   1771

THE | CONSCIOUS LOVERS. | A | COMEDY. | WRITTEN
BY | SIR RICHARD STEELE. | [*quotation, 7 lines*] | GLAS
GOW: | PRINTED BY ROBERT AND ANDREW FOULIS,
| M.DCC.LXXI. | †

FORMULA: Foolscap 8⁰ in fours: A–M⁴ (*signed* ' † ' *on* $1).
    Press-figures: ' 3 ' on A2 Cɪ . . . Mɪ.
PAPER: Medium quality; marks 3/iv.
TYPE: RLP 1, RB 2.
VARIANT: Issue on inferior paper, Foolscap 8⁰:
    Formula: (*without* ' † ' *signatures*).
    Paper: Poor quality, marks 5/?.
COPIES: G⁴ (fine), O (common).

† **534** Storer, John, *De Angina Maligna*, L   1771

TENTAMEN MEDICUM | INAUGURALE | DE | ANGINA
MALIGNA: | QUOD, | ANNUENTE SUMMO NUMINE,
| *Auctoritate Dignissimi Vice-Cancelarii*, | GULIELMI LEECH
MAN, S.S.T.P.P. | ET | COLLEGII GLASG. PRAEFECTI; |
NEC NON | AMPLISSIMI SENATUS ACADEMICI CONSENSU.
| ET NOBILISSIMAE FACULTATIS MEDICAE DECRETO; | PRO
GRADU DOCTORIS, | SUMMISQUE IN MEDICINA
HONORIBUS ET PRIVILEGIIS, | RITE AC LEGITIME
CONSEQUENDIS; | *Eruditorum examini subjicit* | JOANNES
STORER, A.M. *Britannus.* | AD DIEM XI JUNII, HORA XI,

| LOCOQUE SOLITO. | GLASGUAE: | IN AEDIBUS ACA
DEMICIS, | EXCUDEBANT ROBERTUS ET ANDREAS
FOULIS, | ACADEMIAE TYPOGRAPHI. | MDCCLXXI.
FORMULA: [? Crown] 8⁰ in fours: π^2 A–E⁴.
  Press-figures: ' 3 ' on B1 E1.
PAPER: Medium-good quality; marks 9/?.
TYPE: RP 3, RLP 1.
COPIES: G².

1771   Young, Edward, *Poems on Several Occasions* **535**

POEMS | ON | SEVERAL | OCCASIONS, | BY THE REV
EREND | EDWARD YOUNG, D.D. | RECTOR of WELLWYN in
HARTFORDSHIRE, | AND CHAPLAIN IN ORDINARY | TO
HIS MAJESTY. | FROM THE EDITION REVISED AND |
CORRECTED BY THE AUTHOR. | GLASGOW: | PRIN
TED BY ROBERT AND ANDREW FOULIS | M.DCC.
LXXI. | †
FORMULA: Pot 12⁰ in sixes: π^2 A–T⁶ (*signed* ' † ' *on* \$1).
  Press-figures: ' 1 ' on B1 ... H1 K1 M1 N1 Q1 T1. ' 3 ' on I1
L1 O1 R1 S1.
PAPER: Medium quality; marks 3/v.
TYPE: RB 2.
VARIANT: Issue on inferior paper, Pot 12⁰:
  Formula: (*without* ' † ' *signatures*).
  Paper: Medium-poor quality, marks 1/iv.
COPIES: G⁴ (fine), O (common).

1771   Young, Edward, *The Complaint: or Night-* **536**
thoughts, etc.

THE | COMPLAINT: | OR, | NIGHT-THOUGHTS | ON
| LIFE, DEATH, | AND | IMMORTALITY. | TO WHICH
IS ADDED, | A PARAPHRASE ON PART OF THE | BOOK
OF JOB. | [*quotation, 2 lines*] | VOL. I [II]. | GLASGOW: |
PRINTED BY ROBERT & ANDREW FOULIS, | PRINTERS TO THE
UNIVERSITY, | M.DCC.LXXI. [*Different settings.*]
FORMULA: Pot 12⁰ in sixes:
  Vol. I: π^2 A–T⁶ (I2 *unsigned*).
  Vol. II: π^2 A–N⁶ O² (π1 *blank*).
  (*Signed* ' † ' *and* ' VOL. I [II].' *on* \$1 *except title-pages.*)

Press-figures: ' 1 ' on Vol. 1 B1 D1 F1 K1 M1 ... O1 P3 R1 T1, Vol. 11 B1 E1 G1 I1 L1 M1. ' 3 ' on Vol. 1 A2 C1 E1 G1 H1 I3 L1 Q1 S1, Vol. 11 A6ʳ C1 D1 F1 H1 K1 N1 O1.

Plate: frontispiece (poet and Death) faces Vol. 1 title-page, unsigned, plate mark not seen.

PAPER: Medium quality; blue; marks 3/IO in lozenge crowned. Medium quality; marks 1/iv, 1/v.

TYPE: RB 2 RLP 1.

VARIANT: Issue on inferior paper Pot 12⁰:

Formula: (*without* ' † ' *signatures; press-figure* ' 3 ' *on Vol.* 1 N1*; no plate*).

Paper: Medium-poor quality; marks 1/v.

COPIES: G⁴ (both issues), L (fine).

† 537 Bonarelli della Rovere, C. Guidobaldo de, 1772 *Filli di Sciro*, I

FILLI | DI | SCIRO, | FAVOLA PASTORALE | DEL | C. GUIDOBALDO | DE' BONARELLI. | Con le FIGURE di SEBASTIANO LE CLERC. | IN GLASGUA, | DELLA STAMPA DI R. ED A. FOULIS | M.DCC.LXXII. | PRIMIERA MENTE STAMPATA IN FERRARA | M.DC.VII.

FORMULA: Foolscap 8⁰ in fours: a–b⁴ A–X⁴ Y².

Plates: seven plates, numbered ' 1 ' to ' 7 ', No. 1 signed ' *Se. le Clerc f.*'; variously placed, plate marks c. 80 × c. 50.

PAPER: Medium quality; marks 4/?, 5/?ii. The plates on similar paper.

TYPE: RLP 1, RSP 2.

VARIANT: Issue on another sort of paper, not seen (*BQ* 8).

NOTES: *Prices*: Wholesale, ' con figure ': fine, 1*s*. 6*d*.; common, 1*s*. 2*d*. (*BQ* 8). Retail, ' con figure ': (?) fine, 2*s*. (*CP* 6).

Stock in 1777: fine, 244 copies; common, 206 copies (*BQ* 8).

COPIES: G⁴, L (both Foolscap).

538 Burnet, Gilbert, Jr., and Hutcheson, Francis, 1772 *Letters concerning Virtue*

LETTERS | CONCERNING THE | TRUE FOUNDATION | OF | VIRTUE | OR | MORAL GOODNESS, | WROTE IN A CORRESPONDENCE | BETWEEN | MR. GILBERT BUR NET, | AND | MR. FRANCIS HUTCHESON. | GLASGOW: | PRINTED BY ROBERT AND ANDREW FOULIS, | PRINTERS TO THE UNIVERSITY, | M.DCC.LXXII.

FORMULA: Foolscap 8⁰: A–K⁸(–K8).

Press-figures: ' 1 ' on H8ʳ. ' 3 ' on A7 . . . C7 D8ʳ E8ʳ F1 G1 K1.

PAPER. Medium-good quality; marks 4/ ?vii.

TYPE: RLP 1.

VARIANT: Issue in Pot 8⁰:

Paper: Medium-poor quality; marks 1/iv.

NOTES: *Prices*: Wholesale: Foolscap, 1*s*. 2*d*.; Pot, 9*d*. (*BQ* 7).
Stock in 1777: Foolscap, 206 copies; Pot, 234 copies (*BQ* 7).

COPIES: G⁴ (both issues), L (fine).

1772   Cicero, *Orationes Selectae*, L   **539** †

MARCI | TULLII | CICERONIS | ORATIONES | SELEC TAE. | Ex EDITIONE J. OLIVETI. | GLASGUAE: M.DCC.LXXII.

FORMULA: Foolscap 8⁰ in fours: π1 A–M⁴.

PAPER: Medium quality; marks 4/vii.

TYPE: RLP 1.

NOTES: Without the Foulis Press imprint, but almost certainly printed there.
Price: Wholesale: 1*s*. (*BQ* 2).
Stock in 1777: 8 copies (*BQ* 2).

COPIES: G².

c. 1772–4   Foulis, Robert and Andrew, *Books printed*   **540**
                                         by R. and A. Foulis

[*Begins:*] BOOKS | PRINTED BY | ROBERT AND ANDREW FOULIS, | PRINTERS TO THE | UNIVERSITY OF GLAS GOW. | The PRICES of the Books, fewed in Blue Paper, are affixed.

FORMULA: Sheet of Post 2⁰: π² (π2 *blank*).

PAPER: Medium-good quality; thin; marks 6/none; size of sheet 18½ × 15½ in.

TYPE: RP 3.

NOTES: Reads the same as *CP* except: (1) Addison, *on the Christian Religion* (1753) and Argyll's *Instructions to a Son* (1763) listed as 8⁰s, not 12⁰s; (2) omits the following: Euripides, *Medea* (1775), *History of the Feuds among the Clans* (1764); (3) has a smaller list of 12⁰ English poets, but adds to it four books printed in 1771 not included in the list of 1770, No. 505. (Dryden's *Fables*, and Garth, Akenside and Denham).

Since Bonarelli, *Filli di Sciro* (1772) and Hutcheson, *Inquiry* (1772) are included, this list probably dates from the period 1772–4.

The only copy seen was originally sealed as a letter, and is addressed in MS on $\pi 2^r$ 'To | The Reverend Mr Thomas Piercy '.

COPIES: Oxford University Press (John Johnson Memorial).

541 Gay, John, *The Beggar's Opera*   1772

THE | BEGGAR'S | OPERA. | AS IT IS ACTED AT THE | THEATRE-ROYAL | IN | LINCOLNS-INN-FIELDS. | WRITTEN BY | JOHN GAY. | To which is prefixed | THE LIFE OF THE AUTHOR. | [*quotation, 1 line*] | GLASGOW: | PRINTED IN THE YEAR M DCC LXXII. | †

FORMULA: Pot 12° in sixes: A–S^6 T^2 (*signed* ' † ' *on* \$1; H3 *unsigned*).

Press-figures: ' 1 ' on A6^r B1 . . . S1.

PAPER: Medium quality; marks 1/vii.

TYPE: RB 2.

VARIANT: Issue on inferior paper, Pot 12°:

Formula: (*without* ' † ' *signatures*).

Paper: Medium-poor quality; marks 1/?vii.

NOTES: Belongs typographically to the series of 12° poets, though without the Foulis Press imprint.

COPIES: G^4 (common), L (fine).

† **542** Pope's Homer, *Odyssey*, E   1772

THE | ODYSSEY | OF | HOMER. | TRANSLATED BY | ALEXANDER POPE. | VOLUME FIRST [SECOND] [THIRD]. | [*quotation, 2 lines*] | GLASGOW: | PRINTED BY ROBERT & ANDREW FOULIS | M.DCC.LXXII. | † [*Same setting.*]

FORMULA: Pot 12° in sixes:

Vol. I: π^2 A–O^6 (D3, E3, K3 *unsigned*; $\pi 1$ *half-title*).

Vol. II: π^2 A^4 B–P^6 (B2, D2, L2 *unsigned*; $\pi 1$ *half-title*).

Vol. III: π^2 A–N^6 (A2, B3, C3, E2, H2 *unsigned*; $\pi 1$ *half-title*).

(*Signed* ' † ' *on title-pages and* \$1 *except half-titles; signed* ' VOL. I [. . . III].' *on* \$1 *except half-titles.*)

Press figures: ' 1 ' on Vol. I B2 C1 E6 G1 K1 . . . M1. ' 3 ' on Vol. I A1 D2 F1 H1 I1 O1, Vol. II A1 . . . G1 I1 . . . P1, Vol. III B1 . . . F1 I1 . . . L1 N1 (*variant*: no figure on Vol. II F1).

PAPER: Medium quality; marks 1/vii, 1/iv.

TYPE: RB 2.

VARIANT: Issue without ' † ' signatures, Pot 12⁰:
Formula: (without ' † ' signatures).
Paper: Apparently the same as the other issue.

COPIES: G⁴ (both issues), L (issue with ' † ' signatures).

1772   Hutcheson, Francis, *An Essay on the Nature and* **543**
Conduct of the Passions

NOTES: Not seen. Listed by Duncan (p. 72, No. 408) as ' . . .
Third edition, fools. 8vo. fine, 2s. 6d. common, 1s. 2d.' Format
and (wholesale) prices are from *BQ* (p. 8), which lists 213 copies
of the fine and 148 copies of the common in stock in 1777.
Retail price, (?) fine, 3s. (*CP* 7).

1772   Hutcheson, Francis, *Inquiry into our Ideas of* **544**
Beauty and Virtue

AN | INQUIRY | INTO THE | ORIGINAL OF OUR IDEAS
| OF | BEAUTY AND VIRTUE; | IN TWO TREATISES. |
I. Concerning BEAUTY, ORDER, | HARMONY, DESIGN.
| II. Concerning MORAL GOOD and EVIL. | BY FRANCIS
HUTCHESON, LLD. | LATE PROFESSOR OF PHILO
SOPHY IN | THE UNIVERSITY OF GLASGOW. | PRIN
TED FROM | THE FOURTH EDITION, M.DCC.XXXVIII.
| WITH THE AUTHOR'S CORRECTIONS | AND ADDI
TIONS INTERSPERSED | IN THEIR PROPER PLACES.
| GLASGOW: | PRINTED BY ROBERT AND ANDREW
FOULIS, | PRINTERS TO THE UNIVERSITY, |
M.DCC.LXXII.

FORMULA: Foolscap 8⁰: a⁸ A–R⁸ S⁴ (a3, R3 *unsigned;* S4
advertisements).
Press-figures: ' 1 ' on A1 B7 C1 D7 E6ʳ F7 G6ʳ I6ʳ L6ʳ N6ʳ R1.
' 3 ' on P6ʳ.

PAPER: Medium quality; marks 3/ii, 4/vii.

TYPE: RLP 1, RB 2, GB, RP 3.

VARIANT: Issue in Pot 8⁰:
Paper: Medium-poor quality; marks 1/?iv.

NOTES: *Prices:* Wholesale: fine, 2s. 3d.; common, 1s. 2d.
(*BQ* 7–8). Retail: (?) fine, 3s. (*CP* 7).
Stock in 1777: fine, 191 copies; common, 236 copies (*BQ* 7–8).

COPIES: G⁴, L (both Foolscap), O (Pot).

545 Hutcheson, Francis, *Logicae Compendium*, L   1772

LOGICAE | COMPENDIUM. | PRAEFIXA EST | DISSER
TATIO | DE | PHILOSOPHIAE ORIGINE, | EJUSQUE |
INVENTORIBUS aut EXCULTORIBUS | PRAECIPUIS.
| GLASGUAE: | IN AEDIBUS ACADEMICIS | EXCUDE
BANT ROBERTUS ET ANDREAS FOULIS | ACA
DEMIAE TYPOGRAPHI | M.DCC.LXXII.

FORMULA: [? Foolscap] 8° in fours: π^2 A–N^4 (D2 *unsigned;*
π1 *half-title*).

Press-figures: ' 1 ' on B1 C1 F1 H1 L1 N1. ' 3 ' on A1 D4^r E4
G1 I1 K4^r M4^r.

PAPER: Medium-poor quality, no marks.

TYPE: RE 2, RLP 1, RB 2.

NOTES: *Prices*: Wholesale: 9d. (*BQ* 2). Retail: 1s. (*CP* 5).
Stock in 1777: 56 copies (*BQ* 2).

COPIES: G^4.

† **546** Hutcheson, Francis, *A Short Introduction to*   1772
Moral Philosophy

A SHORT | INTRODUCTION | TO | MORAL PHILO
SOPHY, | IN THREE BOOKS; | CONTAINING THE |
ELEMENTS of ETHICKS | AND THE | LAW of NATURE.
| By FRANCIS HUTCHESON, LLD. | LATE PROFESSOR
OF PHILOSOPHY IN | THE UNIVERSITY OF GLASGOW.
| TRANSLATED FROM THE LATIN. | FOURTH EDI
TION. | VOL. I [II]. | GLASGOW: | PRINTED BY ROBERT &
ANDREW FOULIS | PRINTERS TO THE UNIVERSITY |
M DCC LXXII. [*Different settings.*]

FORMULA: Foolscap 8°:

Vol. I: a^8 b^4 A–L^8 M^6 (G4 *signed* ' F4 '; M2, M3 *signed* ' M3 ',
' M4 '; M6 *blank*).

Vol. II: π^2 A^4 B–M^6 N^4 (A2 *signed* ' M4 '; π1 *blank*, N4
advertisements).

(*Signed* ' VOL. I [II].' *on* \$1 *except* Vol. I a1, b1 *and* Vol. II π1.)

Press-figures: ' 1 ' on Vol. I A1 C1 . . . L1, Vol. II A1 C2 E1
E2 F1 H8^r I1 K6^r L1. ' 3 ' on Vol. I B1, Vol. II B3 D1 G2
M6^r N1.

PAPER: Medium quality; marks 5/ii.

TYPE: RLP 1, RB 2, RP 3.

VARIANT: Issue in Pot 8°:

Paper: Medium-poor quality; marks 1/iv.

NOTES: *Prices*: Wholesale: Foolscap, 3*s*.; Pot, 2*s*. 6*d*. (*BQ* 7). Retail: (?) Foolscap, 4*s*. (*CP* 7).
Stock in 1777: Foolscap, 44 copies; Pot, 111 copies (*BQ* 7).
COPIES: G⁴ (Foolscap), L (Pot, lacks Vol. 1 M3.4).

by 1772   Le Sage, Alain René, *The Devil upon Two*   **547** †
                   Sticks (*Le Diable Boiteux*), E

NOTES: Not seen. Advertised in No. 548 (Milton, 1772) as printed by R. and A. Foulis ' in fmall 12mo.'
Prices: Wholesale: ' p[ot]. 12mo. common ', 9*d*. (*BQ* 9). Retail: 1*s*. 6*d*. (*CP* 11, merely specifying 12º; it sounds like fine paper).
Stock in 1777: common, 8 copies (*BQ* 9).

1772   Milton, John, *Paradise Regained, etc.*   **548** †

PARADISE REGAIN'D. | A | POEM, | IN | FOUR BOOKS. | To which is added | SAMSON AGONISTES: | AND | POEMS UPON SEVERAL OCCASIONS, | WITH A TRAC TATE OF | EDUCATION. | THE AUTHOR | JOHN MIL TON. | VOL. I [II]. | GLASGOW: | PRINTED BY ROBERT AND ANDREW FOULIS | M.DCC.LXXII. †

FORMULA: Pot 12º in sixes:
    Vol. I: π² A–P⁶ Q² (*signed* ' † ' *on* π2 *and* A–Q $1; *signed* ' VOL. I.' *on* A–Q $1; π1 *half-title*).
    Vol. II: π⁴ A⁴ B–R⁶ (*signed* ' † ' *on* π2 *and* A–R $1; *signed* ' VOL. II.' *on* A–R $1; π1 *half-title*, R6 *advertisements*).
    Press-figures: ' 1 ' on Vol. 1 A1 . . . E1 H1 K1 L1 O1 P1, Vol. 11 B1 . . . E1 G1 H5 K1 . . . M1 O1 P1 Q 3 R1. ' 3 ' on Vol. 1 F1 G1 I1 M1 N1, Vol. 11 F1 I1 N1.
PAPER: Medium quality; marks 1/vii.
TYPE: RB 2.
VARIANT: Issue on another quality of paper, not seen (' † ' signatures).
COPIES: G⁴, L.

1772   Wight, William, *Heads of a Course on Civil*   **549**
                                    History

HEADS | OF A | COURSE OF | LECTURES | ON | CIVIL HISTORY. | WITH A | CHRONOLOGICAL | TABLE | FROM THE | EARLIEST ACCOUNTS | TO THE | PRE

SENT TIME. | BY | WILLIAM WIGHT, D.D. | PROFESSOR OF HISTORY IN THE | UNIVERSITY OF GLASGOW. | GLASGOW: | PRINTED BY ROBERT & ANDREW FOULIS | M.DCC.LXXII.

FORMULA: Foolscap 8⁰ in fours: π^2 A–G⁴ H².

PAPER: Medium quality; marks 4/vii.

TYPE: RLP 1, RP 3, RSP 2.

VARIANT: Issue in [? Pot] 8⁰, inferior paper:
  Paper: Medium-poor quality; no marks.

NOTES: This is a revision, much altered and with the addition of a chronological table, of Wight's *Heads of a Course on the Study of History*, 1767 (No. 471). It was probably the earlier version, still in print, that was referred to in *GJ* for 27 October 1768, where it was announced that Dr Wight would begin his lectures on Civil History in the College of Glasgow on Tuesday 1 November, and that *Heads* of the course of lectures were to be had at Messrs Foulis's shop.

One of the entries in *BQ* refers to ' Dr. Wight's heads of lectures with the chronological table ', which probably means the book described above. But the other two entries refer simply to ' Dr. Wight's heads of lectures ', fine and common, which may have meant either or both of the earlier *Heads* (No. 471, 1767 and No. 518, 1770).

Prices: Wholesale: fine, 6*d.*; common, 4*d.*; with the chronological table, 6*d.* (*BQ* 11).

Stock in 1777: fine, 8 copies; common, 56 copies; with the chronological table, 134 copies (*BQ* 11).

COPIES: G⁴ (Pot), L (Foolscap).

† **550** Augustine of Hippo, St, *Meditations, etc.*, E   1773

THE | MEDITATIONS | OF | ST. AUGUSTINE, | HIS TREATISE OF THE | LOVE OF GOD, | SOLILOQUIES AND MANUAL. | TRANSLATED BY | GEORGE STAN HOPE, D.D. | LATE DEAN OF CANTERBURY, AND CHAPLAIN IN ORDINARY | TO HER MAJESTY. | GLASGOW: | PRINTED BY ROBERT & ANDREW FOULIS, | M.DCC.LXXIII.

FORMULA: [? Foolscap] 8⁰ in fours: a⁴ b² A–2U⁴ (M2 *signed* ' K2; 2E2 *signed on the verso*).
  Press-figures: ' 1 ' on F1 2I1 2L1 2N1 2P1 2S1. ' 3 ' on 2R1.

PAPER: Medium-poor quality; no marks.

TYPE: RLP 1, RP 3.

VARIANT: Issue on (?) better-quality paper, not seen (*BQ* 8).
NOTES: *Prices*: wholesale: fine, 2*s*.; common, 1*s*. 2*d*. (*BQ* 8).
 Stock in 1777: fine, 36 copies; common, 245 copies (*BQ* 8).
COPIES: G⁴ (? common).

1773   Evans, Samuel, *De Hysteria*, L **551**

DISSERTATIO MEDICA | INAUGURALIS | DE | HYS
TERIA. | QUAM, | ANNUENTE SUMMO NUMINE, |
Auctoritate Digniſſimi Vice-Cancellarii, | GULIELMI LEECH
MAN s.s.t.p.p. | ET COLLEGII GLASG. PRAEFECTI; |
NEC NON | AMPLISSIMI SENATUS ACADEMICI CONSENSU,
| ET NOBILISSIMAE FACULTATIS MEDICAE DECRETO; |
PRO GRADU DOCTORIS, | SUMMISQUE IN MEDICINA
HONORIBUS ET PRIVILEGIIS, | RITE AC LEGITIME
CONSEQUENDIS; | *Eruditorum examini ſubjicit* | SAMUEL
EVANS, HIBERNUS, | SOC. MED. MED-PHYS. ET PHYS-MED.
EDIN. SOD. | AD DIEM XXX. APRILIS, | HORA MERI
DIANA, LOCO SOLITO. | GLASGUAE: | IN AEDIBUS
ACADEMICIS | EXCUDEBANT ROBERTUS ET
ANDREAS FOULIS, | ACADEMIAE TYPOGRAPHI |
M.DCC.LXXIII.

FORMULA: [? Writing Demy] 8⁰ in fours: π^2 A–H⁴ I₁ (C2
signed ' A2 ').
PAPER: Medium-good quality; marks 7/ii.
TYPE: RSP 2.
COPIES: G².

1773   Glasgow University: Academy.   *The Seven* **552**
                                        Cartoons of Raphael

THE | SEVEN CARTOONS | OF | RAPHAEL, | FORMERLY
AT | HAMPTON-COURT, | NOW, FOR THEIR BETTER
PRESERVATION, IN THE | QUEEN'S PALACE, | EN
GRAVED IN THE ACADEMY OF ARTS | IN THE UNI
VERSITY OF GLASGOW, | BY | JAMES MITCHELL, |
AND THE LATE INGENIOUS | WILLIAM BUCHANAN,
| EDUCATED THERE. | GLASGOW: | AT THE EXPENCE
OF ROBERT AND ANDREW FOULIS, | PRINTERS TO
THE UNIVERSITY, | M.DCC.LXXIII.

FORMULA: [? Colombier or Atlas] 2⁰: π1 (*letterpress title-page*)
+ 7 plates, each on a folded whole sheet. Unnumbered, signed
' *G. Buchananus Sculpsit in Academia Glasguae* ' on four of them

(1, 3, 5 and 6), and ' *J. Mitchell Sculpsit in Academia Glasguae* ' on the other three (2, 4 and 7). These are followed in the only copy seen by three more plates, unsigned.

PAPER: Good quality; marks, coat of arms incorporating double ' X '/' D & C BLAUW | IV '; size of sheet at least 32 × 24 in.

TYPE: [No text.]

VARIANT: Issue on Satin, not seen (*CP* 14.)

NOTES: *Prices*: Retail: £3; on satin, £6 (*CP* 14).

COPIES: G⁴.

553 Graham, Thomas, *Poems*　1773

NOTES: Not seen. Listed by Duncan (p. 73, No. 415) as ' Poems by Thomas Graham, 12mo.' I have not been able to discover a poet named Thomas Graham, and Duncan's entry may originally have been intended to refer to Thomas Gray's *Poems*, of which there were two duodecimo editions in 1773. The trouble with this theory is that he did list one of them (p. 72, No. 410, ' Gray and Littleton's Poems, 18mo.', i.e. two of Nos. 554–6 of the present bibliography), and they are so alike that I would not expect him to have told them apart.

554 Gray, Thomas, *Poems*　1773

POEMS | BY | MR. GRAY. | GLASGOW: | PRINTED BY ROBERT AND ANDREW FOULIS | PRINTERS TO THE UNIVERSITY | M.DCC.LXXIII. | †

FORMULA: Pot 12⁰ in sixes: π^2 A–D⁶ E⁴ (*signed* ' † ' *on* $1 *except – sometimes –* A1; E2 *unsigned*).

Press-figures: ' 1 ' on B1 C1. ' 3 ' on D1.

PAPER: Medium quality; marks 1/vii, 1/iv.

TYPE: RB 2.

VARIANT: Although this book is signed with ' † ', the place of a common-paper issue may have been taken by the closely similar edition on medium-poor quality paper also published in 1773 (No. 555).

COPIES: G⁴.

† **555** Gray, Thomas, *Poems* (another edition)　1773

POEMS | BY | MR. GRAY. | GLASGOW: | PRINTED BY ROBERT AND ANDREW FOULIS, | PRINTERS TO THE UNIVERSITY, | M.DCC.LXXIII. | *

FORMULA: Pot 12⁰ in sixes: π^2 A–D^6 E^4 (*signed* ' * ' *on* \$1; D1, E2 *unsigned*).

   Press-figures: ' 1 ' on A1 B1 D1.

PAPER: Medium-poor quality; marks 1/iv.

TYPE: RB 2.

VARIANT: See No. 554, ' VARIANT '.

COPIES: G^4, L.

1773   Lyttelton, George, Baron, *Poems* **556**

POEMS | BY THE | RIGHT HONOURABLE | THE LATE | LORD LYTTLETON. [*sic*] | GLASGOW: | PRINTED BY ROBERT & ANDREW FOULIS, | PRINTERS TO THE UNIVER SITY, | M.DCC.LXXIII. | †

FORMULA: Pot 12⁰ in sixes: π^2 A–G^6 (*signed* ' † ' *on* \$1; E2^v *signed* ' E3 '; A2, B2, G2 *unsigned*).

   Press-figures: ' 1 ' on B6 C1 . . . G1.

PAPER: Medium-good quality; marks 1/(?)PPM.

TYPE: RB 2.

VARIANT: Issue on inferior paper, Pot 12⁰:

   Formula: (*without* ' † ' *signatures*).

   Paper: Medium quality, marks 1/PPM.

COPIES: G^4, L (both fine), O (common).

1773   Millar, John, *Lectures on Government* **557**

A | COURSE | OF | LECTURES | ON | GOVERNMENT; | GIVEN ANNUALLY IN THE | UNIVERSITY. | GLASGOW, M.DCC.LXXIII.

FORMULA: [? Foolscap] 8⁰ in four: π^4.

PAPER: Medium quality; marks ?/vii.

TYPE: RSP 2, RE 4.

NOTES: Without the Foulis Press imprint, but almost certainly printed there.

COPIES: G^4.

1773   Moor, James, *Elementa Linguae Graecae*, L **558**

ELEMENTA | LINGUAE GRAECAE; | NOVIS, PLERUM QUE, REGULIS | TRADITA; | BREVITATE SUA MEMO RIAE FACILIBUS. | PARS PRIMA, | COMPLECTENS |

PARTES ORATIONIS DECLINABILES; | ET | ANALO
GIAM | DUAS IN UNAM SYLLABAS | CONTRAHENDI,
| EX IPSA VOCALIUM NATURA | DEDUCTAM, | ET REGULIS
UNIVERSALIBUS TRADITAM. | IN USUM TYRONUM
JUNIORUM | CLASSIS GRAECAE IN ACADEMIA GLAS
GUENSI. | EDITIO QUINTA PRIORIBUS AUCTIOR ET
EMENDATIOR. | STUDIO JACOBI MOOR L.L.D. | IN
EADEM ACADEMIA LITT. GRAEC. PROF. | [*quotation,
2 lines*] | GLASGUAE: | IN AEDIBUS ACADEMICIS |
EXCUDEBANT ROBERTUS ET ANDREAS FOULIS |
ACADEMIAE TYPOGRAPHI | M.DCC.LXXIII.

FORMULA: [? Crown] 8⁰ in fours: π^2 A–U⁴ X1 (π1 *half-title*).

Plate of abbreviations and contractions faces title-page,
unsigned, plate mark 125 × 95.

PAPER: Poor quality; no marks.

TYPE: RGP 2, GGP, GP, RLP 1.

NOTES: *Prices*: Wholesale: 1s. 3d. (*BQ* 4). Retail: 1s. 8d.
(*CP* 5).

Stock in 1777: 301 copies (*BQ* 4).

COPIES: L.

559 Parnell, Thomas, *Poems on Several Occasions*   1773

POEMS | ON | SEVERAL OCCASIONS; | WRITTEN BY
| DR. THOMAS PARNELL, | LATE ARCH-DEACON OF
CLOGHER: | AND PUBLISHED BY | MR. POPE. | EN
LARGED WITH VARIATIONS AND POEMS. | [*quotation,
2 lines*] | GLASGOW: | PRINTED BY ROBERT & ANDREW FOULIS,
| PRINTERS TO THE UNIVERSITY, | M.DCC.LXXIII. | †

FORMULA: Pot 12⁰ in sixes: π^2 χ1 A–L⁶ M² (*signed* ' † ' *on* $1;
K3 *signed* ' K2 '; χ1 *contents*).

Press-figures: ' 1 ' on A1 . . . G1 I1 . . . L1.

PAPER: Medium quality; marks 1/PPM.

TYPE: RB 2, RSP 2.

VARIANT: Issue without ' † ' signatures, Pot 12⁰:
Formula: (*without* ' † ' *signatures*).
Paper: The same as the other issue.

COPIES: G⁴ (without ' † ' signatures), L (with ' † ' signatures).

† **560** Pope, Alexander, *Poetical Works*   1773

THE | POETICAL | WORKS | OF | ALEXANDER POPE,
Efq. | VOLUME I. | CONTAINING HIS | JUVENILE

POEMS. [II. | CONTAINING | TRANSLATIONS, IMITA
TIONS, | EPISTLES, EPITAPHS, etc.] [III. | CONTAINING
HIS | MORAL ESSAYS, SATIRES, &c.] [IV. | CONTAIN
ING THE | DUNCIAD, | IN | FOUR BOOKS.] | GLASGOW:
| PRINTED BY ROBERT AND ANDREW FOULIS, |
PRINTERS TO THE UNIVERSITY, | M.DCC.LXXIII. †
[*no* ' † ' *in Vol.* III; ' † ' *sometimes on a separate line in Vol.* IV.]

FORMULA: Pot 12⁰ in sixes:
   Vol. I: a⁶ A–N⁶ O⁴ (*signed* ' † ' *on* $1; A2 *unsigned;* O4
advertisements).
   Vol. II: A–P⁶ Q² (*signed* ' † ' *on* $1; D2, E2, G2, I3, L2, M2
unsigned).
   Vol. III: π² A⁴ B–U⁶ X⁴ (*signed* ' † ' *on* A–X $1; O3, S2
unsigned; X4 *blank*).
   Vol. IV: π² A–Q⁶ R⁴ (*signed* ' † ' *on* $1 *except* Q1; *signed* ' † ' *on*
Q6ᵛ; C2ᵛ *signed* ' R3 ', Q 3 *signed* ' Q ' B2, C3, D2, L2, M2,
O2, P2, Q1, Q2 *unsigned;* R4 *blank*).
   (*Signed* ' VOL. I[. . . IV].' *on* $1 *except title-pages*.)
   Press-figures: ' 1 ' on Vol. I A2 D1 H1 . . . M1 O1, Vol. II
B1 F1 I1 K1 O1 P1, Vol. III A4 B1 . . . E1 F6 G1 H6 I1 L1 N1
Q6 S1 T1 . . . X1, Vol. IV E1 . . . O1. ' 3 ' on Vol. II G1.

PAPER: Medium quality; marks 1/PPM.

TYPE: RB 2, RLP 1.

VARIANT: Issue on inferior paper, Pot 12⁰:
   Formula: (*without* ' † ' *signatures; no press-figure on Vol.* III I1).
   Paper: Medium-poor quality; marks 1/PPM, 1/vii.

COPIES: G⁴ (common), L (fine).

1773   Smollett, Tobias, *Ode to Independence* **561**

ODE | TO | INDEPENDENCE. | BY THE LATE | T. SMOL
LETT, M.D. | WITH | NOTES | AND | OBSERVATIONS.
| GLASGOW: | PRINTED BY ROBERT AND ANDREW
FOULIS, | M.DCC.LXXIII.

FORMULA: [? Writing Demy] 4⁰ in twos: π² A–C².

PAPER: Good quality; marks 7/?.

TYPE: RDP, RP 3.

NOTES: Dated 23 February 1773 on C2.

COPIES: L.

562 Watt, James, *Reports relative to Navigation*   1773

REPORTS | TO THE | LORDS COMMISSIONERS | OF | POLICE, | RELATIVE TO THE | NAVIGATION | OF THE RIVERS | FORTH, GUDIE, AND DEVON. | M.DCC.LXXIII. | GLASGOW: | PRINTED BY ROBERT AND ANDREW FOULIS, | PRINTERS TO THE UNIVER SITY, | M.DCC.LXXIII.

FORMULA: Foolscap 4⁰: A–H⁴ I².

PAPER: Medium-good quality; marks 4/vii, 3/v.

TYPE: RP 3, RSP 2.

NOTES: Various dates in the text, the latest being 20 December 1773 (p. 66).

COPIES: L.

† **563** Burrow, Edward, *A New and Compleat Book*   1774
of Rates

A | NEW AND COMPLEAT | BOOK OF RATES; | COM PREHENDING THE | RATES OF MERCHANDIZE | As fettled by the Acts of 12 CAR. II. cap. 4. 11 GEO. I. cap. 7. and fub-|fequent Acts of Parliament; and, | [*contents, 25 lines*] | BY | EDWARD BURROW, | COLLECTOR OF HIS MAJES TY'S CUSTOMS | AT PORT-GLASGOW. | VOL. I. | GLASGOW: | PRINTED BY ROBERT AND ANDREW FOULIS, | PRINTERS TO THE UNIVERSITY, |M.DCC. LXXIV. †

FORMULA: Foolscap 2⁰: π^2 $^2\pi^2$ A^2 B–8H² (*signed* '†' *on* π1, $^2\pi$2, $A2^V$ *and* B–8H $1, *except* M1, 2P1 (*but on* 2P2), 3E1, 6K1 (*but on* 6K2), 6M1, 6U1, 6Y1, 7A1 (*but on* 7A2), 7D1, 7H1, 7S1; *signed* ' § ' *on* 7D1. *The first four leaves, found in various arrangements, are: title-page, dedication, ' advertisement' and contents of chapter the first*).

PAPER: Medium-good quality; marks 4/v.

TYPE: RSP 2, RLP 1, RB 2, RE 4, RP 3, RDP.

VARIANT: Issue on (?) inferior paper, not seen (' † ' signatures).

NOTES: A second volume, containing a ' Law Index ', is advertised on 2π1 as being ' in the prefs', but in fact was never published.

COPIES: L.

1774   Butler, Samuel, *Hudibras* **564**

HUDIBRAS, | IN THREE PARTS. | WRITTEN IN THE |
TIME | OF THE | LATE WARS. | BY | SAMUEL BUTLER.
| WITH | Annotations, and a compleat Index. | VOL. I [II].
| GLASGOW: | PRINTED BY ROBERT AND ANDREW
FOULIS | M.DCC.LXXIV. [*Vol. II adds ' § ' on a separate line.
Different settings.*]

FORMULA: Pot 12° in sixes:
    Vol. I: a⁸ A–T⁶ (*signed* ' § ', ' VOL. I.' *on* A–T $1).
    Vol. II: U–2Q⁶ 2R⁴ (*signed* ' § ' *on* $1; *signed* ' VOL. II.' *on*
X–2R $1; 2M2 *unsigned*).
    Press-figures: ' 1 ' on Vol. I B1 . . . Q1 S1.   Vol. II X1 Y1 2A1
. . . 2C1 2E1 2G1 2I1 2M1 2N1.

PAPER: Medium-good quality; marks 1/v, 1/vii.
TYPE: RB 2, RLP 1.
VARIANT: Issue on (?) inferior paper, not seen (' § ' signatures).
COPIES: G⁴, L.

1774   Glasgow: Printers and Booksellers. *Letter* **565**
              to the Printers and Booksellers of England

[*Begins:*]   A LETTER | FROM THE | PRINTERS AND
BOOKSELLERS OF GLASGOW, | ADDRESSED TO THE
| PRINTERS AND BOOKSELLERS OF ENGLAND | [. . .
Ends, π2ᵛ:] GENTLEMEN, | Your Brethren and Friends, |
THE PRINTERS AND BOOKSELLERS OF GLASGOW. |
Glafgow, | March 28, 1774. [*the last two lines joined by a brace*]

FORMULA: Post 2°: π².
PAPER: Medium-good quality; thin; marks 6/SI.
TYPE: RE 4.
NOTES: Not certainly Foulis Press, but it looks like it, and is
connected with the same controversy as Foulis's *Memorial to
the House of Commons* of April 1774 (No. 566). For a full
account, see Murray, *R. & A. Foulis*, pp. 41–51.
COPIES: G².

1774   Glasgow: Printers and Booksellers. **566**
              Memorial to the House of Commons

[*Begins:*] MEMORIAL | OF THE | PRINTERS AND BOOK
SELLERS OF GLASGOW, | MOST HUMBLY ADDRES

SED TO THE HONOURABLE | THE HOUSE OF COM
MONS, | ASSEMBLED IN PARLIAMENT; | Occaſioned by
a PETITION, given in by Bookſellers of London, | for a New Act
to lengthen out the Monopoly further than | the act of Queen
Anne; [. . . *main text ends*, C4:] We, the Printers and Bookſellers
of Glaſgow, moſt humbly beg par-|don for the length, and all
the other defects of this Memorial; which | we have appointed
Robert Foulis, Printer to the Univerſity, for us, and | in our
name, to ſubſcribe. | [*MS signature of Robert Foulis in one of the
G⁴ copies*] | GLASGOW, | APRIL 25. 1774. [*the last two lines joined
by a brace*]

FORMULA: Post 4⁰: A–C⁴.

PAPER: Medium-good quality; marks 6/i; size of sheet
19 × 15¼ in.

TYPE: RP 3, RE 4.

NOTES: Without the Foulis Press imprint, but almost certainly
printed there.   See *Notes* to No. 565 above.

COPIES: G⁴.

567 Hutcheson, Francis, *Synopsis Metaphysicae*, L   1774

SYNOPSIS | METAPHYSICAE, | ONTOLOGIAM | ET |
PNEUMATOLOGIAM | COMPLECTENS. | EDITIO
SEXTA. | GLASGUAE, | IN AEDIBUS ACADEMICIS |
EXCUDEBANT ROBERTUS ET ANDREAS FOULIS |
M.DCC.LXXIV.

FORMULA: [? Foolscap] 8⁰ in fours: π⁴ A–T⁴ (Q2 unsigned).
Press-figures: ' 1 ' on A1 . . . C1 E1 . . . S1.

PAPER: Medium-poor quality; no marks.

TYPE: RLP 1, RB 2.

VARIANT: Issue on fine paper, Foolscap 8⁰:
Formula: signed ' † ' or ' ‡ ' on $1.
Paper: Medium-good quality; marks 3/v, 5/vii.

NOTES: *Prices*: Wholesale: fine, 1s. 4d.; common, 9d. (*BQ* 2).
Stock in 1777: fine, 82 copies; common, 148 copies (*BQ* 2).

COPIES: G⁴ (common), G² (fine).

568 Mason, William, *Poems*   1774

POEMS | BY | WILLIAM MASON, M.A. | VOLUME I [II]
| GLASGOW: | PRINTED BY ROBERT & ANDREW FOULIS, |
PRINTERS TO THE UNIVERSITY, | M.DCC.LXXIV.
[*Vol. II adds ' § ' on a separate line.   Different settings.*]

FORMULA: Pot 12⁰ in sixes:
    Vol. I: π^2 A–L⁶ M⁴ (*signed* ' § ' *on* A–M $1).
    Vol. II: A² B–L⁶ M⁴ (*signed* ' § ' *on* $1; *signed* 'VOL. II.' *on*
B–L $1; M3 *signed*).
    Press-figures: ' 1 ' on Vol. I A6 B1 C6 D1 E1 G1 H1 K1 L1,
Vol. II C1 D1 F1 G1 I1 M1.

PAPER: Medium quality; marks 1/iv, 1/vii.

TYPE: RB 2.

VARIANT: Issue on (?) inferior paper, not seen (' § ' signatures).

COPIES: G⁴ L.

1774   Richardson, William, *Poems, chiefly Rural* **569**

POEMS, | CHIEFLY | RURAL. | [*quotation, 2 lines*] | GLAS
GOW: | PRINTED BY ROBERT & ANDREW FOULIS, | PRINTERS
TO THE UNIVERSITY, | M.DCC.LXXIV.

FORMULA: Writing Demy 8⁰ in fours: π^4 A–O⁴ (π1 *blank*).

PAPER: Good quality; marks 7/ii; size of sheet 19½ × 15 in.

TYPE: RLP 1.

VARIANT: Issue with the addition of *The Indians*:
    Formula: (*adds*) P–R⁴ S² (*with press-figures* ' 1 ' *on* Q1, ' 3 ' *on*
R1).
    Paper: the additional sections on a similar but slightly
different paper.

COPIES: G⁴ (without *The Indians*), L (with *The Indians*).

1774   Richardson, William, *Poems, chiefly Rural* **570**

POEMS, | CHIEFLY | RURAL. | [*quotation, 2 lines*] | BY |
MR. RICHARDSON, | PROFESSOR OF HUMANITY IN
THE | UNIVERSITY OF GLASGOW. | The SECOND
EDITION, corrected. | GLASGOW: | PRINTED BY ROBERT &
ANDREW FOULIS, | PRINTERS TO THE UNIVERSITY, |
M.DCC.LXXIV.

FORMULA: Pot 12⁰ in sixes: π^4 A–M⁶ (π1 *half-title*).
    Press-figures: ' 1 ' on B1 G1.

PAPER: Medium-poor quality; marks 1/vii.

TYPE: RB 2.

COPIES: G⁴.

† **571** Swift, Jonathan, *Poems*   1774

POEMS | OF | DR. JONATHAN SWIFT, | DEAN OF SAINT PATRICK'S, | DUBLIN. | IN | TWO VOLUMES. | VOL. I [II]. | GLASGOW: | printed by robert & andrew foulis, | PRINTERS TO THE UNIVERSITY, [*this line omitted in Vol.* ii] | M.DCC.LXXIV. | §

FORMULA: Pot 12° in sixes:

Vol. i: π^2 A–P⁶ Q⁴ (*signed* ' § ' *on* \$1*; signed* ' VOL. I.' *on* A1, B1 *and* E–Q $1; C2ᵛ *signed* ' C3 '*;* M2, M3 *signed* ' I2 ', ' I3 ').

Vol. ii: π^2 A–O⁶ P² (*signed* ' § ' *on* \$1*; signed* ' VOL. II.' *on* A–P $1).

Press-figures: ' 1 ' on Vol. i B1 G1 H1 L1 N1, Vol. ii B1 E1 G1 I1 L1 M1 P1. ' 3 ' on Vol. ii C1 D1 F1 H1 K1.

PAPER: Medium quality; marks 1/vii, 1/v.

TYPE: RB 2.

VARIANT: Issue on (?) inferior paper, not seen (' § ' signatures).

COPIES: L.

572 Taylor, Jeremy, *Rules and Advices to the Clergy*   1774

RULES and ADVICES | TO THE | CLERGY | OF THE | DIOCESE OF | DOWN and CONNER: [*sic*] | FOR THEIR DEPORTMENT IN THEIR PER-|SONAL AND PUBLICK CAPACITIES. | Given by JER. TAYLOR, Bifhop of that Diocefs, [*sic*] at | the vifitation at LISNE-GARVEY. | Firft printed fince the Year M.DC.LXI. | GLASGOW: | printed by robert & andrew foulis, | M.DCC.LXXIV.

FORMULA: Pot 8° in fours: A–H⁴ I² (I2 *advertisements*).

PAPER: Medium quality; marks 1/PPM.

TYPE: RE 3.

VARIANT: *BQ* (p. 10) speaks of ' f[oolscap]. 8vo.', so there may have been an issue on better paper.

NOTES: *Price*: Wholesale: ' f[oolscap] ', 4*d*. (*BQ* 10).
  Stock in 1777: 196 copies (*BQ* 10).

COPIES: G⁴ (Pot).

573 Thomas à Kempis, St, *De Imitatione Christi*, E   1774

OF THE | IMITATION | OF | JESUS CHRIST. | IN FOUR BOOKS. | BY | THOMAS à KEMPIS. | GLASGOW: | printed by robert & andrew foulis, | M.DCC.LXXIV. | †

FORMULA: Foolscap 8° in fours: a^4 b^4 c^2 A–$2F^4$ $2G1$ (*signed* '†' *on* \$1).

   Press-figures: '1' on b3 D1 F1 L1 . . . T1 X1 Z1 2B1 . . . 2F1. '3' on I1.

PAPER: Medium quality; marks 4/vii.

TYPE: RLP 1, RB 2.

VARIANT: Issue on inferior paper, [? Foolscap] 8°:
   Title-page: [*without final* '†'].
   Formula: (*without* '†' *signatures; press-figures unaltered*).
   Paper: Medium-poor quality, no marks.

NOTES: *Prices*: Wholesale: fine, 1s. 6d.; common, 1s. (*BQ* 8).
   Stock in 1777: fine, 212 copies; common, 430 copies (*BQ* 8).

COPIES: G^4, L (both fine); G^2 (common).

1774   Thomson, James, *Liberty* **574**

LIBERTY, | A | POEM. | BY | JAMES THOMSON. | [*quotation, 3 lines*] | GLASGOW: | PRINTED BY ROBERT & ANDREW FOULIS, | PRINTERS TO THE UNIVERSITY, | M.DCC.LXXIV.

FORMULA: Pot 12° in sixes: π^2 A–N^6 (*signed* '†' *on* A–N \$1; A5 *signed* 'A3', C4 *signed* 'C3' *or unsigned*, K2 *signed* 'G2'; A3 *and – sometimes –* A4 *and* G3 *unsigned*; $\pi 1$ *half-title*).

   Press-figures: '1' on B1 C2 D2 E1 F1 H1 . . . N1.

PAPER: Medium quality; marks 1/iv.

TYPE: RB 2.

VARIANT: Issue on (very slightly) inferior paper, Pot 12°:
   Formula: (*without* '†' *signatures*).
   Paper: Medium-poor quality; marks 1/vii.

COPIES: G^4 (both issues).

1775   Addison, Joseph, *Poems on Several Occasions* **575** †

POEMS | ON | SEVERAL | OCCASIONS; | BY | THE RIGHT HONOURABLE | JOSEPH ADDISON, ESQ. | GLASGOW: | PRINTED BY ROBERT & ANDREW FOULIS, | M.DCC.LXXV. | §

FORMULA: Pot 12° in sixes: π^2 A–Q^6 R^4 (*signed* '§' *on* \$1; E2 *unsigned*).

   Press-figures: '1' on D1 F1 G1 I1 L1 . . . N1 O2 P1. '3' on C1 H1 K1 R1.

PAPER: Medium quality; marks 1/iv.

TYPE: RB 2.

VARIANT: Issue on (?) inferior paper, not seen (' § ' signatures).

COPIES: G⁴.

† **576** Akenside, Mark, *The Pleasures of Imagination*   1775

THE | PLEASURES | OF | IMAGINATION. | A POEM. | IN | THREE BOOKS. | BY | DR. AIKENSIDE. | [*quotation, 2 lines*] | GLASGOW: | PRINTED BY ROBERT AND ANDREW FOULIS | M.DCC.LXXV.

FORMULA: Pot 12⁰ in sixes: a^2 b^2 A–H⁶ I⁴ (*signed* ' † ' *on* A–I $1).
  Press-figures: ' 1 ' on E1 G1 . . . I1. ' 3 ' on B1 C1.

PAPER: Medium quality; marks 1/iv.

TYPE: RB 2.

VARIANT: Issue on (?) inferior paper, not seen (' † ' signatures).

COPIES: G⁴.

577 Beauvais, Jean-Baptiste de, *The Funeral Oration*   1775
Of Lewis XV, E

THE | FUNERAL ORATION | OF | LEWIS XV | THE WELL-BELOVED, | KING | OF | FRANCE AND NAVARRE. | PRONOUNCED IN THE CHURCH OF THE ROYAL ABBEY OF | SAINT DENIS, THE 27 OF JULY, 1774. | BY MESSIRE DE BEAUVAIS | LORD-BISHOP OF SENEZ. | GLASGOW: | PRINTED BY ROBERT & ANDREW FOULIS, | AND SOLD BY THEM AND | T. CADELL, BOOKSELLER IN LONDON. | M.DCC.LXXV.

FORMULA: Foolscap 8⁰: a⁸ A–F⁸ G⁴ H² (a1 *half-title*).

PAPER: Medium-good quality; marks 4/? monogram in circle; size of sheet $16\frac{1}{2} \times 13$ in.

TYPE: RE 3, RP 3, RSP 2.

VARIANT: Issue on common paper, [? Foolscap] 8⁰:
  Paper: Poor quality; no marks.

NOTES: *Prices*: Wholesale: fine, 8*d.*; common, 4*d.* (*BQ* 10).
  Stock in 1777: fine, 181 copies; common, 115 copies (*BQ* 10).

COPIES: G⁴, L (both common), O (fine).

1775   Buchanan, George, *Jephthes*, L **578**

JEPHTHES, | SIVE | VOTUM, | TRAGOEDIA. | AUCTORE | GEORGIO BUCHANANO | SCOTO. | GLASGUAE, | IN AEDIBUS ACADEMICIS, | EXCUDEBANT ROBER TUS ET ANDREAS FOULIS, | ACADEMIAE TYPO GRAPHI: | M.DCC.LXXV.

FORMULA: [? Crown] 8⁰ in fours: a⁴ A–E⁴ F².

Press-figures: ' 1 ' on A1 . . . E1.

PAPER: Medium-poor quality; no marks.

TYPE: RB 2. Without long f.

VARIANT: Issue on better paper, in (?) Foolscap 8⁰ (*BQ* 2).

NOTES: *Prices*: Wholesale: fine, 4*d.*; common, 3*d.* (*BQ* 2).
Stock in 1777: fine, 80 copies; common, 173 copies (*BQ* 2).

COPIES: L (Crown).

1775   Chandler, Thomas, B., *The American Querist* **579**

THE | AMERICAN QUERIST: | OR, | SOME QUESTIONS PROPOSED | RELATIVE TO | THE PRESENT DISPUTES | BETWEEN | GREAT BRITAIN, | AND HER | AMERICAN COLONIES. | BY A | NORTH-AMERICAN. | [*quotation, 3 lines*] | PRINTED IN NORTH-AMERICA, IN 1774. | LONDON: | Reprinted for T. CADDEL, in the Strand. | M.DCC.LXXV.

FORMULA: [? Foolscap] 8⁰ in fours: A–G⁴ (A1 *half-title*).

PAPER: Medium-poor quality; no marks.

TYPE: RE 3, RSP 2.

VARIANT: Issue on (?) better paper, not seen (*BQ* 11).

NOTES: Without the Foulis Press imprint, but it appears in *BQ*, and was almost certainly printed there. The only copy seen is bound up with No. 577 (Beauvais, 1775, an acknowledged Foulis book); No. 581 (Dalrymple, 1775, ' London: for T. Caddel ', but with the Foulises named as booksellers, and in fact almost certainly printed by them); and with the anonymous *A Letter from a Gentleman in England to his Friend in New-York*, 1775. This last-named book, although its imprint is the same as that of No. 581 (Dalrymple, 1775), is proved beyond doubt by typographical evidence *not* to have been printed at the Foulis Press.

Prices: Wholesale: fine, 4*d.*; common, 2*d.* (*BQ* 11).
Stock in 1777: fine, 30 copies, common, 25 copies (*BQ* 11).

COPIES: G⁴.

580 Collins, William, *Poetical Works,* with   1775
Hammond, James, *Elegies*

THE | POETICAL | WORKS | OF | MR. WILLIAM COL
LINS. | TO WHICH ARE ADDED, | MR. HAMMOND'S
ELEGIES. | GLASGOW: | PRINTED BY ROBERT & ANDREW
FOULIS, | M.DCC.LXXV.

FORMULA: Pot 12⁰ in sixes: π^2 A–I⁶ (16 *advertisements*).
    Press-figures: ' 1 ' on I1. ' 3 ' on D1 F1 H1.

PAPER: Medium quality; marks 1/vii, 1/iv.

TYPE: RB 2.

COPIES: G⁴.

581 Dalrymple, Sir John, *Address to the Inhabitants*   1775
of America, etc.

THE | ADDRESS | OF THE | PEOPLE OF | GREAT-
BRITAIN | TO THE | INHABITANTS OF | AMERICA.
| TO WHICH IS SUBJOINED, | GENERAL BURGOYNE'S
| SPEECH | ON | LORD NORTH'S CONCILIATING
PROPOSITION | RESPECTING AMERICA. | THIRD
EDITION. | LONDON: | Printed for T. CADDEL, in the
Strand, | Sold by W. CREECH, Edinburgh, R. and A. | FOULIS,
Glafgow, | M.DCC.LXXV.

FORMULA: [? Foolscap] 8⁰: π1 A–D⁸ E1.

PAPER: Medium-poor quality; no marks.

TYPE: RLP 1, RB 2.

VARIANT: Issue on (?) better paper, not seen (*BQ* 11).

NOTES: Although R. and A. Foulis appear in the imprint only
as booksellers, they were almost certainly also the printers of
this book. See the NOTES to No. 579 (Chandler, 1775).
    Prices: fine, 6*d*.; common, 3*d*. (*BQ* 11).
    Stock in 1777: fine, 39 copies; common, 108 copies (*BQ* 11).

COPIES: G⁴.

582 Dryden, John, *Original Poems*   1775

ORIGINAL | POEMS, | BY | JOHN DRYDEN, ESQ. | IN
TWO VOLUMES. | VOLUME I [II]. | GLASGOW: | PRINTED
BY ROBERT & ANDREW FOULIS, | PRINTERS TO THE UNI
VERSITY, | M.DCC.LXXV. | §

FORMULA: Pot 12⁰ in sixes:

Vol. I: π^4 A–X⁶ (*signed* ' § ' *on* \$1; *signed* ' VOL. I.' *on* A–X \$1; M2 *signed* ' M3 '; U2 *unsigned;* π1 *half-title*).

Vol. II: a⁴ A–X⁶ Y² (*signed* ' § ' *on* a–X \$1; *signed* ' VOL. II.' *on* A–Y \$1).

Press-figures: ' 1 ' on Vol. I B1 D1 L1 N6 O1 P1 S1 U1 X1, Vol. II B1 E1 F1 O1 P1 R1. ' 3 ' on Vol. I A1 E1 F1 ... K1 M1 Q1 R1. Vol II D1 G6ʳ H1 I1 L1 M1 Q1 S6 T1 X1.

PAPER: Medium quality; marks 1/v.

TYPE: RB 2.

VARIANT: Issue on inferior paper, Pot 12⁰:
Formula: (*without* ' § ' *signatures, except on Vol.* I B1. *No press-figure on Vol.* I F1).
Paper: Medium-poor quality; marks 1/v.

COPIES: G⁴ (fine), L (common).

1775   Epictetus, *Manual*, G and L **583**

ΤΟ ΤΟΥ | ΕΠΙΚΤΗΤΟΥ | ΕΓΧΕΙΡΙΔΙΟΝ. | EX EDI TIONE | JOANNIS UPTON | ACCURATE EXPRESSUM. | GLASGUAE: | IN AEDIBUS ACADEMICIS, | EXCUDE BANT ROBERTUS ET ANDREAS FOULIS, | ACA DEMIAE TYPOGRAPHI: | M.DCC.LXXV.

FORMULA: Foolscap 8⁰: A–D⁸ E² F–G⁸ H².

PAPER: Medium-good quality; marks 4/v.

TYPE: GDP 2, GGP, RP 3, RLP 1. Latin follows Greek.

VARIANT: Issue on (?) inferior paper, not seen (*BQ* 4).

NOTES: *Prices*: Wholesale: fine, 1s. 2d.; common, 9d. (*BQ* 4). Retail: (?) fine, 3s. 6d., together with No. 520 (' Cebes ', 1771) and No. 359 (Theophrastus, 1758) as a set of three (*CP* 4).
Stock in 1777: fine, 227 copies; common, 210 copies (*BQ* 4).

COPIES: C.

1775   Euripides, *Medea*, G and L **584**

'Η ΤΟΥ | ΕΥΡΙΠΙΔΟΥ | ΜΗΔΕΙΑ. | EURIPIDIS | ME DEA. | [*quotation, 5 lines*] | GLASGUAE, | IN AEDIBUS ACA DEMICIS, | EXCUDEBANT ROBERTUS ET ANDREAS FOULIS, | ACADEMIAE TYPOGRAPHI: | M.DCC.LXXV.

FORMULA: Foolscap 8⁰: π^2 A–G⁸ H² (D2, E2 *unsigned*).

PAPER: Medium quality; marks 5/ii; size of sheet $16\frac{1}{2} \times$ 13 in.

TYPE: GP, RLP 1, RSP 2, RB 2. Greek and Latin on facing pages.

VARIANTS: Issue on another quality of paper, 8⁰, not seen (*BQ* 4).

Issue in Foolscap 4⁰:

Formula: Foolscap 4⁰: π^2 A–O⁴ P² (G2, H2, I2, K2 *unsigned*).
Paper: Medium-good quality; marks 4/v, 4/? foolscap.

NOTES: *Prices*: Wholesale: 8⁰, fine, 1*s.* 2*d.*; 8⁰, common, 9*d.*; 4⁰, 2*s.* 6*d.* (*BQ* 4). Retail: 8⁰, (?) fine, 1*s.* 6*d.*; 4⁰, 2*s.* 6*d.* (*CP* 3–4); the price of the quarto probably a mistake; Spotiswood, p. 86, gives 3*s.* 6*d.*

Stock in 1777: 8⁰, fine, 270 copies; 8⁰, common, 127 copies; 4⁰, 93 copies (*BQ* 4).

COPIES: G⁴ (Foolscap 8⁰), L (4⁰).

584A Foulis, Robert and Andrew the Elder, *Prints*   1775
engraved in the Academy at Glasgow

[*Begins:*] PRINTS | ENGRAVED IN THE | ACADEMY AT GLASGOW, | AND SOLD BY | ROBERT AND ANDREW FOULIS, | PRINTERS TO THE UNIVERSITY. | [*ends,* 'π2:*] "ABERBROTHICK." Dr. JOHNSON's Travels in Scotland.

FORMULA: [? size] 2⁰: π^2.

PAPER: Medium quality; no marks; size of cut sheet 10¾ × 14 in.

TYPE: RE 3, with Wilson titling.

NOTES: Undated, and without the Foulis Press imprint although certainly printed there. It can be assigned with equal certainty to 1775: Andrew Foulis the Elder (the younger Andrew was never University Printer at the same time as his father Robert) died on 8 September of that year; while Samuel Johnson's *Journey to the Western Islands*, which is quoted in this catalogue, had been published only eight months earlier, on 18 January 1775 (Maclehose, p. 190; Boswell's *Life* of Johnson, ed. Hill and Powell, vol. ii (Oxford, 1934), pp. 509–10).

COPIES: O.

† **585** Garth, Sir Samuel, *Poetical Works*   1775

THE | POETICAL | WORKS | OF | SIR SAMUEL GARTH, M.D. | GLASGOW: | PRINTED BY ROBERT AND ANDREW FOULIS | M.DCC.LXXV. | †

FORMULA: Pot 12⁰ in sixes: a⁴ A–N⁶ O² (*signed* ' † ' *on* \$1 *except* A1, D1, *which are signed* ' § ').
  Press-figures: ' 1 ' on D1 . . . H1 M1. ' 3 ' on a2 I1.
PAPER: Medium quality; marks 1/vii.
TYPE: RB 2.
VARIANT: Issue on (?) inferior paper, not seen (' † ' and ' § ' signatures).
COPIES: G⁴.

1775 Lyttelton, George, Baron, *Poems* **586**

POEMS | BY THE | RIGHT HONOURABLE | THE LATE | LORD LYTTLETON. [*sic*] | GLASGOW: | PRINTED BY ROBERT AND ANDREW FOULIS | PRINTERS TO THE UNIVERSITY | M.DCC.LXXV. | † [' § ' *in some copies*.]
FORMULA: Pot 12⁰ in sixes: π² A–G⁶ (*signed* ' † ' *on* \$1; G2 *unsigned; sig.* π *vertical chain-lines*).
  Press-figures: ' 1 ' on C1 . . . G1.
PAPER: Medium quality; marks 1/iv.
TYPE: RB 2.
VARIANT: Issue on (?) inferior paper, not seen (' † ' signatures).
COPIES: G⁴.

1775 Miscellany. *Select Poems from a Larger* **587**
Collection

SELECT | POEMS | FROM A | LARGER COLLECTION. | GLASGOW: | PRINTED BY ROBERT & ANDREW FOULIS, | M.DCC.LXXV.
FORMULA: Pot 12⁰ in sixes: π² A–M⁶ N⁴ (*signed* ' § ' *on* \$1 *except* π1, F1; L3 *signed* ' L2 '; B3, D2, H2 *unsigned*).
  Press-figures: ' 1 ' on A1 C1 H6 K1 N1. ' 3 ' on E1 G4ʳ I1 L2 M1.
PAPER: Medium quality; marks 1/iv, 1/v.
TYPE: RB 2, RSP 2.
VARIANT: Issue on another sort of paper, Pot 12⁰:
  Formula: (*without* ' § ' *signatures except – sometimes – on* B1).
  Paper: Medium quality; marks 1/PPM.
NOTES: Selected from Dodsley's *Collection*.
COPIES: G⁴, L (without ' § ' signatures), O (with ' § ' signatures).

588 Richardson, William, *Poems, chiefly Rural* 1775, 1781

[*The original title-page (probably dated 1775, but possibly 1774) not seen. G⁴ has a copy of what is probably the second issue, with a cancel title-page, not printed at the Foulis Press, which reads (in shortened form, and presumably following a cancellandum printed by Foulis):*] Poems, Chiefly Rural. . . . By Mr. Richardson, Professor of Humanity in the University of Glasgow. The Third Edition, corrected. London: Printed for J. Johnson, in St. Paul's Church-yard, and J. Murray, Nᵒ 32 Fleet-street. M.DCC.LXXV.

FORMULA: Post 8ᵒ: π^4 ($\pm\pi$2) A–K⁸ (–K7, K8; π1 *half-title*, π2 *title-page*).

Press-figures: ' 2 ' on B4 (or B5) C3 E3 F8ʳ H1 I8ʳ. ' 3 ' on D2. ' 6 ' on A4 C2 D8ʳ F2 G8 H2.

PAPER: Medium-good quality; marks 6/?i.

TYPE: RLP 1.

VARIANT: [? Third] issue, called ' the fourth edition ', with the addition of *The Indians*, Andrew Foulis, 1781:

Title-page: [*Another cancel, reading:*] POEMS, | CHIEFLY | RURAL: | WITH THE | INDIANS, A TALE. | [*quotation, 2 lines*] | BY MR. RICHARDSON, | PROFESSOR OF HUMAN ITY IN THE UNIVERSITY OF | GLASGOW. | The FOURTH EDITION, enlarged. | GLASGOW: | PRINTED AND SOLD BY ANDREW FOULIS, | PRINTER TO THE UNIVER SITY. | M.DCC.LXXXI.

Formula: (*As above, with the addition of the following sections of* [? *Writing Demy*] *8ᵒ in fours:*) L–O⁴ R1.

Paper: Post (1775) sections: as above. Demy (1781) sections (*cancellans* π2, L–R): Medium-good quality; marks 7/iv.

Type: 1781: adds RLP 2.

COPIES: G⁴ (second and third issues).

† **589** Richardson, William, *Epithalamium*   1775

EPITHALAMIUM | ON THE | MARRIAGES | OF HER GRACE | THE | DUTCHESS OF ATHOL, | AND OF THE HONOURABLE | MRS. GRAHAM | OF | BALGOWAN. | BY | MR. RICHARDSON, | PROFESSOR OF HUMANITY IN THE UNIVERSITY | OF GLASGOW. | GLASGOW: | PRINTED BY ROBERT AND ANDREW FOULIS, | M.DCC.LXXV.

FORMULA: [? Writing Medium] 4ᵒ: π^2 A⁴.

PAPER: Medium-good quality; marks 7/JW.
TYPE: RDP.
COPIES: G².

1775   Shenstone, William, *Select Works* **590** †

THE | SELECT | WORKS | IN | VERSE AND PROSE, | OF | WILLIAM SHENSTONE, | ESQUIRE. | THE THIRD EDITION. | GLASGOW: | PRINTED BY ROBERT & ANDREW FOULIS, | M.DCC.LXXV. | §

FORMULA: Pot 12⁰ in sixes: a⁴ A–K⁶ M² (*signed* ' § ' *on* $1).
Press-figures: ' 1 ' on A4 D3 F2. ' 3 ' on B1 I3.
PAPER: Medium quality; marks 1/iv.
TYPE: RB 2.
VARIANT: Issue on (?) inferior paper, not seen (' § ' signatures).
COPIES: G⁴.

1775   Sherlock, William, *A Practical Discourse* **591**
                                          concerning Death

NOTES: Not seen. Listed by Duncan (p. 74, No. 432) as ' Sherlock on Death, fools. 8vo. fine, 2s. common, 1s. 2d.' Format and (wholesale) prices are taken from *BQ* (p. 6), which records 124 copies of the fine-paper issue and 391 copies of the common remaining in stock in 1777. Retail price, (?) fine, 2s. 6d. (*CP* 8).

1775   Dryden's Virgil, *Works*, E **592**

THE | WORKS | OF | VIRGIL, | TRANSLATED BY | JOHN DRYDEN, ESQ. | IN THREE VOLUMES. | VOL. I [II] [III]. | GLASGOW: | PRINTED BY ROBERT & ANDREW FOULIS, | M.DCC.LXXV. [*Vol.* III *adds* ' § ' *to the last line. Same setting.*]
FORMULA: Pot 12⁰ in sixes:

Vol. I: π^2 a–c⁶ d² A–N⁶ O² (c2, A2, B2, D2, E2 *unsigned;* π1 *half-title*, O2 *advertisements*).

Vol. II: π^2 A–S⁶ T⁴ (I3 *signed* ' 3 '; A2, D2, L2, N2, P2, S2 *unsigned;* π1 *half-title*).

Vol. III: π^2 A–U⁶ X⁴ (L2 *signed* ' L3 '; B2, E2, I2, K2, N2, P2 . . . U2 *unsigned;* π1 *half-title*, X4 *advertisements*).

(*Signed* ' § ' *and* ' VOL. I [. . . III].' *on* $1 *except half-titles; signed* ' § ' *on* Vol. III π2.)

Press-figures: ' 1 ' on Vol. 1 b1 A4 D1 F1 I6 M6 N1, Vol. 11 E6 G2 H6 I6ʳ L1 . . . N1 P3 S3 T1, Vol. 111 D3 H1 M1 . . . O1 Q1. ' 3 ' on Vol. 1 C1 G1 L1, Vol. 11 A6 B1 D1 F1, Vol. 111 A2 C1 F1 P1 R1 U1 X1.

Plates: portrait 'VIRGILIUS.' faces Vol. 1 title-page, unsigned, plate-marks 82 × 65. Folding map at Vol. 11 A1: ' THE | *Voyage* | of Æneas | *As Defcribed by* | VIRGIL ', unsigned, plate marks c. 165 × 235. (These plates are the same as those in No. 497 (Virgil, 1769).)

PAPER: Medium quality; marks 1/iv, 1/vii.

TYPE: RB 2.

VARIANT: Issue on inferior paper, Pot 12° (Vols. 1 and 11 only seen):

Formula: (*without* ' § ' *signatures*).

Paper: Medium-poor quality; marks 1/PPM.

COPIES: G⁴ (fine, lacks plates; common, lacks vol. 111), O (fine, lacks frontispiece).

593 Denham, Sir John, *Poems*   1776

NOTES: Not seen. Listed by Duncan (p. 74, No. 440, a position in the list which implies that it has the imprint of Robert and Andrew Foulis, not of Andrew Foulis alone) as ' Denham's Poems, 12mo.'

594 Edgar, Handaside, *De Peripneumonia*, L   1776

DISSERTATIO MEDICA | INAUGURALIS | DE | PERI PNEUMONIA: | QUAM, | ANNUENTE SUMMO NU MINE, | *Auctoritate Digniſſimi Vice-Cancellarii*, | GULIELMI LEECHMAN, S.S.T.P.P. | ET COLLEGII GLASG. PRAE FECTI; | NEC NON | *Ampliſſimi* SENATUS ACADEMICI *Conſenſu*, | *Et Nobiliſſimae* FACULTATIS MEDICAE *Decreto;* | PRO GRADU DOCTORATUS, | SUMMISQUE IN MEDICINA HONORIBUS ET PRIVILEGIIS | RITE AC LEGITIME CONSEQUENDIS; | IN COMITIIS UNIVER SITATIS GLASGUENSIS, | Eruditorum examini ſubjicit | HANDASIDE EDGAR, A.M. | SCOTO-BRITANNUS. | AD DIEM XXIX FEB. HORA MERIDIANA, | LOCO SOLITO. | [*quotation, 1 line*] | GLASGUAE: | IN AEDIBUS ACADEMI CIS | EXCUDEBANT ROBERTUS ET ANDREAS FOULIS, | ACADEMIAE TYPOGRAPHI, | M.DCC.LXXVI.

FORMULA: [? Writing Demy] 8⁰ in fours: π^2 A–F⁴(–F4).
PAPER: Medium-good quality; marks 7/J WHATMAN.
TYPE: RLP 1, RSP 1.
COPIES: G².

1776   Foulis, Robert, *A Catalogue of Pictures* **595** †

A | CATALOGUE | OF | PICTURES, | COMPOSED AND
PAINTED | CHIEFLY BY THE | MOST ADMIRED MAS
TERS | OF THE | ROMAN, FLORENTINE, PARMAN, |
BOLOGNESE, VENETIAN, | FLEMISH, AND FRENCH
SCHOOLS. | IN WHICH | MANY OF THE MOST CAPITAL
| ARE ILLUSTRATED BY DESCRIPTIONS, | AND CRITI
CAL REMARKS. | HUMBLY OFFERED TO THE | IMPAR
TIAL EXAMINATION OF THE PUBLIC, | BY | ROBERT
FOULIS. | IN THREE VOLUMES. | VOLUME I. | LON
DON: | SOLD AT THE PLACE OF EXHIBITION, AND | BY
T. CADELL AND P. ELMSLY | IN THE STRAND. |
M.DCC.LXXVI. [*Vol. II from a different setting, has minor typo-
graphical changes and omits* ' AT THE PLACE OF EXHIBITION,
AND ' *from line 23; Vol. III from the same setting as Vol. I, changes*
' I ' *to* ' III ' *in line 21.*]

FORMULA: Foolscap 8⁰:
  Vol. I: a–c⁸ d² A–Y⁸ (F3, H3, H4 *unsigned*).
  Vol. II: π^2 a–s⁸ t⁴ u² (b4, l4 *unsigned*).
  Vol. III: π^2 3A–3M⁸ χ1 A–C⁸ D² (*actually signed* ' 3A ', ' 3A2 ',
etc.; 3C3 *unsigned*).

PAPER: Medium-good quality; marks 5/ii; size of sheet
$16\frac{1}{2} \times 13$ in.

TYPE: RE 3, RP 3, RE 4, RSP 2.

VARIANT: Issue on inferior paper, Foolscap 8⁰:
  Paper: Medium-poor quality; no marks; size of sheet
$16\frac{1}{2} \times 13$ in.

NOTES: Without the Foulis Press imprint, but it could scarcely
have been printed elsewhere.
  Vol. III sigs. A–D is the section of the book that is referred to
in this bibliography as *CP*.
  I have a copy of Vol. III of the common-paper issue bound in
mid-nineteenth-century publisher's cloth, unopened.

COPIES: G⁴ (both issues); L (an imperfect copy of Vol. I, with
Robert Foulis's autograph inscription to Lord Charlemont).

596 Knox, Hugh, *Select Sermons*   1776

NOTES: Not seen. Listed by Duncan (p. 74, No. 437, a position in the list which implies that it has the imprint of Robert and Andrew Foulis, not of Andrew Foulis alone) as ' Select Sermons on Interefting Subjects. By Hugh Knox, D.D. &c. 2 vols. 12mo.'

597 Milton, John, *Paradise Lost*   1776

PARADISE | LOST, | A | POEM | IN | TWELVE BOOKS. | THE AUTHOR | JOHN MILTON. | VOLUME I [II]. | GLASGOW: | PRINTED BY ROBERT AND ANDREW FOULIS | PRINTERS TO THE UNIVERSITY, | M.DCC. LXXVI. [*Vol.* II *adds* ' † ' *on a separate line. Same setting.*]

FORMULA: Pot 12⁰ in sixes:
   Vol. I: a⁶ b² A–P⁶ Q² (*signed* ' † ' *on* \$1 *and* ' VOL. I.' *on* b–Q \$1; a1 *half-title*).
   Vol. II: A–O⁶ P⁴ (*signed* ' † ' *on* \$1 *except* H1; *signed* ' VOL. II.' *on* B–P \$1).
   Press-figures: ' 1 ' on Vol. I a4ʳ A1 . . . H1 K1 . . . M1 O1, Vol. II A2 B1 D1 F1 . . . O1. ' 3 ' on Vol. I b1 I1 N1 P1 Q1, Vol. II C1 E1.

PAPER: Medium quality; marks 1/v, 3/ ?v.

TYPE: RB 2, RSP 2.

VARIANT: Issue on another quality of paper, not seen (' † ' signatures).

COPIES: G⁴.

598 Richardson, William, *Poems, chiefly Rural*   1776

POEMS, | CHIEFLY | RURAL. | [*quotation, 2 lines*] | BY | MR. RICHARDSON, | PROFESSOR OF HUMANITY IN THE | UNIVERSITY OF GLASGOW. | The THIRD EDI TION, correcƚed. | GLASGOW: | PRINTED BY ROBERT AND ANDREW FOULIS, | PRINTERS TO THE UNIVER SITY, | M.DCC.LXXVI. | †

FORMULA: Pot 12⁰ in sixes: π⁴ A–M⁶ (*signed* ' † ' *on* π2 *and* A–M \$1 (*sometimes missing from the title-page*); H2 *unsigned*; π1 *half-title*).
   Press-figures: ' 1 ' on B1 G2 M1.

PAPER: Medium quality; marks 1/v.

TYPE: RB 2.

VARIANT: Issue on (?) inferior paper, not seen (' † ' signatures).

COPIES: G4, L.

1776   Shakespeare, William, *Hamlet* **599**

HAMLET, | PRINCE | OF | DENMARK. | THE AUTHOR | MR. WILLIAM SHAKESPEAR. | ACCORDING TO | MR. POPE'S SECOND EDITION. | GLASGOW, | PRINTED AND SOLD BY R. AND A. FOULIS | M DCC LXXVI.

FORMULA: Foolscap 8° fours: A–R4 (P2 *signed* ' P3 ').

Press-figures: ' 3 ' on A3.

PAPER: Medium quality; blue; marks 5/ii.

TYPE: RLP 1, RB 2.

NOTES: Follows the edition of 1756 line for line (No. 460).

COPIES: Birmingham Reference Library.

1776   Simson, Robert, *Works*, L **600** †

ROBERTI SIMSON, M.D. | MATHESEOS NUPER IN ACADEMIA GLASGUENSI | PROFESSORIS | OPERA QUAEDAM RELIQUA, | SCILICET, | [*contents, 9 lines*] | NUNC PRIMUM POST AUCTORIS MORTEM | IN LUCEM EDITA | IMPENSIS QUIDEM PHILIPPI COMI TIS STANHOPE, | CURA VERO JACOBI CLOW IN EADEM ACADEMIA | PHILOSOPHIAE PROFESSORIS, | CUI, AUCTOR OMNIA SUA MANUSCRIPTA TESTA MENTO LEGAVERAT. | GRATUM, UT SPERATUR, GEOMETRIS MUNUS FUTURUM, NEC SCRIPTORIS, | JAM CLARISSIMI, FAMAE OFFECTURUM. | GLAS GUAE: | IN AEDIBUS ACADEMICIS, | EXCUDEBANT ROBERTUS ET ANDREAS FOULIS | ACADEMIAE TYPOGRAPHI, | M.DCC.LXXVI.

FORMULA: Writing Demy 4°: π^2 $^2\pi^2$ a4 b2 A–4E4 4F2 ^{2}A–D4 ^{2}E2 ^{2}F–I4 $^2K^2$ ^{3}A–C4 (π1 *blank*, π2 *half-title*, $^2\pi$1 *title-page*, $^2\pi$2 *foreword; sig*. b, *which is signed* ' b ' *on* b2, *is often found before sig*. a; 4F2, ^2K2 *blank*).

PAPER: Good quality; marks 7/ii; size of sheet 20 × 15 in.

TYPE: RE 4, RSP 2, RSP 1, RB 2, GGP. Numerous woodcut diagrams.

NOTES: A frontispiece portrait of Simson (signed ' *De Nune pinxit 1746 A. Baillie din! et fculp! 1776*') is rarely found, and may not belong to the book.

COPIES: G⁴, L.

601 Thomson, James, *Poems, etc.*   1776

POEMS | BY | JAMES THOMSON. | VIZ. | BRITANNIA, | TO THE MEMORY OF LORD TALBOT, | THE CASTLE OF INDOLENCE, | AND | LESSER POEMS: | WITH | ALFRED, A MASQUE, | BY Mr. THOMSON AND Mr. MALLET. | GLASGOW: | PRINTED BY ROBERT AND ANDREW FOULIS, | PRINTERS TO THE UNIVERSITY, | M.DCC.LXXVI.

FORMULA: Pot 12⁰ in sixes: π^2 A–N⁶ O² (π1 *half-title*).

Press-figures: ' 1 ' on A1 . . . C1 H1 L1. ' 3 ' on D1 . . . G1 16ʳ K1 M1 . . . O1.

PAPER: Medium quality; marks 1/v.

TYPE: RB 2.

COPIES: G⁴.

602 Thomson, James, *The Seasons*   1776

THE | SEASONS. | BY | JAMES THOMSON. | GLASGOW: | PRINTED BY ROBERT AND ANDREW FOULIS | PRINTERS TO THE UNIVERSITY | M.DCC.LXXVI.

FORMULA: Pot 12⁰ in sixes : a–b⁶ c⁴ A–R⁶.

Press-figures: ' 1 ' on A2 C1 E1 G1 . . . N1 P1 R1. ' 3 ' on b1 B1 G1 (*variant*: ' 1 ' on b1, B1).

PAPER: Medium quality; marks 1/v.

TYPE: RB 2, RLP 1.

COPIES: G⁴.

(*Note.*—Andrew Foulis the elder died in September 1775. Books issued between that date and June 1776, when Robert Foulis died, still have the imprint ' Printed by Robert and Andrew Foulis ', possibly referring to the participation of Andrew Foulis the younger.)

PART III

BOOKS PRINTED BY

ANDREW FOULIS

THE YOUNGER

1776–1806

1776   Dryden, John, *Fables Ancient and Modern,* **603** †
etc.

FABLES | ANCIENT AND MODERN; | TRANSLATED INTO | VERSE, | FROM | HOMER, OVID, | BOCCACE AND CHAUCER: | WITH | ORIGINAL POEMS. | BY JOHN DRYDEN ESQ; | VOL. I [II]. | [*quotation, 3 lines; omitted in Vol.* II] | GLASGOW: | PRINTED BY ANDREW FOULIS, | M.DCC.LXXVI. † ['†' *on separate line in Vol.* II.]

FORMULA: Pot 12⁰ in sixes:

    Vol. I: A–U⁶ X⁴ (*signed* '†' *on* \$1; M2 *unsigned*).

    Vol. II: A⁴ B–T⁶ (*signed* '†' *on* \$1 *and* 'VOL. II.' *on* B–T \$1).

    Press-figures: '1' on Vol. I A6ʳ C1 E1 H1 . . . U1, Vol. II C1 D1 F1 I1 K1 L1 N1 O1 Q1 S1 (*variant*: no figure on Vol. I L1). '3' on Vol. I B1 D1 F1 G1, Vol. II B1 G1 H1 M1 P6ʳ R1 T1.

PAPER: Medium quality; marks I/iv, I/v.

TYPE: RB 2.

VARIANT: Issue on another sort of paper Pot 12⁰:

    Formula: (*without* '†' *signatures*).

    Paper: Medium quality; marks I/PPM.

COPIES: O (with '†' signatures), G² (without '†' signatures).

1776   Gay, John, *Poems on Several Occasions* **604** †

POEMS | ON | SEVERAL | OCCASIONS; | BY | MR. JOHN GAY. | [*quotation, 5 lines*] | VOLUME I. | GLASGOW: | PRINTED BY ANDREW FOULIS, | M.DCC.LXXVI. [*Vol.* II:] POEMS | ON | SEVERAL | OCCASIONS. | BY | MR. JOHN GAY. | VOLUME II. | GLASGOW: | PRINTED BY ANDREW FOULIS, | M.DCC.LXXVI. | †

FORMULA: [*Note*: The two volumes of the only copies seen (1 copy of Vol. I, 2 copies of Vol. II, all at G⁴) appear to belong to different issues, Vol. II being on a different – though not noticeably better – paper and having '†' signatures.]

Pot 12⁰ in sixes:

Vol. I: A–Q⁶ R⁴ (*signed* ' VOL. I.' *on* B–R $1; M2 *signed* ' M3 '; R4 *advertisements*).

Vol. II: π² A–Q⁶ (*signed* ' † ' *on* $1; *signed* ' VOL. II '. *on* A–Q $1).

Press-figures: ' 1 ' on Vol. I A2 B1 . . . H1 K1 . . . M1 O6 P1 Q2 R1, Vol. II A2 C1 D6ʳ E1 . . . G1 I1 . . . Q1. ' 3 ' on Vol. I I2 N1.

PAPER: Vol. I: Medium quality; marks 1/PPM.
Vol. II: Medium quality; marks 1/v, 3/?v.

TYPE: RB 2.

VARIANT: see *Note* above.

COPIES: G⁴.

605 Miscellany.   *Modern Poems*   1776

MODERN | POEMS: | SELECTED CHIEFLY | FROM | MISCELLANIES | PUBLISHED LATELY. | GLASGOW: PRINTED BY ANDREW FOULIS. | † M.DCC.LXXVI. [*The obelus sometimes on a separate line.*]

FORMULA: Pot 12⁰ in sixes: π⁴ A–O⁶ P² (*signed* ' † ' *on* π2, C2 *and* A–P $1; A2, H2, I2 *unsigned*; π1 *half-title*).

Press-figures: ' 1 ' on B1 D1 L1 N5 O6ʳ.

PAPER: Medium quality; marks 1/iv.

TYPE: RB 2.

VARIANT: Issue on inferior paper, Pot 12⁰:
Formula: (*without* ' † ' *signatures*).
Paper: Medium-poor quality; marks 1/PPM.

COPIES: G⁴ (common), L (fine).

606 Thomson, James, *Liberty*   1776

LIBERTY, | A | POEM. | BY | JAMES THOMSON. | [*quotation, 3 lines*] | GLASGOW: | PRINTED BY ANDREW FOULIS, | M.DCC.LXXVI.

FORMULA: Pot 12⁰ in sixes: π² A–N⁶ (K2 *signed* ' G2 '; π1 *half-title*).

Press-figures: ' 1 ' on F1 H1 (*variant*: ' 3 ' on F1). ' 3 ' on B1 C2 D2 E1 I1 . . . N1.

PAPER: Medium quality; marks 1/iv.

TYPE: RB 2.

NOTES: Not a reprint from the type of No. 574 (1774), in spite of the coincident mis-signing ' G2 ' for K2.

COPIES: G⁴, L.

1776   Young, Edward, *The Complaint: or Night-* **607**
                                      thoughts, etc.

THE | COMPLAINT: | OR, | NIGHT-THOUGHTS | ON | LIFE, DEATH, | AND | IMMORTALITY. | TO WHICH IS ADDED, | A PARAPHRASE ON PART OF THE | BOOK OF JOB. | [*quotation, 2 lines*] | VOL. I [II]. | GLASGOW: | PRINTED BY ANDREW FOULIS, | M.DCC.LXXVI. | †

FORMULA: Pot 12⁰ in sixes:
  Vol. I: π^2 A–T⁶ (*signed* ' † ' *on* $1; *signed* ' VOL. I.' *on* A–T $1).
  Vol. II: π1 A–N⁶ O² (*signed* ' † ' *on* $1; *signed* ' VOL. II.' *on* A–O $1; G2 *unsigned*).
  Press-figures: ' 1 ' on Vol. I B1 C1 E1 G1 L1 M1 . . . O1 Q1 . . . T1, Vol. II A2 B1 C1 E1 H1 . . . L1 N1. ' 3 ' on Vol. I A6ʳ D1 F1 H1 L6ʳ, Vol. II D1 F1 G1 M1.
PAPER: Medium quality; marks 1/v.
TYPE: RB 2.
VARIANT: Issue on (?) inferior paper, not seen (' † ' signatures).
COPIES: G⁴.

1777   Aeschylus, *Choephorae*, G and L **608**
ʿAI | ΤΟΥ ΑΙΣΧΥΛΟΥ | ΧΟΗΦΟΡΟΙ. | AESCHYLI | CHOE PHORAE. | EX EDITIONE STANLEIANA. | GLASGUAE: | EXCUDEBAT ANDREAS FOULIS, | M DCC LXXVII.
FORMULA: Foolscap 8⁰: π1 A–E⁸ F⁴ G².
PAPER: Medium quality; marks 3/SP; size of sheet $16\frac{1}{2} \times 13$ in.
TYPE: GP, RLP 1.   Greek and Latin on facing pages.
VARIANTS: Issue on inferior paper, [? Foolscap] 8⁰:
  Paper: Poor quality; no marks.
  Issue in Foolscap 4⁰:
  Formula: Foolscap 4⁰: π^2 A–K⁴ M² (π1 *blank*).
  Paper: Same as the fine-paper 8⁰.
COPIES: G⁴ (all three issues), L (fine-paper 8⁰, 4⁰).

1777   Akenside, Mark, *The Pleasures of Imagination* **609**
THE | PLEASURES | OF | IMAGINATION. | A POEM. IN | THREE BOOKS. | BY | DR. AIKENSIDE. | [*quotation, 2 lines*] | GLASGOW: | PRINTED BY ANDREW FOULIS, | M.DCC.LXXVII. | †

FORMULA: Pot 12⁰ in sixes: a^2 b^2 A–H⁶ I⁴ (*signed* ' † ' *on* \$1).
  Press-figures: ' 1 ' on C1 F1 H1. ' 3 ' on B1 E1 G1 I1.
PAPER: Medium quality; marks 1/v.
TYPE: RB 2.
VARIANT: Issue on (?) inferior paper, not seen (' † ' signatures).
COPIES: G⁴, L.

† **610** Anacreon, *Odes*, with Sappho and Alcaeus,   1777
    Remains, G and L

'AI TOΥ | ANAKPEONTOΣ | Ω,ΔAI, | KAI TA THΣ |
ΣAΠΦOΥΣ, | KAI TA TOΥ | AΛKAIOΥ | ΛEIΨANA. |
[*quotation, 1 line*] | GLASGUAE: | EXCUDEBAT ANDREAS
FOULIS, | M DCC LXXVII.
FORMULA: Post 8⁰ in fours: A–M⁴ N² (A1 *half-title*).
  Press-figures: ' 1 ' on D1 E1 ... M1. ' 3 ' on B1 C1.
PAPER: Good quality; thin; marks 6/T & SON.
TYPE: GDP 2, RB 2, RSP 2. Without long f. Latin translation
as footnotes to the text.
COPIES: G⁴.

610A Anderson, John, *Institutes of Physics*   1777

INSTITUTES | OF | PHYSICS. | VOLUME FIRST. |
[*quotation, 3 lines*] | GLASGOW, | PRINTED BY ANDREW
FOULIS, | M.DCC.LXXVII.
FORMULA: [? Writing Medium] 8⁰ in fours: A–S⁴ T² (B2, D2
unsigned).
PAPER: Medium-good quality; marks 7/i.
TYPE: RSP 2, RLP 1, RB 2, GP.
NOTES: Only 'Volume First' seen; it is not certain that any
more of this edition was printed. The Fourth Edition, com-
plete and much enlarged, was printed by Robert Chapman and
Alexander Duncan in 1786. Cf. No. 700, below.
COPIES: G².

† **611** Cicero, *De Oratore*, L   by 1777

NOTES: Not seen. Listed in *BQ* (p. 2) as a Foolscap 12⁰.
Possibly one of the duodecimo Cicero's of 1748–9.
  Prices: Wholesale: fine, 1*s*. 6*d*.; common, 1*s*. 2*d*. (*BQ* 2).
  Stock in 1777: fine, 17 copies; common, 14 copies (*BQ* 2).

1777   Collins, William, *Poetical Works*, with **612**
            Hammond, James, *Elegies*

THE | POETICAL | WORKS | OF | MR. WILLIAM COL
LINS. | TO WHICH ARE ADDED, | MR. HAMMOND'S
ELEGIES. | GLASGOW: | PRINTED BY ANDREW
FOULIS, | M.DCC.LXXVII. | †

FORMULA: Pot 12^0 in sixes: π^2 A–H^6 I^4 (*signed* '†' *on* $1).

   Press-figures: ' 1 ' on C1 E1 G5^r I1 (*variant*: no figure on I1).
' 3 ' on B1 D1 F1 H1.

PAPER: Medium quality; marks 1/vii.

TYPE: RB 2.

VARIANT: Issue on another sort of paper, Pot 12^0:
   Formula: (*without* '†' *signatures*).
   Paper: Medium quality; marks 1/PPM. This paper is
slightly heavier than that of the issue signed '†'.

COPIES: G^4 (without '†' signatures), L (with '†' signatures).

by 1777   Cooper, Anthony Ashley, Lord **613** †
            Shaftesbury, *The Moralists*

NOTES: Not seen. *BQ* (p. 12) lists 54 copies of ' Shaftefbury's
moralift ', Crown 12^0, at 1*s.* wholesale. This immediately
precedes the entry that probably refers to Shaftesbury's
Characteristics, 1743–5 (No. 30); and it seems likely that *The
Moralists* is an extract from Vol. II of that book, in which it has
a separate sub-title and signature series.

1777   Foulis Press.   *A Catalogue of Books in Quires* **614**

A | CATALOGUE | OF | BOOKS, | BEING THE | ENTIRE
STOCK, IN QUIRES, | OF THE LATE MESSIEURS |
ROBERT AND ANDREW FOULIS, | PRINTERS TO THE
UNIVERSITY OF GLASGOW: | CONSISTING OF THEIR
| ELEGANT AND CORRECT EDITIONS | OF THE |
GREEK AND LATIN CLASSICS, | AND OTHER BOOKS
PRINTED BY THEM; | AND LIKEWISE OF | The BOOKS
in QUIRES printed by Others, which were in | their poffeffion;
| Intended to be fold in WHOLESALE by Private Bargain. | Such
as wifh to be Purchafers of this Valuable Colle&tion, are
defired to | lodge their offers, on or before Wednefday the 3d
of December next, with | Mr. JOSHUA JOHNSTON, or Mr.
WILLIAM INGRAM, Merchants in | Glafgow. | GLASGOW,
OCTOBER 1ft, 1777.

FORMULA: Pot 4° in twos: π1 A–G² *H*1.

PAPER: Medium-poor quality; marks 1/iv.

TYPE: RSP 2.   See also NOTES.

NOTES: Without Andrew Foulis's imprint, and perhaps not printed by him.   On π1ᵛ is an 'advertisement' set in what appears to be a late Caslon Long Primer, while the notices on *H*1ᵛ seem to be set in Wilson's English Roman No. 3, which was not a Foulis Press fount.   On the other hand the title-page is in Foulis's style, and he certainly owned RSP 2.

COPIES: G².

615   Foulis Press.   *A Catalogue of Copper-Plates*   *c.* 1777

NOTES: Not seen.   Listed by Duncan (p. 78, No. 515) as ' A Catalogue of a Large Collection of Copper-Plates, [cir. 1777].' Advertised on p. *30* of *BQ*.

616   Foulis Press.   *A Catalogue of Paintings*   *c.* 1777

NOTES: Not seen.   Listed by Duncan (p. 78, No. 516) as ' A Catalogue of Paintings, and of Moulds for cafting Bufts, Statues, &c. in Plaifter of Paris, [cir. 1777].'   Advertised on p. *30* of *BQ*.   (But see No. 692, COPIES, below.)

617   Glasgow: Brewers.   *Representations*   by 1777

NOTES: Not seen.   *BQ* (p. 12) lists 200 copies of 'Reprefenta tions for the brewers in Glafgow ', no price or format given.

† **618**   Gray, Thomas, *Poems*   1777

POEMS | BY | MR. GRAY. | GLASGOW: | PRINTED BY ANDREW FOULIS, | M.DCC.LXXVII. | †

FORMULA: Pot 12° in sixes: π² A–D⁶ E⁴ (*signed* ' † ' *on* $1; E2 *unsigned*).

   Press-figures: ' 1 ' on A1 B1 D1.

PAPER: Medium quality; blue; marks 3/v.

TYPE: RB 2.

VARIANT: Issue on another sort of paper, not seen (' † ' signatures).

COPIES: G⁴, L.

by 1777   Lovell, John, *A Funeral Oration occasioned* **619** †
by the Death of P. Faneuil, Esq.

NOTES: Not seen. *BQ* (p. 12) lists 60 copies of ' Fannuel's funeral oration, f[oolscap]. 4to.', no price given; Spotiswood (p. 86) enters it as a 4⁰, price 3*d*. If my identification of the book with Lovell's *Oration* is correct, this is probably an early Foulis book: Peter Faneuil died in Boston, Mass., in 1743, and the first edition of the *Oration* was published there in the same year.

1777   Lyttelton, George, Baron, *Poems* **620** †

POEMS | BY THE | RIGHT HONOURABLE | THE LATE | LORD LYTTLETON. [*sic*] | GLASGOW: | PRINTED BY ANDREW FOULIS, | M.DCC.LXXVII. | †
[*The title-page is found in two settings, reading the same.*]
FORMULA: Pot 12⁰ in sixes: π² A–G⁶ (*signed ' † ' on \$1 except* C1, *which has ' ‡ '*).
    Press-figures: ' 1 ' on A6ʳ C1 ... G1.
PAPER: Medium quality; blue; marks 1/vii, 3/v.
TYPE: RB 2.
VARIANT: Issue on another sort of paper, not seen (' † ' signatures).
COPIES: G⁴, L.

1777   McCulloch, Michael, *The Character of Daniel* **621**
Campbell

A | SKETCH | OF THE | CHARACTER | OF THE LATE | DANIEL CAMPBELL, | ESQUIRE, OF SHAWFIELD. | [*quotation, 1 line*] | GLASGOW: | PRINTED BY ANDREW FOULIS, | M.DCC.LXXVII.
FORMULA: [? Writing] Royal 4⁰: A–B⁴ C² (C2 *blank*).
PAPER: Good quality; marks 8/J TAYLOR.
TYPE: RDP, RP 3.
COPIES: G⁴.

1777   Mason, William, *Poems* **622**

POEMS | BY | WILLIAM MASON, M.A. | VOLUME I [II]. | GLASGOW: | PRINTED BY ANDREW FOULIS, | M.DCC.LXXVII. | † [*Same setting.*]

FORMULA: Pot 12º:

Vol. I: π^2 A–L⁶ M⁴ (*signed* ' † ' *on* \$1; *signed* ' VOL. I.' *on* A–M \$1; H2 *unsigned*).

Vol. II: A^2 B–L⁶ M⁴ (*signed* ' † ' *on* \$1; *signed* ' VOL. II.' *on* B–M \$1; M4 *contents*).

Press-figures: ' 1 ' on Vol. I A6 B1 H1 I1 L1, Vol. II B3 D1 E6 G1 M1. ' 3 ' on Vol. I C6 D1 E1 F6ʳ K1, Vol. II C1 F1 H1 ... K1.

PAPER: Medium quality; marks 1/?vii.

TYPE: RB 2.

VARIANT: Issue on another sort of paper, Pot 12º:

Formula: (*without* ' † ' *signatures*).

Paper: Medium quality; marks 1/?PPM. This paper is slightly heavier than that of the issue signed ' † ' (cf. No. 612 Collins and Hammond, 1777).

COPIES: L (with ' † ' signatures), C (without ' † ' signatures).

623 Milton, John, *Samson Agonistes*   by 1777

NOTES: Not seen. *BQ* (p. 9) lists 188 copies of ' Milton's Samſon agoniſtes ' as a Pot 12º, price 2*d*. wholesale.

624 Monipennie, John, *The Abridgment or*   by 1777
Summarie of the Scots Chronicle

NOTES: Not seen. *BQ* (p. 10) lists 15 copies, fine, and 14 copies, common, of ' Monnypennie's Scots chronicle ' as a Foolscap 8º. Wholesale prices: fine, 9*d*.; common, 4½*d*.

625 Moor, James, *Elementa Linguae Graecae*   1777

ELEMENTA | LINGUAE GRAECAE; | NOVIS, PLERUM QUE, REGULIS | TRADITA; | BREVITATE SUA MEMO RIAE FACILIBUS. | PARS PRIMA, | COMPLECTENS | PARTES ORATIONIS DECLINABILES; | ET | ANALO GIAM | DUAS IN UNAM SYLLABA | CONTRAHENDI, | EX IPSA VOCALIUM NATURA | DEDUCTAM, | ET REGU LIS UNIVERSALIBUS TRADITAM. | IN USUM TYRONUM JUNIORUM | CLASSIS GRAECAE IN ACADEMIA GLASGUENSI. | EDITIO QUINTA [*sic*] PRIORIBUS AUCTIOR ET EMENDATIOR. | STUDIO JACOBI MOOR L.L.D. | IN EADEM ACADEMIA LITT. GRAEC. PROF. | [*quotation, 2 lines*] | GLASGUAE: | EXCUDEBAT ANDREAS FOULIS, | M.DCC.LXXVII.

FORMULA: Crown 8⁰ in fours: π^2 A–U⁴ X² (π1 *half-title*, X2 *blank*).

Plate of abbreviations and contractions faces title-page, unsigned, plate mark 125 × 95.

PAPER: Poor quality; no marks; size of sheet 19½ × 15½ in.

TYPE: RGP 2, GGP, GP, RLP 1.

COPIES: G⁴.

1777   Nepos, Cornelius, *Lives of the Emperors*, L **626**

CORNELII | NEPOTIS | EXCELLENTIUM | IMPERA TORUM | VITAE. | EDITIO TERTIA. | GLASGUAE: | EXCUDEBAT ANDREAS FOULIS, | M DCC LXXVII.

FORMULA: [? Writing Demy) 8⁰ in fours: a⁴ A–2Q⁴ 2R² (G2 *unsigned*).

Press-figures: ' 1 ' on A4 B1 . . . E1 F2 G1 . . . Q1 U1 . . . 2A1 2D1 . . . 2N1 2P1 . . . 2R1. ' 3 ' on R1 . . . T1 2C1.

PAPER: Good quality; marks 7/ ?i.

TYPE: RE 4, RB 2, RLP 1. Without long f.

VARIANTS: Issue in Foolscap 8⁰:

Formula: (*copies seen with press-figure* ' 1 ' *on* 2B1, *and no figure on* A4).

Paper: Medium-good quality; marks 4/vii.

Issue in Pot 8⁰:

Formula: (*as* Foolscap 8⁰).

Paper: Medium-poor quality; marks 1/PPM.

COPIES: G⁴ (all three issues), L (Demy and Foolscap).

1777   Sallust, *Works*, L **627** †

C. CRISPI | SALLUSTII | OPERA | QUAE SUPERSUNT, | OMNIA. | EX RECENSIONE | GOTTLIEB CORTII. | GLASGUAE: | EXCUDEBAT ANDREAS FOULIS, | M DCC LXXVII.

FORMULA: [? Writing Demy] 8⁰ in fours: π^2 A–2R⁴ 2S² 2Q2 *unsigned;* π1 *half-title*).

Press-figures: ' 1 ' on 2L1; ' 3 ' on A1 . . . 2I1 2M1 . . . 2P1 2R1.

PAPER: Good quality; marks 7/ ?i.

TYPE: RSP 2, RB 2, GB. Without long f.

VARIANTS: Issue in Post 8⁰:
Paper: Medium-good quality; thin; marks 6/?T & SON, Issue in Pot 8⁰:
Paper: Medium quality; marks 1/PPM.

COPIES: G⁴ (Post and Pot), L (Demy).

628 [Anon.], *Sermon on Early Piety* by 1777

NOTES: Not seen. *BQ* (p. 12) lists 48 copies of a ' Sermon on early piety, 8vo ', price not given. Possibly an edition of *The Beauty and Benefit of Early Piety* by David Jennings (London, 1731).

629 Sophocles, *Oedipus Tyrannus*, G and L 1777

'Ο ΤΟΥ | ΣΟΦΟΚΛΕΟΥΣ | Ο'ΙΔΙΠΟΥΣ | ΤΥΡΑΝΝΟΣ. | SOPHOCLIS | OEDIPUS | TYRANNUS. | GLASGUAE: | EXCUDEBAT ANDREAS FOULIS, | M.DCC.LXXVII.

FORMULA: Foolscap 8⁰: π² A–H⁸ (A3, B4, C3, D3, F3, G4, H3, H4 *unsigned*).
   Press-figures: ' 3 ' on A1.
PAPER: Medium quality; blue; marks 5/ii.
TYPE: GP, RLP 1, RSP 2. Greek and Latin on facing pages.
VARIANT: Issue on common paper, [? Foolscap] 8⁰:
   Paper: Medium-poor quality; no marks.
   Issue in Foolscap 4⁰:
   Formula: Foolscap 4⁰: π² A–Q⁴ (Q2 *unsigned*). *Press-figures*: ' 3 ' on A1.
   Paper: Medium-good quality; marks 4/foolscap, 4/vi, 4/v.
COPIES: G⁴ (8⁰ fine, and 4⁰); L (8⁰ fine); G² (8⁰ common).

630 Tacitus, *Agricola*, L 1777

JULII AGRICOLAE | VITA, | SCRIPTORE | C. CORNELIO TACITO. | EX EDITIONE | JACOBI GRONOVII | FIDE LITER EXPRESSA. | GLASGUAE: | EXCUDEBAT ANDREAS FOULIS, | M DCC LXXVII.

FORMULA: Foolscap 8⁰ in fours: π1 A–G⁴.
   Press-figures: ' 1 ' on F1 G1.
PAPER: Medium-good quality; marks 3/?vii, 4/?iv.
TYPE: RSP 2.
NOTES: Probably retailing at 1*s*. (Spotiswood, p. 87).
COPIES: G⁴.

by 1777   Voltaire, *The History of Charles XII*, E **631** †

NOTES: Not seen. *BQ* (p. 10), lists 1 copy of ' Voltaire's Charles the XII ' as a Foolscap 8⁰, common, at the wholesale price of 1*s*.

1778   Cicero, *Pro Archia*, L **632**

MARCII [*sic*] TULLII | CICERONIS | PRO | A. LICINIO ARCHIA | POETA | ORATIO. | Ex EDITIONE J. OLIVETI. | | GLASGUAE: | EXCUDEBAT ANDREAS FOULIS, | M DCC LXXVIII.

FORMULA: Foolscap 8⁰ in fours: π^2 A–D⁴ E^2 (π1, E2 *blank*).

PAPER: Medium-good quality; marks 3/JB or JC in double circle.

TYPE: RE 4.

COPIES: G².

1778   Cicero, *Pro Ligario*, L **633**

MARCII [*sic*] TULLII | CICERONIS | PRO | Q. LIGARIO. | AD C. CAESAREM. | ORATIO. | Ex EDITIONE J. OLIVETI. | GLASGUAE: | EXCUDEBAT ANDREAS FOULIS, | M DCC LXXVIII.

FORMULA: Foolscap 8⁰ in fours: π^2 A–D⁴ E^2 (π1, E2 *blank*).

PAPER: Medium-good quality; marks 3/JB or JC in double circle.

TYPE: RE 4.

COPIES: G².

1778   Homer, *Iliad*, G and L **634**

H TOY | OMHPOY | IΛIAΣ. | HOMERI | ILIAS. | VOL. I [II]. | [*quotation, 2 lines*] | GLASGUAE: | EXCUDEBAT ANDREAS FOULIS, | M DCC LXXVIII.

FORMULA: Foolscap 8⁰ in fours:

   Vol. I: π^2 A–2I⁴ ²A–2C⁴ (P1 *unsigned;* π1 *half-title*, 2I4 *blank*).

   Vol. II: π^2 A–2L⁴ 2M² ²A–2E⁴ (*signed* ' VOL. II.' *on* A–²2E $1; π1 *half-title*, 2M2 *blank*).

   Press-figures: ' 1 ' on Vol. I A1 . . . M1 O1 . . . 2I1 ²A1 . . . ²M1 ²P1 . . . ²2C1, Vol. II A1 . . . S1 T2 U1 . . . 2L1 ²A1 . . . ²I1 ²L1 . . . ²2E1. ' 3 ' on Vol. I N1 ²N1 ²O1.

PAPER: Medium quality; blue; marks 3/?JC in double circle.

TYPE: GP RB 2.   Latin follows Greek in each volume.

VARIANT: Issue on inferior paper, [? Foolscap] 8⁰:
   Paper: Poor quality; no marks.
   Sometimes found without the Latin translation, and may
have been issued thus.

NOTES: Spotiswood offers what are probably the two issues
of this edition at 4s. and 3s. 6d. respectively (p. 86).

COPIES: G⁴ (both issues).

634A Hutcheson, Francis, *Logicae Compendium*, L   1778

LOGICAE | COMPENDIUM. | PRAEFIXA EST | DISSER
TATIO | DE | PHILOSOPHIAE ORIGINE, | EJUSQUE |
INVENTORIBUS AUT EXCULTORIBUS | PRAECIPUIS.
| GLASGUAE: | EXCUDEBAT ANDREAS FOULIS, |
M.DCC.LXXVIII.

FORMULA: Foolscap 8⁰ in fours: π² A–N⁴ (π1 *half-title*).

PAPER: Medium-good quality; blue; marks 3/?.

TYPE: RP 2, RLP 1.

COPIES: G².

635 Isocrates, *Panegyricus*, G and L   1778

ʽΟΤΟΥ | ΙΣΟΚΡΑΤΟΥΣ | ΠΑΝΗΓΥΡΙΚΟΣ. | ISOCRATIS |
PANEGYRICA. | GLASGUAE: | EXCUDEBAT ANDREAS
FOULIS, | M DCC LXXVIII.

FORMULA: Foolscap 8⁰ in fours: π² A–N⁴ (π1, N4 *blank*).
   Press-figures: ' 1 ' on A1 . . . F1 I1 . . . N1. ' 3 ' on H1.

PAPER: Medium-good quality; blue, marks 3/?; white,
marks 6/?, 4/?vii; size of sheet 16½ × 13 in. (the paper with
mark 6 cut down).

TYPE: GP, RLP 1.   Latin follows Greek.

VARIANT: Issue on common paper, [? Foolscap] 8⁰:
   Paper: Medium-poor quality; no marks.

COPIES: G⁴ (Fine); G² (both issues).

636 Lucian, *Excerpts*, G and L   1778

EXCERPTA | EX | LUCIANI | OPERIBUS. | IN USUM
JUVENTUTIS | ACADEMICAE. | GLASGUAE: | IN

AEDIBUS ACADEMICIS, | EXCUDEBAT ANDREAS FOULIS, | ACADEMIAE TYPOGRAPHUS. | M.DCC. LXXVIII.

FORMULA: Foolscap 8⁰ in fours: π1 A–O⁴ ²A–O⁴ ²P1 (O4 *blank*).

PAPER: Medium good quality; blue; marks 3/?JC in double circle; size of sheet 16½ × 13¼ in.

TYPE: GP, RLP 1. Latin follows Greek.

COPIES: G⁴.

1778 Plautus, *Aulularia*, L **637**

MARCI | ACCII | PLAUTI | AULULARIA. | EX EDITIONE | JOH. FREDERICI GRONOVII. | GLASGUAE: | IN AEDIBUS ACADEMICIS, | EXCUDEBAT ANDREAS FOULIS, | ACADEMIAE TYPOGRAPHUS, | M DCC LXXVIII.

FORMULA: Foolscap 8⁰ in fours: A⁴(–A1) B–E⁴.
Press-figures: ' 1 ' on C1 . . . E1. ' 3 ' on B1.

PAPER: Medium-good quality; marks 4/?vii, 3/?vii.

TYPE: RB 2.

COPIES: G².

1778 Tacitus, *Germania*, L **638**

C. CORNELII TACITI | DE | SITU, MORIBUS, | ET | POPULIS | GERMANIAE | LIBELLUS. | EX EDITIONE | JACOBI GRONOVII | FIDELITER EXPRESSA. | GLAS GUAE: | IN AEDIBUS ACADEMICIS, | EXCUDEBAT ANDREAS FOULIS, | ACADEMIAE TYPOGRAPHUS, | M.DCC.LXXVIII.

FORMULA: Foolscap 8⁰ in fours: π² A–F⁴ (π1 *half-title*, F4 *blank*).

PAPER: Medium quality; marks 3/?JB in double circle.

TYPE: RSP 2.

COPIES: G⁴, L.

1778 Virgil, *Works*, L **639** †

PUBLII | VIRGILII | MARONIS | BUCOLICA, | GEOR GICA, | ET | AENEIS. | EX EDITIONE | PETRI BUR

MANNI. | TOMUS PRIMUS [SECUNDUS]. | GLASGUAE: | IN AEDIBUS ACADEMICIS, | EXCUDEBAT ANDREAS FOULIS, | ACADEMIAE TYPOGRAPHUS, | M.DCC. LXXVIII.

FORMULA: Writing Demy 2⁰:

Vol. I: π^2 $^2\pi^2$ A^2 B–4A² (signed ' VOL. I.' on B1; π1 half-title, π2 title-page, $^2\pi$1 dedication, $^2\pi$2 note from Quintilian, 4A2 blank).

Vol. II: π^2 a–4h² 4i² (π1 half-title, 4i1 subscribers, 4i2 blank).

PAPER: Good quality; marks 7/JB in double circle, 7/C TAYLOR, 7/iv, 7/i; size of sheet 19¾ × 15½ in.

TYPE: RDP, RSP 2.

VARIANT: Issue in Foolscap 2⁰:

Paper: Medium-good quality; marks 3/SP, 3/JC in double circle.

NOTES: Spotiswood (p. 85) lists what is presumably this book at £1. 11s. 6d., large paper, and 17s., small, in 1779.

COPIES: G⁴ (both issues), L (Demy).

† **640** Aeschines, *Against Ctesiphon*, G and L   1779

ΑΙΣΧΙΝΟΥ | 'Ο ΚΑΤΑ | ΚΤΗΣΙΦΩΝΤΟΣ | ΛΟΓΟΣ. | AESCHINIS | IN CTESIPHONTEM | ORATIO. | GLAS GUAE: | IN AEDIBUS ACADEMICIS, | EXCUDEBAT ANDREAS FOULIS, | ACADEMIAE TYPOGRAPHUS. | M.DCC.LXXIX.

FORMULA: Foolscap 8⁰ in fours: π^4 A–L⁴ M² a² ²A–N⁴ ²O² (π1 half-title).

PAPER: Medium quality; blue; marks 3/ ?JB in double circle; size of sheet 16½ × 13 in. The prelims on Post paper, marks 6/vii, cut down.

TYPE: GP, RLP 1. Latin follows Greek.

COPIES: G⁴, L.

641 Callander, John, *Essay towards a Literal English* 1779
Version of the New Testament

ESSAY | TOWARDS A | LITERAL ENGLISH VERSION | OF THE | NEW TESTAMENT, | IN THE | EPISTLE OF THE APOSTLE PAUL | DIRECTED TO | THE EPHE SIANS. | [copper-plate vignette, unsigned, plate mark 57 × 56] | GLASGOW: | PRINTED BY ANDREW FOULIS, PRIN TER TO THE UNIVERSITY, | M.DCC.LXXIX.

FORMULA: [? Writing Demy] 4º: *A*⁴ B–D⁴.
PAPER: Medium-good quality; marks 7/iv.
TYPE: GDP 2, GP, RSP 2, RE 4.
COPIES: G⁴.

1779   Drummond, William, *Polemo-middinia* **642**

POLEMO-MIDDINIA | INTER | VITARVAM | ET | NEBERNAM. | GLASGOW: | PRINTED BY ANDREW FOULIS, | M.DCC.LXXIX.
FORMULA: Pot 4º in twos: A–C² *D*² (*D2 blank*).
PAPER: Medium-poor quality; marks 1/PPM.
TYPE: RGP 2.
COPIES: G⁴.

1779   Ebeling, J. T. P. C., *De Quassia et Lichene* **643**
                                        Islandico, L

DISSERTATIO MEDICA | INAUGURALIS | DE | QUAS SIA | ET | LICHENE ISLANDICO: | QUAM, | ANNUENTE SUMMO NUMINE, | *Auctoritate Digniſſimi Vice-Cancellarii*, | GULIELMI LEECHMAN, S.S.T.P.P. | ET COLLEGII GLASG. PRAEFECTI; | NEC NON | *Ampliſſimi* SENATUS ACADEMICI *Conſenſu;* | *Et Nobiliſſimae* FACULTATIS MEDICAE *Decreto;* | PRO GRADU DOCTORATUS, | SUMMISQUE IN MEDICINA HONORIBUS ET PRIVI LEGIIS | RITE AC LEGITIME CONSEQUENDIS; | IN COMITIIS | UNIVERSITATIS GLASGUENSIS, | Erudi torum examini ſubjicit | JOH. THEOD. PHIL. CHRIST. EBELING, | LUNEBURGENSIS. | AD DIEM XIII MAII, HORA PRIMA P.M. | LOCO SOLITO. | GLASGUAE: | IN AEDI BUS ACADEMICIS, | EXCUDEBAT ANDREAS FOULIS, | ACADEMIAE TYPOGRAPHUS, | M.DCC.LXXIX.
FORMULA: [? Writing Demy] 8º in fours: π² A–G⁴ H1.
PAPER: Medium-good quality; marks 7/iv.
TYPE: RLP 1, RB 2.
COPIES: G².

1780   Cicero, *Somnium Scipionis* and *Paradoxa* **644**
                                        Stoicorum, L

MARCI TULLII | CICERONIS | SOMNIUM | SCIPIONIS | ET | PARADOXA. | EX EDITIONE J. OLIVETI. | GLASGUAE:

| IN AEDIBUS ACADEMICIS, | EXCUDEBAT ANDREAS FOULIS, | ACADEMIAE TYPOGRAPHUS, | M.D.CC. LXXX. [*The first word probably printed* 'MARCII' *and the second* 'I' *scratched out by hand.*]

FORMULA: Foolscap 8⁰ in fours: π^2 A–F⁴ G1.

PAPER: Medium-good quality; marks 4/vii.

TYPE: RSP 2.

COPIES: G⁴.

645 Hutcheson, Francis, *Synopsis Metaphysicae*, L   1780

SYNOPSIS | METAPHYSICAE, | ONTOLOGIAM | ET | PNEUMATOLOGIAM | COMPLECTENS. | EDITIO SEPTIMA. | GLASGUAE: | IN AEDIBUS ACADEMICIS, | EXCUDEBAT ANDREAS FOULIS, | M.DCC.LXXX.

FORMULA: Small Crown 8⁰ in fours: a⁴ A–T⁴.

PAPER: Poor quality; no marks; size of sheet $17\frac{1}{4} \times 14\frac{1}{2}$ in.

TYPE: RLP 1, RB 2.

COPIES: G⁴.

646 Moor, James, *Elementa Linguae Graecae*, L   1780

ELEMENTA | LINGUAE GRAECAE; | NOVIS, PLERUM QUE, REGULIS | TRADITA; | BREVITATE SUA MEMO RIAE FACILIBUS. | PARS PRIMA, | COMPLECTENS | PARTES ORATIONIS DECLINABILES; | ET | ANALO GIAM | DUAS IN UNAM SYLLABAS | CONTRAHENDI, | EX IPSA VOCALIUM NATURA | DEDUCTAM, | ET REGULIS UNIVERSALIBUS TRADITAM. | IN USUM TYRONUM JUNIORUM | CLASSIS GRAECAE IN ACADEMIA GLASGUENSI. | EDITIO SEXTA PRIORIBUS AUCTIOR ET EMENDATIOR. | STUDIO JACOBI MOOR L.L.D. | IN EADEM ACADEMIA LITT. GRAEC. PROF. | [*quotation, 2 lines*] | GLASGUAE: | EXCUDEBAT ANDREAS FOULIS. | EDINBURGI: | VENEUNT APUD W. GRAYE, ET J. DICKSON. | M DCC LXXX.

FORMULA: [? Crown] 8⁰ in fours: π1 ²π1 A–U⁴ X1 (O2 *unsigned;* π1 *half-title,* ²π1 *title-page*).

PAPER: Poor quality; no marks. ²π1 (only) horizontal chain lines.

TYPE: RGP 2, GGP, GP, RLP 1. (This is a new setting, not a re-issue of the edition of 1777, in spite of the fact that the title-page might be a cancel.)

COPIES: G⁴.

1780   [Anon.], *Series Titulorum qui in Pandectis con-* **646A**
       tinentur [*Heads of Lectures on Roman Law*], L

SERIES | TITULORUM | QUI IN | PANDECTIS CON
TINENTUR; | SECUNDUM PRAELECTIONUM, | IN |
UNIVERSITATE GLASGUENSI, | ORDINEM. | GLAS
GUAE, M D CC LXXX.

FORMULA: Foolscap 4⁰ in two: π1 A–D².

PAPER: Medium quality; marks 4/?.

TYPE: RP 3.

NOTES: Probably, although not certainly, printed by Andrew Foulis.

COPIES: G²

1780   Spence, William, *De Opio*, L **647**

DISSERTATIO MEDICA | INAUGURALIS | DE | OPIO.
| QUAM, | ANNUENTE SUMMO NUMINE, | *Auctoritate*
Digniffimi Vice-Cancellarii, | GULIELMI LEECHMAN,
S.S.T.P.P. | ET COLLEGII GLASG. PRAEFECTI; | NEC
NON | *Ampliffimi* SENATUS ACADEMICI *Confenfu;* | *Et*
Nobiliffimae FACULTATIS MEDICAE *Decreto;* | PRO
GRADU DOCTORATUS, | SUMMISQUE IN MEDICINA
HONORIBUS ET PRIVILEGIIS | RITE AC LEGITIME
CONSEQUENDIS; | IN COMITIIS | UNIVERSITATIS
GLASGUENSIS, | Eruditorum examini fubjicit | GULIEL
MUS SPENCE | VIRGINIENSIS. | SOCIETATIS MEDI
CAE EDINENSIS SOCIUS, | NEC NON | SOCIETATIS
PHYSICO-CHIRURGICAE EDIN. SODALIS. | AD DIEM
XXXI MAII, HORA PRIMA P.M. | LOCO SOLITO. |
GLASGUAE: | EXCUDEBAT ANDREAS FOULIS. |
M.DCC.LXXX.

FORMULA: [? Printing Demy] 8⁰ in fours: π² A–F⁴ G1 (A2, B2, C2 *unsigned*).

PAPER: Medium quality; marks 9/?.

TYPE: RP 3.

COPIES: G⁴.

† **648** Euclid, *Elements I-VI, XI-XII and Data*, E,   1781
with *Elements of Trigonometry*

THE | ELEMENTS | OF | EUCLID, | VIZ. | THE FIRST
SIX BOOKS, | TOGETHER WITH THE | ELEVENTH
AND TWELFTH. | The Errors, by which THEON, or others,
have long ago Vitiated | thefe Books, are Corrected, | And
fome of EUCLID's Demonftrations are Reftored. | ALSO, | THE
BOOK OF | EUCLID'S DATA, | In like manner Corrected.
| BY | ROBERT SIMSON, M.D. | Emeritus Profeffor of Mathe-
matics in the Univerfity of Glafgow. | TO THIS EDITION
ARE ALSO ANNEXED, | ELEMENTS of PLANE and
SPHERICAL TRIGONOMETRY. | GLASGOW: | PRIN
TED AND SOLD BY ANDREW FOULIS, PRINTER TO
THE UNIVERSITY; | SOLD ALSO BY ROBERT CROSS,
NEAR THE COLLEGE; JAMES | DUNCAN, DUNLOP
AND WILSON, AND BY J. AND | W. SHAWS, BOOK
SELLERS. | M.DCC.LXXXI.

FORMULA: [? Printing Demy] 8^0: π^4 A–2F^8 2G^2 a–b^8 c^4 (a2, a4
unsigned; c4 *blank*).

Plates: three copper-plates of trigonometrical diagrams at
a6^v and c3^v (two); unsigned, plate marks 190×195, 187×173,
125×187.

PAPER: Medium quality; no marks. (Some copies appear to be
on slightly better paper than others; there may be two issues.)

TYPE: RP 3, RSP 1. Numerous woodcut diagrams.

COPIES: G^4 (worse paper), O (better paper).

† **649** Le Sage, Alain René, *Le Diable Boiteux*, F   1781

LE | DIABLE | BOITEUX. | PAR M. LE SAGE. | NOUVELLE
E'DITION, CORRIGE'E | AVEC SOIN. | TOME PREMIER
[II]. | A GLASGOW: | DE L'IMPRIMERIE DE A. FOULIS,
| A L'UNIVERSITE'. | M.DCC.LXXXI.

FORMULA: Foolscap 12^0 in sixes:
    Vol. I: a^6 A–Y^6 Z4(– Z4; *signed* 'TOME. I.' *on* A–Z $1; a1
half-title).
    Vol. II: a^4 A–2C^6 2D^2 (a2 *signed* ' a3';* *signed* 'TOME. II.' *on*
A–2D $1).

PAPER: Medium quality; blue; marks 3/HB.

TYPE: RLP 1.

COPIES: G^2.

1781   Lysias, *Against Eratosthenes*, G and L **650**

'Ο ΤΟΥ | ΛΥΣΙΟΥ, | ΚΑΤΑ ΤΟΥ ΕΡΑΤΟΣΘΕΝΟΥΣ, | ΛΟΓΟΣ. | LYSIAE, | CONTRA ERATOSTHENEM, | ORATIO. | GLASGUAE: | IN AEDIBUS ACADEMICIS, | EXCUDEBAT ANDREAS FOULIS, | ACADEMIAE TYPO GRAPHUS. | M. DCC. LXXXI.

FORMULA: Foolscap 8⁰ in fours: π^2 A–C⁴ ²A–C⁴ (π1 *half-title*).

PAPER: Medium-good quality; marks 4/vii.

TYPE: GP, RLP 1. Latin follows Greek.

VARIANT: Issue on inferior paper, Foolscap 8⁰:
  Paper: Medium quality; marks 5/PPM; size of sheet 16½ × 13 in.

COPIES: G⁴ (common), O (fine).

1782   Cicero, *In Catilinam I*, L **650A**

MARCI TULLII | CICERONIS | IN CATILINAM | ORATIO. | Ex EDITIONE J. Oliveti. | GLASGUAE: | IN AEDIBUS ACADEMICIS | EXCUDEBAT ANDREAS FOULIS, | ACADEMIAE TYPOGRAPHUS. | M. DCC. LXXXII.

FORMULA: Foolscap 8⁰ in fours: π1 A–C⁴ *D*1.

PAPER: Medium quality; marks (?)/letters in double circle.

TYPE: RSP 2.

COPIES: G².

1782   Demosthenes, *On the Crown*, G and L **651**

ΔΗΜΟΣΘΕΝΟΥΣ | 'Ο ΠΕΡΙ ΣΤΕΦΑΝΟΥ | ΛΟΓΟΣ. | DEMOSTHENIS | DE CORONA | ORATIO. | GLASGUAE: | IN AEDIBUS ACADEMICIS, | EXCUDEBAT ANDREAS FOULIS, | ACADEMIAE TYPOGRAPHUS. | M.DCC. LXXXII.

FORMULA: Foolscap 8⁰ in fours: a⁴ A–N⁴ O² ²a² ²*b*1 ²A–M⁴ ²N1.

PAPER: Medium quality; marks 3/S·LAY.

TYPE: GP, RB 2. Latin follows Greek.

VARIANT: Issue on inferior paper, Foolscap 8⁰:
  Paper: Poor quality; no marks; size of sheet 16½ × 14½ in. (i.e. rather large for Foolscap).

COPIES: G⁴ (both issues), L (fine paper, lacking the Latin).

651A   Douglas, Francis, *The Birthday*   1782

THE | BIRTH-DAY; | WITH A | FEW STRICTURES ON THE TIMES; | A POEM, | IN THREE CANTOS. | WITH | The Preface and Notes of an Edition to be publiſhed in the Year | 1982. | BY A FARMER. | GLASGOW: | Printed by A. Foulis for the Author; and fold by W. Creech, | Edin burgh; A. Angus and Son, Aberdeen; and by the | faid A. Foulis, Glaſgow. | [PRICE TWO SHILLINGS AND SIX PENCE.] | M.DCC.LXXXII.

FORMULA: [? Writing Demy] 4º: A–I⁴ K².

PAPER: Medium-good quality; marks 7/iv.

TYPE: RE 3, RP 4, RSP 2, RLP 1.

NOTES: Price (retail) 2*s*. 6*d*. (title-page).

COPIES: L.

652   Gray, Thomas, *Poems*   1782

POEMS | BY | MR. GRAY. | GLASGOW: | PRINTED AND SOLD BY ANDREW FOULIS, | PRINTER TO THE UNI VERSITY. | M.DCC.LXXXII.

FORMULA: Pot 8º in fours: π^2 A–F⁴ G².

PAPER: Medium quality; marks 1/iv, v.

TYPE: RB 2.

COPIES: L.

652A   Plautus, *Curculio*, L   1782

MARCI ACCII | PLAUTI | CURCULIO. | EX EDITIONE | JOH. FREDERICI GRONOVII. | GLASGUAE: | IN AEDI BUS ACADEMICIS, | EXCUDEBAT ANDREAS FOULIS, | ACADEMIAE TYPOGRAPHUS. | M. DCC. LXXXII.

FORMULA: [? Foolscap] 8º in fours: *A*⁴ B–D⁴ (*A*1 *half-title; torn leaf* D4 *mended with paper and paste before printing in the only copy seen*).

PAPER: Medium-poor quality; no marks.

TYPE: RB 2.

COPIES: G².

1783   Anacreon, *Odes*, with Sappho and Alcaeus, **653**
Remains, G and L

'ΑΙ ΤΟΥ | ΑΝΑΚΡΕΟΝΤΟΣ | Ω,ΔΑΙ, | ΚΑΙ ΤΑ ΤΗΣ |
ΣΑΠΦΟΥΣ, | ΚΑΙ ΤΑ ΤΟΥ | ΑΛΚΑΙΟΥ | ΛΕΙΨΑΝΑ. |
[*quotation, 1 line*] | GLASGUAE: | IN AEDIBUS ACA
DEMICIS, | EXCUDEBAT ANDREAS FOULIS, | ACA
DEMIAE TYPOGRAPHUS. | M.DCC.LXXXIII.

FORMULA: Foolscap 8⁰ in fours: A–M⁴ N² (A1 *half-title*).

PAPER: Medium quality; blue; marks 3/?JC in double circle.

TYPE: GDP 2, RB 2. Without long f. Latin translation as
footnotes to the text.

VARIANT: Issue on inferior paper, Foolscap 8⁰:
Paper: Poor quality; horizontal chain-lines; no marks;
size of half-sheet 16½ × 14¼ in. (One of a number of books
printed from 1783 to 1793 by Andrew Foulis on half sheets –
themselves halved for 'half-sheet imposition' – of Double
Foolscap and Double Crown. The other books were: *Foolscap*:
Nos. 655 (Cicero, 1783), 657 (Eutropius, 1783), 662 (Phaedrus,
1783), 665 (Cicero, 1784), 668 (Euripides, 1784), 673 (Virgil,
1784), 676 (Lucan, 1785), 679 (Theophrastus, 1785), 685A
(Hutcheson, 1787), 687 (Pindar, 1788), 690 (Longinus, 1790),
693 (Anacreon, 1792), 694 (Xenophon, 1792), 695 (Aristophanes,
1793); *Crown*: 660 (Moor, 1783), 682 (Riddell, 1786), 696
(Moor, 1793).)

COPIES: G⁴ (common), L (fine).

1783   Anacreon, *Odes*, with Sappho and Alcaeus, **654** †
Remains, G and L

'ΑΙ ΤΟΥ | ΑΝΑΚΡΕΟΝΤΟΣ | Ω,ΔΑΙ, | ΚΑΙ ΤΑ ΤΗΣ |
ΣΑΠΦΟΥΣ, | ΚΑΙ ΤΑ ΤΟΥ | ΑΛΚΑΙΟΥ | ΛΕΙΨΑΝΑ. |
[*quotation, 1 line*] | GLASGUAE: | IN AEDIBUS ACA
DEMICIS, EXCUDEBAT | ANDREAS FOULIS, | ACA
DEMIAE TYPOGRAPHUS. | M.DCC.LXXXIII.

FORMULA: Foolscap 8⁰ in fours: A⁴ B–L⁴ (A1, I1 *and* L4 *missing
in the only copy seen, but its condition suggests that they were torn
out by an owner rather than removed by the printer*).

PAPER: Medium quality; blue; marks 3/i.

TYPE: GGP, RB 2. Latin follows Greek.

COPIES: G⁴.

655 Cicero, *De Finibus Bonorum et Malorum*, L   1783

M. T. | CICERONIS | DE | FINIBUS | BONORUM ET
MALORUM, | AD | MARCUM BRUTUM, | LIBRI QUIN
QUE: | EX EDITIONE J. OLIVETI: | ADJECTIS | VARI
ANTIBUS QUIBUSDAM LECTIONIBUS. | GLASGUAE:
| IN AEDIBUS ACADEMICIS | EXCUDEBAT ANDREAS
FOULIS. | M.DCC.LXXXIII.

FORMULA: Foolscap 12⁰ in sixes: a^2 b^6 c^2 A–Y^6 Z^4.

PAPER: Medium-good quality; marks 3/JC in double circle.

TYPE: RB 2.

VARIANT: Issue on inferior paper, Foolscap 12⁰:
Paper: Poor quality; vertical chain-lines; no marks; size
of half-sheet $16\frac{1}{2} \times 14\frac{1}{4}$ in. (half-sheets of Double Foolscap; see
No. 653 (Anacreon, 1783), VARIANT).

COPIES: G^4 (common), L (fine).

655A Cicero, *Pro Caelio*, L   1783

MARCI TULLII | CICERONIS | PRO | MARCO CAELIO |
ORATIO. | EX EDITIONE J. OLIVETI. | GLASGUAE: | IN
AEDIBUS ACADEMICIS | EXCUDEBAT ANDREAS
FOULIS, | ACADEMIAE TYPOGRAPHUS. | M. DCC.
LXXXIII.

FORMULA: Foolscap 8⁰ in fours: A–H^4 I^1.

PAPER: Medium quality; marks 3/letters in double circle.

TYPE: RSP 2.

NOTES: Advertised in No. 673 (Virgil, 1784) as printed and
sold by A. Foulis and A. Tilloch.

COPIES: G^2.

656 Dalrymple, David, Lord Hailes, *The Antiquities* 1783
of the Christian Church

ᴺCERNING | THE ANTIQUITIES
ᴺ CHURCH. | GLASGOW: |
ᴵ.IS, PRINTER | TO THE

B2.

PAPER: Medium-good quality; blue; marks 3/?iv, 3/ . . . M, 3/?JB in circle.
TYPE: RP 4, RLP 1, GB.
COPIES: G⁴.

1783   Eutropius, *Breviarium ab Urbe Condita*, L **657**

EUTROPII | HISTORIAE ROMANAE | BREVIARIUM | AB URBE | CONDITA USQUE AD VALENTINIANUM ET | VALENTEM AUGUSTOS. | GLASGUAE: | IN AEDIBUS ACADEMICIS, EXCUDEBAT | ANDREAS FOULIS, | ACADEMIAE TYPOGRAPHUS. | M.DCC. LXXXIII.
FORMULA: Foolscap 8⁰ in fours: a² A–N⁴ O² (O2 *signed;* C2 *sometimes unsigned*).
PAPER: Medium quality; blue; 3/vii, 3/M.
TYPE: RB 2, RLP 1.
VARIANT: Issue on inferior paper, [? Foolscap] 12⁰:
Formula: [? Foolscap] 12⁰ in sixes: a² A–I⁶ K⁴.
Paper: Poor quality; vertical chain-lines; no marks (probably half-sheets of Double Foolscap; see No. 653 (Anacreon, 1783), VARIANT).
COPIES: G⁴ (both issues).

1783–4   Foulis, Andrew the younger and Tilloch, **658** †
             Alexander, [Stereotyped Books]

NOTES: From 1783 to 1786 Foulis was in partnership with Alexander Tilloch, a fellow-Scotchman who had re-invented the stereotype process and who needed the assistance of a printer to help him put his invention into practice.* Several books were actually set, stereotyped and issued, according to Tilloch's own interesting account in his *Philosophical Magazine* (Vol. x (1801), pp. 267–77). He says:
'. . . several small volumes were actually printed from plates made by myself and Mr. Foulis, and the editions were sold to the trade without any intimation of their being printed out of the common way ! We had heard whispers that our work

---

* The patent for ' Foulis and Tillock's Plates for Letterprinting ' (No. 1431 of 1784) is quoted by John Carter in *The Library*, Fifth Series, Vol. xv, p. 162, n. 3.

could not possibly be such as would pass for *common printing* !
The trade knew what we were at, and would *take care* of any
thing done in the *new-fangled* way! The first essays, therefore,
were in the lowest sense of the word common: one or two
histories,* and a cheap edition of the Economy of Human Life.
We also printed a Greek volume, *Xenophon's Anabasis*, 1783, and
had plates for several small volumes of the English Poets
almost finished, but the latter were never put to press. Having
preserved two or three of the plates made along with Mr.
Foulis, I shall subjoin to the present account a specimen of
one or two' (pp. 274–5).

The plates which Tilloch prints as specimens are: (1) p. 91
of an 8⁰ Xenophon, *Anabasis* (B), set in GGP; unfortunately
the surviving fragment of the *Anabasis* of 1792 (No. 694) does
not include this page. (2) The ' Argument ' of Book xiii of
a small edition of Pope's Homer's *Iliad*; it is not the same setting as that of the equivalent page in the Foulis 12⁰ of 1784
(No. 669).

I have not found copies of any of the books mentioned by
Tilloch in his article. The following edition of Salomon
Gessner's *Death of Abel*, with the imprint ' Glasgow: printed
by Alex. Tilloch and Co. 1784 ', is puzzling. It belongs to the
period when Tilloch and Foulis were in partnership, yet it was
not mentioned in Tilloch's article of 1801, and on typographical
grounds it does not appear to have been set by Foulis, though
of course he may have printed it off.

THE | DEATH | OF | ABEL. | IN FIVE BOOKS. | AT
TEMPTED FROM THE | GERMAN of Mr GESSNER. |
The EIGHT [*sic*] EDITION. | GLASGOW: | PRINTED BY
ALEX. TILLOCH AND COMPANY. | M.DCC.LXXXIV.

FORMULA: [? Crown] 12⁰ in sixes: A–L² (I2 *unsigned*).

PAPER: Poor quality; no marks; vertical chain-lines (probably half-sheets of Double Crown).

TYPE: Apparently a Caslon-type Long Primer.

NOTES: Presumably one of Tilloch's stereotype editions,
although he does not mention it as one of the books printed

'* A kind of books technically so called, such as *The Seven
Champions of Christendom*; *The Twelve Caesars*; *The History of
Valentine and Orson*; *The French Convert*; and such scientific
and classical performances, of which great numbers are
annually exported to America.'

by Andrew Foulis and himself in his article in *The Philo-sophical Magazine* (see above). Perhaps, in view of the type used, it was not printed at the Foulis Press.

COPIES: G².

Advertisements for books printed and sold by A. Foulis and A. Tilloch do not mean that they were stereotyped; one such notice in No. 673 (Virgil, 1784) refers to a book (No. 637) which had been printed in 1778; nor does Tilloch's signature to the dedication of Vols. II and III of the folio Pope, of 1785 (No. 678) and of the folio Parnell of 1786 (No. 681) indicate that those great tomes were stereotyped.

1783   Miscellany. *Select Poems* **659**

SELECT | POEMS; | VIZ. | [*two columns, 4 and 3 lines, separated by a vertical plain double rule, 13; left;*] | HAMMOND's Love ele-|gies. | STILLINGFLEET's Eſſay | on converſation. | [*right:*] AIKENSIDE's Odes. | And | PHILIPS' Paſtorals. | GLASGOW: | PRINTED BY ANDREW FOULIS, PRINTER | TO THE UNIVERSITY. | M.DCC.LXXXIII.

FORMULA: Pot 12⁰ in sixes: πI A–C⁶ ²A–E⁶ ²F² ³A⁴ ³B–C⁶ (πI *general title-page*. AI *sub-title to Hammond*, C6 *blank*, ²AI *text of Stillingfleet and Akenside begins* (*no separate sub-title*), ³AI *sub-title to Philips*).

PAPER: Medium-poor quality; marks I/?R WILLIAMS, I/iv.

TYPE: RB 2.

COPIES: G⁴, L.

1783   Moor, James, *Elementa Linguae Graecae*, L **660**

ELEMENTA | LINGUAE GRAECAE; | NOVIS, PLERUM QUE, REGULIS | TRADITA; | BREVITATE SUA MEMO RIAE FACILIBUS. | PARS PRIMA, | COMPLECTENS | PARTES ORATIONIS DECLINABILES; | ET | ANA LOGIAM | DUAS IN UNAM SYLLABAS | CONTRA HENDI, | EX IPSA VOCALIUM NATURA | DEDUCTAM, | ET REGULIS UNIVERSALIBUS TRADITAM. | IN USUM TYRONUM JUNIORUM | CLASSIS GRAECAE IN ACA DEMIA GLASGUENSI. | EDITIO SEPTIMA PRIORI BUS AUCTIOR ET EMENDATIOR. | STUDIO JACOBI MOOR L.L.D. | IN EADEM ACADEMIA LITT. GRAEC. PROF. | [*quotation, 2 lines*] | GLASGUAE: | EXCUDEBAT ANDREAS FOULIS, | M.DCC.LXXXIII.

FORMULA: [? Crown] 8⁰ in fours: π^2 A–U⁴ X1.

PAPER: Medium-poor quality; no marks; horizontal chain-lines (probably printed on half-sheets of Double Crown; see No. 653 (Anacreon, 1783), VARIANT).

TYPE: RGP 2, GGP, GP, RLP 1.

COPIES: C.

661 Musaeus Grammaticus, *Hero and Leander*, E   1783

HERO AND LEANDER. | A POEM. | TRANSLATED FROM THE GREEK OF MUSAEUS. | [*quotation, 5 lines*] | GLASGOW: | PRINTED BY ANDREW FOULIS. | M.DCC. LXXXIII.

FORMULA: [? Writing Demy] 4⁰: π^2 A–C⁴.
Plate: copper-plate frontispiece (suicide of Hero), unsigned, plate mark 177 × 130. There is another version, signed ' *Ralſton ſc.*', plate mark 177 × 133.

PAPER: Medium-good quality; marks 7/I. TAYLOR.

TYPE: RE 3, RP 4.

NOTES: Translated by Edward Taylor.

COPIES: G⁴, L (lacks frontispiece).

662 Phaedrus, *Aesop's Fables*, L   1783

PHAEDRI, | AUGUSTI LIBERTI | FABULARUM | AESOPIARUM | LIBRI QUINQUE: | EX RECENSIONE | PETRI BURMANNI. | GLASGUAE: | IN AEDIBUS ACADEMICIS | EXCUDEBAT ANDREAS FOULIS, | ACADEMIAE TYPOGRAPHUS. | M.DCC.LXXXIII.

FORMULA: Foolscap 8⁰ in fours: A–M⁴ *N*² (C2 *signed*, ' B2 '; *N*2 *blank*).

PAPER: Medium-good quality; blue; marks 3/M.

TYPE: RLP 1, RB 2.

VARIANT: Issue on inferior paper, [? Foolscap] 8⁰:
Paper: Poor quality; horizontal chain-lines; no marks (probably half-sheets of Double Foolscap; see No. 653 (Ana-creon, 1783), VARIANT).

COPIES: G⁴ (both issues).

1783   Simpson, John, *De Catarrho*, L **663** †

TENTAMEN MEDICUM | INAUGURALE | DE | CATAR
RHO. | QUOD, | ANNUENTE SUMMO NUMINE, |
Auctoritate Dignissimi Vice-Cancellarii, | GULIELMI LEECH
MAN, S.S.T.P.P. | ET COLLEGII GLASG. PRAEFECTI;
| NEC NON | *Amplissimi* SENATUS ACADEMICI *Consensu;*
| *Et Nobilissimae* FACULTATIS MEDICAE *Decreto;* | PRO
GRADU DOCTORATUS, | SUMMISQUE IN MEDICINA
HONORIBUS ET PRIVILEGIIS | RITE AC LEGITIME
CONSEQUENDIS; | IN COMITIIS | UNIVERSITATIS
GLASGUENSIS, | Eruditorum examini subjicit | JOANNIS
SIMPSON, | ANGLO-BRITANNUS. | AD DIEM IV.
NOVEMBRIS, HORA PRIMA P.M. | LOCO SOLITO. |
GLASGUAE: | IN AEDIBUS ACADEMICIS, | EXCUDE
BAT ANDREAS FOULIS, | ACADEMIAE TYPOGRA
PHUS | M.DCC.LXXXIII.

FORMULA: [? Writing Demy] 8⁰ in fours: π^2 A–D⁴ ($2 *unsigned;*
D4 *blank*).

PAPER: Medium-good quality; marks (not seen)/I TAYLOR.

TYPE: RE 4, RLP 1.

COPIES: G².

[Entry deleted.]   **664**

1784   Cicero, *De Officiis*, L **665** †

MARCI TULLII | CICERONIS | DE | OFFICIIS | AD |
MARCUM FILIUM | LIBRI TRES. | GLASGUAE: | IN
AEDIBUS ACADEMICIS, EXCUDEBAT | ANDREAS
FOULIS, | ACADEMIAE TYPOGRAPHUS. | M.DCC.
LXXXIV.

FORMULA: Foolscap 8⁰ in fours: a⁴ b² A–2H⁴ 2I² (2H2 *unsigned*)
Press-figures: ' 1 ' on P1. ' 3 ' on K1 . . . M1 O4 T1 . . . X1 Y4.

PAPER: Medium-good quality; blue; marks 3/M, 3/i.

TYPE: RSP 2, RLP 1, RB 2.

VARIANT: Issue on inferior paper, [? Foolscap] 8⁰:
Paper: Medium-poor quality; horizontal chain-lines; no
marks (probably half-sheets of Double Foolscap; see No. 653
(Anacreon, 1783), VARIANT).

COPIES: G⁴ (common), L (fine).

666 Cochrane, Thomas, *De Tetano*, L   1784

DISSERTATIO MEDICA | INAUGURALIS | DE | TE
TANO. | QUAM, | ANNUENTE SUMMO NUMINE, |
Auctoritate Digniſſimi Vice-Cancellarii, | GULIELMI LEECH
MAN, S.S.T.P.P. | ET COLLEGII GLASG. PRAEFECTI; |
NEC NON | *Ampliſſimi* SENATUS ACADEMICI *Conſenſu;* |
Et Nobiliſſimae FACULTATIS MEDICAE *Decreto;* | PRO
GRADU DOCTORATUS, | SUMMISQUE IN MEDICINA
HONORIBUS ET PRIVILEGIIS | RITE AC LEGITIME
CONSEQUENDIS; | IN COMITIIS | UNIVERSITATIS
GLASGUENSIS, | Eruditorum examini ſubjicit | THOMAS
COCHRANE, A. M. | BRITANNUS. | SOCIET. PHYSICO-
CHIRURG. EDIN. SOC. HONOR. | AD DIEM XXVII.
DECEMBRIS, HORA PRIMA P.M. | LOCO SOLITO. |
GLASGUAE: | IN AEDIBUS ACADEMICIS, | EXCUDE
BAT ANDREAS FOULIS, | ACADEMIAE TYPOGRA
PHUS. | M.DCC.LXXXIV.

FORMULA: [? Printing Demy] 8⁰ in fours: π^2 A–E⁴ ($2 *unsigned*).

PAPER: Medium-poor quality; marks (not seen)/?1.

TYPE: RP 3.

COPIES: G⁴.

666A Dixon, William M., *De Hepatitide*, L   1784

DISSERTATIO MEDICA | INAUGURALIS | DE | HEPA
TITIDE. | QUAM, | ANNUENTE SUMMO NUMINE, |
Auctoritate Digniſſimi Vice-Cancellarii, | GULIELMI LEECH
MAN, S.S.T.P.P. | ET COLLEGII GLASG. PRAEFECTI; |
NEC NON | *Ampliſſimi* SENATUS ACADEMICI *Conſenſu;* |
Et Nobiliſſimae FACULTATIS MEDICAE *Decreto;* | PRO
GRADU DOCTORATUS, | SUMMISQUE IN MEDICINA
HONORIBUS ET PRIVILEGIIS | RITE AC LEGITIME
CONSEQUENDIS; | IN COMITIIS | UNIVERSITATIS
GLASGUENSIS, | Eruditorum examini ſubjicit | GULIEL
MUS MAJOR DIXON, A.M. | CIVIS VIRGINIENSIS. |
SOC. REG. MED. EDIN. SODAL. | NEC NON | SOCIET.
PHYSIC. EDINEN. SOC. | AD DIEM XX. SEPTEMBRIS,
HORA PRIMA P.M. | LOCO SOLITO. | GLASGUAE: |
IN AEDIBUS ACADEMICIS, | EXCUDEBAT ANDREAS
FOULIS, | ACADEMIAE TYPOGRAPHUS. | M.DCC.
LXXXIV.

FORMULA: [? Printing Demy] 8⁰ in fours: π^2 A–E⁴ (2$ *unsigned*).
PAPER: Medium quality; marks 9/?.
TYPE: RP 3.
COPIES: G².

by 1784 Dyche, Thomas, *Spelling Book* **667**

NOTES: Not seen. Advertised in No. 673 (Virgil, 1784) as
' Dyche's Spelling Book ', printed and sold by A. Foulis and
A. Tilloch. Probably an edition of Dyche's *The Spelling Dic-
tionary.*

1784 Euripides, *Medea*, G and L **668**

'H TOϒ | EϒPIΠIΔOϒ | MHΔEIA. | EURIPIDIS | MEDEA.
| EX EDITIONE MUSGRAVIANA. | [*quotation, 5 lines*] |
GLASGUAE: | IN AEDIBUS ACADEMICIS, EXCUDEBAT
| ANDREAS FOULIS, | ACADEMIAE TYPOGRAPHUS. |
M.DCC.LXXXIV.

FORMULA: [? Foolscap] 8⁰ in fours: A^4 B–U⁴ (G2 . . . O2, U2
unsigned; A2, U4 *blank;* A4 *possibly meant to be used as a half-
title*).

PAPER: Poor quality; horizontal chain-lines (except B and C
which are vertical); no marks; size of half sheet $16\frac{3}{4} \times 14$ in
(half-sheets of Double Foolscap; see No. 653 (Anacreon, 1783),
VARIANT).

TYPE: GGP GP RSP 1, RSP 2. Greek and Latin on facing
pages.

VARIANT: Issue on fine paper, Foolscap 8⁰:
  Paper: Medium-good quality; blue; marks 3/?.
COPIES: G⁴ (common), G² (fine).

1784 Pope's Homer, *Iliad*, E **669**

THE | ILIAD | OF | HOMER. | TRANSLATED BY | ALEX
ANDER POPE. | VOLUME FIRST [SECOND] [THIRD]
[FOURTH]. | [*quotations, 4 lines (Vol.* i), *4 lines (Vol.* ii), *5 lines
(Vol.* iii) *and 2 lines (Vol.* iv)] | GLASGOW: | PRINTED BY
ANDREW FOULIS, | M.DCC.LXXXIV.

FORMULA: Pot 12⁰ in sixes:
  Vol. i: π^2 A–O⁶ P⁴ (*signed* ' † ' *on* A1, B1; π1 *half-title*).
  Vol. ii: π^2 A² B–O⁶ (π1 *half-title,* O6 *blank*).

Vol. III: π1 A–P⁶ Q².
Vol. IV: π1 A⁴ B–O⁶.
(*Signed* ' Vol. I[. . . IV].' *on* $1 *except* π *sigs.*)
Press-figures: ' 1 ' on Vol. I D1 F1 H1 L1 N1 P1, Vol. II B1 C1
E1 F1. ' 3 ' on Vol. I A1 . . . C1 E1 G1 I1 K1 O1, Vol. II D2
G2 I1 . . . L1.
PAPER: Medium-poor quality; marks 1/iv, 1/letters in circle.
TYPE: RB 2.
VARIANT: The two ' † ' signatures in Vol. I may be relics of
an issue on (?) better-quality paper, not seen.
COPIES: G⁴.

670 Plautus, *Mostellaria*, L   by 1784

NOTES: Not seen. Advertised in No. 673 (Virgil, 1784) as
printed and sold by A. Foulis and A. Tilloch. Possibly *c.* 1778,
when the *Aulularia* (No. 637), similarly advertised, appeared.

671 Plautus, *Trinummus*, L   by 1784

NOTES: Not seen. Advertised in No. 673 (Virgil, 1784) as
printed and sold by A. Foulis and A. Tilloch. Possibly *c.* 1778,
when the *Aulularia* (No. 637), similarly advertised, appeared.

† **672** Thomson, James, *Poetical Works*   1784

THE | POETICAL WORKS | OF | JAMES THOMSON. |
IN TWO VOLUMES. | VOL. I [II]. | GLASGOW: | PRINTED
BY ANDREW FOULIS, PRINTER | TO THE UNIVER
SITY. | M.DCC.LXXXIV. [*Same setting.*]
FORMULA: Writing Demy 2⁰:
    Vol. I: *a*1 b–h² χ² ²χ1 ³χ1 *A*² B–3S² 3*T*² (χ1 *title-page to* The
Seasons (*dated 1783*), χ2 *dedication*, ²χ1 *To Amanda*, ³χ1 (*signed
' i '*) *The Arguments*; 3*T*², *the subscribers list, may also be found
elsewhere*).
    Vol. II: π1 *A*² B–4M² 4N1.
PAPER: Medium-good quality; marks 7/C. TAYLOR, 7/I.
TAYLOR; size of sheet 19¾ × 12½ in.
TYPE: RDP, RE 4, RP 4, RSP 2, RGP 2.
NOTES: The dedication signed by Andrew Foulis.
COPIES: G⁴, L.

1784   Virgil, *Works*, L **673** †

PUBLII | VIRGILII | MARONIS | BUCOLICA, | GEORGI
CA, | ET | AENEIS. | EX EDITIONE | PETRI BURMANNI.
| GLASGUAE: | IN AEDIBUS ACADEMICIS, EXCUDE
BAT | ANDREAS   FOULIS, | ACADEMIAE   TYPO
GRAPHUS. | M.DCC.LXXXIV.

FORMULA: Foolscap 8º in fours: π^2 A–2G⁴ ²A–U⁴ (E2 *signed*
' D2 '; ²U4 *advertisements; pagination as well as signing begins
anew on* ²A1, *the beginning of Aeneid VII*).

PAPER: Medium-good quality; blue; marks 3/ ?i, 3/ ?M.

TYPE: RB 2, RLP 2. Without long ſ.

VARIANT: Issue on inferior paper, [? Foolscap] 8º:
  Paper: Poor quality; vertical chain-lines in sigs. A–C,
horizontal in the rest; no marks (the sections with horizontal
chain-lines probably printed on half-sheets of Double Foolscap; see No. 653 (Anacreon, 1783), VARIANT).

NOTES: The advertisements on ²U4 are for books printed and
sold by A. Foulis and A. Tilloch.

COPIES: G⁴ (both issues).

by 1784   Watts, Isaac, *Hymns and Spiritual Songs* **674**

NOTES: Not seen.   Advertised in No. 673 (Virgil, 1784) as
printed and sold by A. Foulis and A. Tilloch.

by 1784   Watts, Isaac, *The Psalms of David Imitated* **675**

NOTES: Not seen.   Advertised in No. 673 (Virgil, 1784) as
printed and sold by A. Foulis and A. Tilloch.

1785   Erskine, David Steuart, Earl of Buchan, **675A**
          Memorable Occurences in the History of Scotland

A | DISSERTATION | ON CERTAIN | MEMORABLE
OCCURENCES | IN THE | HISTORY OF SCOTLAND. |
READ BEFORE THE | SOCIETY OF ANTIQUARIES OF
SCOTLAND, | 5th April, 1785: | THE EARL OF BUCHAN,
| FIRST VICE PRESIDENT, | IN THE CHAIR. | GLAS
GOW: | PRINTED BY ANDREW FOULIS. | M.DCC.
LXXXV.

FORMULA: Foolscap 4⁰ in twos: A^2 B–E^2 F1.

PAPER: Medium-good quality; marks 3/iv.

TYPE: RDP.

COPIES: G^2.

676 Lucan, *Pharsalia*, L   1785

MARCI ANNAEI | LUCANI | PHARSALIA, | SIVE DE | BELLO CIVILI, | LIBRI X. | Ad Editionem Cortii fideliter expressi. | GLASGUAE: | IN AEDIBUS ACADEMICIS EXCUDEBAT | ANDREAS FOULIS ACADEMIAE TYPO GRAPHUS. | MDCCLXXXV.

FORMULA: [? Writing Demy] 8⁰ in fours: π^2 A–2I⁴ (π1 *half-title*).

PAPER: Good quality; marks 7/C Taylor.

TYPE: RB 2. Without long f.

VARIANTS: Issue in Foolscap 8⁰:
  Paper: Medium quality; marks 3/F HAYES, 3/monogram. Issue in [? Foolscap] 12⁰:
  Formula: [? Foolscap] 12⁰ in sixes: π^2 A–X^6 Y^2 (π1 *half-title*).
  Paper: Poor quality; vertical chain-lines; no marks; size of half-sheet 17 × 14¾ in. (probably half-sheets of Double Foolscap, though the size is large); see No. 653 (Anacreon, 1783) VARIANT).

COPIES: G^4 (all three issues), L (Demy).

† 677 M'Nab, Henry, *Heads of a Course of Elocution*   1785

HEADS | OF A COURSE OF | ELOCUTION. | WITH EXERCISES; | PARTLY FROM | MANUSCRIPTS. | FOR THE PURPOSE OF | IMPROVEMENT IN READING AND | SPEAKING. | BY | HENRY M'NAB. | [*quotation, 2 lines*] | GLASGOW: | PRINTED BY A. FOULIS, FOR THE AUTHOR. | M.DCC.LXXXV.

FORMULA: Printing Demy 12⁰ in sixes: π^2 A–2F⁶(–2F5, 2F6; *the text of the only copy seen is interrupted at* 2F4, *so that it is not clear how much of the book is missing*).

PAPER: Medium-poor quality; marks 9/monogram JB, 9/B; size of sheet 21¼ × 17¼ in.

TYPE: RLP 1, RSP 2.

NOTES: The dedication is dated 30 March 1785.

COPIES: G^4.

1785 Pope, Alexander, *Poetical Works* **678** †

THE | POETICAL WORKS | OF | ALEXANDER POPE, ESQ. | IN THREE VOLUMES. | VOL. I [II] [III]]. | GLAS GOW: | PRINTED BY ANDREW FOULIS, PRINTER TO | THE UNIVERSITY. | M.DCC.LXXXV. [*Different settings.*]

FORMULA: [? Writing Demy] 2⁰:

Vol. I: a^2 χI b–h² A–4K² (aI *title-page*, a2 *dedication*, χI *contents*).

Vol. II: π^2 χI A–4Y² 4ZI (*signed* ' VOL. II.' *on* A *to* 4Z $1; πI *title-page*, π2 *dedication*, χI *contents*).

Vol. III: π^2 A^2 B–5H² 5II 5K^2 (*signed* ' VOL. III.' *on* B–5I $1; πI *title-page*, π2 *dedication*, A^2 *contents*, 5K^2 *subscribers*).

PAPER: Medium-good quality; marks 7 with the following alternative countermarks: C TAYLOR, I TAYLOR, T BUDGEN, T WILMOTT, CURTEIS & SONS.

TYPE: RDP, RE 4, RP 4, RLP I. Block 14.

VARIANT: The copy at C has two versions of the subscribers list, reading the same as each other, bound at the end of Vol. III. Each is printed on an unsigned conjugate pair, one (set in RP 4) occupying all four pages, the other (set in RSP 2) occupying only three.

NOTES: The dedications are signed Andrew Foulis (Vol. I), and A. Foulis and A. Tilloch (Vol. II and III).

COPIES: G⁴, L (no subscribers lists), C (two subscribers lists), O (subscribers list in RP 4).

1785 Theophrastus, *Characters*, G and L **679**

ΘΕΟΦΡΑΣΤΟΥ | ΧΑΡΑΚΤΗΡΕΣ | ΗΘΙΚΟΙ. | THEO PHRASTI | CHARACTERES | ETHICI. | EX RECEN SIONE | PETRI NEEDHAM, | ET VERSIONE LATINA | ISAACI CASAUBONI. | GLASGUAE: | IN AEDIBUS ACADEMICIS, | EXCUDEBAT ANDREAS FOULIS, | ACADEMIAE TYPOGRAPHUS. | MDCCLXXXV.

FORMULA: Foolscap 8⁰: A–H⁸ I².

PAPER: Medium-good quality; blue; marks 3/. . . D . . . AND, 3/iv, 5/?.

TYPE: GDP 2, RP 3. Latin follows Greek.

VARIANT: Issue on common paper, [? Foolscap] 8⁰:

Paper: Medium-poor quality; horizontal chain lines; no marks (probably half-sheets of Double Foolscap; see No. 653 (Anacreon, 1783), VARIANT).

COPIES: G⁴, L (fine); G² (common).

† **680**   MacNab, Henry, *A Plan of Reform in Instruction*   1786
in English Schools

A | PLAN OF REFORM, | IN THE | MODE OF INSTRUC
TION, | AT PRESENT PRACTISED IN | ENGLISH
SCHOOLS. | ALSO | A PROPOSAL FOR THE | IMPROVE
MENT OF PUBLIC SPEAKING. | BY | HENRY MACNAB.
| GLASGOW. | PRINTED BY ANDREW FOULIS, FOR
THE AUTHOR. | M.DCC.LXXXVI.

FORMULA: Foolscap 4° in twos: π^2 A–F^2.

PAPER: Medium quality; marks 3/CURTEIS & SONS.

TYPE: RP 4, RE 4, RLP 2.

NOTES: The dedication is dated 28 October 1786. There are
advertisements on $F2^v$ for three books by MacNab shortly to
be published, but there is no suggestion that they were being
printed at the Foulis Press (*The Philosophy of Natural and
Artificial Language*; *The Director, in teaching English*; and *The
Reader and Speaker*).

COPIES: L.

680A   MacNab, Henry, *A Synopsis of a Course of*   1786
Elocution

A | SYNOPSIS | OF A | COURSE OF ELOCUTION. | BY |
HENRY M'NAB. | GLASGOW: | Printed by A. FOULIS,
Printer to the Univerſity. | M.DCC.LXXXVI.

FORMULA: Foolscap 8° in fours: π1 A–C^4 D1.

PAPER: Medium-good quality; marks 3/?.

TYPE: RLP 1.

COPIES: G^2.

681   Parnell, Thomas, *Poetical Works*   1786

THE | POETICAL WORKS | OF | DR. THOMAS PARNELL,
| LATE ARCHDEACON OF CLOGHER. | GLASGOW: |
PRINTED BY ANDREW FOULIS, PRINTER TO | THE
UNIVERSITY. | M.DCC.LXXXVI.

FORMULA: [? Writing Demy] 2°: a^2 χ1 b–c^2 A–$5E^2$ $5F^2$ (*a*1
*title-page, a*2 *contents,* χ1 *dedication,* $5F^2$ *subscribers*).

PAPER: Medium-good quality; marks 7/T WILMOTT, 7/C
TAYLOR.

TYPE: RDP, RE 4, RSP 2.

NOTES: The dedication is signed A. Foulis and A. Tilloch.

COPIES: G⁴, L.

1786   Riddell, John, *Malvina* **682**

MALVINA, | A | TRAGEDY. | GLASGOW; | PRINTED BY
ANDREW FOULIS. | M.DCC.LXXXVI.

FORMULA: [? Crown] 8⁰ in fours: $\pi 1$ A–H⁴ I² ($2 *unsigned*).

PAPER: Medium-poor quality; horizontal chain-lines; blue;
no marks (probably half-sheets of Double Crown). See No. 653
(Anacreon, 1783), VARIANT.

TYPE: RLP 2.

COPIES: G⁴.

1787   Collins, William, *Poetical Works* **683**

THE | POETICAL WORKS | OF | WILLIAM COLLINS. |
GLASGOW: | PRINTED BY ANDREW FOULIS, PRINTER
| TO THE UNIVERSITY. | M.DCC.LXXXVII.

FORMULA: [? Writing Demy] 2⁰: π2 a–b² c1 A–E² F² G–T²
U1 ²a² ²b² (*sig.* A *signed on* A2; $\pi 1$ *half-title;* ²b² *subscribers*).

PAPER: Medium-good quality; marks 7/C TAYLOR, 7/IA.

TYPE: RDP, RE 4, RSP 1.

COPIES: G⁴, L.

1787   Gray, Thomas, *Poetical Works* **684**

THE | POETICAL WORKS | OF | THOMAS GRAY. |
GLASGOW: | PRINTED BY ANDREW FOULIS, PRINTER
| TO THE UNIVERSITY. | M.DCC.LXXXVII. [*There are two
settings of the title-page, reading the same.*]

FORMULA: [? Writing Demy] 2⁰: π2 χ1 a–f² ²a² A–2F² ³a–e²
(2A1 . . . 2F1 *signed* 'A2 . . . F2'; $\pi 1$ *half-title,* π2 *title-page,* χ1
dedication).

PAPER: Medium-good quality; marks 7, with the alternative
countermarks T BUDGEN, C TAYLOR, I TAYLOR, IA.

TYPE: RDP, RE 4, GDP 2, RLP 2.

NOTES: The dedication is signed Andrew Foulis.

COPIES: G⁴, L.

† **685** Hammond, James, *Poetical Works* 1787

THE | POETICAL WORKS | OF | JAMES HAMMOND. | GLASGOW: | PRINTED BY ANDREW FOULIS, PRINTER | TO THE UNIVERSITY. | M.DCC.LXXXVII.

FORMULA: [? Writing Demy] 2⁰: π^2 a–b² ²b² A–M² N1 (*sig.* A *signed on* A2; π1 *half-title*).

PAPER: Medium-good quality; marks 7 with the alternative countermarks T BUDGEN, I TAYLOR, C TAYLOR, IA.

TYPE: RDP.

COPIES: G⁴, L.

685A Hutcheson, Francis, *Logicae Compendium,* L 1787

LOGICAE | COMPENDIUM. | PRAEFIXA EST | DISSER TATIO | DE | PHILOSOPHIAE ORIGINE, | EJUSQUE | INVENTORIBUS AUT EXCULTORIBUS | PRAECIPUIS. | GLASGUAE: | IN AEDIBUS ACADEMICIS | EXCUDE BAT ANDREAS FOULIS | ACADEMIAE TYPOGRAPHUS | M DCC LXXXVII.

FORMULA: [? Foolscap] 8⁰ in fours: π1 A–L⁴ (L2 *signed* ' K2 '; B2, G2, H2 *unsigned*).

PAPER: Medium-poor quality; horizontal chain-lines; no marks (probably half-sheets of Double Foolscap; see No. 653 (Anacreon, 1783), VARIANT).

TYPE: RP 4, RLP 1.

COPIES: G².

† **686** Lyttelton, George, Baron, *Poetical Works* 1787

THE | POETICAL WORKS | OF | GEORGE LORD LYT TELTON. | GLASGOW: | PRINTED BY ANDREW FOULIS, PRINTER | TO THE UNIVERSITY. | M.DCC. LXXXVII.

FORMULA: [? Writing Demy] 2⁰: π^2 a^2 b–c² ²a² A–2I² 2K1 (2A1 . . . 2I1 *signed* ' A2 . . . I2 ', 2K1 *signed normally;* π1 *half-title*).

PAPER: Medium-good quality; marks 7 with the alternative countermarks I TAYLOR, C TAYLOR, R WILLIAMS, IA, IV.

TYPE: RDP.

NOTES: The dedication is signed Andrew Foulis.

COPIES: G⁴, L.

1788   Pindar, *Olympia*, G and L **687**

ΤΑ ΤΟΥ | ΠΙΝΔΑΡΟΥ | ΟΛΥΜΠΙΑ. | PINDARI |
OLYMPIA. | CUM INTERPRETATIONE LATINA: | EX
EDITIONE S.G.HEYNE. | GLASGUAE: | IN AEDIBUS
ACADEMICIS, | EXCUDEBAT ANDREAS FOULIS, |
ACADEMIAE TYPOGRAPHUS, | M.DCC.LXXXVIII.

FORMULA: [? Foolscap] 8⁰ in fours: π² A–L⁴ M² ²A–C⁴ ²D²
(G2, L2 *signed* ' G3 ', ' L3 '; ²C2 *unsigned;* π1 *half-title*).

PAPER: Poor quality; horizontal chain-lines; no marks (probably half-sheets of Double Foolscap; see No. 653 (Anacreon,
1783), VARIANT).

TYPE: GGP, GP, RB 2. Without long f. Latin follows Greek.

COPIES: G⁴.

1788   Ramsay, Allan, *The Gentle Shepherd* **688** †

THE | GENTLE SHEPHERD, | A | PASTORAL COMEDY;
| BY | ALLAN RAMSAY. | GLASGOW: | PRINTED BY
A. FOULIS, AND SOLD BY D. ALLAN, DICKSON'S |
CLOSS, EDINBURGH, ALSO BY J. MURRAY, N⁰. 32. |
FLEET-STREET, AND C. ELLIOT, | STRAND, LONDON.
| M.DCC.LXXXVIII.

FORMULA: [? Writing] Royal 4⁰: π² a² b⁴ A–O⁴ ²A–E² (²B2,
²C2 *signed;* b2 *unsigned;* π1 *half-title*).

Plates: Aquatints; frontispiece portrait and 12 numbered
plates (the second plate unnumbered) facing π2 A2, C2, C3,
D2ᵛ, E3ᵛ, G2ᵛ, G3ᵛ, I4ᵛ, K4ᵛ, L4ᵛ, M2ᵛ, N4ᵛ; dark brown
or grey, except for No. 4, which is usually reddish. Engraved
by David Allan, with his imprint as publisher dated Edinburgh
1788 (12 July 1788 in plates 1, 2, 3, 5, 8, 10 and frontispiece).
(See *The Times Literary Supplement*, 4 May 1951, 'An Eighteenth-
Century Illustrator ', for a note on these plates.) Nine leaves
of engraved music, pp. 1–18, bound at the end; unsigned, plate
marks c. 260 × 200.

PAPER: Good quality; marks 8/?JW. Plates on a heavier laid
paper, marks indistinguishable.

TYPE: RDP, RP 4, RE 4.

VARIANT: G⁴ has a copy in which the plates are coloured, very
successfully, by hand. The quantity and colour of the ink
used does not differ markedly from that of normal copies of
the plates, and it is hard to be sure when the colouring was
done. The present binding dates from the second half of the
nineteenth century.

NOTES: The dedication is dated 3 October 1788.

COPIES: G⁴ (plates uncoloured and coloured), L (plates uncoloured).

688A Crawford, Andrew, *De Vita Animali*, L   1789

DISSERTATIO | DE | VITA ANIMALI. | QUAM, | ANNUENTE SUMMO NUMINE, | EX AUCTORITATE DIGNISSIMI VICE-CANCELLARII, | ARCHIBALDI DAVIDSON, S.S.T.P.P. | ET COLLEGII GLASG. *Praefecti;* | NEC NON | *Amplissimi* SENATUS ACADEMICI *Consensu,* | *Et Nobilissimae* FACULTATIS MEDICAE *Decreto;* | PRO GRADU DOCTORIS, | SUMMISQUE IN MEDICINA HONORIBUS ET PRIVILEGIIS, | RITE AC LEGITIME CONSE QUENDIS; | IN COMITIIS | UNIVERSITATIS GLAS GUENSIS, | ERUDITORUM EXAMINI SUBJICIT | ANDREAS CRAWFORD, A.M. | SCOTO-BRITANNUS, | SOCIET. REG. PHYS. EDIN. SOC. | ET | AD ACTA EDENDA AB ELECTIS. | NEC NON | SOCIET. PHYS. AMERICAN. SOC. EXTR. | Prid. Calendar. Maii [*30 April*], hora locoque folitis. | GLASGUAE: | IN AEDIBUS ACA DEMICIS | EXCUDEBAT ANDREAS FOULIS, | ACA DEMIAE TYPOGRAPHUS. | M.DCC.LXXXIX.

FORMULA: [? Printing Demy] 8⁰ in fours: $\pi 1$ $^{2}\pi^{2}$ A–E⁴ $F1$ (C2 *signed* ' A2 ', A1 *unsigned;* $\pi 1$ *title-page,* $^{2}\pi^{2}$ *two dedications*).

PAPER: A–E: medium quality; blue; marks 9/i. π, F; and $^{2}\pi$: two sorts of medium-quality white paper, showing mark 9 on $F1$.

TYPE: RLP 2.

COPIES: York Medical Society Library.

689 Plato, *Apology*, G and L   1789

ΠΛΑΤΩΝΟΣ | ΑΠΟΛΟΓΙΑ | ΣΩΚΡΑΤΟΥΣ. | PLATONIS | APOLOGIA | SOCRATIS. | GLASGUAE: | IN AEDIBUS ACADEMICIS | EXCUDEBAT ANDREAS FOULIS | ACADEMIAE TYPOGRAPHUS | M.DCC.LXXXIX.

FORMULA: Foolscap 8⁰ in fours: $\pi 1$ A–O⁴(–O4; A3 *signed*).

PAPER: Medium-poor quality; blue, marks, 4/? letters in circle; white, marks 3/? letters in circle.

TYPE: GGP, RLP 2. Latin follows Greek.

VARIANT: Issue on inferior paper, [? Foolscap] 8⁰:
  Paper: Poor quality; no marks.

COPIES: G⁴ (both issues).

1790   Cuninghame, William, *De Cynanche* **689A**
                                    Tracheali, L

TENTAMEN MEDICUM | INAUGURALE | DE |
CYNANCHE TRACHEALI. | QUOD, | ANNUENTE
SUMMO NUMINE, | EX AUCTORITATE DIGNISSIMI
VICE-CANCELLARII, | ARCHIBALDI DAVIDSON,
S.S.T.P.P. | ET COLLEGII GLASG. *Praefecti;* | NEC NON
| *Ampliſſimi* SENATUS ACADEMICI *Confenſu,* | *Et Nobili
ſſimae* FACULTATIS MEDICAE *Decreto;* | PRO GRADU
DOCTORIS, | SUMMISQUE IN MEDICINA HONORIBUS
ET PRIVILEGIIS | RITE AC LEGITIME CONSEQUEN
DIS; | IN COMITIIS | UNIVERSITATIS GLASGUENSIS,
| ERUDITORUM EXAMINI SUBJICIT | GULIELMUS
CUNINGHAME, A.M. | SCOTO-BRITANNUS. | SOCIET.
AMER. PHYSIC. EDIN. | PRAESES ANNUUS ET SOC.
EXTRAORD. | NEC NON | SOCIET. REG. PHYSIC. SOC.
HON. | Ad diem iii. Junii, hora locoque folitis. | GLASGUAE:
| IN AEDIBUS ACADEMICIS, | EXCUDEBAT ANDREAS
FOULIS, | ACADEMIAE TYPOGRAPHUS. | M.D.CC.XC.

FORMULA: Royal 8⁰ in fours: π^4 A–C⁴ D² ($2 *unsigned;* π1
half-title, π2 *title-page,* π3–4 *dedications*).

PAPER: Medium-good quality; marks 8/?.

TYPE: RSP 2.

COPIES: G².

1790   Longinus, *On the Sublime*, G and L **690**

ΤΟ ΤΟΥ | ΔΙΟΝΥΣΙΟΥ | ΛΟΓΓΙΝΟΥ | ΠΕΡΙ | ΥΨΟΥΣ |
ΥΠΟΜΝΗΜΑ. | EX EDITIONE | JOANNIS TOUPII, |
EXPRESSUM. | GLASGUAE: | IN AEDIBUS ACA
DEMICIS | EXCUDEBAT ANDREAS FOULIS, | ACA
DEMIAE TYPOGRAPHUS. | M.DCC.XC.

FORMULA: Foolscap 8⁰ in fours: π1 A–X⁴ Y1 (B2, C2, F2,
G2, I2 . . . L2 *unsigned*).

PAPER: Medium quality; blue; marks 3/iv.

TYPE: GGP, GP, RLP 2. Latin follows Greek.

VARIANT: Issue on common paper, Foolscap 8⁰.
    Formula: (E2, M2 *unsigned*.)
    Paper: Sigs. A–L, π, Y: Poor quality; horizontal chain-
lines; no marks. Sigs. M–X: Poor quality: vertical chain-
lines; marks 5/iv. (The paper with the horizontal chain-lines
is almost certainly half-sheets of Double Foolscap, themselves

printed by ' half-sheet imposition '. The paper with the vertical chain-lines is an ordinary Foolscap, watermarked as such. See No. 653 (Anacreon, 1783), VARIANT).

COPIES: Philip Gaskell (fine), G⁴ (common).

691 Glasgow University: Library. *Catalogus* 1791
Impressorum Librorum (author catalogue), by Arthur, Archibald

CATALOGUS | IMPRESSORUM LIBRORUM | IN | BIBLIOTHECA | UNIVERSITATIS | GLASGUENSIS, | SECUNDUM LITERARUM ORDINEM DISPOSITUS. | IMPENSIS ACADEMIAE, | LABORE ET STUDIO | ARCHIBALDI ARTHUR, A.M. | PHILOSOPHIAE MORA LIS PROFESSORIS. | GLASGUAE: | IN AEDIBUS ACADEMICIS | EXCUDEBAT ANDREAS FOULIS, | ACADEMIAE TYPOGRAPHUS. | M,DCC,XCI.

FORMULA: Writing Demy 2⁰: π^2 A–6I² (X2 *signed* ' U2 ';
B2 . . . 2B2 *signed;* π1 *half-title*).

PAPER: Medium-good quality; marks 7 with the alternative countermarks C TAYLOR, I TAYLOR, T BUDGEN, CURTEIS & SONS, IV; size of sheet 19½ × 15½ in.

TYPE: RP 4.

COPIES: G⁴.

691A Glasgow University: Library. *Catalogus* 1791
Impressorum Librorum (shelf list), by Arthur, Archibald

[*Title-page printed from the same type as No. 691, with line 7 altered to read:*] SECUNDUM PLUTEORUM ORDINEM DISPOSITUS.

FORMULA: Writing Demy 2⁰: π^2 A–5E² 5E1 (π1 *half-title*).

PAPER: Good quality; marks 7/iv.

TYPE: RP 4.

COPIES: G².

692 Foulis, Andrew the younger, *The Origin of* 1791
the Glasgow Press

[*Begins:*] A | SLIGHT SKETCH | OF THE ORIGIN OF THE | GLASGOW PRESS, | AND | ACADEMY OF THE FINE ARTS. | [*followed by text.*]

FORMULA: Medium 4⁰: A⁴.

PAPER: Medium quality; wove; no marks.

TYPE: RE 4.

NOTES: See Maclehose, p. 200, for an account of this pamphlet, with which Foulis hoped to obtain subscriptions for the failing Press. The copy described is a proof, and it is likely that no edition was ever printed.

COPIES: Edinburgh University Library, inserted in Laing MSS, III.363. (Note that a printed *Catalogue of Pictures*, 1776, laid down in the same volume of MSS, is not a Foulis Book, although it is an epitome of part of *CP*.)

1792   Anacreon, *Odes*, with Sappho and Alcaeus, **693**
Remains, G and L

'ΑΙ ΤΟΥ | ΑΝΑΚΡΕΟΝΤΟΣ | Ω῾ΔΑΙ, | ΚΑΙ ΤΑ ΤΗΣ | ΣΑΠΦΟΥΣ, | ΚΑΙ ΤΑ ΤΟΥ | ΑΛΚΑΙΟΥ | ΛΕΙΨΑΝΑ. | [*quotation, 1 line*] | GLASGUAE: | IN AEDIBUS ACA DEMICIS, | EXCUDEBAT ANDREAS FOULIS, | ACA DEMIAE TYPOGRAPHUS. | M.DCC.XCII.

FORMULA: [? Foolscap] 8⁰ in fours: π^2 A–M⁴ (G2, I2 . . . M2 *unsigned; π1 half-title*).

PAPER: Poor quality; horizontal chain-lines; no marks (probably half-sheets of Double Foolscap. See No. 653 (Anacreon, 1783), VARIANT).

TYPE: GDP 2, RB 2. Without long f. Latin translation as footnotes to the text.

COPIES: G⁴.

1792   Shapter, William R., *De Scorbuto*, L **693A**

DISPUTATIO MEDICA | INAUGURALIS | DE | SCOR BUTO. | QUAM, | ANNUENTE SUMMO NUMINE, | EX AUCTORITATE DIGNISSIMI VICE-CANCELLARII, | ARCHIBALDI DAVIDSON, S.S.T.P.P. | ET COLLEGII GLASG. PRAEFECTI: | NEC NON | Ampliffimi SENATUS ACADEMICI Confenfu, | Et Nobiliffimae FACULTATIS MEDICAE Decreto; | PRO GRADU DOCTORIS, | SUM MISQUE IN MEDICINA HONORIBUS ET PRIVILE-| GIIS RITE AC LEGITIME CONSEQUENDIS; | IN COMI TIIS | UNIVERSITATIS GLASGUENSIS, | ERUDITO RUM EXAMINI SUBJICIT | GULIELMUS RANDLE

SHAPTER, A.M. | ANGLUS. | COLLEG. CHIRURG.
LONDIN. SOC. | SOCIET. PHYSIC. LONDIN. SOC. HON.
| ET, | LEG. EQUIT. BRIT. SEPTENT. REG. | CHIRUR
GUS. | Ad diem vi Aprilis hora locoque folitis. | [*quotation, 3
lines*] | GLASGUAE: | IN AEDIBUS ACADEMICIS |
EXCUDEBAT ANDREAS FOULIS, | ACADEMIAE
TYPOGRAPHUS. | M.DCC.XCII.

FORMULA: [? Writing Demy] 8⁰ in fours: A^2 χ1 B–C⁴ ²C⁴
(*A*1 *half-title*, *A*2 *title-page*, χ1 *dedication*, ²C4 *blank*).

PAPER:·Medium-good quality; marks 7/J WHATMAN.

TYPE: RSP 1, RB (?)2.

COPIES: G^2.

† **694** Xenophon, *Anabasis*, G and L   1792

[*Note: Vols.* I, III *and* IV *not seen.*]
ΤΟΥ | ΞΕΝΟΦΩΝΤΟΣ | 'Η ΤΟΥ | ΚΥΡΟΥ | ΑΝΑΒΑΣΙΣ.
| XENOPHONTIS | EXPEDITIO | CYRI. | TOMIS QUA
TUOR. | EX EDITIONE T. HUTCHINSON | TOM. II. | GLAS
GUAE: | IN AEDIBUS ACADEMICIS, | EXCUDEBAT
ANDREAS FOULIS, | ACADEMIAE TYPOGRAPHUS. |
M DCC.XCII.

FORMULA: Foolscap 8⁰ in fours: Vol. II: π1 A–2B⁴ (A2, B2,
D2, G2, H2, L2, N2, O2, P2 *signed* ' A3 ', ' B3 ' *etc.*; C2 *signed*
' O3 ', M2 *signed* ' K3 '*; E2, F2, Q2 *unsigned; other* $2 *signatures
normal;* 2B4 *blank*).

PAPER: Poor quality; horizontal chain-lines; no marks; size
of half sheet 16½ × 14 in. (half-sheets of Double Foolscap. See
No. 653 (Anacreon, 1783), VARIANT).

TYPE: GGP, RLP 1. Latin follows Greek.

COPIES: G⁴ (Vol. II only).

695 Aristophanes, *Clouds*, G and L   1793

'ΑΙ ΤΟΥ | ΑΡΙΣΤΟΦΑΝΟΥΣ | ΝΕΦΕΛΑΙ· | ΚΩΜΩιΔΙΑ.
| ARISTOPHANIS | NUBES, | COMOEDIA. | GLAS
GUAE: | IN AEDIBUS ACADEMICIS | EXCUDEBAT
ANDREAS FOULIS | ACADEMIAE TYPOGRAPHUS |
M.DCC.XCIII.

FORMULA: [? Foolscap] 8⁰ in fours: π² A–Q⁴ (I2, L2, M2, P2,
Q2 *unsigned*).

PAPER: Medium-poor quality; blue; horizontal chain-lines; no marks (probably half-sheets of Double Foolscap. See No. 653 (Anacreon, 1783), VARIANT).

TYPE: GP, RSP 1, RLP 1. Greek and Latin on facing pages. The first two pages of the translation (pp. 5–6) are set in RSP 1, the rest in RLP 1.

COPIES: G⁴.

Moor, James, *Elementa Linguae Graecae*, L   1793 **696**

ELEMENTA | LINGUAE GRAECAE; | NOVIS, PLERUM
QUE, REGULIS | TRADITA; | BREVITATE SUA MEMO
RIAE FACILIBUS. | PARS PRIMA, | COMPLECTENS |
PARTES ORATIONIS DECLINABILES; | ET | ANALO
GIAM | DUAS IN UNAM SYLLABAS | CONTRAHENDI, |
EX IPSA VOCALIUM NATURA | DEDUCTAM, | ET REGULIS
UNIVERSALIBUS TRADITAM. | IN USUM TYRONUM
JUNIORUM | CLASSIS GRAECAE IN ACADEMIA GLAS
GUENSI. | STUDIO JACOBI MOOR L.L.D. | IN EADEM
ACADEMIA LITT. GRAEC. PROF. | [*quotation, 2 lines*] |
GLASGUAE: | EXCUDEBAT ANDREAS FOULIS, |
M.DCC.XCIII.

FORMULA: [? Crown] 8⁰ in fours: π^2 A–U⁴ X1 (π1 *half-title*).

Plate of abbreviations and contractions faces A1, signed
' *Mᶜ.Intyre fc.*', plate mark 160 × ?.

PAPER: Medium-poor quality; blue; horizontal chain-lines; no marks (probably half-sheets of Double Crown. See No. 653 (Anacreon, 1783), VARIANT). Sig. O only: vertical chain-lines.

TYPE: Sigs. π, G, O–X: RE 2, GGP, RLP 1, GP. Sigs. A–F, H–N: RE 4 and three Wilson types not found in any other book printed at the Foulis Press (the English and Small Pica greeks of the *Specimen* of 1786, and the Long Primer roman No. 3 of the *Specimen* of 1772). The press-work in these sections printed in strange type is different from that of the rest of the book (it is rather better); and it may be inferred that they were not printed at the Foulis Press, while sigs. π, G and O–X were printed there.

COPIES: G⁴.

1794   Moor, James, *On the End of Tragedy* **697**

ON THE | END | OF | TRAGEDY, | ACCORDING TO |
ARISTOTLE; | AN ESSAY, | IN TWO PARTS; | READ
TO A LITERARY SOCIETY IN | GLASGOW, AT THEIR

WEEKLY | MEETINGs WITHIN THE | COLLEGE. | By
JAMES MOOR LLD. | GLASGOW, | PRINTED AND SOLD
BY A. FOULIS PRINTER TO | THE UNIVERSITY |
M.DCC.XCIV.

FORMULA: Post 12⁰ in sixes: π^2 A–C⁶ D⁴ (B2 *unsigned;* π1
half-title).

PAPER: Medium quality; marks 6/i; size of sheet 18¾ × 15½ in.

TYPE: RE 4, GGP, RLP 2, GB.

COPIES: L.

698 1794 Smollett, Tobias, *Ode to Independence*

ODE | TO | INDEPENDENCE. | BY THE LATE | T.
SMOLLETT, M.D. | [*quotation, 5 lines*] | GLASGOW: |
PRINTED AND SOLD BY A. FOULIS, | WILSON STREET
| MDCC.XCIV.

FORMULA: [? Pot] 8⁰ in four: π^4.

PAPER: Medium-poor quality; marks ?6/not seen.

TYPE: RSP 1, RLP 2.

COPIES: G⁴.

† **699** Aeschylus, *Tragedies*, G 1795

ΑΙ ΤΟΥ | ΑΙΣΧΥΛΟΥ | ΤΡΑΓΩΔΙΑΙ | ΕΠΤΑ. | [*quotation,
1 line*] | GLASGUAE; | IN AEDIBUS ACADEMICIS, | EX
CUDEBAT ANDREAS FOULIS ACADEMIAE TYPO
GRAPHUS. | EDINBURGI, PROSTANT VENALES APUD
GULIELMUM LAING: | LONDINI, APUD T. PAYNE,
B. ET I. WHITE, | ET T. EGERTON. | MDCCXCV.

FORMULA: Post 2⁰: π1 ²π^2 a–c² A–4X² (2A1, 2B1 *signed* ' A2 ',
' B2 '; π1 *half-title,* ²π1 *title-page,* ²π2 *sub-title to* Prometheus –
which should be placed after c2 – 4X2 *blank*).

PAPER: Medium-good quality; marks 6/i, 6/ii; size of sheet
18¾ × 15¼ in.

TYPE: GDP 2, GGP, RP 4.

VARIANT: Issue on large paper, [? Writing Royal] 2⁰:
Formula: (−π1, *half-title*).
Paper: Good quality; wove; mark J. WHATMAN at edge of
sheet; no uncut copy seen, but size of sheet at least 23¼ × 18½in.

NOTES: Copies of the Post issue, and (according to Murray)
of the large-paper issue, sometimes have a set of plates by
Flaxman, with imprints dated 12 January 1795.

The following details are from Murray, *R. & A. Foulis*, p. 122: small paper, 52 copies printed, retailed at 3 guineas; large paper, 11 copies retailed at 10 guineas, or £20 with the plates. Edited by Porson.

COPIES: G⁴ (Post), L (both issues, the Post with plates).

Anderson, John, *Institutes of Physics*   1795 **700**

NOTES: Not seen. Murray, *R. & A. Foulis*, pp. 123–4, says ' In 1795 he [Andrew Foulis the younger] had printed the fifth edition of Professor Anderson's *Institutes of Physics* '; there does not appear to be a copy, however, in the Murray Collection at G².

1795   Moor, James, *Elementa Linguae Graecae*, L **701**

ELEMENTA | LINGUAE GRAECAE; | NOVIS, PLERUMQUE REGULIS | TRADITA; | BREVITATE SUA MEMORIAE FACILIBUS | PARS PRIMA, | COMPLECTENS | PARTES ORATIONIS DECLINABILES; | ET | ANALOGIAM | DUAS IN UNAM SYLLABAS | CONTRAHENDI, | EX IPSA VOCALIUM NATURA | DEDUCTAM, | ET REGULIS UNI VERSALIBUS TRADITAM | IN USUM TYRONUM JUNI ORUM | CLASSIS GRAECAE IN ACADEMIA GLAS GUENSI. | EDITIO NOVA PRIORIBUS AUCTIOR ET EMENDATIOR. | STUDIO JACOBI MOOR L.L.D. | IN EADEM ACADEMIA LITT. GRAEC. PROF. | [*quotation*, *2 lines*] | GLASGUAE: | IN AEDIBUS ACADEMICIS | EXCUDEBAT ANDREAS FOULIS, | M.DCC.XCV.

FORMULA: [? Printing Demy] 8⁰ in fours: π1 A–R⁴ (B1 *signed* ' A | B '; $2 *unsigned*).
    Plate of contractions and abbreviations faces B1, signed ' *Mᶜ.Intyre fc.*', plate mark 160 × 97.

PAPER: Poor quality; no marks.

TYPE: GGP, GP, RE 2, RLP 1.

NOTES: The two copies seen (both at G⁴) both have *Fragmenta Grammatices Graecae: ad usum Tironum in Literis Graecis in Academia Edinensi* (n.d.), a separate book not printed at the Foulis Press, bound at the end.

COPIES: G⁴.

† **702** Aeschylus, *Tragedies*, G and L 1796, ' 1794 ', 1806

AESCHYLI | TRAGOEDIAE | QUAE SUPERSUNT. |
TOMUS PRIMUS [SECUNDUS]. | GLASGUAE: | EXCUDE
BAT ANDREAS FOULIS. | MDCCXCVI.

FORMULA: Post 8⁰:

Vol. I: π1 ²π² A–2F⁸ 2G1 (B4 *signed* ' B2 '; 2A2, 2A3 *signed*
' A2 ', ' A3 '; 2F1 *signed* ' F '; B2 *unsigned* ²π² *prelims to* Prometheus Bound).

Vol. II: π1 A–2B⁸ 2C² (*signed* ' VOL. II.' *on* A–2C $1 *except*
C1, G1, H1, I1).

PAPER: Vol. I A–2G, Vol. II A–F: Medium-good quality;
marks 6/?.

Vol. I π1, Vol. II π1, G–2C: Medium-good quality; wove;
mark WC & C⁰ at edge of sheet.

Vol. I ²π on another laid paper, mark not seen.

TYPE: GGP, GB, RSP 1.

VARIANT: Issue in [? Writing Royal] 8⁰, with cancel title-pages
dated 1806 (*Note*: this fine-paper issue no doubt appeared
originally in 1796, with the title-pages uncancelled, but no
such copy has been seen):

Title-pages: [*Cancel title-pages, not printed at the Foulis Press,
reading in shortened form:*] Aeschyli Tragoediae Septem, cum
Versione Latina. Volumen I [II]. Glasguae: excudebat
Foulis, M,DCC,LXXXXIV. [*sic*] Veneunt Londini, apud T.
Payne; Payne & Mackinlay: Oxoniae, apud Jos. Cooke.
M,DCC,VI.

Formula: Vol. I: (*begins*) π² (*etc., ends*) 2G² (π1 *half-title conjugate with new cancel title-page, 2G2 blank*). Vol. II: (*begins*) π²
(*etc.;* π1 *half-title conjugate with new cancel title-page;* C1 *signed*
' VOL. II.').

Paper: Good quality; wove; mark J WHATMAN at edge of
the sheet; no uncut copy seen, but size of sheet at least
21¾ × 18 in.

NOTES: Same text as No. 699, edited by Porson.

COPIES: G⁴ (both issues described).

† **703** Ramsay, Allan, *The Gentle Shepherd* 1796

THE | GENTLE SHEPHERD. | A | PASTORAL COMEDY;
| BY | ALLAN RAMSAY | GLASGOW: | PRINTED AND
SOLD BY ANDREW FOULIS, | M.DCC.XCVI.

FORMULA: Post 2⁰: π^2 A–Y² a–c² d1 (π1 *half-title;* Y1 *and* Y2 *are sometimes separated by the engraved music*).

Plates: Aquatints: the same frontispiece and twelve plates used in No. 688 (Ramsay, 1788), imprints etc. unchanged. Also the same nine leaves of engraved music.

PAPER: Medium quality; marks 6/i; size of sheet $18\frac{3}{4} \times 15\frac{1}{4}$ in. Plates on a medium-quality wove paper, no marks.

TYPE: RDP, RE 2.

VARIANTS: Issue in Writing Royal 2⁰:

Paper: Good quality; wove; mark J. WHATMAN at edge of sheet; size of sheet $23\frac{3}{4} \times 19$ in. Plates on the same paper.

A copy of the Post issue at G² has a variant title-page, and contains, in addition to the plates, David Allan's original pencil and chalk sketches for the plates mounted and bound in. The binding is modern.

Title-page: [*From the same type as the usual title-page, but with the addition of the following stanza between lines 6 and 7:*] O! bonny are our greenfward howes, | Whar, thro' the birks, the burny rows, | And the bee bums, and the ox lows, | And faft winds rufle. | And SHEPHERD LADS on funny knows | Blaw the blyth whufle.

COPIES: G⁴ (Post and Royal), L (Post), G² (Post with variant title-page).

1797, 1806   Euripides, *Tragedies*, G and L **704** †

'ΑΙ ΤΟΥ | ΕΥΡΙΠΙΔΟΥ | ΤΡΑΓΩΔΙΑΙ | ΣΩZOMENAI. | EURIPIDIS | TRAGOEDIAE | QUAE SUPERSUNT, | EX RECENSIONE SAMUELIS MUSGRAVII. | TOMUS PRIMUS [. . . DECIMUS]. | GLASGUAE: | EXCUDEBAT ANDREAS FOULIS. | EDINBURGI PROSTANT VEN ALES APUD G. LAING, | ET APUD D. BREMNER LONDINI. | MDCC.XCVII. [*also another setting reading* 'M. DCC.XCVII.' *in the last line; in the* L *copy this other setting is used in Vols.* II–IV *and Vol.* VI, *in the* G⁴ *copy it is used in Vols.* I–III *and Vol.* IX.]

FORMULA: Post 8⁰ in fours:

Vol. I: π1 a^2 A–2O⁴ 2P².
Vol. II: π1 a^2 A–2P⁴ 2Q².
Vol. III: π1 a^2 A–2H⁴ 2I².
Vol. IV: π1 a1 A–2G⁴ 2H1 (a1 printed as 2H2).
Vol. V: π1 a^2 A–2P⁴ 2Q².
Vol. VI: π1 a^2 A–2E⁴.
Vol. VII: π1 a^2 A–2B⁴.

Vol. VIII: $\pi 1$ A^2 ^{2}A–2I^4 ^{2}2K^2.

Vol. IX: $\pi 1$ a1 A–2O^4(–2O4).

Vol. X: $\pi 1$ a^2 A–R^4 ^{2}R^4 S^4 ^{2}a^4 ^{2}b–g^4 ^{2}h^2.

Signed ' TOM. I.' *on Vol.* 1 a1, *and* ' VOL. II [. . . X].' *on Vols.* II–X $1 *except title-pages.*)

Plate: vignette portrait frontispiece faces Vol. 1 $\pi 1$, signed ' *Walker sculp^t*.', plate mark 115 × 90.

PAPER: Medium-good quality; wove; marks WC & Co at edge of sheet; size of sheet 19$\frac{1}{4}$ × 15 in.

TYPE: GGP, GB, RLP 2, RLP 1, RB 2.

VARIANTS: Issue on large, inferior-quality paper, [? Printing Demy] 8° (Vols. 1 and II only seen):

Title-pages: [*Re-set, reading the same except:* ' MUSGRAVE ' *for* ' MUSGRAVII ' *in line 8; lines 12 and 13* (' EDINBURGI . . . LONDINI.') *omitted; last line reads* ' M.DCC.XCVII.']

Formula: (*both vols. begin*) π^2 ($\pi 1$ *half-title; no plate*).

Paper: Medium-quality; laid, marks 9/WC & Co (dated 1795 at edge of sheet); laid, no marks; wove, no marks.

The Demy issue (Vols. 1 and II) with cancel title-pages dated 1806:

Title-pages: EURIPIDIS | TRAGOEDIAE | SELECTAE. | TOM. I [II]. | GLASGUAE: | EXCUDEBAT ANDREAS FOULIS. | 1806. [*These title-pages poorly and amateurishly printed.*]

Formula: (*No half-titles; no plate. The only copy seen lacks* Vol. 1 A1; *it also has Vol.* 1 a^2 *in position as the central fold of* 2P *and Vol.* II a^2 *as the central fold of* 2Q.)

Paper: As the Demy issue described above, but dated 1797 on the marked laid paper, and 1796 on the otherwise unmarked wove.

NOTES: The Demy issue with title-pages dated 1797 presumably included all the original ten volumes; so, at any rate, the title-pages would imply, although only the first two volumes have been seen. The Demy issue with title-pages dated 1806, on the other hand, quite possibly consisted only of the first two volumes, since it is called *Tragoediae Selectae.*

COPIES: G^4 (all three issues), L (Post, 1797).

705 Anderson, John, *Observations upon Roman*   1800
Antiquities

OBSERVATIONS | UPON | ROMAN ANTIQUITIES, | DISCOVERED BETWEEN THE | *FORTH & CLYDE.* |

|*plain double rule, 123*] | BY THE LATE | JOHN ANDERSON, | PROFESSOR OF NATURAL PHILOSOPHY IN THE UNIVERSITY OF GLASGOW. | [*plain double rule, 123*] | EDINBURGH: | PRINTED BY ANDREW FOULIS. | [*swelled rule, 10*] | 1800.

FORMULA: Writing Royal 4⁰: π^2 A⁴ + 4 leaves of plates (π1 *half-title*).

PAPER: Good quality; wove; marks J WHATMAN 1794 at edge of sheet; size of sheet 24 × 19 in.

TYPE: Very worn founts of (?) Caslon Pica and Caslon Long Primer; more Caslon type on the title-page and half-title, including some ' Open '.

NOTES: Although probably printed by Andrew Foulis (the shoddy setting and appalling press-work match his worst work of the seventeen-nineties), the Edinburgh imprint and the Caslon type make it clear that this is not strictly speaking a Foulis Press book.

COPIES: G⁴, L.

n.d.   [Anon.], *A Hymn fit to be sung on days of* **706** †
                                        Humiliation and Prayer

[*The following leaf at* L (11602. i. 5 (7)) *appears from its typography to have been printed at the Foulis Press in the seventeen-forties. Begins:*] A | HYMN, | Fit to be fung on Days of *Humilia tion* and *Prayer.* | [*followed by 8 stanzas.*]

FORMULA: [? size] 2⁰: [*single leaf*].

PAPER: Medium quality; marks ?/ii.

TYPE: RGP 1, RE 1; Two-line English titling; Four-line Pica ' W '.

COPIES: L.

APPENDIX A

PROPOSALS FOR PLATO, 1751

The following Proposals were printed on M11–M12^v of Thomas à Kempis, *De Imitatione*, 1751 (No. 218), which was published by 27 May 1751. For a note on all the Plato Proposals of 1750–1751, see No. 164.

GLASGOW, *January* 7, 1751

ROBERT & ANDREW
FOULIS,

PRINTERS TO THE UNIVERSITY
Propofe to print by fubfcription

THE

WORKS OF PLATO.

On a new Type, the largeft of the Louvre fizes,[1] juft now cut by Alexander Wilfon, M.A. Type-founder to the Univerfity:

In QUARTO, and in FOLIO.

I. In IX volumes in quarto, of which the Greek in 6 volumes, and the Latin tranflation, with the notes, in 3. the price to fubfcribers, one penny fterling per fheet. the whole will be contained in about 500 fheets; fo the price will be about 2l. 1s. 8d. in quires; on a fair paper.

A number will be printed on a fine large paper, at two-pence fterling per fheet.

II. In VI volumes in folio, with the tranflation on the fame page, below; likewife at one penny per fheet; and in about 740 fheets; which will amount to about 3l. 1s. 8d.

---

1. I.e. Garamond's Gros Parangon *grec du roi* of c. 1550, the equivalent of Double Pica. GDP 1 was actually used in 1751 in No. 182.

A number also on the fineſt writing paper, (the ſame on which we printed Cicero,[1]) at three half-pence per ſheet; which will amount to about 4l. 12s. 6d.

The GREEK ſhall be accurately printed from the edition of H. Stephens.[2]

The various readings, and his own conjeċtures, printed on the margin of his edition, ſhall be printed at the bottom of each page.

Any other readings we can procure, or conjeċtural emendations, ſhall alſo be printed at the bottom of each page, or at the end of the work, with proper distinċtions.

The NOTES of H. Stephens, relating to the Greek text, which are printed at the end of his edition, ſhall alſo be printed at the end of this.

Alſo all other notes of any merit, publiſhed ſince his edition, and all which we can procure beſides.[3]

The TRANSLATION will be that of FICINUS;[4] but with ſeveral correċtions publiſhed ſince, and all others which we can procure.

The PUBLISHERS propoſe to demand no money at ſubſcription: only beg leave to reſerve it in their own choice, to call for, at delivery of the volume firſt printed, which will contain the LAWS and EPINOMIS, ONE GUINEA of the whole price, upon their note to deliver the reſt of the work according to the above terms. N.B. The LAWS and EPINOMIS make about a fifth part of the whole of Plato's works.

GENTLEMEN who chuſe to favour this undertaking, and are at a diſtance, will very much oblige the printers if they take the trouble themſelves of tranſmitting their names to Glaſgow, and as quickly as poſſible; or if, at leaſt, they give notice to the printers, of the perſon with whom they have ſubſcribed. by either of theſe means, but eſpecially by the former, the

---

1. A good-quality Foolscap; see No. 101.

2. Henri Estienne II (Plato, *Works*, G and L, Paris, 1578).

3. See Duncan, pp. 54-5; Murray, *R. & A. Foulis*, p. 24; Maclehose, pp. 168-9; and Buchan MSS at Baillie's Institution, Glasgow.

4. Plato, *Works*, L., Florence, 1484-5.

undertakers will both have the fatiffaction of knowing their encouragers, and of having it in their power to prevent gentlemen from being difappointed of their copies, or in the fize or paper they had chofen.

As the undertakers are to do their utmoft to render this edition the most extenfively ufeful, they take this occafion of inviting gentlemen of learning every where to communicate what helps they can, either for eftablifhing the text, correcting the verfion, or illuftrating the philofophy. whatever of this kind is received fhall be gratefully acknowledged, printed with the author's name, if not forbid, and his labour fuitably rewarded.

APPENDIX B

ROBERT FOULIS AND JAMES BOSWELL,
1767–8

Several letters which passed between Robert Foulis and James
Boswell, concerning the printing and publication of Boswell's
Dorando, 1767 (No. 462) and *An Account of Corsica*, 1768 (No.
473), are preserved at Yale. By the generous permission of the
Editorial Committee of the Yale Edition of the Private Papers
of James Boswell and of William Heinemann Ltd. I reproduce
here extracts from the letters which illuminate what a modern
publisher would call the ' production ', as opposed to the
' editorial ', side of the Foulis Press. But the complete letters
should be consulted when the research edition appears,[1] since
they throw, in their entirety, an invaluable light upon the
relationship between Robert Foulis and one of his clients.

The letters concerned are as follows:

1. *Dorando*: Foulis to Boswell, 24 April 1767

2.   Foulis to Boswell, 8 May 1767

3.   Foulis to Boswell, 29 June 1767

4. *Corsica*: Boswell to Foulis, c. 15 August 1767

5.   Boswell to Foulis, c. 15 August 1767

6.   Foulis to Boswell, 21 August 1767

7.   Foulis to Boswell, 30 December 1767

8.   Foulis to Boswell, 2 March 1768

---

1. The Foulis–Boswell letters are to be included in the section edited by Professor A. F. Falconer, who kindly drew my
attention to them.

1. *Robert Foulis at Glasgow to James Boswell at Auchinleck.*
   24 April 1767
   ' Your Letter with the Spanish Tale came safe to hand; but
   it will not come into less than two Sheets and an half.[1]   I
   had set up half a Sheet of it with a loaded[2] page; but I found
   it both look'd ill, and yet wou'd not come in.' . . . [Foulis then
   explains how Boswell, as the anonymous author, may pre-
   serve the copyright by instructing John Wilkie or Thomas
   Davies – two of the booksellers mentioned in the imprint – to
   give in ' 9 Copies and a sixpence, and sign himself as Pro-
   prietor with consent of the Author ' at Stationer's Hall.]

2. *Robert Foulis to James Boswell.   8 May 1767*
   ' You'll receive inclos'd two half Sheets.   The whole will
   be finish'd this day.' . . . ' I shall immediately send 300 to
   M^r [John] Wilkie, & send him the Carron-Receipt.[3]   With
   respect to Edinburgh, I think you might manage it, without
   trusting anybody with the Secret: In that view, the Copies
   might be sent from Glasgow directly to yourself at Edinburgh.   M^r [Alexander] Kincaid, or any other Bookseller
   to whom you intrusted the management, needed not be
   informed by whom it was writ; And might be allowed
   to take it for granted, that it was printed where the Title-
   page says [*i.e.* London], and come to the care of a friend.
   No more might be put into the hands of the Bookseller
   at Ed^r. but 200; if these are suddenly sold off, there are
   300 more printed, with the words on the Title-page, ' The
   second edition '.   These last are on a different paper, not
   so large, but very fair, the same on which Sir David
   Dalrymple printed his Copies for presents of all the Books
   he has printed, and on which he would have printed

---

1. Foulis eventually used three sheets and a quarter, including a half-title and a final blank leaf.

2. ' Loaded ' presumably means here ' set solid, with reduced
margins '.

3. I.e. the receipt from the Carron Wharf, whence the books
were shipped to London.

The Escape, if it could have been had.[1]   I have restrain'd the Number to 700,[2] not only because I think these will serve, but because the expence of Composition will be between 30 and 40 shillings, And there is a great chance of its being put into News-papers & Magazeens, and even of its being pirated.' . . .

3. *Robert Foulis at Glasgow to James Boswell at Auchinleck.*
    29 June 1767
    ' The Parcel for London was sent off for Carron on the 26th of May, and sail'd from Carron for London on the 4th of June, and arrived at London soon after; ' . . . ' The were only nine [copies] sent by Land, that number serving for Stationers-Hall,' . . .

    ' There has been no Copies call'd for from us, because the Students are gone, & we live in a desart,' . . .

    ' The persons proper to promote the sale here are the Booksellers near the center of the Town, for there are few that wou'd take the trouble of coming up to the College for them if they were to receive them in presents; The chief of which Booksellers are, above the Cross, Mr J. Barry; On the Exchange, Mr Stalker; and in the Salt mercat, Mr Dan. Baxter, and Mr J. Gilmour who publishes the Glasgow Chronicle.   But you must allow them to them for 9 pence, which is the ordinary allowance.[3] ' . . .

---

1. In fact the fine-paper copies of Lord Hailes's books printed at the Foulis Press were printed on a good quality Post paper, not on the Crown paper of the ' second edition ' of *Dorando.* (see Nos. 405, 447 and 448).

If *The Escape* was *An Account of the Preservation of Charles II* (1766, No. 449), it actually appeared on a medium-good quality Printing Demy paper.

2. Earlier in this letter, however, Foulis has mentioned 300 copies to be sent to Wilkie in London, 200 for the bookseller at Edinburgh, and 300 more of the ' second edition ' held in reserve;   which totals 800, not 700.

3. I.e. the booksellers were to have threepence in the shilling, or twenty-five per cent.

4. *James Boswell to Robert Foulis* (*copy*).
   About the middle of August 1767

   ' I like Your large Type[1] best, but think you have printed
   it too closs. The English[2] is also a pretty Type, but a little
   Worn. I wish Mr Dilly May choose the large Type When
   once We are fairly set agoing. You must if possible let
   me have three Sheets a Week ' . . . ' Mr Dilly is to have
   the arms of Corsica engraved upon the Title page. I sup-
   pose You can do it very Well at Your Academy.' . . .

5. *James Boswell to Robert Foulis* (*copy*).
   About the middle of August 1767

   ' General directions for the printing of an Acco[t] of
   Corsica.' [Eight directions concerned chiefly with spelling
   and typographical style, of which the last two are:]

   7 Be very exact as to the pointings Which is left to you.
   8 Send Mr Boswell the proof Sheets and the Copy along
      with them.

6. *Robert Foulis at Glasgow to James Boswell at Edinburgh.*
   21 August 1767
   [Foulis's receipt for the first three chapters of the *Account of
   Corsica* by the hand of Boswell's clerk.]

7. *Robert Foulis at Glasgow to James Boswell at Edinburgh.*
   30 December 1767

   ' You will receive inclosed a Title of the Acco[t]. of Corsica.
   The leaf you ordered last to be cancell'd, was accordingly
   done: and 500 Copies with the Titles & cancell'd leaves
   are carefully gather'd, collated, & packt up into two bales,
   Directed for M[r] Dilly at London; and the rest are preparing.
   The Distribution you mention'd of 500 only for London,
   & 1000 for Scotland, is different from what he [? Dilly]
   had formerly mention'd to us, which was one thousand

   ---

   1. Foulis must have sent Boswell some sort of specimen.
   The ' large Type ' may be RE 3, which is almost as big as
   Great Primer, and was used in the book.
   2. Possibly RE 2, which was the main text type eventually
   chosen.

for London in two different ships. However, we will obey your order, as it is the last, if you are quite sure. It is quite the same to us. We only want to make a complete delivery, And then we order what we have occasion for, on the same footing with the other Booksellers.' . . .

[Postscript, following Foulis's signature:] ' Cause the Map to be immediately sent to Mr Dilly.'[1]

8. *Robert Foulis at Glasgow to James Boswell at Edinburgh.*
2 March 1768

. . . ' I am glad the fine copies of Corsica & the Manuscript[2] came safe to your hand.' . . .

' I rejoice to hear of the success of the History of Corsica, . . . I expect to hear of its being soon in French & Italian, and that it has been burnt by the hand of the hangman at Genoa, which, in my opinion, it well deserves: ' . . .

. . . ' I do not know whether the Pope is on the Genoese or Corsican side, or a neutral. I have no doubt but the Genoese will have interest enough with him to get your Book put among the Libri prohibiti, and in due time have an honourable place in the Index Expurgatorius. Wishing you health & fortitude to bear these misfortunes in an edifying manner, I have the honour to be, Dear Sir, yours, &c.   Robert Foulis.'

---

1. Possibly a sketch for the folding copper-plate map placed at the beginning of No. 473, which has Dilly's imprint as publisher dated 4 February 1768.

2. Not the MS copy of *An Account of Corsica*, but apparently a manuscript book for which Boswell had sent in a bid to one of the Foulises' auctions.

ADDITIONS AND

AMENDMENTS

(1986)

White, Jeremiah, *A Persuasive to Mutual Love* **0**
and Charity

INTRODUCTION: Mr John Stephens has kindly drawn the following material to my attention. On 5 March 1739 Francis Hutcheson wrote to the Rev. Thomas Drennan of Belfast: 'A worthy lad of this town [Glasgow], one Robt Foulis, out of a true public spirit, undertook to reprint, for the populace, an old excellent book, *A Persuasive to Mutual Love and Charity*, wrote by [Jeremiah] White, Oliver Cromwell's Chaplain, it is a divine, old fashioned thing. Some are cast off, in better paper and sold at 9*d*., in marble paper, the coarse ones are sold at 5*d*. in blue paper and at 4*d*. to booksellers. I wish your bookseller would commission a parcel of both sorts. . . . The *Persuasive* is, in the old edition, an half-crown book.' (James McCosh, *The Scottish Philosophy*, London 1875, p. 464, and W. R. Scott, *Francis Hutcheson*, Cambridge 1900, p. 81.) There is in O what is apparently a copy, dated 1739, of the book reprinted by Foulis, which turns out to be an abbreviated version of Jeremiah White's *A Perswasive to Moderation and Forbearance in Love among the divided forms of Christians*, London 1708 (2nd ed. 1725):

A | *PERSUASIVE* | TO | MUTUAL LOVE | AND | CHARITY | AMONG | *CHRISTIANS* | Who *differ* in OPINION. | Drawn from the MOTIVES of the GOSPEL, and | proper for healing the PRESENT DIVISIONS | among us. | [*plain rule*, 70] | By a MINISTER of the GOSPEL. | [*plain rule*, 70] | [*quotation*, 5 *lines*] | [*plain rule*, 72] | [*plain rule*, 70] | Printed in the Year MDCCXXXIX.

FORMULA: Foolscap 8°: π1 A–F⁸ G1 (F3, 4 *signed* 'F4, 5').

COPIES: O.

NOTES: Probably but not certainly printed for Robert Foulis; six of the other eight items bound in the same volume (Vet A 4 f 505) are Foulis books (items 147, 324, 429, 450, 469, and 478), and of the other two one was printed in Edinburgh and the other in Belfast. For prices, see INTRODUCTION above.

Burnet, Gilbert, *Life of Rochester* **2**

SOME | PASSAGES | OF THE | *LIFE AND DEATH* | OF | JOHN | EARL OF *ROCHESTER*. | [*plain rule*, 60] | *Written at his Defire, on his Death-bed*, | By *GILBERT BURNET*, D.D. | Sometime *Profeffor of Divinity* in the Univerfity | of *Glafgow*, and afterwards

Bifhop of *Sarum*. | [*plain rule,* 65] | Containing more amply their Converfations | on the great Principles of NATURAL and | REVEALED RELIGION. | [*plain rule,* 61] | To which is fubjoined, a further Account of his | CONVERSION, and Penitential Sentiments, by | *Robert Parfons,* M.A. Chaplain to the Countefs | Dowager of *Rochef ter.* | [*two plain rules,* 63] | Printed in the YEAR, M.DCC.XLI. | AND | Sold by the Bookfellers in Town and Country.

FORMULA: Pot 8° in fours: A⁴ ²A⁴ B–N⁴ (B2, D2, G2, K2, M2 *unsigned*; N4 *not seen*).

NOTES: Probably but not certainly a variant of Duncan, p. 49, No. 4, ('Bifhop Burnet's Life of John, Earl of Rochefter, 12mo.'), and probably printed for Robert Foulis. Cf. the virtually identical wording of the title-page of No. 223; there is also a typographical similarity with the title-page of additional No. 0. Advertised in *GJ* for 26 October 1761 at 1*s.* 2*d.*, bound.

COPIES: Brian Gerrard (who supplied this description); New York Public Library; both of which lack leaf N4.

3 Cicero, *De Natura Deorum,* L   1741

FORMULA: (π1 *advertisement for No.* 8; I3 *unsigned*) (information from B. J. McMullin).

11 Mears, John, *A Catechism*   1742

TITLE-PAGE: [*Line 8 up: insert a comma after* 'MEARS'; *line 6 up: insert* '|' *before* '*The THIRD EDITION.*']

13 Terence, *Comedies,* L   1742

VARIANTS: *Title-page:* (1) [*reads as the* 'MILLAR' *state of the original Urie title-page down to line* 16, *then:*] [*plain rule* 12] | MDCCXLII. | In hanc Chartam maximam quadraginta Exemplaria folum-|modo funt excufa. (2) [*reads as the* '*Robert & Andrew Foulis*' *cancel title-page down to its last line, then:*] | In hanc Chartam maximam quadraginta Exemplaria folum-|modo funt excufa.

Formula: Royal 8° in fours: (*as the Crown* 8°, *but* 2I4 *not a cancel; mis-signed* 2K *not corrected in MS*).

Paper: Good quality; marks 8/?.

Copies: (1) Brian Gerrard (who supplied this description); (2) McMaster University Library (described by B. J. McMullin in *The Book Collector,* 28(1979)573).

1742   'Cebes', *Table*, E **18**

VARIANT: Isue on better-quality paper, Demy 18°:
Paper: Medium-good quality; marks 9/i.
Copies: Brian Gerrard (who supplied this description).

1742   Leechman, William, *The Temper of a Minister,* **23**
                                       a Sermon

VARIANT: Mr A. S. Fotheringham reports a copy which has
'[PRICE, FOUR-PENCE.]' instead of '[PRICE, SIX-PENCE.]' on the
title-page, but which accords otherwise with the description of
No. 23.

1742   A.M., *The State of Religion in New England* **25**

TITLE-PAGE: [*Line 6 ends in a full stop; in line 2 of the right-hand column
for 'TURRELL,' read 'TURELL,'; the length of the plain rule (line 5 up) is*
79.]
FORMULA: [? Crown] 8° in fours: A^4 B–E^4 F^2 (B3 *signed* 'B2').
PAPER: Medium quality; no marks.
TYPE: RP X, RE 1.
VARIANT: Issue on inferior paper:
    Formula: (B3 *not signed* 'B2'.)
    Paper: Poor quality; no marks; size of sheet 15¾ × 14 in.
COPIES: G^2 (both issues).

1742   A.M., *The State of Religion in New England,* **26**
                                 second edition

TITLE-PAGE: [*Line 6, 'NEW-ENGLAND,' hyphenated; line 9, for
'friend' read 'Friend'; line 13, for 'Various' read 'various'; line 16, for
'Chauncey' read 'Chauncy'; line 7 up, for 'EDITION' read 'Edition';
line 3 up, for ' Edinburgh' read 'Edinburgh'.*]
VARIANT: Issue on fine paper:
    Title-page: [*Last line, for 'Six Pence.' read 'One Shilling.'*]
    Formula: Crown 8° in fours (a2 *signed* 'a3', *not* 'A3').
    Paper: Medium quality; marks 9/i.
COPIES: G^2 (both issues).

30 Cooper, Anthony Ashley, Lord Shaftesbury,   1743–5
Characteristics

TITLE-PAGE: [*Vol.* III, *line* 2, *for* 'IIII.' *read* 'III.'; *line 9 ends with a comma in the ?Crown* 12° *issue.*]

VARIANT: Separate issue of part of vol. II (*The Moralists*).
Formula: Post 12° in sixes: π^2 A–S^6 (*i.e.* χ^2 ^{2}A–S^6 *of Vol.* II).
Paper: Medium quality; marks 6/HR.
Notes: *BQ* (p. 12) lists 54 copies of 'Shaftefury's moralift', Crown 12°, at 1*s.* wholesale.

(Described by H. E. Meyer in *The Book Collector*, 21(1972)272–3. See No. 613.)

36A Lovell, John, *A Funeral Oration occasioned*   1743
by the Death of Peter Faneuil

A | FUNERAL ORATION | DELIVER'D | At the Opening | OF THE | *Annual Meeting* of the TOWN, *March* 14$^{th.}$ 1742. | IN | *Faneuil-Hall* in BOSTON: | Occafion'd by the DEATH of the FOUNDER, | PETER FANUEIL, Efq; | [*plain rule*, 103] | By *JOHN LOVELL*, A. M. Mafter of the | South *Grammar-School* in BOSTON. | [*plain rule*, 103] | [*quotation*, 1 *line*] | *BOSTON* Printed: *Glafgow* reprinted, and fold by | ROBERT FOULIS. MDCCXLIII.

FORMULA: Foolscap 4° in twos: A^2 B^2.

PAPER: Medium quality; marks 4/?.

TYPE: RE 1. Block: rectangular headpiece in double frame, landscape medallion with cornucopias on either side, 29 × 109.

NOTES: *Price*: 3*d.* (Spotiswood 86).
Stock in 1777: 60 copies (*BQ* 12).

COPIES: G^2, C.

39 Shenstone, William [actually Lowth, Robert],   1743
The Judgment of Hercules, etc.

VARIANT: Issue on common paper:
Title-page: Price Three Pence.
Paper: No marks.
Copies: L.

NOTES: Foxon L293–4.

1743   Theophrastus, *Characters*, G and L **40**

VARIANT: The 12° issue is also found with Greek on the versos and Latin on the rectos of each opening (copy at G^4).

1744   Cicero, *Tusculanae Quaestiones*, L **45**

FORMULA: 8°: (2C1 *signed* 'C', 2C2 *signed* 'C2').
    12°: (H2, K2, and $^+_+$2 *unsigned*; $^+_+$6 *may be bound after* a4).
(Information from Brian Gerrard and B. J. McMullin.)
PAPER: 12°: marks 9/i, eagle/CM over T (Brian Gerrard; possibly another issue).

1744   Epictetus, *Manual*, etc., G and L **47**

FORMULA: (*B. J. McMullin reports that in the Sydney University Library copy of the consecutive-text issue* E1 *and* F1 *are conjugate.*)

1744   Steele, Sir Richard, *The Conscious Lovers* **56**

FORMULA: (*Signature G originally had four leaves, not two.*)
VARIANT: Issue in Post 12°:
   Paper: Medium-poor quality; marks 6/i.
   Copies: Canberra (ANL). Described by B. J. McMullin.

c. 1745   Addison, Joseph, *Cato* **57**

Entry renumbered 70A (1746).

1745   Aristotle, *Poetics*, G and L **58**

VARIANT: Intermediate issue in Pot 8°:
   Formula: (*Signed* '*' *on* $1.)
   Paper: Medium-poor quality, marks 1/iv, 1/v.
   Copies: Canberra (ANL), Brian Gerrard; described by B. J. McMullin (*The Book Collector*, 28(1979)574).

61 Hoadly, Benjamin, *An Abridgment of the Plain*　　　1745
Account of the Lord's Supper

VARIANT: Issue on inferior paper:
　Formula: (*Without* '*' *signatures*.)
　Paper: Marks 1/iv, 1/v.
　Copies: Brian Gerrard (who supplied this description).

68 Sophocles, *Tragedies*, G and L　　　1745

VARIANTS: (1) There were two Pot 8°, Greek and Latin, issues, one
(described in the main entry) on poorer-quality paper than the
other:
　Title-pages: [*Both issues are found with either the* 'Edinburgh' *or the*
'ROBERTUS FOULIS' *title-page*.]
　Formula: (*The issue on better-quality paper is signed* '*' *on* \$1.)
　Paper: Issue on better-quality paper: medium quality; marks 1/iv,
1/v.
　Notes: Copies of the issue on poorer-quality paper are found with
some gatherings signed '*'.
　Copies: Better quality: Canberra (ANL); poorer quality; L, C^2,
Otago University Library.
(2) Issue in Foolscap 4°, Greek only:
　Formula: (*William Poole's Catalogue* 2 *(*1980*), item* 317, *described a*
copy with two extra preliminary leaves – i.e. a^2 *of vol.* 1 *of the Foolscap* 8°,
Greek and Latin issue.)
NOTES: A. S. Fotheringham reports a hybrid made up of sections of
No. 68, Sophocles, and sections of No. 71, Aeschylus (one-volume
issues in Foolscap 4°, Greek only); this was probably the result of
an error in the warehouse.

70 Xenophon, *Hieron*, G and L　　　1745

VARIANT: Issue in Pot 8° in fours:
　Paper: Medium quality; marks 1/v.
　Copies: Ian Grant.

70A Addison, Joseph, *Cato*　　　1746

CATO | A | TRAGEDY | BY | JOSEPH ADDISON Efq; | [*quotation*, 7
lines] | *GLASGOW:* |Printed and fold by ROBERT FOULIS. |
MDCCXLVI.

FORMULA: [? Crown] 12° in sixes: π1 A–E^6 F^4 G1.

PAPER: Medium-poor quality; no marks; vertical chain-lines, probably from half sheets of Double Crown.

TYPE: RB 1.

VARIANT: Issue on better-quality paper; not seen (*GC* 31 March 1746).

NOTES: Advertised in *GC* for 10 and 31 March 1746, the latter giving the prices 4*d*. and, fine, 6*d*.

COPIES: E.

1746   Aeschylus, *Tragedies*, G and L **71**

TITLE-PAGES: [*Line* 12, *for* 'LECTIONES' *read* 'LECTIONIBUS'.]

VARIANTS: The issue described on pp. 106–7 as a Pot 4° in twos is in fact a Foolscap 4° in twos; but there was also an issue of the two-volume Greek and Latin version in Pot 4° in twos:

 Paper: Good-quality; marks 1/iv, 1/v.

 Copies: MEL (described by B. J. McMullin in *The Book Collector* (28(1979)574).

NOTES: The advertisement naming Andrew as well as Robert Foulis also appears on 2O4 of the 8° issues. See also No. 68, Addenda, NOTES.

1746–70   Foulis, Robert and Andrew, *Auction* **75**
                    Catalogues

There are four more catalogues in G²:

(1) A | CATALOGUE OF BOOKS | Unfold of the late | MR. WILLIAM FORBES's LIBRARY, | To be offered again to Sale by AUCTION on Friday and Saturday Nights, | being the 5th and 6th of December 1746, in the Back-Common-Hall | within the College, beginning at the ufual Hour.

FORMULA: [? size] 2°: A1.

PAPER: Medium-poor quality; no marks.

TYPE: RE 1, RLP 1.

(2) A CATALOGUE of the entire LIBRARIES | of the two late LEARNED and WORTHY GENTLEMEN, | FATHER AND SON, | MR. ALEXANDER DUNLOP, | PROFESSOR of GREEK, | and MR. ALEXANDER DUNLOP, | PROFESSOR of the ORIENTAL LAN GUAGES, | Both in the UNIVERSITY of GLASGOW; | Befides many curious and valuable Books, either lately imported from abroad, or Selections | of valuable Libraries, for the moft part not

hitherto expofed to Sale. | Gentlemen are defired to direct their Commiffions to Robert & Andrew Foulis Bookfellers in Glasgow.

FORMULA: Crown 2°: A^2.

PAPER: Medium quality; no marks; size of sheet 18 × 14 in.

TYPE: RE 2, RLP 1.

NOTES: Alexander Dunlop the elder died in April 1747; Alexander Dunlop the younger died in September 1750.

(3) on WEDNESDAY, being JULY 15th, 1752 | Continues to be fold by R. and A. Foulis at their Auction-room near the Crofs, | A Valuable Collection of Books, chiefly Englifh. | Time of Sale from Seven o'Clock at Night.

FORMULA: [? size] 2°: A1.

PAPER: Medium-poor quality; no marks.

TYPE: RE 1.

(4) On WEDNESDAY, being December 20th, 1752 | Will continue to be fold by R. and A. Foulis at their Auction-room near the Crofs, | A Valuable Collection of Books. | Time of Sale from Six o'Clock at Night.

FORMULA: Crown 2°: A1.

PAPER: Medium quality; no marks; size of sheet 18 × 14½ in.

TYPE: RE 1.

NOTES: Advertisement on A1 for Nos. 246, 237, 233, and 245, 'This day publifhed and fold by R. and A. Foulis'.

76 Montgomery, Capt. Alexander, *The Cherrie and the Slae*   1746

FORMULA: (Should include D6, *advertisements*.)

76A Philips, Ambrose, *The Distressed Mother*   1746

THE | DISTREST | MOTHER. | A | TRAGEDY. | BY | AMBROSE PHILIPS. | GLASGOW: | PRINTED AND SOLD BY ROBERT FOULIS. | MDCCXLVI.

FORMULA: Foolscap 12° in sixes: $A^6(-A6)$ $B^6(-B1)$ $C-E^6$ F^2.

PAPER: Medium-poor quality; no marks; size of sheet 17 × 14 in.

TYPE: RB 1, RLP 1.

VARIANT: Issue on another quality of paper, not seen (*GC*, 23 March 1747).

NOTES: Advertised in *GC*, 23 March 1747.
  Prices: Retail, fine, 6*d*; common, 4*d*.

COPIES: E (as described).

1746   Steele, Sir Richard, *The Guardian* **77**

TITLE-PAGE: [*Reads '* GLASGOW:*', not '*GLASGOW:*'.*]
FORMULAE: 8° vol. I: a^2 b1 A–2U^4 (–2U4; b1 *signed* 'a3').
12° vol. I: a^2 b1 A–2E6 2F^4(–2F4; b1 *signed* 'a3'; R3 *signed* 'Q3').

1746   Theocritus, *Works*, G and L **78**

VARIANT: Issue in Pot 4°, Greek only:
  Formula: (*As for the Foolscap 4°, Greek only, but signed '***' on* A1, B1.)
  Paper: Medium quality; marks 1/iv, 2/iv.
  Copies: Brian Gerrard (who supplied this description).

1747   Homer, *Iliad*, G and L **84**

VARIANTS: Issue in Pot 8°, Greek and Latin.
  Title-pages: [*As in the Foolscap 8°, Greek only, issue, with '*'H TOY' *in both, with lines 6 and 7 omitted, and with a comma after '*GLAS GUAE'.]
  Formula: As in the Foolscap 8°, Greek and Latin.
  Vol. I: (*signed '***' on* \$1 *except* π1, Q1).
  Vol. II: (π1 *blank; signed '***' on* \$1 *except* π1, ^{2}L1).
  Paper: Medium-good quality, marks 1/v.
  Type: As in the Foolscap 8°, Greek and Latin.
  Copies: Loaned by Messrs Deval and Muir.

1747   Hutcheson, Francis, *A Short Introduction to* **85**
                            Moral Philosphy

TITLE-PAGE: [*Line 3 up ends with a comma, not a full stop.*]

1747   Old Poem. *Chevy Chace* **92**

TITLE-PAGE: [*No new line between '*FOULIS,*' and '*ACCORDING*'.*]

94 Philips, Ambrose, *The Distressed Mother*,   1747

Entry deleted. See No. 76A.

98 Worthington, John *A Scripture Catechism*   1747

A | SCRIPTURE | CATECHISM, | SHEWING | WHAT A
CHRISTIAN IS TO BELIEVE AND | PRACTISE IN ORDER
TO SALVATION. | VERY USEFUL FOR PERSONS OF ALL
AGES AND | CAPACITIES AS WELL AS CHILDREN. | COM
POSED BY THE PIOUS AND LEARNED | JOHN WORTH
INGTON, D. D. | *GLASGOW,* | PRINTED AND SOLD BY
R. FOULIS. | MDCCXLVII.

FORMULA: Crown 12° in sixes: A–D⁶.

PAPER: Medium-poor quality, vertical chain lines; no marks; size of
sheet 19½ in. × 15 in., so probably half sheets of Double Crown.

TYPE: RLP Cas, RE 1, RLP 1.

COPIES: L.

101–6, The Duodecimo Ciceros   1748–9
611
INTRODUCTION: Twenty-four copies of No. 101 (Cicero, *Works*, L, 20
vols, 1748–9) have been examined and exhaustively analysed, with
reproductions, by B. J. McMullin in *Papers of the Bibliographical
Society of America*, 74(1980)177–200. The notes that follow give first
the major amendments made by Dr McMullin to the entry for
No. 101 itself, and then summarise his findings regarding the
various separate editions and issues of parts of the twenty-volume
set.

GENERAL: DATES: The list should read:
    1748: Vols. II, III, XI–XVII.
    1749: Vols. I, IV–X, XVIII–XX.

COLOPHONS: Line 2 has a comma after 'FRATRES'.

PAPER: Foolscap issue, add 4/v; Pot issue, add 1/iv.

INDIVIDUAL VOLUMES: Vol. 1: *General title-page*: ['DILIGENTER
EXPRESSA' set in one line.]

Formula: (²a⁴–²b1, *which contain the title and preface to George Rosse's*
Notes, *should be placed between sig.* R *and* S. π⁶ *exists in three states: in the*

second π3.4 *are reset; in the third* π1.2, 5.6 *are also reset (for illustrations see McMullin* 186–8*): the punctuated date – which has no internal spacing – is the resetting*).

Vol. II: *Title-page*: ['AD + M. BRUTUM.' *set in two lines.*]

Vol. III: *Formula: (An extra leaf* (?=²H12) *containing an added title is placed between sig.* K *and* ²A.)

Vol. IV: *Colophon*: The colophon transcribed for Vol. IV properly belongs to Vol. XI.

Formula: (The first gathering is π^2, *not* π^4. *The volume is found in three states; see McMullin* 177–80*):* (i) π^2 A–Q^{12}; (ii) π^2 A–O^{12} P^{12}(–P6–12); (iii) π^2 A–O^{12} P^6.)

Vol. V: *Formula: (The volume is found in four states; see McMullin* 177–80*):* (i) π^2 R–2I^{12}; (ii) π^2 P^{12}(–P1–5) Q–2H^{12} 2I^{12}(–2I8–12); (iiia) π^4 P^6 Q–2H^{12} 2I^6 χ^2 (π1, χ2 *blank*); (iiib) π^4 P^6 Q–2H^{12} 2I^8 (π1, 2I8 *blank*).

Vol. VI: *Formula: (The volume is found in three states; see McMullin* 177–80*):* (i) π^2 2K–3B^{12} 3C^6; (ii) π^2 2I^{12}(–2I1–7) 2K–3B^{12} 3C^6; (iii) π^2 2i^6 2K–3B^{12} 3C^6 (π1 *blank*).

Vol. XI: *Formula:* π^2 a^6 A–I^{12} K^6 ²π1 ²A–C^{12}(²C4 + χ1) ²D–F^{12} ²G^8 (χ1 *added title to* 'Laelius'.

Vol. XII: *Title-page*: ['GLASGUAE' *followed by a colon, not a comma.*]

Vol. XIX: *Title-page*: [*Last line reads* 'M.DCC.XLIX'.]

With regard to the various separate editions and issues of parts of this twenty-volume set, Dr McMullin suggests that those that were printed from different settings of type (Nos. 102, 103, 105, and 106) were produced to make good shortages in No. 101 but were sold separately as well; that the separate settings of *De Oratore*, 1749 (No. 611), comes into the same category; and he suggests that No. 104 represents part of Vol. III of No. 101, not a separate edition. He has found a separate issue of *In Verrem*, 1749, which is an extract, reimposed with new signatures and pagination, from Vols. IV, V, and VI of No. 101. He believes, finally, that the four other works mentioned at the end of my Note on the duodecimo Ciceros on p. 121 above (*De Lege Agraria; in M. Antonium; in Vatinium*; and *Lucullus*) are probably volumes, or parts of volumes, of No. 101 (respectively Vols. VII, X, part of IX, part of XV), not separate editions.

1748   Hamilton, William, *Poems on Several Occasions* **110**

FORMULA: Brian Gerrard notes a copy with an errata slip pasted at the bottom of π3.

112A M'Michan, John, *De Dysenteria* 1748

DISSERTATIO MEDICA | INAUGURALIS, | DE | DYSEN
TERIA: | [8 *lines*] | PRO GRADU DOCTORATUS, | summisque
in MEDICINA honoribus ac privilegiis | RITE ET LEGITIME
CONSEQUENDIS, | ERUDITORUM EXAMINI SUBJICIT |
JOHANNES M'MICHAN HIBERNUS A.M. | ad diem tertium
Maii, hora locoque folitis. | [2 *lines*] | Ex officina roberti foulis.
M. DCC. XLVIII.

FORMULA: Foolscap 4° in twos: A^2 B–D^2.

PAPER: Medium-good quality; marks 5/iv.

TYPE: RE 2.

COPIES: Ian Grant.

119 Rowe, Nicholas, *Lady Jane Gray* 1748

VARIANT: Issue on inferior paper, Pot 8° in fours:
Formula: (*Without* '*' *signatures*.)
Paper: Medium-poor quality; marks 1/v.
Copies: Ian Grant.

125 Apollonius of Perga, *Plane Loci*, L 1749

VARIANT: Issue on inferior paper:
Formula: (*B. J. McMullin reports that the McMaster University Library
copy is signed* '*' *on* O1, *and that* F2 *and probably* M4 *are not cancels*.)
NOTES: About 700 copies were printed, apparently in 1746 (though
they were not released until 1749); about one-third of them were on
'the best' paper, and the remainder on the cheaper paper, retailing
at about 11s. and 9s. respectively. Some of the diagrams appear to
have been printed from metal, not from wood blocks. (From an
article by John Burnett on Simson's Euclid, to be published in *The
Bibliotheck*).

126 Aurelius Antoninus, Marcus, *Meditations*, E 1749

TITLE-PAGE: [*Line 6, for* 'greek' *read* 'Greek'.]

128 Davies, Sir John, *The Original, Nature and* 1749
Immortality of the Soul

TITLE-PAGE: [*line* 14, *insert* '|' *after* 'GLASGOW,'.]

1749   Hamilton, William, *Poems on Several Occasions* **131**

VARIANT: Brian Gerrard reports that the version without the comma after 'FOULIS' on the title-page also has the Preface reset on one page, rather than on two as in the other version.

1749   Rogers, Bayly, *De Haemorrhoidibus* **136A**

DISSERTATIO MEDICA | INAUGURALIS, | DE | HAEMOR RHOIDIBUS: | [8 *lines*] | PRO GRADU DOCTORATUS, | SUMMISQUE IN M E D I C I N A HONORIBUS ET PRIVI LEGIIS | RITE ET LEGITIME CONSEQUENDIS | ERUDI TORUM EXAMINI SUBJICIT | BAYLY ROGERS HIBERNUS A. et R. | ad diem 1['0' *in manuscript*] Martis, hora locoque folitis. | [*quotation, 4 lines*] | EX OFFICINA ROBERTI FOULIS. M. DCC. XLIX.

FORMULA: Foolscap 4°: π1 A^2 B–D^2 E1 (π1 *half-title*)

PAPER: Medium-good quality; marks 4/v.

TYPE: RE 2, GGP.

COPIES: Ian Grant.

1750   Caesar, *Works*, L **140**

VARIANT: The copy in Melbourne University Library is printed on a medium quality paper, marks 1/v, and is presumably from an issue in Pot 12° (B. J. McMullin in *The Book Collector*, 28 (1979)574).

NOTES: A1 of vol. II is a title-page covering vols. II and III, which have continuous pagination; it is likely that the set was sometimes bound in two volumes, not three.

1750   Fleming, Samuel, *De Incremento Ossium* **149A**

DISSERTATIO | MEDICA INAUGURALIS | DE | INCREMENTO | OSSIUM. | [8 *lines*] | PRO GRADU DOC TORATUS, | SUMMISQUE IN MEDICINA PRIVILEGIIS ET HONORIBUS, | RITE AC LEGITIME CONSEQUENDIS, | ERUDITORUM EXAMINI SUBMITTIT | SAMUEL FLEM-ING, HIBERNUS, A.M. | Ad diem 27 Junii, hora 11ma, ante meridiem, | LOCO SOLITO. | GLASGUAE, | IN AEDIBUS ACADEMICIS | EXCUDEBANT ROB. ET AND. FOULIS ACADEMIAE TYPOGRAPHI | MDCCL.

FORMULA: [? Demy] $4°$ in twos: A^2 B–F^2.
PAPER: Medium-good quality; marks 7/1.
TYPE: RE 2.
COPIES: G^2.

150 Garth, Sir Samuel, *The Dispensary*   1750

VARIANT: David Foxon reports copies on better-quality paper, signed '*' in the direction line, but also with marks 4 (Foxon G33–4).

152 Gay, John, *Fables*   1750

FORMULA: Pot $8°$ in fours: π^4 A–$2A^4$ (O1, O2 *unsigned*).
PAPER: Medium-good quality; marks 1/v.
TYPE: RLP 1.
COPIES: E, G^4.

153 Gee, Joshua, *The Trade and Navigation*   1750
of Great Britain

VARIANT: Issue in (?)Pot $8°$ in fours:
  Paper: Medium-poor quality; marks 1/iv, 1/v (but D on 5/?).
  Copies: Sydney University Library (noted by B. J. McMullin in *The Book Collector*, 28(1979)574).

154A Hutcheson, Francis, *De Concoctione Ciborum*   1750

DISSERTATIO | MEDICA INAUGURALIS | DE | CONCOC TIONE | CIBORUM. | [8 *lines*] | PRO GRADU DOCTOR ATUS, | SUMMISQUE IN MEDICINA PRIVILEGIIS ET HONORIBUS, | RITE AC LEGITIME CONSEQUENDIS, | EUDITORUM EXAMINI SUBMITTIT | FRANSISCUS HUTCHESON, HIBERNUS, A.M. | Ad diem 27 Junii, hora 11ma, ante meridiem, | LOCO SOLITO. | GLASGUAE, | IN AEDIBUS ACADEMICIS | EXCUDEBANT ROB. ET AND. FOULIS ACADEMIAE TYPOGRAPHI | MDCCL.

FORMULA: [? Demy] $4°$ in twos: A^2 B–E^2 F1.
PAPER: Good quality; marks 7/?.
TYPE: RE 2.
COPIES: G^2.

1750   Jerningham, Edward, *The Epistle of Yarico to Inkle* **157**

NOTES: This poem is by Edward Moore, not by Jerningham.

1750–51   Plato, [Proposals for editions, E and L, **164**
                                        with specimens]

There are two copies of the Latin proposals, with one copy of a specimen, in the Bibliothèque Nationale in Paris: photocopies only seen.

(1) PROPOSALS

[P. 1 begins] Ex AEDIBUS ACADEMIAE GLASGUENSIS, vii Januarii 1751 | ROBERTUS ET ANDREAS FOULIS, | ACADEMIAE GLASGUENSIS | TYPOGRAPHI, | ORBI LITERATO PRO PONUNT; | SE, FAVENTE SUBSCRIPTIONE, | EDITIONEM SUSCEPISSE | PLATONIS; | TYPIS NOVIS, GRANDIORI BUS, PULCHERRIMIS; | QUOS, IN HUNC FINEM, | AD EXEMPLAR TYPORUM REGIORUM | QUIBUS EDIDIT NOVUM TESTAMENTUM IN FOLIO | ROBERTUS STEPHANUS, | ELEGANTISSIME SCULPSIT | ALEXANDER WILSON A.M. | ACADEMIAE GLASGUENSIS TYPORUM ARTIFEX. | PRODIBIT OPUS, ET IN QUARTO, ET IN FOLIO.

FORMULA: Two leaves of Foolscap folio, printed on the rectos only.

PAPER: Marks 5/?.

TYPE: RP2, RB2.

NOTES: This is a Latin version of the proposals printed in Appendix A, pp. 393–5.

(2) SPECIMEN

[Four pages from the *Crito* in Greek, with a two-column footnote translation into Latin.]

FORMULA: Two leaves of Foolscap folio, printed on all four pages.

PAPER: Marks 5/?.

TYPE: GDP 1, GP, RLP 1.

NOTES: BN Rés. Atlas Q.21, (1) and (2) described by Jeanne Veyrin-Forrer in *Bulletin des bibliothèques de France*, 2S, 8(1966).

1750   Pope, Alexander, *An Essay on Man* **164A**

AN | ESSAY | ON | MAN. | IN FOUR EPISTLES. | BY | ALEXANDER POPE Efq; | *GLASGOW,* | PRINTED AND SOLD BY R. & A. FOULIS | MDCCL.

FORMULA: Foolscap 8° in fours: a⁴ A–G⁴.

PAPER: Marks 3/iv.

TYPE: RLP 1, RB 2.

NOTES: Not seen; description from a photocopy and information from Mr W. H. Bond. See NOTES to No. 210.

COPIES: HD.

176 Young, Edward, *Love of Fame*   1750

> VARIANT: Issue in Foolscap 8°:
> *Paper*: Medium quality; marks 4/iv, 5/iv.
> *Copies*: Brian Gerrard.
> *Notes*: Foxon Y175.

176A [Title-page for a 16th-century Cicero]   c.1750

FRAGMENTA | M. TULLII | CICERONIS | VARIIS IN LOCIS DISPERSA, | CAROLI SIGONII diligentia collecta et Scholiis | illuftrata. | *VENETIIS,* | Apud J. ZILLETUM. MDLVIIII.

NOTES: A title-page specially printed to replace the presumably missing title-page of a copy of Adams C1669 belonging to Lawrence Dinwiddie (1696–1764, Provost of Glasgow 1742, 1743); probably printed at the Foulis Press and bound into the book at the Foulises' bindery.

COPIES: Philip Gaskell.

193 Gay, John, *Poems on Several Occasions*   1751

> VARIANTS: *Formula*: B. J. McMullin reports that in the Otago University (Selwyn Collection) copy of Vol. I of the 12° issue D6 is present, containing the same text as E1, except that E1ᵛ has only the first 12 lines of 'Monday' plus 10 lines of notes not included on D6ᵛ.
> Separate issue of *Dione*, 1752:
> *Title-page*: DIONE, | A | PASTORAL TRAGEDY. | BY | MR. JOHN GAY. | [*quotation, 3 lines*] | GLASGOW, | PRINTED BY ROBERT AND ANDREW FOULIS | M DCC LII.
> *Formula*: [? Crown] 12° in sixes: π1 A–F⁶ G⁴ (G4 *advertisements*).
> *Paper*: Medium-poor quality, no marks.
> *Notes*: Apart from the new title-page this is from the same setting as Vol. II P3–Z2 (8°), K1–Q4 (12°).
> *Copies*: O.

1751   Pliny the Younger, *Works*, L   **208**

FORMULA: Copies at G^2 (and elsewhere) bound in three volumes, with an extra pair of leaves preceding sig. Z, so that Vol. III collates: π^2 Z–2D^{12} 2E^6 2F^{12} (π1 *half-title*, π2 *volume title*).

     B. J. McMullin reports copies of the Pot 12° issue with the two extra leaves but bound in two volumes; with Y6 missing; and with 2A2 signed 'A2', 2C5 signed 'C5'.

1751   Pope, Alexander, *An Essay on Man*   **210**

NOTES: The Advertisements in Nos. 141 and 175 probably refer to No. 164A, not to No. 210.

1751   Prior, Matthew, *Poems on several occasions*   **211**

TITLE-PAGE: [*No full stop after* 'FOULIS' *in the imprint of vol.* II.]
VARIANT:
    Paper: Medium-poor quality; no marks.
    Copies: O.

1751   Steele, Sir Richard, *The Conscious Lovers*   **216**

THE | CONSCIOUS LOVERS. | A | COMEDY. | WRITTEN BY | SIR RICHARD STEELE. [*quotation, 9 lines*] | GLASGOW, | PRINTED AND SOLD BY ROBERT & ANDREW FOULIS. | MDCCLI.
FORMULA: Post 12° in sixes: A^2 B–F^6 G1.
PAPER: Medium quality; marks 6/vii.
TYPE: RB 1.
COPIES: E.

1751   Temple, Sir William, *A letter of consolation*   **217**
                           to the Countess of Essex

A | LETTER | OF | CONSOLATION | TO THE | COUNTESS OF ESSEX, | UPON | HER GRIEF | OCCASIONED BY THE LOSS OF | HER ONLY DAUGHTER. | BY | SIR WILLIAM TEMPLE BART. | GLASGOW, | PRINTED AND SOLD BY ROBERT & ANDREW FOULIS | MDCC LI.
FORMULA: Foolscap 8° in fours: π^2 A–C^4 D^2 (π1 *half-title*).
PAPER: Medium-good quality; marks 4/v.

TYPE: RE 2.

NOTES: *Price*: Foolscap 8°, 2½d. (*BQ* 10).
  Stock in 1777: 210 copies (*BQ* 10).

COPIES: C.

225 Denham, Sir John, *The Sophy*   1752

THE | SOPHY. | A | TRAGEDY. | As it was Acted at the | PRIVATE HOUSE | IN | *BLACK FRYARS.* | BY | His MAJESTY's Servants. | *The AUTHOR* | SIR JOHN DENHAM. | GLASGOW: | Printed in the YEAR MDCCLII.

FORMULA: Pot 8° in fours: A^4 B–L^4 M^2 (*A*1 *half-title*).

PAPER: Medium-poor quality; marks 1/v.

TYPE: RLP 1.

COPIES: E.

228 Dryden, John, *The Spanish Friar*   1752

VARIANT: Issue in Pot 8° in fours:
  Formula: A–N^4 O^2 (o2 *advertisements*).
  Paper: Medium quality; marks 1/v, 1/?.

COPIES: C (8°), G^4 (12°).

244 Sheffield, John, Duke of Buckingham, *Poems on*   1752
Several Occasions, etc.: Julius Caesar

VARIANT: Separate issue of *Julius Caesar*:
  Title-page: THE | TRAGEDY | OF | JULIUS CAESAR, | ALTERED: | WITH A | PROLOGUE AND CHORUS; | BY HIS GRACE | JOHN DUKE OF BUCKINGHAM. | GLASGOW, | PRINTED BY ROBERT AND ANDREW FOULIS | M DCC LII.
  Formula: Pot 8° in fours: A^4 B–I^4 K1 (*A*1 *half-title*).
  Paper: Medium-poor quality; marks 1/v, size of sheet 15 × 12¼ in.
  Type: RLP 1, RB1.
  Copies: E.

247 Waller, Edmund, *Works*   1752

VARIANT: Issue in Pot 8°:
  Paper: For 'marks 5/v' read 'marks 1/v'.

1752   Young, Edward, *The Revenge* **248A**

THE | REVENGE, | A | TRAGEDY. | BY THE REVEREND | EDWARD YOUNG, LL.D. | Rector of *Wellwyn* in *Hertfordſhire,* | AND | Chaplain in Ordinary to His MAJESTY. | [*quotation,* 1 *line*] | *GLASGOW,* | PRINTED AND SOLD BY ROBERT & ANDREW FOULIS | M DCC LII.

FORMULA: Pot 8° in fours: A–K^4 L^2.
PAPER: Medium quality; marks 1/v.
TYPE: RB 1, RLP 1.
COPIES: E.

1753   Addison, Joseph, *Of the Christian Religion* **250**

VARIANT: The issue on inferior paper is a Pot 8° in fours:
  Paper: Medium-poor quality; marks 1/v.
  Copies: Brian Gerrard (who supplied this description).

1753   Cibber, Colley, *The Careless Husband* **250A**

THE | CARELESS HUSBAND. | A | COMEDY. | *Written by* C. CIBBER. | [*quotations,* 4 *lines*] | GLASGOW, | PRINTED AND SOLD BY R. AND A. FOULIS | M DCC LIII.

FORMULA: Post 12° in sixes: A–F^6 G^4 H^2.
PAPER: Medium quality; marks 6/?.
TYPE: RB 1.
COPIES: E.

1753   Dick, Robert, *Experiments and Lectures* **252A**
                                     on Mechanics

A | COURSE | OF | EXPERIMENTS | AND | LECTURES | ON | MECHANICS, HYDROSTATICS, | PNEUMATICS and OPTICS; | To be begun on Tueſday the ſixth of November, and continued | during the Seſſion of the College, | BY | *ROBERT DICK* M.D.P.N.P. | GLASGOW: | PRINTED BY ROBERT AND ANDREW FOULIS | PRINTERS TO THE UNIVERSITY | M DCC LIII.

FORMULA: Pot 4°: A–B^4 C^2.
PAPER: Medium-poor quality; marks 1/v.
TYPE: RE 2.
COPIES: Glasgow, University of Strathclyde Library (Andersonian Library).

264 Steele, Sir Richard, *The Funeral* 1753

VARIANT: Issue in Post 12°:
Formula: Post 12° in sixes: A–G^6 H^2.
Paper: Medium quality; marks 6/?.
Copies: D.

265 Tacitus, *Works*, L 1753

VARIANT: The issue on inferior paper is a Pot 12°:
Paper: Medium quality; marks 1/v.
Copies: Brian Gerrard (who supplied this description).

269A Young, Edward, *Love of Fame* 1753

LOVE OF FAME, | THE | UNIVERSAL PASSION. | IN | SEVEN CHARACTERISTICAL | SATIRES. | [*quotation, 2 lines*] | BY THE REVEREND | EDWARD YOUNG, LL.D. | RECTOR OF WELLWYN IN HARTFORDSHIRE, | AND CHAPLAIN IN ORDINARY TO | HIS MAJESTY. | PRINTED IN THE YEAR M.DCC.LIII.

FORMULA: Foolscap 8° in fours: π^4 $^2\pi$1 A–L^4 M^2.

PAPER: Medium quality; marks 5/v.

TYPE: RLP 1, RE 1.

NOTES: This is probably Duncan's '1754' edition (entry 279). Certainly a Foulis book, notwithstanding the imprint.

COPIES: Brian Gerrard (who supplied this description).

276A Steele, Sir Richard, *The Tender Husband* 1754

THE | TENDER HUSBAND: | OR, THE | ACCOMPLISH'D FOOLS. | A | COMEDY. | Written by | Sir RICHARD STEELE. | [*quotation, 2 lines*] | GLASGOW, | PRINTED AND SOLD BY R. AND A. FOULIS | M DCC LIV.*

FORMULA: Pot 8° in fours: A–G^4 H^2 (*signed* '*' *on* $1 *except* H1)

PAPER: Medium-good quality; marks 1/iv.

TYPE: RB 1.

VARIANT: Common-paper issue, Pot 8°:
Formula: (*Without* '*' *signatures.*)
Paper: Medium-poor quality; marks 1/v.

COPIES: G^2 (better-quality paper); Brian Gerrard (common paper; description supplied by Mr Gerrard).

THE FOULIS PRESS

1754   Vanbrugh, Sir John, *The Provoked Wife* **278**

VARIANT: Issue on better-quality paper, Pot 8°:
Formula: (*With '*' signatures on* $1 B–F H I L.)
Paper: Medium quality; marks 1/v.
COPIES: Brian Gerrard (who supplied this description).

1754   Voltaire, *The History of Charles XII*, E **278A**

THE | HISTORY | OF | CHARLES XII. | KING OF SWEDEN. |
BY | MR. DE VOLTAIRE. | TRANSLATED FROM THE
FRENCH. | GLASGOW, | PRINTED AND SOLD BY ROBERT
AND ANDREW FOULIS | MDCCLIV.
FORMULA: Foolscap 8° in fours: A–2I⁴ 2K1.
PAPER: Medium-good quality; marks 4/ii; and medium quality;
marks 3/iii, v.
TYPE: RLP1, RB2.
NOTES: *Price*: Wholesale: 1s. (*BQ* 10).
Stock in 1777: 1 copy, common (*BQ* 10). The copy seen is on
paper of mixed quality.
COPIES: O.

1754   Young, Edward, *Love of Fame* **279**

Entry renumbered 269A (1753).

1755   Aristophanes, *Clouds*, G and L **281**

VARIANTS: Issue in Pot 8°, Greek and Latin:
Formula: Same as the Foolscap 8° issue.
Paper: Medium-poor quality; marks 1/v.
Copies: Brian Gerrard (who supplied this description).

1755   Boileau-Despréaux, Nicolas, *L'Art Poétique*, E **282**

VARIANT: Issue on common paper, Pot 8°:
Formula: (*Without '*' signatures.*)
Paper: Medium-quality; marks 1/v.
Copies: Brian Gerrard (who supplied this description).

283 Callimachus, *Hymns and Epigrams*, G   1755

VARIANTS: Foolscap 2°:
Formula: (*B. J. McMullin reports copies with the first two preliminary leaves conjugate; and with an extra blank conjugate with the last preliminary leaf.*)
NOTES: See Hillyard, Brian, 'The Edinburgh Society's silver medals for printing', *PBSA*, 78(1984)300.

288 Farquhar, George, *The Beaux' Stratagem*   1755

THE | BEAuX strATAGEM: | A | COMEDY. | BY | MR. GEORGE FARQUHAR. | GLASGOW: | PRINTED AND SOLD BY ROBERT AND ANDREW FOULIS | M.DCC.LV.
FORMULA: Pot 8° in fours: A–L^4 (L4 *advertisements*).
PAPER: Medium quality; marks i/iv.
TYPE: RB 1, RLP 1.
COPIES: Glasgow, Baillie's Library.

289A Farquhar, George, *Love and a Bottle*, another edition   1755

LOVE AND A BOTTLE. | A | COMEDY. | BY | MR. GEORGE FARQUHAR. | [*quotation, 2 lines*] | GLASGOW: | PRINTED AND SOLD BY ROBERT AND ANDREW FOULIS | M.DCC.LV.
FORMULA: Pot 8° in fours: A–L^4 (L4 *blank*).
PAPER: Medium quality; marks i/v.
TYPE: RB 1, RB 2.
COPIES: G^2.

294 Gay, John, *Dione*   by 1755

Entry deleted. See p. 418, No. 193.

297 Hutcheson, Francis, *A System of Moral Philosophy*   1755

TITLE-PAGE: [Vol. II *imprint reads* 'GLASGOW,', *not* 'GLASGOW:'.]

1755   Somerville, William, *The Chace*   **306**

VARIANT: Issue in [? Small Crown] 12°:
  Formula: [? Small Crown] 12° in sixes: A–G^6 (G6 *advertisements*).
  Paper: Medium-poor quality, thin; no marks, vertical chain lines
(probably from half sheets of Double Crown).
  Copies: G^2.

by 1755   Steele, Sir Richard, *The Tender Husband*   **308**

Entry renumbered 276A (1754).

by 1755   Young, Edward, *The Revenge*   **310**

Entry renumbered 248A (1752)

1756   Euclid, *Elements I–VI, XI–XII*, L and E   **315–6**

NOTES: A full account of the production and distribution of these
two editions of Simson's Euclid is given in a article by John
Burnett, to be published in *The Bibliotheck*. Amongst other things, it
appears that of the Latin edition 66 copies were printed on 'royal
perfect' paper and 477 on 'fine thick demy', total 543; and that of
the English edition the quantities were 93 and 710 copies respectively, total 803. Some of the diagrams appear to have been printed
from metal, not from wood blocks.

1756   Euclid, *Elements I–VI, XI–XII*, E   **316**

FORMULA: (*Watermarks suggest that either* A1.4 *or* A2.3 *is a cancel in a
Royal* 4° *copy reported by B. J. McMullin.*)
VARIANT: Issue in [? Printing Demy] 4°:
  Paper: Medium-poor quality; no marks.
  Copies: Brian Gerrard (who supplied this description).

1756–8   Homer, *Works*, G   **319**

NOTES: See Hillyard, Brian, 'The Edinburgh Society's silver medals
for printing', *PBSA*, 78(1984)308, 311, 314.

320 Horace, *Works*, L   1756

FORMULA: John Sibbald reports a copy with the formula: $a^8(a^2+\chi^2)$ A–R^8 (a1 *half-title*, χ1 *dedication*, χ2 *blank*). Melbourne University has a copy in which N4.5 is a cancel.

VARIANT: The McMaster University Library copy is signed '§' on $1 A–I, P, but the quality of the paper is not distinguishably different and the marks are the same (B. J. McMullin in *The Book Collector* 28(1979)574).

NOTES: See Hillyard, Brian, 'The Edinburgh Society's silver medals for printing', *PBSA* 78(1984)307.

329 Anacreon, *Odes*, with Sappho and Alcaeus,   1757
Remains, G

TITLE-PAGE: ['KAI TA TOY' *is set in one line, not two.*]

332 Cicero, *De Officiis*, L   1757

FORMULA: B. J. McMullin (*Papers of the Bibliographical Society of America*, 72(1978)161–8) shows that the cancellation of conjugate pairs of leaves certainly or probably took place in a majority of the sections. The pairs thus cancelled appear to have been A4,5, B3.6, D2.7, E1.8, F4.5, I1.8, I2.7, I3.6, I4.5, L1.8, M1.8, N2.7, O1.8, O3.6, P2.7, Q1.8, Q2.7 (the whole of I being apparently cancelled piecemeal by pairs).

VARIANT: Issue on different paper, Foolscap 8°:
Formula: (*With '*' signatures. Of seven copies with '*' reported by B. J. McMullin, none had '*' on $1 throughout, each one having a different group of '*' signatures.*)
Paper: Marks 4/iv, 4/vi.
Copies: G^2 (4), E, E^2, L.

NOTES: See Hillyard, Brian, 'The Edinburgh Society's silver medals for printing', *PBSA* 78(1984)311.

340A [Anon.], *The Seven Champions of the Stage*   1757

THE | SEVEN CHAMPIONS | OF THE | STAGE: | In imitation of GILL MORICE. | An excellent new old faſhion'd | SONG | All to the melancholy Tune of *Gill* | *Morice*; except the 17$^{th.}$ 18$^{th.}$ and | 19$^{th.}$ Stanzas which ought to be Sung | to the merry Tune of the C---s | are coming O ho! | Printed in the Year MDCCLVII.

FORMULA: Pot 8° in fours: $\pi 1$ A⁴.

PAPER: Medium-good quality; marks 1/?.

TYPE: RLP 1, RP 2.

NOTES: Without the Foulis Press imprint, but certainly printed there. (The next tract in the same volume at E², press mark Df.8.19, is catalogued as part of this item, but it is actually a different book, not printed at the Foulis Press.)

COPIES: E².

1758   Frederick II of Prussia, *La Délassement*   **351**
        de la Guerre, F and E

THE | RELAXATION | OF | WAR, | OR, THE | HERO'S PHILOSOPHY. | A | POEM | IN | FRENCH AND ENGLISH. | WROTE BY THE | KING OF PRUSSIA, | DURING HIS RESI DENCE AT BRESLAW. | THE SECOND EDITION. | GLAS GOW: | PRINTED AND SOLD BY R. AND A. FOULIS | M DCC LVIII.

FORMULA: Foolscap 4° in twos: $A1$ B² (B2 + 2 *disjunct leaves, the second of them signed* 'B') C².

PAPER: Medium-good quality; marks 4/iv.

TYPE: RE 2; French and English on facing pages.

COPIES: E.

1758   Hamilton, William, *Poems on Several Occasions*   **354**

NOTES: There is a copy at G⁴ which has another setting of this 1758 title-page (but reading 'sold' for 'fold' in the penultimate line), which is then followed by the contents leaf and sigs B3 to the end of the 1749 edition (No. 131).

1758   Ray, John, *The Wisdom of God manifested in*   **357A**
        the Works of the Creation

THE | WISDOM OF GOD | MANIFESTED IN THE | WORKS | OF THE | CREATION. | IN TWO PARTS. | VIZ. | [9 *lines*] | BY | JOHN RAY, F.R.S. | GLASGOW: | PRINTED IN THE YEAR M.DCC.LVIII.

FORMULA: Demy 12° in sixes: $a-b^6$ A–2C⁶ 2D².

PAPER: Medium-poor quality; marks 9/i.

TYPE: RLP 1, GP, RP 2, RB 2.

COPIES: G⁴.

360 Virgil, *Works*, L   1758

NOTES: Ian Grant has a copy in which F1 and M3 are cancellantia.
See Hillyard, Brian, 'The Edinburgh Society's silver medals for
printing', *PBSA* 78(1984)314.

362 Addison, Joseph, *A Discourse on Ancient and*   1759
Modern Learning

VARIANT: Issue in Pot 8°:
Paper: Medium-good quality; marks 1/v.
Copies: E.

370 Lucretius, *De Rerum Natura*   1759

NOTES: See Hillyard, Brian, 'The Edinburgh Society's silver medals
for printing', *PBSA* 78(1984)315.

373A Plomer, James, *De Iliaca Passione*   1759

DISSERTATIO MEDICA | INAUGURALIS, | DE | ILIACA
PASSIONE; | [8 *lines*] | PRO GRADU DOCTORATUS, | SUM
MISQUE IN MEDICINA PRIVILEGIIS, ET HONORIBUS, |
RITE AC LEGITIME CONSEQUENDIS, | ERUDITORUM
EXAMINI SUBJICIT | JACOBUS PLOMER, Anglus, | Ad
diem 15 Maii, hora locoque solitis. | GLASGUAE, | IN AEDIBUS
ACADEMICIS | EXCUDEBANT ROB. ET AND. FOULIS,
ACADEMIAE TYPOGRAPHI | M DCC LIX.
FORMULA: [? size] 4° in twos: π^2 A–I^2.
PAPER: Good quality; marks 7/?.
TYPE: RGP 2.
COPIES: G^2.

375 Thucydides, *The Peloponnesian War*, G and L   1759

NOTES: See Hillyard, Brian, 'The Edinburgh Society's silver medals
for printing', *PBSA* 78(1984)316.

1760   Anderson, John, *A Compend of Experimental* **377**
Philosophy

[Variant title-page] A | COMPEND | OF | EXPERIMENTAL |
PHILOSOPHY. | FOR THE USE OF THE | PRIVATE STU
DENTS | OF | NATURAL PHILOSOPHY | IN THE |
UNIVERSITY OF GLASGOW. | GLASGOW: | PRINTED BY
ROBERT AND ANDREW FOULIS | M.DCC.LX.

FORMULA: (instead of a⁴) π^2 $^2\pi$1 (π1 *title-page*, π2 'advertisement',
$^2\pi$1 *contents*).

COPIES: Glasgow, University of Strathclyde.

1760   Horace, *Works*, L **383**

FORMULA: The dedication (χ1) is found in various places in π; and it
is sometimes found as a conjugate pair with a blank leaf (thus
becoming χ^2). But χ is not printed on the same paper as π^6 or U^2.

NOTES: See Hillyard, Brian, 'The Edinburgh Society's silver medals
for printing', *PBSA* 78(1984)317.

1760   Le Sage, Alain René, *The Devil upon Two* **384A**
Sticks (Le Diable Boiteux). E

LE | *Diable Boiteux*: | OR, THE | DEVIL | UPON | TWO STICKS.
| Tranflated from the French of | MONSIEUR LE SAGE, | Author
of the Adventures of GIL BLAS. | GLASGOW: | PRINTED IN
THE YEAR M.DCC.LX.

FORMULA: Pot 12°: π^2 2π1 A–N¹² O².

Plate: copper-plate frontispiece ('*EL DIABLO COIUELO*'),
unsigned.

PAPER: Medium-good quality; marks 1/iv.

TYPE: RLP 1.

NOTES: See also No. 477A.

COPIES: Mr David Murray.

1761   Butler, Samuel, *Hudibras* **388**

VARIANT: Issue on slightly better paper, Pot 12°:
Formula: (With '' signatures on $1 A–X, except* G *which is signed*
'†'.)
Paper: Medium-good quality; marks 1/v.
Copies: Brian Gerrard (who supplied this description).

395 Herodotus, *History*, G and L   1761

VARIANT: Issue on better paper, Foolscap 8°, Greek only:
Formula: Foolscap 8° in fours:
Vol. I: π^2 A–2G^4 (−2G4, *?blank*; A2 *signed* 'A3'; *signed* '*' *on* I1).
Vol. II: πI A–2B^4.
Vol. III: πI A–Y^4 (R2 *signed* 'R3').
Vol. IV: πI A–Z^4 (−Z4, *?blank*; *signed* 'TOM. V.' *on* I1).
Vol. V: πI A–Q^4 (−Q4, *?blank*).
Vol. VI: πI A–Q^4 R^2.
Vol. VII: πI A–2E^4 2F^2.
Vol. VIII: πI A–R^4.
Vol. IX: πI A–T^4 U^2 (U1 *signed* 'T'; U2 *advertisements*).
(B. J. McMullin, who supplies these details in *The Book Collector*, 28(1979)574–5, also notes a copy with vol. I O1.8, P1.8, and 2F2.7 cancelled.)
Paper: Good to medium quality; marks 4/i, 4/ii, 4/v, 4/vi, 5/i, 5/ii, 5/v, 5/vi.
Copies: Melbourne University Library (the variant described here); MEL (the conjugate pair cancels).

396 Milton, John, *Paradise Lost*   1761

PARADISE | LOST, | A | POEM | IN | TWELVE BOOKS. | THE AUTHOR | JOHN MILTON. | ACCORDING TO THE AUTHOR'S LAST | EDITION, IN THE YEAR 1674. | GLASGOW: | PRINTED AND SOLD BY R. & A. FOULIS | PRINTERS TO THE UNIVERSITY | M.DCC.LXI.

FORMULA: Pot 12°: A^8 B–G^{12} H^6 I–P^{12} Q^4 (A1 *half-title*, Q3–4 *advertisements*).

PAPER: Medium quality; marks 1/iv.

TYPE: RB 2.

COPIES: Glasgow, Baillie's Library.

397 Nepos, Cornelius, *Lives of the Emperors*, L   1761

VARIANT: Post 8° issue:
Formula: (*B. J. McMullin reports a copy with* N8 *as well as* G4 *cancelled*.)

NOTES: See Hillyard, Brian, 'The Edinburgh Society's silver medals for printing', *PBSA* 78(1984)318.

by 1761   Ray, John, *The Wisdom of God manifested* **398**
                  in the Works of Creation

Entry renumbered 357A (1758).

1761   Wright, James, *De Summo Bono* **399A**

DISSERTATIO PHILOSOPHICA | INAUGURALIS, | DE |
SUMMO BONO. | [8 *lines*] | PRO GRADU MAGISTERII, |
SUMMISQUE IN PHILOSOPHIA ET ARTIBUS LIBERALI
BUS, | PRIVILEGIIS, ET HONORIBUS, | RITE AC LEGI
TIME CONSEQUENDIS, | IN AUDITORIO PUBLICO ACADEMIAE
GLASGUENSIS, | Ad diem 28. FEBRUARII, hora 11$^{\text{ma,}}$ | PROPUGNA
BIT | JACOBUS WRIGHT. | [*quotation, 3 lines*] | GLASGUAE, |
IN AEDIBUS ACADEMICIS | EXCUDEBANT ROB. ET AND.
FOULIS, ACADEMIAE TYPOGRAPHI | M DCC LXI.

FORMULA: Post 4° in twos: π^2 A–F^2.
PAPER: Good quality; marks 6/?.
TYPE: RP 2.
COPIES: G^2.

1762   Cicero, *In M. Antonium I–II*, L **404**

VARIANT: Common-paper issue, Pot 8° in fours:
Paper: Medium-poor quality; marks 1/v.
Copies: E.

1762   Dalrymple, David, Lord Hailes, *Memorials* **405**
                           and Letters: James I

VARIANT: Issue on poorer-quality paper, Foolscap 8°:
Formula: (D1.8 *cancelled*.)
Paper: Medium quality; marks 5/ii.
Copies: Sydney University Library (reported by B. J. McMullin
in *The Book Collector*, 28(1979)575).

1762   Thomas More, St, *Utopia*, E **412**

VARIANT: Issue on common paper, Pot 8°:
Paper: Poor quality; marks 1/v.
Copies: Brian Gerrard (who supplied this description).

413 Xenophon, *Hellenica and Agesilaus*, G and L $\quad$ 1762

FORMULA: (*B. J. McMullin reports cancels in Vol.* III *at* B1, B5, C1, D5.)

415 Bell, John, *Travels from St Petersburg* $\quad$ 1763

TITLE-PAGES: [*Vol.* I: *no full stops following the two initials* 'A' *in line* 5 *of the imprint (present in vol.* II). *Vol.* II: *the two columns of contents are separated by a vertical plain double rule. Both vols: line* 3, *for* 'S^T.' *read* 'S^T.']

426 Tasso, Torquato, *La Gierusalemme Liberata* $\quad$ 1763

VARIANT: Vol. 1 of the Foolscap 8° issue, 'Con le Figure', with the title-page imprint 'IN PARIGI: DAVIDTS. | [*plain rule,* 21] | M DCC LXIV.' in place of the five-line Foulis imprint which appears as usual in vol. 2 of the same set. This appears to have been printed specially for Rombaut Davidts (bookseller in Paris from 1751 to 1772; Lottin, *Librairies de Paris,* 1789, IIe partie, p. 36), who presumably acted as agent for the Foulises.

COPIES: Mr Alex Fotheringham.

427 Aurelius Antoninus, Marcus, *Meditations*, E $\quad$ 1764

NOTES: B. J. McMullin reports that the McMaster University Library copy of this book has a leaf of advertisements added at the end of vol. II; it is from the same setting as No. 435 (Xenophon), vol. 1 R4 and vol. III Q4.

432 Hutcheson, Francis, *A Short Introduction to* $\quad$ 1764
Moral Philosophy

FORMULA: Vol. 1: (*after* a^8 *add* b^4.)

435 Xenophon, *Anabasis*, G and L $\quad$ 1764

VARIANTS: Issue in Foolscap 8°, Greek only:
$\quad$ *Formula*: Foolscap 8° in fours:
$\quad\quad$ Vol. 1: π^2 A–R^4 (π1 *half-title*, R4 *advertisements; signed* 'TOM. I[...IV].' *on* \$1 *except half-titles, and Vol.* II A1)
$\quad\quad$ Vol. II: π^2 A–Q^4 R1 (π1 *half-title*).

Vol. III: π^2 A–Q^4 (π1 *half-title*; Q4 *advertisements*).
Vol. IV: π^2 A–R^4 S^2 (π1 *half-title*).
Paper: Medium-good quality; marks 4/vi, 5/v, 5/large crown.
Copies: Brian Gerrard (who supplied this description).

[c.1765]   [Anon.], *A succinct Description of the*   **441A**
                                                 Microcosm

A SUCCINCT | DESCRIPTION | OF THAT | Elaborate and
Matchlefs Pile of Art, | CALLED, THE | MICROCOSM. |
WITH A SHORT ACCOUNT OF THE | SOLAR SYSTEM, |
INTERSPERSED WITH | POETICAL SENTIMENTS, | ON
THE | PLANETS. | Extracted from the moft approved AUTH
ORS | on that SUBJECT. | THE SEVENTH EDITION, WITH
ADDITIONS. | GLASGOW: | Printed by R. and A. Foulis, for
the Proprietor, | Mr. EDWARD DAVIES. | (Price 6d.)

formula: Demy 8° in fours: A^4 B–D^4.

paper: Medium-poor quality; marks 9/?.

type: RE 2, RLP 1, RGP italic.

copies: L.

1765   Swift, Jonathan, *Directions to Servants*   **446A**

DIRECTIONS | TO | SERVANTS | IN GENERAL; | And in
Particular to the | [*two columns, 8 lines each, separated by a vertical plain
rule*, 29] | By the Reverend | Dr. SWIFT, D.S.P.D. | GLASGOW: |
PRINTED IN THE YEAR, M.DCC.LXV.

formula: [? Demy] 12° in sixes: A–H^6.

paper: Poor quality, no marks; vertical chain-lines, probably from
half sheets of Double Demy.

type: RP 2.

notes: Poorly printed, this may or may not be a Foulis reprint of
the 1762 edition noted by Duncan (see no. 411).

copies: E.

1766   Dalrymple, David, Lord Hailes, *Memorials*   **447**
                                              and Letters: Charles I

formula: (Should read a–b^8 c^4 A–M^8.)

449 Dalrymple, David, Lord Hailes, *The*   1766
Preservation of Charles II

NOTES: Although only seven copies of this book were listed in *BQ* in 1777, enough copies remained elsewhere (Dalrymple's own stock, perhaps) for John Scott to re-issue the book in 1803 with a cancel title-page and four inserted plates (A new edition: London: Printed by S. Gosnell, Little Queen Street, Holborn, for John Scott, No. 447, Strand; E. Harding, No. 100, Pall Mall; and T. Ostell, No. 3, Ave Maria Lane. 1803).

A second cancel title-page, also of the early nineteenth-century but following the wording of the original Foulis title page less the date, is reported and reproduced by B. N. Gerrard in *Bibliographical Society of Australia and New Zealand Bulletin*, 4(1979–80)223–6.

COPIES: (1803) G^2; (undated) B. N. Gerrard.

451 Epictetus, *Discourses*, E   1766

Probably printed by Urie, not by Foulis; entry deleted.

454 Milton, John, *Paradise Lost*   1766

VARIANT: Issue on inferior paper, Pot 12°:
Formula: (G3, M5 *unsigned*.)
Paper: Medium-poor quality; marks 1/iv, 1/v, 3/v.
Copies: Brian Gerrard (who supplied this description).

458 Moor, James, *Vindication of Virgil*   1766

FORMULA: Copy reported by William Poole (Catalogue 2, 1980, item 311) lacking A2.3, and with the 'note' from A3 printed on *E*1.

458A Nooth, John Mervin, *De Rachitide*   1766

TENTAMEN MEDICUM | INAUGURALE | DE | RACHI TIDE, | [8 *lines*] | PRO GRADU DOCTORIS, | SUMMISQUE IN MEDICINA HONORIBUS ET PRIVILEGIIS, | RITE AC LEGITIME CONSEQUENDIS; | *Eruditorum judicio subjicit* | JOHANNES MERVIN NOOTH, | BRITANNUS. | Ad diem   Julii, hora locoque folitis. | [4 *lines*] | EDINBURGI. | EX OFFICINA ROBERTI ET ANDREAE FOULIS | M.DCC.LXVI. |

FORMULA: [? Medium] 8° in fours: A^4 B–E^4 F^2 (A1 half-title).
PAPER: Good quality; marks 7/?.
TYPE: RP 2, RLP 1.
COPIES: G^2.

1767   Boswell, James, *Dorando* **462**

VARIANTS: Issue in 4°:
  Title-page: (*not* 'SECOND EDITION.')
  Formula: [?Writing Demy] 4° in twos: A^2 B–M^2 N1 (A1 half-title).
  Paper: Good quality; marks 9/i.
  Copies: C^2 (presentation copy from the author).
NOTES: There was a 'third' (=second) edition of *Dorando* (Edinburgh, printed for J. Wilkie, London; sold also by Drummond, Edinburgh, and by all the booksellers in Scotland, 1767), but it appears not to have been printed at the Foulis Press.

1767   Somerset, Edward, Marquis of Worcester, **470**
                                  A Century of Inventions

VARIANT: 'Dickson' issue:
  Formula: (*The* 'Dickson' *title-page is a cancel*: a1 *was removed and replaced by* π^2, π1 *half-title*, π2 *title-page: copy at MEL reported by B. J. McMullin*).

1768   Boswell, James, *An Account of Corsica* **473**

FORMULA: (D2 *is also a cancel in some copies, the cancellans having been printed not at the Foulis Press but probably at Edinburgh by Neill & Co. (see R. H. Carnie in* The Book Collector, *26(1977)186–9).*)

1768   Gray, Thomas, *Poems* **475**

VARIANTS: There does appear to have been an issue of intermediate quality, as suggested by *BQ*. Copies at MEL and McMaster University Library are on a medium-quality paper, marks 8/i, with '*' signatures throughout (B. J. McMullin in *The Book Collector*, 28(1979)575–6).
NOTES: See R. H. Carnie, 'The letters of Robert Foulis to James Beattie', *The Bibliothek*, 9(1978)33–46.

477A Le Sage, Alain René, *The Devil upon Two*   1768
Sticks (Le Diable Boiteux), E

LE | *Diable Boiteux*: | OR, THE | DEVIL | UPON | TWO STICKS. | Tranſlated from the French of | MONSIEUR LE SAGE, | Author of the Adventures of GIL BLAS. | GLASGOW: | PRINTED BY R. AND A. FOULIS, | M.DCC.LXVIII.

FORMULA: Pot 12° in sixes: π^4 A–2B^6.

PAPER: Medium-poor quality; marks 1/v.

TYPE: RSP 1.

NOTES: Probably the book advertised in No. 548 (Milton, 1772) as printed by R. and A. Foulis 'in ſmall 12mo'.

    Prices: Wholesale 'p[ot]. 12mo. common', 9*d.* (*BQ* 9). Retail: 1*s.* 6*d.* (*CP* 11, specifying 12°, which sounds like fine paper). There may have been two issues.

    Stock in 1777: common 8 copies (*BQ* 9).

COPIES: E.

481A Ramsay, Allan, *The Gentle Shepherd*   1768

THE | GENTLE | SHEPHERD: | A SCOTS | PASTORAL | COMEDY. | BY | ALLAN RAMSAY. | GLASGOW: | PRINTED BY ROBERT & ANDREW FOULIS, | M.DCC.LXVIII. | *

FORMULA: [? Foolscap] 8°: A–F^8 G^4 H^2 (H2 *advertisements*).

    Press-figures: '2' on B1, G1. '3' on F1.

PAPER: Poor quality; no marks.

TYPE: RLP 1 RSP 1.

COPIES: E.

482 Ramsay, Allan, *The Tea-table Miscellany*   1768

VARIANT: Copy reported by William Poole (Catalogue 6, 1982, item 52) with '*' signatures in Vol. II, O–U.

483 Shenstone, William, *Select Works*   1768

VARIANT: Issue on common paper:
    Formula: Without '*' signatures.
    Paper: Medium-poor quality; marks 1/?.
    Copies: Ian Grant.

1769   Butler, Samuel, *Hudibras* **485**

VARIANTS: B. J. McMullin reports copies with '†' signatures that are printed on 1/v paper.

1769   Cicero, *Pro Marcello* and *Pro Ligario*, L **486**

VARIANT: Issue on inferior paper, [? size] 8°:
Formula: (*Without* '†' *signatures.*)
Paper: Poor quality; no marks.
Copies: E.

1769, 1770   Thom, William, *The happiness of* **494A,**
Dead Clergymen and *A Vindication of* **516A**
Doctor Tail

NOTES: These two books have the imprint 'Glasgow: Typis Academicis', but appear on typographical grounds not to be Foulis Press books.

1769   Thomson, James, *The Seasons* **495**

FORMULA: There is a copy at Aberystwyth, College of Librarianship Library, (reported by L. J. Harris) that is signed '†' on K1, and has the press figure '3' on a4^v.

1769   Thomson, James, *The Seasons* (another **496**
edition)

VARIANT: Issue on better-quality paper:
Formula: (*Signed* '†' *on* $1.)
Paper: Medium quality; marks 1/vii.
Copies: G^2.

1770   Addison, Joseph, *Poems on Several Occasions* **499**

VARIANT: Issue on better quality paper, Pot 12°:
Formula: (*Signed* '†' *on* A–Q $1.)
Press-figures (*both* issues): '1' also on D1 E1.
Paper: Medium quality; marks 1/v.
Copies: Brian Gerrard (who supplied this description).

502 [Anon.], *A Compend of Physics* 1770

TITLE-PAGE: [*Line* 9 *should read* 'CADEL', *not* 'CADEL'.]
NOTES: Attributed to John Anderson.

503 Dryden, John, *Original Poems* 1770

FORMULA: Vol. II: (*For* 'π^4' *read* 'a^4'; *for* 'Y^4' *read* 'Y^2'; S2 *signed* 'S3'.)
VARIANT: Issue on (?) better-quality paper:
  Formula: (*Signed* '†' *on* $1 *throughout* (*the copy reported lacking Vol.* IIπ1).)
  Paper: Medium-poor quality; marks 1/v, 3/?v, 3/crown, 3/LO in lozenge.
  Copies: Monash University Library (reported by B. J. McMullin in *The Book Collector*, 28(1979)576).

505 Foulis, Robert and Andrew, *Books printed* 1770
by R. and A. Foulis

NOTES: Amongst the papers of Andrew Stuart, W.S. M.P. (d. 1801) in E is a manuscript 'A List of Books printed by Robt & And^w Foulis with the prices unbound.' (E MS. 8325, ff. 91a–b, presented in 1961 by Madam H. Stuart-Stevenson.) Dating probably from 1770, it is very similar to 505 but is not copied from it.

506 Gay, John, *Poems on Several Occasions* 1770

TITLE-PAGE: [*Line* 6, *for* 'GAY,' *read* 'GAY.'.]
VARIANT: Issue on better-quality paper, Pot 12°:
  Formula: (*Signed* '†' *on* $1.)
  Paper: Medium-good quality; marks 3/'IO' in a crowned lozenge, 1/v.
  Copies: Brian Gerrard (who supplied this description).

509 [Anon.], *Military Instructions for Officers* 1770

MILITARY INSTRUCTIONS | FOR | OFFICERS | DETACHED IN THE FIELD: | CONTAINING | A SCHEME | FOR FORMING | A CORPS OF A PARTISAN. | ILLUS TRATED WITH | P L A N S of the M A N Œ U V R E S | Neceſſary in carrying on the PETITE GUERRE. | [*quotation*, 1 *line*] | [*plain rule*,

69] By an OFFICER. | [*plain double rule*, 68] | LONDON: | Sold by Meffrs. D.WILSON; | And T.CADELL, Succeffor to Mr. MILLAR; | in the Strand: | T.PAYNE, at the Mews-Gate: | And by Meffrs. FOULIS, Glasgow. | M.DCC.LXX. | †

formula: Foolscap 8°: π^2 A–R^8 (*signed* '†' *on* $1).

Press-figures: '3' on A4^r C1 D1 E1 G1 I1 L1 N1, '1' on F1 H1 K1 M1 O1 P1 Q1 R1. Twelve folding plates, variously placed.

paper: Medium-good quality; marks 4/v.

type: RP 3.

variant: Issue on (?) another quality of paper:
Formula: (*Without* '†' *signatures*). Press-figure '3' on π2^r and B1, but not on A4^r.
Paper: no apparent difference.

copies: With '†' signatures, E; without '†' signatures, Glasgow, Baillie's Library.

1770   Milton, John, *Paradise Lost* **510**

notes: See R. H. Carnie, 'The letters of Robert Foulis to James Beattie', *The Bibliothek*, 9(1978)33–46. There may have been printed Proposals for this book in 1769 (loc. cit. 37).

1770   Montgomery Family. *Memorables of the* **511**
                                        Montgomeries

notes: Brian Gerrard has a copy of an early nineteenth-century type-facsimile of this book, complete with Foulis imprint dated 1770.

1770   Shenstone, William, *Select Works* **515**

variant: Issue with '†' signatures, recorded in William Poole's Catalogue 8 (1983), item 334.

1770   Thom, William, *A Vindication of Doctor Tail* **516A**

See entry 494A.

517 Waller, Edmund, *Poems on Several Occasions*　　　1770

TITLE-PAGE: ['SEVERAL | OCCASIONS;' (*two lines, not one*).]
VARIANT: Issue on better-quality paper, Pot 12°:
　Formula: (*Signed* '†' *on* $1; Q2, R2, *and* T3 *unsigned*.)
　Press-figures: '1' on B1 E1 . . . M1 O1 P1 S1 U1 . . . Y1; '2' on R1;
'3' on N1 T1.
　Paper: Medium-quality; marks 1/v.
　Copies: Brian Gerrard (who supplied this description).

521 Cervantes Saavedra, Miguel de, *Don Quixote*, E　　　1771

TITLE-PAGES: Vols. I-IV: [*Line* 11, *for* 'a new' *read* 'a-new'.] Vols. II,
IV: [*Penultimate line, for* 'FOULIS' *read* 'FOULIS,'.]
FORMULA: *Plates*: There was also a plate for Vol. I, with a direction
for placing at Vol. I p. 220.
COPIES: McMaster University (described by B. J. McMullin).

522 Collins, William, *Poetical Works*, with　　　1771
　　　 Hammond, James, *Elegies*

VARIANT: Issue on inferior paper, Pot 12°:
　Formula: (*Without* '†' *signatures*.)
　Paper: Medium-poor quality; marks 1/iv, 1/v.
　Copies: Brian Gerrard (who supplied this description).

529 Millar, John, *Lectures on Government*　　　1771

A | COURSE | OF | LECTURES | ON | GOVERNMENT; |
GIVEN ANNUALLY IN THE | UNIVERSITY. | GLASGOW,
M.DCC.LXXI.
FORMULA: Foolscap 8° in fours: A^4.
PAPER: Medium-good quality; marks 4/?.
TYPE: RE3, RSP2.
NOTES: Without the Foulis Press imprint, but certainly printed
there.
COPIES: O.

531 Milton, John, *Paradise Lost*　　　1771

FORMULA: Vol. II: (*For* '$P^6(-P_5, P6)$' *read* 'P^4'.)

1771 Prior, Matthew, *Poems on Several Occasions* **532**

VARIANT: Issue on inferior paper, Pot 12°:
Formula: (*without* '†' *signatures*).
Paper: Medium-poor quality; marks 1/v.
Copies: MEL (noted by B. J. McMullin in *The Book Collector*, 28(1979)576).

1771 Storer, John, *De Angine Maligna*, L **534**

TITLE-PAGE: [*Line* 7, *for* '*Cancelarii*' *read* '*Cancellarii*'.]

1772 Aird, John, *De Dysenteria* **536A**

DISSERTATIO MEDICA | INAUGURALIS | DE | DYSEN
TERIA: | [9 *lines*] | PRO GRADU DOCTORIS, | SUMMISQUE
IN MEDICINA HONORIBUS ET PRIVILEGIIS | RITE AC
LEGITIME CONSEQUENDIS; | *Eruditorum examini fubjicit* |
JOANNES AIRD, *Britannus*, | AD DIEM XXV, JUNII, HORA 1ma P.M. |
LOCOQUE SOLITO. | GLASGUAE: | IN AEDIBUS ACADE
MICIS | EXCUDEBANT ROBERTUS ET ANDREAS
FOULIS, | ACADEMIAE TYPOGRAPHI | M.DCC.LXXII.
FORMULA: Demy 8° in fours: π^2 A–E^4 (C2 signed 'C3'; E4 *blank*).
PAPER: Good quality; marks 7/?.
TYPE: RE 4 (apparently its earliest appearance at the Foulis Press).
COPIES: G^2.

1772 Bonarelli della Rovere, C. Guidobaldo de, **537**
Filli di Sciro, I

TITLE-PAGE: [*line* 6, *for* 'GUIDOBALDO' *read* 'GUIDUBALDO'.]
VARIANT: Issue on inferior paper, Pot 8°:
Paper: Poor quality; marks 1/iv.
Copies: Brian Gerrard (who supplied this description).

1772 Cicero, *Orationes Selectæ*, L **539**

VARIANT: Issue on inferior paper, [? size] 8°:
Title-page: [*Line* 4, *for* 'ORATIONES' *read* 'ORATIONES.'.]
Formula: (*The first gathering is* π^2, (π1 *half-title*).)
Paper: Medium-poor quality; no marks.
Copies: E.

542 Pope's Homer, *Odyssey*, E   1772

FORMULA: Vol. I: (*Should end* 'P²'.)

546 Hutcheson, Francis, *A Short Introduction to*   1772
Moral Philosophy

TITLE-PAGES: [*Both vols., line* 7, *for* 'ETHICKS' *read* 'ETHICS'.]
FORMULA: Vol. II: (*For* 'A⁴' *read* 'A²'; *the other two leaves were probably
Vol.* I M3.4 (*information from B. J. McMullin*).)

546A Leader, Henry, *De Origine ac Natura Dysenteriae*,   1772
L

OBSERVATIONES QUAEDAM | INAUGURALES | DE | ORI
GINE AC NATURA | DYSENTERIAE, | ET | USU EVACUAN
TIUM | IN ILLA CURANDA. | [8 *lines*] | PRO GRADU DOC
TORIS, | SUMMISQUE IN MEDICINA HONORIBUS ET
PRIVILEGIIS | RITE AC LEGITIME CONSEQUENDIS; |
Eruditorum examini fubjicit | HENRICUS LEADER, A.M. | AB
INSULA OCCIDENTALI, BARBADOS. | AD DIEM XIV. OCTOB
RIS, | HORA MERIDIANA, LOCO SOLITO. | GLASGUAE:
| IN AEDIBUS ACADEMICIS | EXCUDEBANT ROBERTUS
ET ANDREAS FOULIS, | ACADEMIAE TYPOGRAPHI |
M.DCC.LXXII.

FORMULA: Medium 8° in fours: π² A–D⁴.
PAPER: Good quality; marks 7/J WHATMAN.
TYPE: RLP 1.
COPIES: G².

547 Le Sage, Alain René, *The Devil upon Two*   by 1772
Sticks (Le Diable Boiteux), E

See entries 384A (1760) and 477A (1768).

548 Milton, John, *Paradise Regained, etc.*   1772

VARIANT: Issue on inferior paper, Pot 12°:
  Formula: (*without* '†' *signatures*).
  Paper: Medium-poor quality; marks 1/iv.
  Copies: MEL (noted by B. J. McMullin in *The Book Collector*,
  28(1979)576).

1773   Augustine of Hippo, St, *Meditations, etc.*, E **550**

VARIANT: Issue on better-quality paper, Foolscap 8°:
Formula: *Press-figures*: add ' 1 ' on E1.
Paper: Medium-quality; marks 5/ii, 4/vii.
Copies: Brian Gerrard (who supplied this description).

1773   Gray, Thomas, *Poems* (another edition) **555**

VARIANT: Issue on inferior paper, Pot 12°:
Formula: (*Without* '*' *signatures*.)
Paper: Poor quality; marks 1/vii.
Copies: Brian Gerrard (who supplied this description).

1773   Pope, Alexander, *Poetical Works* **560**

FORMULA: William Poole's Catalogue 8 (1983), item 338, reports a
copy with four frontispieces.

1774   Burrow, Edward, *A New and Compleat Book* **563**
of Rates

NOTES: Proofs of what appears to be part of the projected volume 2
are in L^{30} (Goldsmith's Library), comprising 44 pages of a reprint
of a seventeenth-century Book of Rates, and matching 563 in
typography and paper. The first page reads: 'THE | RATES | OF |
HIS MAJESTIES CUSTOMES, | [11 *lines*] | Edinburgh, printed
by ANDREW ANDERSON, Anno Dom. 1670. | Cum Privilegio. | VOL.
II. †'

1774   Swift, Jonathan, *Poems* **571**

VARIANT: Issue on inferior paper, Pot 12°:
Title-page: [*Vol.* 1 *also omits* 'PRINTERS TO THE
UNIVERSITY,.]
Formula: (*without* '§' *signatures*).
Paper: Medium-poor quality; marks 1/v, 1/PPM.
Copies: MEL (noted by B. J. McMullin in *The Book Collector*,
28(1979)576).

574A Thomson, James, *Poems* 1774

POEMS | BY | JAMES THOMSON. | VIZ. | BRITANNIA, | TO THE MEMORY OF LORD TALBOT, | THE CASTLE OF INDOLENCE, | AND | LESSER POEMS: | WITH | ALFRED, A MASQUE, | BY | Mr. THOMSON AND Mr. MALLET. | GLAS GOW: | PRINTED BY ROBERT AND ANDREW FOULIS, | PRINTERS TO THE UNIVERSITY, | M.DCC.LXXIV. | †

FORMULA: Pot 12° in sixes: π^2 A–N^6 O^2 (*signed* '†' *on* π2 *and* A–O $1). *Press-figures*: '1' on D1 G1 L1 M1 N1 O1.

PAPER: Medium-good quality; marks 1/W.

TYPE: RB 2.

VARIANT: Issue on inferior paper, Pot 12°:
Formula: (*Without* '†' *signatures*.)
Press-figures: '1' on D1 G1 K1 . . . O1.
Paper: Medium-poor quality; marks 1/vii.

COPIES: G^2, G^4 (fine); Brian Gerrard (common, description supplied by Mr Gerrard).

575 Addison, Joseph, *Poems upon Several* 1775
Occasions

VARIANT: Issue on common paper:
Formula: (*Without* '†' *signatures*.)
Paper: Medium-poor quality; marks 1/PPM; size of sheet 14¾ × 12½ in.

COPIES: G^2.

576 Akenside, Mark, *The Pleasures of Imagination* 1775

VARIANT: Issue on inferior paper, Pot 12°:
Formula: (*Without* '†' *signatures except on* b1.)
Paper: Medium-poor quality; marks 1/iv, 1/v.
Copies: Brian Gerrard (who supplied this description).

577A Blair, John, *De Somno et Vigilia* 1775

TENTAMEN PHYSIOLOGICUM | INAUGURALE | DE | SOMNO ET VIGILIA: | [8 *lines*] | PRO GRADU DOCTOR ATUS, | SUMMISQUE IN MEDICINA HONORIBUS ET PRIVILEGIIS | RITE AC LEGITIME CONSEQUENDIS; | Eruditorum examini fubjicit | JOHANNES BLAIR, HIBERNUS. | AD DIEM VIII JUNII, HORA XII, MERIDIANA, | LOCO

QUE SOLITO. | GLASGUAE: | IN AEDIBUS ACADEM
ICIS | EXCUDEBANT ROBERTUS ET ANDREAS FOULIS, |
ACADEMIAE TYPOGRAPHI, | M.DCC.LXXV.

FORMULA: Demy 8° in fours: π^2 A–C^4 D^2.

PAPER: Medium-good quality; marks 7/ii.

TYPE: RSP2.

COPIES: Brian Gerrard; description by John Stephens.

1775   Garth, Sir Samuel, *Poetical Works* **585**

VARIANT: Issue on inferior paper, Pot 12°:
  Formula: (*Without* '†', '§' *signatures; with press figure* '1' *on* A6^v).
  Paper: Medium-poor quality; marks 1/vii, 1/v.
  Copies: MEL (noted by B.J. McMullin in *The Book Collector*,
28(1979)576).

1775   Langhorne, John, *De Argento Vivo* **585A**

DISSERTATIO | CHEMICO-MEDICA | INAUGURALIS | DE
| ARGENTO VIVO. | [8 *lines*] | PRO GRADU DOCTORIS, |
SUMMISQUE IN MEDICINA HONORIBUS ET PRI
VILEGIIS | RITE AC LEGITIME CONSEQUENDIS; | Erudi
torum examini fubjicit | JOANNES LANGHORNE. | GLAS
GUAE: | IN AEDIBUS ACADEMICIS | EXCUDEBANT
ROBERTUS ET ANDREAS FOULIS, | ACADEMIAE TYPO
GRAPHI | M.DCC.LXXV.

FORMULA: Demy 8° in fours: π1 A–I^4 K1.

PAPER: Good quality; marks 7/?ii.

TYPE: RE 3.

COPIES: G^2.

1775   Richardson, William, *Epithalamium* **589**

TITLE-PAGE: [*Line 7 is also found with the variant spelling* 'HONOR
ABLE'.]

1775   Shenstone, William, *Select Works* **590**

VARIANT: Issue on inferior paper, Pot 12°:
  Formula: (*Without* '§' *signatures*.)
  Paper: Medium-poor quality; marks 1/PPM.
COPIES: Brian Gerrard (who supplied this description).

595 Foulis, Robert, *A Catalogue of Pictures*   1776

FORMULA: Vol. I: [±a2.]

600 Simson, Robert, *Works*, L   1776

COLOPHON: (*on* ²E2ʳ) GLASGUAE: | IN AEDIBUS ACADE
MICIS, | EXCUDEBANT ROBERTUS ET ANDREAS FOUL
IS, | ACADEMIAE TYPOGRAPHI, | M.DCC.LXXIV.

603 Dryden, John, *Fables, Ancient and Modern, etc.*   1776

TITLE-PAGE: ['†' *is sometimes on a separate line in vol. I as well as in vol.*
II.]
FORMULA: Vol. I: (*signed* 'VOL. I.' *on* B C E–I L $1.)

604 Gay, John, *Poems on Several Occasions*   1776

NOTE: When the original entry was made only mixed copies of this
book had been seen, Vol. I being on a medium-quality Pot paper
without '†' signatures, and Vol. II on a medium-quality Pot paper
with '†' signatures. Now Brian Gerrard describes a copy with '†'
signatures in both volumes, and G² has two copies without '†'
signatures in both volumes.

VARIANTS: (1) With '†' signatures:
Formula: (*Signed* '†' *on* $1 *except for the title-page of* Vol. I.)
Paper: Medium quality; marks 1/v, 3/v.
(2) Without '†' signatures:
Formula: (*Without* '†' *signatures*.)
Paper: Medium quality; marks 1/PPM, 1/iv.
Copies: See NOTE above.

605A Steele, Sir Richard, *The Lying Lover*   1776

THE | LYING LOVER: | OR, THE | LADIES FRIENDSHIP. |
A | COMEDY. | WRITTEN BY | SIR RICHARD STEELE. |
[*quotation, 1 line*] | GLASGOW: | PRINTED BY ROBERT & ANDREW
FOULIS | M.DCC.LXXVI.

FORMULA: Foolscap 8° in fours: a⁴ B² A–K⁴ L² (*signed* '†' *on* $1
A–B, D–I).
Press-figures: '3' on A1.
PAPER: Medium quality; marks 5/?, size of sheet 15¾ × 12½ in.
TYPE: RLP 1.
COPIES: E.

THE FOULIS PRESS

1777 Aeschylus, *Choephoræ*. G and L (another **608A**
edition)

TITLE-PAGE: [*As no. 608, except that* 'EX EDITIONE STAN
LEIANA' *is omitted, and that the last line reads* 'M.DCC.LXXVII.']
FORMULA: [? Demy] 8°: A–G⁸ H1 (A1 half-title).
PAPER: Medium-good quality, wove; marks 'WC & Cᵒ', and no
marks.
TYPE: GGP, RSP 1; Greek and Latin on facing pages.
COPIES: Ian Grant.

1777 Anacreon, *Odes*, with Sappho and Alcaeus, **610**
Remains, G and L

VARIANT: Issue in foolscap 8° in fours:
Formula: (*signed* '†' *on* $1 *except* E1, N1).
Press figures: as Post 8°.
Paper: Medium quality; marks 4/vii, 4/SR.
Copies: Brian Gerrard.

by 1777 Cicero, *De Oratore*, L **611**

See entries 101–106 (1748–9), pp. 412–13.

by 1777 Cooper, Anthony Ashley, Lord Shaftesbury, **613**
The Moralists

This is a separate issue of part of No. 30 (1743), q.v. p. 406.

1777 Gray, Thomas, *Poems* **618,**
1777 Lyttelton, George, Baron, *Poems* **620**

VARIANTS: Copies of each of these two books at G² are on common
paper, bound together, with the prelims transposed:
Formula: (*Without* '†' *signatures*.)
Paper: Medium-poor quality; marks 1/?.
Copies: G².

by 1777 Lovell, John, *A funeral Oration occasioned* **619**
by the Death of Peter Faneuil

Renumbered 36A (1743).

620 Lyttelton, George, Baron, *Poems*   1777

See No. 618, Addenda.

622A Millar, John, *Heads of the Lectures*   1777
on the Law of Scotland

HEADS | OF THE | LECTURES | ON THE | LAW of SCOT
LAND, | IN THE | UNIVERSITY of GLASGOW, | M DCC
LXXVII. | PRINTED BY ANDREW FOULIS.

FORMULA: Foolscap 8° in fours: A–C⁴.

PAPER: Medium-good quality; marks 3/v.

TYPE: RSP 1, RLP 1.

COPIES: E.

626A Parnell, Thomas, *Poems on Several*   1777
Occasions

POEMS | ON | SEVERAL OCCASIONS; | WRITTEN BY | DR.
THOMAS PARNELL, | LATE ARCH-DEACON of
CLOGHER: | AND PUBLISHED BY | MR. POPE. |
ENLARGED WITH VARIATIONS AND POEMS. | [*quotation, 2
lines*] | GLASGOW: | PRINTED BY ANDREW FOULIS, |
M.DCC.LXXVII.

FORMULA: Pot 12° in sixes: π^4 A–L⁶ M² (π1 *blank*)
   Press-figures: '1' on A1 C1 D1 F1 ... I1 L1 M1, '3' on E1

PAPER: Medium quality; marks 1/PPM.

TYPE: RB 2.

VARIANT: Issue on another paper, Pot 12°:
   Formula: (*Signed* '†' *on* $1.)
   Paper: Medium quality; marks 1/vii, 3/v.

COPIES: E (without '†' signatures), Brian Gerrard (with '†' signatures, description supplied by Mr Gerrard).

627 Sallust, *Works*, L   1777

VARIANTS: Issue in Foolscap 8°:
   Paper: William Poole's Catalogue 8 (1983), item 342, reports a
copy with marks 4.

1777   Shenstone, William, *Select Works* **628A**

THE | SELECT | WORKS, | IN | VERSE AND PROSE, | OF | WILLIAM SHENSTONE, | ESQUIRE. | THE FOURTH EDI TION. | GLASGOW: | PRINTED BY ANDREW FOULIS, | M.DCC.LXXVII.

FORMULA: Pot $12°$ in sixes: a^4 $A-L^6$ M^2 (E_3 *signed* 'C_3').

   Press-figures: '1' on A4 E3 F1 G6 H1 I3 L4, '3' on B1 D3

PAPER: Medium quality; marks 1/PPM.

TYPE: RB 2.

COPIES: E.

by 1777   Voltaire, *The History of Charles XII*, E **631**

Entry renumbered 278A (1754).

1778   Millar, John, *Lectures on Government* **636A**

A | COURSE | OF | LECTURES | ON | GOVERNMENT; | GIVEN ANNUALLY IN THE | UNIVERSITY. | GLASGOW, M.DCC.LXXVIII.

FORMULA: [? Foolscap] $8°$ in fours: A^4.

PAPER: Medium-good quality; no marks seen.

TYPE: RP 3, RSP 1.

COPIES: E.

1778   Virgil, *Works*, L **639**

FORMULA: Vol. II: ($\pm$3y1 *or* 3y2).

1779   Aeschines, *Against Ctesiphon*, G and L **640**

VARIANT: Issue on common paper, [?] Foolscap $8°$ in fours:

   Paper: Medium-poor quality; no marks.

   Copies: Brian Gerrard.

1781   Euclid, *Elements I–VI, XI–XII and Data*, E **648**
                         with *Elements of Trigonometry*

NOTES: Brian Gerrard has a copy with the formula: A^8 ($\pm$A1) B–2I^8 $2K^4$. Mr Gerrard is uncertain of its status; he thinks that it is probably a Foulis book, but that it may be stereotyped.

649 Le Sage, Alain René, *Le Diable Boiteux*, F   1781

FORMULA: (*No full stop after* 'TOME' *in either volume.*)

652B Knox, Hugh, *The Transitory and evanescent*   1782
Nature of all Sublunary Things

THE TRANSITORY AND EVANESCENT NATURE OF | ALL SUBLUNARY THINGS. | BEING | THE SUBSTANCE OF | TWO DISCOURSES | DELIVERED IN THE PRESBY TERIAN CHURCH | OF ST. CROIX; | On the fixth and thirteenth days of January | 1782, from 1 Cor. vii. 31. | BY | HUGH KNOX, D.D. | PASTOR OF THAT CHURCH. | AND PUBLISHED | At the particular requeſt of one of the HEARERS. | GLAS GOW: | PRINTED BY ANDREW FOULIS, PRINTER | TO THE UNIVERSITY. | M.DCC.LXXXII.

FORMULA: Demy 8° in fours: A–I⁴.

PAPER: Medium-good quality; marks 7/J WHATMAN; size of sheet 21¼ × 16¾ in.

TYPE: RP 4.

COPIES: G⁴.

654 Anacreon, *Odes*, with Sappho and Alcaeus,   1783
Remains, G and L

FORMULA: There is now a copy at E, which collates: A^4 B–G^4 H^2 I–L^4 (*A*1 *half title*).

COPIES: E; the G⁴ copy is now missing.

658 Foulis, Andrew the younger, and Tilloch,   1783–4
Alexander, [Stereotyped books]

There is in the Bibliothèque Nationale, Paris, a two-leaf folio specimen of Cicero, *De senectute* (*Cato major*), which is described in contemporary notes as having been sterotyped by Foulis some time before May 1785. Set in RDP, two pages are printed on two separate leaves of paper watermarked 'I. TAYLOR', countermark 'GR'. A faint pencil note on the first leaf of the specimen reads 'Il y a 80 ans à Londres, fondue tout entière. Foulis Glascuuae.' A separate note attached reads '11 May 1785. Rapporté de Londres par M. Anisson. Pages fondues d'un seul jet par les Foulis de Glascow, par un procédé usité et connu depuis il y a 80 ans.' The cover sheet is endorsed 'Pages fondues d'un seul jet.' The period of eighty years before 1785 takes us back to 1705, when stereotype plates were in indeed being made in Holland by the Müller process (not of course in London, as the first note might seem to suggest). BN Rés.g.V.51, photocopy only seen, described by Jeanne Veyrin-Forrer in *Bulletin des bibliothèques de France*, 2S, 8(1966).

See also the addendum to Entry 673.

1783   Millar, John, *Lectures on Government* **658A**

A | COURSE | OF | LECTURES | ON | GOVERNMENT; | GIVEN ANNUALLY IN THE | UNIVERSITY. | GLASGOW: M.DCC.LXXXIII.

FORMULA: [? Foolscap] 8° in fours: A^4.
PAPER: Medium quality; ? marks.
TYPE: RP 3, RSP 1.
COPIES: G^2.

1783   Simpson, John, *De Catarrho*, L **663**

TITLE-PAGE: [*Line* 9 *up, for* 'JOANNIS' *read* 'JOANNES'.]

1783   Thomson, James, [Proposals for *The* **664A** *Seasons*, 1783]

HEADING: UNIVERSITY OF GLASGOW, Jan. 6th, 1783.
TEXT: A.FOULIS, Printer to the University of Glasgow, lately published an edition of VIRGIL, in two volumes folio, dedicated, by permission, to his Royal Highness GEORGE PRINCE OF WALES. From the approbation and encouragement which that work has received from the lovers of learning and of the arts, the Printer is induced to publish the following proposals, for an edition of THOMSON'S SEASONS, on the same plan.

Copies on the finest demy writing paper will be delivered to subscribers, in boards, at one guinea per copy.

The edition will be put to the press as soon as 200 are subscribed for.

The names of the encouragers are to be printed.

No money taken till the book is delivered.

FORMULA: [? Demy] 2°: A^2.
PAPER: Medium-good quality; marks 7/C TAYLOR.
TYPE: RDP.
COPIES: E.

665 Cicero, *De Officiis* 1784

VARIANT: Issue on large paper, [? Demy] 8°:
Formula: [2H2 *signed*.]
Paper: Medium-good quality, slightly blue; marks 7/C. TAYLOR,
I. TAYLOR.
Copies: Ian Grant, Brian Gerrard.

671A Robinson, James Templeton, *De Electricitate* 1784
Medica

TENTAMEN | PHILOSOPHICO-MEDICUM, | DE | ELEC
TRICITATE MEDICA. | [8 *lines*] | PRO GRADU DOCTOR
ATUS, | SUMMISQUE IN MEDICINA HONORIBUS ET
PRIVILEGIIS | RITE AC LEGITIME CONSEQUENDIS; | IN
COMITIIS | UNIVERSITATIS GLASGUENSIS, | Eruditorum
examini fubjicit | JACOBUS TEMPLETON ROBINSON, |
HIBERNUS. | SOC. PHYSIC. EDINEN. S. | AD DIEM XXX.
JULII, HORA PRIMA P.M. | LOCO SOLITO. | GLASGUAE:
| IN AEDIBUS ACADEMICIS, | EXCUDEBAT ANDREAS
FOULIS, | ACADEMIAE TYPOGRAPHUS. |
M.DCC.LXXXIV.
FORMULA: [? Demy] 8° in fours: π^2 A–D^4 E1.
PAPER: Medium-good quality; marks 7/?.
TYPE: RP 3.
COPIES: G^2.

672 Thomson, James, *Poetical Works* 1784

VARIANT: Separate issue of *The Seasons*, 1783

Title-page: THE | SEASONS. | BY | JAMES THOMSON. |
GLASGOW: | PRINTED BY ANDREW FOULIS, PRINTER |
TO THE UNIVERSITY. | M.DCC.LXXXIII. (Otherwise as no.
672, vol. 1)
Copies: E.

673 Virgil, *Works*, L 1784

VARIANT: Issue on fine paper, Demy 8°:
Formula: Press-figure: '3' *on* H1.
Paper: Good quality, white; marks 7/I TAYLOR, 7/C TAYLOR,
7/i.

Copies: Brian Gerrard (who supplied this description).

NOTES: A.G. Camus notes in *Histoire et Procédes du Polytypage et de la Stéréotypie*, Paris, An X, p. 37:

Le citoyen Reth . . . m'a communiqué les 216 premières pages d'un *Virgile* petit in-8° ou in-12, avec la note suivante: "Ce *Virgile* a été polytypé vers 1780, en metal ordinaire de caractères, par André Foulis, de Glascow, qui obtint, pour ses procédés, une patente ou privilége exclusif de quinze années." J'ai facilement reconnu les caractères de Foulis; j'ai aperçu les défauts qui se trouvent ordinairement dans les éditions stéréotypes, tels que des caractères déformés lors de la pression, et d'autres inégalement empreints: mais, dans le nombre des feuilles qui m'ont été remises, il n'y a ni frontispice ni avertissement; rien, par conséquent, qui fixe la date précise de l'édition, ni qui indique les procédés par lesquels elle a été exécutée. Je fais des recherches ultérieures sur cette édition: s'il m'arrive quelques renseignemens, je les publierai. Je remarque seulement que l'édition dont je parle est reconnoissable à une faute au premier mot du dix-huitième vers de la sixième éclogue, page 15, ligne 4. On lit *adgresti* au lieu de *adgressi*.

P.15, l.4 of No. 673 does read 'Adgresti', not 'Adgressi', and it is presumably this edition that was stereotyped; it is not clear whether the copies seen were printed from type or plates.

1785   Lynch, Samuel, *De Stimulantium Natura* **676A**

TRACTATUS PHYSICO-MEDICUS, | DE | STIMULAN TIUM NATURA, | IN CORPORA VIVENTIA AGENTIUM. | AUCTORE | SAMUELE LYNCH, M.D. | EX INSULA ANTI GUA. | GLASGUAE: | IN AEDIBUS ACADEMICIS, EX CUDEBAT | ANDREAS FOULIS, | ACADEMIAE TYPO GRAPHUS. | M.DCC.LXXXV.

FORMULA: [? Demy] 8° in fours: π^2 A–E^4.
PAPER: Medium quality; ? marks.
TYPE: RLP 1.
COPIES: G^2.

1785   McNab, Henry, *Heads of a Course of Elocution* **677**

TITLE-PAGE: [*Line* 11: *for* 'M'NAB' *read* 'M^{c}NAB'.]
FORMULA: Printing Demy 12° in sixes: π^2 A–2F^6 (2F6 *blank*).
TYPE: *add* RP4.
COPIES: G^2 (complete).

677A M'Pherson, Alexander, *De Framboesia* 1785

DISSERTATIO MEDICA INAUGURALIS | DE | FRAM
BOESIA. | [8 *lines*] | PRO GRADU DOCTORATUS, | SUMMIS
QUE IN MEDICINA HONORIBUS ET PRIVILEGIIS | RITE
AC LEGITIME CONSEQUENDIS; | IN COMITIIS |
UNIVERSITATIS GLASGUENSIS, | Eruditorum examini fub
jicit | ALEXANDER M'PHERSON, | ANTIGUENSIS, | SOC.
PHYSIC. EDINEN. SOC. | NEC NON | SOC. NATUR.
STUDIOS. ED. SOC. | [*quotation, 2 lines*] | AD DIEM XXIX.
DEC. HORA PRIMA P.M. LOCO SOLITO. | GLASGUAE: | IN
AEDIBUS ACADEMICIS, | EXCUDEBAT ANDREAS
FOULIS, | ACADEMIAE TYPOGRAPHUS. |
M.DCC.LXXXV.

FORMULA: Demy 8° in fours: π^4 A–D^4 (π1 *half-title*).
Corrigenda slip pasted on $\pi 4^v$.

PAPER: Good quality; marks 7/C *or* I TAYLOR.

TYPE: RE 3, RLP 2.

COPIES: E.

678 Pope, Alexander, *Poetical Works* 1785

FORMULA: Vol. II: (± 2U1.)

VARIANT: Separate issue of vol. III as *Select Poetical Works*:
  Title-page: SELECT | POETICAL WORKS | OF | ALEXAN
DER POPE, ESQ. | [*thick and thin rule*, 66] | MISCELLANIES, ON
VARIOUS SUBJECTS. | SATIRES AND EPISTLES OF
HORACE IMITATED. | THE DUNCIAD, WITH NOTES
AND INDEX. | [*thin and thick rule*, 67] | [*quotations, 7 lines*] | [*plain
double rule*, 146] | GLASGOW: | PRINTED BY ANDREW
FOULIS, PRINTER TO | THE UNIVERSITY. |
M.DCC.LXXXV. | [*thin and thick rule*, 43] | ONE GUINEA IN
BOARDS.
  (Otherwise as No. 678 vol. III.)
  Copies: E.

679A Carey, George Saville, *Poetical Efforts* 1786

POETICAL EFFORTS | BY | GEORGE SAVILLE CAREY.
[*copper-plate of poet in landscape, signed ' Ralfton fculp.', plate-mark* 52 ×
65] | *GLASGOW*: | Printed by A. FOULIS; and Sold by R. JAMESON, |
No. 227, Strand, London; and J. WHITEFIELD, | Newcaftle. |
M.DCC.LXXXVI. | ⟦Price Two Shillings.⟧

FORMULA: Medium 12° in sixes: π^2 $^2\pi_1$ A–E^6 F^4.
PAPER: Medium-poor quality; marks 9/B; size of sheet 21¾ ×
17¼ in.
TYPE: RLP 1, RP 2.
COPIES: E.

1786   MacNab, Henry, *A Plan of Reform in Instruction* **680**
                                        in English Schools

TITLE-PAGE: [Line 7, comma after 'ALSO'.]

1786   Maywood, Robert, *De Actione Mercurii in* **680B**
                                        Corpus Humanum

CONAMEN MEDICUM | DE | ACTIONE MERCURII | IN
CORPUS HUMANUM. | [8 *lines*] | PRO GRADU DOCTORIS, |
SUMMISQUE IN MEDICINA HONORIBUS ET PRI
VILEGIIS | RITE AC LEGITIME CONSEQUENDIS; | IN
COMITIIS | UNIVERSITATIS GLASGUENSIS, | Eruditorum
examini fubjicit | ROBERTUS MAYWOOD, A.M. | HIBER
NUS. | AD IPSAS IDUS JULII, HORA LOCOQUE SOLITIS. |
GLASGUAE: | IN AEDIBUS ACADEMICIS, | EXCUDEBAT
ANDREAS FOULIS. | M.DCC.LXXXVI.
FORMULA: [? Medium] 8° in fours: π^2 A–E^4.
PAPER: Medium quality; marks 9/?.
TYPE: RP 4.
COPIES: L.

1787   Hammond, James, *Poetical Works* **685**

FORMULA: (*There are cancels at* E1 *or* E2, D1 *or* D2, *and possibly* C2;
information from B. J. McMullin).

1787   Lyttelton, George, Baron, *Poetical Works* **686**

FORMULA: (*There are cancels in* D, S, R, *and* 2C; *information from*
B. J. McMullin).

686A Millar, John, *Lectures on Government* 1787

A | COURSE | OF | LECTURES | ON | GOVERNMENT; | GIVEN ANNUALLY IN THE | UNIVERSITY. | GLASGOW: M.DCC.LXXXVII.

FORMULA: [? size] 8° in fours: A^4.

PAPER: Medium-good quality; marks ?/C TAYLOR.

TYPE: RP 3, RSP 1.

COPIES: G^2.

686B Richardson, William, *Elegiac Verses* 1787

ELEGIAC VERSES, | OCCASIONED | BY | THE DEATH OF | DOCTOR IRVINE, | LECTURER IN CHYMISTRY | AND | MATERIA MEDICA, | IN THE | UNIVERSITY OF GLAS GOW. | BY | MR. RICHARDSON. | GLASGOW: | PRINTED BY ANDREW FOULIS, PRINTER TO THE | UNIVERSITY. | M.DCC.LXXXVII.

FORMULA: [? Demy] 8° in fours: A^4 (*A4 blank*).

PAPER: Medium quality; no marks; horizontal chain lines, so probably a quarter sheet of Double Demy.

TYPE: RLP 1.

COPIES: E.

688 Ramsay, Allan, *The Gentle Shepherd* 1788

PAPER: Good quality; marks 8/J WHATMAN; size of sheet 24 × 19 in., = Writing Royal. *Plates*: Dovecote (cf. Heawood 1233–4)/AUVERGNE 1742 T DUPUY FIN (cf. Heawood 1317). Reported from the McMaster University copy by B. J. McMullin.

688B Millar, Richard, *De Morbi Venerei Natura* 1789

DISSERTATIO MEDICA | INAUGURALIS, | DE | MORBI VENEREI NATURA, | ATQUE DE | FACULTATE PROPRIA, | QUA IN HUNC | MORBUM POLLEAT | ARGENTUM VIVUM, | QUAEDAM PROPONENS. | [8 *lines*] | PRO GRADU DOCTORIS, | SUMMISQUE IN MEDICINA HONORIBUS ET PRIVILEGIIS | RITE AC LEGITIME CONSEQUENDIS; | IN COMITIIS | UNIVERSITATIS GLASCUENSIS, | ERU DITORUM EXAMINI SUBJICIT | RICARDUS MILLAR, | EX VALLE GLOTTIANA | SCOTUS. | SOC. REG. MED.

EDIN. SOC. EXTRAORD. | NEC NON | SOC. NAT. STUD.
SOD. | Ad iv Id. Mart. hora locoque folitis. | [*quotation, 2 lines*] |
GLASCUAE: | IN AEDIBUS ACADEMICIS | EXCUDEBAT
ANDREAS FOULIS, | ACADEMIAE TYPOGRAPHUS, |
M.DCC.LXXXIX.

FORMULA: [? Demy] 8° in fours: π1 a² A–F⁴ G². Errata slip pasted
on a2ᵛ.

PAPER: Medium-poor quality; marks 9/–.

TYPE: RP 4.

COPIES: G⁴.

1790   Darbey, Robert, *De Moschi et Salis* **689B**
                                               Alk. Volat. Usu

DISSERTATIO MEDICA | QUAEDAM DE | MOSCHI ET
SALIS ALK. VOLAT. | USU, | IN FEBRE NERVOSA ET
GANGRAENA, | PROPONENS. | [*8 lines*] | PRO GRADU DOC
TORIS, | SUMMISQUE IN MEDICINA HONORIBUS ET
PRIVILEGIIS | RITE AC LEGITIME CONSEQUENDIS; | IN
COMITIIS | UNIVERSITATIS GLASGUENSIS, | ERUDI
TORUM EXAMINI SUBJICIT | ROBERTUS DARBEY, A.M.
| SOCIET. LIT. ET PHIL. MANCUNIENSIS SOCIUS. | Ad
diem i. Aprilis, hora locoque folitis. | GLASGUAE: | IN AEDIBUS
ACADEMICIS, | EXCUDEBAT ANDREAS FOULIS, | ACA
DEMIAE TYPOGRAPHUS | M.DCC.XC.

FORMULA: [? Royal] 8° in fours: π² A–C⁴ D1.

PAPER: Good quality; marks 8/?.

TYPE: RLP 2.

COPIES: G².

1790   Muir, John, *De Tetano* **690A**

NOTES: A copy of this medical dissertation at G² has the imprint 'Ex
ed. quam Glasguae in aedibus Academicis, excudebat Andreas
Foulis, Academiae Typographus. Apud Mundell et filium, Edin
burgi.' It is not itself a Foulis book, but the imprint suggests that
Andrew Foulis printed (or perhaps intended to print) an edition.

1790   Tacitus, *Agricola*, L **690B**

JULII AGRICOLAE | VITA, | ET | DE SITU, MORIBUS, ET |
POPULIS | GERMANIAE | LIBELLUS, SCRIPTORE | C. COR

NELIO TACITO. | EX EDITIONE | JACOBI GRONOVII | FIDELITER EXPRESSA. | GLASGUAE: | IN AEDIBUS ACADEMICIS | EXCUDEBAT ANDREAS FOULIS, | ACA DEMIAE TYPOGRAPHUS. | M.DCC.XC.

FORMULA: Pot 8° in fours: π1 A–H4 *I*1.

PAPER: Medium-poor quality; marks 3/?; size of sheet 15 × 12¼ in.

TYPE: RB 2.

COPIES: E.

690C Craufuird, G K , *De Submersis*　　　　　1791
Exsuscitandis

DISPUTATIO | PHYSICO-MEDICA, | DE | SUBMERSIS EXSUSCITANDIS. | [8 *lines*] | PRO GRADU DOCTORIS, | SUMMISQUE IN MEDICINA HONORIBUS ET PRIVILE-|GIIS RITE AC LEGITIME CONSEQUENDIS; | IN COM ITIIS | UNIVERSITATIS GLASGUENSIS, | ERUDITORUM EXAMINI SUBJICIT | G. K. CRAUFUIRD, A.M. | BRITAN NUS, | SOCIET. REG. PHYS. EDIN. SOD. HON. | Ad diem xxiv Junii, hora prima P.M. locoque folitis. | [*quotation, 4 lines*] | GLAS GUAE | IN AEDIBUS ACADEMICIS | EXCUDEBAT ANDREAS FOULIS, | ACADEMIAE TYPOGRAPHUS. | M.DCC.XCI.

FORMULA: [? Demy] 8° in fours: π² A–H⁴ (–H4; π1 *half-title*).

PAPER: Medium-good quality, wove; no marks.

TYPE: RSP 1.

COPIES: G².

690D Daniel, J M , *De Ophthalmia*　　　　　1791

DISPUTATIO MEDICA | INAUGURALIS | DE | OPHTHAL MIA. | [8 *lines*] | PRO GRADU DOCTORIS, | SUMMISQUE IN MEDICINA HONORIBUS ET PRIVILE-|GIIS RITE AC LEGITIME CONSEQUENDIS; | IN COMITIIS | UNIVERSI TATIS GLASGUENSIS, | ERUDITORUM EXAMINI SUB JICIT | J. M. DANIEL, A.M. | VIRGINIENSIS. | SOCIET. AMER. PHYSIC. | SOC. EXTRAORD. AC PRAESES ANNUUS. | Ad diem iv Octobris hora locoque folitis. | [*plain rule, 73*] | [*quotation, 2 lines*] | [*plain rule, 70*] | GLASGUAE: | IN AEDIBUS ACADEMICIS | EXCUDEBAT ANDREAS FOULIS, | ACADEMIAE TYPOGRAPHUS. | M.DCC.XCI.

FORMULA: [? Demy] 8° in fours: π² ²π² ³π1 A–C⁴ D² (π1 *half-title*; ²π, ³π *dedications*).

PAPER: Medium quality, wove; no marks; medium-good quality, laid, no marks.

TYPE: RSP 1.

COPIES: G^2.

1791   Langslow, Richard, *De Vitabis Variolosae* **692A**

TENTAMEN MEDICUM | INAUGURALE | QUASDAM | OBSERVATIONES EXPERIMENTAQUE | DE | VITABIS VARIOLOSAE, | IN STADIIS | MORBI DIVERSIS; | ET DE | USU MERCURII | AD MORBUM MITIGANDUM, | COM PREHENDENS: | [8 *lines*] | PRO GRADU DOCTORIS, | SUM MISQUE IN MEDICINA HONORIBUS ET PRIVILE-|GIIS RITE AC LEGITIME CONSEQUENDIS; | IN COMITIIS | UNIVERSITATIS GLASGUENSIS, | ERUDITORUM EXAMINI SUBJICIT | RICHARDUS LANGSLOW, A.M. | ANGLUS, | SOCIET. REG. MED. EDIN. SOD. | Ad diem xviii Maii, hora prima P.M. locoque folito. | GLASGUAE: | IN AEDI BUS ACADEMICIS | EXCUDEBAT ANDREAS FOULIS, | ACADEMIAE TYPOGRAPHUS. | M.DCC.XCI.

FORMULA: Royal 8° in fours: π^2 $^2\pi^2$ A–B^4.

PAPER: Good quality; marks 8/J WHATMAN.

TYPE: RSP 1.

COPIES: G^2.

1792   Caunce, William, *De Rheumatismo acuto* **692B**

TENTAMEN MEDICUM | INAUGURALE | DE | RHEUMA TISMO ACUTO. | [8 *lines*] | PRO GRADU DOCTORIS, | SUMMISQUE IN MEDICINA HONORIBUS ET PRIVILE-|GIIS RITE AC LEGITIME CONSEQUENDIS; | IN COM ITIIS | UNIVERSITATIS GLASGUENSIS, | ERUDITORUM EXAMINI SUBJICIT | GULIELMUS CAUNCE, A.M. | ANGLUS. | Ad diem xiv Maii hora locoque folitis. | [*quotation,* 1 *line*] | GLASGUAE: | IN AEDIBUS ACADEMICIS | EXCUDE BAT ANDREAS FOULIS, | ACADEMIAE TYPOGRAPHUS. | M.DCC.XCII.

FORMULA: [? Demy] 8° in fours: A1 B–E^4.

PAPER: Medium quality; no marks; with horizontal chain lines, so probably from half sheets of Double Demy.

TYPE: RP 4.

COPIES: G^2.

693B Winterbottom, T M , *De Morbo*   1792
Puerperali

DISSERTATIO MEDICA | DE | MORBO PUERPERALI. | [8 *lines*] | PRO GRADU DOCTORIS, | SUMMISQUE IN MEDI CINA HONORIBUS ET PRIVILE-|GIIS RITE AC LEGI TIME CONSEQUENDIS; | IN COMITIIS | UNIVERSITATIS GLASGUENSIS, | ERUDITORUM EXAMINI SUBJICIT | T.M. WINTERBOTTOM. A.M. | ANGLUS. | Ad diem vii Martii hora locoque folitis. | [*quotation, 4 lines*] | GLASGUAE: | IN AEDI BUS ACADEMICIS | EXCUDEBAT ANDREAS FOULIS, | ACADEMIAE TYPOGRAPHUS. | M.DCC.XCII.

FORMULA: [? Demy] 8° in fours: A^2 B–D^4 (A1 *half-title*, D4 *blank*).

PAPER: Medium quality; no marks; horizontal chain lines, so probably from half sheets of Double Demy.

TYPE: RSP 1.

COPIES: G^2.

694 Xenophon, *Anabasis*, G and L   1792

B. J. McMullin describes a copy of Vol. III in *Bibliographical Society of Australia and New Zealand Bulletin* 6(1982)77–8:

TITLE-PAGE: [*As vol.* II, *except line* 10 *is followed by a three-line quotation; line* 6 *up, for* 'II.' *read* 'III.'; *line* 2 *up, ends with a comma, not a full stop; last line reads* 'M, DCC, XCIII.']

FORMULA: (*Greek*:) π^2 A–P^4 Q^2; (*Latin*:) ^{2}A–H^4 (I1 *signed* 'H'; *signed* 'TOM. III. *on* $1).

PAPER: As Vol. II, but horizontal chain lines in Greek sigs. A and B only.

COPIES: Canberra (ANL).

695A Cumming, John, *De Pleuritide*   1793

TENTAMEN MEDICUM | INAUGURALE | DE | PLEURI TIDE. | [8 *lines*] | PRO GRADU DOCTORIS, | SUMMISQUE IN MEDICINA HONORIBUS ET PRIVILE-| GIIS RITE AC LEGITIME CONSEQUENDIS; | IN COMITIIS | UNIVERSI TATIS GLASGUENSIS, | ERUDITORUM EXAMINI SUB JICIT | JOANNES CUMMING, A.M. | MARYLANDINENSIS | SOCIET. REG. PHYS. EDIN. SOC. HON. | ET PRAESES ANNUUS | SOCIET. AMER. PHYS. EDIN. SOC. EXT. | ET PRAESES ANNUUS. | Ad diem XXII, Aprilis, hora locoque folitis. | [*quotation, 3 lines*] | GLASGUAE: | IN AEDIBUS ACADE-MICIS | EXCUDEBAT ANDREAS FOULIS | ACADEMIAE TYPOGRAPHUS. | MD.CC.XCIII.

FORMULA: [? Demy] 8° in fours: π^2 A–E^4 F^2 G1.

PAPER: Medium quality; marks 9/?.

TYPE: RE 4.

COPIES: G^2.

1794   Kinglake, Robert, *De Vitae Principio* **696A**

DISSERTATIO PHYSIOLOGICA | INAUGURALIS, | QUAEDAM DE | VITAE PRINCIPIO, | SANITATE ET MORBO | COMPLECTENS: | [*8 lines*] | PRO GRADU DOC TORIS, | SUMMISQUE IN MEDICINA HONORIBUS ET PRIVILE-|GIIS RITE AC LEGITIME CONSEQUENDIS; | IN COMITIIS | UNIVERSITATIS GLASGUENSIS, | ERUDI TORUM EXAMINI SUBJICIT | ROBERTUS KINGLAKE, A.M. | ANGLUS, | Societ. Reg. Med. necnon, Societ. Phyfic. Americ. Edin. Soc. | et Lycei Med. Lond. Sod. | Ad diem v. Junii, hora locoque folitis. | [*quotations, 4 lines*] | GLASGUAE: | IN AEDIBUS ACADEMICIS | EXCUDEBAT ANDREAS FOULIS | ACADEMIAE TYPOGRAPHUS. | M.DCC.XCIV.

FORMULA: [? Royal] 8° in fours: A^4 B–E^4 F^2.

PAPER: Good quality, wove; no marks.

TYPE: RSP 1.

COPIES: G^2.

1795   Aeschylus, *Tragedies*, G **699**

NOTES: See R. H. Carnie, 'Andrew Foulis the younger: some illustrative letters', *The Bibliothek*, 6(1972)93–104.

1796, '1794', 1806   Aeschylus, *Tragedies*, G and L **702**

VARIANT: 1806 issue in Post 8°:
   Paper: Medium good quality; marks 6/?.
   Copies: G^2.

1796   Ramsay, Allan, *The Gentle Shepherd* **703**

TITLE-PAGE: [*Line 6, 'ALLAN RAMSAY', ends with a full stop.*]

704 Euripides, *Tragedies*, G and L   1797

FORMULA: Vol. I: (*For* 'a²' *read* 'a²'.)

VARIANTS: MEL has a copy of vols. I–VI of the issue on large, inferior quality paper, (?Demy) 8°, 1797. All the title-pages are reset. Noted by B. J. McMullin in *The Book Collector*, 28(1979)576–7, who describes the paper in detail. See also R. H. Carnie, 'Andrew Foulis the younger: some illustrative letters', *The Bibliothek*, 6(1972)93–104.

704A Campbell, Alexander, *An Introduction to the History of Poetry in Scotland*, with *Sangs of the Lowlands of Scotland*   1798, 1799

AN | INTRODUCTION | TO THE | HISTORY OF POETRY | IN | SCOTLAND, | FROM THE BEGINNING OF THE THIR TEENTH CENTURY | DOWN TO THE PRESENT TIME; | TOGETHER WITH | A CONVERSATION ON SCOTISH SONG, | BY | ALEXANDER CAMPBELL, | AUTHOR OF ODES AND MISCELLANEOUS POEMS, &c. | TO WHICH ARE SUBJOINED, | SANGS OF THE LOWLANDS OF SCOT LAND, | CAREFULLY COMPARED WITH THE ORIGINAL EDITIONS, AND EMBELLISHED | WITH CHARACTERIS TIC DESIGNS, COMPOSED AND | ENGRAVED BY THE LATE | DAVID ALLAN, | HISTORICAL PAINTER. | EDIN BURGH: | SOLD BY ANDREW FOULIS, AT HIS SHOP, OPPOSITE THE TURF | COFFEE-HOUSE ST. ANDREW'S STREET. | M,DCC,XCVIII.

FORMULA: Medium 4°: π^4 A–$2Z^4$ $3A^2$ 3B1 ^{2}A–B^2 ($\pm$ B⁴; 2Y1 *signed* 'Y'; 3B1 *signed* 'Bb').

PAPER: π-2K (except B): medium quality wove; marks '1796', '1797'; B, 2L-²B: medium quality laid; same marks.

TYPE: ? RP 4, RB 2, RLP 1; movable music type on ²A–B. Possibly not printed at the Foulis Press.

COPIES: Ian Grant.

704B Campbell, Alexander, *Sangs of the Lowlands of Scotland*   1798, 1799

SANGS | OF THE | LOWLANDS OF SCOTLAND | CAREFULLY COMPARED WITH THE ORIGINAL EDI TIONS, | AND EMBELLISHED WITH | CHARACTERISTIC DESIGNS COMPOSED AND ENGRAVED | BY THE LATE |

DAVID ALLAN ESQ. | HISTORICAL PAINTER. | EDIN
BURGH: | PRINTED AND SOLD BY ANDREW FOULIS |
STRICHENS CLOSE HIGH-STREET. | M.DCC.XCIX.

FORMULA: Medium 4°: π1 A–2D⁴ 2E² 2F1.

PAPER: All except π1: Medium quality laid; marks '1797'; π1:
medium quality wove; marks '1796'.

TYPE: ? RE 4. Possibly not printed at the Foulis Press.

PLATES: Frontispiece by Weir and Bengosc; eight plates by David
Allan, variously placed.

VARIANT: Separate issues in Medium and [? Crown] 4° dated 1799:
Title-page: dated 'M.DCC.XCIX.'
Paper: Medium issue: Medium-poor quality, laid; mark '1797'.
[? Crown] issue: Medium quality, wove; marks 'WC&Co',
'1794'.

COPIES: Ian Grant (both issues).

n.d.   [Anon.], *A Hymn fit to be sung on days of* **706**
                                    Humiliation and Prayer

NOTES: Dated by David Foxon [174–?] (Foxon H421).

INDEX

Translators, and most editors, of books printed at the Foulis Press are indexed, but not the editors of the classical texts used by the Foulises. The additions and amendments (1986) are included in the index. **References are to page numbers, not to entry numbers.**

ABBREVIATIONS, general, 9; languages, 10; libraries, 10; paper (watermarks), 60; type, 32, 33–48, 60

ABÉLARD, Pierre, *Letters of the celebrated Abélard and Héloïse*, E (trs. Hughes, John; *with* POPE, Alexander, *Eloisa to Abelard*), 1751, 151

ADDISON, Joseph, *Cato, c.* 1745, 99, 407, 408; 1748, 118; 1746, 408; 1753, 179; 1765, 259 *Discourse on ancient and modern learning*, 1759, 226, 428; *Dramatic works* (title leaf), 1752, 168; *Drummer*, 1749, 130; 1751, 152; *Of the Christian religion*, 1753, 179, 421; *Poems on several occasions*, 1751, 151; 1770, 292, 437; 1775, 327, 444; *Remarks on several parts of Italy*, 1755, 192; *Rosamond, c.* 1749, 130; 1751, 152; 1758, 218

ADDISON, Joseph, *and* STEELE, Sir Richard, *The Tatler*, 1747–9, 118

ADDITIONS and amendments, 403–63

Ad Gulielmum Cumbriae ducem ode, L, *c.* 1748, 126

AESCHINES, *Against Ctesiphon*, G and L, 1779, 356, 449

AESCHYLUS, *Choephorae*, G and L, 1777, 345; 1777, another edition, 447; *Tragedies*, G and L, 1746, 106, 409; G, 1795, 386, 461; G and L, '1794', 1796, 388, 461; G and L, 1806, 388, 461

AESOP. *See* PHAEDRUS, *Aesop's Fables*

AIRD, John, *De dysenteria*, 1772, 441

À KEMPIS, Thomas. *See* THOMAS à Kempis, St

AKENSIDE, Mark, *Odes* (in *Select Poems*), 1783, 367; *Pleasures of Imagination*, 1771, 301; 1775, 328, 444; 1777, 345

ALCAEUS, *Remains*, G, 1750, 135; G, 1751, 152; G, 1757, 213; G, 1761, 238; G *and* L, 1770, 293; G *and* L, 1777, 346; G *and* L, 1783, 363; G *and* L, 1783 another ed., 363; G *and* L, 1792, 383

ALEMBERT, Jean le Rond d'. *See* D'ALEMBERT, Jean le Rond

ALLAN, David (artist, engraver, plate-publisher, bookseller; Edinburgh), 379, 389

A. M., *The state of religion in New England*, 1742, 80, 405; 2 *ed.*, 1742, 81, 405

AMORY, Thomas, *A dialogue on devotion after the manner of Xenophon*, 1749, 132

ANACREON, *Lyrics* (*with* SAPPHO, *Lyrics*), G and L, 1744, 91; *Odes* (*with* SAPPHO *and* ALCAEUS, *Remains*), G, 1750, 135; G, 1751, 152; G, 1757, 213, 426; G, 1761, 238; G *and* L, 1770, 293; G *and* L, 1777, 346, 447; G *and* L, 1783, 363; G *and* L, 1783, another ed., 363, 450; G *and* L, 1792, 383

ANDERSON, John, *A compend of experimental philosophy, and heads of lectures*, 1760, 234, 429; *Institutes of physics*, 1777, 346; 1795, 387; *Observations upon Roman antiquities*, 1800, 390

ANGUS, Alexander (bookseller; Aberdeen), 362

ANISSON-DUPERRON, E. A. J., and stereotype, 450

ANONYMOUS, *Ad Gulielmum Cumbriae ducem ode, c.* 1748, 126; *Compend of Physics*, 1767, 274; 1770, 294, 438; *Confession of faith*, 1765, 1766, 261; *Considerations upon a bankrupt law for*

Scotland, 1771, 304; *Dialogue on Devotion*, 1749, 132; *Essay on religion and morality*, 1707, 274; *Essay on the theory of agriculture*, 1760, 235; 1761, 235; *Extract of orders and regulations*, 1761, 240; *Flax-husbandman instructed*, 1756, 205; *Fragmenta grammatices Graecae*, n.d., 387; *French convert*, 1783–4, 366; *History of the feuds and conflicts among the clans*, 1764, 257; *History of Valentine and Orson*, 1783–1784, 366; *Hymn fit to be sung on days of humiliation and prayer*, n.d., 391, 463; *Military instructions for officers*, 1770, 297, 438; *Lady's religion*, 1748, 126; *Letter from a gentleman in England to his friend in New York*, 1775, 329; *Memorables of the Montgomeries*, 1770, 297; *Military instructions for forming a partisan*, by 1768, 282; *Modern farmer's guide*, 1768, 282; *Odes by a lady*, 1748, 126; *Plain Reasons for being a Christian*, by 1749, 131; *Series titulorum qui in pandectis continentur*, 1780, 359; *Sermon on early piety*, by 1777, 352; *Seven champions of Christendom*, 1783–4, 366; *Seven champions of the stage*, 1757, 426; *State of religion in New England*, 1742, 80; 2 ed., 1742, 81; *Succinct description of the microcosm, c.* 1765, 433; *True religion, a mystery*, 1746, 111; *Twelve Caesars*, 1783–4, 366; *Virtue's expostulation with the British poets*, 1757, 218; see OLD POEM

APOLLONIUS of Perga, *Plane loci*, L, 1749, 131, 414

ARCHIMEDES, *The sand reckoner* (with *The theorem of Eudoxus*), G, c. 1751, 153

ARGYLL, Duke of. See CAMPBELL, Archibald, 3rd Duke of Argyll

ARGYLL, Marquis of. See CAMPBELL, Archibald, Marquis of Argyll

ARISTOPHANES, *Clouds*, G and L, 1755, 193, 423; G and L, 1793, 384

ARISTOTLE, *Poetics*, G and L, 1745, 99, 407; see MOOR, James, *On the end of tragedy*

'ARISTOTLE', *De mundo*, G and L, 1745, 100

ARTHUR, Archibald, *Catalogus impressorum librorum in bibliotheca universitatis Glasguensis*, L, 1791, 382; L, 1791, another ed., 382

AUBERT de Vertot d'Aubeuf, René, *The History of the revolutions of* *Portugal*, E, 1758, 218

AUGUSTINE of Hippo St, *Meditations, etc.*, E (trs. Stanhope, George), 1773, 316, 443

AURELIUS Antoninus, Marcus, *Meditations*, G and L, 1744, 92; E (trs. Moor, James *and* Hutcheson, Francis), 1742, 75; 1749, 131, 414; 1752, 168; 1764, 255, 432

AUTHOR, printed for the. See FOULIS PRESS, printing for authors

BAILLIE, A. (engraver), 340

BAINE, John (typefounder), 32

BALFOUR, John (bookseller; Edinburgh), 51, 251, 255, 262, 263, 265, 274, 287, 294; see HAMILTON, Gavin *and* BALFOUR, John; HAMILTON, Gavin, BALFOUR, John and NEILL

Banishment of Poverty, The, in *The Speech of a Fife Laird, etc.*, 1751, 161

BANKS, Robert (bookseller; Stirling), 221

BARNARD, John, *A zeal for good works, a sermon*, 1742, 75

BARNARD, Sir John, *A present for an apprentice*, 1765, 260

BARNWELL, C.F., note on Archimedes, 153

BARR, James, *An easy introduction to Latin grammar*, 1763, 249

BARRY, John (bookseller; Glasgow), 287, 288, 289, 292, 295, 398

BASKERVILLE, John (typefounder), 42

Battle of Harlaw, The, 1748, 127

BAXTER, Daniel (bookseller; Glasgow), 257, 274, 282, 287, 288, 289, 292, 398

BAXTER, Richard, *A call to the unconverted*, Gaelic, 1750, 135

BEATTIE, James (editor of Gray), 280

BEAUVAIS, Jean-Baptiste de, *The funeral oration of Lewis XV*, E, 1775, 328

BECKET, Thomas (bookseller; London), 233, 234, 235; see MILLER, A., NOURSE, J., BECKET, T., and DE HONDT, P. A.

BELL, John, of Antermony, *Travels from St Petersburg*, 1763, 249, 432

BELL, John, *A system of English grammar*, 1769, 285

BELL, William (printer; Glasgow), 51

BELL (bookseller; Edinburgh). See KINCAID, Alexander, and BELL

BELLENDEN, John, *Virtue and vice; with* Dunbar, William, *The Thistle and the Rose*; 1750, 138

BELLOY, P.-L. B. de. *See* BUIRETTE de Belloy, Pierre-Laurent

BENNET, Benjamin, *The persecution and cruelty of the church of Rome*, 1746, 107

BERKELEY, George, *The querist*, and *A word to the wise*, 1751, 154

BIBLE, Old Testament, Psalms. Buchanan, George, *Paraphrasis psalmorum Davidis*, L, 1765, 260; Watts, Isaac, *The Psalms of David imitated*, by 1784, 373

BIBLE, New Testament, G, 1759, 226; L (*trs.* Castellion, Sébastien), 1758, 219; Callander, John, *Essay toward a literal English version*, 1779, 356

BIBLIOGRAPHICAL notation in the bibliography explained, 57–62

BINDING of Foulis Press books, 54–5

BLAIR, John, *De somno et vigilia*, 1775, 444

BLOCKS, printing, 49, 61

BOETHIUS, *De consolatione philosophiae*, L, 1751, 154

BOILEAU-DESPRÉAUX, Nicolas, *L'art poétique*, F, 1758, 219; E (*trs.* Soames, Sir William), 1755, 193, 423; *Le Lutrin*, E (*trs.* Rowe, Nicholas), 1752, 169; *Works*, F, 1759, 227

BOLINGBROKE, Lord. *See* SAINT JOHN, Henry, Lord Bolingbroke

BONARELLI della Rovere, C. Guidobaldo de, *Filli di sciro*, I, 1772, 310, 441

Book of the Foulis Exhibition, The, 1913, 13

BOOKSELLERS AND PRINTERS, Copyright controversy 1774, 323

BOOKSELLERS AND PRINTERS mentioned in imprints, etc. (*see* references under names):

Aberdeen: ANGUS, Alexander

Bath: FREDERICK, J.; LEAKE, J.

Bristol: CADELL, Thomas the elder

Edinburgh: ALLAN, David; BALFOUR, John; BELL; COCHRANE; CREECH, William; DICKSON, J.; DONALDSON, (?) Alexander; DRUMMOND, (?) William; FLEMING, Robert; GORDON, William; GRAYE, W.; HAMILTON, Gavin; KINCAID, Alexander; LAING, William; MUNDELL and son; MURRAY; NEILL; PATON, John; Ross (or ROSSE), John; SANDS,

William; SPOTISWOOD (or SPOTTISWOOD), James; YAIR, John

Glasgow: BARRY, John; BAXTER, Daniel; BELL, William; CARLILE, Alexander; CHAPMAN, Robert; CROSS, Robert; DUNCAN, Alexander; DUNCAN, James; DUNLOP; GILMOUR, John, and son; MILLER, Alexander; ORR, John; SHAWS, J. and W.; SIMSON, Matthew; SMITH, Robert; STALKER, Andrew; TILLOCH, Alexander; URIE, Robert; WILSON

Liverpool: FLEETWOOD, R.

London: BECKET, Thomas; BOWLES Carrington; BREMNER, D.; CADELL, Thomas the younger; DAVIES, T.; DE HONDT, P. A.; DILLY, Edward and Charles; DODSLEY, James; DURHAM, J.; EGERTON, T.; ELLIOTT, C.; ELMSLY, P.; GOSNELL, S.; HARDING, E.; HENDERSON, C.; JOHNSON, Joseph; LONGMAN, Thomas; MACKINLAY; MILLAR, Andrew; MILLER, A.; MURRAY, John; NOURSE, J.; OSTELL, T.; PAYNE, T.; SANDBY, William; SCOTT, John; TONSON, Jacob; WHITE, B. and I.; WILKIE, J.; WILSON, D.

Newcastle: CHARNLEY, William

Oxford: COOKE, Joseph; FLETCHER, James

Paris: DAVIDTS, Rombaut

Stirling: BANKS, Robert

Wigton, Cumberland: THOMLINSON

BOSSUET, Jacques-Bénigne, *An account of the edition of the Dauphine*, etc., E (*trs.* Phillips, J.T.), 1743, 82

BOSWELL, Alexander, of the Edinburgh Society, 209

BOSWELL, James, *An account of Corsica*, 1768, 278, 396, 399–400, 435; *Dorando*, 1767, 273, 396–8, 435; correspondence with Robert Foulis, 1767–8, 396–400

BOWERS, Fredson T., *Principles of bibliographical description*, 1949, 58

BOWLES, Carrington (bookseller; London), 279

BOYER, Abel (translator of Fénelon), 197

BOYSE, Samuel (translator of 'Cebes)', 137, 302

BREKELL, John, *Free and candid remarks on Mottershead's discourse of baptizing*, 1760, 234

BREMNER, D. (bookseller; London), 389

BUCHAN, Lord. *See* ERSKINE, David Steuart, 11th Earl of Buchan

BUCHANAN, George, *Francisci Valesii et Mariae Stuartae epithalamium*, L, *c.* 1745, 100; *Jepthes*, L, 1775, 329; *Paraphrasis psalmorum Davidis*, L, 1765, 260

BUCHANAN, William (engraver), 317

BUCKINGHAM, Duke of. *See* SHEFFIELD, John, 1st Duke of Buckingham

BUDGELL, Eustace (translator of Theophrastus), 90

BUIRETTE de Belloy, Pierre-Laurent, *La siège de Calais*, F, 1765, 261

BURNET, Gilbert, *A discourse of pastoral care*, 1762, 244; *Life of Rochester* (i.e. *Some passages of the life and death of Rochester*), 1741, 65, 403; 1752, 169; *Select Sermons*, 1742, 76; *A treatise concerning the truth of the Christian religion* with Locke, John, *A discourse on miracles*, 1743, 82; Preface to Scougal, 1751, 166; 1770, 299; translator of Lactantius, 1765, 263; 1766, 267; translator of St Thomas More, 1743, 91; 1762, 248

BURNET, Gilbert, son of the Bishop of Salisbury, and HUTCHESON, Francis, *Letters concerning the true foundation of virtue*, 1772, 310

BURNETT, James, of the Edinburgh Society, 209

BURROW, Edward, *A new and compleat book of rates*, 1774, 322, 443

BUSHE, Amyas, *Socrates*, 1762, 244

BUTLER, Joseph, *The analogy of religion*, 1764, 256; *Fifteen sermons*, 1759, 227

BUTLER, Samuel, *Hudibras*, 1747, 111; 1761, 239, 429; 1769, 286, 437; 1774, 323

CAESAR, *Works*, L, 1750, 136; 1750, another ed., 136, 415

CADELL, Thomas the elder (bookseller; Bristol), 249

CADELL, Thomas the younger (bookseller; London), 274, 287, 294, 328, 329, 330, 337

CALDWELL, John, *An impartial trial of the spirit, a sermon*, 1742, 76

CALLANDER, John, *Essay towards a literal English version of the New Testament*, 1779, 356; commentary on *Paradise Lost*, 145

CALLIMACHUS, *Hymns and Epigrams*, G, 1755, 194, 424

CAMPBELL, Alexander, *Introduction to the history of poetry in Scotland*, with *Sangs*, 1798–9, 462; *Sangs of the Lowlands of Scotland*, 1798–9, 462

CAMPBELL, the Rev. Alexander, auction catalogue of his library, 1765, 109

CAMPBELL, Archibald, Marquis of Argyll, *Instructions to a son*, 1743, 83; 1762, 244

CAMPBELL, Archibald, 3rd Duke of Argyll, *Catalogus librorum*, L, 1758, 220

CAMPBELL, Daniel, of Shawfield, *Sketch* of his life, 1777, 349

CAMUS, Armand Gaston, and sterotype, 453

CAPELL, Edward, *Prolusions*, 1760, 49

CAPPE, Newcome, *The voice of rejoicing, a sermon*, 1758, 220

CARDROSS, Lord. *See* ERSKINE, David Steuart, 11th Earl of Buchan

CAREY, George Saville, *Poetical efforts*, 1786, 454

CARLILE, Alexander (bookseller; Glasgow), 71

CASTELLION, Sébastien (translator of the Bible), 219

CATALOGUE. CAMPBELL, Archibald, Duke of Argyll, *Catalogus librorum*, 1758, 220; FOULIS PRESS, *A catalogue of books in quires*, 1777, 347; *A catalogue of copper-plates*, *c.* 1777, 348; *A catalogue of paintings*, *c.* 1777, 348; FOULIS, Robert, *A catalogue of books imported*, 1740, 65; 1744–5, 94; *A catalogue of pictures*, 1776, 337, 446; epitome, 383; FOULIS, Robert and Andrew, *Auction catalogues*, 1746–70, 108, 409; *Books printed by R. and A. Foulis*, 1770, 295, 438; *c.* 1772–4, 311; *A catalogue of books* (*Greek authors*), 1754, 189; *A catalogue of books of various ages*, 1771, 305; *A catalogue of books, with prices*, 1751, 158; *Prints engraved in the Academy at Glasgow*, 1775, 332; GLASGOW University, Academy, *A catalogue of pictures, etc.*, 1758, 222; GLASGOW University, Library, *Catalogus impressorum librorum*, 1791, 383

CATCHWORDS, 49

CAUNCE, William, *De rhematismo acuto*, 1792, 459

'CEBES', *Table*, G and L, 1744, 93; 1747, 111; 1757, 213; 1771, 301;

E, 1742, 77; E (trs. Boyse, Samuel), 1750, 137; 1771, 302
CELSUS, De re medica, L, 1766, 51
CERVANTES Saavedra, Miguel de, Don Quixote, E (trs. Motteux, Peter Anthony, rev. Ozell, John), 1757, 213; 1771, 302, 440
CHANDLER, Samuel, Plain reasons for being a Christian, by 1749, 131
CHANDLER, Thomas B., The American querist, 1775, 329
CHAPMAN, Robert, and DUNCAN, Alexander (printers; Glasgow), 346
CHARNLEY, William (bookseller; Newcastle), 226
CHARTERIS, Laurence, The corruption of this age, etc., 1761, 239
CHAUNCY, Charles, The wonderful narrative, 1742, 77
Chevy Chace, 1747, 116, 411
CHILD, Sir Josiah, Bart., A new discourse of trade, etc., 1751, 155
CIBBER, Colley, The careless husband, 1753, 421
CICERO, Cato major, etc., L, 1748, 121, 413; De inventione, L, 1748, 122, 413; De finibus bonorum et malorum, L, 1748, 122, 413; 364; De lege agraria, etc.; L, by 1777, 121, 413; De natura deorum, L, 1741, 66, 404; De officiis, L, 1748, 122, 413; 1757, 214, 426; 1784, 369, 452; De oratore, L, 1749, 346, 413, 447; De senectute (i.e. Cato major), L, 1748, 121; 1783-4, 450; Fragmenta, c. 1750, 418; In Catilinam I–IV, L, 1756, 204; I, L, 1782, 361; In M. Antonium, L, by 1777, 121, 413; I–II, L, 1762, 245, 431; In Vatinium, L, by 1777, 121, 413; In Verrem, 1749, 413; Laelius, L, 1748 (linen); 120; L, 1748, 121; E, 1759, 227; Lucullus, L, by 1777, 121, 413; Orationes selectae, L, 1772, 311, 441; Orator, L, 1748, 123, 413; Paradoxa Stoicorum, L, 1748, 121; L, 1780, 357; Pro Archia, L, 1778, 353; Pro Caelio, L, 1783, 364; Pro Ligario, L, 1778, 353; Pro Marcello and Pro Ligario, L, 1769, 286, 437; Pro Milone, L, 1761, 239; Somnium Scipionis (from De republica), L, 1748, 121; and Paradoxa Stoicorum, L, 1780, 357; Tusculanae quaestiones, L, 1744, 92, 407; Works, Proposals, 1748, 119; Works, L, 1749, 119, 412-13; note on the duodecimo Ciceros, 1748-9, 121, 412-13

CLARENDON, Lord. See HYDE, Edward, 1st Earl of Clarendon
CLEANTHES, Hymn to Zeus, G and L, 1744, 93
CLOW, James (editor of Simson), 339
COCHRANE, Thomas, De tetano, L, 1784, 370
COCHRANE (bookseller; Edinburgh). See SANDS, William, MURRAY and COCHRANE
COLLINS, Clear Type Press, Glasgow, commissions Fontana, 8
COLLINS, Edward, (papermaker), 27
COLLINS, William, Poetical Works, with Hammond, James, Elegies, 1770, 293; 1771, 303, 440; 1775, 330; 1777, 347; (without Hammond), 1787, 377
Compend of Experimental Philosophy, A, (by ANDERSON, John), 1760, 234
Compend of Physics, A, 1767, 274; 1770, 294, 438
Confession of Faith, etc., The, 1765, 1766, 261
CONGREVE, William, Dramatic Works, 1751, 155; The mourning bride, 1747, 112; 1755, 195; Poems upon several occasions, 1752, 170
Considerations upon a bankrupt law for Scotland, 1771, 304
COOKE, Joseph (bookseller; Oxford), 388
COOPER, Anthony Ashley, 3rd Earl of Shaftesbury, Characteristics, 1743-5, 84, 406; Letters, 1746, 108; The moralists, by 1777, 347, 406, 447
CORNARO, Luigi, Sure methods of attaining a long life, E, 1753, 180
CORNELIUS Nepos. See NEPOS, Cornelius
Corsica: a poetical address (by RICHARDSON, William), 1769, 290
COYPEL, Charles, Dialogue sur la connoissance de la peinture, F, 1753-4, 180
CRAIG, William, The character and obligations of a minister, a sermon, 1764, 256; An essay on the life of Jesus Christ, 1767, 274; 1769, 287; The reverence due to the name of God, a sermon, 1761, 240
CRAUFUIRD, G. K., De submersis exsuscitandis, 1791, 458
CRAWFORD, Andrew, De vita animali, L, 1789, 380
CREECH, William (bookseller; Edinburgh), 330, 362

CROSS, Robert (bookseller; Glasgow), 360

CUDWORTH, Ralph, *The life of Christ, a sermon*, 1744, 93

CUMBERLAND, Duke of. *Ode to the Duke of Cumberland*, c. 1748, 126

CUMMING, John, *De pleuritide*, 1793, 460

CUNINGHAME, William, *De cynanche tracheali*, L, 1790, 381

D'ALEMBERT, Jean le Rond, *Sur la destruction des Jésuites en France*, F, 1765, 262

DALRYMPLE, Sir David, Lord Hailes, *An account of the preservation of King Charles II, with his Letters*, 1766, 265, 398, 434; *Disquisitions concerning the antiquities of the Christian church*, 1783, 364; *Memorials and letters relating to the reign of Charles I*, 1766, 264, 433; *Memorials and letters relating to the reign of James I*, 1762, 245, 431; 1766, 264; editor of Gordon, 198

DALRYMPLE, Sir John, Bart., *The address of the people of Great Britain to the inhabitants of America, etc.*, 1775, 330; *An essay towards a general history of feudal property*, 1758, 221

DALRYMPLE, William, *Christian unity illustrated, a sermon*, 1766, 265; 1767, 266

DANIEL, J. M., *De opthalmia*, 1791, 458

DANIEL, Samuel, *Cleopatra*, 1751, 156

DARBEY, Robert, *De moschi et salis alk. volat. usu*, 1790, 457

DAVIDTS, Rombaut (bookseller; Paris), 432

DAVIES, Sir John, *The original, nature and immortality of the soul*, 1749, 132, 414; 1759, 228

DAVIES, T. (bookseller; London), 273, 397

Death of Artho and the death of Fraoch, The, 1769, 289

DE BEAUVAIS, Messire. *See* BEAUVAIS, Jean-Baptiste de

DE BELLOY, Buirette. *See* BUIRETTE de Belloy, Pierre-Laurent

DE HONDT, P. A. (bookseller; London). *See* MILLER, A., NOURSE, J., BECKET, T. and DE HONDT, P. A.

DEMETRIUS 'of Phalerum', *De elocutione*, G and L, 1743, 85

DEMOSTHENES, *De pace, etc.*, (?)G and L, 1750, 137; *On the crown*, G and L, 1782, 361; *Philippics and Olynthiacs*, G and L, 1747, 112; 1750, 137; *Philippics alone*, G, 1762, 246

DENHAM, Sir John, *Poems and translations, with The sophy*, 1751, 156; 1771, 304; *Poems*, 1776, 336; *The sophy*, 1752, 170, 420

DENINA, Carlo, *Discorso sopra le vicende della letteratura*, I, 1763, 250

DERHAM, William, *Astro-theology*, 1757, 214

Dialogue on devotion, after the manner of Xenophon, A, (by AMORY, Thomas), 1749, 132

DICK, Robert, *Experiments and lectures on mechanics*, 1753, 421

DICK, William. *See* STAYLEY, George, *An elegy on Mr William Dick*, 1770, 299

DICKSON, J. (bookseller; Edinburgh), 274, 277, 287, 358

DILLON, Wentworth, 4th Earl of Roscommon, *Works*, 1753, 181

DILLY, Edward and Charles (booksellers; London), 278, 279, 399, 400

DINWIDDIE, Lawrence (Provost of Glasgow), 418

DIXON, William Major, *De hepatitide*, L, 1784, 370

DODSLEY, James (bookseller; London), 273

DODSLEY, Robert, *A Collection of poems by several hands. See* MISCELLANY, *Select poems from a larger collection*, 1775, 333; *The Economy of Human Life*, c. 1783–4, 366

DONALDSON, (?) Alexander (bookseller; Edinburgh and London), 51

Dorando (by BOSWELL, James), 1767, 273, 396–8

DOUGLAS, Francis, *The birthday*, 1782, 362

DRUMMOND, William, *Polemo-middinia*, 1748, 123; 1750, 138; 1757, 215; 1768, 279; 1779, 357

DRUMMOND, (?) William (bookseller; Edinburgh), 51

DRYDEN, John, *Aureng-Zebe*, 1752, 171; *The conquest of Granada*, by 1755, 195; '*The conquest of Mexico*', by 1755, 195; *Fables ancient and modern, etc.*, 1752, 170; 1771, 305; 1776, 343, 446; *Original Poems*, 1756, 204; 1770, 294, 438; 1775, 330; *The Spanish friar*, 1752, 171, 420; *The works of Virgil*, E, 1769, 291; 1775, 335

DUBLIN Society, Royal. *The Dublin Society's weekly observations for the advancement of agriculture and manufactures*, 1756, 205; *The Flaxhusbandman instructed*, 1756, 205

DUFRESNOY, Charles-Alphonse, *A judgment on the work of the painters of the last two ages*, E, 1755, 195

DUNBAR, William, *The thistle and the rose* (with BELLENDEN, John, *Virtue and vice*), 1750, 138

DUNCAN, Alexander (printer; Glasgow). *See* CHAPMAN, Robert and DUNCAN, Alexander

DUNCAN, James (bookseller; Glasgow), 51

DUNCAN, James, DUNLOP and WILSON (booksellers; Glasgow), 360

DUNCAN, John, *The defects and dangers of a pharisaical righteousness, a sermon*, 1751, 156

DUNCAN, William James, Glasgow bibliographer, 11–12; *The literary history of Glasgow*, 1831, 1886, 11–12

DUNLOP, Alexander (father and son), their libraries auctioned, c. 1750, 409

DUNLOP (bookseller; Glasgow). *See* DUNCAN, James, DUNLOP and WILSON

DURHAM, James (bookseller; London). *See* WILSON, D. and DURHAM, J.

DYCHE, Thomas, *Spelling book* (?=*The spelling dictionary*), by 1784, 371

EARLY, Piety. *Sermon on early piety*, by 1777, 352

EBELING, Johann T. P. C., *De quassia et lichene islandico*, L, 1779, 357

EDGAR, Handaside, *De peri-pneumonia*, L, 1776, 336

EDINBURGH, the Edinburgh Society, awards prizes to Foulis books, 194, 209, 210, 230

EDINBURGH, University of Edinburgh, *Fragmenta Grammatices Graecae*, n.d., 387

EGERTON, T. (bookseller; London), 386

ELLIOTT, C. (bookseller; London), 379

ELMSLY, P. (bookseller; London), 337

ELPHINSTON (or ELPHINGSTON), James (translator of Fénelon), 157, 188, 236

ENGRAVERS. *See* ALLAN, David; BAILLIE, A.; BUCHANAN, William; FLAXMAN; LE CLERC, Sébastien; MCINTYRE; MITCHELL, James; RALSTON; RAMSAY, A. Junior; RIDDELL, John; SMITH, T.; STRANGE, R.; TAYLOR, Samuel; WALKER

EPICTETUS, *Discourses*, E, 1766, 266, 434; *Manual* (with works by 'Cebes', Prodicus and Cleanthes), G and L, 1744, 93, 407; *Manual* alone, G and L, 1751, 157; G and L, 1758, 221; G, 1765, 262; G and L, 1775, 331; L (trs. Ivie, Edward), 1744, 94; E, 1743, 85; E (trs. Stanhope, George), 1750, 138

Epistle of Yarico to Inkle, The (by JERNINGHAM, Edward), 1750, 143

ERSKINE, David Steuart, 11th Earl of Buchan, formerly Lord Cardross, 12, 241; *Memorable occurrences in the history of Scotland*, 1785, 373

Essay on religion and morality, An, 1767, 274

Essay on the theory of agriculture, by a farmer, An, 1760, 1761, 235

EUCLID, *Elements*, Proposals, 1755, 195; *Elements I–VI, XI–XII*, L, (ed. Simson, Robert), 1756, 206, 425; E (ed. and trs. Simson, Robert), 1756, 206, 425; 1762, 246; with *Elements of Trigonometry*, 1781, 360, 449

EUDOXUS of Cnidos. *See* ARCHIMEDES, *the sand-reckoner*, c. 1751, 153

EUGENE Francis, Prince of Savoy, *Prayer*; with *King Henry's Prayer*, E, by 1761, 240

EURIPIDES, *Medea*, G and L, 1775, 331; 1784, 371; *Orestes*, G and L, 1753, 181; *Tragedies*, G and L, 1797, 1806, 389–90

EUSDEN, Laurence (translator of Musaeus), 145

EUTROPIUS, *Breviarium ab urbe condita*, L, 1783, 365

EVANS, Samuel, *De Hysteria*, L, 1773, 317

EXHIBITION. Foulis exhibition, 1913, 13; *Catalogue*, 1913, 13; Foulis exhibition, 1958, 13

Extract of orders and regulations for garrison and camp duties, 1761, 240

FALCONER, Professor A. F., 198, 396

FANEUIL, Peter. *See* LOVELL, John, *A funeral oration*, by 1777, 349, 401

FARMER, A, *An essay on the theory of agriculture*, 1760, 1761, 235

FARMER, A. *See* DOUGLAS, Francis, *The birthday*, 1782, 362

FARMER, A real, *The modern farmer's guide*, 1768, 282

FARQUHAR, George, *The beaux' stratagem*, 1755, 196, 424; *The constant couple*, 1756, 207; *Love and a bottle*, 1755, 196; 1755, another ed., 424; *The recruiting officer*, 1755, 196; *The twin-rivals*, 1755, 196

FÉNELON, François de Salignac de la Mothe-, *Advice and consolation for a person in distress and dejection of mind*, E, 1750, 139; *A demonstration of the existence and attributes of God*, E (*trs.* Boyer, Abel), 1755, 197; *Dialogues concerning eloquence, with a letter on rhetoric and poetry, etc.*, E, 1750, 139; 1760, 235; *Dialogues of the dead, and fables*, E, 1752, 171; É (*trs.* Elphinston, James), 1754, 188; *Fables composed for the Duke of Burgundy*, E (*trs.* Elphinson, James), 1751, 157; 1760, 236; *Instructions for the education of daughters*, E (*trs.* Hickes, George), 1750, 140; *A letter concerning rhetoric, poetry, history*, E, 1750, 139; *Letters to the Duke of Burgundy*, E, 1746, 108; *Philosophical discourse on the love of God*, E (*trs.* Ramsay, A.M.), 1767, 276; *Pious thoughts concerning the knowledge and love of God, etc.*, E, 1763, 250; *Télémaque*, É (*trs.* Littlebury, Isaac and Boyer, Abel), 1755, 197

FINDLAY, Robert, *A vindication of the sacred books*, 1770, 294

Flax-husbandman instructed, The, 1756, 205

FLAXMAN, John (artist and engraver), 386

FLEETWOOD, R. (bookseller; Liverpool), 234

FLEMING, the Reverend Robert, *The confirming work of religion*, 1743, 86; *A description of the confirmed state of a Christian*, 1743, 86

FLEMING, Robert (bookseller; Edinburgh), 51, 222

FLEMING, Samuel, *De incremento ossium*, 1750, 415

FLETCHER, James (bookseller; Oxford), 79

FLOWERS, printers', 49, 61

FONTANA, Monotype Series 403, based on RE3, 8

FORBES, William, his library auctioned, 1746, 109, 409

FORDYCE, James, *The delusive and persecuting spirit of popery, a sermon*, 1758, 221; *The eloquence of the pulpit*, 222; *The methods of promoting edification by public institutions*, 1755, 222

FOULIS, Andrew the elder, printer with Robert Foulis, 1746, 107; University Printer, 1746, 111; *see* FOULIS, Robert and Andrew the elder.

FOULIS, Andrew the younger, bookseller in College, 51; dedications signed by, 372, 375, 377, 378; imprints, University Printer, 1778, 355–6; Wilson Street, Glasgow, 1794, 386; Edinburgh, 1800, 391; *A slight sketch of the origin of the Glasgow Press*, 1791, 382; and TILLOCH, Alexander, stereotyped books, 1783–4, 365, 450; *see* TILLOCH, Alexander

FOULIS Exhibition, 1913, 13; 1958, 13

FOULIS Press
Bindery and binding, 54–5
A catalogue of books, being the entire stock in quires, 1777, 347; *A catalogue of copper-plates, c.* 1777, 348; *A catalogue of paintings, c.* 1777, 348; *A catalogue of pictures*, 1776, 383
Editions: awarded prizes by the Edinburgh Society, 194, 209, 210, 230; duodecimo English poets, 62; edition quantities, 15, 273, 387, 397, 399, 414, 425; extent and character, 15–19; miniature editions, 152, 157, 190, 238, 262; number of editions, 15–17, 24–5; part of a book printed at another press, 385; texts, choice of titles, 18; texts, classical, 18; texts, classical, first in Greek, 85; texts, for schools, 137; texts, most often printed, 18; texts, other languages, 18; texts, other languages, first in French, 180, Gaelic, 135, Italian, 186; variant issues, 18–19
Illustrations. *See* ILLUSTRATIONS
Printing. *See* PRINTING, methods of
Printing equipment, presses, 21–2; rolling press, 19; type in short supply, 22
Printing for authors, 216, 234, 249, 282, 285, 362, 374, 376, 397
Printing for booksellers, etc., 117, 221, 226, 261, 273, 274, 278, 294, 397–400

Publication. *See* PUBLICATION, methods of

Size, in terms of plant and employees, 21

Slight sketch of the origins of the Glasgow Press, A (by FOULIS, Andrew the younger), 1791, 382

Typographical style, 29, 399; catchwords dropped, 49; G *and* L parallel-text layout, 90; long f dropped, 49 *See* BOOKSELLERS AND PRINTERS mentioned in imprints, etc.

FOULIS, Robert, bookseller in College, 51; bookseller, terms of trade, 65, 95; correspondence with James Boswell, 1767–8, 396–400; *A catalogue of books imported*, 1740, 65; 1744–5, 94; *A catalogue of pictures*, 1776, 337, 446; represents Glasgow printers and booksellers, 324; University Printer, 1743, 90

FOULIS, Robert and Andrew the elder, *Auction catalogues*, 1746–70, 108, 409; book auctions, 108, 400; books printed for, 51; booksellers, terms of trade, 65, 95, 109; *Books printed by R. and A. Foulis*, 1770, 295, 438; *c.* 1772–4, 311; *A catalogue of books, with prices*, Parts 1 and 2, 1751, 158; *A catalogue of books (Greek authors)*, 1754, 189; *A catalogue of books of various ages*, 1771, 305; *Prints engraved in the Academy at Glasgow*, 1775, 332; *see* FOULIS Press, *A catalogue of books in quires*, 1777, 347

Fragmenta grammatices Graecae (Edinburgh University), 387

FREDERICK II of Prussia, *La délassement de la guerre*, F *and* E, 1758, 222, 427

FREDERICK, J. (bookseller; Bath), 249

French Convert, The, 1783–4, 366

GAIRDEN, George, *Scougal's funeral sermon*, 1751, 166

GARDEN, James, *Comparative theology*, 1752, 172

GARTH, Sir Samuel, *The dispensary*, 1750, 141, 416; *Poetical works*, 1771, 306; 1775, 332, 445

GASKELL, Philip, 'Early work of the Foulis Press and the Wilson Foundry', 1952, 13

GATAKER, Thomas, *Maxims of the Stoics, etc.*, 1742, 75

GAY, John, *The beggar's opera*, 1750, 141; 1753, 182; 1772, 312; *Dione*, 1752, 198, 418, 424; *Fables*, 1750, 141, 416; 1761, 241; 1762, 247; *Poems on several occasions*, 1751, 158, 418; 1757, 215; 1770, 295, 438; 1776, 343, 446; *The what d'ye call it*, 1749, 132

GEDDES, James, *An essay on the composition of the antients, particularly Plato*, 1748, 124

GEE, Joshua, *The trade and navigation of Great Britain*, 1750, 142, 416; 1760, 236

GENTLEMAN, Francis, and SOUTHERNE, Thomas, *Oroonoko*, 1760, 238

GEORGE III, King, *His Majesty's speech to Parliament, 25 November 1762*, 1762, 247; 1776, 247

GESSNER, Salomon, *The death of Abel*, 1784, 366

GILLIES, John, *Historical Collections*, Proposals, 1752, 172; *Historical collections relating to the success of the gospels*, 1754, 189

Gill Morice, 1755, 201

GILMOUR, John (bookseller; Glasgow), 51, 102, 257, 282, 288, 289, 292, 398

GILMOUR, John and son (booksellers; Glasgow), 295

GLASGOW Academy. *See* GLASGOW, University of Glasgow, Academy

GLASGOW, Brewers, *Representations for the Brewers in Glasgow*, by 1777, 348

Glasgow Courant, The, 1745–60, 102

GLASGOW, Printers and booksellers, *A letter to the printers and booksellers of England*, 1774, 323; *Memorial to the House of Commons*, 1774, 323

GLASGOW, University of Glasgow Doctoral and magisterial dissertations: AIRD, John, 441; BLAIR, John, 444; CAUNCE, William, 459; COCHRANE, Thomas, 370; CRAUFUIRD, G. K., 458; CRAWFORD, Andrew, 380; CUMMING, John, 460; CUNINGHAME, William, 381; DANIEL, J. M., 458; DARBEY, Robert, 457; DIXON, William M., 370; EBELING, J. T. P. C., 357; EDGAR, Handaside, 336; EVANS, Samuel, 317; FLEMING, Samuel, 415; HUTCHESON, Francis, 'Hibernus', 416; KINGLAKE, Robert, 461; LANGHORNE, John, 445; LANGSLOW, Richard, 459; LEADER, Henry, 442; LYNCH, Samuel, 453;

M'MICHAN, John, 414; M'PHERSON, Alexander, 454; MAYWOOD, Robert, 455; MILLAR, Richard, 456; MUIR, John, 457; NOOTH, John Mervin, 434; PLOMER, James, 428; ROBINSON, James T., 452; ROGERS, Bayley, 415; SHAPTER, William R., 383; SIMPSON, John, 369; SPENCE, William, 359; STORER, John, 308; WEBB, Bernard, 149; WINTERBOTTOM, T. M., 460; WRIGHT, James, 431
Lecture notes, etc.: ANDERSON, John, 234, 429; *A compend of physics*, 274, 294; DICK, Robert, 421; MACNAB, Henry, 374, 453; MILLAR, John, 307, 319, 440, 448, 449, 451, 456; *Series titulorum*, 359; WIGHT, William, 277, 301, 315
Official papers, etc., 1766–90, 266
[*Vacation exercise for students*], L, 1753, 182
GLASGOW, University of Glasgow, Academy: *A catalogue of pictures, etc., done at the Academy in the University of Glasgow*, 1758, 222; *The gallery of Raphael, being fifty-two prints*, 1770, 296; *Prints engraved in the Academy at Glasgow*, 1775, 332; *A proposal for encouraging an Academy*, [? 1753], 182; *The seven cartoons of Raphael, engraved by James Mitchell and William Buchanan*, 1773, 317; *A slight sketch of the origin of the Glasgow Press, and Academy of the fine arts* (by FOULIS, Andrew the younger), 1791, 382
GLASGOW, University of Glasgow, Library: *Catalogus impressorum librorum* (author catalogue), (by ARTHUR, Archibald), 1791, 382; (shelf list), 1791, 382
GLOVER, Richard, *Leonidas*, 1769, 287
GORDON, Sir Adam, *Edom of Gordon*, 1755, 198
GORDON, George, *De natura rerum quaestiones philosophicae*, L, 1758, 222
GORDON, William (bookseller; Edinburgh), 147
GOSNELL, S. (printer; London), 434
GRAHAM, George, *Telemachus*, 1767, 274
GRAHAM, Thmas, *Poems*, 1773, 318
GRANVILLE, George, Baron Lansdowne, *Plays*, 1752, 173

GRAY, John, *The art of land-measuring explained*, 1757, 215
GRAY, Thomas, *Poems*, 1768, 279, 435; 1770, 297; 1773, 318; (another edition), 1773, 318, 443; 1777, 348; 1782, 362; *Poetical works*, 1787, 377, 447; *see* GRAHAM, Thomas, *Poems*, 1773, 318
GRAYE, W. (bookseller; Edinburgh), 358
Guardian, The, 1746, 110
GUARINI, Giambattista, *Il pastor fido*, I, 1763, 251

HAILES, Lord. *See* DALRYMPLE, Sir David, Lord Hailes
HALE, Sir Matthew, *Some thoughts on true religion*; with RALEIGH, Sir Walter, *A letter to his lady*, 1742, 78
HALES, John, *Letters from the synod of Dort*, 1765, 262; *Works*, 1765, 262
HAMILTON, Gavin (bookseller; Edinburgh), 65; *see* HAMILTON, Gavin, and BALFOUR, John; *see* HAMILTON, Gavin, BALFOUR, John and NEILL
HAMILTON, Gavin, and BALFOUR, John (booksellers; Edinburgh), 67, 68, 69, 70, 75, 76, 78, 80, 82, 83, 88, 89, 91, 96, 104, 216
HAMILTON, Gavin, BALFOUR, John, and NEILL (booksellers; Edinburgh), 224
HAMILTON of Bangour, William, *Poems on several occasions*, 1748, 125, 413; 1749, 133, 415; 1758, 223, 427; (?) 1767, 276
HAMMOND, James, *Elegies*; *with* Collins, William, *Poetical Works*, 1770, 293; 1771, 303; 1775, 330; 1777, 347; in *Select Poems*, 1783, 367; *Poetical Works*, 1787, 378, 455
HARDING, E. (bookseller, London), 434
Hardyknute (by WARDLAW, Elizabeth, Lady), 1745, 105; 1748, 129
HELIODORUS, *Theagenes and Chariclea*, E, 1753, 183
HENDERSON, C. (bookseller; London), 249
HENRY, King. *See* EUGENE Francis, Prince of Savoy, *Prayer*, E, by 1761, 240
HERODOTUS, *History*, Proposals, *c.* 1750, 142; G *and* L, 1761, 241, 430
HICKES, George (translator of Fénelon), 140
HIEROCLES, *Commentary on the Pythagoreans' Golden verses*, E, 1756, 207

474

INDEX

'HIPPOCRATES', *Aphorisms*, G and L, 1748, 125

'*Histories*' (i.e. chapbooks), 366

History of the feuds and conflicts among the clans, The, 1764, 257

History of Valentine and Orson, The, 1783–4, 366

HOADLY, Benjamin, *An abridgment of the Plain account of the sacrament of the Lord's supper*, 1745, 100, 408; *Several discourses concerning the terms of acceptance with God*, 1759, 228

HOMER, *Iliad*, G and L, 1747, 113, 411; G, 1756, 208; G and L, 1778, 353; E (*trs.* Pope, Alexander), 1767, 275; 1771, 306; 1783–4, 366; 1784, 371; *Odyssey*, G, 1757, 1758, 208; E (*trs.* Pope, Alexander), 1768, 280; 1772, 312, 442; *Works*, G, 1756–8, 208, 425

HORACE, *Works*, L, 1744 (the 'immaculate Horace'), 95; 1750, 142; 1756, 210, 426; 1760, 237, 429

HUGHES, John (translator of Abélard), 151

HUTCHESON, Francis, *De naturali hominum socialitate (oratio inauguralis)*, L, 1756, 210; *An Essay on the nature and conduct of the passions*, 1769, 288; 1772, 313; *An Inquiry into the original of our ideas of beauty and virtue*, 1772, 313; *Logicae compendium*, L, 1756, 210; 1759, 229; 1764, 257; 1772, 314; 1778, 354; 1787, 378; *Metaphysicae synopsis*, L, 1742, 79; *Oratio inauguralis (de naturali hominum socialitate)*, L, 1756, 210; *Philosophiae moralis institutio compendiaria*, 1742, L, 79; 1745, 101; 1755, 198; (in E as) *A short introduction to moral philosophy*, 1747, 114, 411; 1753, 183; 1764, 258; 1772, 314, 432; *Synopsis metaphysicae* (as *Metaphysicae synopsis*), L, 1742, 79; *Synopsis metaphysicae*, L, '1743', 96; 1744, 96; 1749, 133; 1756, 211; 1762, 247; 1774, 324; 1780, 358; *A System of moral philosophy*, Proposals, 1753, 184; 1755, 199, 424; *Thoughts on laughter*, 1750, 143; 1758, 223; (translator of Aurelius Antoninus, Marcus), 75, 131, 168, 255; and BURNET, Gilbert (son of the Bishop of Salisbury), *Letters concerning the foundation of virtue*, 1772, 310; quoted, 403

HUTCHESON, Francis, 'Hibernus', *De concoctione ciborum*, 1750, 416

HUYGENS, Christiaan, *Cosmotheoros*, E, 1757, 216

HYDE, Edward, 1st Earl of Clarendon, *Essays*, 1764, 258

Hymn fit to be sung on days of humiliation and prayer, A, n.d. 391

ILLUSTRATIONS, coloured plates, 379; copper-plate, 19, 399; original drawings for, 389; woodcut, 19

INGRAM, William (merchant; Glasgow), 347

Institutes of Physics, 1777, 346; 1795, 387

Instructions for officers, 1770, 297

ISOCRATES, *Panegyricus*, G and L, 1778, 354

IVIE, Edward (translator of Epictetus), 94

JAMES I, King of Scotland, and RAMSAY, Allan, *Christ's kirk on the green*, 1768, 281

JENNINGS, David, *The Beauty and benefit of early piety*, 1731, 352

JERNINGHAM, Edward, *The epistle of Yarico to Inkle*, 1750, 143, 417

JESUS CHRIST. *See* THOMAS à Kempis, St, *De imitatione Christi*

JOHNSON, Joseph (bookseller; London), 334

JOHNSON, Samuel, *Journey to the Western Islands*, 1775, 332

JOHNSTON, Joshua (merchant; Glasgow), 347

Judgment of Hercules, The (by SHENSTONE, William), 1743, 89

JULIUS CAESAR. *See* CAESAR, Julius

JUVENAL, *Satires*; *with* PERSIUS, *Satires*; L, 1742, 68; 1750, 143

KEMPIS, Thomas à. *See* THOMAS à Kempis, St

KEYNES, Sir Geoffrey, 230

KINCAID, Alexander (bookseller; Edinburgh), 104, 397; *see* KINCAID, Alexander, and BELL

KINCAID, Alexander, and BELL (booksellers; Edinburgh), 51, 249

KINGLAKE, Robert, *De vitae principio*, 1794, 461

KNOX, Hugh, *Select sermons*, 1776, 338; *Transitory and evanescent nature of all sublunary things*, 1782, 450

LACTANTIUS, *De mortibus persecutorum*, E (*trs.* Burnet, Gilbert), 1765, 263; 1766, 267

Lady's religion, A, 1748, 126

LAING, William (bookseller; Edinburgh), 386, 389

LANGHORNE, John, *De argento vivo*, 1775, 445

LANGSLOW, Richard, *De vitabis variolosae*, 1791, 459

LANGUAGES, abbreviations for, 10

LANSDOWNE, Lord. *See* GRANVILLE, George, Baron Lansdowne

LATIN POETS, *Poetae latini minores*, L, 1752, 174

LAW, John, *Money and trade considered*, 1750, 143; 1760, 237

'LAW, John', *Proposals and reasons for constituting a Council of Trade in Scotland*, 1751, 158

LEADER, Henry, *De origine ac natura dysenteriae*, 1772, 442

LEAKE, J. (bookseller; Bath), 249

LE CLERC, Sébastien (engraver), 186, 251, 255, 310

LEECHMAN, William, *Account* of Francis Hutcheson's life, 1755, 199; *The nature of prayer, a sermon*, 1743, 87; 1743 (second edition), 87; 1745, 101; 1749, 133; 1755, 199; 1769, 288; *The temper of a minister, a sermon*, 1741, 66; 1741 (another edition), 67; 1742, 80, 405; 1744, 96; 1749, 134; 1755, 199; 1769, 289; *The wisdom of God in the gospel revelation, a sermon*, 1758, 224

LEIGHTON, Robert, *Rules and instructions for a holy life*, 1751, 166; 1770, 299

LE SAGE, Alain René, *Le diable boiteux*, F, 1781, 360, 450; E (as *The devil upon two sticks*), 1760, 429; 1768, 315, 436, 442

LESLIE, John (correspondent of Robert Foulis, 1753), 184

Letter from a gentleman in England to his friend in New-York, A, 1775, 329

LIBRARIES, abbreviations for, 10; Bodleian Library, Oxford, 11; British Museum Library, 11; Cambridge University Library, 12; Edinburgh University Library, 12; Glasgow University Library, 11; Hunterian Library, Glasgow University, 11; Harvard University Library, 12; Mitchell Library, Glasgow, 11; Murray Collection, Glasgow University Library, 11; National Library of Scotland, Edinburgh, 12; Signet Library, Edinburgh, 12

LINEN, printing on. *See* PRINTING, materials other than paper

LITTLEBURY, Isaac (translator of Fénelon), 197

LOCKE, John, *A discourse on miracles*, 1743, 82; *Elements of natural philosophy* with *Thoughts concerning reading and study*, 1751, 159; *Essay concerning human understanding* (abr. Wynne, John), 1744, 97; 1752, 173; *Thoughts concerning reading and study*, 1751, 159

LONGINUS, *On the sublime*, (?) G and L, 1747, 115; G and L, 1751, 159; 1763, 251; 1790, 381

LONGMAN, Thomas (bookseller; London), 199

LONG f, dropped, 49

LOVELL, John, *A funeral oration occasioned by the death of P. Faneuil, Esq.*, 1743, 349, 406, 447

LOWTH, Robert, *The judgment of Hercules*, etc., 1743, 89, 406

LUCAN, *Pharsalia*, L, 1751, 160; 1785, 374

LUCIAN, *Excerpts*, G and L, 1778, 354

LUCRETIUS, *De rerum natura*, L, 1749, 134; 1759, 229, 428

LYNCH, Samuel, *De stimulantium natura*, 1785, 453

LYSIAS, *Against Eratosthenes*, G and L, 1781, 361

LYTTELTON, George, Baron, *Poems*, 1773, 319; 1775, 333; 1777, 349, 447, 448; *Poetical works*, 1787, 378, 455

M., A., *The state of religion in New England*, 1742, 80; second edition, 1742, 81

MCCULLOCH, Michael, *A sketch of the character of the late Daniel Campbell*, 1777, 349

MACFARLANE, Rev. Alexander (translator of Baxter), 135

M'GILL, William, *The prayer of our Saviour, a sermon*, 1768, 281

M'ILHOSE, William, his library auctioned, 1768, 109

MCINTYRE (engraver), 385, 387

MACKINLAY (bookseller; London). *See* PAYNE, T. and MACKINLAY

MACLEHOSE, James, *The Glasgow University Press*, 1931, 13

M'MICHAN, John, *De dysenteria*, 1748, 414

MACNAB (or M'NAB), Henry, *The director, in teaching English*, 376; *Heads of a course of elocution*, 1785, 374, 453; *The philosophy of natural and artificial language*, 376; *A plan of*

INDEX

reform in the mode of instruction prac-
tised in English schools, 1786, 376,
455; *The reader and speaker,* 376; *A*
synopsis of a course of elocution, 1786,
376

M'PHERSON, Alexander, *De fram-*
boesia, 1785, 454

MALLET, David, and THOMSON,
James, *Alfred, a masque,* 1776, 340

MARCUS AURELIUS. *See* AURELIUS
Antoninus, Marcus

MARDERSTEIG, Dr Giovanni,
designs Fontana, 8

Mare of Collingtoun, The, 1751, 161

MASON, William, *Poems,* 1774, 324;
1777, 349

MAXWELL, Patrick, his library
auctioned, 1750, 109

MAYWOOD, Robert, *De actione mer-*
curii in corpus humanum, 1786, 455

MEARS, John, *A catechism,* 1741, 67;
1741–2, 67; 1742, 69, 404

Metaphysicae synopsis. See HUTCHESON,
Francis

MILITARY. *Extract of orders and regula-*
tions, 1761, 240; *Military instructions*
for forming a partisan, by 1768, 282;
Military instructions for officers, 1770,
297, 438

MILLAR, Andrew (bookseller;
London), 51, 66, 67, 69, 70, 75, 79,
80, 81, 87, 88, 102, 199, 263. *See*
MILLER, A. (bookseller; London)

MILLAR, John, *A course of lectures on*
government, 1771, 307, 440; 1773,
319; 1778, 449; 1783, 451; 1787,
456; *A course of lectures on the private*
law of Scotland, 1771, 307; *Heads of*
the lectures on the law of Scotland,
1777, 448

MILLAR, Richard, *De morbi venerei*
natura, 1789, 456

MILLER, Alexander (University
Printer; Glasgow), 66

MILLER, A., NOURSE, J., BECKET, T
and DE HONDT, P. A. (booksellers; London), 249

MILTON, John, *Comus,* 1747, 116;
L'allegro and il penseroso, 1747–9,
115; 1751, 160; *Minor poems,* 1765,
264; *Paradise lost,* 1747, 115; 1750,
144; 1752, 173; 1761, 242, 430;
1766, 268, 434; 1770, 297, 439;
1771, 307, 440; 1776, 338; *Paradise*
Lost Book I (with a commentary by
John Callander), 1750, 144; *Para-*
dise regained, with Samson agonistes,
Poems on several occasions and a trac-
tate of education, 1747, 115; 1752,

174; 1765, 263; 1772, 315, 442;
Poems on several occasions, 1752, 174;
Samson agonistes, by 1777, 350; *A*
tractate of education, 1747, 116

MINUCIUS FELIX, *Octavius,* L, 1750,
145

MISCELLANY. *Modern poems,* 1776,
344; *Poems in the Scottish dialect,*
1748, 126; *Poems on moral and divine*
subjects, 1751, 160; *Poetae latini*
minores, L, 1752, 174; *Select poems*
(by AKENSIDE, Mark, HAMMOND,
James, PHILIPS, Ambrose and
STILLINGFLEET, Benjamin), 1783,
367; *Select poems from a larger collec-*
tion, 1775, 333; *The speech of a Fife*
laird, etc., three Scots poems, 1751,
161; *The tea-table miscellany* (by
RAMSAY, Allan), 1768, 284

MITCHELL, James (engraver), 317

Modern farmer's guide, by a real farmer,
The, 1768, 282

MONIPENNIE, John, *The abridgment or*
summarie of the Scots chronicle, by
1777, 350

MONOTYPE Fontana, based on RE3,
8

MONTGOMERIE, Hugh. *See* MONT-
GOMERY FAMILY, *Memorables of the*
Montgomeries, 1770, 297

MONTGOMERY, Capt. Alexander, *The*
cherry and the slae, 1746, 109, 410;
1751, 161

MONTGOMERY FAMILY, *Memorables*
of the Montgomeries, 1770, 297, 439

MOOR, James, *De analogia contrac-*
tionum linguae Graecae regulae gener-
ales, L, 1753, 184; 1755, 200; 1759,
230; (*De analogiea* continued as)
Elementa linguae Graecae, L, 1766,
268; 1770, 298; 1773, 319; 1777,
350; 1780, 358; 1783, 367; 1793,
385; 1795, 387; *Essays read to a*
literary society, 1759, 230; *On the end*
of tragedy, according to Aristotle, 1763,
252; 1794, 385; *On the praepositions*
of the Greek language, 1766, 268;
1766 (another edition), 269;
Vindication of Virgil from a charge of a
puerility, 1766, 269, 434; (editor of
Archimedes), 153; (of 'Cebes'),
112; (of Homer), 209; (of Tyrtaeus), 234; (translator of Marcus
Aurelius), 75, 131, 168, 255; notes
on Demosthenes, 238

MOORE, Edward, *The epistle of Yari-*
koto Inkle, 1750, 143, 417

MORE, Henry, *Divine dialogues,* 1743,
88; *An essay on disinterested love,*

1756, 211

MORE, Sir Thomas. *See* THOMAS More, St

MOTTERSHEAD, Joseph, *Religious discourses*, 1759, 231; 1760, 238; *see* BREKELL, John, *Free and candid remarks*, 1760, 234

MOTTEUX, Peter Anthony, (translator of Cervantes), 214, 302

MOYLE, Walter (translator of Xenophon), 162

MUIR, John, *De tetano*, 1790, 457

MUIRHEAD, George (editor of Homer), 209

MUN, Thomas, *England's treasure by foreign trade*, 1755, 200

MUNDELL and son (booksellers; Edinburgh), 457

MURDOCH, Robert, his library auctioned, 1754, 109

MURRAY, David, *Robert & Andrew Foulis*, 1913, 13; *Some letters of Robert Foulis*, 1917, 13

MURRAY, John (bookseller; London), 334, 379

MURRAY (bookseller; Edinburgh). *See* SANDS, William, MURRAY and COCHRANE

MUSAEUS Grammaticus, *Hero and Leander*, E (*trs.* Eusden, Laurence), 1750, 145; E (*trs.* Taylor, Edward), 1783, 368

NEILL (bookseller; Edinburgh). *See* HAMILTON, Gavin, BALFOUR, John and NEILL

NEPOS, Cornelius, *Lives of the emperors*, L, 1742, 70; 1749, 135; 1761, 242, 430; 1777, 351

NETTLETON, Thomas, *Treatise on virtue and happiness*, 1751, 161; *see* CHANDLER, Samuel, *Plain reasons for being a Christian*, by 1749, 132

NOOTH, John Mervin, *De rachitide*, 1766, 434

NORTHUP, C. S. (bibliographer of Gray), 297

NOURSE, J. (bookseller; London). *See* MILLER, A., NOURSE, J., BECKET, T. and DE HONDT, P. A.

NYE, Stephen, *A discourse concerning natural and revealed religion*, 1752, 175

Odes by a lady, by 1748, 126

OLD POEM. *The battle of Harlaw* (with *The red squair*), 1748, 127; *Chevy chace*, 1747, 116, 411; *The death of Artho and the death of Fraoch*, 1769,

289; *Gill Morice*, 1755, 201, 426; *Young Waters*, 1755, 201; *see* DUNBAR, William, *The Thistle and the rose, etc.*, 1750, 138; GORDON, Sir Adam, *Edom of Gordon*, 1755, 198; JAMES I of Scotland, *Christ's Kirk on the green*, 1768, 281; MISCELLANY, *Poems in the Scottish dialect*, 1748, 126; *The speech of a Fife laird, etc.*, 1751, 161; MONTGOMERY FAMILY, *Memorables of the Montgomeries*, 1770, 297; MONTGOMERY, Capt. Alexander, *The cherry and the slae*, 1746, 109; 1751, 161; *seven champions of the stage*, 1757, 426

ORR, John (bookseller; Glasgow), 261

OSTELL, T. (bookseller; London), 434

OSTERWALD, Jean-Frédéric, *Theologiae Christianae compendium*, L, 1757, 217

OTWAY, Thomas, *The orphan*, 1745, 102; 1751, 162; 1758, 224; *Venice preserved*, 1747, 117; 1752, 175

OVID, (?) *Works*, L, *c.* 1751, 162

OZELL, John (translator of Cervantes), 214, 302

PAPER. *See* PRINTING PAPER

PARNELL, Thomas, *Poems on several occasions*, 1773, 320; 1777, 448; *Poetical works*, 1786, 376; *Works*, 1755, 201; 1767, 275

PARSONS, Robert, *Account of Rochester's conversion*, 1741, 65, 403; 1752, 169

PATERSON, William ('LAW, John', *Proposals and reasons for constituting a council of trade in Scotland*, 1751, 159

PATON, John (bookseller; Edinburgh), 88

PAYNE, T. (bookseller; London), 386; *see* PAYNE, T. and MACKINLAY

PAYNE, T. and MACKINLAY (booksellers; London), 388

PERIODICAL. *The Glasgow courant*, 1745–60, 102; *The guardian*, 1746, 110; *The tatler*, 1747–9, 118

PERSIUS, *Satires* (with JUVENAL, *Satires*(, L, 1742, 68; 1750, 143

PETTY, Sir William, *Political arithmetic* (with XENOPHON, *Ways and means*, E), 1751, 162

PHAEDRUS, *Aesop's fables*, L, 1741, 68; 1751, 163; 1754, 190; 1783, 368

PHILIPS, Ambrose, *The distressed mother*, 1746, 410; 1747, 117, 412; 1752, 175; *Pastorals*, 1763, 252,

253; *Pastorals* in *Select poems*, 1783, 367

PHILIPS, John, *Poems on several occasions*, 1763, 253

PHILLIPS, J. T. (translator of Bossuet), 82

PINDAR, *Olympia*, G and L, 1788, 379; *Works*, G and L, 1744, 97; G, 1754–8, 190; G and L, 1770, 298

Plain reasons for being a Christian (by CHANDLER, Samuel), by 1749, 131

PLATO, *Alcibiades secundus*, G and L, 1744, 98; *Apology*, G and L, 1789, 380; E (*trs.* Gataker, Thomas), 1742, 75; *Republic*, E (*trs.* Spens, Hary), 1763, 253; *Works*, Proposals and specimens, 1750–51, 146, 393–5, 417. *See* GEDDES, James, *An essay on the composition of the antients, particularly Plato*, 1748, 124

PLAUTUS, *Aulularia*, L, 1778, 355; *Comedies*, L, 1763, 254; *Curculio*, L, 1782, 362; *Mostellaria*, L, by 1784, 372; *Trinummus*, L, by 1784, 372

PLINY the younger, *Works*, L, 1751, 163; 1751 (another edition), 163, 419

PLOMER, James, *De iliaca passione*, 1759, 428

PLUTARCH, *De superstitione* (with XENOPHON, *Socrates and Aristodemus*; PLATO, *Alcibiades secundus*), G and L, 1744, 98; *How the young should hear poetry*, G and L, 1753, 184

POMFRET, John, *Poems on several occasions*, 1751, 164; 1757, 217

POMPONIUS MELA, *De situ orbis*, L, 1752, 176

POPE, Alexander, *Eloisa to Abelard*, 1751, 151; *An essay on man*, 1750, 417; 1751, 164, 419; 1754, 191; *Homer's Iliad*, 1767, 275; 1771, 306; 1783–4, 366; 1784, 371; *Homer's Odyssey*, 1768, 280; 1772, 312, 442; *Poems on several occasions*, 1752, 176; *Poetical works*, 1768, 283; 1773, 320, 443; 1785, 375, 454; *The universal prayer*, 1750, 146; (editor of Shakespeare), 270, 339

PORSON, Richard (editor of Aeschylus), 387, 388

POTTLE, F. A. (bibliographer of Boswell), 273, 279

PRICES. *See* PUBLICATION, methods of

PRINTERS. *See* BOOKSELLERS AND PRINTERS mentioned in imprints, etc.; BOOKSELLERS AND PRINTERS, Copyright controversy, 1774, 323

PRINTER'S FLOWERS, 49, 61

PRINTING INK, 22; red, 71

PRINTING MATERIALS other than paper, 26; linen, 120, 124; silk or satin, 153, 190, 318; vellum, 68, 112, 113–14, 124, 145

PRINTING, methods of, 21–2

Cancels, 22, 299, 426; cancels set in duplicate, 279

Composition, duplicate setting, 268–9, 290–91, 318–19; MS copy, 199, 399; pointing left to the printer, 399; speed of composition, 399

Correction, proofs, 96, 209, 234, 399, 443; 'purgation' by errata list, 98–9

Imposition, 'half sheet', 22; G and L parallel-text scheme, 90; unusual impositions, 79, 86, 211, 220, 222, 234

Parts of books not printed at the Foulis Press, 116, 279, 385

'Press figures', 21; early example, 272; regular use from 1768, 279, 282–5

Press work, standard of, 22

Proofs. *See* Correction

Signatures, 22; for variant issues 22; unusual signatures, 84, 337

Stereotype, 365–7, 450–1

Type kept standing for long periods, 187, 305

Variants, order of printing of, 22, 145, 252

PRINTING PAPER, 23–7

Blue-tinted, 23; first use of, 304, 310

Collins, Edward, supplies, 27

Duty on paper, 15

Half double-sized sheets used, 112, 117, 128, 147, 156, 161, 205, 211, 303, 363, 364, 365, 368, 369, 371, 373, 374, 375, 377, 378, 379, 381, 383, 384, 385

Qualities used at the Foulis Press, 23

Sizes used at the Foulis Press, 23

Sources of the Foulises' paper, 26–27

Special-paper issues, 18–19

'Variant' issues on the same paper, 313, 320

Watermarks, 26–7; abbreviations for, 60; unusual watermarks, 114, 162, 178, 180, 204, 208, 220, 230, 246, 250, 254, 265, 269, 274, 293, 318

Whatman, 26–7; IW mark first

used, 114; JW mark first used, 148

Wove, 23, 383, 386, 388, 389, 390, 391 *See* PRINTING MATERIALS other than paper

PRINTING TYPE, 29–49
Abbreviations for, 32, 33–48, 60
Baskerville's influence on Wilson's, 42
Blocks, 49, 61
Flowers, 49, 61
Foulis Press types, 33–48
Groups of type at the Foulis Press, 32
Hebrew, 295
Long f dropped, 49
Non-Wilson type, Caslon, 34, 279, 348, 366, 391; Dutch or German, 37
Ornaments, 49, 61
Stereotype, 365–7
Unusual founts, 127, 279
Wilson's founts, chronology, 30–32; gradually revised, 29–31, 38; modern approach of, 48
Wilson's italic, 49
See FOULIS PRESS, Typographical style

PRIOR, Matthew, *Poems on several occasions*, 1751, 165, 419; 1759, 231; 1769, 289; 1771, 307, 441

Process of Declarator, 1775, 1778, 267

PRODICUS, *The choice of Heracles*, G and L, 1774, 93

PROOFS. *See* PRINTING, methods of, Correction

PROPERTIUS, *Works*, L, 1753, 187

PROPOSALS, 52; 1748, for Cicero, 119; *c.* 1750, for Herodotus, 142; 1750–51, for Plato, 146, 393–5, 417; 1752, for Gillies, 172; 1753, for Hutcheson, 184; 1755, for Euclid, 195; 1760–61, for Thucydides, 233; *c.* 1766, for Spenser, 273; for Thomson, 451

PRUSSIA, King of. *See* FREDERICK II of Prussia

PUBLICATION, methods of, 51–5, 396–400
Advertisements, in Glasgow newspapers, 52–3; in other newspapers, 53; title-page as advertisement, 132, 187
Copyright, 323, 397–8
False imprint, 52, 235, 265, 273, 330, 397; concealing reprint, 272

False edition number, 52, 201, 273, 334, 397
Foulises' auction-room, 51
Foulises' bookshop, 51
Luxury editions, 54
Prices, 53–4, 403; of duodecimo poets, 62; luxury edition, 387; one price for several books, 162, 188; 221, 225, 302, 331; 275, 281; 288, 289; price raised after a period, 110; sources, 53
Re-issues, 434, 435
Shared publication, 51–2; *see* BOOKSELLERS AND PRINTERS mentioned in imprints, etc.
Stock catalogue, 1777 (*BQ*), 54, 347
Stock-in-trade, 54, 347
Subscription, 52, 233, 283, 393–5; after publication, 233; *see* PROPOSALS
See FOULIS PRESS, editions; PROPOSALS; SPECIMENS

PYTHAGOREANS, *Golden verses*, E (*trs.* Rowe, Nicholas; with SHENSTONE, William, *The judgment of Hercules*), 1743, 89; (with POPE, Alexander, *The universal prayer*), 1750, 146; *see* HIEROCLES, *Commentary on the golden verses*, E, 1756, 207

QUINTILIAN,(?) *Works*, L, *c.* 1751, 165

RALEIGH, Sir Walter, *Instructions of a father to his son, etc.*, 1754, 191; *A letter to his lady* (with HALE, Sir Matthew, *Some thoughts on true religion*), 1742, 78
RALSTON (engraver), 368
RAMSAY, Allan, *Christ's kirk on the green* (after James I of Scotland), 1768, 281; *A collection of Scots proverbs*, 1750, 147; *The gentle shepherd*, 1743, 89; 1745, 103; 1747, 117; 1750, 147; 1752, 176; 1768, 436; 1788, 379, 456; 1796, 388, 461; *The tea-table miscellany*, 1768, 284, 436
RAMSAY, Allan Jr (engraver), 284
RAMSAY, Andrew Michael, Chevalier, *The philosophical principles of natural and revealed religion*, 1748–1749, 127; *A plan of education*, 1741, 68; 1742, 80; 1766, 270; *A translation of the philosophical discourse on the love of God* (by Fénelon), 1767, 276; *The travels of Cyrus, etc.*, 1755, 202

RAPHAEL, *The gallery of Raphael, being fifty-two prints*, 1770, 296; *The seven cartoons of Raphael, engraved*, 1773, 317

RAY, John, *The wisdom of God manifested in the works of creation*, 1758, 243, 427, 431

Red squair, The, 1748, 127

RELPH, Josiah, *A miscellany of poems*, 1747, 117

RICHARDSON, Samuel, editions printed by, 17

RICHARDSON, William, *Corsica: a poetical address*, 1769, 290; *Elegiac verses occasioned by the death of Dr Irvine*, 1787, 456; *Epithalamium on the marriages of the Duchess of Athol and of Mrs Graham*, 1775, 334, 445; *The indians*, added to *Poems*, 1774, 325; to *Poems*, 1775, 334; *Poems, chiefly rural*, 1774, 325; 1774 (another edition), 325; 1774, *see* 334; 1775, 334; 1776, 338; 1781, 334

RIDDELL, John, dramatist, *Malvina*, 1786, 377

RIDDELL, J. (?=John, dramatist), *An elegy in memory of Mr George Stayley*, 1778, 300

RIDDELL, John (engraver), 250

ROBINSON, James Templeton, *De electricitate medica*, 1784, 452

ROCHESTER, Lord. *See* BURNET, Gilbert, *Some passages of the life and death of Rochester*, 1741, 65; 1752, 169; PARSONS, Robert, *Account of Rochester's conversion*, 1752, 169

ROGERS, Bayly, *De haemorrhoidibus*, 1749, 415

ROSCOMMON, Lord. *See* DILLON, Wentworth, 4th Earl of Roscommon

ROSS (or ROSSE), John (bookseller; Edinburgh), 141, 143, 145

ROWE, Nicholas, *The fair penitent*, 1748, 128; *Jane Shore*, 1748, 128; *Lady Jane Gray*, 1748, 129, 414; *Tamerlane*, 1750, 147; 1758, 224; (translator of Boileau), 169; (of Pythagoreans), 89, 146

SAINT JOHN, Henry, Viscount Bolingbroke, *The freeholder's political catechism*, 1757, 217

ST RÉAL, Abbot de. *See* VISCHARD DE ST RÉAL, César

SALLUST, *Works*, L, 1751, 165; 1777, 351, 448

SANDBY, William (bookseller; London), 265

SANDS, William (Bookseller; Edinburgh), 196; *see* SANDS, William, MURRAY and COCHRANE

SANDS, William, MURRAY and COCHRANE (booksellers; Edinburgh), 148

SAPPHO, *Lyrics*, G and L, 1744, 91; *Remains*, G, 1750, 135; G, 1751, 152; G, 1757, 123; G, 1761, 238; G and L, 1770, 293; G and L, 1777, 346; G and L, 1783, 363; G and L, 1783 (another edition), 363; G and L, 1792, 383

SATIN, printing on. *See* PRINTING MATERIALS other than paper

SCOTT, John (bookseller; London), 434

SCOUGAL, Henry, *Discourses on important subjects* (with GAIRDEN, George, *Scougal's funeral sermon*), 1751, 166; *The life of God in the soul of man* (with LEIGHTON, Robert, *Rules and instructions for a holy life*), 1751, 166; 1770, 299

SELDEN, John, *Table-talk*, 1755, 202

Series titulorum qui in pandectis continentur, L, 1780, 359

Sermon on early piety, by 1777, 352

Seven champions of Christendom, The, 1783–4, 366

Seven champions of the stage, The, 1757, 426

SHAFTESBURY, Lord. *See* COOPER, Anthony Ashley, 3rd Earl of Shaftesbury

SHAKESPEARE, William, [*Dramatic*] *Works* (ed. Pope, Alexander), 1766 (individual plays dated 1752–66), 270; *Hamlet* (ed. Pope, Alexander), 1776, 339

SHAPTER, William Randle, *De scorbuto*, L, 1792, 383

SHAWS, J. and W. (booksellers; Glasgow), 360

SHEFFIELD, John, 1st Duke of Buckingham, *Julius Caesar*, 1752, 177; *Marcus Brutus*, 1752, 177; *Poems on several occasions, with Julius Caesar and Marcus Brutus*, 1752, 177, 420

SHENSTONE, William, *The judgment of Hercules* (with PYTHAGOREANS, *Golden verses*), 1743, 89, 406; *Select works*, 1768, 284, 436, 439; 1775, 335, 445; 1777, 449

SHERLOCK, Thomas, *A letter on occasion of the late earthquakes*, 1750, 148

SHERLOCK, William, *A discourse con-*

cerning the happiness of good men, 1764, 258; *A discourse of the immortality of the soul and a future state*, by 1768, 285; *A practical discourse concerning death*, by 1761, 243; 1775, 335

SILK, printing on. *See* PRINTING MATERIALS other than paper

SIMPSON, John, *De catarrho*, L, 1783, 369, 451

SIMSON, Matthew (bookseller; Glasgow), 102

SIMSON, Robert, *Works*, L, 1776, 339, 446; (editor of Apollonius of Perga), 131; (of Euclid), 195, 206, 246, 360, 425, 449

SMITH, Adam, Preface to Hamilton's *Poems*, 125

SMITH, Edmund, *Phaedra and Hippolitus*, 1750, 148

SMITH, John, *The excellency and nobleness of true religion*, 1745, 104

SMITH, Robert (bookseller; Glasgow), 78

SMITH, T. (engraver), 215

SMOLLETT, Tobias, *Ode to independence*, 1773, 321; 1794, 386

SOAMES, Sir William (translator of Boileau), 193

SOMERSET, Edward, 2nd Marquis of Worcester, *A century of names and scantlings of inventions*, 1767, 277, 435

SOMERVILLE, William, *The chace*, 1755, 203, 425; *Hobbinol*, 1755, 203; *Poems*, 1766, 273

SOPHOCLES, *Oedipus Tyrannus*, G and L, 1777, 352; *Tragedies*, G and L, 1745, 104, 408

SOUTHERNE, Thomas, *Oroonoko*, 1753, 185; (adapted by Gentleman, Francis), 1760, 238

SPECIMENS, 1750–51, of Plato, 146, 417; 1767–8, of Boswell, 399

Speech of a Fife laird, etc., The, 1751, 161

SPENCE, William, *De opio*, L, 1780, 359

SPENS, Hary (translator of Plato), 253

SPENSER, Edmund, *The Faerie Queen*, intention to publish Proposals for an edition, 1766, 273

SPOTISWOOD (or SPOTTISWOOD), James (bookseller and paper-warehouseman; Edinburgh), 53; buys stock of Foulis Press, 53

STALKER, Andrew (bookseller; Glasgow), 191, 222, 249, 398

STANHOPE, George (translator of Augustine), 316; (of Epictetus), 138

STANHOPE, Philip, Lord, and Simson's *Works*, 1776, 339

STARR, H. W. (bibliographer of Gray), 297

State of religion in New England (by 'A.M.'), 1742, 80; second edition, 1742, 81

STAYLEY, George, *An elegy on Mr William Dick*, 1770, 299; *A moral enquiry*, 1778, 300; *see* RIDDELL, J., *An elegy in memory of Mr George Stayley*, 1778, 300

STEEL, William, *Memorial concerning small stipends in Scotland*, 1750, 148

STEELE, Sir, Richard, *The conscious lovers*, 1744, 99, 407; 1751, 166, 419; 1771, 308; *The funeral*, 1753, 185, 422; *The guardian*, 1746, 110, 411; *The lying lover*, 1776, 446; *The tender husband*, 1754, 203, 422, 425

STEELE, Sir Richard, and ADDISON, Joseph, *The tatler*, 1747–9, 118

STILLINGFLEET, Benjamin, *Essay on conversation*, in *Select poems*, 1783, 367

STOICS, *Maxims of the Stoics*, E, 1742, 75

STONEHOUSE, James, *Spiritual directions*, 1770, 300

STORER, John, *De angina maligna*, L, 1771, 308, 441

STOWER, Caleb, *The printer's grammar*, 1808, 79

STRANGE, R. (engraver), 97

Succinct description of the microcosm, A, c. 1765, 433

Sur la destruction des Jésuites en France (by D'ALEMBERT, Jean le Rond), 1765, 262

SWIFT, Jonathan, *Directions to servants*, 1762, 247; 1765, 433; *Poems*, 1774, 326, 443

Synopsis Metaphysicae. See HUTCHESON, Francis

TACITUS, *Agricola*, L, 1777, 352; 1790, 457; *Germania*, L, 1778, 355; *Works*, L, 1753, 186, 422

TASSO, Torquato, *Aminta*, I, 1753, 186; 1763, 254; *La Gierusalemme liberata*, I, 1763, 255, 432

Tatler, The, 1747–9, 118

TAYLOR, Edward (translator of Musaeus), 368

TAYLOR, Jeremy, *Rules and advices to the clergy of Down and Conner*, 1774, 326

TAYLOR, Samuel (engraver), 91

TEMPLE, Sir William, *Letter of consolation to the Countess of Essex*, 1751, 167

TERENCE, *Comedies*, L, 1742, 70, 404

THEOCRITUS, *Works*, G and L, 1746, 110, 411; 1753, 187

THEOPHRASTUS, *Characters*, G and L, 1743, 89, 407; 1748, 129; 1758, 224; 1785, 375; E (*trs.* Budgell, Eustace), 1743, 90

Thistle and the rose, The (by DUNBAR, William), 1750, 138

THOM, William, *Happiness of dead clergymen* and *Vindication of Dr Tail*, 1769-70, 437, 439

THOMAS à Kempis, St, *De imitatione Christi*, L, 1751, 167, 393; E, 1774, 326

THOMAS More, St, *Utopia*, L, 1750, 149; E (*trs.* Burnet, Gilbert), 1743, 91; 1762, 248, 431

THOMLINSON ((?) bookseller; Wigton, Cumberland), 117

THOMSON, James, *Liberty*, 1774, 327; 1776, 344; *Poems* (with *Alfred, a masque*, by THOMSON and MALLET, David), 1774, 444; 1776, 340; *Poetical Works*, 1784, 372, 452; *The seasons*, 1769, 290, 437; 1769 (another edition), 291, 437; 1776, 340; proposals for *The seasons*, 1783, 451

THUCYDIDES, *Funeral orations, etc.* (from *The Peleponnesian war*), G and L, 1755, 203; *The Peleponnesian war*, G and L, 1759, 232, 428

TIBULLUS, *Works* (with PROPERTIUS, *Works*, L, 1753, 187

TILLOCH, Alexander (printer and bookseller; Glasgow), in partnership with Foulis, Andrew the younger, 364, 371, 372, 373; dedications signed by, 375, 377; stereotyped books, 365-7, 450-1

TONSON, Jacob (bookseller; London), 263

TRANSCRIPTIONS of title-pages, conventions used, 58

True religion, a mystery, 1746, 111

TUCKER, Josiah, *A letter to a friend concerning naturalisations*, 1753, 187

TWEEDIE, James (proof reader), 209

Twelve Caesars, The, 1783-4, 366

TYPE. See PRINTING TYPE

TYPOGRAPHICAL STYLE. See FOULIS PRESS, Typographical style; PRINTING INK, red

TYRTAEUS, *Spartan lessons*, G and L, 1759, 233

URIE, Robert (printer and bookseller; Glasgow), 68, 70, 222

VANBRUGH, Sir John, *Aesop*, 1756, 212; *The provoked husband*, 1754, 191; *The provoked wife*, 1754, 192, 423; *The relapse*, 1756, 212

VELLEIUS PATERCULUS, *Historiae Romanae*, L, 1752, 177

VELLUM, printing on. See PRINTING MATERIALS other than paper

VERTOT, Abbé de. See AUBERT de Vertot d'Aubeuf, René

VIRGIL, *Works*, L, 1758, 225, 428; 1778, 355, 449; 1784, 373, 452; E (*trs.* Dryden, John), 1769, 291; 1775, 335; *see* MOOR, James, *Vindication of Virgil*, 1766, 269

Virtue and vice (by BELLENDEN, John), 1750, 138

Virtue's expostulation with the British poets, 1757, 218

VISCHARD de St Réal, César, *The history of the conspiracy of the Spaniards*, E, 1752, 178

VOLTAIRE, *The history of Charles XII*, E, 1754, 353, 423, 449; *La pucelle d'Orléans*, F, 1756, 212

WALKER, Capt. Thomas, his library auctioned, 1768, 109

WALKER (engraver), 390

WALLER, Edmund, *Poems on several occasions*, 1770, 300, 440; *Works*, 1752, 178, 420

WARDLAW, Elizabeth, Lady, *Hardyknute*, 1745, 105; 1748, 129

WATT, James, *Report to the Lords Commissioners of police relative to navigation*, 1773, 322

WATTS, Isaac, *Hymns and spiritual songs*, by 1784, 373; *The psalms of David imitated*, by 1784, 373

WEBB, Barnard, *De imperii civilis origine et causis*, L, 1750, 149

WELWOOD, James (translator and editor of Xenophon), 150

WHATMAN paper, 26-7; *see* PRINTING PAPER, Whatman

WHITE, B. and I. (booksellers; London), 386

WHITE, Jeremiah, *A persuasive to mutual love and charity*, 1739, 403

WIGHT, William, *Heads of a course of lectures on ancient and modern history*, 1770, 301; *on civil history*, 1772, 315; *on the study of history*, 1767, 277

WILKIE, J. (bookseller; London), 273, 397

WILSON, Alexander, his types. *See* PRINTING TYPE, *passim*

WILSON, D. (bookseller; London), 51, 263

WILSON, D. and DURHAM, J. (booksellers; London), 216

WILSON (bookseller; Glasgow). *See* DUNCAN, James, DUNLOP and WILSON

WILSON REID, D. J. (Glasgow University Archivist), 13

WINTERBOTTOM, T. M., *De morbo puerperali*, 1792, 460

Wonderful narrative, The (by CHAUNCY, Charles), 1742, 77

WORCESTER, Marquis of. *See* SOMERSET, Edward, 2nd Marquis of Somerset

WORTHINGTON, John, *A scripture catechism*, 1747, 118, 412

WRIGHT, James, *De summo bono*, 1761, 431

WYNNE, John (editor of Locke), 97, 173

XENOPHON, *Agesilaus*, G *and* L, 1748, 130; *Anabasis*, G *and* L, 1764, 259, 432; G, 1783, 366; G *and* L, 1792, 384, 460; *Cyropaedia*, G *and* L, 1767, 278; *Discourse upon improving the revenue of Athens*, see *Ways and means*; *Hellenica and Agesilaus*, G *and* L, 1762, 248, 432; *Hieron*, G *and* L, 1745, 106, 408; E, 1750, 150; *Memorabilia*, G, 1761, 243; *Polity of the Lacedaemonians*, G *and* L, 1756, 212; *Socrates and Aristodemus*, G *and* L, 1744, 98; *Symposium*, E (*trs.* Welwood, James), 1750, 150; *Ways and means*, E (*trs.* Moyle, Walter), 1751, 162; *see A dialogue on devotion after the manner of Xenophon*, 1749, 132

YAIR, John (bookseller; Edinburgh), 222

Yarico to Inkle, The epistle of (by JERNINGHAM, Edward), 1750, 143

YOUNG, Edward, *The Complaint, or Night-thoughts, etc.*, 1769, 292; 1771, 309; 1776, 345; *The force of religion*, 1751, 167; *Love of fame*, 1750, 150, 418; 1753, 422; 1754, 192, 423; 1758, 225; *A poem on the last day*, 1752, 179; *Poems on several occasions*, 1771, 309; *Revenge*, 1752, 204, 421, 425

Young Waters, 1755, 201